THE R

YUGOSLAVIA

REAL GUIDE CREDITS

Series Editor: Mark Ellingham.
Editorial: Martin Dunford, John Fisher, Jack Holland, Jonathan Buckley.
US Text Editors: Marc Dubin, Jamie Jensen.
Production: Susanne Hillen, Kate Berens, Andy Hilliard.
Typesetting: Gail Jammy and Greg Ward.
Design: Andrew Oliver.

Thanks for help, information and encouragement with this edition to: the Yugoslav National Tourist Office in London, JAT, Victor Rudez at Pan Adriatic Travel, Jasminka Stanojčic at the Tourist Association of Serbia, Nigel Dudley and Pete Raine for the piece on wildlife, Elizabeth Fosner, Alan Ambrose, Bridget Bouch, John Hodgson, Eve and Chris, Kim Burton, Karmen Balaško, Marc Dubin, Tricia Murphy, Miša and Debi, Igor and Milena, Bora Dimitrijevic, Želimir, Alen and Jovo.

Grateful **acknowledgement** is also made for permission to use a quotation from *The Mountains of Serbia* by Anne Kindersley (John Murray) on p.337; translation from the original by Anne Kindersley.

Illustrations in Part One and Part Three by Ed Briant;
Basics illustration by Tommy Yamaha; Contexts illustration by David Loftus.

Published in the United States and Canada by Prentice Hall Trade Division
A division of Simon & Schuster, Inc., 15 Columbus Circle, New York, NY 10023.

Typeset in Linotron Univers and Century Old Style.
Printed in the United States by R.R. Donnelley & Sons.

Library of Congress Cataloging-in-Publication Data

The Real Guide Yugoslavia/ written and researched by Martin Dunford, Jack Holland, Jonathan Bousfield, and Phil Lee; edited by Martin Dunford and Jack Holland.

464pp includes index
ISBN 0–13–783838–7 : $12.95
Rev. ed. of: The rough guide to Yugoslavia. 1985
1. Yugoslavia—Description and Travel—1981—Guide-books
  I. Holland, Jack, 1959– II. Dunford, Martin III. Bousfield, Jonathan IV. Lee, Phil
DR1213.D85 1990
914.9704'24—dc20   89–28765
                                                                         CIP

THE REAL GUIDE

YUGOSLAVIA

Written and Researched by

**MARTIN DUNFORD, JACK HOLLAND,
JONATHAN BOUSFIELD, and PHIL LEE**

With additional contributions by
Janet Goring, Ruth Ayliffe, Dave Robson,
John McGhie, and Simon Palmour

Edited by
Martin Dunford and Jack Holland

■ PRENTICE HALL ■
NEW YORK LONDON TORONTO SYDNEY TOKYO SINGAPORE

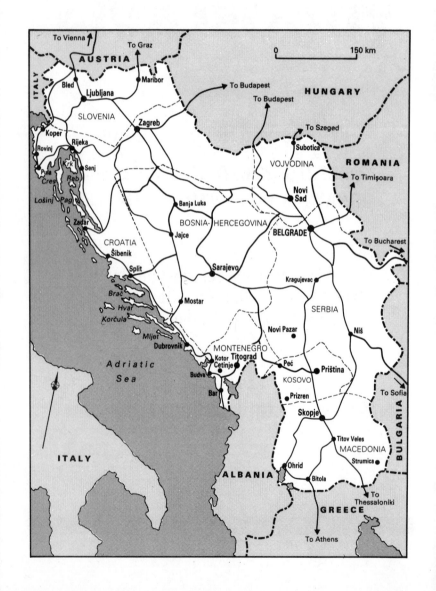

CONTENTS

Introduction *vii*

This book is dedicated to the survival of Yugoslavia as an independent, non-aligned, and federal state.

INTRODUCTION

Most people think of **Yugoslavia** as one country: no Yugoslav ever does. Dominated by the Turks for five hundred years, plundered by the Venetians and Austrians for almost as long, and bordered by more countries than any other European nation, Yugoslavia sports a mixture of cultures, religions, and nationalities unrivaled in Europe. Though Yugoslavia was officially formed earlier this century as a monarchy, it only took on its present form, as a federation of different republics, after World War II, knocked into shape by the wartime Partisan leader Tito, who saw to it that the traditional conflicts of the nations that made up the area were submerged in favor of forging a new Socialist, southern Slav state.

Since Tito's death in 1980, the federation and the economic legacy that went with it has seemed increasingly fragile, and today, with hyper inflation, wages among the lowest in Europe, and an agricultural system that sometimes seems a vestige from the last century, the country is facing big problems. The fiercely protected individuality of each of the republics persists— only four percent of Yugoslavs describe themselves as such on their passport, the vast majority preferring to be considered Macedonian, Montenegrin, or whatever their republic of birth. And this, exacerbated by the stark divergence in living standards between the wealthy north and poorer south, has led to conflict. Strikes, demonstrations, and a resurgence of nationalism, especially in Serbia, have for the first time since the war threatened the future of the alliance. Nationalist differences, too, have been manifest in attitudes to the political system. Despite liberalizing moves in the northern republics, and the abandonment of the Marixst-Leninist ideology in the rest of central Europe, Yugoslavia as a whole has been slow to reform, the Belgrade-based government even now hanging on to outmoded systems of Socialist self-management. Dissenters, for their part, are unsure of what to put in its place. Even now, with free elections sanctioned by the Party and on the agenda for 1990, there's a danger that new political parties will organize along nationalist lines, further threatening the stability of the federation.

Yet the variety and disparateness that threatens Yugoslavia's existence is in many ways its draw. The country has three official religions (Roman Catholic, Orthodox Christian, and Muslim), and innumerable nationalities, with sizable populations of Albanians, Hungarians, and Romanians alongside the core Slav majority of Serbs, Croatians, Macedonians, and Slovenians, making up the total population of 22 million; and its landscape is spectacular, riven with high mountains and deep gorges and valleys running down to the grand starkness of the coastal karst. For years backpackers have rarely given the country a second glance as they hurry down to Greece, and eighty percent of those who do vacation here are swallowed up by a handful of coastal resorts, making for a popular impression that's far from the truth. That said, the **Adriatic coast** is one of the most beautiful in Europe, and, despite its popularity with the package tour trade, is long enough to make avoiding busy patches easy. A coast road and plentiful ferries make touring simple enough, and there are a number of appealing centers to structure travel around. Though technically part of the republic of Croatia, the old province of Dalmatia forms the coast's heartland, its capital **Split** an essential stop, with an ancient center molded around the palace of Diocletian—and home to some of the best classical architecture you'll find anywhere. Split is an atmospheric, vibrant city, and gives access to some of the best of the country's offshore **islands**—places like Hvar, Korčula, and Brac, which, notwithstanding the tourist invasion of the last couple of decades, have managed to preserve distinctive characters. The two islands of Vis and Lastovo, closed to foreign traffic until the late 1980s, are particularly unspoilt, though the highlight of the coast remains **Dubrovnik**, a walled city that figures in all travel brochures—and which, despite its popularity, has also managed to retain some semblance of its old feel.

Inland, the distinctiveness of each of the six republics comes as a surprise after the relative homogeneity of the coast. If you're heading into Yugoslavia from the north, **Slovenia** provides a gentle transition—the richest of the republics, Austrian in flavor, with, in **Ljubljana,** arguably the liveliest of the country's regional capitals. To the north, the rugged alpine scenery splashed with lakes is magnificent, and popular skiing territory during winter. East of Slovenia, the capital of Croatia, **Zagreb**, provides an elegant focus before the long haul east across the plain of Slavonia to **Belgrade**, the drab, if vigorous, capital of **Serbia.** This, the largest and for years the most powerful of Yugoslavia's republics, has a legacy of medieval Serbian-Orthodox monasteries that date from the days of medieval Serbian independence, which was arrested by the fourteenth-century Turkish invasion. Several monasteries—Manasija, Sopoćani, and Mileševa—have superb frescoes, and almost all are magnificently sited, though in spite of this Serbia remains one of the least visited parts of the country. Within its formal boundaries, to the south, the ethnically Albanian autonomous province of **Kosovo** boasts more monasteries, despite its predominantly Muslim population, though it is perhaps more renowned for the ethnic tensions current there; the **Vojvodina**, towards Hungary in the north, is a land of rolling fields dotted with yet more monasteries—though this again is a part of the country few travelers get to unless heading into Hungary itself. West of Serbia, the republic of **Bosnia-Hercegovina** most fully absorbed the Turkish invaders, and is still deeply influenced by the remains of the Ottoman Empire: Islam is the dominant religion, mosques are still active, and the capital **Sarajevo** retains an Islamic university. Outside Sarajevo, the landscape is one of mountains and fertile valleys, becoming barer the closer you get to the coast. To the south of Bosnia, **Montenegro** straddles some of the country's highest mountains, in an impressive range that falls down to a picturesque stretch of coast. In the far south of Yugoslavia, bordering Greece, **Macedonia** has a blisteringly hot, impoverished landscape once again spotted with Serbian-Orthodox monasteries. Its capital, **Skopje**, is a worthwhile stop-off, once again with remnants of Turkish times in its old bazaar quarter; and the lakes of the republic's southwestern corner, **Ohrid** and **Prespa**, are some of the country's great (though increasingly discovered) delights.

Climate and When to Go

Yugoslavia's **climate** follows two patterns: Mediterranean on the coast, with warm summers and mild winters, and Continental inland—much hotter during summer, extremely cold in winter. Come to the coast in July or August and you'll find almost everywhere full of tourists; arrive in May, early or late September, and you'll avoid the crowds, a little of the heat, and the high season prices. The interior, particularly Bosnia-Hercegovina and Macedonia, can swelter in summer—you need to start your travels early to avoid midday meltdown. From late autumn onwards the mountain ranges of Montenegro, Bosnia, and Macedonia become impassable, though in some areas, especially in Slovenia, the skiing season begins in November and can last until early May.

AVERAGE TEMPERATURES (C)							
	Jan	Apr	May	June	July	Aug	Sept	Oct
Belgrade	0	9.5	17.8	20.5	22.7	22.8	18.9	13.3
Bled	0.3	6.7	17.2	21.0	23.3	23.0	21.7	16.0
Budva	8.6	13.9	17.4	21.7	23.9	24.0	21.1	17.2
Dubrovnik	8.3	13.4	17.8	22.2	25.6	25.0	22.3	17.8
Hvar	8.4	13.9	18.3	22.8	25.0	25.0	22.5	18.3
Ljubljana	1.0	9.2	14.3	17.5	19.5	18.5	14.4	9.7
Opatija	5.5	10.0	16.7	21.2	23.8	24.0	20.6	15.0
Sarajevo	-1.6	9.6	14.7	18.0	19.2	17.8	13.4	8.8
Split	7.5	12.8	18.9	23.9	26.7	26.1	22.8	16.7

°F = °C multiplied by 5/9, plus 32

PART ONE

THE

BASICS

JUGOSLAVIJA

GETTING THERE

The only direct scheduled flights from North America to Yugoslavia are with *JAT*, the Yugoslav national airline. They fly into Zagreb and Belgrade from New York, Chicago, Los Angeles, Cleveland and Detroit in the US, and from Toronto and Montreal in Canada. While several US carriers also fly to the country, they entail making European connections en route.

FLYING TO YUGOSLAVIA

Flying to either **Belgrade** or **Zagreb** with *JAT* (☎800/752-6528) costs the same, and both destinations allow for connections to be made to other cities. Flying **from New York** is the cheapest option, Apex fares starting at $701 in the low season, rising to $1044 in the high season. **From Chicago** the fares are $840 low season and $1084 high season, and **from Los Angeles** $969 low season, rising to $1224 in the high. Flying from Canada, a low season Apex fare **from Montreal** with *JAT* will cost $CDN748, and $CDN1110 in the high season. If you're eligible, take advantage of one of *JAT*'s **youth discount** tickets, with which considerable savings can be made. This type of fare from New York, for instance, is only $486, though they are available only in the low season.

Traveling with a US carrier will be a cheaper option than a regular flight with *JAT*, but also more time-consuming due to the necessity of making a connection at one of several European cities. *Pan Am* (☎800/221-1111), for example,

offers an Apex fare from New York for $599 in the low season, $1001 in high. Other US carriers are comparable, offering similar fares and connections from various European centres.

If you're flying to Yugoslavia as part of a wider European travel itinerary, or decide to make your own arrangements for a connecting flight from the US, your point of arrival can be any one of a number of cities, including **Ljubljana**, **Belgrade**, **Zagreb**, **Pula**, **Dubrovnik**, and **Split**. Obviously this is a matter of choice depending on your travel plans, and shouldn't be counted on to save you any money. See below for details on travel via the United Kingdom.

STUDENT AND DISCOUNT FLIGHTS

Students can take advantage of the array of specialist operators who offer flights at fares below the regular scheduled rates. *STA*, for instance, offer a low season Apex fare from **New York to Belgrade** for only $630, rising to $790 in the high season. Alternatively, *Council Travel* (☎212/661-1450) have low season fares starting at $623. Other companies in this field to try include *Nouvelles Frontieres*, *Access International* (☎800/333-7280), *McTravel* (☎800/333-3335), *International Travel Specialists* (☎800/444-6064), and *Travel Cuts* in Canada (known as *Voyages Cuts* in Quebec). See overleaf for addresses throughout the USA and Canada.

If you're not a student, one way of picking up a **discount flight** is to check the Sunday travel sections of the *New York Times* and *Los Angeles Times* for discount/charter flights. These generally work out a little cheaper than using a scheduled flight, and if you're able to be flexible in your travel plans can offer some genuine bargains.

There are also many **discount travel clubs**, which charge an annual fee for membership and sell unsold airline tickets at discounts ranging from fifteen to sixty percent. Travelers call a hotline number for information on what's available. *Airhitch* are one such organization, and sell last-minute stand-bys to Europe from several US cities for one low price—currently $160 from New York, and $229 from Los Angeles. However, precise dates and destinations cannot be guaranteed. Instead you tell them what range of days you want to fly on, and where you want to fly to, and a few days prior to the time you wanted to

CIEE IN THE US

Head Office: 205 E. 42nd St., New York, NY 10017; ☎800/223-7401

CALIFORNIA
2511 Channing Way, Berkeley, CA 94704; ☎415/848-8604
UCSD Student Center, B-023, La Jolla, CA 92093; ☎619/452-0630
5500 Atherton St., Suite 212, Long Beach, CA 90815; ☎213/598-3338
1093 Broxton Ave., Los Angeles, CA 90024; ☎213/208-3551
4429 Cass St., San Diego, CA 92109; ☎619/270-6401
312 Sutter St., San Francisco, CA 94108; ☎415/421-3473
919 Irving St., San Francisco, CA 94122; ☎415/566-6222
14515 Ventura Blvd., Suite 250, Sherman Oaks, CA 91403; ☎818/905-5777

GEORGIA
12 Park Place South, Atlanta, GA 30303; ☎404/577-1678

ILLINOIS
29 E. Delaware Place, Chicago, IL 60611; ☎312/951-0585

MASSACHUSETTS
79 South Pleasant St., 2nd Floor, Amherst, MA 01002; ☎413/256-1261

729 Boylston St., Suite 201, Boston, MA 02116; ☎617/266-1926
1384 Massachusetts Ave., Suite 206, Cambridge, MA 02138; ☎617/497-1497

MINNESOTA
1501 University Ave. SE, Room 300, Minneapolis, MN 55414; ☎612/379-2323

NEW YORK
35 W. 8th St., New York, NY 10011; ☎212/254-2525
Student Center, 356 West 34th St., New York, NY 10001; ☎212/661-1450

OREGON
715SW Morrison, Suite 1020, Portland, OR 97205; ☎503/228-1900

RHODE ISLAND
171 Angell St., Suite 212, Providence, RI 02906; ☎401/331-5810

TEXAS
1904 Guadalupe St., Suite 6, Austin, TX 78705; ☎512/472-4931
The Executive Tower, 3300 W. Mockingbird, Suite 101, Dallas,TX 75235; ☎214/350-6166

WASHINGTON
1314 Northeast 43rd St., Suite 210, Seattle, WA 98105; ☎206/632-2448

STA IN THE US

BOSTON
273 Newbury St., Boston, MA 02116; ☎617/266-6014

HONOLULU
1831 S. King St., Suite 202, Honolulu, HI 96826; ☎808/942-7755

LOS ANGELES
920 Westwood Blvd., Los Angeles, CA 90024; ☎213/824-1574
7204 Melrose Ave., Los Angeles, CA 90046; ☎213/934-8722

2500 Wilshire Blvd., Los Angeles, CA 90057; ☎213/380-2184

NEW YORK
17 E. 45th St., Suite 805, New York, NY 10017; ☎212/986-9470;☎ 800/777-0112

SAN DIEGO
6447 El Cajon Blvd., San Diego, CA 92115; ☎619/286-1322

SAN FRANCISCO
166 Geary St., Suite 702, San Francisco, CA 94108; ☎415/391-8407

NOUVELLES FRONTIÈRES

In the United States
NEW YORK 19 W. 44th St., Suite 1702, New York, NY 10036; ☎212/764-6494
LOS ANGELES 6363 Wilshire Blvd., Suite 200, Los Angeles, CA 90048; ☎213/658-8955
SAN FRANCISCO 209 Post St., Suite 1121, San Francisco, CA 94108; ☎415/781-4480

In Canada
MONTREAL 1130 ouest, bd de Maisonneuve, Montréal, P.Q. H3A 1M8; ☎514/842-1450
QUEBEC 176 Grande Allée Ouest, Québec, P.Q. G1R 2G9; ☎418/525-5255

leave you will be offered a choice of flights.

Naturally this form of travel is very uncertain—while you're almost sure to leave when you wanted, it can't be guaranteed that you'll fly to your chosen destination. It should also be remembered that discount ticket availability is very sensitive to seasonal demand. *Airhitch*, for example, close down for the two weeks over Christmas, as most flights are too full to have standbys.

VIA GREAT BRITAIN

If you're traveling to Yugoslavia **via Britain** as part of a wider European tour, the simplest option is to take one of the frequent scheduled flights, taking just two to four hours from a variety of British regional airports. However, if you have the time it's worth considering traveling overland, which takes a minimum of 36 hours, but can also allow an unlimited number of stop-offs en route, depending on the method of travel you choose.

TRAINS

There are two **principal rail routes** to Yugoslavia, both of which take around 30 hours. The most direct is through Belgium, Germany and Austria, and involves one change, usually in Munich, while the second, through France, Switzerland and Italy, involves changes in Paris and Venice. Unless you're under 26 however, standard fares don't compare well with flying, and can even work out more expensive: a round-trip ticket from London to Ljubljana costs £222.

If you're **under 26** and want to travel by train you could buy an **InterRail** pass. This costs £155 and entitles the holder to a month's unlimited travel on all European trains, and on selected European ferries. Available through student/youth travel agents, or direct from *British Rail*, it is, however, strictly only available to those resident in Europe for six months or more—though some agents may bend the rules if you're persuasive. The official North American alternative, **Eurail**, is much more expensive and not worth it unless you intend to virtually live on trains while in Europe. Either ticket will in any case be of limited use in Yugoslavia, where the rail system is scant.

An alternative to rail passes for under-26's is a **BIJ ticket**, available to most Yugoslav destinations through *Eurotrain* (52 Grosvenor Gardens, London SW1; ☎01-730 34902). These allow unlimited stopovers on their given routes over a two-month period of validity. A round-trip *BIJ* fare from London to Zagreb will cost around £150.

TRAVEL CUTS IN CANADA

Head Office: 187 College St., Toronto, Ontario M5T 1P7; ☎416/979-2406

ALBERTA
1708 12th St. NW, Calgary T2M 3M7; ☎403/282-7687. 10424A 118th Ave., Edmonton T6G 0P7; ☎403/471-8054

BRITISH COLUMBIA
Room 326, T.C., Student Rotunda, Simon Fraser University, Burnaby, British Columbia V5A 1S6; ☎604/291-1204. 1516 Duranleau St., Granville Island, Vancouver V6H 3S4; ☎604/689-2887. Student Union Building, University of British Columbia, Vancouver V6T 1W5; ☎604/228-6890 Student Union Building, University of Victoria, Victoria V8W 2Y2; ☎604/721-8352

MANITOBA
University Centre, University of Manitoba, Winnipeg R3T 2N2; ☎204/269-9530

NOVA SCOTIA
Student Union Building, Dalhousie University, Halifax B3H 4J2; ☎902/424-2054. 6139 South St., Halifax B3H 4J2; ☎902/424-7027

ONTARIO
University Centre, University of Guelph, Guelph N1G 2W1; ☎519/763-1660. Fourth Level Unicentre, Carleton University, Ottawa, K1S5B6; ☎613/238-5493. 60 Laurier Ave. E, Ottawa K1N 6N4; ☎613/238-8222. Student Street, Room G27, Laurentian University, Sudbury P3E 2C6; ☎705/673-1401. 96 Gerrard St. E, Toronto M5B 1G7; ☎(416) 977-0441. University Shops Plaza, 170 University Ave. W, Waterloo N2L 3E9; ☎519/886-0400.

QUÉBEC (Known as *Voyages CUTS*)
Université McGill, 3480 rue McTavish, Montréal H3A 1X9; ☎514/398-0647. 1613 rue St. Denis, Montréal H2X 3K3; ☎514/843-8511. Université Concordia, Edifice Hall, Suite 643, S.G.W. Campus, 1455 bd de Maisonneuve Ouest, Montréal H3G 1M8; ☎514/288-1130. 19 rue Ste. Ursule, Québec G1R 4E1; ☎418/692-3971

SASKATCHEWAN
Place Riel Campus Centre, University of Saskatchewan, Saskatoon S7N 0W0; ☎306/343-1601

BUSES

Taking a **long-distance bus** is the cheapest but also the most uncomfortable way of getting to Yugoslavia. *Eurolines* (52 Grosvenor Gdns, London SW1; ☎01-730 8235), operate a weekly service, currently leaving London on Fridays, to Zagreb for £66 one-way, £114 round-trip (changing in Germany), and a summer service to Istanbul which stops at Ljubljana and Niš. Journey-time is roughly 36 hours, London–Zagreb. A less expensive (but less reliable) option are the independent Greek operators, who sometimes stop off on their way down to Greece. Use only as a last resort.

FERRIES

Yugoslavia is well connected to Italy and Greece by a series of regular **ferries**, which can make for a painless, if relatively expensive, way to arrive in the country. *Jadrolinija*, Yugoslavia's national line (c/o *Yugotours*, Chesham House, 150 Regent Street, London W1; ☎01-439 7233), run services **from Corfu** to Yugoslavia's larger coastal towns, offering deck-passenger fares at $40–50, depending on your destination. Add around $20 for the cheapest sort of cabin, upwards of $60 if you have a car. *Jadrolinija* and *Adriatica* (c/o Sealink Travel Centre, Platform Two, Victoria Station, London SW1; ☎01-828 1940) also operate services between the **Italian coast and Yugoslavia**, linking most of the main ports on both sides of the Adriatic at least once a week in

season. Expect to pay around $40 one-way as a deck passenger, about $50 for a cabin, another $25 if you're driving. Journey times vary, but to give some idea, Ancona to Split is about an eight-hour trip. For further information see the "Travel Details" at the end of each coastal chapter.

PACKAGES AND ORGANIZED TOURS

There are many companies operating **group travel and tours** in Yugoslavia, ranging from full-blown luxury tours to small groups following specialized itineraries, though one factor most have in common is that they tend to be escorted. Needless to say, prices can vary a great deal, so it's important to check what you're getting for your money—some packages for instance don't include airfares.

Kompas Travel (630 Fifth Avenue, Suite 219, New York, NY10111; ☎212/265-8210) are the largest organizers of tours in the US. They offer a fourteen-day "Best of Yugoslavia" package for between $798 and $948, depending on the season, which includes two meals a day, but not the cost of the airfare. They also offer a "Wonderful Yugoslavia Panorama" eight-day tour, for around $469–538, again depending on the season. *Love Holidays/Uniworld* (15315 Magnolia Boulevard, Sherman Oaks, CA 91402; ☎800/456-5683) also operate tours in Eastern Europe, including an eight-day "Yugoslavia Discovery" package, for $1198–1398.

RED TAPE AND VISAS

passport and disappear; don't panic if this happens—you'll get it back later, stamped with the visa. Usually the date stamp on these is illegible, and if you leave with a recently expired visa no one is going to kick up a fuss. But if you do need an **extension**, the choice is between hopping over the border for a fresh stamp or facing the bureaucracy of the local *Opštinski SUP* (*sekretarijat za unutrašnje poslove*, or interior ministry). Usually this just means the main district police station, which you can find by asking at your accommodation for the local *milicija*. They will expect good reasons for you wanting to prolong your visit. While in Yugoslavia you're required to carry your passport at all times.

CUSTOMS

When entering the country by rail or road, you might be asked to declare any radios, tape recorders, cameras, or other consumer items that you have with you for personal use, details of which will be scribbled into your passport. This will be checked on leaving the country to make sure that you didn't sell them while you were in Yugoslavia. Attention to such details is often lax, however, especially at minor crossing points.

American and Canadian citizens require a visa to enter Yugoslavia, which permits a stay of up to one year. The multiple entry visa is issued free at any Yugoslav consulate, usually on the spot.

As an alternative you can obtain a visa on the border, but this is unpopular with officials and likely to be time consuming. If you do so, you're given a stamp that entitles you to a stay of 90 days. Arrive by train and an official may take your

YUGOSLAV CONSULATES

In the US (all open 10am–1pm Mon–Fri)
Washington 2410 California Street, NW Washington DC 20008 (☎202/462-6566).
Cleveland Suite 4R, Park Center, 1700 East 13th Street, OH 44114 (☎216/621-2093).
New York 17th Floor, 767 Third Avenue, NY 10017 (☎212/838-2300).
Chicago Suite 1600, 307 North Michigan Avenue, IL 60601 (☎312/332-0169).

Pittsburgh Suite 1605, 625 Stanwix Street, PA 15222 (☎412/471-6191).
San Francisco Suite 406, 1375 Sutter Street, CA 94709 (☎415/776-4961).
In Canada:
Ottawa 17 Blackburn Avenue, Ontario K1N 8A2 (☎613/233-6289).
Toronto 377 Spadine Road, Ontario N5P 2V7. (☎416/481-7279).

HEALTH AND INSURANCE

No inoculations are required for travel in Yugoslavia, but an up-to-date typhoid booster is a good idea, especially if you're heading for out-of-the-way places where food preparation isn't always over-careful. Along these lines, diarrhea is likely to be the most immediate and unavoidable problem, so stock up on remedies before you leave.

HEALTH CARE AND HOSPITALS

Minor complaints can be solved at a drug store or *Apoteka* (in Croatian, *Ljekarna*), where you'll also find other essentials and often someone who speaks English. In larger towns there's usually a **24-hour pharmacy**, details of which are given in the "Listings" sections of the guide. For serious medical attention, phone ☎94 for the ambulance service. Outpatient and emergency wards are found in most **hospitals** or *Bolnica*, signposted by a white H on a blue background. The local *Turist Biro* will put you on to English-speaking doctors.

INSURANCE

Travel insurance can buy you peace of mind as well as save you money. Before you purchase any insurance, however, check what you have already, whether as part of a family or student policy. You may find yourself covered for medical expenses and loss, and possibly loss of or damage to valuables, while abroad.

For example, **Canadians** are usually covered for medical expenses by their provincial health plans (but may only be reimbursed after the fact). Holders of **ISIC** cards are entitled to $2000 worth of accident coverage and 60 days ($100 per diem) of hospital in-patient benefits for the period during which the card is valid. University **students** will often find that their student health coverage extends for one term beyond the date of last enrollment.

Bank and charge **accounts** (particularly *American Express*) often have certain levels of medical or other insurance included. **Home-owners' or renters'** insurance may cover theft or loss of documents, money, and valuables while overseas, though exact conditions and maximum amounts vary from company to company.

SPECIALIST INSURANCE

Only after exhausting the possibilities above might you want to contact a **specialist travel insurance** company; your travel agent can usually recommend one—*Travelguard* and *The Travelers* are good policies.

Travel insurance offerings are quite comprehensive, anticipating everything from charter companies going bankrupt to delayed (as well as lost) baggage, by way of sundry illnesses and accidents. **Premiums** vary widely—from the very reasonable ones offered primarily through student/youth agencies (though available to anyone), to those so expensive that the cost for two or three months of coverage will probably equal the cost of the worst possible combination of disasters.

A most important thing to keep in mind—and a source of major disappointment to would be claimants—is that *none* of the currently available policies insures against **theft** of anything while overseas. North American travel policies apply only to items lost from, or damaged in, the custody of an identifiable, responsible third party, i.e. hotel porter, airline, luggage consignment, etc. Even in these cases you will still have to contact the local police to make out a complete report so that your insurer can process the claim.

BRITISH POLICIES

If you are **transiting through Britain**, policies there cost considerably less (under £20/$32 for a month) and include routine cover for theft. You can take out a British policy at almost any travel agency or major bank; check agencies detailed in the "Getting There" section for addresses. ISIS, a "student" policy but open to everyone, is reliable and fairly good value; it is operated by a company called *Endsleigh*, and is available through any student/youth travel agency.

REIMBURSEMENT

All insurance policies—American or Canadian—work by **reimbursing you** once you return home, so be sure to keep all your receipts from doctors and pharmacists. Any thefts should immediately be reported to the nearest police station and a police report obtained; no report, no refund.

If you have had to undergo serious medical treatment, with major hospital bills, contact your consulate. They can normally arrange for an insurance company, or possibly relatives, to cover the fees, pending a claim.

HEALTH INFORMATION

The *International Association for Medical Assistance to Travelers* informs its members about health care abroad, including the names of English-speaking doctors who are affiliated with the organization. For further information write to *IAMAT*, 417 Center St., Lewiston, NY 14092 (☎716/754-4883).

International SOS Assistance also offers medical assistance to travelers abroad, especially emegency transportation. Write to Box 11568, Philadelphia PA 19116 (☎800/523-8930).

COSTS, MONEY, AND BANKS

A poor country by western standards, Yugoslavia sees the annual tourist invasion as its main opportunity to earn badly needed hard currency, with prices upped accordingly for visitors .

But in spite of this the country remains one of Europe's least expensive destinations. Prices in the north and on the coast have risen significantly in response to the tourist boom, but life's essentials still come cheaply, especially so in the rest of the country. The main problem is to keep up with the sudden and unannounced price-hikes that accompany Yugoslavia's ever-worsening inflation (2000 percent at the last count). However, confusion is the worst of this, since your hard currency will retain its value against the falling dinar. Prices for accommodation are quoted throughout the country in **US dollars** or **West German marks**, and in order to maintain a degree of continuity in the guide, we've followed this system to some extent, listing all prices in US dollars.

COSTS

As for a **daily budget**, if you're camping, using local buses, and buying your food from markets and supermarkets you can get by on as little as $13–16 a day; for around $25–33 a day you could be living fairly well.

Everywhere, **accommodation** is the major expense, with the prices for foreign visitors several times the rates for Yugoslavs. Nevertheless, student hostels open over the summer in major cities, and private rooms are reasonable, starting at about $10–15 for a double, even in the well-touristed areas.

Food is a negligible expense, with a basic filling meal weighing in at around $5 a head, sometimes less in the less visited interior, with wine, beer, or heady spirits as cheap accompaniment. **Transportation**, is also relatively inexpensive, and you can cover long distances by trains or (more usually) bus for next to nothing; as a broad guide, reckon on paying around $8 for a one-way bus journey from Split to Rijeka, a roughly 250-kilometer trip.

MONEY AND BANKS

With the Yugoslav **currency**, the *dinar*, beset by hyperinflation, even the simplest expenditure can run into hundreds of thousands. Notes currently come in 10, 20, 50, 100, 500, 1000, 5000, 20,000, 50,000, 100,000 and 500,000 denominations, but expect new ones to be added as the dinar continues to fall. Worthless 10-, 20-, 50- and 100-dinar coins are still in circulation, and you may be burdened with them in change. To make matters worse, despite the revaluation of the currency in the 1960s* (knocking two zeros off), many Yugoslavs persist in talking in old dinars, adding a surreal quality to the constant price rises. Listen out for people totting up expenses in millions of old dinars, and for the tendency in popular speech to omit the word for a "thousand"; if someone tells you that something costs "six hundred," this could mean either 600,000 dinars or 600,000 old dinars, namely 6000 new. When confronted with prices in old dinars, simply divide by 100 to get the new dinar figure. If you're too confused to work it out at all, don't worry—many of the locals can't make heads or tails of it any more either.

CURRENCY RESTRICTIONS AND THE BLACK MARKET

You're only allowed to buy around $16 worth of dinars before you enter Yugoslavia. There's little point, in any case, in stocking up with too much Yugoslav currency before you travel: you'll get a better rate once inside the country itself and be charged negligible commission, and you won't lose out on the constantly falling exchange rate.

---

*As we went to press plans were afoot to revalue the dinar again, one new dinar being worth 10,000 old ones. This may now have happened, though it's likely only to have added to the confusion.

Indeed, it's best to change small amounts at regular intervals, thus avoiding being saddled with an unwieldy wad of rapidly-depreciating cash. If you're coming from Greece it's worth knowing that 1000-drachma notes aren't exchangeable anywhere in Yugoslavia.

It's also prohibited to take more than $16 worth of dinars **out of the country**. Since you can't spend them at airports or frontiers—duty-free shops only take sterling, US dollars, and other strong currencies—and most Yugoslav banks refuse to change dinars back into hard currency, it's best to budget carefully so you're not left with a lot of useless dinars. Even if you can get them out of the country, most banks abroad will give you a very poor rate for them.

You may be offered **black market rates** for your hard cash; many Yugoslavs resort to hard-currency dealing as a means of survival. Whether you take advantage of this is up to you, but bear three things in mind: first, it's still technically illegal (although so widespread that the authorities turn a blind eye); second, you'll have to change a lot of cash before it's worth it, since the going rate on the black market is only ten percent higher than in a bank; third, assume that anyone who approaches you (rather than vice versa) is out to fleece you—and beware.

TRAVELLER'S CHECKS AND CREDIT CARDS

The best way of carrying the bulk of your money is in **traveler's checks**, available from any downtown bank for (usually) one percent commission, whether or not you have an account, and cashable in almost all Yugoslav banks, tourist offices, post offices, and most major stores, for a small commission. Even on a Sunday you should always be able to find somewhere to change money, and don't worry about getting ripped off—exchange rates are standard across the country. *American Express*, *Thomas Cook*, and *Visa* are the most widely accepted brands of check.

You may be offered **Dinar Checks** in return, for which you're given a ten-percent bonus in shops and restaurants displaying the sign. Although theoretically welcomed, the scheme has proved unpopular, and many proprietors are reluctant to take them. Where they're most useful is in paying larger bills (eg at a hotel where it's clearly stated they'll be accepted). Don't get stuck with your unused ones either—they're notoriously difficult to re-exchange.

Credit cards like *American Express*, *Mastercard* and *Visa* can also be used to get cash, but very often only in major banks (*Jugobanka* is one) and larger towns. Cards are readily accepted in larger shops, stores, and more upscale restaurants across the country, although rural areas are lagging behind in this respect. There don't seem to be any hard and fast rules on this, so don't depend on your card too much when out in the wilds. In the few places where you're not billed in dollars or Deutschmarks, using credit cards to pay for major expenses such as hotel and restaurant bills is a good way to save money—bills paid by credit card often take a couple of months to reach your account at home, by which time the dinar will have fallen dramatically.

COMMUNICATIONS: POST AND PHONES

In larger cities, main **post offices** (*pošta* or PTT) are open Monday to Saturday from 7am until 7pm, with occasional Sunday hours in larger cities. Most newspaper kiosks sell stamps (*marke*) too—more convenient and you avoid lengthy lines. Every post office has a **poste restante** (general delivery) desk; to claim your mail produce your passport and a small fee. To send a letter to Yugoslavia poste restante, address the envelope "Poste Restante, Pošta," followed by the name of the town.

Post offices are also the best places to make **phone calls**. Line up at the relevant desk, state the number you want, and either take the call or dial it from a booth. Be warned, however, that you may have quite a wait, normally due to the long lines of army conscripts waiting to call their home town.

Due to the increasing worthlessness of Yugoslav coins, most **public phone booths** are now being converted to tokens or *žetoni*, although a few remaining older phones still take 100-dinar coins. Available from post offices and kiosks, *žetoni* come in three sizes, A, B, and C. One A is sufficient for a local call, B for longer distance, C for international calls. One word of warning: phones in Slovenia belong to a different system and tokens bought here can't be used elsewhere in the country. Phonecards are also

being introduced in some major centers, but for the time being don't expect to find very many of them outside Belgrade. The price of a local call is minimal, but for anything long-distance charges rise steeply and the quality of the system becomes more dubious. Dialling for fifteen minutes before being connected is not an uncommon experience. If the post office is closed and all available public phones are besieged, most **hotels** will allow you to make calls from the lobby, though you have to pay over the norm for the privilege. To dial a number abroad first use the international code, then the area code, omitting any initial zeros.

INTERNATIONAL TELEPHONE CODES

UNITED STATES and CANADA ☎99 1
BRITAIN ☎99 44

IRISH REPUBLIC ☎99 353
AUSTRALIA only through operator (☎901)

INFORMATION AND MAPS

Before you set off, visit the Yugoslav National Tourist Office at 630 Fifth Avenue, New York, NY 10111 (☎212/757-2801) for a supply of their copious promo. As well as the usual glossy rhapsodizing, their details on major campgrounds, private rooms and hotels, and their tourist map, are useful. They also have maps of larger cities, and ferry timetables.

TOURIST OFFICES

In Yugoslavia itself, most places of any size have some kind of office where you can pick up infor-

mation and in most cases town maps—though in smaller places these outlets can be neglected and poky, with very little to offer, often no more than a desk in the lobby of a hotel. Tourist offices tend to be organized locally and trade under a variety of titles—**Turist Biro** or **Turističko Društvo** are the most common, though there are any number of other, regional travel agents who often offer the same services. Names to look out for include *Kompas*, *Putnik*, *Kvarner Express*, *Dalmacijaturist*, *Generalturist*, and many others, all of whom will change money, stock information and maps of the local area, and sometimes act as an agency for private rooms. At many you can also buy train and bus tickets, and air tickets on *Adria Airways*. The other offices you'll see everywhere are *Atlas*, which is the agent for *American Express* in Yugoslavia—though only the larger branches will provide cash on production of your card.

MAPS

The city and island plans printed in the guide should be fine for most purposes, but if you're going to be doing a lot of moving about you'll need something more detailed on the country as a whole. Certainly you should invest in a large-scale **road map**: *Michelin* produces the best-value and most widely available one ($6), though you may find the slightly pricier but marginally larger scale *Daily Telegraph* map ($8) clearer to read. For the coast, *Kummerley & Frey* produce a map of western Yugoslavia ($9). Also on the coast, watch out in Yugoslavia for *The Yugoslav Coast*, a series of five booklets (published by the Yugoslav Lexicographical Institute) with detailed maps, town plans and lots of in-depth—if rather dated—information on every town, village, and monument bar none. You can get most of these, together with detailed plans of Belgrade and the other large cities, through *Pacific Travellers Supply*, 529 State St, Santa Barbara, CA93101 (☎805/963-4438).

For **hiking**, there's much less available. Detailed 1:20,000-scale maps of the Julian Alps are to be found in most Ljubljana bookshops, and the Slovenian mountains are well covered by the indispensable *Alpine Guide* by Robin Collomb, published by West Col in the UK at £5.25. Route information on the rest of Yugoslavia can be more of a problem. A range of 1:50,000 and 1:100,000 British and German military maps, drawn up during World War II, were recently released and may be available for reference and photocopying at major university and public libraries in the US and Canada—though in lieu of these you're dependent on the charts occasionally available from the tourist board in New York.

GETTING AROUND

You can get just about everywhere in Yugoslavia by some form of public transit. The train system is scanty but does serve the major cities; buses go everywhere, and are how most people get around, with costs around the lowest in Europe. The road system, too, is both comprehensive and of reasonable quality.

BUSES

Though **buses** are cheap, the system might seem initially confusing, with numerous bus companies, each of which decides its own routes. However, although they're not especially quick, buses generally leave on time, undaunted by distance or natural barriers, and at rates everyone can afford. Keep in mind that prices can vary, and journeys cost proportionately less in the poorer east of the country than in Slovenia and on the coast. You can normally pay on the bus but not always, so wherever possible buy a ticket in advance and reserve a seat; use the phrase *ima li*

rezervacija to do so (although be prepared to deal with constant double reservations and fellow passengers who refuse to sit in their allotted seats). During the tourist season, especially on the coast, it's often a good idea to reserve seats a day or two before you plan to travel. Always remember, too, which company you're traveling with—your ticket won't be valid for any other. On top of the price of your ticket, there's usually a small charge for stashing your gear in the hold.

TRAINS

Trains, by contrast, are not such an efficient way to get around the country: aside from the northwest, the network is patchy (and getting more so) and even on the major routes travel can be excruciatingly slow, stopping and starting every few minutes, waiting hours in dead-end stations for no obvious reason. Fares are usually significantly cheaper than buses, but conditions in second-class carriages are more often than not overcrowded and dirty.

You can at times escape from this by paying a little extra to travel on the faster, more luxurious **business** and **"green" trains** (*poslovni voz* and *zeleni vlak* respectively), which link major cities; if possible you should avoid the slower *putnički voz* and *ubrzani voz*. Also, the rail system can be a useful way of covering long distances at night, taking advantage of the reasonably cheap couchette prices and saving yourself the cost of an overnight stop in the process. Given the nature

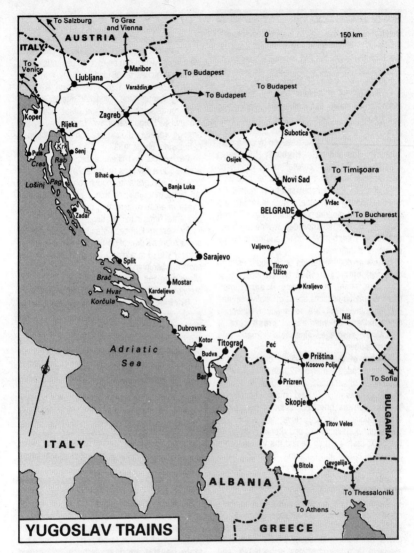

YUGOSLAV TRAINS

of the country, many train journeys are worth making for the sheer spectacle of the scenery—you invariably have plenty of time to admire the views. One journey you should especially try and make is the **Belgrade–Bar line**, a feat of engineering of which the Yugoslavs are justifiably proud, linking coast and capital by way of some of the most wild and enchanting mountain scen-ery the country has to offer. The **Sarajevo–Kardeljevo run** is a good second choice.

Rail **timings and routes** are listed in *Vozni Red*, the nationwide annual train timetable, which you can buy from tourist offices and travel agents. Always buy **tickets** in advance, prefera-bly from an authorized travel agent—the lines tend to be shorter than at stations.

DRIVING AND HITCHING

Driving in Yugoslavia gives obvious advantages. However, although there's been a vast improvement in the road system in recent years, the expressway (*autoput*, or *autocesta* in Slovenia) system is still a bit of a con, featuring only limited stretches of divided highway, and lesser roads can be poorly surfaced, often deteriorating into rutted tracks when you make a side turn. This, together with the sometimes dubious standards of driving, can make traveling by car a risky business. The **Adriatic Highway** (*Jadranska Magistrala*), the main coastal route, is littered with wrecks, and passing seems to be done with little concern for personal safety or regard for what's heading the other way. Rockfalls are frequent on mountain roads, causing real dangers. In the countryside, wandering farm animals and inattentive horses and carts create problems of their own.

As far as documentation goes, you'll need to carry **vehicle registration** (which must be in your own name), your **driving licence** (international driving licences aren't officially required for Yugoslavia, but are for many neighboring countries) and an international **green card** of insurance coverage, available from your insurance agent.

Rules of the road include driving on the right, and speed limits of 120kph on freeways, 100kph on other roads, 80 or 60kph in towns; speeding **fines** must be paid on the spot. Though Yugoslav drivers often don't bother, **seatbelts** are compulsory for both driver and front seat passenger. Kids under 12 and drunks must sit in the back; drunks sitting behind the wheel face a steep fine and/or imprisonment. A warning triangle should always be carried and if you pass an **accident** you're legally required to stop and offer assistance.

Petrol Coupons, known as *Bonovi*, sometimes come in useful for **fuel** (which costs around $2.50 a gallon right now). Buy them on the border and get a ten percent discount; otherwise they're available from tourist offices, some hotels, and the Yugoslav *AAA* equivalent *Auto Moto Savez Jugoslavije*, or **AMSJ**, addresses of whom you'll find in the guide, but *never* from filling stations. Remember that you *have* to pay for coupons in foreign currency; unused coupons can be cashed at the border. It's also worth noting that gas stations aren't as frequent as elsewhere in western Europe, and you should remember to fill up if you're heading into the wilds. Unleaded gas is still hard to find; don't expect to run into any outside major cities and resorts. The AMSJ have also just introduced toll coupons, purchased at the border, which can be used to pay tolls on the limited stretches of divided highway north and south of Belgrade. They'll be useful if you're plowing through the Yugoslav interior on the main route south. Should you break down, the national **SPI** organization will tow you away and arrange repairs, though it won't be cheap—nationwide, phone ☎987.

Car rental isn't cheap either; prices start at around $30 a day for a thrashed Žastava two-door compact in Yugoslavia, though you may be able to cut costs by organizing things before you leave. Those interested in renting by the day will find city rental firms in our "Listings" sections.

By western European standards, **taxis** can be an inexpensive way of getting around town, especially if you're in a group, although spiraling fuel costs are beginning to make this less economical. Make sure the driver starts the meter immediately or you'll face overcharging.

Hitching, just about anywhere in the country, is fairly dire; only on out-of-the-way rural roads is there any chance of lifts, and then they'll just be short local hops. Long lifts are out—Yugoslavs tend to regard foreign hitchhikers with a certain amount of suspicion, and the main coast road is so jam-packed with vacation traffic throughout the season so as to not make it worth the bother. Anyway, given the prices of buses and trains it shouldn't be necessary to hitch too often. If you do, bear in mind that hitching on anything termed an *autoput* (or *autocesta* in Slovenia) is illegal.

FERRIES

Traveling on the Adriatic coast, you'll certainly need to use the **ferries**. Run by *Jadrolinija*, the main Yugoslav ferry operator, these are inexpensive, punctual, and extremely comprehensive. Just about every inhabited island is connected by some kind of regular **local ferry**, and there's a **main coastal service** which cruises up and down the coast from Rijeka to Dubrovnik around six times a week throughout the summer season, calling at most of the major ports and islands, supplemented by ferries to Greece, which stop at many of the same Yugoslav ports and resorts. For more details on coastal ferries, see the "Coastal Practicalities" section in *The Adriatic Coast and Islands*, p.119, and the "Travel Details" at the end of the chapter. Or contact *Jadrolinija* direct at Obala Jugoslovenske Mornarice 16, Rijeka (☎058/25-203), which can send you timetables for the coastal ferry, and for international and local services.

PLANES

JAT and *Adria Airways* between them link Yugoslavia's major cities in a broad network of **domestic flights**—not especially cheap (tourists pay two to three times over the domestic rate), but extremely reliable, and, in a country where bus and train travel can be so wearingly slow, often a positive alternative if you can afford it.

Planes are best for long strides from the coast up to Belgrade or Zagreb, or for getting to the north from the south of the country quickly: Dubrovnik to Belgrade, for example, works out at about $60 at present, well over double the price of the bus but taking 45 minutes as opposed to the best part of a day and a night. If you do consider taking a plane, make sure of your seat well in advance—demand is high, and many flights booked solid in high season. Get further details from travel agents, and be sure to ask about the *Adria Airways* services as well as those run by *JAT*, since they are often a bit cheaper. Travel agents also handle reservations for *Adria* flights; for *JAT* details and reservations you need to go to a *JAT* office, which you can find in most large towns (we've listed addresses in the guide).

SLEEPING

Finding a bed for the night isn't as cheap as you might expect. For all kinds of accommodation two rates are levied: one for Yugoslavs (*domaće*), another for foreigners (*stranci*), which can be several times what Yugoslavs pay.

For easy reference the Yugoslav National Tourist Office produce annual foreigners' price lists for hotels, private rooms, and campgrounds nationwide. Prices are always quoted in dollars or Deutschmarks, but, while on the whole correct, shouldn't be taken too literally; in general we've used these prices in the guide but it's often the case that hotels have a handful of rooms available for a cheaper rate, especially outside the high season. One point to remember: for each night's accommodation you should be given a coupon. Although hotel authorities are increasingly lax on this matter, you should make sure you get one and keep it on your person. If you are stopped by the police it's your only proof you're not sleeping rough or in unlicensed rooms—both illegal.

HOTELS

Yugoslav **hotels** are classified A to D. Prices are strictly controlled and must be displayed clearly in your room, so there's little chance of getting ripped off—though the categories and price ranges can vary greatly from one part of the country to another. In general, expect to pay over the norm in the larger centers, while the same category room in a more rural area may offer more luxury for a lower price. Nowhere, however, are there any real bargains. As a general guide, reckon on spending $20–30 for a double room in the average C or D category hotel; facilities will be basic—a shared bathroom and infrequent supplies of hot water—but standards are generally kept well above the acceptable minimum. The more common B category hotels work out at $30–40 for a double. Room prices everywhere normally include the standard Yugoslav hotel breakfast of bread roll, triangle of cheese (or optional boiled egg), and coffee or teabag dunked in water.

Yugoslavia's burgeoning private enterprise culture has not yet produced very much in the way of **privately-run hotels**, but a few smaller *pansions* are springing up in the provinces, especially in the north. In Slovenia, particularly, there's much more of a tradition of wayside farmhouse inns keeping a few spare rooms for the occasional traveler straying off the beaten track.

We've quoted all hotel **prices** in US dollars. Although these figures are "official," out of the summer months, or when a hotel is empty, you may find things cheaper—especially if you're prepared to do a little under-the-counter bargaining.

PRIVATE ROOMS, YOUTH AND STUDENT HOSTELS

Private rooms (*sobe*) are a cheaper, more intimate option than hotels. Well organized and reliable, they will set you back $10–15 for a double room (single rooms are hard to come by and can cost almost as much), though it's wise to realize they can disappear at an alarming rate in season; if necessary book in advance. They're plentiful everywhere on the coast, and in the larger or more touristy centers countrywide, though many of the more remote places won't have any at all, the only local option being a hotel. They're available from the main local tourist office or travel agency, but in many places you might be offered one at the bus or train station, or on the coast at the ferry terminal. Don't be afraid to take a room offered in this manner—you avoid the tourist office surcharges and restrictions—but be sure to establish the price (bargain strenuously) and location clearly beforehand. In many coastal areas you'll also see signs for rooms in windows, often in German (*zimmer frei*). Freelance room-hunting in this manner is an especially good idea on the coast, where you're charged a thirty percent surcharge on the price of the room for staying less than four days.

Tourist offices also deal in **apartments**, which can work out slightly cheaper if there's a group of you—a four-person apartment goes for, very roughly, $30 a night. Also, in the countryside the renting of private rooms is often organized by local tourist offices under the title of *seoski turizam* (or in Slovenia *kmečki turizem*)—literally **village tourism**—by which local families are encouraged to take foreign visitors into their homes and offer them a slice of rural hospitality.

There are around thirty **youth hostels** (*FSJ Doms*) in Yugoslavia. They're mainly confined to larger cities, coastal resorts and more popular places inland, and can be a good way of cutting accommodation costs, though beware that many, especially on the coast, are filled up well in advance during the summer season.

Prices vary, but reckon on paying $5–8 per person per night. Technically you need to be a member of the Youth Hostel Association (YHA); however, if there's space most hostels will waive the rule and let you in for a few extra dinars. Curfews are common and strictly observed—you'll rarely be let in after midnight. For up-to-date details on Yugoslav hostels contact either the YHA in North America or the head office of the Yugoslav Youth Hostel Association, *Ferijalni Savez Jugoslavije*, Moše Pijade 12/V, Belgrade 11000.

An alternative to youth hostels is **student accommodation**, whereby student rooms are rented out cheap to travelers during the summer vacation—usually mid-July until the end of August. This varies from a bed in a student dormitory to a double room which can be up to the standard of a C-category hotel. Prices vary too: dormitory beds can cost under $10 a night; a double room in a student apartment might cost double that. It's a service largely aimed at Yugoslavs, and you might find raised eyebrows when you ask about it in tourist offices. But it's worth insisting, as in some towns it can be by far the least expensive alternative—it helps if you can wave a student card of some description. Whether the accommodation is actually available also tends to change from year to year; where it's reasonably constant we've listed details in the guide.

CAMPING AND OTHER OPTIONS

Campgrounds, known as *autocamps*, are plentiful on the coast and in the mountainous areas of the northwest, but again, outside of really touristy spots, are few and far between in the rest of the country. Where they exist at all, they're often huge affairs, with space for thousands of trailers, masses of facilities, stores, and so forth. The Yugoslav National Tourist Office publishes an annual booklet detailing grounds, facilities and prices, though there are many grounds not actually listed in here. Most tend to be open from around April until September/October, and you won't find much open at all during the winter months. As for prices, two people traveling with a tent can expect to pay a total of about $7; traveling with a car or motorcycle, add about $2 to that figure. **Camping rough** is illegal, and the police don't take too kindly to those they catch in the act—it's not worth taking the risk unless you have to.

If **staying with friends**, you are in theory supposed to register with the local *SUP* (or police) within 24 hours of arrival—a tedious bureaucratic procedure whereby your host must submit documents proving that they are the legal occupants of the house/flat in question. You are also supposed to sign out on departure. Attitudes to this differ; most Yugoslavs either don't know that such regulations exist or simply can't be bothered to abide by them. Should you be stopped and asked where you're staying, the chances are that the police will be similarly lax. However, if you're likely to be staying long-term, and are likely to attract the attention of a bored cop, it's best to register and save your hosts any potential embarrassment.

EATING AND DRINKING

Yugoslav food tends to be cheap and filling, with a distinctive variety of dishes that is one of the country's most enduring holdovers from its complex past.

Plenty of dishes are found nationwide—kebabs and goulash are well-known examples—but it's a cuisine spiced everywhere with regional variation: in Slovenia and northern Croatia the Austrian influence prevails, with starchy main courses and strudels; the Vojvodina sports a clear Hungarian strain; and in Serbia, Bosnia, and Macedonia, menus are tinged with Turkish flavors. Dalmatia and Istria remain firmly fishy—squid is cheap and delicious all the way down the coast with plentiful pasta pointing to the long-standing Italian connection. Prices vary from region to region: north of an invisible line between Dubrovnik and Belgrade things are likely to be more expensive; south of this—in Serbia and Macedonia—food gets markedly cheaper.

Either way, even on a tight budget you should be able to afford to eat in all but the really classy or heavily touristed restaurants.

SNACKS AND STREET FOOD

The most common Yugoslav **street snack** is the *burek*, a greasy Turkish-style pastry on which a good proportion of the nation starts the day. Sold at street kiosks in the mornings, and widespread in Serbia, Macedonia, and Bosnia, it comes most commonly with cheese (*sa sirom*) and meat (*sa mesom*), occasionally with apple (*sa jabukom*). In the north, hot dogs and sausages predominate; in Slovenia especially look out for *hrenovke* (hot dogs) or *klobase* (larger sausages). Other fast foods include the ubiquitous *ćevapčići*—little wads of spiced ground meat served in groups of ten with copious sprigs of green onion, *pljeskavica* (hamburger basically), and *ražnjići* (shish kebab). All of these are available from street stalls, but you'll find them equally on restaurant menus countrywide. Watch out also for *kukuruz* or corn on the cob, available from charcoal grills on street corners all over the country.

The number of **western-style fast-food** joints is on the increase: *McDonalds* opened its first outlet in Belgrade in 1988 and plans many more, and domestic chains are springing up in competition. If you've a preference for things less greasy, buy your own bread and cheese, meat, or pâté (in little plastic tubs marked *pašteta*) from a **supermarket**, or, failing that, get the delicatessen counter to make you up a sandwich—they normally oblige. Remember, too, that local **markets** contain a wealth of ridiculously cheap home-grown fruit and vegetables.

RESTAURANT FOOD

Sit-down eating is more expensive—though not much. The cheapest places to do it are a *bife* (a small snack-bar), *krčma* (traditional inn), or, more usually, an *Express Restaurant*—a self-service restaurant, not especially hospitable in look or feel, but which often serves much the same food as far more upscale places but at a fraction of the cost. Don't be put off by the dried-up look of most of the dishes laid out for display—just ask for a fresh plateful, the quality isn't bad for the prices.

More common is the *gostiona* or simple *restoran* (in Slovene, *gostilna* and *restavracija* respectively), where you can get a straight two-course meal for $5–8 with wine. On the menu, or *jelovnik*, starters are often described as *predjela*, and main courses sometimes divided into *gotova jela*, quickly-prepared dishes which are available in a few minutes, and *jela po narudžbini*—literally "dishes to order"—for which you have to wait a little longer.

WHAT TO EAT

Regular **appetizers** include *pršut* (Dalmatian smoked ham), delicious but expensive, a rich array of different broths, and *čorba*, a thick soup imported from Turkey many moons ago and now found mainly in the eastern reaches of the country—with bread, a meal in itself. Another staple starter-as-main meal is *pasulj*, a dense bean soup dotted with pieces of bacon or sausage.

Meat dishes predominate for the **main course**, with the grilled pork, lamb, and beef dishes traditionally associated with Serbian cuisine widespread throughout the country, the ubiquitous *pljeskavica* and *ćevapčiči* joined by a host of other rich, fatty dishes more often than not garnished with incendiary peppers and tomato-and-onion sauces. In Slovenia and northern Croatia, schnitzels and similar meat cutlets predominate, and everywhere inland the trout is good if you can find it. On the coast, the fish is excellent, with deep-fried squid an inexpensive standby all the way up the coast, and a range of grilled fish available in most restaurants. Whatever you choose, it'll almost invariably come with a handful of french fries (or in Serbia, a large bread cake called a *pogača*), to which you can add a couple of side salads for all to dig in. If at all possible, avoid eating in coastal hotels, where conventional wisdom maintains that tourists only want to eat what they have at home.

Pizzas are found in the larger centers more or less everywhere, and aren't bad generally, but these aside, **vegetarians** are going to have a hard time of it in much of the country. Specifically vegetarian restaurants as such don't exist at all in Yugoslavia, although most will make the effort to juggle the items on their menu to suit your needs if you ask them nicely. There are a number of meatless Yugoslav dishes, though most are little more than glorified starters: *gibanica* is a layered cheese pie, *pohovani sir* deep-fried cheese in breadcrumbs, *gljive na žaru* are grilled mushrooms (often served as a main course). There are also a number of eggplant- and pepper-based dishes found in Bosnia.

ICE CREAM AND DESSERTS

For sweeter teeth, there's Yugoslav **ice cream**, which enjoys a popularity here on a par with Italy. Every street corner has its *slastičarnica* or ice-cream parlor, dolloping out a kaleidoscopic range of flavors; a *kugla* is a scoop, a *kornet* a cone.

Slastičarnice also sell soft drinks, *burek*, yogurt, and **cakes and pastries**. The latter are usually very good, and again differ considerably from region to region—*strudels* to the north, Turkish *baklava* in the east, *palačinke* or crepes just about nationwide—but all share a characteristic Balkan sweetness and richness.

DRINKING

Recreational **drinking** is mainly done in a *kafana*, unpretentious places that serve both soft and alcoholic drinks. More expensive is a *caffe-bar* or *konoba*—dimly-lit young peoples' haunts, with loud music and standing room only.

COFFEE, TEA, SOFT DRINKS

Coffee is Turkish-style in Bosnia, Serbia, and Macedonia, thick with the grounds at the bottom, while in Croatia and Slovenia espresso or cappuccino are served.

Tea is normally served straight (with milk is *sa mlekom*, with lemon *sa limunom*), and although it's rarely more than a teabag dunked in hot water, it can be very good. Look out especially for the many herbal teas sold in supermarkets: *lipov čaj* (made from the leaves of the linden tree) and *planinski čaj* (literally "mountain tea," containing a variety of highland herbs) are two favorites.

A FOOD AND DRINK GLOSSARY

Basics

Hleb (Serb)	Bread	*Puter/Maslac*	Butter	*Biber*	Pepper
Kruh (Croat)		*Sečer*	Sugar	*Riba*	Fish
Voče	Fruit	*Sir*	Cheese	*Ulje*	Oil
Povrće	Vegetables	*So*	Salt	*Jaje*	Egg
Jogurt	Yoghurt	*Meso*	Meat	*Sirce*	Vinegar

Soups and starters

Supa/Juha	Soup (broth)	*Juha od povrča*	Vegetable soup	*Burek*	Cheese pastry
Čorba	Thick soup	*Pileča juha*	Chicken soup	*Prsut*	Smoked ham
Riblja čorba	Fish soup	*Govedja juha sa*	Beef soup with	*Kajgana*	Scrambled eggs
Borsč	Borscht	*jajem*	egg	*Pašteta*	Pate
	(Beetroot soup)				

Meat and poultry

Govedjina	Beef	*Jagnjetina*	Lamb	*Dzigerica/jetra*	Liver
Teletina	Veal	*Ovcetina*	Mutton	*Cufte*	Meatballs
Svinjetina	Pork	*Slanina*	Bacon	*Gulas*	Goulash
Piletina	Chicken	*Kobasice*	Sausages	*Bubrezi*	Kidneys
Šunka	Ham				

Fish

Barbun	Red mullet	*Pastrmka*	Trout	*Skusa*	Mackerel
Skampi	Shrimp	*Zubatac*	Bream	*Tunj*	Tuna
Lignji	Squid	*Bakalar*	Cod	*Skoljka*	Mussels
		Sardele	Sardines		

Dishes

Ćulbastija	Grilled veal or pork with pepper and onions	*Čevapčići*	Spiced ground meat rolls
		Mučkalica	Cubed steak in a hot, spicy sauce
Pljeskavica	Hamburger	*Pasticada*	Beef with dumplings, cooked with wine and plums
Ražnjici	Shish kebab		
Musaka	Layers of meat and eggplant	*Vesalice*	Intertwined strips of pork, sometimes *dimljene*, or smoked
Djuveć	Lamb or pork casserole with rice and tomatoes	*Odrezak*	Chop or cutlet, usually veal or pork
Punjene	Peppers stuffed with minced meat	*Snicla*	Breaded cutlet, or schnitzel
paprike	and tomato	*Karadjordje*	Breaded veal cutlet, rolled and
Sarme	Cabbage leaves stuffed with ground meat and rice	*va snicla*	stuffed with cheese (a Serbian specialty)

Vegetables

(Prženi)	(Fried)	*Kupus*	Cabbage	*Paprike*	Green peppers
Krompir	Potatoes	*Krastavac*	Pickle	*Grašak*	Peas
Beli Luk	Garlic	*Kiseli kupus*	Sauerkraut	*Paradajz*	Tomatoes
Pomfrit	French fries	*Kukuruz*	Corn on the Cob	*Pirinač/Risa*	Rice
Gljive/Pecurke/	Mushrooms	*Pasulj*	Beans, bean	*Plavi paradajz*	Eggplant
Sampinjons			soup	*Luk*	Onion

Salads

Salata	Salad	*Pržene paprike*	Grilled red and green peppers (usually pickled)
Zelena salata	Green salad	*Ljute papricice*	Smaller, hotter red peppers.
Mešana salata	Mixed salad	*Kiseli krastavci*	Pickled.
Srpska salata	"Serbian" salad; usually tomato, raw onion, and hot peppers.	*Ajvar*	Purée made from eggplant and red peppers
Šopska salata	Similar to "Serbian" salad, topped with a piquant soft cheese.		

Terms

Doručak	Breakfast	*Kuvano*	Boiled	*Peceno*	Roast
Ručak	Lunch	*Na rostilju/na*	Grilled	*Prženo*	Fried
Večera	Dinner	*zaru*		*Vruče/Hladno*	Hot/Cold

Basics

Narandza	Oranges	*Šljive*	Plums	*Lubenica*	Watermelon
Limun	Lemon	*Ananas*	Pineapple	*Visnja*	Sour cherry
Breskve	Peaches	*Grožđje*	Grapes	*Tresnja*	Sweet cherry
Krujške	Pears	*Dinja*	Melon	*Kajsija*	Apricot

Cheeses and Desserts

Kajmak	Curd cheese	*Krofna*	Doughnut
Gibanica	Layered cheese pie	*Pogača*	Dainty, slightly salty pastry, often eaten at breakfast
Vlasić	Mild sheep's cheese from Bosnia		
Paški Sir	Hard strong cheese from Pag	*Potica*	Traditional Slovene flaky pastry (usually filled with nuts or raisins)
Baklava	Turkish pastry with syrup		
Palačinke	Crepes		
Strudla	Strudel	*Struklji*	Slovene dumplings
Sladoled	Ice cream	*Sirovi struklji*	Cheese dumplings
Torta	Cake	*Slatko*	Exceptionally sweet fruit preserve, often served as accompaniment to coffee
Čokolada	Chocolate		
Kompot	Stewed fruit		

Drinks

(Mineralna)Voda	(Mineral) water	*Rakija*	Spirits	*Oporo*	Dry
Mleko	Milk	*Pivo*	Beer	*Prosek*	Aperitif
Kafa	Coffee	*Vino*	Wine	*Spricer*	White wine with soda/
Turska cava	Turkish coffee	*Crno vino*	Red wine		mineral water
Čaj	Tea	*Bijelo vino*	White wine		
Voćni sok	Fruit Juice	*Slatko*	Sweet	*Živeli*	Cheers!

Of other **nonalcoholic** refreshments, there are the usual international soft-drink brands like Pepsi, Coca-Cola and Schweppes, all made under license in Yugoslavia. Better than these, though, is the indigenous fruit juice or *voćni sok*. Ask for for *gusti* or "thick" *sok*, a natural, dense fruit pulp. Less widespread now, but still available in some parts of Macedonia and the south, is *boza*, a refreshing drink made from millet. Mineral water, known as *mineralna voda* and usually fizzy, is available everywhere, either by the bottle or the glass.

BEER

Beer normally comes by the half-liter bottle—either *domaće*, the local brew, or an international brand made under license such as *Tuborg*. Yugoslav beers are light, thirst-quenching, and deceptively strong: brands to look out for are the Slovene beers *Union* and *Zlatorog*, *Nikšičko* from Nikšič in Montenegro, *Karlovačko* in Croatia, and *Apatinsko* in Vojvodina. *Crno pivo*, a dark brew not unlike a mild ale, is occasionally found in the north. In Slovenia, beer is usually served in large glass tankards in Teutonic fashion—ask for *točeno pivo* for beer on tap, *steklenica* for a bottle. Wherever you're drinking, you'll find the beer brewed to near-German standards of purity, with little in the way of synthetic additives or preservatives.

WINE

Yugoslav wines are consistently good and very cheap, drunk by the *dva deci* (20cl) if you're just tasting, *pola litra* (50cl) or *litro* (1 liter); ask for a *flaša* if you want a bottle. Local rotgut (*domače vino*) costs $1.50–3.50 a bottle in a restaurant, less if bought from a supermarket, and in Slovenia, Croatia, and parts of northern Serbia—the more established wine-growing areas—it's rare that you'll get anything undrinkable.

In the north, of worldwide and *Liquor Barn* fame, there are the Slovenian *Rieslings*: *Laski*, a delicate wine, verging on the sweet, and *Renski*—drier, less fruity and by far the better of the two. In Dalmatia there are some pleasant whites, crisp dry wines like *Kaštelet*, *Grk*, and *Pošip*, as well as reds like the dark, heady *Dingač* from the Pelješac peninsula and *Babić* from Primošten. Istrian wines are excellent too—*Semion*, a bone-dry white, and *Teran*, a light, fresh red, are two of the best—and you should also try *Žlavka*, a medium-sweet white from Mostar, and Yugoslavia's most popular red wine, the Montenegrin *Vranac*. Of a number of sweet wines, there is *prošek*, a dessert wine that's best, they say, from Rab, but is found almost everywhere. A popular wine-based drink is *spricer*, white wine with soda or fizzy mineral water—

delicious and refreshing in the heat of the day; you can buy it by the glass or simply ask for a jug of mineral water with your wine.

SPIRITS AND FIREWATERS

You'll notice people starting the day with a down-in-one shot of strong **spirit** (*rakija*)—common practice just about everywhere. There's a strikingly complete array, best known of which is *Šljivovica*, a sharp, clear brandy made from plums—*Manastirka* is the brand-name to look out for if you're buying from a supermarket. *Prepečenica* is a double-strength version. In addition to *Šljivovica*, there are any number of other aromatic herb-infused spirits, many of them with medicinal properties. *Klekovača*—and its Slovene cousin *Brinjevec*—are juniper-based firewaters; *Travarica* is a blend of many different herbs and berries. *Vinjak* is the blanket term for locally-produced copies of French-style cognac, generally a little more expensive and smoother than the plum brandies but varying greatly from brand to brand. *Rubin* and *Slovin* are two good ones, but there are cheaper, rougher varieties. More authentic is *Lozovača*, a mind-frying brandy drunk in Montenegro and Dalmatia in preference to *Šljivovica*, and the widely drunk *Mastika*, distilled from mastic resin—a flavorsome drop, not unlike Greek ouzo. Well known too is *Maraskino*—from Zadar—a velvety smooth, very sweet cherry liqueur.

All spirits are very inexpensive, broadly around $2.50 a bottle from the supermarket, 35 cents a glass in a bar; home-distilled stuff on market stalls comes even cheaper—if you're adventurous enough to try it. The locally-produced ersatz rums and vodkas are generally not worth touching, but if you do need the solace of non-Yugoslav spirits remember that they're all cheaply available from the now widespread **duty-free shops**, though only for hard currency.

POLICE, TROUBLE, AND SEXUAL HARASSMENT

Known as Milicija— МИЛИЦИА **—Yugoslav police are generally easygoing and helpful. Stations are signposted and ☎92 is the universal emergency telephone number.**

Since tourism took off on the coast, Yugoslavia has lost much of its false image as a

dour land where the police wait to pounce on erring visitors. A few **guidelines** should be followed, however. Don't take photos of military camps or installations (usually indicated by a no-photography symbol), railroad stations, or bridges—if you're caught you may lose your film, possibly your camera, and go through all the attendant hassles. Carry your **passport** at all times—checking your entry visa often gives a bored cop something to do. At all official accommodation your passport should be exchanged for a daily *potvrda*, a date-stamped card that should be carried until you get your passport back, and then held on to until you leave the country—though many hotels and tourist agencies no longer bother with this, so don't panic if you never receive one. On the whole it's normally the case that the police are being no more than mildly inquisitive if they stop you. Be polite and friendly and ructions won't arise. If you do find yourself in trouble, wait until you can explain things to someone in English—a few ill-chosen words in a foreign language can cause a lot of misunderstanding.

Consulates vary in the amount of help they can offer; all the American consulate will do is refer you to local attornies, and only then very begrudgingly. They'll never—repeat never—lend you any cash if you've run out or been ripped off. You'll find addresses in our town listings.

SEXUAL HARASSMENT

Despite a social system which guarantees women equal wages and equal rights in the workplace, Yugoslavia is still very much a male-dominated country. Women traveling alone can expect to bump into familiar southern Mediterranean machismo almost everywhere – usually nothing too sinister but irritating enough at the best of times. Attitudes vary from the package vacation mentality of the Adriatic resorts, where all women travelers on their own are automatically regarded as "available" (the locals who swoop down on them are nicknamed *galebovi*, or seagulls), to the Islamic and more backward regions inland where women are treated with almost reverential respect one minute, and as mere peasant chattels the next. A suitably firm response should be enough to cope with most situations, although trying to answer back or trading comments only encourages farther hassle. Bear in mind that the local women have to put up with this all the time, copy what they do, and ignore the offenders in stony silence.

CHURCHES, MOSQUES, AND MUSEUMS

Yugoslavia's mixture of Orthodox, Catholic, and Muslim faiths provides a good variety of places of worship to explore. Freedom of religious belief is guaranteed by law, and although each of the faiths experienced a waning of worship during the postwar period, the resurgence in national identity in the 1980s has made them popular once more with the young.

CHURCHES AND MOSQUES

Concentrated in Macedonia, Montenegro, the Vojvodina, and Kosovo, and of course Serbia itself, the ancient **Serbian Orthodox** churches and monasteries have lost much of their monastic function and are open to visitors these days—though you'll find that the tradition of building them in the most beautiful and remote places has left many inaccessible today, at least without a car. In the Orthodox churches of the Middle Ages, elaborate **frescoes** formed an aid to worship, depicting biblical stories and fierce portraits of patron saints and the medieval monarchs. You'll

find an in-depth account of the churches and their art in the *Contexts* section at the end of the book, and individual monasteries are described throughout the guide.

The republics of Croatia and Slovenia practice the **Catholic** faith. Built during the Venetian occupation, many of the churches on the coast follow trends then current in Italy; scaled-down Romanesque, Gothic and Renaissance churches are one of the delights of the Adriatic, and everywhere you go Venetian-Gothic *campanili* dominate the skyline. Slovenia's churches went up when the Baroque style was in full swing, under the Austrians, and consequently don't pull any decorative punches. As in other parts of Catholic Europe, women are expected not to show too much bare flesh when entering churches.

Turkish domination of the Balkans means that there are also **mosques** dotted around the country, though you'll find by far the greatest concentrations in Bosnia, Kosovo, and Macedonia. The basic layout of a mosque is a carpet-covered square with a *mihrab* cut into the eastern end facing Mecca; from this niche the *imam* or priest leads the congregation in prayer, the women grouped behind the men on a balcony or behind a low balustrade. Occasionally, particularly in Bosnia where the Muslim faith is still dominant, you'll hear the *muezzin* singing the *ezan* or call to prayer from a minaret, though these days it's more usually relayed by a loudspeaker. The Islamic faith prohibits reproduction of the human form, with the result that the richest mosques are covered in passages from the Koran and non-figurative decoration of tiles and ornamented plaster. Normally it's only this and the size that distinguishes one mosque from the next. Visitors are allowed in major mosques, but are expected to observe certain proprieties: shoes should be removed before entering, women must cover their heads, and you may be asked to leave a small donation.

MUSEUMS AND GALLERIES

Yugoslavia's **museums** all too often go for collections of quantity rather than quality, and exclusively Serbo-Croatian labeling doesn't help matters. Generally speaking you'll find three main types. A **Narodni Muzej** or national museum is normally an archaeological or art collection gathered from around the republic; each republic usually has several such museums. A **Gradski (Mestni) Muzej** or town museum gives an account of a town's history through artifacts, fine art, and photos. Thirdly, there are **Liberation Museums**, which proliferate in almost every town and village, each relating World War II events with reference to the locality. They vary greatly in quality, layout, and accessibility, but

you should certainly see at least one—the best are in Belgrade and Sarajevo. Designed as much for didactic impact as historical record—you often pass phalanxes of schoolkids gaping at photos of Nazi atrocities—they are meant as a constant reminder of the Partisans' sacrifices during the war years.

After the war Yugoslavia laid heavy emphasis on the social function of art, initially giving rise to the dreary and poorly executed themes of Socialist Realism. Subsequent artists have expanded these techniques to encompass more liberal and experimental styles, but much of what you find in **modern galleries** tends to be heavily derivative, watered-down imitations of whatever was going on elsewhere in Europe at the time. To find something you enjoy you'll need to be very selective. **Naive art**, on the other hand, has become a peculiarly Yugoslav development, formally encouraged by the state and the country's major postwar movement. You'll see work by Generalić and Kovačić, the best-known of these artists, scattered around the galleries, and at its best in Zagreb and the village of Hlebine in northern Croatia.

Opening times of museums and galleries vary greatly, but as a rough rule they close on Monday, sometimes Sunday, and open 9am or 10am until noon or 1pm, and a couple of days a week for a few hours in the afternoon—4pm or 5pm until 6pm or 7pm. Ticket costs are negligible, but can often be halved by flashing a valid ISIC card. Full opening hours for each museum are detailed in the guide, though we've omitted mentioning entry fees.

MEDIA

Although many Yugoslav news kiosks seem increasingly well stocked with German titles, particularly women's fashion magazines, British and American newspapers are few and far between, mainly found in quickly sold quantities at the major coastal resorts and luxury hotels inland. Week-old copies of *Newsweek* are regularly sighted on one or two newsstands in Belgrade, Zagreb, and Ljubljana, but don't bank on getting your hands on anything else.

The Yugoslavs themselves produce two main English-language publications: *Yugoslav Review*,

a glossy magazine devoted to tourism and culture, though this now only appears sporadically; and *Yugoslav Life*, an unspeakably dull news monthly.

NEWSPAPERS AND MAGAZINES

Yugoslavia enjoyed something of a media explosion in the 1980s. Erosion of confidence in party and state has been accompanied by a gradual breakdown of **censorship**, making way for an increasingly rebellious and free-speaking press. This loosening of the reins hasn't been without its down-side: the local party bosses encourage the regionally-based magazines and newspapers to promote local issues, thus fanning the flames of the increasing inter-republican conflicts.

Of the "heavies," *Borba* is the only pan-Yugoslav daily **newspaper**, and as such offends everyone and pleases no one. Published by the Communist Party's front organization, the Socialist Alliance, its front page alternates between the Latin and Cyrillic scripts on a day-to-day basis.

All the other major dailies have a republican or even narrower regional base. The purely Cyrillic-script *Politika* — ПОЛИТИКА —acts as the voice of Serbia, waging constant polemical disputes with rivals like Zagreb's *Vjesnik*, Ljubljana's *Delo*, and the Split-based *Slobodna Dalmacija*.

Similarly, the country's two major **news magazines**, the Serbian *NIN (Nedeljne Informativne Novine* or "Weekly Informative News") and the Croatian *Danas* ("Today"), indulge in weekly mudslinging matches. In general, political control of the press is much fought over. Party bosses in Slovenia and Croatia have found it convenient to encourage the new atmosphere of liberalism, while in the south— and especially in problem areas like Kosovo— journalists are under much more pressure to toe the official line.

Yugoslavia's **youth press** has played a major role in breaking down censorship, opening up hitherto taboo subjects and leading campaigns against corrupt officials. Most important among them, and the only one so far to attain any real independence, is the weekly organ of the Slovene youth movement, *Mladina*. This still functions ostensibly as a youth-oriented countercultural rag, but its support for new social movements and democratic forces has allowed it to play a major role in influencing the political agenda of the last few years. Successive waves of provocative and stinging articles (revelations about the lifestyles of top party functionaries, criticism of the Yugoslav arms industry for its exports to Third World dictatorships, and attacks on the Yugoslav army for the potential threat it represented to the newly won Slovene liberalism) eventually persuaded the Slovene authorities that to try and silence *Mladina* would only serve to make it more popular—a public abandonment of censorship that was a watershed in the politics of the northern republic.

Belgrade's response to this was ham-fisted, putting three *Mladina* journalists and an army corporal on trial for allegedly handling military secrets in June 1988. The accused were found guilty and each sentenced to a few months in prison, and the trial aroused indignation in Slovenia, considerably worsening relations with the rest of the federation. Since then, *Mladina* has continued to thrive, and has been joined by other reform-minded publications, most prominently *Demokracija*, an independent weekly.

The other branch of the media which has taken advantage of the relaxation of censorship is the **pornography** industry. A new generation of harder, more exploitative titles has hit the newsstands in the last year or two, headed by the glossy and unimaginatively titled *Sexy-Erotika*. There's also talk of a Yugoslav-language version of *Playboy*.

Fashion and style magazines are thin on the ground, but it's well worth tracking down the Ljubljana-based *AV*, a glossy quarterly devoted to fashion, architecture, photography, and design, which backs up its plans to become a Europe-wide title of the *Vogue* variety by producing an English-language edition. Elsewhere, the cultural pages of Zagreb's *Start* present a passable rip-off of western style magazines, although its distinctly retrograde front cover invariably features an unclad female.

TELEVISION AND RADIO

The dubious delights of pan-European porn have also found their way into the country's **television** schedules, with Yugoslavia's main two channels now joined by a third station largely devoted to foreign cable and satellite sources. The nightly melange of pop videos, variety programs, and Italian porno flicks does sometimes yield a few welcome surprises—such as CNN news in English in some areas. Some major TV stations in Belgrade, Zagreb, and Ljubljana have also begun to broadcast nightly **news bulletins in English** over the summer. Timings vary from one evening to the next, but they usually fall somewhere between 8pm and 10pm.

Yugoslav **radio** is hard to categorize. The major regional stations, dominated by talk and middlebrow culture, are supplemented by an extensive local network—often the best places to catch the indigenous folk music. The number of FM stations, funded by advertising and concentrating on western pop, is increasing sharply. A major feature of the airwaves in Ljubljana and Zagreb is student radio, offering a popular mixture of more "alternative" music and pungent political comment. Details of **English broadcasts** in major towns and cities are given in the "Listings" sections throughout the guide. Failing that you can pick up the BBC World Service throughout the day on a variety of short wave bands.

FESTIVALS AND OTHER ENTERTAINMENT

Yugoslavia is home to a staggering number of festivals and annual celebrations, some of them traditional, others more recently invented arts binges. Most take place during the summer and are centered around the country's most beautiful towns or buildings.

FESTIVALS AND ANNUAL CELEBRATIONS

One of the most important of Yugoslavia's **festivals** is the **Dubrovnik Festival**, which runs from July 10 until August 25, a series of concerts, ballet, and drama played against a backdrop of the city's historic monuments. If artists are not exactly in the top line internationally, the performances are usually first-rate, though inevitably the main magic is the settings, which utilize the city's loveliest courtyards and palaces. The Yugoslav National Tourist Office can normally provide details of the Dubrovnik schedule well in advance.

Ohrid's Summer Festival, held between July 12 and August 20, is not nearly so prestigious, but still worth catching: concerts are held in the old churches and the Balkan Festival of Folk Music and Dance finds an outlet in Ohrid's

fortress. **Struga**, nearby, hosts a **Poetry Festival** at the end of August—an event invariably attended by poets of international repute. Also worth looking out for if you're in pursuit of high culture are the **Ljubljana Summer Festival**, a series of opera, classical music, and ballet events running from mid-June until mid-September; the **Zagreb Summer**, a series of plays and concerts in the squares and courtyards of the old town from June through to August; and **Zadar's** concerts in St Donat's Church and **Šibenik's** concerts in the cathedral, both in July and August. And from mid-July until mid-August, the **Split Summer Festival**, a mixed bag of music, opera, ballet, and folklore happenings, is worth checking out if you're in the vicinity.

FOLKLORE AND ANCIENT CUSTOMS

Of festivals devoted solely to folklore, Zagreb's **International Folklore Festival** in July is probably the biggest. In addition there are a host of other **traditional events**, including some specifically tourist-geared, and designed to slot into vacation schedules. "Peasant" weddings, mass ceremonies in full costume, are most common: you come across them in **Plitvice** in the last week of May, **Ljubljana** in late June, and **Bohinj Galičnik** in the second week of July. Other **ancient customs and ceremonies** abound, though it's true that many are sustained by the tourist dollar. Each Thursday between May and September in **Korčula**, *Moreška* sword dances take place, lively, colorful dance theater from the sixteenth century; **Sinj's** *Alka Sinjska*, a furious joust-like competition, happens on August 15; and **Ptuj's** Kurenti Processions, weird ceremonies dating from pre-Christian times, take to the streets in late February–early March. Exact times and forums can be found in local tourist offices.

AGRICULTURAL FAIRS AND FEASTS

For more direct contact with local traditions and customs, there's a whole series of autumn agricultural fairs, often connected with the harvest.

They usually feature processions in traditional costume, but also provide a good excuse for excessive outdoor eating, drinking and dancing. In **Subotica**, the grain harvest in mid-September is marked by the **Dužijanca**, a festival linked with a distinct community of Vojvodina Catholics, the *bunjevci*. Elsewhere in Vojvodina, the **Vršac fair** celebrates the grape harvest in an atmosphere of unrestrained hedonism. The two biggest and most famous agricultural fairs in Serbia are at **Negotin** in the last two weeks of September (again marking the grape harvest), and at **Šabac**, usually around September 21.

In Slovenia the onset of autumn is marked by a series of *veselice*, or **public feasts**, another excuse for outdoor revelry organized in small towns by local guilds and professional organizations—more often than not the town fire brigade, which proudly turns out in antiquated uniforms. Look out for roadside posters advertising precise dates.

CARNIVAL AND NEW YEAR

In Catholic areas of Yugoslavia many towns also still observe the tradition of the **Carnival** immediately prior to Lent. While not as spectacular as similar events elsewhere in Europe or Latin America, they feature a wealth of masks, costumes, and the usual orgy of over consumption. In **Ljubljana** the carnival is known as *Pust*, and covers a long weekend finishing on *pustni torek* or Shrove Tuesday. In Croatia, the best-attended carnivals are in **Gorica** and **Samobor**, two small market towns within easy reach of Zagreb.

If you're in Yugoslavia over the **New Year** (*nova godina*), most large hotels and restaurants organize big New Year's Eve parties, kitschy affairs featuring a live dance band and a sit-down meal. These are advertised as *silvestrovanje* in Slovenia, and *doček nove godine* in the rest of the country. In Orthodox areas, seasonal merry-making is supplemented by further celebrations on January 6 and 13—Christmas Eve and New Year's Eve according to the Julian calendar.

MUSIC AND DANCE

A fuller account of Yugoslavia's diverse music appears in the *Contexts* section of the guide, where you'll also find details on venues, festivals, and available records. Suffice it to say here that the music you're likely to encounter on your travels is as colorful and varied as Yugoslavia's complex past and regional differences suggest.

Much of the country's grassroots **musical tradition** has been sacrificed to the likes of Michael Jackson and U2, but folk singing and dancing have proved surprisingly resilient in almost all areas. Whenever you chance upon a wedding or saint's day celebration there's bound to be much festivity; even the performances put on by the tourist board are a lot less contrived and more enjoyable than you might imagine. Near Eastern influences predominate in the folk music of much of the interior, with fast-running codas on wind instruments and notes rising in quarter tones. Everywhere the accordion has all but replaced traditional instruments, but the melodies and rhythms of ethnic music have to some extent been preserved in a modern, popular variant, *novokomponovana narodna muzika*, or "newly composed folk music," which can be heard in bars and buses all over the southern republics, and enjoys a role and popularity similar to that of Country and Western in the USA.

Most Yugoslavs beyond kindergarten age know at least the rudiments of **dance**, and it's been part of the folk idiom for so long that it's quick to surface at any celebration. The **kolo** (*oro* in Macedonia) is almost the national dance. A linking of hands and moving slowly in a line or circle, it has myriad permutations and complexities, and though often accompanied by Turkish-style music, the leader of the *kolo* clenches his right fist behind his back—a symbol of secret defiance against Turkish rule. In each region, practically in each village, the *kolo* developed along individual lines, often for a specific purpose; as well as celebration, it was danced to ward off evil spirits, to bring fertility to a newly married couple, to bless the sowing of a spring crop, or celebrate the harvest. The more frenetic, syncopated *cocek* is also found in many areas of the south, a dance of hedonistic abandon which has its roots in Middle Eastern belly dancing.

The best place to find music and dance nearest the original is **Macedonia**: Macedonians seem to burst into song at the slightest excuse, and dancing is an inevitable accompaniment to an evening's drinking. Express any interest and you'll be dragged in. Before you fall over, remember that, for the Macedonians, to dance well is a sign of honor.

Yugoslav **rock and pop** is largely a pale imitation of the west, what originality there is coming from the Slavic lyricism of the local word-smiths rather than the music itself. On the whole the domestic scene is surprisingly inward-looking, and leaving aside the odd one hit wonder, Ljubljana is the only city to have thrown up groups (notably Laibach and Borghesia) capable of competing with the western music industry on its own terms. Western music dominates the airwaves, and major western acts do occasionally get this far, playing the big sports halls in Ljubljana, Zagreb, and to a lesser extent Belgrade. Check listings details throughout the guide for more pointers.

Jazz has a wide and knowledgeable following among urban Yugoslavs, but places to catch live music are few and far between. The country's main international jazz festival is probably the one in Zagreb in mid-October, after which many of the participants move on to the festival in Belgrade during mid-November.

FILM

Going to the **movies** is the main source of recreation for young urban Yugoslavs. Theaters are cheap, but often overcrowded and extremely noisy. Major international films usually arrive two or three months after release elsewhere in Europe, but they are almost invariably subtitled rather than overdubbed, so you can easily follow the (usually) Anglo-American original. Major cities often have a *kinoteka*, which programs Hollywood classics, art-house movies, and cult films. The rest of Yugoslavia's film diet always includes a large slice of soft porn, usually from Italy or Scandinavia.

Domestic production has fallen off in recent years due to financial restrictions imposed by the crisis, and the Yugoslav film industry has been largely relegated to the position of cut-price location for European and American productions. However there's still a great deal of quality—and it can be an excellent introduction to Yugoslav mores and mentality if you can deal with the language barrier. Like other branches of Yugoslav culture, the cinema has benefited from the gradual breakdown of censorship throughout the

1980s, and has played a significant part in opening up areas of the country's past previously considered to have been taboo. The dark days of the late 1940s, when many innocents fell victim to an overly-paranoid secret police, have been revisited by films like **Živko Nikolić**'s *U imenu naroda* (*In the Name of the People*). However, it's in poignant, earthy domestic dramas that the industry's real strengths lie. Unfortunately little of this really travels well. The Sarajevo-based director, **Emir Kusturica**, is perhaps the only Yugoslav filmmaker whose work has enjoyed international success over the last decade; his *Otac na službenom putu* (*When Father Was Away on Business*), the story of a painful childhood spent in the Sarajevo of the 1950s, was declared best film at the Cannes film festival in 1985. He also won the prize for best director at Cannes in 1989, with his most recent movie, *Dom za vešanje* (*The Time of the Gypsies*)—a long, at times dream like parable about the international trade in gypsy children, transported across the Italian-Yugoslav border to be sold into virtual slavery as pickpockets.

Yugoslavia's **film festivals** are largely concerned with domestic work and don't offer much to the foreign visitor. Major home-produced films compete every year at the Pula festival in August, shown to vast audiences inside the Roman amphitheater. Tickets, however, are hard to come by.

THEATER

Theater in Yugoslavia is subsidized and cheap, and there are very few towns without a major program. There is, however, aside from major festivals, precious little in English, although a lot of modern Yugoslav drama is accessible to non-speakers of the language through its progression away from text-based theater towards a much wider spectacle of music and movement. Best known exponents of the avantgarde are the *Slovene Youth Theater* and *Red Pilot*, both based in Ljubljana; Sarajevo's *Tattoo Theater* (regular visitors to the Edinburgh Festival); and the Dubrovnik-based *Lero*—all of whom travel extensively.

SPORTS

Yugoslavia consistently enjoys Olympic success in team events such as basketball, waterpolo, and handball—sports which are played in most schools and given wide coverage on television. However, it is the country's biggest spectator sport, soccer, which provides Yugoslavs with the main arena in which to express their regional rivalries and tensions.

SOCCER

Most of the major honors in the Yugoslav soccer league are shared out by the **big four** clubs: *Dinamo Zagreb, Hajduk Split*, and the two Belgrade teams, *Crvena zvezda* (Red Star) and *Partizan* (the army team). Games between them are colorful, noisy, passionate affairs not to be missed. Matches usually take place on Sunday afternoons—although major contests are sometimes switched to Saturday.

However, despite receiving a morale boost from the national team's qualification for the 1990 World Cup, the domestic game has been in the doldrums for some time. One problem has been the extent of **bribery and corruption** in the sport, which is known incontrovertibly to exist but has proven hard to eliminate. The 1986 season ended with no less than ten first division clubs being penalized for agreeing their end-of-season results in advance, a dispute which dragged on through the courts for months. A similar saga occurred in 1988, when the *Čelik* squad, from the steeltown of Zenica in Bosnia, tried to avoid relegation to a lower division by paying their adversaries to lose. Unfortunately, with soccer's ruling body composed of two delegates each from the six republics and two autonomous provinces, the controversies are never satisfactorily resolved, local pride usually taking the place of desire for justice.

In recent seasons, a spate of **hooliganism** has added to soccer's woes. Some of the worst offenders are from Split, where *Hajduk* are soon to finish a three-year ban from European competition. Fans of the big four teams tend to model themselves on their western European counterparts, with hard-core *Red Star* supporters even calling themselves the *Ultras* in imitation of followers of *Real Madrid*. Nationalist tensions have played their part in exacerbating the problem; groups of fans traveling between matches are nowadays accompanied by the kind of police presence that in other countries is reserved for the visiting English.

SKIING

Yugoslavia's **ski resorts** offer all the amenities of neighboring Austria and Italy at a fraction of the cost. Well-appointed complexes are dotted throughout Slovenia, the major one being at Kranjska Gora, while in Bosnia the Olympic leftovers at Sarajevo have suffered from a lack of investment since the 1984 games. Recent developments in Serbia, notably the showpiece resort of Kopaonik, are also worth investigating. Local tourist offices will rent out equipment and sell bargain "season tickets" for ski-lifts, etc. For a full lowdown on all Slovenia's winter resorts, see p.60.

HIKING

Although the Yugoslavs aren't great hikers themselves, the country offers some of the finest and most unspoiled **walking and hiking** terrain in Europe. The most popular and best-equipped area is western Slovenia's Julian Alps, with the Triglav National Park pulling in hordes of walkers all year round. But the mountains of Bosnia, Montenegro, and Macedonia are no less rewarding, and here you'll be much more on your own. Snow can stay on the Julian Alps well into July, making walking on the upper reaches without ice axe and crampons difficult but not impossible. The central Yugoslav mountains are generally free of snow by June/July. As you proceed south, the heat can get pretty oppressive during the summer, so always carry plenty of water.

In Slovenia, the **mountain huts** are efficiently run and thick on the ground (*planinarski dom* is the phrase to look out for). Elsewhere, except for in a major national park such as Durmitor in Montenegro, they're something of a rarity. Although camping rough is technically illegal, up in the mountains it seems to be accepted by police and villagers alike. **Water** in the highlands is generally safe to drink—often coming from wells sunk in the limestone, where the knack of swinging the bucket is not as easy as it looks.

You'll find specific details of the suggested **hiking routes** throughout the guide. These are intended more as pointers than a definitive guide, and you'll certainly need much larger-scale maps than the ones we've been able to print. For details of hiking maps, see "Information and Maps."

OTHER PARTICIPATORY SPORTS

Facilities for **windsurfing, sailing, tennis, and other recreational sports** are well provided on the coast throughout the summer. Many of the larger vacation complexes have these facilities on site. Most major towns and cities inland have indoor sports and swimming facilities, mentioned in city "Listings" sections throughout the guide. **Hunting**, if it can be called a sport, is eagerly pushed by tourist offices in inland Yugoslavia (especially Slovenia and Vojvodina) desperate to attract big-spending groups. You're more likely to be enticed by outdoor pursuits such as **canoeing, kayaking, and rafting;** the Slovene whitewater rivers Soca, upper Sava and Krka are popular sites. For information on the first two, contact the tourist offices in Bled, Bohinj, Bovec, and Radovljica; for details on the Krka River, write to Turističko Društvo Kajak-kanu, 68360 Žužemberk. For rafting on the rivers Drina and Tara farther south, see p.277.

DIRECTORY

ADDRESSES The street name always comes before the number. The Serbo-Croatian word for street, *ulica*, is either abbreviated to *ul*, or, more often than not (as in our text), omitted altogether. In some cases you will come across the name of the street followed by the letters bb, which simply means *bez broja* or "without a number" – this usually refers to a newly constructed building which hasn't been fitted into the street's numbering system.

AIRPORT TAX This is charged at all Yugoslav airports as you leave, unless you're on a package charter flight, so keep $2–3 worth of local currency handy.

BEACHES Yugoslavia's rocky coastline isn't well blessed with beaches, and you'll find that when tourist offices refer to a beach, they frequently mean rocks; at best beaches are pebbles or shingle, and expanses of sand are very rare, confined more to the south end of the coast. On the plus side, the rocks are often concreted over for comfort, and the water is always clean and clear. See also "Nudism," below.

CAMPING GAS Cartridges for the smallest camping stoves are sometimes difficult to find in Yugoslavia. Bring your own supply or a large-cylinder stove.

CIGARETTES Turkish-type tobaccos grown in Macedonia and Serbia make for some flavorsome and very cheap cigarettes, although regulations governing quality control and tar content are far from stringent. Popular local brands are *Drina*, *57*, and the milder *Ronhill*. Western cigarettes such as *Kent*, *Winston*, *Marlboro*, and *Dunhill* are made here under license but they're more expensive—though most towns have a duty free shop on the main commercial street where you can get the original article at half the cost.

CONTRACEPTIVES Barbaric-looking, Czech-produced condoms (*kondomi*, or more colloquially, *gumice*) are sold in kiosks, less openly so in Catholic areas, although the onset of the AIDS era has rendered such things more visible. The Pill (*pilula*) is hard to get hold of without a prescription; bring your own.

ELECTRIC POWER 220 volts, out of round, two-pin plugs of the continental variety. Equip yourself with an adaptor and transformer before leaving home.

EMERGENCIES Countrywide, the numbers to phone for Police and Ambulance are respectively ☎92 and ☎94. The breakdown number for the Yugoslav auto club (AMSJ) is ☎987.

FILM Domestic color films are poor in quality, imported ones expensive, so stock up before you leave. Bear in mind that you're only officially allowed to import five rolls, but the ubiquitous duty-free shops are good places to replenish your stocks.

GAY LIFE No real "scene" as such, and the fact that homosexuality is illegal in all but two of the republics—Slovenia and Croatia—means that places to make contacts are few and usually outdoors. In Ljubljana, gay and lesbian groups have come to the fore in recent years, fighting for recognition under the aegis of the Slovene youth movement (see Ljubljana "Listings" on p.48). In the traditionally-minded south and east, however, the existence of homosexuality is hardly acknowledged at all.

LAUNDRY Laundromats don't exist, and you're confined to utilizing your landlady's sink or washing machine (in private rooms) or getting it done in your hotel—an expensive business.

NUDISM A Big Thing in Yugoslavia, and long officially encouraged in an attempt to open up the country to the West and dispel all myths of socialist puritanism. Every resort has its official naturist beach—denoted by the intials FKK—and stripping off in secluded places is rarely frowned upon. The biggest nudist campground is at Vrsar in Istria; others are scattered up and down the entire coast.

PUBLIC HOLIDAYS Almost all stores, offices, and banks, along with many museums, are closed nationwide on the following days: January 2; May 1 and 2; July 4 (Partisan Day); November 29 and 30 (Republic Day). Each of the republics celebrates the day of its uprising in 1941 with a holiday: Serbia, July 7; Montenegro, July 13; Slovenia, July 22; Croatia and Bosnia-Hercegovina, July 22; Macedonia, August 2 and October 11. December 25 is a public holiday in Slovenia only.

RAZORS Time was when you could pay your hotel bills in Yugoslavia with a few packets of Gillette razor-blades: even today the domestic brands (marketed with such endearingly naive names as Gilbert) are pretty useless and twin blades a rarity—best to bring your own. As an alternative, getting a shave at a barber shop isn't expensive and is wonderfully luxurious.

STORES AND OPENING HOURS Big-city stores and supermarkets have taken to western ways and open Monday to Friday 8am to 8pm ("Non-Stop" they proclaim), Saturday 8am to 3pm. In smaller places, and as you head south, shops tend to follow the tradition of early morning and late afternoon hours: roughly 7am to noon and 5 to 8pm. Markets kick off at around 5:30am. Banking hours are 7am to 7pm, Saturday 7am to 1pm, but can vary locally. Post offices open Monday–Saturday 7am to 7pm, with variable Sunday hours in big cities. Recent years have seen an incredible mushrooming of so-called duty-free shops, and now almost every town has one. Here you can stock up on any amount of western smokes, booze, toiletries, and film at genuinely duty free prices, providing you've got the hard currency to pay for it—dinars are not accepted. Incidentally, the initials "VI" next to the name of the shop denotes a privately owned (as opposed to state-owned) shop.

TAMPONS Only sporadically available from pharmacies and large city department stores, so it's a good idea to bring supplies. Feminine hygiene products manufactured in Slovenia, available throughout the country, are beginning to approach western standards of quality and comfort.

PART TWO

THE
GUIDE

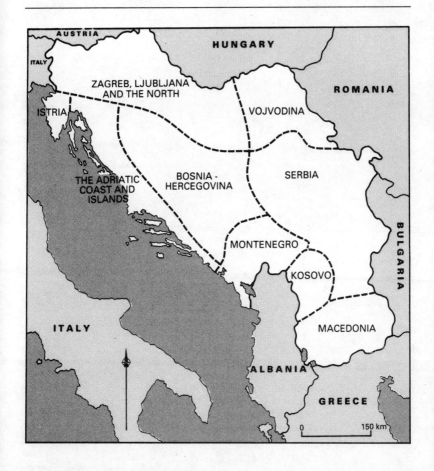

CHAPTER ONE

LJUBLJANA, ZAGREB, AND THE NORTH

A rriving by road or rail, **the North**—a serviceable label for the stretch of land that takes in most of Slovenia and the top of Croatia—is the first most people see of Yugoslavia. Initially **Slovenia** doesn't seem that different from northern Italy or Austria, yet historically and culturally the Slovenes are a people apart. While much of the rest of the country was under Turkish control, what's now Slovenia was a feudal state administered by Austrian and German overlords, eventually becoming part of the Austro-Hungarian Empire. The Slovenes absorbed the culture of their captors but maintained a strong sense of regional identity through the Slovene language, which was (and is) rather different from Serbo-Croat.

Economically and industrially the North is miles ahead of the rest of Yugoslavia, with higher wages, lower unemployment, and a more westernized lifestyle. That they're rich uncle to the other republics leads to disgruntled complaints from Slovenes in particular that their taxes are channeled into development programs for poorer areas like Kosovo, but by and large things progress smoothly and efficiently here: shops are well stocked, tourist facilities are excellent, and buying a bus ticket isn't the ugly brawl often experienced elsewhere.

The political scene is the most liberal in the country, and in recent years "alternative" political parties have mushroomed. However Slovenia is currently at loggerheads with Serbia, reacting to what it sees as Serbian expansionism; in 1989 the Republic's parliament voted itself the right to secede from the federation of republics that constitutes Yugoslavia—a grandiose gesture that made international news, and one not ignored in Belgrade. Similarly, Serbian nationalism has alienated the Croatians, dangerously re-awakening an old enmity. In the final analysis, while Slovenia feels itself pulled towards Austria and membership of the European Community, its wealth is created by having a captive economic hinterland in Yugoslavia for the electrical and technical goods it manufactures (*Gorenje*, makers of washing machines and domestic appliances, and *Iskra*, manufacturers of telephones and computers, are both Slovenia-based). The financial reality is that Slovenia would find life outside the federation far more competitive and difficult than some of its separatist apologists believe.

On a more superficial level, the North is a useful introduction to the country as a whole. The landscape is as varied as it is beautiful: along the Austrian

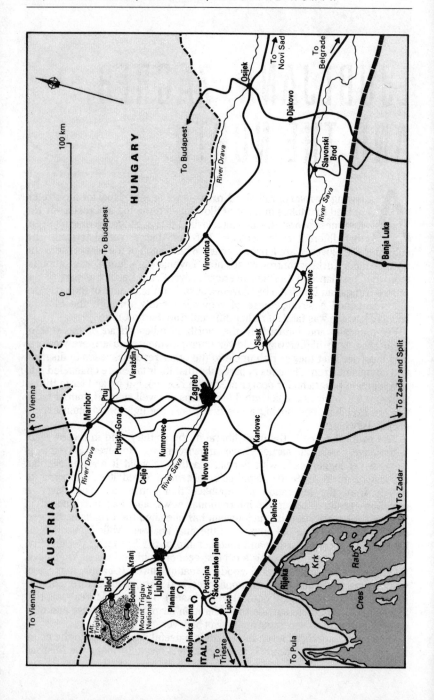

border the **Julian Alps** provide stunning mountain scenery and skiing at a fraction of Austrian or Swiss prices; farther south is the brittle, dry karst landscape riddled with spectacular caves like those at **Postojna**. Slovenia's capital **Ljubljana** is best of the cities, a vital, youthful place cluttered with Baroque and Hapsburg buildings, followed closely by **Zagreb**, the urbane capital of Croatia with a bristling nightlife and an explorable old core. Between runs a broad corridor of lush hills dunked in the plain, dotted with white-walled farmhouses and acres of vineyards—industry remaining thankfully and carefully hidden away.

Ljubljana

LJUBLJANA curls under its castle-topped hill, an old quarter marooned in the shapeless modernity that stretches out across the plain. It's most people's favorite place in the North, which in a way is odd: Ptuj is prettier, Maribor is equally old, Zagreb has finer museums and churches. Where Ljubljana tops them is in its vitality, and self-conscious air of being the growing capital of a rich and industrious republic. At first glance it seems Austrian, a few strands of Vienna pulled out of place, typically exuberant and refined; but Ljubljana is really Slovenian through and through, with outside influences absorbed and tinkered with over the years. What follows is an account of the center, but that is only part of the picture; first and foremost Ljubljana is a place to meet people, to get involved in the nightlife—the buildings just provide the backdrop.

Orientation and Getting Around

Ljubljana's main point of reference is **Titova Cesta**, a busy north–south thoroughfare that slices the city down the middle. Most of the sights are within easy walking distance from here, with the **Old Town** straddling the River Ljubljanica to the south and east, and sedate nineteenth-century squares with the principal museums and galleries to the west.

Ljubljana's **buses** are cheap, frequent, and usually overcrowded. Payment is made by thrusting a wad of notes into a box next to the driver (the price of a flat fare is constantly rising but clearly marked), or by using the slightly cheaper **tokens** (*žetoni*) available from most kiosks.

> The Ljubljana area telephone code is ☎061

Arrival, Information, and Accommodation

Your likely point of arrival (and the drop-off point for the *JAT* bus from Brnik airport) is the city's main **train and bus station**, ten minutes' walk to the north and east of Titova Cesta on Trg Osvobodilne Fronte. In the train station there's an **information office** run by *Slovenijaturist* (daily 6am–10pm), only useful for getting a town map, changing money, or buying international rail tickets. Far better to head straight for the **Tourist Information Center** (TIC) at Titova Cesta 11 (April–Sept Mon–Fri 8am–9pm, Sat & Sun 8am–noon & 5–9pm; Oct–March Mon–Fri 8am–7pm, Sat & Sun 8am–noon & 4–7pm; ☎224-222 or ☎215-412), a short #2 or #9 bus ride or fifteen-minute walk away.

The TIC can provide **private rooms** for $11 a double, though these tend to be in high-rise projects well out of the center of town: a much better option, from the beginning of July to the end of August, is to utilize rooms in **student hostels**. The main outlet for these is usually the *Studentsko Naselje* (Student Village) at Cesta 27 Aprila 31 (☎223-811; bus #14 or a twenty-minute walk), in a suburb to the west of town. It's important that you check at the TIC first, as host facilities change regularly. One that may provide rooms all year is the *Zvezni Center za Izobraževanje Gradbenih Instruktorjev* at Kardeljeva Ploščad 27 (☎342-671), north of downtown in Bežigrad (buses #6, #8, #21).

Farther out in the same direction, the **campground** can be reached by taking bus #8 north along Titova until it reaches its terminal at JEŽICA (☎371-382; May–Sept; $6 per person). It's situated in a pleasant recreation area and has a few bungalows with double rooms for $33.

Hotels

Should you arrive out of the season for student rooms, or want something a little more luxurious, Ljubljana is well stocked with hotels. The following are listed in order of expense.

Ilirija, Trg Prekomorskih Brigad 4 (☎551-162). Basic no-frills accommodation 2.5km northwest of the city center off Celovška Cesta; check with the TIC for directions and room availability. Double rooms $18.

Park, Tabor 9 (☎316-777). Basic, but conveniently near the station. Doubles $25.

Bellevue, Pod Gozdom 12 (☎313-133). Very small, and with few amenities, but occupying a beautiful old building above Tivoli Park with a breathtaking view across Ljubljana. Doubles $32.

Pansion Mrak, Rimska 4 (☎223-412). Cheapest place downtown. Doubles $34.

Union, Miklošičeva 1 (☎212-133), and the *Slon*, Titova 10 (☎211-232). Two B category hotels that retain a little of the old Central European atmosphere. Doubles $55.

Kompas, Miklošičeva 9 (☎326-061). Central modern hotel. Doubles from $55.

Tourist, Dalmatinova 13 (☎322-043). Well situated near the heart of things, but a little bland. Doubles $55.

Lev, Vošnjakova 1 (☎310-555). Ljubljana's most affordable luxury hotel. Doubles from $55.

Holiday Inn, Miklošičeva 3 (☎211-434). International luxury at unjustifiable prices. From $80 single, $122 double.

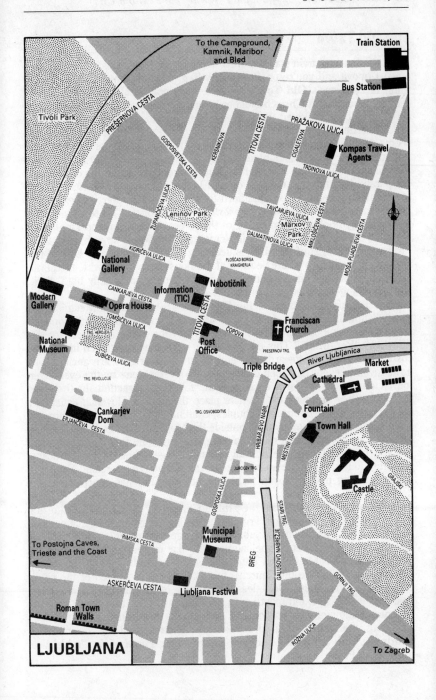

LJUBLJANA

The Old Town

From the bus and train stations, walk south down Titova Cesta, then cut left down Copova and you're on **Prešernov Trg**, the hub around which everything in Ljubljana's **Old Town** revolves. Overlooking all, the seventeenth-century **Franciscan Church** blushes a sandy red above the bustling square and the Ljubljanica River: in its tired-feeling interior the old wall paintings look like faded photographs, and even Francesco Robba's Baroque high altar seems a little weary. Robba was an Italian architect and sculptor brought in to remodel the city in its eighteenth-century heyday. Ljubljana lay between Austria and Italy on one side, Central Europe and the East on the other; traders passed through and stopped off and Ljubljana got rich—so rich that by the eighteenth century it could afford to indulge itself in Baroque excesses. Across the nineteenth-century *Tromostovje* ("triple bridge") a **fountain**, also by Robba, symbolizes the meeting of the rivers Sava, Krka, and Ljubljanica (he stole the idea from a Bernini in Rome), and the whole stretch down from Prešernov Trg west of the river is decaying Baroque grandeur. East of the river along Gallusovo Nabrežje most of the houses are ramshackle medieval, occasionally slicked up as clothes shops and stores but mainly high, dark, and crumbling—memories of an earlier, less fanciful past.

Opposite Robba's fountain is the **Magistrat** (Town Hall) on Mestni Trg—an undistinguished Baroque building around a courtyard (which contains another, more modest fountain by Robba), and the scene each year for the **"Country Weddings."** This mass wedding ceremony conducted in peasant costume takes place towards the end of June; its origins are ancient, but nowadays the event has been dragged out to over a week by the ever-eager tourist authorities to form a convenient "folklore" attraction. In the days preceding the ceremony events take place throughout Slovenia, usually in the presence of the bethrothed couples, culminating in a procession through Ljubljana and the ceremony itself outside the Magistrat. It's undeniably colorful and good-natured, with much dancing, drinking, and folk-music concerts, yet you can't help but feel it's all a fraud, staged more for the vidcam-clutching tourists than the unfortunate couples. If you're interested—and it *is* worth catching if you happen to be around—the TIC has exact dates and details.

A little east of the Magistrat the **Stolna Cerkev Sv Nikolaja** (St Nikolas's Cathedral) on Ciril-Metodov Trg is, depending on your tastes, the most sumptuous or overblown of Ljubljana's Baroque statements, all whimsical ostentation and elaborate embellishment, its size more than anything inducing hushed reverence as you enter. Designed by Andrea Pozzo (architect also of Dubrovnik's Jesuit Church), this is the best preserved of the city's ecclesiastical buildings. Doubtless Ljubljana's other churches were once nearly as impressive, but most have gone the way of the Franciscan church; Baroque buildings are particularly sad when they fall on hard times. Adjoining the cathedral is the **Bishop's Palace**, and to the north a **Seminary**, with a dramatic doorway known as the *Portal of the Giants*, also the work of Pozzo.

Just to the west of the cathedral buildings you can't fail to miss the **general market** (Mon–Sat) on Vodnikov Trg, a brash free-for-all as everyone competes to sell their particular produce. Lining the river side, the herb sellers have a bewildering Macbethian selection—stock up on what you can identify as prices are minimal. As a sort of unofficial adjunct, old women sell poisonous-looking medicinal mushrooms. Purchase at your peril.

Opposite the market, Studentska winds up the thickly wooded hillside to the **castle**, visible from everywhere in town and currently being restored to the glory it had when protecting Ljubljana's defensive position in earlier times—what's left today dates mainly from a sixteenth-century rebuilding. Climb the clocktower (8am–7pm) for a wide and superlative view of the old town crowded below, the urban sprawl of high-rises beyond and the Kamniški Alps to the north. Best time to be here is towards sunset, when the haze across the plains burns red and golden, suffusing the town in a sensual light.

Central Ljubljana and Beyond

Back on the western side of the river, the broad slash of **Titova Cesta** forms the commercial heart of Ljubljana. Dominated by grimy nineteenth- and twentieth-century shops and offices, it's a place to do business rather than sightsee—except perhaps for its only real landmark, **Nebotičnik**, a gaudily painted provincial response to the American Art Deco skyscrapers of the 1930s. Nebotičnik's rather humble fourteen storys are crowned with a penthouse café and an excellent view.

At Titova's southern end, the modern concrete-paved expanse of **Trg Revolucije**, a few steps away to the west, is something of a monument to the postwar order. The **Ljudska Skupščina**, the Slovene parliament building, crouches on one side (the sculpted relief framing the entrance is a fine example of 1950s Socialist Realism), and two symbols of the Republic's financial and economic power—the headquarters of the *Ljubljanska Banka* and the industrial giant *Iskra*—towering above it on the other. Below, the chic, matt-black exterior of the **Maximart department store** does its best to pander to Ljubljana's nascent consumerism, while outside street sellers hawk copies of the iconoclastic youth magazine *Mladina* * and the independent newspaper *Demokracija*, or hand out information on recently formed political movements.

Returning across Titova Cesta, the grubby park of Trg Osvoboditve leads back down towards the river. The eye-catching building at the Trg's western end is the early-eighteenth-century **Ursulinska Cerkev** or Ursuline church, whose looming Baroque coffee-cake exterior is one of the city's most imposing: should you manage to gain entry there's another florid high altar by

---

* The weekly *Mladina* is one of the most influential magazines in the country. Originally a youth magazine devoted to music, film, and book reviews, it soon outgrew its confines to become a forum for investigative reporting and scathing political commentary. Though exclusively written in Slovene, you only have to flip through its pages to get an idea of its importance as a document of changing times. See "Media" in *Basics*.

Robba. Lower down, by the side of the main university building, Vegova Ulica leads southward from Trg Osvoboditve towards Trg Francoske Revolucije, passing on the way the checkered pink-green-and-gray brickwork of the **University Library**. This was designed in the late 1930s by **Jože Plečnik**, the architect who more than any other determined the appearance of present-day Ljubljana. The library is one of the few Plečnik projects that ever saw completion; his lasting contribution to the image of the city was in the form of renovation carried out during the 1930s, a tidying-up operation for a town still showing the effects of an 1895 earthquake. The whole atmosphere around the River Ljubljanica, including the riverbanks and several bridges, is the result of rebuilding work by Plečnik. His legacy, in the shape of Neoclassical columns, pillars, and minature brick pyramids scattered all over the city, is impossible to avoid.

One such oddity is the **Illyrian Monument** on Trg Francoske Revolucije, erected in 1930 in belated recognition of Napoleon's failure to create a fiefdom of the same name centered on Ljubljana. Virtually next door is the seventeenth-century monastery complex of **Križanke**; originally the seat of a thirteenth-century order of Teutonic Knights, its delightful colonnaded courtyard was restored by Plečnik to form a permanent home for the Ljubljana Summer Festival (see "Entertainment and Culture" on p.40). The beer-cellar atmosphere of the aptly-named café *Plečnikov Hram* ("Plečnik's Shrine"), inside the ivy-covered courtyard, is a good place to sit back and admire the man's handiwork. Across Gosposka, at no. 15, a seventeenth-century palace contains the **Municipal Museum** (Tues & Thurs 9am–noon & 4–6pm, Sun 9am–noon), which has dull furniture and duller statuary.

Beyond Trg Francoske Revolucije there's little to see, except for a remaining stretch of the town's **Roman Walls** (again rearranged by Plečnik) on Mirje, and, a little farther on, Plečnik's old house—now an **Architectural Museum** (Karunova 4; Mon & Thurs 10am–2pm, Wed 3–5pm) where you can wander around Plečnik's ascetic living quarters.

PLEČNIK, POST-MODERNISM, AND GRAVEYARDS

For further exposure to Plečnik, and a real insight into why he's now so highly regarded, it's worth heading out to the municipal cemetery, **Žale**. Stretching between Žalska and Tomačevska in the northeast of the city, Žale can be reached by buses #7, #9, and #22 from Titova Cesta. Plečnik designed a monumental colonnaded archway at the cemetery's entrance that leads on to a cluster of small chapels devoted to individual saints, each constructed in a style or mélange of styles that show Plečnik's eclecticism. Classical Greek and Roman elements are mixed with Byzantine, Islamic, and even ancient Egyptian motifs, all filtered through a mixture of folk craftwork and twentieth-century construction techniques. It was work like this that alienated Plečnik from the dominant trends in modern architecture during his own lifetime, only to be rediscovered in the 1980s and hailed as a prophet of the latest "ism," Post-Modernism. The Ljubljana authorities have tried to continue the relationship between graveyards and great architecture with the building of a luxurious new cemetery across the road: a geometrically laid-out, high-tech necropolis, dotted, rather curiously, with inverted pink marble pyramids.

West of Titova: Museums and Tivoli Park

West of Titova, Cankarjeva leads to a neatly ordered corner of town that contains the city's main **museums**. Under Austrian control, all attempts by the town to make itself the cultural and political capital of Slovenia were repressed, leaving it with an enforced provincialism that took years to wear off. Another legacy was the sedate Neoclassical mansions the Austrians built; two of the three museums are housed in buildings of this period, and to be honest that's the best thing about them. Listen to the tourist office and you'd think each was a meeting of the British Museum and the Louvre—don't be fooled. In a roughly descending order of mediocrity, the **Modern Gallery**, Cankarjeva 15 (Tues–Sat 10am–6pm, Sun 10am–1pm), has twentieth-century Slovenian art, uniformly hack save for paintings by the Kralj brothers; the **National Museum**, Trg Herojev 1 (Tues–Sat 10am–6pm, Sun 10am–1pm), is notable only for having the one complete mammoth skeleton found in Europe; the **National Gallery**, Cankarjeva 20 (Tues–Sat 10am–6pm, Sun 10am–1pm), however, is housed in a building of some historic interest. Formerly the *Narodni Dom*, it was built in the 1890s to accommodate Slovene cultural institutions in defiance of the Hapsburgs. Today, the whole question of Ljubljana's long standing provincialism can be reviewed in the last few rooms of the gallery's collection, which are devoted to the Sloveneian Impressionists Rihard Jakopič, Ivan Grohar, Matija Jama, and Matej Sternen. Although they were painting impressionist works some thirty years after the French artists they slavishly emulated, the movement they represented nevertheless had considerable importance for the development of the Slovene national consciousness, extolling the virtues of rural Slovene peasantry and elevating them to the status of a subject fit for art.

Beyond the National and Modern Art galleries, Cankarjeva leads past an unobtrusive twentieth-century Serbian Orthodox church to **Tivoli Park**, an expanse of lawns and tree-lined walkways laid out by the ubiquitous Plečnik. Most of Ljubljana's recreational and sporting facilities can be found in the sports center at the northern end of the park (for details of which see "Sports"; p.47), but much more engaging is the **Muzej Ljudske Revolucije Slovenije** (Slovenian Museum of the People's Revolution) at Celovška 23 (Tues–Fri 10am–6pm, Sat 10am–1pm & 3–6pm, Sun 10am–1pm). As well as the usual displays of photos and guns there are puppets from a Partisan theater, with grinning Partisan dolls victoriously leading away the swastika-laden baddies.

At the top of the park's main avenue, the puce nineteenth-century **Villa Tivolski Grad** is now the center of an international graphic arts association, and, during summers of odd-numbered years, plays host to the winners of the Ljubljana **Graphics Biennial**, the one event that puts the city on the European arts map. From here a succession of pathways winds up into the **Rožnik Hills**—a beautiful, tranquil woodland region only ten minutes from the city center. Tracks lead to the not-too-distant summit of Cankarjev Vhr, where there's a small **inn** (1–8pm, often closed in August) and a memorial room dedicated to the turn-of-the-century novelist **Ivan Cankar** (summer only, 10am–2pm). Other tracks lead north to the *Bellevue* hotel, whose terrace café commands a panoramic view of the city.

Eating

Snacks and Lunches

For **snacks**, the numerous *burek* kiosks near the station, along with stands throughout town selling hot-dogs and local *gorenjska* sausages, are the quickest and cheapest choice for on-your-feet eating. The quality of Ljubljana's **delicatessens** makes them a good option for putting together picnics from locally produced cheeses, sausages, and hams, washed down with a bottle of decent Slovene wine (see p.70).

Cheap if rather uninspiring self-service or "Express" restaurants are *Daj-Dam*, Cankarjeva 4; *Emona*, Cankarjeva 2; and in the underground passage below the *Maximarket* department store on Trg Revolucije (Mon–Fri 9am–6pm, Sat 9am–2pm). The *Maximarket Grill* (Mon–Fri 9am–10pm, Sat 9am–3pm), immediately above ground, serves standard Yugoslav fare. An alternative is the local version of *McDonald's*, *Ham Ham Rio*, at Titova 4.

For **lunches**, there's a wealth of inexpensive and reasonably decent pizza places: *Parma*, underneath *Maximarket*, is popular, lively, and quick; *Mercator Pizzeria and Konditorei* halfway down Čopova, is very cheap and has a mouthwatering selection of cakes.

Restaurants . . . and Slovene Cuisine

As befits its sophisticated image, Ljubljana has a tight concentration of restaurants, most of which offer excellent value for money. While the larger hotel restaurants dish out standard fare, the range of cooking is perhaps broader than in any other Yugoslav city, and the compact nature of Ljubljana's center means that interesting options are always close to hand. One slight exception to this is authentic **Slovene cooking**, a tradition which isn't sufficiently cultivated in the city—Ljubljančans themselves are more likely to head out to neighboring villages in search of *zlikrofi*, ravioli filled with potato, onion, and bacon; *žganci*, buckwheat porridge served sprinkled with chitlins, and *gorenjska* sausages.

Figovec, Gosposvetska 1. Serves local specialties, including (yum yum) horsemeat.

Ljubljanski Dvor, Dvorni Trg. Inexpensive, atmospheric pizza restaurant with outdoor seating on a square overlooking the Ljubljanica River.

Maček, Cankarjevo Nabrežje 15. The best and most expensive (though by no means prohibitively so) of the city's fish restaurants. Traditional decor, good service; closed Sun.

Maxim, underneath *Maximarket* store on Trg Revolucije. Expensive international cuisine; a place for impressing guests and doing business. Closed Sat evening and all day Sun.

Operna Klet, Zupančičeva 2. Lurking behind an uninviting doorway opposite the Opera House, but one of the city's better restaurants specializing in fish dishes. Closed Sun.

Pri Mraku, Rimska 4. In an unfashionable part of town and rather drab in decor, but with a good reputation for its Sloveneian dishes. Closed Sun.

Pri Vitezu, Breg 18–20. Popular riverside location with outdoor seating. A mixed menu, but more authentically Slovene than the others in town.

Sechuan, Gorni Trg 23. First-rate Szechuan Chinese restaurant, and a popular meeting place for a youngish crowd.

Šestica, Large open-air restaurant-café that draws a broad mixture of Ljubljana's youth to its pleasant setting.

Union Klet, Miklošičeva 1. Hotel restaurant with a good selection of wines and an interesting menu of meats—it occasionally serves bear.

Zlata Ribica, Cankarjevo Nabrezje. Next door to *Maček* (see above) and not quite as stylish—or as pricey.

Cafés and Patisseries

There's little of *Mittel Europa* café society left in Ljubljana, but a few places on and around Titova present a convenient daytime refuge from the city center's noise and bustle. *Evropa*, on the corner of Titova and Gosposvetska, serves pizzas and drinks along with sweets and ice creams, and is indecently plush and palatial, like a nineteenth-century ballroom. The *Slon* hotel on the corner of Titova and Čopova has a couple of street-level café areas as well as a swish restaurant, but the kitsch atmosphere detracts from the indisputable quality of the cake trolley. The café-patisserie *Tivoli*, at Cankarjeva 6, has a cool dark marble interior and an extensive selection of pastries. In comparison, the café of the *Union* hotel, Miklošičeva 1, is decidedly down-at-heel but does good lunches. Its beer garden is a popular nighttime watering hole and meeting point.

Drinking

Ljubljana has a nightlife second to none in Yugoslavia; on a summer's evening the cafés around Prešernov Trg spill out on to the streets with the hectic atmosphere of a mass open-air bar. In fact there *are* several outdoor **bars**, the best-known being *Pri Konjskem Repu* ("At the Sign of the Horse's Tail"), at the top of Hribarjevo Nabrežje beside the triple bridge—a good place to get into conversation with the locals or just to hang out. From here, a wander up and down the banks of the Ljubljanica through the old town will yield an interesting locale every fifty yards or so. On the eastern side, *Rotovž*, outside the Magistrat on Mestni Trg, is a sedate venue for outdoor eating and drinking. Continuing south down Stari Trg, bars come in quick succession, the first and least characterful being *Dnevni Bar Julija*. At *Valvasor* next door you can lounge in deep wicker armchairs; *Bistro Romeo* immediately opposite is busy and trendy, and *Pri Vejici* slightly lower down is similar. Following the bottom of castle hill round to Gornji Trg, *Amerikanec* at no. 20 attracts a more self-consciously stylish crowd, and employs a harmless bouncer at the door to create an air of exclusivity. On the opposite bank of the river, Juričičev Trg is home to at least three popular cafés with outdoor seating, of which the quiet and relaxed *Bistro Roža* at Židovska 6 is best for an intimate drink.

Back up towards Titova Cesta, *Mali Slonček* on Čopova serves excellent draft beer, and around the corner on Titova's southern end at no. 4, *Rio* fills a massive courtyard packed with a noisy cross-section of locals from poets to punks. The food's good here too—try the spiced beans or *pasulj*. Some ten minutes' walk south of the main booze trail but well worth the extra effort, *Sax Pub* at Eipprova 7 (11pm–late, closed Mondays) stands beside the willow-lined banks of the Gradaščica canal which then flows into the Ljubljanica. Finally, if you're in search of late-night drinking, other than joining the midnight diehards at the *Holiday Inn Bar* at Miklošičeva 3, the only place worth heading for is *K4*—about which see below.

Entertainment and Culture

Ljubljana's main **venue** is the impressive *Cankarjev Dom* cultural center (usually known as the "CD"), a palatial, marble-floored bunker built below street level on Trg Revolucije. With a number of auditoriums as well as conference centers and exhibition spaces, it's here that the major orchestral and theatrical events take place, along with a whole range of pop, folk, jazz, and big-band concerts. The CD information center in the passage below *Maximarket* handles all information and reservations (Mon–Fri 1–8pm, Sat 9am–noon, and one hour before each performance). Details of **what's playing** at the CD (and anywhere else in town) can be found in the monthly *Calendar of Events* (in English) given out by the TIC, or at the back of the daily newspaper *Delo*—if you're prepared to wade through the Sloveneian.

The Contemporary Music Scene
Ljubljana is one of the few places in Yugoslavia that developed a strong **domestic rock** scene after the punk explosion of the late 1970s. Constant nurturing by local student radio and the Student Cultural Center (ŠKUC—which also has it's own record label, *FV*) kept the scene alive, although the deepening financial crisis has in recent years led to a definite tapering off in the scope of musical activities. Most famous—and controversial—of the bands to come out of Ljubljana in the mid-1980s were **Laibach**. Irritating the local authorities by calling themselves after the German name for the city, and subsequently raising temperatures across Europe by what was seen as the "Fascist chic" of their highly theatrical concerts, Laibach's supreme achievement was to record a complete cover version of the Beatles' *Let it Be* LP that has to be heard to be believed. Though now mainly resident in the United States, their concerts, which contain references to the more recondite elements of Slovene folk culture, are well worth catching. (For more on music, see *Contexts*.)

VENUES, NIGHTCLUBS, AND DISCOS
Ljubljana's proximity to western Europe means that there's a constant procession of foreign bands through the city. Artists as diverse as The Jesus and Mary Chain, The Sugarcubes, Black Sabbath, The Pixies, and Stevie Wonder have all played Ljubljana in recent times. Other than the CD, the main **music halls** to look out for on posters or in the pages of the local press are the *Tivoli*

Sports Center, or on occasion the smaller *KUD France Prešeren* (Karunova 14, in the suburb of Trnovo just south of the center). However, the essential Ljubljana **nightclub** is *K4*, Keršnikova 4 (Sun–Wed 10pm–3am, Thurs–Sat 10pm–4am), in the basement offices of Slovenia's youth organization. The program changes frequently, with different nights devoted to different tastes in music (pick up a copy of the schedule at the door), but *K4* serves up a basic menu of good "alternative" dance music, regular live bands, and a reasonably priced bar—and all for a measly entrance fee. Because *K4* is the best place to go after 11pm, it draws a very mixed crowd; no one feels out of place.

For something a little more mainstream, there's a choice of **discos**. Best is *Disco Turist*, below the *Turist* hotel on Dalmatinova 15 (Mon–Sat 9:30pm–3am), a fashionable hangout whose Monday-night discos have for years been a regular meeting point for the city's arty and "alternative" crowd. The *Palma* disco at Celovška 25, beneath the *Tivoli Sports Center* (nightly 10pm–3am), is tacky inside but has a varied program of music—reggae, rock and roll, punk, Latin, etc.—on different nights of the week. Inside the sports center, *Valentino* (Mon–Sat 10pm–4am, Sun 5pm–1am) offers more traditional disco fodder, but seems to be introducing a more "alternative" program in response to competition. Ljubljana's other discos such as *Nebotičnik*, in the skyscraper at Kidričeva 1, and *Babilon*, at Volfova 12, entrance on Trg Osvobitve, have a tawdry meat-market atmosphere best avoided.

FESTIVALS

The city hosts two important **contemporary music festivals** each year, both using the outdoor stage at *Križanke* on Trg Francoske Revolucije. *Druga Godba* ("Another Music") runs from the last week in May to the first week in June, and features a broad spectrum of world music, jazz, experimental noises, and rock from all over Europe. In the first or second weekend of September *Novi Rock* ("New Rock") is a showcase for the best new Yugoslav acts, whenever possible featuring a selection from each republic and a headlining guest from abroad. Details of both events can be found at the Križanke Information Center opposite the venue itself. A lesser gathering of open-air music events under the banner *Izrez Poletja* (roughly, "Pastiche of Summer") takes place throughout July and August beneath the Metalka building on Titova. Usually this includes performances by domestic rock bands twice a week in July (daily 8–10pm), but precise dates change from year to year; check with the TIC for further details.

Classical Music, Opera, and Ballet

Ljubljana's energetic **symphony orchestra**, the *Slovenska Filharmonia*, hangs out at Trg Osovobitve 9 (☎213-554), and while not of international standards is still well worth hearing. The Republic's **opera and ballet** companies are housed in the *Slovensko Narodno Gledališče* (Slovene National Theater), a sumptuous nineteenth-century Neoclassical building at Zupančičeva 1 (ticket office 11am–1pm and one hour before each performance; or reserve by phone between 10 and 11am on ☎331-930). The major classical music event of the year is the Ljubljana **Summer Festival** in June and August, when a variety of high-brow cultural events take place at Križanke.

Drama and Dance

The two principal mainstream **theater companies** are the *Slovene National Theater*, which performs at *Drama*, Erjavčeva 1 (box office 11am–noon and 6pm until start of performance; ☎221-511); and *Mestno Gledališče Ljubljansko*, Čopova 4, entrance in the passage between Čopova and Nazorjeva (☎214-111). The *Slovensko Mladinsko Gledališče* (Slovene Youth Theater), Trg VIII Kongresa ZKJ 1 (☎310-010), behind the exhibition grounds on Titova Cesta, has a strong reputation for high quality and original avant-garde work. A smaller, independent, experimental fringe theater is *Glej*, Gregorčičeva 2 (☎216-679). Note, however, that it's rare for any of these companies to perform in English.

The very young but highly regarded modern **dance** theater, *Plesni Teater Ljubljane*, have no permanent home but is a name to look out for—likely as not cropping up in the program of the *Cankarjev Dom*. Finally, for kids (and not presenting much of a language problem), there's the Ljubljana puppet theater, *Lutkovno Gledališče Ljubljane*, Kregov Trg 2 (☎314-789).

Film

The principal places to catch current **international films** in central Ljubljana are *Kino Komuna*, Cankarjeva 1, and *Union Kino*, Nažororjeva 2. Really big hit films, as well as the occasional art-house movie, play at the *Cankarjev Dom*, while *Kinoteka*, Miklošičeva 28, shows a mix of cult films and classics. In summer, an outdoor cinema at Križanke takes over. Films are invariably subtitled rather than dubbed—though the soundtracks are often indistinct.

Shopping

Ljubljana's **stores** are better stocked than anywhere else in the country, with a wide range of domestically produced consumer goods which aspire to western European standards of reliability and design. Most of the main stores are on or around Titova Cesta, while more specialized clothes shops with luxury items—such as jewelry, souvenirs, and objets d'art—are concentrated in the old town.

The city's two main **department stores** are the modern, lavish *Maximarket* on Trg Revolucije, and the slightly scruffier *Nama* on Titova, opposite the post office; both have large food sections in their basements, and are open Monday to Friday from 8am to 8pm and on Saturday from 8am until 2pm. For other culinary needs, don't forget the **market** on Vodnikov Trg (Mon–Sat).

The best **bookshop** is the branch of the *Mladinska Kniga* chain at Titova 3. The first floor has a good selection of maps, guidebooks, and detailed street-plans of Ljubljana and other Slovene cities, as well as a useful English-language guide, "How to Climb Triglav." There's a decent choice, too, of English novels and Penguin Classics. For more of the latter, as well as occasional rarities, two secondhand bookstores worth checking out are *Trubarjev Antikvariat* on Mestni Trg (Mon–Fri 8am–noon & 5–8pm, Sat 8am–noon), and *Mladinska Knjiga*, Nazorjeva 1 (Mon–Fri 9am–7pm, Sat 9am–1pm). For **magazines**, head for any of the kiosks in the city center. These stock all sorts of German titles, mostly fashion and women's magazines; material in other languages is harder to find. The newsstands of *Maximarket* and *Nama* occasionally have copies of British newspapers, as well as *Time* and *Newsweek*.

Records and tapes are comparatively cheap throughout Yugoslavia, and there's a wide selection of classical music and mainstream pop in the shop in Emona Passage beneath *Maximarket* on Trg Revolucije. For "alternative" releases from the domestic avant-garde, the main outlet is *Galerija ŠKUC*, Stari Trg 21 (Mon–Fri 4–9pm). If you're after a smarter sort of Sloveneian **souvenir**, try the rather pricey folk and craft stores of the *Dom* chain: outlets at Titova 4, Mestni Trg 24, Cankarjeva 6, and Trg Osvoboditve 5.

Sports

There's an adage that Ljubljana is the only city in Europe where more people go to the opera than visit soccer matches, and while the local team *Olympia* has recently been elevated to the first division for the first time in years, Ljubljana is not much of a soccer town. *Olympia* play at the austere, poorly appointed Bežigrad stadium, north of the center on Titova Cesta (buses #6, #8, #21). The forum for almost all other sports is the **Tivoli Sports Center**, where people get marginally more excited about the fortunes of the local basketball team, *Smelt*. The sports center has an indoor pool (daily 9–11am & 5:30–9pm) as well as an indoor skating rink, tennis courts, sauna, and gym.

Virtually everyone in Ljubljana **skis**—schoolkids are given a month's holiday each winter in order to learn—and with mountain resorts within easy striking distance of the city, a day on the piste is a popular form of recreation throughout the winter months. The most accessible slopes are 25km away at KRVAVEC, a half-hour bus ride from the city. If you want to buy skiing equipment, *Slovenijašport* are Ljubljana's best specialists: their branch at Titova 26 has a complete range of skiing accessories.

Listings

Airline offices *JAT*, Miklošičeva 34 (☎317-077); *Adria*, Kuzmičeva 7 (☎313-366).

Airport Brnik, 20km north of the city (information ☎064/22-844). The *JAT* coach from the bus station takes the better part of an hour to reach it.

American Center Cankarjeva Cesta 11 (Mon, Wed, & Fri 9am–4pm, Tues & Thurs 10am–5pm) has up-to-date US newspapers and magazines, and a well-stocked library.

American Express *Atlas*, Mestni Trg (Mon–Fri 8am–7pm; ☎222-711) will hold mail but does not offer cardholder cash-advance services.

Bus station Trg Osvobodilne Fronte. For timetable information (in Slovene only), phone ☎325-885.

Car rent *Avis*, Rimska 2 (☎223-428 & ☎223 388) and at Brnik airport (☎064/26-680); *Emona Globtour-Budget*, Kidričeva 13 (☎213-840), Vegova 2 (☎321-980); *Kompas-Hertz*, Celovška 206 (☎57-004), Miklošičeva 11 (☎26-655), and Brnik airport (☎064/22-113).

Car repairs Mercedes, Audi, VW at *Autocommerce*, Titova 146 (☎343 061); Opel and Vauxhall at *Autotehna*, Celovška 288 (☎556-997); Fiat and Zaštava at *Slovenija-Auto*, Tržaška 133 (☎261-785); Ford at *Dolenc-Gorjup*, Trzin (☎721-720).

Driving information *Auto-Motorska Zveza Slovenije* (*AMZS*, the Slovene Automobile Association), Titova 138 (☎342-378).

Ecology *Zveza Zelenih na Slovenskem* (Slovene Green Association), Cesta v Rožno Dolino 45 (☎577-109).

Feminism *Lilit*, the women's section of the ŠKUC (see below), acts as an umbrella group for meetings, groups and women's studies.

Flea market Sunday mornings at the general market on Vodnikov Trg. Lively market with a vast selection of junk and the occasional bargain.

French Cultural Center Trg Osvobitve 16 (Mon–Fri 8am–3pm). French newspapers, magazines and pompous exhibitions devoted to Gallic culture.

Galleries *Galerija ŠKUC*, Stari Trg 21 (Mon–Fri 4–9pm), has the best reputation for showcasing the younger, more avant-garde, and adventurous of Slovene artists. It also hosts a wide range of concerts, film evenings, talks and happenings, as well as selling books, records, and cassettes published by ŠKUC (see below). Other galleries worth checking out are *Mala Galerija*, Titova 11 (Tue–Sat 10am–6pm, Sun 10am–1pm), and *Equrna*, Gregorčičeva 3 (Mon–Fri 10am–1pm & 5–7pm, Sat 10am–noon).

Gay and lesbian groups ŠKUC (see below) has both lesbian and gay sections, and organizes occasional evenings at the *K4* nightclub (see "Entertainment and culture," p.44). Check with ŠKUC or *K4* for details and happenings.

Kompas Miklošičeva 11, for the speedy issue of domestic and international train and coach tickets. English-speaking and helpful.

Laundromat *Pralnica*, on Vrtača near the junction with Prešernova (daily 7am–3pm; attendant washes must be left overnight).

Listings *Calendar of Events*, a leaflet in English put out by the TIC with full details of what's on each month. Useful and free. *Where to in Slovenia*, a small booklet with patchy listings of what's on over the summer. Though its choice of detail is arbitrary, it's packed with oddball information unobtainable elsewhere: where to get lead-free gas, lists of obscure local festivals, etc.

Maps *Ljubljana: Maps, Tourist Guide, Information*, published in English by Mladinska Knjiga, has a useful set of street maps and an alphabetical index. It's pretty much essential if you're staying here for any length of time.

Medical assistance ☎323-060.

Pharmacies *Lekarna Miklošič*, Miklošičeva 24, offers a 24-hour service.

Police Emergency number ☎92. Headquarters at Prešernova 18.

Post office Main office at Titova 8 (Mon–Fri 8am 8pm, Sat 8am–2pm). 24-hour service at Cigaletova 15.

Radio *Radio Student* (89.3 and 104.3FM) belts out hard-core punk and other "alternative" sounds. *Radio Glas Ljubljane* (102.4 and 105.1FM) carries a more commercial diet of popular music.

ŠKUC Keršnikova 4. Housed in the offices of the Slovene Youth Movement, this began life as the student cultural center, but has grown into an umbrella organization covering a whole range of "alternative" social and cultural activities.

Slovene Alpine Association (*Planinska Zveza Slovenije*), Dvoržakova 9 (☎312-556). Useful source of info if you're heading up into the Julian Alps; their detailed hiking and mountaineering maps are also widely available in Ljubljana's bookshops.

Taxis ☎311-583 and ☎323-094.

Telephones *PTT* office (for pay later/international calls), Pražakova 3 (Mon–Fri 7am–8pm, Sat 7am–2pm, Sun 7am–1pm). Public phones in Slovenia use tokens (*žetoni*) which are different from those used in the rest of Yugoslavia. Buy them from post offices or most kiosks.

Tours Guided walking tours of central sights depart from the town hall steps every day from July 1 to Aug 31 at 5pm.

Zoo *Večna Pot*, 3km west of center in Rožna Dolina, bus #14 (Tues–Sun 8am–4pm, 8am–7pm in summer). A humble selection of animals, but interesting for its collection of wildlife indigenous to central Europe and the Balkans, such as wild cats and water buffalo.

Around Ljubljana: the Postojna Caves and Lipica

Emphatically not to be missed while you're in Ljubljana is a visit to the **Postojna Caves**—easily managed either as a day-trip or en route to Koper, Opatija, or Trieste in Italy. Postojna is on the main rail route between Ljubljana and Trieste, but as the walk to the caves from Postojna train station is farther than from the bus stop, most people go by one of the regular buses. Once in the town, signs direct you to the caves and their suitably cavernous entrance. Daily **tours** run every half hour in the season (last tours: May–Sept 6pm, April & Oct 5pm, Nov–March 1pm weekdays, 3pm Sat & Sun; dress warmly; entrance fee $12), and once inside a railroad whizzes you helter-skelter through 2km of preliminary systems before the guided tour starts. It's little use trying to describe the vast and fantastic jungles of rock formations; the point is to see them for yourself—breathtaking stuff. Postojna's caves are about four million years old and provide a chilly home for *Proteus anguineus*, a weird creature that looks like a cross between a bloated sperm and a prawn. Actually it's a sort of salamander, one of whose odd capabilities is to give birth to live young in temperatures above 16°F but lay eggs if it's colder. They live their seventy-year lives down here in total darkness and hence are blind—and very confused at being put on display to inquisitive tourists.

Discovered in 1818, Postojna's 27-kilometer system wasn't explored for years, and large sections are still uncharted. During the last war Italian occupying forces used the entrance caves as a fuel dump without having a map of the system; the local partisans, however, did, and worked their way through a side passage to blow up the stores—you can still see the walls blackened by the explosion.

Practical Details

The **tourist office** at Tržaška 4 can reserve private **rooms** and give directions to the local **campground**. The cheapest hotel, with doubles at $40, is the *Pansion Erazem* (067/59-185). Best places to eat are those in the town used by locals—anything near the cave entrance or plastered with credit card stickers is tourist-geared and, not surprisingly, overpriced.

Predjamski Grad

The other site you're steered to near Postojna is **Predjamski Grad**, a castle 9km out and only reachable with your own transportation or by an organized trip—we tried bumming a ride with the tour buses from Postojna but it wasn't happening; you might be luckier. Pushed up high against a cave entrance in the midst of dramatic karst landscape, the sixteenth-century castle is a damp and melancholy sort of place, unimproved by a lackluster collection of odds and ends from this and an earlier castle that stood nearby. The previous castle was the home of one **Erasmus**, a colorful brigand knight of the fifteenth century who spent his days waylaying the merchant caravans that passed through the region. Sheriff of Nottingham to his Robin Hood was the governor of Trieste, who laid exasperated siege to the castle for over a year. Secure in his defensive position and supplied by a secret passage to the outside world, Erasmus taunted the governor by tossing fresh cherries and the occasional roast ox over the wall to show he was far from beaten. Such hubris couldn't go unnoticed, and Erasmus finally met with one of the more ignominious deaths on record: blown to bits by a cannon ball while sitting in the castle outhouse.

The Škocjanska and Other Caves

Caves abound in the limestone karst around Postojna. A seven-kilometer bus trip away, the **Planina** caves are little visited and provide a good contrast to Postojna—fewer rock formations but dramatic arched river passages. Four kilometers from Postojna, **Pivka** is the cave nearest the only campground in the area. Nowhere near as dramatic as Postojna and considerably smaller, should you be passing it's just about worth going on one of the two daily tours that include entrance to the **Crna** cave.

Thirty-three kilometers southwest of Postojna the **Škocjanska** cave is debatably the most spectacular of all the systems in the region, though as it's little advertised and considerably more difficult to reach by public transit, it's a far quieter, more relaxed alternative to joining the scrimmage at Postojna.

THE KARST

Named after the Karst, the barren limestone plateau around Trieste, **karst** land-scapes are formed by the action of rainwater on limestone. Rain picks up small amounts of carbon dioxide from the atmosphere, which, when it falls on limestone rock, slowly dissolves it. Gradually, over millions of years, the action of rain attacking the rock causes hairline cracks in the limestone, which are steadily enlarged by running water. In it's early stages, karst scenery is characterized by thin, narrow ridges and fissures; as these grow and deepen, the dry limestone is raked into wild, sharp-edged fragments, practically bare of vegetation since any topsoil is blown away—and bleached bright white, like shards of bone. Karst scenery is found throughout Yugoslavia, particularly in **Slovenia** and **Montenegro**, and in practically all of the mountains ranges that line **the coast** from Istria south.

Rivers do odd things in karst landscapes: they disappear down holes where the limestone is weakest, and flow for miles underground, suddenly bursting from rocks when the geology changes. If an underground river widens and forms a cavern, the drips of rainwater percolating through the soil above will deposit minuscule amounts of the calcium bicarbonate that the rain has dissolved from the limestone above. Over millions of years the deposits form stalactites hanging from the roof of the cavern; the drips on the floor form columns called stalagmites. Traces of other minerals such as iron and copper color the stalactites and stalagmites, and the whole process forms cave systems like those at **Postojna**.

When an underground cavern collapses, the land on the surface subsides and often accumulates river-borne or wind-blown soils and, eventually, vegetation, which thickens the soil and makes the depression fertile. These can then be cleared of rocks and the land, known in Yugoslavia as a *polje*, cultivated; *poljes* can be miles long, and tend to absorb water slowly, leading to flooding after heavy rain. A good example of a *polje* is **Trebinje** in Bosnia-Hercegovina (see p.278): the *polje* here is 60km long, and fills with water every September.

From DIVAČA, the nearest town, turn right out of the combined bus and train station (it's on the Ljubljana–Koper rail route), along the road parallel to the rail lines as far as the bridge. Take the main road to Koper, and after about a kilometer the caves are signposted; all told, it's around a five-kilometer walk. From the beginning of June to the end of September guided tours start daily at 10 and 11:30am, 1, 2, 3:30, and 5pm; tours fall to two a day in April, May, and October, and two a day on Sundays only in other months; they last for about 90 minutes and cost $10. Beginning with the **Tiha Jama** ("Quiet Cave"), filled with monstrous stalactites and stalagmites, you cross over the nerve-wrackingly narrow and rickety **Hankarjev Bridge** towards the source of the river Reka, which plunges down, via a waterfall, to a lake, before disappearing to emerge 50km southeast in the Bay of Trieste.

Practical Details

The most important point is a negative one: there's no **accommodation** at the Škocjanska caves. The nearest is at Postojna, so you'll need to time your visit carefully. All the **information bureau** outside the entrance to the caves can do is give help on tour times. If you've worked up an appetite underground there's a **gostilna**, again near the entrance.

Lipica

A less spectacular alternative to the cave visit is **LIPICA**, near the Italian border; buses run from DIVAČA or, if you're reading this on the coast, tour coaches ply the route. Very much the "oasis in the barren karst," as it's always described, Lipica gave its name to the **Lippizaners** horses you associate with the Spanish Riding School of Vienna. There are 300 horses here, the results of fastidious breeding that can be dated back two centuries. The Austrian Archduke Charles established the stud farm in 1580, adding Spanish and Arab blood to the Lippizaner strain that was first used by the Romans for chariot races, and it's been breeding the graceful white horses ever since. Though the school is not as grand as the one at Vienna, tours are given around the stud (8:30am–5pm: mornings half-hourly, afternoons hourly), and twice a day the horses give the elegant displays for which they're famous (Mon–Fri 11am and 2:30pm; Sat & Sun 3pm), with a more elaborate display daily at 11am in July and August. If you've any horseback-riding ability, it's also possible to go on rides around the region—a wonderfully relaxing way to explore. A week's riding costs around $134, and there are also beginners' and advanced riding courses. Neither of the local **hotels** are cheap: rooms in the *Club* (☎067/73-597) or *Maestoso* (☎067/73-541) cost around $65 for a double.

North of Ljubljana: the Road to Bled

Heading north from Ljubljana to Lake Bled and the **Julian Alps**, the tail end of the Alps that extends into northwest Yugoslavia from Austria and Italy, most travelers' priority is to cover the ground as quickly as possible. However, if you're not in a hurry, three towns en route deserve a stop-off, both as a contrast to the big city excitement of Ljubljana, and as a prelude to the attractions of the mountains and lakes to the north. While it's possible to catch trains from Ljubljana to each, buses offer easier (and often faster) connections.

ŠKOFJA LOKA is just twenty minutes' bus ride from Ljubljana. Arriving at the station you're dumped in the middle of the town's firmly unappetizing industrial park, but walk from the station across the footbridge over the river and you reach the sleepy **Old Town**—arguably the best preserved medieval town center in Slovenia. Its nucleus is **Mestni Trg**, a beautifully arranged square with Gothic and Baroque houses and a fifteenth-century church. It's also home to the **tourist office** at no. 10 (Mon–Fri 3–6pm, Mon, Wed, & Fri also 10–11:30am), which can arrange private rooms, or there's a **hotel**, the *Transturist* (☎064/61-261), with doubles at $50. Really though, the single thing to see is **Loški Castle** atop the hill. Built following an earthquake in 1511, it has a small museum (daily 9am–5pm), with some unusual peasant glass-paintings, mostly of biblical subjects, and good examples of Slovene peasant wood-carving. The castle is also the setting for a random assortment of evening concerts and events.

Škofja Loka's other attraction is its *gostilne*, which serve Slovene country food. The best of these is that in the **Homan House** on Mestni Trg, decorated on the outside with early-sixteenth-century frescoes. Less adventurously there's also a pizzeria, *Pivnica*, just over the footbridge from the bus station.

From Škofja Loka buses run every half hour to **KRANJ**, a fifteen-minute trip. Kranj is very much a mixed-up place, and, although it has several old and attractive buildings hidden among the greenery and dramatically backed by mountains, it's primarily an industrial center. That the town is best known in the rest of the country for its local sausage—an overgrown frankfurter known as *kranjska klobasa*—probably says it all.

Kranj's center, the pedestrianized main square of Titov Trg, is a little under a kilometer away from the bus station, via an uphill walk along Koroška past the **tourist office** at no. 29 (Mon–Fri 9am–noon). The Gothic **Cathedral of Sv Kancijan** dominates Titov Trg and the old part of town, a mainly fourteenth-century hall church decorated inside with frescoes showing angels playing lyres, painted around 1460. Next door, the **Prešeren Theater** was built in tribute to the Slovene lyric poet France Prešeren, who died in the town in 1849. He's also commemorated by an oversized statue outside, and in a small **museum** at Ulica Prešernova 7—one of many streets in Slovenia that bear his name.

Of Kranj's other museums, the **Gorenjski Muzej** at Tavcarjeva is worth popping into if it's raining; ethnography and archaeology are its main thrusts, along with work by local painters. Though it's hard to think of a reason why you'd want to stay, **rooms** are available from *Kompas* in the shopping center, *Koroška*, or there's a rather crummy **hotel**, the *Jelen* (☎064/21-466), with doubles at $30.

Just a couple of kilometers before the road swings east to Bled, **RADOVLJICA** also has a Baroque castle and Gothic church, with the castle containing the main reason for coming here—the **Čebelarski Musej** (Apicultural Museum; Tues–Sun 10am–1pm & 3–6pm). Beekeeping has long been a source of income in this part of Slovenia, and the museum details just about every aspect of it, from bee biology to the social history of the beehive. Of real interest are the painted **beehive fronts** from the eighteenth century onwards: cartoon-like figures in morality skits, political jibes, or religious scenes. Look out for the frequent appearance of Job; the patron of beekeepers.

Bled and Bohinj

At the tail end of the Julian Alps and in easy reach from Ljubljana, the **mountain lakes** of **Bled** and **Bohinj** are Slovenia's number-one tourist pull. And for good reason: all the delights and trappings of their Austrian and Italian neighbors are here—but at affordable prices. Tour operators have been quick to include the lakes in their brochures, and while Bled, surrounded by Olympian mountains and busily oozing charm, lives up to expectations it's also chock-full of English and German tourists, which can't help but temper its delights. Bohinj, in contrast, is less visited, more beautiful, and cheaper—and, should you want to explore the imposing and exhilarating mountains around Mt Triglav, at 2864m Yugoslavia's highest peak, this is the place to head for.

Getting There

Buses are the easiest way to reach both Bled and Bohinj: they're frequent (hourly from Ljubljana; journey time 1hr to Bled, 2hr to Bohinj), reliable, and cheap, and link most of the small villages in the area. **Trains** from Bled arrive at LESCE, 5km to the east of town, and though you can catch a connection down to Ljubljana, it's far easier to take a bus. The line is only really of use if you want to continue farther afield—say to Zagreb or Austria.

At the western end of Lake Bled, **Bled-Jezero** train station lies on the JESENICE to NOVA GORICA rail line—a smaller, secondary system that runs to Bohinjska Jezero and on towards Italy and the coast. The trip from Jesenice, chugging steadily through the mountains and karst, is as impressive as you'd imagine. Train buffs should note that a **steam train**, the *Old Timer*, is laid on in summer months, at considerable additional expense.

Bled

There's no denying that **BLED** has all the right ingredients—a placid mirror lake with romantic island, a fairy-tale castle high on a bluff, leafy lakeside lanes, and a backdrop of snow-capped mountains. As such it's worth a day of anyone's time, and one advantage of the tourist trade is that everything is efficiently packaged. The **tourist office** staff (Ljubljanska Cesta 7; Mon–Sat 8am–5pm) fall over themselves to supply information: their free English-language *Bled Information* booklet has every practical detail you need from bike rental to acupuncture facilities, and their *Alpine Guide* gives comprehensive hiking routes for the whole area including Triglav (though to attempt this you need the help of mountain guides). In summer the lake, fed by warm-water springs that take the water temperature up to 76°F, forms the setting for a whole host of watersports—there's a major international rowing contest held on May 1 each year—and in winter the surface becomes a giant skating rink. Again, consult the tourist office for full details of events and equipment rental.

Somewhere to Stay

The best option for accommodation in Bled are private **rooms** from the tourist office or *Alpetour* at Ljubljanska 11 (stays under 3 nights $8, otherwise $7). The similarly priced **youth hostel** is straight up Grajska from the bus station, past farmyards and a small shrine until you reach the hostel at Grajska 17—where dormitory accommodation and a strict 10:30pm curfew/lockout may persuade you to reconsider a private room. The nearest **campground**, *Zaka*, is beautifully placed, sheltered at the western end of the lake amid the pines and with its own stretch of beach; catch a bus towards Bohinj and get off the

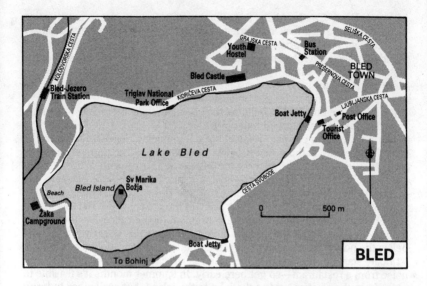

Kidričeva street stop. Should the campground be full, head for the *Šobec* site, 2km east of Bled on the road to LESCE; note that it's strictly illegal to camp anywhere other than an official site—a rule rigorously upheld by the local police. Another rustic alternative, at prices broadly similar to private rooms, is accommodation in a local **farmhouse**; reservations are handled exclusively by the tourist office. The majority of the **hotels** in Bled are group-booked and overpriced; if you do need to stay in one, *Hotel Krim* and *Hotel Lovex* are the least expensive, with doubles from $65. Outside of the summer and winter seasons, it's worth asking at the tourist office for any bargains or "special prices."

Eating
One downside of the all-embracing tourist industry is that there are few cheap places **to eat** in Bled—the only budget options are the earthy *Gostilna* at the bottom of Grajska, or the *Hram* pizzeria next to the *Park Hotel* at the eastern end of the lake. Alternatively you could hit the supermarkets for picnic ingredients. Of the restaurants, *Okarina*, Rikljeva 9, around the back of the castle, has the reputation of being one of the best in the country. At $15 and up for a meal it's also one of the most expensive, but if you feel like a blow-out this is the place to do it, and its excellent menu includes vegetarian options.

The Town and Lake
Even if you don't stay there it's a good idea to observe the youth hostel's curfew: rise early while the hotels are still sleeping and Bled is all yours, and at its most atmospheric. A path just behind the youth hostel runs up to the

fairy-tale **Bled Castle** (daily 8am–8pm)—which upon closer examination turns out to be a pricey restaurant with a fine view and a very ordinary museum, its only surprise a small sixteenth-century chapel. The castle was founded in the eleventh century and for the next 800 years was the seat of the bishops in whose South Tyrol see Bled stood. Ignac Novak, one of Bled's more enterprising sons, was castellan here in the eighteenth century; his great plan was to drain the lake and use the residual clay as raw material for a brick factory he intended to build on the shore. With an astute eye to tourism even then, the council turned him down.

During the day a constant relay of stretch gondolas* leave from below the *Park Hotel* or the bathing resort below the castle, ferrying tourists back and forth to Bled's intensely picturesque **island** ($2.50 return). With an early start (and by renting your own rowboat or canoe from the same places as the gondolas) you can beat them to it. Crowning the island, the natty Baroque **Church of Sv Marika Božja** ("Our Lady of the Lake") is the last in a line of churches on a spot that's long held religious significance for the people around the lake: under the present building are remains of early graves and, below the north chapel, a very early (pre-Roman) temple. As soon as the tourist boats start up, the peace of the island is wrecked by over-amplified disco noise from a restaurant—so get here early. In summer months it's feasible to swim from the western end of the lake to the island, but remember to bring some light clothes in a watertight bag if you want to get into the church. During winter, under the snug muffle of alpine snow, you can walk or skate across.

Lake Bohinj

It's 30km from Bled to Lake Bohinj and buses run every half hour through the **Sava Bohinjka valley**—dense, verdant, and often laden with mist and low cloud. Dotted along its sides are *kozolecs*, wooden frames for drying hay and wheat that are found all over Slovenia. On the damp alpine ground crops don't dry well; hanging them on a *kozolec* lets the sharp winds do the work. Around Bohinj the double *kozolec* with a workroom above and high-pitched roof is usual; farther northwest they become much more decorative, with patterned animals and figures cut into the weatherboards; near Ljubljana long ranks of single *kozolec*s are common. It was from a *kozolec* that Tomaž Hostnik, erstwhile lead singer with the contentious Ljubljana group Laibach, hanged himself in 1983. Considering how much the band pride themselves on the more recherché elements of their Slovene identity, he couldn't have chosen a more fitting end . . .

---

*It's reassuring to note that the tourist authorities have gone Green when it comes to this form of lake transportation: the gondolas (which rely on muscle power) are used in preference to motor boats in an attempt to keep the lakewater clean. However, in 1989 the authorities blotted their environmental copybook in throwing up some disgusting buildings for the annual rowing regatta: with luck, the outcry these have provoked will ensure they don't last too long.

In appearance and character **Lake Bohinj** is utterly different from Bled: the lake crooks a narrow finger under the wild mountains, woods slope gently down to the water enclosing it in secretive tranquillity, and a lazy stillness hangs over all—in comparison to Bled it feels almost uninhabited.

A number of places take their name from the lake. **Bohinjska Bistrica**, 4km before Bohinj on the Bled–Bohinj bus route, has little except a few rooms. **Bohinjska Jezero** (often just referred to as Jezero), at the eastern end of the lake, is where most facilities are based, including the **tourist office** (Sept–June Mon–Fri 7am–6pm; July & Aug daily 7am–8pm), which offers rooms, apartments, and bike rental. Pride of place here goes to the **Church of Sv Janez** (July & Aug daily, 9am–noon & 3–6pm), a solid-looking structure whose nave and frescoes date back to the fourteenth century: but once you've seen this and arranged a room there's no reason to hang around. To the west of the lake is the area known as **Zlatorog**, named after "Goldenhorn," a fearsome immortal chamois-goat of local legend who guards the golden treasure of Mount Triglav. The Zlatorog **campground** is at this end of the lake and there are a limited number of private **rooms**—try asking around or at the reception of the *Zlateoog Hotel* (☎064/723-331)—which, incidentally, has doubles from $42 and is a convenient place to eat and drink.

An easy walk back east takes you to the **cable car** (daily 7:30am–6pm, every half hour) at the foot of **Mt Vogel** (1540m). If the Alps look dramatic from the lakeside, from Vogel's summit they're breathtaking. As the cable car briskly climbs the 1000 meter difference—not for the fainthearted this—the panorama is gradually revealed, with Triglav the crest of a line of pale red mountains, looking more like a clenched claw than the three-headed god after which it's named. Finally, if you're around at the end of September, the return of the cattle from the higher alpine pastures is celebrated in the mass debauch called the *Kravji Bal* or "Cow Dance." This is a great opportunity to meet local people, most of whom still make their living off the land. Thankfully, tourism hasn't completely obliterated real life here, and the people of Bohinj preserve their own individuality, reflected in the mass of folklore and unusual customs you begin to notice if you spend any time in the region. One such odd tradition concerns mourning: the death of a mother is mourned for two years by her children, a father for just eighteen months—which, considering the patriarchal tradition of Yugoslavia, is surprising.

An hour's walk north from Zlatorog, the **Savica Waterfalls** make a good hiking target, a photogenic ribbon of water falling into the lake that marks the beginnings of the river Sava—though if you've looked out from Belgrade's Kalemegdan Fortress at the broad and powerful river as it joins the Danube, it's hard to reconcile it with the bubbling stream here. Set in the foothills of the the Triglav range are the beginnings of a spectacular beech- and fir-packed national park known as the **Valley of the Seven Lakes**. From here, briefed with the notes on the next page, and armed with a copy of *How to Climb Triglav* and a guide, you could begin your ascent of Triglav. It's a comparatively easy (if strenuous) hike amid magnificent scenery. When you reach the top, expect your companions to indulge in a little mild flagellation—tradition has it that on first scaling the summit of Triglav, initiates have to be beaten on the bottom with a birch stick.

HOW TO CLIMB MOUNT TRIGLAV

What follows is only the barest-boned description of one of many routes up Mount Triglav. It's not intended as a definitive guide, nor should you rely on it as your sole source of information. You may read elsewhere that it's easy to climb Triglav, with only a little general hiking experience; this is nonsense. At least one person is killed on the mountain each year because they were inexperienced, went alone, got lost, or didn't pay attention to that day's weather forecast. Our advice is to climb with an official guide recommended by the tourist office in Bled: not only will you be safe, but you'll also climb more efficiently and learn masses about the mountain and its folklore, flora, and fauna. This account is designed to give you some hints on how to approach the climb—and to whet your appetite for a trip that's one of the most rewarding experiences Yugoslavia has to offer.

Before you start you'll need:
● A copy of *How to Climb Mount Triglav*, the definitive **guide** to the climb and packed with essential additional information. It's available from the tourist office in Bled, and (more reliably) bookshops in Ljubljana.
● The 1:20,000 **map** of Triglav published by the Slovene Alpine Association (*Planinska Zveza Slovenije*), Dvoržakova 9, Ljubljana (☎061/312-556), and available from *Pacific Travelers Supply*, 529 State Street, Santa Barbara CA93101.
● Basic **hiking gear**—tough walking boots, warm and waterproof clothing (not jeans), a compass, and light rations. There's no need to take food supplies since you can eat at the mountain refuges. These are also the places to sleep; they supply bedding and cost about $10 per person.
● A **weather forecast** from the tourist office. August, September and, occasionally, early October are the best months; climbing between the end of October and late June is impossible. Even on clear, sunny days the weather can change abruptly: it's common for temperatures to drop by 18°F in half an hour, and snow falls can be very heavy. Should you be caught in a storm, make your own shelter or head for the nearest refuge.
● Strong **legs**.

The Route
From the **Savica waterfall** (see previous page) a marked path curls up to **Komarca Crag**, from where it's a little over three hours' steady hiking to the first **refuge**, *Koča pri Triglavskih Jezerih* (1683m). This is the place to spend your first night. Note that it's not possible to make reservations in the refuges, though you won't be turned away if the weather is deteriorating. Refuges are most crowded at weekends. Alternatively, if you've made an early start and still have the energy, you can make a side trip to **Mt Tičarica** (2091m).
On day two, head along the wonderful Valley of the Seven Lakes, then northeast to the **Hibrace Plateau**. From here, walk down through the **Dolic Saddle** (2164m) to the *Trzaska Koca na Dolicu* refuge, a total of four to five hours' hiking. You can either opt for spending the night here or continuing for another hour and a half to the *Dom Planika* refuge. This leaves day three for the final hour-and-a-half's trek, past the well-equipped *Triglavski Dom* refuge beside **Mt Kredarica**, to Triglav's **summit** (2864m), where, after gulping in the stunning views across spectacular snow-covered ranges, you can indulge in the tradition of walloping your partner's rump with a birch twig.
Along the route you're bound to fall into conversation with other climbers who can suggest alternative routes down. If you're here in September, you may bump into the annual climb by one hundred women led by ten guides. Passing itself off as an old tradition, this oddly sexist stunt was in fact dreamed up as a publicity gimmick by a local magazine a few years back.

North of Bled: towards Austria

JESENICE, the next major roadside town north of Bled, is the name stamped on your passport if you arrive from western Europe by train. Indeed the town's train station is its biggest landmark; unless you're into steel works, it's not the best of introductions to the country. Via a marvelous secondary rail line, Jesenice is linked to Bled and Bohinj and, eventually, to Nova Gorica on the coast.

Roughly halfway between Jesenice and the border, **KRANJSKA GORA** is a particularly well-equipped ski resort ideal for beginners; out of season it's a decent enough town, if a little clinical. On its outskirts, **GOZD MARTULJEK** is also developing as a ski center.

Northwest Slovenia

Unless you're into serious hiking and climbing, it's unlikely that you'll be heading for the towns of **northwest Slovenia** from Bled or Bohinj; the Julian Alps form an insurmountable obstacle to road and rail links, and the usual approach is the road that runs south to the coast from VILLACH in Austria or TARVISIO in Italy. An alternative is to travel west from Ljubljana via ŠKOFJA LOKA, but even this road degenerates into a rough track at times. Once here, you really need a car to absorb what is some of the Republic's finest scenery; buses are few and practically nonexistent on the most beautiful routes, such as the **Soča valley** from Bovec to Nova Gorica, through which the main north–south road runs.

Starting in Slovenia's northwestern corner, **BOVEC** is better as a jumping-off point for the region than as a base, linked as it is by six trains a day to Ljubljana (journey time 6hr). With a pretty, village-like center that's grown up around its skiing industry, Bovec is new on the tourist scene, with limited numbers of private **rooms** available through the **tourist office** (☎050/86-064) or *Kompas* (☎050/86-101); cheapest of the town's **hotels** is the *Alp* (☎065/86-040), whose double rooms are a bargain at $27. Unaccountably, Bovec also boasts three campgrounds, of which the best is *Polovnik*, near the center. Twenty-three kilometers south of Bovec and a few kilometers from the Italian border crossing, **KOBARID** (**Caporetto** in Italian) became well-known during World War I as the scene of a major battle where the Austrian army broke through into Italy (an event described in Hemingway's *A Farewell to Arms*). Hemingway's description of Caporetto was "... a little white town with a campanile in a valley. It was a clean little town and there was a fine fountain in the square"—and it's much unchanged. The next place of any size is **TOLMIN**, though this again is little more than an expansion of a compact village. It's typically Slovene and totally uninteresting, as is its side-kick MOST NA SOČI.

The last major town before crossing into Italy is **NOVA GORICA**, which, as the name suggests, is a recently built adjunct to the town of GORICA, today in Italy. Yugoslavia was denied possession of Gorica after World War II, and the new, unlikable industrial town sprung up soon after. A three-foot

AN A-Z OF SLOVENIAN SKI RESORTS

Slovenia's ski resorts are uniformly well equipped and inexpensive. All have rescue facilities and stores where you can buy or rent equipment, and many have ski schools of varying size. The majority also have on-site accommodation in hotels or private rooms, but it's advisable to check availability with the tourist office in the nearest large town before you set off. Bear in mind too that you will invariably save money by buying a package skiing vacation through a travel agent; see the Yugoslav Tourist Office's Ski Yugoslavia *brochure for further details.*

KALIČ (765–981m), 6km from POSTOJNA. A small resort with no accommodation —you'll need to rely on the hotels and pensions of nearby Postojna. Four ski lifts; the magnificent **Postojna Caves** are close by (see p.49).

KANIN (483–2300m), near BOVEC. Slopes are suitable for all abilities and there's a ski school with a good reputation. Six kilometers of runs, one cable car, three chair lifts, and one ski lift.

KOBLA (543–1530m), near BOHINJ. A good beginners' course and medium inclines, all well organized. Bohinj Bistrica train station lies at the foot of the slopes.

KOPE (1250–1400m), 15km from SLOVENJ GRADEC. Dramatic scenery, plentiful accommodation, seven ski lifts, and floodlit night skiing. A large resort, and one that will probably continue to grow.

KRANJSKA GORA (810m), 83km northwest of Ljubljana. One of Yugoslavia's largest ski centers, and probably the best equipped after Sarajevo. A good supply of private rooms, a ski school, five chair lifts, fifteen ski lifts, a toboggan course, and excellent mixed-ability skiing from December to mid-March.

KRVAVEC (1853m), between LJUBLJANA (32km) and KRANJ (15km). With magnificent views over Ljubljana, Krvavec has thirty kilometers of runs, six chair lifts, six ski lifts, a ski school, and floodlit night skiing. Regular buses from Ljubljana and Kranj arrive by the ski lifts. Highly popular with weekending Ljubljanc̆ ans.

MARIBORSKO POHORJE (1050–1250m), 5km from MARIBOR. Thirty kilometers of runs and fifteen ski lifts.

MT VOGEL (1500–1800m), near BOHINJ. Sixteen kilometers of runs, numerous ski lifts, and easy slopes amid spectacular scenery—its season usually stretches from November to early May, and it's the best resort for intermediate-level skiing. Accommodation is readily found around Bohinj.

PLANICA, 7km to the west of Kranjska Gora. Fine cross-country courses and a TV-familiar ski jump.

ROGLA (1517m), 17km from ZREČE, 50km from MARIBOR. A well-equipped winter sports center with very gentle beginners' slopes and a tobogganing course. Other facilities include fifteen ski lifts and private rooms.

ZATRNIK (880–1270m), 9km from BLED, accessible by half-hourly ski buses. Nineteen kilometers of runs, five lifts. Very popular.

border fence runs through the town just to underline the point. The only reason you'd want to be here is to pick up one of four daily trains on the scenic route to Jesenice via Bled; for accommodation, try the *Hotel Park* (☎065/21-422), which has doubles from $40.

East of Ljubljana: Kamnik, Šempeter, and Celje

With the more dramatic scenery situated in the west, most people limit their experience of central and eastern Slovenia to the inadequate, congested E-93 highway that crawls across the lowlands towards Maribor, Gratz, and Vienna. Yet it's best to get off the beaten track and explore the towns and villages along the way—most of which make easy day-trips from Ljubljana itself.

Kamnik

KAMNIK is just to the north of the E-93, 22km northeast of Ljubljana and half an hour's drive across a sun-dried plain of wheat and maize fields, with the **Kamniški Alps** rearing majestically in the background. Nestling at the foot of the mountains, it was an important political capital in the Middle Ages before trade routes shifted southwards and left it stranded. Nowadays it's a tranquil market town, and a major staging post on the way to hiking and skiing destinations beyond.

Kamnik's medieval overlords left it with two **castles**, both dating from the twelfth century. Overlooking the town from a hill, the **Gornji Grad** (upper castle) is a somber ruin, deserted for over 400 years. It's a good two-hour walk away from town, or a bone-shaking car ride via a gravel track, but you can reward yourself with a drink at the adjacent restaurant and a panoramic view of the distant peaks. The equally derelict but more accessible **Mali Grad** (lower castle) occupies a hillock in the center of town. Standing at the summit is a gleamingly whitewashed two-story chapel of which the Romanesque lower floor (now a crypt) dates from the late eleventh century, one of the earliest surviving ecclesiastical structures in Slovenia. Frustratingly, the chapel is usually closed, but if you manage to gain access look out for the remanants of Gothic frescoes from the 1400s.

Below the Mali Grad stretch the medieval houses of **Titov Trg**, a small but busy town square taken over by café tables in summer. Descending from the castle in the other direction, a stroll down Kamnik's sleepy main street, **Kidričeva**, takes you past unassuming two-story eighteenth-century houses and the parish church—a fairly standard example of eighteenth-century Baroque save for a separate bell tower. Farther down, on a hillside about 100m to your left, is the sixteenth-century chateau **Zaprice**. Once the refuge of Lutherans fleeing the Counter-Reformation, it's now the home of the town **museum** (Tues–Thurs 9am–noon & 4–6pm, Sun 9am–noon), a gloomy, forlorn place which combines the usual pictures of partisans with an unenticing display of bent wood furniture. Much more interesting is the traditional peasant architecture on the lawn outside, where a selection of *kašče* or granaries have been brought down from their original homes in the mountain valleys high above. These squat structures with thatched roofs served as storehouses on the higher pastures, keeping the alpine herdsmen well-supplied during their prolonged absences from the villages lower down.

More *kašče* can be seen in their original habitat in the upper reaches of the Tuhinje valley just beyond Kamnik to the northeast. This lies at the base of a large walking and skiing area, **Velika Planina**, well served by a chair lift from the valley floor 5km north of Kamnik. Five kilometers farther on at the head of the valley, the idyllic recreation spot of **KAMINŠKA BISTRICA** is the starting point for hikes up into the surrounding mountains. Information on **accommodation**, largely in outlying farms and *gostilne*, can be obtained from the **Golftourist office** at Titov Trg 20 in Kamnik (Mon–Fri 8am–3pm, Sat–Sun 8–11am). There are also mountain huts in Kaminška Bistrica, and one on the col above KAMINŠKO SEDLO, the main destination for mountaineers. Kamnik itself possesses a **campground** at Maistrova 32, 500m east of the town center.

Šempeter

From Kamnik it's back to the E-93, the main eastbound highway, which after winding its way among wooded hills between Lucovica and Trojane drops down into the Savinja basin, where the valley floor is lined with row upon row of hop plantations. Just short of Celje, the otherwise unremarkable village of ŠEMPETER conceals an intriguing **Roman Necropolis** (daily 8am–noon & 2–6pm), a series of monumental gravestones uncovered in 1952 and set down in a grassy park that's signposted from the main road. There are 24 stones, some as much as eight meters high, dating from the first century onwards when the area served as an exclusive cemetery for well-to-do nobles of **Celeia** or Roman Celje. It remained in use until about AD 270, when a flood covered the whole site in a thick layer of ooze and gravel. Many of the tombs are richly decorated, with relief portraits of the families they commemorate and scenes from classical mythology (the reliefs of *Europa Riding the Bull* on the second-century tomb of Ennius, and that of the *Legend of Iphigenia* curving round the lower half of the largest of the tombs, that of the Priscianus family, are the best).

Opposite the entrance to the necropolis, the **Šempeter Tourist Association** (daily 8am–noon) can help with local information, while on the other side of the road it's worth seeing if the bright yellow parish church of **Sv Petra** is open—the altar contains a small Gothic sculpture of the Virgin .

Just north of Šempeter, the **Pekel cavern** (April–Oct daily; tours roughly every half hour, last tour about 5pm) is very modest indeed compared to the much more dramatic affairs at Postojna and Škocjan, but nevertheless offers an interesting if brief upward climb through stalactite-infested galleries. Pekel is a well-signposted three-kilometer drive from the town itself, followed by a short walk through the forest.

Before leaving Šempeter altogether it's worth sampling Yugoslavia's new taste for private enterprise in the shape of Slovenia's most renowned *gostilna*, *Štorman*. On the highway to Celje 1km east of town, it's typical of many of the new privately-run family restaurants serving Slovene food. Enormously popular with the local nouveau riche, it's chaotically busy, and has prices to match its reputation.

Celje

The largely modern city of **CELJE** has the air of a calm, civilized, and sober place in which nothing much ever really happens. Traces of the town's history, first as a Roman trading post on the road between Ptuj and Ljubljana, then as a key medieval power base for German feudal magnates, make it worth an hour or two of your time—but it's not a place to get caught in for long.

Practicalities

Both the railroad station and bus terminal are on the eastern side of the center on Titov Trg, five minutes' walk away from parallel Stanetova Ulica, the pedestrianized high street. A bustling shopping area with well-patronized cafés and ice-cream parlors by day, it soon empties as evenings and week-ends approach. Stanetova opens out into Tomšičev Trg, where the Celje Tourist Association (*Turistično Društvo Celje*; Mon–Sat 9–11:30am) has maps and private rooms—should you need them. Three modern hotels (the *Celeia*, ☎063/22-041; *Europa*, ☎063/21-233 and *Merx*, ☎063/21-917) each have double rooms for around $45.

The center

To the right of Tomšičev Trg is Muzejski Trg, where the sixteenth-century **County Hall** (begun in Renaissance style, finished in Baroque) is home to a mediocre **Regional Museum** (Tues–Sun 9am–1pm, Wed also 2–4pm) which contains a few Roman bits and pieces and precious little else, save for a ceiling painting on the first floor. Completed in around 1600 by an unknown artist, this so-called "Celje Ceiling" creates an illusion of height, with painted pillars and columns seemingly leading ever upwards to an imaginary sky filled with frolicking cherubs.

On the other side of Tomšičev Trg is Šlomskov Trg, and the parish church of Sv Danijela. Inside is one of the most important surviving examples of Gothic art in Slovenia, the **Kapela Žalostne Materje Boze** (Chapel of Our Lady of the Sorrows), where exquisitely painted angels wheel across the vaults in frescoes dating from the early fifteenth century.

From here it's a stone's throw to the river and the Capuchin monastery on the opposite bank. Founded in the thirteenth century, the monastery has not enjoyed a happy fate in recent times. The majority of the Slovene intelligentsia was locked up here between 1941 and 1945, when the occupying Germans evicted the monks and turned the place into a prison. During the war, two successive fires reduced to ashes a historic library rich in volumes dating from the Counter-Reformation, and after the war the buildings were converted into flats. Still functioning, however, is the **monastery church** (open daily; hours vary), a straightforward eighteenth-century Baroque structure with a largely modern interior—rebuilt after the aforementioned fire.

A hundred meters to the right as you face the monastery, the remains of the **Roman Temple of Hercules** lie in an unmarked field on the hillside. There's nothing much to look at apart from the foundations and a reconstructed pillar or two—but this is probably all there is to see of Roman Celje.

What makes Celje really worthwhile is the fourteenth-century **castle** that dominates the valley from a hilltop southeast of the city center; you should allow two hours for the well signposted journey on foot. The masters of the castle were the counts of Celje, a massively rich German family who stayed top dogs of the region for well over two centuries, owning a string of castles—those at Samobor, Trakošćan, Varaždin, and Vitrovica among them—that stretched down into what is now Croatia. With the murder of Ulrich II of Celje in 1456, the male line came to an abrupt end, and the castle and the territories that went with it fell conveniently into the lap of the Hapsburgs.

What remains is a glorious windswept ruin, the main feature of which is the 35-meter-high **Friderikov Stolp** or "Friedrich's Tower." Ascendable for a small fee (opening times vary: Fri–Sun 10am–5pm at time of writing), the tower offers a stupendous panorama of Celje, the Savinja valley, and the surrounding hills. Elsewhere in the castle there's a *gostilna* (closed Mon and Tues) with a limited menu but a similarly breathtaking view.

From Celje the eastbound highway leads onwards to MARIBOR, climbing over the low hills of the **Konjiška Gora** range before dropping into the Drava basin.

Northeast Slovenia

North of the E-93 Ljubljana–Maribor highway, minor roads head off into areas relatively untouched by the hand of tourism. Although there's nothing to compare with the majesty of the Julian Alps here, there's much that is typical of old rural Slovenia: quiet valleys with forgotten hamlets and wayside chapels, wooden barns, and hayricks in picturesque abundance. Despite being off the beaten track **accommodation** shouldn't be too much of a problem: local tourist offices can usually find rooms in private farmhouses and *gostilne*.

One of the best ways to experience this region is to head west up the **Savinja Valley** from Šempeter towards SOLČAVA and the silent, sparsely inhabited valley of **Logarska Dolina**, just short of the Austrian border. This has long been a popular hiking destination for Slovenes, but the lack of regular bus links from Ljubljana and other major centers makes it a difficult trip to contemplate unless you have your own vehicle. Should you make it, the natural beauty of the region is supposed to be stunning.

Titovo Velenje, Slovenj Gradec, and Around

About 18km north of Celje is **TITOVO VELENJE**, which, despite some craggy medieval ruins and a ski jump that puts it on the winter-sports map, is an unwelcoming industrial town dominated by the machine industry and regimented rows of apartment blocks. The surrounding area is blighted by a vast lignite mine that snakes up the valley to the grim mining town of Šoštanj. The bus station contains a **tourist office** which has rooms, but the best advice is to press on northward to the dark forests and highland meadows of the Koroška region.

The road over the hills towards Slovenj Gradec takes you through beautiful stretches of limestone gorge and densely wooded subalpine sceney before dropping down into the verdant pastures and sleepy villages of the Mislinja valley. **SLOVENJ GRADEC** itself is scarred by wood- and paper-mills on the northern side, but the center retains the ambience of a rural market town. Lively and vibrant it certainly isn't, but it could be a useful base for exploring the Pohorje Hills to the east—for those who want to get away from it all.

The town's main attraction is the **Art Gallery** on Glavni Trg 24 (9am–noon & 3–6pm), which houses Slovenia's largest collection of works by the highly regarded naive painter **Jože Tisnikar**, whose dark obsessions with death, funeral processions, and corpses are reflected in the sombre but gripping canvases here. Adjoining the picture gallery is a slightly incongruous collection of African sculptures, while next door lurks the inevitable museum of revolution.

On nearby Trg Svobode the parish church of **Sv Elizabete** is stern, gray, and Gothic on the outside, but inside has a sumptuous Baroque altar with fine gilded statuary, completed by Gratz-based craftsman Janez Jakob Šoj in 1733. In the presbyterium on the same square is the **Soklič Museum** (Trg Svobode 5; daily 8am–3pm), a private collection amassed by local priest Jakob Soklič between 1935 and 1972. It's an eccentric hodgepodge of furniture, ceramics, figurines, and mediocre genre paintings by obscure artists.

If you're dallying in Slovenj Gradec for any length of time, take a look at the church of **Sv Duha**, with Gothic frescoes dating from the 1460s, and the medieval settlement of **Stari Trg** just south of the town, above which the part-Gothic, part-Baroque church of **Sv Pankrac** has been built into a ruined castle.

The **bus station** is five minutes' walk from the market square of Glavini Trg, where the *Kompas* **tourist office** at no. 38 doles out advice on the region's beauty spots and rooms in outlying farms. The *Hotel Kompas Pohorje* next door (☎062/842-291) has doubles from $35.

Fifteen kilometers away from Slovenj Gradec up in the hills to the east is the ski center of KOPE (see p.58), the main winter resort in the western Pohorje. The whole region is an up-and-coming winter sports area, earmarked for farther development.

Ten kilometers north of Slovenj Gradec the river Mislinja flows into the river Drava at **DRAVOGRAD**, a dour little place with little to tempt you save for the ancient Romanesque church of Sv Vida, and the stern lessons to be learned from the **Museum of Nazi Terror** (Trg 4 Jula 7; Mon–Fri 8am–noon), housed in what was once a Gestapo jail. From here the road leads westward along the lonely, unspoiled border-hugging route to SOLČAVA and LOGARSKA DOLINA, or eastward down the valley to Maribor.

The road down the Drava closely follows the placid waters of the river, slowed down by a series of hydroelectric projects stretching from Dravograd itself as far as Ptuj. The route passes through a string of quaint villages with ancient churches, notably at VUZENICA, 15km beyond Dravograd and slightly off the main road where the twelfth-century church of **Sv Miklavža** displays the whole gamut of styles from Romanesque onward. A little farther on the beautifully whitewashed, wooden-roofed church of Sv Janez Krstnika stands by the roadside at Spodnja Muta. Beyond the characterless frontier town of RADLJE steep densely wooded hills begin to give way to a more gentle landscape covered with vineyards. The widening of the river (and occasional sightings of yachts and pleasure craft) is a sign that you're approaching a major dam above Maribor, and the western suburbs of the city itself.

Maribor

Five buses a day run from Slovenj Gradec, taking a couple of hours to reach **MARIBOR**, which began life as the eleventh-century castle of Marchburg, defending the German Empire's lonely southeastern frontier against incursions by belligerent Magyars. The town came into its own in the eighteenth century, when the Austrian emperor Charles VI decided to build a new road to Trieste; it then replaced Varaždin as the main beneficiary of Vienna's trade route to the Adriatic.

Nowadays Slovenia's second city is a dull industrial sprawl which rejoices in having the highest suicide rate in Yugoslavia; it's uninspiring save for a compact, Austrianate center and the nearby winter resort of the **Mariborsko Pohorje**. Furthermore, its proximity to Austria seems to have forced prices up in recent years, so it's no longer the conveniently cheap stopping-off point it used to be. At night especially, central Maribor can be a miserable place; deserted, dimly lit streets echo either to the sounds of stray drunks or the heavy trucks thundering through town on the quick route down from Austria.

From the bus and rail stations on the east of town, a ten-minute walk down Partizanska brings you face to face with the forbidding redbrick bulk of the **Franciscan church**—fortunately, a reasonably pretty town center lies behind it. Immediately beyond the church—past a disturbingly ugly war memorial—**Grajski Trg** is home to an eighteenth-century castle that today contains the **Regional Museum** (*Pokrajnski Muzej*, Grajski 2; Tues–Sat 9am–5pm, Sun 10am–noon). It's a large collection with a little of everything, including costumes used in the *Kurenti* dances of Ptuj (of which more later) and one of the most inept ceiling paintings in Europe.

Opposite the museum, Grajski Trg funnels into the largely pedestrianized **Old Town**, with the dark, narrow streets of Vetrinjska, Jurčičeva, and Gosposka forming the core. A few steps away to the west is the lumpish, largely sixteenth-century Gothic **Cathedral** on Slomškov Trg—its mostly Baroque interior unremarkable save for some surviving Gothic stone pews. From here, Poštna leads down to **Glavni Trg**, a pleasing Renaissance square with a sixteenth-century town hall and a Baroque plague column. Beyond Glavni Trg, steps lead down to the river. There's not much to see on the waterfront save for the town's two remaining medieval landmarks; the curious whitewashed fifteenth-century **Sodni Stolp** (judge's tower), 200m to the right, and the sixteenth-century **Vodni Stolp** (water tower), now a *vinoteka* where you can sample local wines. For the rest, there's little except for a couple of uninspiring **museums**: the **Museum of the National Liberation Struggle**, Heroja Tomsica 5 (Mon–Fri 8am–1pm), is a waste of a fine nineteenth-century mansion, and the **Art Gallery** (*Umetnostna Galerija*), Strossmayerjeva 6, two blocks west of Slomškov Trg (Tues–Sat 9am–1pm & 3–6pm, Sun 9am–3pm), has a modest collection of modern works by local artists.

One relaxing place to explore if you've got time on your hands is the **town park**, due north from the museum along Grajska. Even so it's an oddly sterile place, with well-regimented stretches of lawn bisected by concrete strips of pathway. Things get marginally better as the park climbs up into the foothills of the **Mariborske Gorice**, with vineyards rolling down into the town's northern suburbs.

Accommodation, Eating, and Drinking

The helpful **Maribor Tourist Information Center** (*MATIC*, Grajski Trg 1; Mon–Fri 8am–7pm, Sat 8am–1pm) distributes maps, and will seek out private **rooms** (usually well out of the center) or, from beginning of July to the end of August, organize you a place at one of the **student hostels**. Of centrally located **hotels**, *Zamorec* (Gosposka; ☎062/26-171) is the cheapest and most basic with doubles at $28. There's also a **campground and motel** at JEZERO (☎062/621-103), way out on the Dravograd route near the village of Bresternica.

Virtually all the **restaurants** in central Maribor are owned by the same monolithic hotel and catering organization, *Pohorje*, and as such tend to be characterless places run by uninterested staff. Most locals wisely head for inns in outlying villages. Hence Maribor doesn't have much of an outdoor eating and drinking scene, although the café in the courtyard behind the town hall is adequate; the terrace of the *Hotel Orel* on Grajski Trg comes close to being a sidewalk café-restaurant (although the *Astoria Self-service* immediately opposite serves much the same food at half the cost). One restaurant with a reasonable reputation is *Novi Svet* at Jurčičeva 7, with quite expensive fish specialties and a predominantly Austrian clientele. Otherwise, the privately run bistro and bar *Amadeus* on Slovenska (the main road leading westward from Grajski Trg) appears to be the only sign of life in the center.

Far better to head straight for the banks of the river Drava below Glavni Trg, where a string of five or six privately owned **bars** (with names such as *Capucino*, *Brut*, and *Picolo*) occupy a short stretch of the recently renovated riverfront—it's here that the local youth congregate. But, in all honesty, Maribor offers little by way of cultural diversions and is tomb-quiet at night*. It lacks regular club or concert outlets, a state of affairs partially explained by the fact that the town's university is oriented towards technical subjects; youngsters with a penchant for the arts invariably leave town for Ljubljana.

The best time to be in Maribor is mid-September, when the grape harvest is marked by a ten-day festival known as *Vesela Jesen*—"Merry Autumn." Usually running from September 14 to 25, this is the one event guaranteed to breath of life into Maribor and its normally comatose citizens.

---

*The last word on swinging Maribor goes to one of its disenchanted locals: "In Maribor," she said, "we drink all day and watch TV at night. It is all very depressing."

Ptuj

Twenty-five kilometers down the road and an easy local bus ride from Maribor, **PTUJ** is the antidote to all this. Usually billed as the oldest town in Slovenia, it's about the most attractive as well, rising up from the Drava valley in a flutter of red roofs and topped by a friendly-looking castle. But the best thing is its streets, scaled-down mansions standing shoulder to shoulder on scaled-down boulevards, medieval fantasies crumbling next to Baroque extravagances. Out of the windows hang plants and the locals; watching the world go by is a major occupation here.

The town doesn't have a center as such, but if it did it would be **Trg Mladinskih Brigad**, with an Austrian-style town hall at one end, and the **Priory Church** (open mornings only) at the other. Begun in the twelfth century, this is mainly Gothic, though splashed with Baroque; there's a fine carved choir of 1446. Nearby, its rather unambitious **tower** started life in the sixteenth century as a bell tower, became city watchtower in the seventeenth century, and was retired in the eighteenth, when it was given an onion-bulb spire for decoration. Roman tombstones have been embedded in its lower reaches, but a more noticeable holdover of Roman times is the **tablet** that stands below like an oversize tooth, actually a funeral monument to a Roman mayor. It's just possible to make out its carvings of Orpheus entertaining assembled fauna; in medieval times local ne'er-do-wells and petty criminals were chained to the tablet and publicly humiliated.

Right at the other end of the street the **Archaeological Museum** (mid–April–Nov Tues–Sun 10am–1pm) lives in what was once a Dominican monastery, a mustardy building gutted in the eighteenth century and now hung with spidery decoration, and worth a look for the carvings and statuary around its likably disheveled cloisters.

A path opposite the monastery winds up to the **Castle** (mid–April–Nov Tues–Sun, obligatory guided tours on the hour 9am–3pm). There's been a castle of sorts here for as long as there's been a town, since Ptuj was the only fording point across the Drava for miles around, holding the defenses against the tribes of the north. The Romans maintained a large base here and the fleeing Slavs fought off the Hungarians in the sixth-century migrations. An agglomeration of styles from the fourteenth to the eighteenth centuries, the castle was home to a succession of noble families who struck it rich in the town. Last of these were the **Herbensteins**, who lived here until 1945; of Austro-Scottish descent, they'd welcomed the Nazi invaders in 1941, and only their wealth and influence rescued them from just desserts at the end of the war. Their portraits hang on the walls of the **museum** the castle now holds, a collection mixed in theme and quality. On the first floor you will find period rooms, the usual stuff, with original tapestries and wallpaper; on the second are a few excellent pieces of medieval carving—Saint George unconcernedly killing a rather homey dragon, Saints Barbara and Catherine delicately and exquisitely crafted. There's also armor, furniture, and, if you're interested, a collection of musical instruments, all of which seem to have twanged or tooted their last.

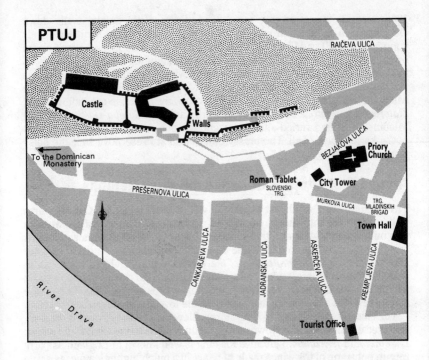

At Shrovetide (late February/early March) Ptuj is host to one of the oldest and most unusual customs in Yugoslavia. The **Kurenti processions** are a sort of fertility rite and celebration of the dead combined: participants wear sinister masks of sheepskin and feathers with a colored beak for a nose and white beads for teeth, and possibly represent ancestral spirits—have a look at a picture and you'll see that there is something deeply and primitively frightening about them. So dressed, the *Kurenti* move in hopping procession from house to house, scaring off evil spirits with the din from the cowbells tied to their costumes. At the head of the procession is the Devil, wrapped in a net to symbolize his capture: behind the *Kurenti* the *Orači*—"the plowers"—pull a small wooden plow, scattering sand around to represent the sowing of seed, and housewives smash clay pots at their feet—possibly the leftovers of a sacrifice tradition—in the hope that this will bring health and luck to their households. Lenten rituals like this were once widespread in Europe's farming communities; perhaps because of its oddness the *Kurenti* procession is one of few to survive in anything like its original form.

Practicalities

Ptuj is linked by (painfully slow) train to Ljubljana and Varazdin; the **train station** is 500m northeast of the center on Osojnikova Cesta, the **bus station**

100m nearer town on the same road. From both points, walk down Osojnikova to its junction with Ulica Heroja Lacka; a right turn here lands you straight on Trg Mladinskih Brigad. **Private rooms** in Ptuj aren't cheap or central—and for about the same price you might as well stay at the *Hotel Poetovio* (☎062/772-640) at Trstenjakova 13, whose doubles cost $27. If this is full the **tourist office** at Trg Svobode 4 (Mon–Fri 8am–3pm, Sat 8am–1pm) will point you toward the rooms. For **food** you fare better: in ascending order: *Zlatorog* at Bezjakoca 10 is cheap and ordinary, the *Evropa Gostilna* on Trg Mladinskih Brigad varied and boozy, and the fish restaurant at the river end of Cankarjeva best of all. The brassy *Café Gloria* at Presernova 20 is the noisy hangout of Ptuj's youth.

Around Ptuj: Ptujska Gora and the Wine Regions

Twelve kilometers southeast of Ptuj the village of **PTUJSKA GORA** is worth visiting if you're into things Gothic. Its pocket-sized **Church of Sv Marika** was built around 1415, and though altered over the years retains some of its fine original carvings, most likable of which is a relief above the high altar showing the *Virgin as Protectress of the World*. Seven angels lift her cloak to reveal ranks of figures, each drawn with the detail and attention of a portrait; which is indeed what they were, depicting the assembled families of the counts of Celje. The church itself is one of the loveliest in Slovenia.

The rolling hills east of Ptuj form Slovenia's **wine-growing region**, centered around two small towns that give their name to the local white wines: *Ljutomer* and *Jeruzalem*. Ljutomer Riesling is well known in England as party rotgut, but some of the wines made here are in a much higher league; as a rule of thumb go for the bottles with a numbered circular black label, indication of a sort of Slovenian *appelation controlé*. *Sipon* and *Halozan* are among the best, and try the *Renski Risling*—smooth, dry, and not too fruity.

Southeast from Ljubljana: Novo Mesto, the Krka Valley, and Samobor

The road south of Ljubljana towards Zagreb is likely to be your first experience of a quintessentially Yugoslav phenomenon, the *autocesta* (*autoput* in Serbo-Croatian), which conveys traffic from the north right down through Belgrade and Serbia to Macedonia and the Greek border. Although it literally translates as "expressway," the *autoput/autocesta* is often anything but—a slow-moving single line of traffic occasionally relieved by stretches of true expressway on the approaches to major cities (the most extensive bits of divided highway are south of Zagreb, and both north and south of Belgrade). So from Ljubljana onwards you'd better get used to the idea of spending a great deal of your time either crawling behind caravans of heavy freight, or narrowly avoiding head-on collisions with those recklessly passing in the opposite direction.

The area between Zagreb and Ljubljana is one of gentle hills and pastoral greens and yellows, dotted with vineyards, monasteries, and castles. The provincial capital **Novo Mesto** is a good base for exploring further, but most of the places in the account below (each of them just off the main autocesta by a few kilometers) are easily accessible in short hops by **bus**.

Taking the **train** for the Ljubljana to Zagreb run means you'll see little of the towns of the region, since the route passes north of the *autocesta*, winding down the wooded Sava valley past the grim mining town of Trbovlje. However it is possible to reach Novo Mesto by train, on a lesser line which heads due south from Ljubljana towards Karlovac.

Novo Mesto

Occupying a rocky promontory on the Krka River, **NOVO MESTO** is essentially an ancient market town onto which the twentieth century has been unceremoniously grafted in a rush of postwar development. To be fair, the industrial zones (producing among other things Renault cars made under license by the local firm IMV) are isolated to the north and south of the old center, but the traffic and general bustle created by recent urban expansion daily reduces Novo Mesto's narrow streets to noisy, exhaust fume-filled chaos.

The **train station** is way out to the north, and reaching the center entails a lengthy half-hour walk down Ljubljanska Cesta or a short local bus ride. The **bus station** is more conveniently situated on Novi Trg; turn right at the exit into Cesta Komandanta Staneta and either follow this all the way to the main square **Glavni Trg**, or take the next right up a narrow street to Prešernov Trg and the **Chapter Church of Sv Miklavza**, built at the summit of the hill around which the medieval town grew. The church has a checkered architectural history typical of many of the region, passing through Gothic, Baroque and neo-Gothic phases—but it's the gray stone exterior of the fourteenth-century Gothic original which shines through. Inside, the picture of Saint Nicholas above the main altar is attributed by all the local tourist literature to the Venetian master Tintoretto, but it's much more likely to be the work of one of his school.

Below the church is the **Museum of the Dolenjska Region** (Muzejska Ulica; Tues–Fri 9am–3pm & 5–7pm, Sat 9am–noon & 5–7pm, Sun 9am–noon), a modern, well-lit gallery containing a small but fascinating collection of trinkets from the Iron Age. Novo Mesto was the center of thriving Bronze- and Iron-Age cultures from at least 1000 BC onward, as the number of rich local grave-finds bears witness. The Celts in particular were prolific in their use of large grave urns built in imitation of the dwellings of the deceased; unfortunately, many locally-found treasures were carted off to Vienna and Ljubljana, leaving the museum with leftovers belatedly unearthed after 1950. However, there's much of value here, including a splendid Celtic suit of armor.

From the museum, narrow alleyways descend through the oldest part of town to the river Krka on the south side or, passing a small market on the way, to Glavni Trg to the east. A cobbled market square surrounded by arcades, Glavni Trg is dominated by an eccentric, mock-Renaissance **Town Hall**, built by ostentatious provincial burghers at the turn of the century. Overlooking the square a few steps behind the town hall, the Franciscan monastery church of **Sv Lenart** echoes the chapter church. The basic Gothic structure was built in 1472 by Franciscan monks fleeing from Bosnia in the wake of Turkish advances. (Novo Mesto was at that time fast emerging as an important line of defense against the Ottomans, remaining so until the fortress of Karlovac was built farther south in 1579.) A Baroque exterior was added later in 1664 after a fire, only to undergo complete neo-Gothification in the nineteenth century when tastes changed once again. The resulting creamy yellow facade, with its arches and columns surmounted by swirling, almost Moorish molded patterns, resembles an extravagantly iced cake. Opposite the church, an old **gymnasium**, founded in 1743 during the educational reforms of Empress Maria Theresa, now functions as a music school.

At the bottom of Glavni Trg, the bridge spanning the river leads to featureless residential suburbs on the other side; but it's worth a quick trip across just to look back at the town's impressive location, hovering above a bend in the river.

Practicalities

Novo Mesto's **tourist office** is at Breg 1, at the bottom of Glavni Trg just before the bridge, and has a supply of private **rooms**. If they're all taken, cheapest alternative is the *Prenočišča pri Vodnjaku* pension (☎068/21-584) at Dilančeva 1 on the corner of Glavni Trg, with rooms at $33 a double. The smart, modern *Hotel Metropol* (☎068/22-226) on Novi Trg has doubles for $45, while doubles at the slightly less salubrious *Hotel Kandija* (Zagrebška 2—just over the bridge) go for $42.

The most convenient places to **eat** are on Glavni Trg. The *Goščišča na Trgu* has a sidewalk café as well as a self-service (Mon–Sat 8am–8pm) and a slightly classier restaurant. Across the road is another café with a basement pizzeria. A little more expensive but with a good reputation for local recipes is *Breg* on the narrow street of the same name, 100m beyond the tourist office; its outdoor terrace in the warren of alleyways below the Chapter church is also a pleasant place for a drink. Almost all places to eat in town are closed on Sundays; the single exception is the *Expres-Restoran* at the bus station—and even this closes at 6pm. If you want to assemble your own picnic, Glavni Trg has a couple of delicatessens and supermarkets.

Due west of Novo Mesto are the dark, impenetrable forests of **Kočevski Rog**. During the war, these wooded hills provided excellent cover for the Slovene partisans, who concealed a string of secret field hospitals here along with a major administrative center, known as **Baza 20**. This encampment of log cabins, 20km southwest of Novo Mesto, was the seat of the Slovene Central Committee from April 1943 until the beginning of 1945; it remained completely undetected by the Germans throughout the war. Unfortunately the same can't be said of other more long-standing denizens of the forests: stags, wild boar, lynx, and bears provide upwardly-mobile Yugoslav functionaries and their monied foreign guests with much exclusive hunting.

The Lower Krka

Continuing southeast from Novo Mesto, the E-94 *autocesta* follows the course of the Krka towards Zagreb. The preponderance of late-medieval castles and *chateaux* is a sign that you're entering the old *Vojna Krajina* or **Military Frontier**, a band of territory designated by the Hapsburgs into a defensive buffer zone to guard against Turkish incursions. From the early 1500s onwards, the Military Frontier shifted back and forth across the Balkans for almost three centuries, before the northern half of what is now Yugoslavia finally stabilized under Austrian rule. Most of the warlords and adventurers who held sway over the frontier region were taken from the indigenous Slav population; many were Serbs, who after fleeing northward to escape Turkish atrocities were welcomed by the Hapsburgs in recognition of their warlike qualities.

Seven kilometers beyond Novo Mesto, on an island on the River Krka, is the sixteenth-century citadel of **Otočec**. The castle here lost its military importance almost as soon as it was built (with the frontier shifting southwards), and it was purchased in 1560 by the supreme commander of the Military Frontier, Ivan Lenkovič. Otočec is now heavily commercialized: the castle has become a luxury hotel (where a double room costs anything between $75 and $170), and it's surrounded by sport, and leisure facilities.

More picturesque is the town of **KOSTANJEVICA**, 15km farther on. Again it occupies a small island created by a loop in the river Krka, accessible across quaint wooden bridges. Billed as one of Slovenia's most ancient towns, Kostanjevica was a thriving commercial center in the Middle Ages, and in the thirteenth century minted its own coins. Nowadays it's no more than a sleepy village backwater, visited primarily for its quiet rural beauty and the impressive **Cistercian Monastery** (Tues–Sun 9am–6pm) which lies a kilometer to the west. Founded in 1234, but largely rebuilt in the Baroque era, the monastery was abandoned in 1782 and further damaged by fire in this century, and the long and painstaking process of restoration is still only half complete. However, the austere, crumbling off-white appearance of the monastery buildings (enlivened only by the Baroque facade added to an earlier, thirteenth-century church) conceals a beautiful and spacious courtyard lined with three storys of arcades. These are now home to an extensive **art gallery** (times as above) containing fragments of Gothic frescoes found in the church below, and gloomy portraits of monastic worthies brought here from the neighboring (and still functioning) Carthusian monastery of PLETERJE. Most space is devoted to major figures of twentieth-century Slovene art: the local painter **Božidar Jakac**, who as a young man documented life with the partisans in a series of line drawings and sketches; and the **Kralj** brothers Tone and France, key figures in the interwar Slovene avant-garde, who later opted for a more politically committed socialist realism (and thus became the beneficiaries of much official praise). The lawns outside the monastery serve as a sculpture park for *Forma Viva*, a colony of artists who assemble here every three years to sculpt specifically in wood.

A short stroll round Kostanjevica itself is worthwhile. There's a small Gothic church at each end of this tiny town; the one at the southern end being noted for modern frescoes painted by the local expressionist painter Janez Gorjup in 1931.

Fifteen kilometers farther east, to the north of the *autocesta*, the Krka joins the Sava at **BREŽICE**, another one-horse town which nevertheless contains one of Yugoslavia's better provincial **museums** (Mon–Sat 8am–1pm, Sun 9am–noon), housed in a sixteenth-century castle at the bottom of the town's main street, **Cesta Prvih Borcev**.

Built in the mid-1500s when the combined threats of Turkish raids and local peasant rebellions were at their height, the castle's solid blockhouse structure with conical, red-tiled defensive towers at each corner was very much the norm for sixteenth-century fortifications in this neck of the woods—others at Otočec (see above) and Mokrice (see below) do not greatly differ. The museum has some fascinating tenth-century BC skeletons, weapons, and jewelry extricated from Celtic graves in the nearby village of DOBOVA. The rest of the museum is a treasure trove of nineteenth-century peasant culture—unfortunately badly labeled with little guidance even in Slovene—but there's a rich collection of self-explanatory spinning machines, weaving machines, and wine-presses. Centerpiece of the museum is the **Knight's Hall**, decorated at the end of the sixteenth century in the florid, ostentatious style of the Italian Baroque. The result is a vertigo-inducing array of scenes from classical myth and legend.

Ten kilometers farther on en route for Zagreb, the last item of interest before reaching the Slovene-Croat border is another Renaissance stronghold at **MOKRICE**. The fate of Mokrice Castle is typical of many: initially a strongpoint in the defense against marauding Turks and unruly peasants, it subsequently became a stately residence in more peaceful times, and was finally converted into an upscale hotel. The gilded pseudo-aristocratic kitsch of the luxury dining room makes this a popular weekend recreation spot for the local middle classes.

Samobor

From Mokrice the green flatlands of the Sava valley take over as you pass from Slovenia into Croatia about 20km west of Zagreb. Worth a detour, or indeed a day trip out from Zagreb itself, is the delightful historic town of **SAMOBOR**, 3km to the west of the autoput. Nestling among wooded hills, Samobor was well established as a trade and craft center during the Middle Ages, and preceded neighboring Zagreb in being granted the privileges of a free royal town. Nowadays it presents a well-preserved nucleus of prosperous nineteenth-century provincial life, and is a popular starting point for gentle hikes into the surrounding hills.

The town center revolves around the long, extended triangle of **Trg Kralja Tomislava**, lined with pale yellow whitewashed eighteenth- and nineteenth-century buildings and overlooked by an unassuming seventeenth-century parish church. Along the western side of the square flows the Gradna (here more of an swollen brook than a river), spanned by a succession of slender bridges.

Livadićeva Ulica leads you out of the northern end of the square to the **Town Museum** (Livadićeva 7; Mon–Fri 9am–3pm, Sat & Sun 9am–1pm, closed Thurs), a modest collection of furniture, ceramics, and fusty portraits of local burghers. The rather more interesting ethnographical collection is currently languishing in storage, awaiting the renovation of an adjacent outbuilding to which it will be transferred. The museum is housed in **Livadićev Dvor**, the nineteenth-century home of composer **Ferdinand Weisner**, whose enthusiasm for the liberation of Slavdom from the Hapsburg yoke led him to change his name to its Slavic form, Ferdo Livadić. During the 1830s and 1840s his home became an important meeting place for the leaders of the **Illyrian movement**, who aimed to raise the national consciousness of the Slavs within the Hapsburg Empire, displaying a particular interest in the unity of the southern Slavs—a kind of prototype Yugoslavism. Vienna initially tolerated the movement as a politically useful counterweight against the boisterous nationalism of the Hungarians, but eventually became alarmed and reacted severely, banning any mention of the word "Illyria" in 1843.

Continuing up Livadićeva, Samobor's oldest quarter, **Taborec** (now an anonymous residential district) cowers below the medieval **castle**, a bleak romantic ruin dating from 1260. Passing through the hands of many a feudal baron, it remained a fine aristocratic seat (as a scale model in the local museum attests) right up until this century, but after being abandoned on the eve of World War I it rapidly fell into disrepair—its decline hastened by locals plundering the derelict castle for building materials. From here the road continues up a progressively narrowing valley—the start of a popular hiking area with trails leading up to the castle itself.

A more popular starting point for ventures into the great outdoors is **Anindol**, a local beauty spot overlooking the town. It's a 25-minute walk up Maršala Tita, which winds up into the hills from the west side of Trg Kralja Tomislava. It was on Anindol that Tito organized the founding congress of the Croatian Communist Party on August 1, 1937, in an attempt to persuade the Croats that Yugoslav Communists shared their nationalist aspirations. An annual hiking festival was used as a cover; with the whole area filling up with weekend visitors, party activists could infiltrate without arousing suspicion. Tito himself even took the precaution of joining a hiking organization some months in advance. Only sixteen Communist agents actually made it to the "congress," and Tito was reduced to scratching the resolutions of the meeting on the back of a Catholic calendar with a penknife—well, so the story goes. Despite the presence of a stone plinth marking the spot, the real reason for most pilgrimages here is to enjoy the scenery and embark on the many walks radiating outwards from Anindol. If you lack the energy to make it all the way up to Anindol itself, the town cemetery, ten minutes up Maršala Tita, is a good place to savor a panoramic view of the town.

Leaving Trg Kralja Tomislava from the south end, Langova Ulica curls its way up to a **Franciscan Monastery** with an adjoining eighteenth-century church. Despite the dull exterior, the church contains some worthwhile Baroque art by two of the most prolific local painters of the period: a monumental *Dormition of the Virgin* by France Jelovšek, and altar paintings by Valentin Metzinger.

Practicalities

Samobor's **bus station** is five minutes east of the main square. As it's one of the remotest outposts of Zagreb's municipal transit system, tickets bought here are valid for one and a half hours in any direction within Zagreb itself. Buses leave every twenty minutes for one of two tram terminals in western Zagreb—Remiza or Černomerec—at which you change for central Zagreb and the train/bus stations.

The *Kvarner* **tourist office** on Trg Kralja Tomislava (Mon–Fri 8am–4pm, Sat 8am–noon) is mostly intended for locals trying to get out rather than tourists coming in, but it may be able to supply the occasional private room. Otherwise *Hotel Lavica* (Livadićeva, at the end of the main Trg and next door to the museum) has doubles for $35.

For **food and drink**, the café on the main Trg is the best place for an early-morning coffee or afternoon drink, while the narrow streets leading south from the Trg are well supplied with privately owned cafés and bars. One of these streets, Kleščićeva, has three café-restaurants relaxingly situated alongside the river Gradna. The best time to be in Samobor is undoubtedly during the February **Karneval** immediately preceding Lent, when visitors pour in from Zagreb to join in the general atmosphere of hedonism and excess.

Zagreb

Yugoslavia's second city and the capital of the Republic of Croatia, **ZAGREB** runs close to Ljubljana as the country's most vibrant and youthful center. Approaching from the east, Zagreb certainly feels a long way from gray Belgrade— its people better clothed, better fed, and generally more comfortable than their compatriots in the southern republics. It's a good-looking city, too. As capital of the wartime puppet state of the Croat fascist Ante Pavelić, the city center suffered less than many other places in the last war, and the majority of its buildings are relatively well-preserved, grand peach-colored monuments to the self-esteem of the Austro-Hungarian Empire. Much of it has also, like Belgrade, recently benefited from a thorough facelift, spurred by its role as host of the 1987 Student Olympic Games. Two days here are well spent; in fact, a handful of good museums, side trips to the nearby Zagorje hills, and the above-average nightlife, should keep you occupied for at least that.

Arrival, Getting Around, and Information

Arriving by **plane**, Zagreb's airport is about 10km southeast of the city, connected with the center by half-hourly *JAT* bus between 7:30am and 8pm; after that time buses simply connect with flights. The buses drop you behind the *Hotel Esplanade*, close to the central **railroad station**, or *Glavni Kolodvor*, on Tomislava Trg, on the edge of the city center ten minutes' walk from Trg Republike. Coming in by **bus**, Zagreb's main bus station is about ten minutes' walk east of the railroad station at the junction of Branimirova and Avenija Marina Držića. Trams #2, #3, and #6 run down to the railroad station from here; get off at the second stop.

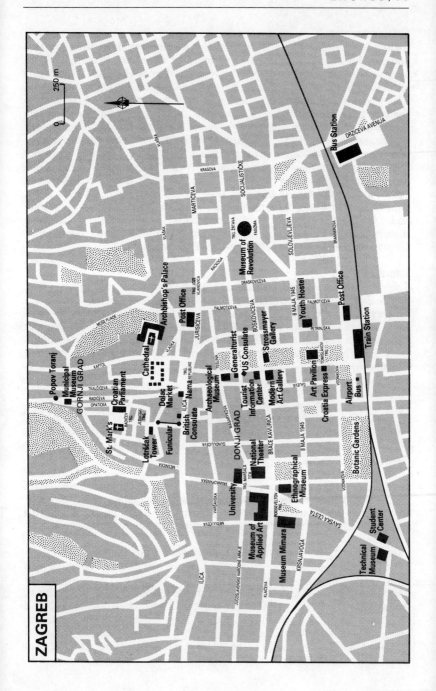

Getting Around

Zagreb has an efficient and comprehensive **public transit** network of trams and to a lesser extent buses, though much of downtown is easily seen on foot, and the old upper town only thinly covered by public transit. Use trams for getting from the bus station to the rail station or city center north of here, out to your accommodation, or for quick hops from one side of the town to the other. There's a flat fare per journey on both buses and trams; tickets (*tramvajske kartice*) are valid for ninety minutes and are sold from newspaper kiosks and sometimes the back carriage of the tram by a conductor. Validate your ticket by punching it in the machines on board the trams. Newspaper kiosks also sell day tickets, which can work out cheaper if you intend to use public transit a lot—they're valid from the moment they're punched. For information, a diagram of the main tram routes is posted up at tram stops, which, together with a decent map, is about all you need. The railroad station and Trg Republike are the two main hubs of the tram system. The main termini of local buses are at Britanski Trg, Kaptol, Mihaljevac, Ljubljnaica, Črnomerec, and Dubrava, behind the main railroad station.

Information

There are two main **tourist information centers** in central Zagreb: one at Trg N. Zrinjskog 14 (Mon–Fri 8am–8pm, Sat & Sun 9am–6pm; ☎411-833) and another at Trg Republike 11 (same times; ☎278-910 or ☎278-855). Both of these offices have maps and up-to-date leaflets on events, and can help out with general queries, though neither has private rooms or can book accommodation. There's a third information office in the upper town, close to where the funicular stops on Strossmajerov Šetalište, though its information is restricted to the immediate neighborhood.

> The Zagreb area telephone code is ☎041

Finding a Place to Stay

It's difficult to find **accommodation** in Zagreb, especially during the summer. For a city of its size it has few hotels, pitiful stocks of private rooms, and beds in its hostels are often reserved way in advance. Between June and August, it's not a good idea to turn up without having reserved something beforehand.

Private Rooms, Hostels, Student Accommodation, and Camping

What **private rooms** there are, however, can be had from two offices, both a short walk from the railroad station: *Generalturist*, Trg N. Zrinjskog 18 (Mon–Fri 7:30am–7:30pm, Sat 7:30am–1pm; ☎425-566) and *Croatiaturist*, Tomislavov Trg 17 (Mon–Fri 6:30am–7:30pm, Sat 6:30am–1pm; ☎411-436). If they have run out and you don't care about being smack in the center, try for rooms at the *Turiŝtiĉko Druŝtvo* at Trnsko 15e in Novi Zagreb (Mon–Fri 8am–3pm; ☎521-523), though be warned that this is some way out. Take tram #6 from the railroad station.

There's a **youth hostel** conveniently placed at Petrinjska 77 (open 5am–1am; ☎434-964), five minutes' walk from the railroad station, which has dormitory accommodation for $5–8 per person depending on age and IYHF membership, and double rooms in an adjoining D Category hotel for around $26 a double room. Failing that, in summer a stand is set up in the main railroad station giving information about rooms in **student hostels**, usually available between mid-July and the end of September and costing around $20 per night. There are two student hostels: the *Sava*, Horvaćanski Zavoj (☎318-255), and *Cvjetno*, Ljubice Gerovac 8 (☎534-524), both of which are within reasonable distance of the city center. Information and reservations through the student tourist bureau at Savska Cesta 25 (☎274-674).

If you're **camping**, the *Mladost* campground, on the corner of Horvaćanski (☎319-071), is the closest to downtown, on the banks of the river Sava. Take tram #4 from the railroad station to the terminal just before the Savski Most (Sava Bridge), or tram #14, #5, or #17 and get off at the bridge.

Hotels

You have to pay a premium price for **hotel accommodation** in the center of the city. Most of the hotels are B category and following the 1987 student Olympiade many have been spruced up. The cheapest is probably the *Jadran*, Vlaška 50 (☎414-600), fifteen minutes' walk from the station at the top end of Draškovićeva, which has doubles for around $35. More conveniently, there's the *Central*, Branimirova 3 (☎425-777), right opposite the railroad station, with double rooms for around $50, or the *Beograd*, a couple of minutes' away at Petrinjska 71 (☎430-444), which charges a little less—count on about $40.

You can cut costs drastically by lodging **out of the city center**, or even out of town altogether. The *Park*, Ivanićgradska 52 (☎233-422), has doubles for $28, but is way east of the center, about half an hour's walk from the railroad station or a #2 or #3 tram-ride. Outside the city altogether, and only really feasible if you have a car, the *Motel Zagreb*, Dubrovačka Aleja 1 (☎533-055), in Novi Zagreb near the Velasejam trade fair center, has double rooms for about $25. There are also two hotels at the top of Mount Sljeme, north of the city: the *Tomislavov Dom*, close by the cable-car terminal (☎449-821), has double rooms for upwards of $38 and is in a lovely location. Take tram #14 to its terminal, then tram #15, walk for ten minutes and it's twenty minutes from there by cable car to the top. Failing that, local buses run regularly from Kaptol to Sljeme direct.

The City

Zagreb was originally two cities, **Kaptol** to the east and **Gradec** to the west, each sited on a hill and divided by a river long since dried up but nowadays marked by a street known as Tkalčićeva. Kaptol was a religious community—its name means "cathedral chapter" in Croatian—and as seat of the archbishop had more power; Gradec was ruled by a group of Croatian nobles, and only became a free city after providing refuge for King Bela IV in 1242 as he fled the Tartars. He returned the favor by bestowing on Gradec its own charter and thus its freedom from the authority of the parish of Kaptol. The two communities became bitter rivals, which they remained until the sixteenth century, when the threat of Turkish invasion caused them to unite against the common enemy and take the name Zagreb—which means, literally, "behind the hill."

Nowadays, the city splits neatly into three. The original quarter of Gradec, also known as the **Gornji Grad** or "Upper Town," and **Kaptol**, to the east, which runs down to Trg Republike, are both peaceful districts of ancient mansions, quiet squares and leafy parks. The **Donji Grad** or "Lower Town," the modern core of the city, bustling with trams and shoppers, extends south from Trg Republike and Ilica to the railroad station. The city center effectively ends at the railroad station. Beyond here, despite some limited gentrification of some of the old warehouses and industrial buildings, there's not much of interest, at least for the casual visitor—the principal impression one of a mixture of broad boulevards and bland modern buildings extending down to the Sava, and, beyond that, the planned suburb of Novi Zagreb.

Donji Grad

There's a better-than-even chance that you'll arrive at the **railroad station**, which is as good a place as any to get your bearings and start on an exploration of the city. More or less everything you're likely to want to see lies north of here, the backbone of the lower town leading directly up from the station in a series of connected shady green squares.

Tomislava Trg, across the street, is the first of these, its name taken from the tenth-century Croatian king remembered on horseback in the center. At the far end, the **Umjetnički Paviljon** was built in 1898 and hosts regular temporary art exhibitions in its gilded stucco-and-mock-marble interior. Behind the pavilion lies the second of the three squares, **Strossmayerov Trg**, at the end of which a similarly palatial nineteenth-century building is the former home of the Yugoslav Academy of Science and Arts, an organization founded by one Bishop Strossmayer, whose statue, the work of Ivan Meštrović, sits among the trees behind the building.

Strossmayer was something of a Croatian hero. An accomplished linguist, art connoisseur, horse-breeder, and raconteur, he led Croat resistance to the tyranny of Austria-Hungary during the nineteenth century, and fought for the union of Croats and Serbs in a Yugoslav state—not a belief dear to many Croat hearts at the time. As a fierce pro-Yugoslav himself, this statue must have an important piece of work for Meštrović, and certainly the figure, depicted with long bony fingers and a gown spread tightly over akimbo knees, is one of his more successful works, a careful blend of the firmness and humanism for which Strossmayer was known.

The academy itself also remembers the bishop, housing as it does the **Strossmayer Gallery of Old Masters** (Wed–Fri 10am–1pm, Sun 5–7pm). Occupying the second floor of the building, this is a good museum, instigated by Bishop Strossmayer's donation in 1867, from which it has since grown several-fold. Among a host of Italian works, there are pieces by prominent Venetians—Veronese, Tintoretto—together with a small *Mary Magdalen* by

El Greco, some early Flemish canvases by Joos van Cleve and the Master of the Virgin among the Virgins, and French paintings by Fragonard and Boucher. The building also houses, in its archives, the world's largest collection of manuscripts in the Glagolitic script—the ancient Slavic alphabet which after medieval battles with Rome for its use in the Catholic liturgy became symbolic of the Croatian struggle for independence—and displays in the courtyard the **Baška Stone**, the oldest Glagolitic insciption ever found, from Baška on the island of Krk (see *The Adriatic Coast and Islands*).

Across the street from the Strossmayer Gallery, there's another museum—the **Modern Gallery** (Tues–Sun 10am–1pm & 5–8pm), which comprises a vast collection of late-nineteenth-century and twentieth-century Croatian art, including more stuff by Meštrović as well as the odd French Impressionist. **Trg N. Zrinjskog**, the last of the three squares which form the lower town's spine, holds on its west side the **Archaeological Museum** (Mon–Fri 8:30am–1:30pm, Mon, Wed, & Fri also 4:30–7:30pm, Sun 10am–1pm; free on Mon) which displays antiquities from prehistoric times up to the Middle Ages. The prehistoric section is good, with fragments from the so-called "Krapina Man," found in northern Croatia; other departments hold early Croatian finds, ancient Roman and Greek artifacts, and what ranks as Yugoslavia's largest selection of Egyptian antiquities, with a set of mummies, sarcophagi, and tomb inscriptions.

Walk up from here and you're on **Trg Republike**, the heart of the city and its busiest intersection, flanked by cafés, hotels, and department stores and hectic with the whizz of trams and hurrying pedestrians. This square, a large open space that was given a thorough overhaul for the student games in 1987, has marked the center of Zagreb for over a hundred years; the pastel blues and pinks of its surrounding buildings, restored to their former Austro-Hungarian elegance, provide a suitable backdrop for the street musicians and impromptu events which take place here during the summer months. The fountain in the middle represents the remains of a well, the **Manduševać**, which was uncovered during the refurbishment of the square (it had been paved over in 1895), and left open due to public demand—though the water no longer flows and the works have been replaced by a stone block.

The tall clock on the eastern side of the square is where half the city seem to agree to meet in the evening. Beyond, Jurišićeva runs towards Trg Žrtava Fašizma, where the **Museum of the Revolution of the People of Croatia** (Tues–Fri 10am–5pm, Sat 9am–4pm, Sun 9am–1pm) occupies a graffitied modern round building in the center, and holds the usual items relating to the liberation from the Nazi occupiers with particular reference to Croatia. There's not much else to bring you to this part of town, except for the **Maksimir Park** much farther east, which is Zagreb's largest and lushest open space, reachable by taking a #4, #7, #11, or #12 tram. The park was founded in 1794, and is a carefully landscaped enclosure, with various attractions, including a belvedere and mock Swiss chalet dating from the mid-eighteenth century, the *Dinamo Zagreb* stadium, and five lakes—on one of which an islet holds the city's **zoo**.

In the other direction from Trg Republike, **Ilica** is the city's main shopping street, running just below the hill of Gradec. A little way down, off to the right, you can take a **funicular** up to the top at Strossmayerovo Šetalište, or cut down via **Trg Bratstva i Jedinstva**, a small, lively square where there's a flower market, to **Trg Maršala Tita**. This is a grandiose open space, focussed on the late-nineteenth-century **Croatian National Theater**, a solid peach-colored bulk behind yet another work by Ivan Meštrović, the strangely erotic *Well of Life*. This neighborhood is home to a good many of the city's best museums. Across the square, a long gabled building houses the **Museum of Arts and Crafts** (Mon–Sat 10am–7pm, Sun 10am–1pm), an impressive display of furniture, ceramics, clothes, and textiles from the Renaissance to the present day. On the southern side of the square, on Trg Ivana Mažuranića, the **Ethnographic Museum** (Tues, Wed, & Thurs 9am–1pm & 5–7pm, Fri, Sat & Sun 9am–1pm) offers a colorful cultural insight into Yugoslavia as a whole, with farm implements and costumes from every corner of the country, as well as a down-at-heel heap of artifacts brought back from the South Pacific, Asia, and Africa by obscure but intrepid Yugoslav explorers.

If museum fatigue is beginning to get to you, there's a antidote close by in the **Botanical Gardens**, south across Mihanovićeva. If you're not burned out, walk a couple of minutes west to the most important—and compelling— museum in the area, on Rooseveltov Trg, the **Mimara Museum of Fine Arts** (Tues–Sun 10am–8pm, Mon 2–8pm), housed in an elegant neo-Renaissance structure that used to be a secondary school. Only opened a couple of years ago, this is made up of the art and archaeological collection of one Ante Topić Mimara, a native of Zagreb who spent much of his life in Austria. Apart from a brief showing of a few items on Brioni in the early 1980s, the collection had been kept under wraps for years, and the opening of the museum gave the first chance for Mimara's attributions to be tested by other experts. There's no English labeling, but you can buy an English-language guide to the exhibits at the entrance.

There are around 4000 items on display in all, about a third of the entire collection, and as a whole it makes a quite remarkable impression. Mimara's tastes were nothing if not eclectic. On the ground floor there are exhibits of ancient glassworks from Egypt, Greece, Syria, and the Roman Empire, together with later examples of glass from Venice and most of the rest of Europe. Close by are oriental carpets from the seventeenth century to the nineteenth century, Chinese art from the Shang through to the Song dynasty, and Indian Khmer and Japanese art through the ages. Upstairs there's more ancient material (pre-Columbian artifacts, Etruscan sculpture), assorted European sculpture, and, perhaps the crowning section of the museum, the collection of European paintings. If Mimara's attributions are to be believed, this is as good an array of canvases as you'll see anywhere in Europe, concentrating on art up to (but not beyond) the nineteenth century. Raphael, Veronese, and other Italian artists show the flag, as do Rubens and Rembrandt, and the Dutch and Flemish painters, as well as later artists like Manet—though this is about as modern as Mimara's preferences got.

If you've still not had your fill of museums, one more remains in the lower town—the **Technical Museum**, not far from the Mimara at Savska Cesta 18 (Mon, Tues, Thurs, & Fri 8am–2:30pm, Wed 8am–noon & 2–4:30pm, Sat & Sun 8am–noon). From the outside this looks like a military base, but it's actually one of the city's best museums, with displays on the harnessing of energy, transportation and mining that include a mock-up of an underground mine. There's also a small planetarium with regular film showings.

Kaptol and Gradec

Behind Trg Republike, the filigree spires of Zagreb's **Cathedral** mark the edge of the district (and street) known as **KAPTOL**, ringed by the ivy-cloaked turrets of the eighteenth-century **Archbishop's Palace**—"a sumptuous Kremlin" according to the archaeologist Arthur Evans before its decimation by earthquake in 1880. After the disaster, the cathedral was rebuilt in an enthusiastic neo-Gothic style, a high, bare structure inside with very little left from the years before the earthquake—only four Renaissance benches from the early sixteenth century and a painting of the *Passion* from about 1500, part of which has been ascribed to Durer. But the church is the symbolic center of Croatian Catholicism—and, as such, of Croatian nationalism. Behind the altar lies the final resting-place of Archbishop Stepinac, head of the Croat church in the Forties and a virulent anti-Communist who encouraged the creation of the fascist Uštase state of Ante Pavelić during the war. When the partisans took power, he was tried for collaboration, but despite being found guilty was given a soft sentence and allowed to die in peace in 1960, since when his grave has become something of a shrine for Croatian Catholics.

Kaptol is the home of all of Zagreb's other Catholic institutions, but otherwise is not so much a district these days as one long street, becoming Nova Ves in its northern reaches. After leaving the cathedral, it's a good idea to head up to **GRADEC**, the most ancient and atmospheric part of Zagreb, a leafy, tranquil backwater of tiny streets, small squares and Baroque palaces, whose mottled brown roofs peek out from the hill to the west. Make your way to the **Dolac** market, which occupies several tiers immediately behind Trg Republike; this is the main city food market, a feast of fruit, vegetables, meat and fish held every morning but at its best on Fridays and Saturdays. From the far side, **Tkalčićeva** strikes north, following the course of the river which once formed the boundary between Kaptol and Gradec. The **Mark Virius Gallery** at no. 14 (Mon–Sat 10am–1pm & 5–7pm) has a collection of Croatian naive art if you're keen on the genre, though Tkalčićeva is better known as the home of some of Zagreb's best bars and nightlife.

Entry to Gradec proper from here is by way of the so-called **Krvavi Most** or "Bloody Bridge," which connects the street with Radićeva—a reminder of the former animosity felt betwen the two communities of Kaptol and Gradec. On the far side of Radićeva, the **Kamenita Vrata**—literally the "stone gate"—is a gloomy tunnel with a small shrine that formed part of Gradec's original fortifications. Just to the south, **Jezuitski Trg** is flanked on the left by a seventeenth-century Jesuit monastery, a forum for regular temporary art exhibitions containing a small café and courtyard that hosts regular summer concerts. The Mimara collection was originally supposed to have been housed here, but the collector rejected it as being too small.

Beyond the square, **Katerinski Trg** has another small gallery, the **Gallery of Modern Art**, which mounts imaginative temporary shows from home and abroad. Close by, the **Lotrščak Tower** or "Burglars' Tower," marking the top station of the funicular railroad down to Ilica in the lower town, is another remainder of the upper town's fortifications, from which a bell was once sounded every evening before the city gates were closed. Nowadays a cannon is fired every day at noon, supposedly to commemorate a victory against the Turks. The views, incidentally, over the rest of the city and the plains beyond, are terrific.

Back in the heart of the upper town, **Radićev Trg** is the core of Gradec—a restrained golden-brown square fringed by solid government offices that focuses on the squat church of **Sv Marko**, a much-renovated structure whose colored tiled roof shows the coats of arms of the constituent parts of Croatia to the sky and, it would seem from opening any book on Zagreb, thousands of enterprising photographers. In many ways the symbolic heart of Croatia, the square was the site of the ruthless putting-down of the sixteenth-century peasants' revolt, whose leader, Matija Gubec, in a mock ceremony arranged by the Austrian authorities, was seated in a throne here after considerable torture in 1573 and crowned with a band of white-hot steel. His remains were hung from a gibbet as a warning to other would-be revolutionaries.

Gubec is remembered by a small sculpture of his head on the corner of Kamenita and Čirilmetodska. As for the church, it's a small, homey, Gothic building, originally fourteenth-century, but like the cathedral since ravaged by earthquake and fire and modified with nineteenth-century skin—though some parts, including the south portal, are original. The Baroque bell tower was added in the seventeenth century, and the interior decorations completed in the 1930s by the painter Jozo Kljaković and the sculptor Ivan Meštrović. The frescoes are typically Slav works, huge, musclebound figures caught in dramatic mid-gesture; Meštrović's crucifix is more sensitive, merging more responsively with the rest of the church.

You can see more work by Ivan Meštrović just north of Radićev Trg, at Mletačka 8, where the **Meštrović Atelier** (Tues–Sat 10am–1pm & 5–7pm, Sun 10am–1pm) occupies the sculptor's former home and studio. This is a delightful museum, and one which you don't have to be a Meštrović fan to enjoy, with an intimacy that the artist's other combined former home and museum, in Split, lacks. On display are sketches, photographs, memorabilia from exhibitions worldwide, and small-scale studies for his more familiar public creations: there's a miniature of his *Grgur Ninski* (the giant version is in Split), studies for the *Crucifixion* in Sv Marko, and some lovely female statuettes in the small atrium.

There are other museums in Gradec, and though none are particularly scintillating, they might provide a target for your wandering around the quarter. Left off Radićev Trg, the **Historical Museum of Croatia**, at Matoševa 9, in one of the more crumbly of Gradac's Baroque mansions, houses portraits of various Croatian bigwigs over the years, together with an aimless variety of weapons, photographs, ecclesiastical bits and pieces, and the like. North of the square, the **Natural History Museum** (Tues–Sun 9am–1pm, Tues & Fri also 4–7pm) is much as you would expect, with displays on the animal life of Yugoslavia, collections of fossils and minerals, and an exhibit on Krapina Man and his animal contemporaries. The **Museum of Zagreb**, at Opatička 20 (Tues–Sat 10am–1pm, Tues & Thurs also 4–7pm, Sun 10am–1pm), close to the thirteenth-century **Popov Toranj** or "Priest's Tower," is better, telling the tale of Zagreb's development from medieval times to the early twentieth century with the help of paintings and lumber from the city's wealthier households, not to mention an array of instruments of torture used against witches. Consider also a trip to the **Gallery of Primitive Art**, Čirolometodska 3 (Tues–Sat 10am–1pm & 5–7pm, Sun 10am–1pm), one of Europe's largest collections of naive art from Yugoslavia and elsewhere.

Eating, Drinking, and Nightlife

Whatever your budget, there's no shortage of places to **eat** in Zagreb, and the city is one of Yugoslavia's best when it comes to **cafés and bars**, with a drinking scene that's much more established than in the south of the country. There are any number of places for outdoor sipping; plenty of places, too, for late-night revelry. Indeed **nightlife** in general can measure up with the best of Europe—there are several established clubs and discos, and when foreign bands come to Yugoslavia it's here (and in Ljubljana) that they tend to play.

Breakfast, Snacks, and Street Food

All the central hotels will serve you **breakfast** for a set fee, though don't expect it to be cheap. If money is no object, the buffet affair served up at the *Esplanade* is the best way to start the day. If it is, use the café-bar at Ilica 1, or the corner café on Trg Republike, both of which serve coffee and pastries.

For **food on your feet** later in the day, there are lots of places serving *bureks* and/or *čevapčići*. Try the place at the bottom end of Tkalčićeva, near Trg Republike, for burgers; the one at Ilica 23 for *bureks*—open until 2am. If you want hamburgers, *Hamby*, Draškovićeva 3, is the Zagreb version of *McDonald's*. **Picnic supplies** can be purchased from the supermarket on the ground floor of the *Nama* department store, on the corner of Trg Republike. For fresh fruit and vegetables use the Dolac market, just above the square. If you need to eat in the middle of the night, the café at the bus station is open 24 hours.

Restaurants

Even if you want to sit down, it's not difficult to eat cheaply. **Self-service restaurants** abound in the city center. Of them, *Astoria*, is central, at Draškovićeva 15, as are *Turist Express* at Masarykova 7, and *Petrinjska*, just around the corner from the youth hostel at Petrinjska 79. For ultra-cheap food, there's also the student dining hall in the university complex at Savska Cesta 25; the food isn't great here and you might have an hour's wait, but if you're desperate . . .

Pizza places are everywhere. One of the best is the long-established *Kamenita Vrata*, next door to the gate of the same name at Kamenita 2a, in the upper town (open until 1am). *Dvojica*, Nova Ves 2, is also popular, and its pizzas are enormous. Try also *As*, Vlaška 62, which serves a decent pizza. There are also various pizzerias along Tkalčićeva, though don't expect terrific quality at most of these.

Up a bracket in price, the *Splendid* on Strossmayerov Trg has waiter service and is not overpriced. The *Medulić* restaurant at Medulićeva 2, just off Ilica, has a varied menu that actually includes some vegetarian dishes—virtually without precedent in Yugoslavia. *Stari Fijaker*, Mesnička 6, is a dimly lit, intimate restaurant serving local cuisine. *Brno*, Frankopansko 1, has both Croatian and more international dishes, as does the *Vinodol*, with tables outside in a small courtyard just off Nikola Tesle. The *Drina*, too, is not expensive and serves Bosnian specialties. For fish, try the *Korčula* restaurant, at Nikola Tesle 17, which serves excellent squid. If you're catching a train, the *Hotel Central* restaurant, opposite the railroad station, serves very reasonably priced meals in large portions.

More expensive, but worth it if you have the money, the *Stara Vura* at Opatička 20, is a cosy restaurant with music and candle-lit tables up in the old town; the food is excellent. The *Dubravkin Put*, on Dubravkin Put, the road running down the west side of Gradec through the green, park-like area of Tuškanac, has delicious roast meat and an outdoor terrace. The *Grički Top*, Zakardijeve 2, on the steps leading down from Strossmayerovo Šetalište to Trg Republike, is good too, a small restaurant with a terrace overlooking the lower town.

Cafés and Bars

One of the best places to **drink** in the lower town is the *Pivnica Tomislav* on Tomislava Trg, which has outside tables and serves food as well as large glasses of draft beer. North of here, *Blato*, on Masarykova, is a lively bar with restaurant attached, though the really trendy place to hang out in the lower town is *Kavkaz*, on the corner of Trg Maršala Tita opposite the National Theater (from which it derives its name). The terrace here is the watering-hole of the city's self-consciously chic types, though most people skip paying the inflated prices and just hang out on the corner, which is probably the most vibrant section of Zagreb youth's evening *korso*. If you get thirsty, the bar a little way along Masarykova does beer at half the price of *Kavkaz*.

There's a wider selection of bars in the upper town, especially along Tkalčićeva, which boasts a number of cafés that ignite with activity at night. *Melin*, just off the main drag, is one of the best bars. Down towards Trg Republike, *Matejna* at Kaptol 4 has a warm, cosy atmosphere, with the tables pushed close together; *Palainkova*, farther north at Ilirska Trg 1, is one of the oldest cafés in Zagreb, with a terrace in summer and an intimate basement feel inside. Also in the upper town, *Lapidarij* at Habdelićeva is an amiable bar and nightclub; *Točkica*, at Mesnička 34, functions as a crowded post-modernist bar popular with young Zagreb—though unfortunately the lack of a liquor license means the only available alchohol comes in the form of surreptitious shots of whisky.

Clubs, Discos, and Live Music

The most central place to **dance** in Zagreb is *Neboder*, on the fourteenth floor of the high-rise on Trg Republike—a well-known haunt of tourists and a renowned pick-up joint. There are also a couple of discos up on the Tuškanac hill, west of Gradac: *Jabuka*, at Jabukovac 28, is the less exclusive of the two, a divey hangout with videos and a young clientele; *Saloon*, at Tuškenac 1a, is more upscale, possibly the city's most popular disco.

For **live music**, a number of bars and restaurants around town host bands, notably *Lapidarij* and *Stara Vura* (see above). Check out also *La Bamba*, on Vlaška, not far from the cathedral, though you should get there early as it fills up fast. The *Omladinski Centar*, on Nikola Tesle, has interesting programs, both live music and youth theater, plus other events, as does *Kulušić*, Hrvojeva 6, which stages pop, rock, and jazz performances plus sporadic drama. The *Lisinski* is the city's main concert hall, south of the railroad station—the forum for big names but a rather clinical place to see anyone.

Listings

Airlines *Adria*, Praška 9 (☎433-333); *JAT*, Trg N. Zrinjskog 17 (☎421-555).

Airport inquiries ☎525-511 or ☎516-200.

American Center Zrinjevac 13 (Mon–Sat 11am–4:30pm; ☎444-800). Library, newspapers, reading room.

American Express Zrin Jevac 17 (☎427-623).

AMSJ Siget 17 (☎522-522).

Books *Mladost*, Gundulićeva 7, has a good selection of English books.

British Council Ilica 12 (Mon–Fri 7:30am–2:30pm; ☎425-244). Library, newpapers, reading room.

Bus inquiries ☎515-037 or ☎512-331.

Car rent *InterRent*, Gajeva 40 (☎446-316); *Kompas-Hertz*, Kršnjavoga 13 (☎415-699); *Putnik*, Hotel Esplanade, Mihanovićeva 1 (☎257-777); *Unis*, Gajeva 29a (☎449-421).

Car repair Ford, Audi, VW, Fiat at *Autodubrava*, Maksimirska 282; Opel, GM at *Automehanika*, Vlaška 79; Renault at *Taksi Remont*, Kate Dumbović 9; Peugeot, Talbot at *Peugeot Servis*, Kraljevićeva 24.

Consulates *Netherlands*, Proleterskih Brigada 72 (☎537-282), *UK*, Ilica 12 (☎424-888); *USA*, Braće Kavurića 2 (☎444-800).

Dental problems The clinic at Perkovčeva 3 (☎423-666) has a 24-hour service.

Exchange There's a 24-hour exchange office at the main railroad station. You can also change money on the black market, for a slightly better rate, from traders outside the student center at Savska Cesta 25; it's technically illegal but the police rarely move in to stop it.

Festivals One of Zagreb's biggest annual events is its folklore festival, held at the end of July, with performances of ethnic music and dance from the world over. Venues include the *Lisinski* concert hall and outdoor stages all over town. If you're here in October, try to catch the city's jazz festival, staged at a number of outlets during the middle two weeks of the month. Other events include the *biennale*, a modern music festival held every other year in April; the "Summer in Zagreb" arts festival, held in tandem with the Dubrovnik Festival in August and usually involving the same performers; and a June cartoon film festival, staged in the years when the biennale isn't running.

Funicular Runs regularly from Tomasićeva, just off Ilica, up to the Lotršćak tower on Strossmayerovo Šetalište in the upper town.

Guidebooks *Grafički Zavod Hrvatske* publishes an excellent city guide to Zagreb, with more detail than we could ever hope to include here and available from most good city bookstores. The snag is it's only available in the original Serbo-Croatian or German. It's worth it, though, if you have the languages.

Hospital There's a 24-hour emergency medical service at Djordjevića 26. Or phone ☎94.

Local bus information Call ☎685-207 or ☎685-208.

Luggage consignment At the railroad station.

Pharmacy 24-hour pharmacies at Trg Republike 3 and Ilica 103.

Plitvice Lakes Information Office Trg Tomislava 19 (Mon–Fri 7am–7pm, Sat 8am–1pm; ☎442-448).

Police ☎92.

Post offices The two main post offices in the city center are at Jurišićeva 13 (Mon–Fri 7am–8pm, Sat 7am–7pm) and Branimirova 4, next door to the railroad station (Mon–Fri 7am–8pm, Sat 7am–7:30pm). Both have international telephone services, at Jurišićeva open 24hr, at Branimirova 4 open Mon–Sat 7am–8pm, Sun 1–8pm.

Radio *Radio Zagreb 1* broadcasts in English every day except Saturday on 90.5, 98.1 or 99.7 MHz. Tune in also to Zagreb Youth Radio, *Omladisnki Radio 101*, one of the country's most controversial radio stations, threatened with closure many times but still broadcasting its mixture of investigative journalism and good music.

Sport Zagreb's soccer team, *Dinamo Zagreb*, plays every other Sunday during the season at the Dinamo stadium in the Maksimir Park, east of the city center, reachable by tram #4, #7, #11, or #12. Local people favor basketball: the Zagreb team, *Cibona*, is one of the best squads in the country and tickets to their matches are like gold dust. If you can get one, their stadium is west of downtown on Rade Končara, accessible on tram #3, #9, or #12.

Swimming Take tram #5 or #17 to their terminal at Jarun on the north bank of the Sava, where there's a (popular) artificial lake and beaches for sunbathing and swimming. Central swimming pools include *Šalata*, an outdoor pool ten minutes' walk north from Trg Republike on the street of the same name, and *Mladost*, a sports center which has an indoor and outdoor pool, on the north bank of the Sava near the Savski Most, at Horvaćanski Zavoj bb—tram #4, #5, or #17.

Taxis Ranks outside the railroad station, on Gajeva and Praška near Trg Republike. Or call, for journeys north of the station, ☎684-444; south of the station ☎682-211. Waiting time should be about five minutes.

Telephones International telephone calls can be made at either of the main post offices (see above).

Tours Tours of the city can be arranged through the *Turističko Društvo* on Trg Republike.

Train inquiries ☎272-244 or ☎272-245. Train tickets can be bought either direct from the railroad station, or from *Croatia Express*, Tomislavov Trg 17 (Mon–Sat 7am–8pm).

Travel agents *Narom Travel*, Tomašićeva 3 (☎411-280), have discount flights, *BIJ* tickets, *ISIC* cards, etc.

North of Zagreb: the Zagorje and Varaždin

Spread roughly between Zagreb and Varaždin, the **Zagorje** is an area that deserves two over-used adjectives—delightful and charming. It's a land of chocolate-box enchantment: miniature wooded hills are crowned with the castles they seem designed for, streams tumble through lush ground sprinkled with vineyards. It's also an important region historically. **Varaždin**, just north of the Zagorje, was for a short period in the middle of the eighteenth century the capital of Croatia, and the area as a whole remained stolidly independent of both the Turks and Hungarians for much of the colonial period.

The Zagorje

The wooded slopes of **Medvenica** or Bear Mountain offer the easiest escape from the city, the highest peak of **Sljeme**, 1035m up, accessible by cable car (*žičara*) and easily seen on a day trip. There's not much to see, but the walking is good and there's skiing and tobogganing in winter—and there are wonderful views from the top over to Zagreb and the Zagorje proper beyond. To get there, take a #14 tram to the end of the line, then #15 to its terminal, and walk for ten minutes through the tunnel until you're at the cable car station. These cars are small, with room for just four people at a time; they leave frequently throughout the day and take twenty minutes to reach Sljeme. If you don't like the look of these delicate contraptions, you can walk up in around two hours. Eat in one of the hotels at the top, which serve cheap, filling food.

About 30km northwest, close to the border with Slovenia, **KUMROVEC** was the birthplace of Josip Broz—**Tito**—and is accordingly a place of pilgrimage for many Yugoslavs. Born in 1892, Josip Broz was the seventh son of a Slovenian mother and Croat father, who, after rising from the deep poverty of his childhood by toiling as a metalworker, became an officer in the Austrian army (Croatia was then part of Austria-Hungary). In 1915 he was captured by the Russians, and joined the Red Army two years later, beginning his involvement with Communism. Part of the simple peasant house in which he was born has been turned into a museum, with photos, mementoes, and lifelike recreations of the 1890s rooms. It's a predictable display, and you might come expecting more, though in a country where celebrations of the man, his life, and works are nearly-ubiquitous, perhaps Kumrovec is admirable for its restraint.

If you're heading north to Ptuj, Maribor, or Austria, Kumrovec is a stopover manageable by bus; other towns in the Zagorje are only easily reached with your own wheels. **BELEC**, near Zlatar in the Ivancice hills, has a couple of impressive churches: one medieval, alongside the ruins of a thirteenth-century castle; the other, deceptively ordinary from the outside, containing a fantastic riot of frothy Baroque furniture and ornament. Apparently it was commissioned by a local countess after she'd had a nightmarish vision.

There are over a hundred castles in the Zagorje region, enduring evidence of its long feudal past. Many are now museums or hotels, but **Tracošćan**, 10km east of the main Zagreb–Ptuj road, is perhaps the most visited. It's actually a bit of a fake. The original, the property of a series of feudal families from the locality, dated from the fourteenth century originally, but was much cut about in the nineteenth century to provide what you see today. Inside there are a number of rooms decorated in nineteenth-century style, together with a collection of weapons and armor through the ages, but really it's the castle's mock-Norman posture and lakeside setting that succeed best. There's a hotel in the grounds, the *Trakošćan*, which has rooms for a very reasonable $15 and all the facilities you could possibly want—a restaurant, bar, sauna, swimming pool, even a bowling alley.

Varaždin and Around

Further north from Trakošćan the countryside levels out, the Drava River winding through featureless lowlands dotted with light industry and criss-crossed by electricity pylons. In the midst of this uninspiring landscape, **VARAŽDIN** comes as a pleasant surprise, perhaps the best preserved of Croatia's inland towns and well worth a day trip from Zagreb to see.

Varaždin has always been a crucial center. In the Middle Ages it occupied a key position on the nascent Hungarian kingdom's route to the sea, becoming the military stronghold of successive Hungarian and Hapsburg rulers in the face of rapid Turkish expansion, and growing fat on the profits of the super-powers' military campaigns. During the eighteenth century it was actually capital of Croatia for a while, though a disastrous fire in 1776 forced relocation to Zagreb, leaving a vacuum in the town which was filled with opulent Baroque palaces, mansions, and villas—buildings which have recently bene-fited from a thorough refurbishment, making Varaždin ripe for discovery.

The Town

The heart of the old town, reached by way of Gundulićeva, the eighteenth-century trading quarter lined with old shops, is largely pedestrianized, modern boutiques and cafés hiding behind shuttered windows and carved doorways. Trg Božidara Adžije, at the end of Gundulićeva, is flanked by the mansions of wealthy merchants, their ostentatious arched portals surmounted by family crests and heavy stone balconies. The seventeenth-century

Franciscan church and monastery are fairly standard Baroque, outside of which is a copy of Ivan Meštrović's *Grgur Ninski*, the original of which is in Split. The Palača Herczer, next door, is now home to an **Entomological Museum** (Tues–Sun 9am–noon), which, in addition to displays of insects impaled on pins, sports a mildly diverting history of bee-keeping in the region.

At the eastern end of the street, **Trg Narodnih Heroja** is the main town square, similarly surrounded by elegant palaces and overlooked by the clock tower of the sixteenth-century town hall. A block away, the bright orange exterior of the seventeenth-century Palača Šermage conceals the town's **picture gallery** (Tues–Fri 9am–noon & 6–8pm, Sat & Sun 9am–noon), which holds a few old Dutch and French paintings by lesser masters, as well as a fair amount of obscure Yugoslav output. Immediately opposite, a wooden drawbridge and gatehouse marks the entrance to the **Castle**, an irregular rectangle surrounded by a grassy earthwork pallisade. Dating from the mid-1500s, when Varaždin was in the front line against the advancing Turks, this stood its ground well and was eventually transformed into an elegant residence by the powerful Erdödy family, who lorded it over the region for several centuries. The courtyard, with its three tiers of balustrades, has been beautifully restored; the inside, where there's the usual display of weaponry and period furniture, is currently being restored and should be open from the summer of 1990.

About 400m west of the castle, down Hinka Hinkovića, there's one final thing you shouldn't miss, the **Municipal Cemetery**—laid out at the beginning of the last century, and a minor horticultural masterpiece, with sculpted hedges surrounding (sometimes even incorporating) the graves. The memorials which adorn the family plots are worth at least a few minutes, being great Baroque monstrosities that give a fine insight into the provincial middle classes' view of themselves and their world.

Practical Details

Arriving by **bus**, the town center is a five-minute walk along Augusta Cezarca and then Maršala Tita. The **train station** is slightly farther out, on the eastern fringes of town, a ten-minute hike down Moše Pijade and right onto Maršala Tita.

Once here, the **Turističko Društvo**, Gundulićeva 2 (Mon–Fri 7am–9pm, Sat 8am–3pm), is well organized and helpful, and has **private rooms** both in the town and outlying villages. Of Varaždin's **hotels**, the centrally located *Turist*, at Aleja 8 Maja bb (☎042/491-44), has doubles for about $35–40; the **motel** and **campground** at Izletište, east of the town on the banks of the Drava, has doubles for about $25. There's also a new privately run pension due to open soon opposite the *Hotel Turist*, which might be a cheap alternative.

There are plenty of places to **eat**, though not much difference between any of them. The *Janje* and *Istre*, both on Kukuljevića, just off Trg Narodnih Heroja, have a fairly standard selection of grills and schnitzels; the *Šibenik*, Kranjčevićeva 12, has good fish; and the *Snack Bar Centar*, Božidara Adžije 5, serves pizzas. To **drink**, try the *Kula*, which occupies the old guardhouse next to the castle; or there's the *Gradska Kafana*, on Gundulićeva—more down-to-earth and with a useful patisserie attached.

On from Varaždin

First impressions of ČAKOVEC, 15km northeast towards the Hungarian border, suggest a smaller version of Varaždin, with a quaint historic core and a seventeenth-century **castle** that was once the home of the Zrinjskis. The Zrinjski family were, along with the Frankopans (see p.121), awkward subjects of the Austro-Hungarians, feudal barons who attempted to maintain a degree of independence from the colonial occupier. The seventeenth-century ban of Croatia, Petar Zrinjski, was so annoyed at the failure of the Hapsburgs to fully reward the family for their efforts in the defense of Christendom that in 1670 he concluded a pact with the Turks making Croatia an independent vassal of Turkey with the Zrinjskis at the helm, in return for Ottoman support against the Austrians. This support never materialized, however, and Zrinjski was captured and executed soon after.

There's not much else of appeal in the region, but the village of **HLEBINE**, about 30km to the southeast, was the base of an important naive school of painters in the 1930s, which, under the guidance of the Zagreb-based artist, Krsto Hegedušić, exalted the crafts and culture of the Croatian peasantry in their art, giving themselves the group name *Zemlja* or "Earth." Hegedušić introduced young men to painting early, teaching them the old-fashioned technique of painting in tempera on glass. His best pupils, Ivan Generalić and Franjo Mraz, are now naive painters of world renown, but there's still an established colony of "peasant" artists in Hlebine, and an art gallery with their work.

South of Zagreb: Karlovac to the Coast

From Zagreb, the *autoput* runs south as far as **KARLOVAC**, less than an hour away from the city, the site of one of the most important fortresses on the Hapsburgs' military frontier. Built in 1579, the castle was deliberately sited in a malarial swamp prone to seasonal flooding in order to discourage enemies from laying siege. Not much remains of the castle, though its shape, a six-pointed star, is discernible in the street-plan of the town center, the moat filled in by public gardens. Otherwise Karlovac is a spacious, industrial town, famous for its beer, *Karlevačko*, which is found over much of the north of the country. There's a small **museum** in the Baroque-style Frankopan winter palace on Strossmajerov Trg, which gives the lowdown on the growth of the town from the citadel, and there are a number of other solid seventeenth- and eighteenth-century buildings around the old quarter. But after seeing these you might as well push straight on west.

An *autoput* link from Karlovac to Rijeka, completing the expressway route between the two main cities of Croatia, is under construction, and when finished should cut the journey-time considerably if you're in a hurry to get to the coast. The existing road, however, is fine, and follows an increasingly scenic route through the hills and mountains of the **Gorski Kotar**—a spectacular landscape of green, dimpled river valleys and wooded hillsides, cascades of slender evergreens thrusting high to catch the light. **DELNICE**, about 60km beyond Karlovac, at a height of 2000m, is the region's main ski resort and a good base for both winter sports and hiking into the mountains of the

---

HIKING ROUTE: JASENAK TO OSILNICA (3–4 DAYS)

This hike takes you through the richly forested hills of the Croatian interior, beginning south of Delnice at **Jasenak**, where there's a hotel but little else. Leave the village on a track which leads northwest into the **Bjelolasica Mountains**, in which there are marked paths and huts; this is a wooded area, but punctuated now and then by high, jagged outcrops of coast. The main track climbs to a plateau which is an important tree-felling area. Lumberjacks, working up here for a week at a time in camps, still use horses to drag logs to the trail for collection. You can camp on the grassy pastures above **Tuk**, where there's a hut, before following the track into **Mrkopalj**, center of a region that's a favorite with Zagreb's second-home owners. There are some shops here. From Mrkopalj, a series of tracks leads to **Delnice** and then once more into thick forest. Work your way north on the track and then drop steeply down to **Razloge**, where the river emerges from the limestone. Follow the rich river valley north on a good path through pasture and haystacks to **Osilnica** and Slovenia.

Risnjak National Park to the west. There are no private rooms but there's a **hotel**, the *Delnice* (☎051/811-266), with double rooms for around $30. The local tourist office has maps of the region. Beyond Delnice, it's not long before the green, wooded nature of the scenery changes, and you're descending through an increasingly barren karst landscape to Rijeka and the coast.

East from Zagreb: Slavonia

East of Zagreb, the *autoput* cuts through the harrowingly dull plain of **Slavonia**, the strongest contender for the most unceasingly boring of all Yugoslav regions. It's this area more than any other that has given Yugoslavia a bad name among back-packing cognoscenti; as Greece-bound travelers gaze out at the vistas of flat, checkered farmland fading drearily into the distance they not surprisingly feel in no hurry to come back. In part this is unfair— while Slavonia is never going to be the focal point of anybody's holiday plans, there are one or two places of interest worth a stop if you're with a car and in no hurry. Indeed, if you're following the busy and notoriously perilous *autoput*, a few detours might be in order merely to preserve your sanity.

Sisak and Around

Not far out of Zagreb, **SISAK**, 20km south of the autoput, is typical of many of the larger centers you'll encounter in Slavonia. An historically interesting town, sited at the junction of the Sava, Odra, and Kupa rivers, Sisak has always been strategically important, though there's little to suggest this now. The Roman emperor Diocletian made it a base for his river fleet, and it was the seat of an influential Croatian prince, Ljudevit Posavski, in medieval times. The splendid triangular **fortress**, dating from the sixteenth century, is about the only thing worth seeing, though even this is 2km south of the center of town on the banks of the Kupa River, and there's no local transit link.

The countryside around Sisak is more inspiring. The villages of **ZAŽINA**, 12km west, and **LEKENIK**, another 10km on, preserve a large quantity of the nineteenth-century wooden architecture peculiar to the region, most commonly two-story houses with thatched roofs and overhanging eaves, with an entrance on the first floor accessible by an outside staircase. Many also have elaborately carved porches or balconies. You can see more of these houses, a number of which play host to migrating storks, in and around the **Lonjsko Polje** nature reserve east of Sisak—a marshy floodplain which is a haven for wading birds and aquatic wildlife.

Jasenovac

Forty or so kilometers on down the autoput, a right turn leads to **JASENOVAC**, a small town 10km away on the banks of the Sava. During World War II this was the site of a grouping of concentration camps, renowned for their viciousness, at which the Croatian Uštase, who ran the "independent" state of Croatia on behalf of their German masters, are believed to have murdered as many as 700,000 Serbs, Jews, Gypsies, and assorted left-wingers. The site of the main camp has been turned into an enormous memorial park centered on a modern sculpture resembling an giant concrete orchid, the work of the architect and sculptor Bogdan Bogdanović. It's a stark place, the bleakness of the marshes only adding to the grim feel, not to mention the memorial museum, which displays macabre implements of torture used during the occupation. Incidentally, on a more contemporary note, Bogdanović went on to become mayor of Belgrade in the 1980s but was recently purged under Slobodan Milošević's "anti bureaucratic revolution."

Slavonska Požega

Farther down the *autoput*, across the small, lumpish hills of the **Požeška Gora**, lies the market town of **SLAVONSKA POŽEGA**, an appealing little place that's a welcome antidote to the tedium of the main road. The town was occupied by the Turks between 1536 and 1691, but today the look of the place is overwhelmingly baroque, with its main square, Trg Maršala Tita, surrounded by elegant, arcaded yellow-ocher buildings. The streets leading off here merit a wander. At the western end of the square, opposite the dazzling white facade of the eighteenth-century **Terezinska** church, a statue remembers one Luka Ibrišimović Sokol, a Franciscan friar and fierce-looking warrior priest who was instrumental in winning a famous victory over the Turks at nearby Sokolovec and thereby liberating Požega in the process. To the north, the Gothic Franciscan church of **Sv Duha** was used as a mosque by the Turks and has been recently spruced up, while the older church of **Sv Lovre** is said to contain some fine Gothic frescoes, though it's currently undergoing restoration and is inaccessible. At the east end of the main square stands the **town museum** which has a limited display of local archaeological finds.

Požega makes a good place to break a journey between Zagreb and Belgrade. The **tourist office** on Trg Maršala Tita has no private rooms in the town itself, but it organizes so-called *seoski turizam* (literally "village tourism")—farmhouse accommodation in the more rural setting of Velika, 16km northwest in the rolling Papuk hills. In Požega itself, the D category *Grgin Dol* (☎055/72-222) has the cheapest **hotel** beds but is often full; failing that, the *Bufet kod Kralja*, on the main road to Slavonski Brod, has a few rooms above the café.

Slavonski Brod, Djakovo, and Osijek

Around 30km closer to Belgrade, and almost exactly halfway between the capital and Zagreb, **SLAVONSKI BROD** is a tidy modern town of tree-lined boulevards and extensive parks. It was an important center for both the Romans and the Hapsburgs, but there's nothing to see here now—though again it's an obvious place to stop over if it's late and you want to break your journey down the *autoput*, or before you head on south into Bosnia, which lies just across the river. The tourist office has no private rooms and not much of anything else, but the B-category **hotel** *Park* (☎055/241-566), opposite, normally has room and is not too expensive at about $30 for a double.

Half an hour beyond Slavonski Brod, a road forges north towards the Hungarian border, reaching, after 20km, **DJAKOVO**, the former episcopal seat of Archbishop Strossmayer and home of his prodigious, red-brick, neo-Gothic **Cathedral**. This is a vast building, designed and constructed in 1882 by the renowned Gothic Revival architect Baron Schmidt, and it forms the final resting place of the archbishop, who lies in the crypt.

Beyond Djakovo, the road enters an area known as the **Baranja**, a region of flat, reedy marshlands where the Drava River peters out into swamp and its waters join the Danube. The Baranja's main center is the spacious garden city of **OSIJEK**, about 30km from the Hungarian border, an important crossing-point on the Drava River in Roman times and more recently a crucial garrison town for Austria after the expulsion of the Turks in 1670. It's nowadays known for its cosmetic and timber industries (Osijek is Yugoslavia's main producer of matches), though most of the industry is located well east of the center and the town makes a pleasant stop-off on the way into Hungary.

There's nothing much to see, but downtown is nice enough to stroll through. The heart of modern Osijek is **Gornji Grad**, centered around the neat Trg Slobode, a short walk from the rail and bus stations and dominated by the town's preposterous neo-Gothic cathedral. The buildings around here are mainly nineteenth-century Neoclassical, and the more interesting part of town is **Trvdja**, the area originally enclosed by the Turkish and then Hapsburg fortifications. Glavni Trg is its heart, flanked by eighteenth-century Baroque-style buildings, one of which, the old town hall, houses the **Museum of Slavonia**, which displays what's been recovered from the Roman colony here.

Practical details . . . and on into Hungary

Osijek's **bus and train stations** are located next door to each other on Karadžićeva on the south side of the town center, ten minutes' walk from Trg Slobode (follow Radićeva). The **tourist office** is at Augusta Cezarca 2, and has a stock of (relatively expensive) **private rooms**. Moving on **to Hungary**, whose frontier is about 40km away, there are four buses and two trains daily to Pécs, regional capital of the Hungarian Baranja, making Osijek much better connected to Hungary than most other towns in this part of the country.

travel details

Buses

From Ljubljana: to Zagreb (hourly; 2hr 45min); Belgrade (6 daily; 9hr); Bled (half hourly; 1hr 30min); Maribor (hourly; 3hr 45min); Ptuj (4 daily; 4hr); Postojna (hourly; 1hr 45min); Škofja Loka (half hourly; 20min); Slovenj Gradec (3 daily; 3hr); Novo Mesto (every 45min); Rijeka (4 daily; 2hr 45min); Opatija (3 daily; 3hr); Koper (hourly; 2hr).

From Kranj: to Jesenice (6 daily; 2hr); Bled (hourly; 1hr); Bovec (2 daily; 4hr); Kamnik (8 daily; 45min); Škofja Loka (half hourly; 15min).

From Maribor: to Ptuj (hourly; 45min); Slovenj Gradec (4 daily; 2hr); Varaždin (hourly; 1hr 45min); Zagreb (hourly; 2hr).

From Slovenj Gradec: to Celje (5 daily; 2hr); (Maribor (5 daily; 2hr).

From Novo Mesto: to Kostanjevica (hourly; 50min); Otočec (half hourly; 30min).

From Zagreb: to Bled (3 daily; 4hr 30min); Slavonski Brod (hourly; 3hr 15min); Osijek (6 daily; 5hr 30min); Trakošćan (hourly; 1hr 45min); Sisak (hourly; 1hr 30min); Slavonska Požega (5 daily; 3hr); Varaždin (hourly; 1hr 45min); Belgrade (10 daily; 7hr); Novi Sad (3 daily; 6hr 30min); Karlovac (hourly; 1hr 45min); Kumrovec (8 daily; 1hr); Krapina (hourly; 1hr); Kranj (4 daily; 3hr); Dubrovnik (3 daily; 12hr); Maribor (hourly; 3hr);

Plitvice (half hourly; 3hr); Rijeka (hourly; 4hr); Sarajevo (4 daily; 8hr); Split (3 daily; 9hr); Zadar (hourly; 5hr).

From Slavonski Brod: to Belgrade (hourly; 3hr 30min); Osijek (hourly; 2hr); Banja Luka (hourly 2hr); Slavonska Požega (7 daily; 45min).

From Osijek: to Belgrade (6 daily; 2hr 45min); Novi Sad (6 daily; 3hr).

Trains

From Ljubljana: to Zagreb (hourly; 2hr); Trieste (3 daily; 4hr); Maribor (hourly; 3hr); Postojna (hourly; 1hr); Slavonski Brod (5 daily; Rijeka (4 daily; 2hr).

From Zagreb: to Belgrade (hourly; 6hr); Slavonski Brod (8 daily; 3hr); Rijeka (4 daily; 4hr); Sarajevo (1 daily; 8hr 30min); Kardeljevo (1 daily; 11hr); Split (8 daily; 7hr).

From Slavonski Brod: Ljubljana (5 daily; 3hr 30min); Belgrade (14 daily; 3hr 30min); Sarajevo (3 daily; 5hr).

International trains

From Ljubljana: to Munich (7 daily; 8hr); Salzburg (6 daily; 6hr); Venice (2 daily; 6hr).

From Zagreb to Venice (2 daily; 9hr); Vienna (3 daily; 7hr 30min); Budapest (2 daily; 7hr 30min).

CHAPTER TWO

ISTRIA

stria is Yugoslavia at its most developed. Many of the towns here were tourist resorts back in the last century, and in recent years their proximity to northern Europe has proved a tempting target for exploitation. The coast, particularly the western side, is infested with *autocamps* and hotels; the beaches (concrete mainly) tend to be bloated with people; and in July or August finding a room can be impossible without advance booking.

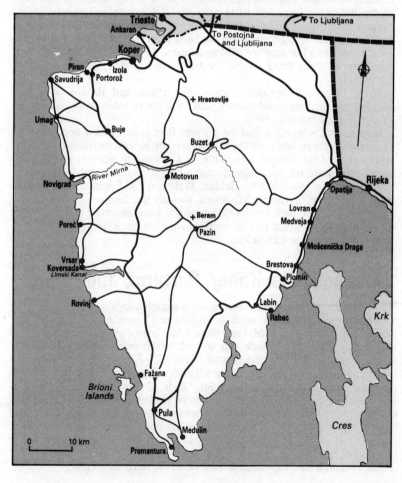

All of which may sound horrendous, as Istria, at its worst, can be. But through all the crowds, concrete and tourist settlements, it has managed to retain a charm and identity which make much of the region well worth exploring. As with the coast farther south, development has on the whole been kept well clear of the beautiful Venetian towns, and even in the largest resorts it is possible to get away from the real gluts of people. The interior, with its villages pitched high in the mountains, is still amazingly unexplored, and where the Spanish *costa* fleshpots had nothing much to start with, Istria can draw on a rich historical and cultural legacy.

The basis of this is Italian, from the 400 years of Venetian rule that preceded the region's incorporation into the Austro-Hungarian Empire, and eventually into the Yugoslav federation. There's still a fair-sized Italian minority here, and Italian is very much the second language, although many of the Italian-speakers left Istria after the last war, afraid of what might happen once the Communists took control. In response, the Yugoslav government encouraged emigration to Istria from the rest of the country, and today there are a fair number of Macedonians, Albanians, and Bosnians here too, many of them living on the coast and coining their fortune out of the tourist industry.

Along the coast, diminutive towns like **Piran** and **Rovinj**, with their cobbled piazzas, shuttered houses, and back alleys laden with laundry, are almost overwhelmingly pretty.

Koper, too, is worth a look, more port than resort and a good base for exploring northern Istria. By the same token, **Pula**, with its amphitheater and other relics of the Roman occupation, is a rewarding place to spend a few days—rooms are relatively easy to come by and most of Istria's interesting spots are only a bus ride away. Inland, **Motovun** and **Pazin** are perhaps the most impressive of Istria's hill towns, though the former is in danger of becoming a theme park for day-excursionists from the coast; and the village of **Beram**, between the two, is worth visiting for the fifteenth-century frescoes in the church just outside.

Slovene Istria: Koper, Portorož, and Piran

The **northern part** of Istria has long been a contentious area. The subject of bitter postwar wrangles between the Italians and Yugoslavia, it didn't become part of Yugoslavia until 1954. Until then, it had been divided by the Allies into two zones: "Zone A," Trieste and around, which came under a temporary Anglo-American administration; and "Zone B"—Koper, Piran, Umag, and Novigrad—which for the time being fell under Yugoslav control. In a compromise designed to appease both parties, "Zone A" was finally handed over to the Italians (principally to keep the crucial port of Trieste from falling into Soviet hands) and "Zone B" formally became part of Yugoslavia. It was the sort of diplomatic fudging which pleased no one; indeed both parties were incensed at losing pieces of territory to which they believed they had a historic right. Tito had always regarded Trieste as a Yugoslav city, and the Italians found it hard to renounce their claims on Istria as a whole.

With the absorption of northern Istria into Yugoslavia, Umag and Novigrad joined the Republic of Croatia like the rest of the peninsula; the towns of the northern coast, however, became part of Slovenia. The reasons for this are unclear—it was, perhaps, to give the republic an outlet to the sea—and there's still debate as to whether it's a truly Slovene part of the country. Aside from this, it is, not surprisingly, one of the most Italianate parts of the region: there's a steady flow of traffic to and fro across the border, Italian is fairly widely spoken, and road signs are in Italian as well as Slovene.

Koper and Around

Arriving from Italy, **KOPER**, or *Capodistria* in Italian, is the first large town you reach, a prosperous place and one of the largest Istrian centers, sited on what was originally a small island but is now incorporated into the mainland. From the main road, it's an unalluring spectacle, dominated by tower blocks, cranes, and industrial zones. But within this surge of development, Koper is a rickety old Venetian town, crowded with a dense lattice of narrow streets.

Arrival and Practical Details

Koper's **bus** and **train stations** are located next door to each other, twenty minutes' walk from downtown, or a short ride on one of the frequent yellow buses. These drop you just outside the city center, inside which only residents are allowed to drive.

Accommodation is pricey in Koper but if you're eager to stay, **private rooms** are plentifully available through an office at the bus station (though these are more expensive) or from Koper's **tourist office** at Ukmarjev Trg 7 (daily 7am–8pm), by the harbor. The least expensive **hotel** is the *Žustarna* (☎066/34-112), which has rooms for about $40. The closest **campground** is in Izola (see below) about 5km west, ten minutes away by half-hourly bus from the station, though it's said to be noisy.

The Town

All of Koper's streets and paved alleys lead to **Titov Trg**, the fulcrum of the old city, flanked by a Venetian **loggia** dating from 1463 and now a café. At the opposite end is the **Praetor's Palace**, Koper's most enduring symbol, with its battlements, balconies, busts, and coats of arms like the stage backdrop for a Renaissance drama. Built originally in the thirteenth century, and added to and adapted 200 years later (the battlements were actually added in 1664 and only ever served a decorative purpose), this was the seat of the mayor and Venetian governor, evidenced by the facade's Lion of St Mark. Also on the square, Koper's **Cathedral** is a mixture of architectural styles, its facade blending a Venetian Gothic lower story with an upper level completed a hundred years later in Renaissance fashion. Dedicated to Saint Nazarius, an unknown martyr who is patron saint of the town, the interior is large and imposing, and holds several paintings by Vittore Carpaccio, said to be a native of Koper—though this is disputed. Two of these, a *Massacre of the Innocents* and a *Presentation in the Temple*, hang on the high altar, the latter oddly shaped due to its originally having been painted for an organ panel.

Behind the cathedral, the Romanesque **Rotunda Carmine**, from the thirteenth century, is the cathedral baptistery. On the other side of the square, an arch through the Praetor's Palace leads on to **Čevljarska** or "shoemakers" street, the main shopping thoroughfare of the city. This eventually joins up with the **Prešernov Trg** on the southern fringe of the center, where there's a Renaissance well from 1423, shaped like a bridge, and the only surviving town gate, the **Vrata Muda**, from 1516. In the other direction from Titov Trg, following Kidričeva, the **Civic Museum** (Tues–Fri 9am–1pm, Sat 9am–noon) holds more paintings, including works by Correggio, together with archaeological fragments, ancient maps, and the like.

Around Koper: Trieste, Izola, and Hrastovjle

There's not much else to see in Koper, but it makes a good base for seeing the rest of Slovene Istria—a lack of beaches and its busy working harbor have kept it relatively untouristed. It's also handy for popping **over the Italian border**, 10km away. The traffic both ways is almost constant—the Italians come here for cheap goods, the Yugoslavs hop across for classy clothes and consumer items—and there are departures to Trieste almost hourly from the bus station. If you do go across, remember that you'll need your passport, and that you must pay in *lire* for the return journey.

In the opposite direction lies **IZOLA**, a pretty, red-roofed, and belfried fishing town, like Koper jutting out into the sea on a rounded promontory. There's nothing here really, but it's the closest place to Koper where you might be able to swim, though frankly the cleanliness of the water, well within range of Koper's (and Trieste's) industrial installations, is open to question. Izola also has Koper's nearest campground (see above).

Inland from Koper might prove a more rewarding direction to travel in, though if you don't make the one train a day you'll need a car to get to its one major attraction, the village of **HRASTOVJLE**, where the church of **Sv Trojice** (Holy Trinity) has the best preserved set of Gothic Istrian frescoes in existence. Set in a wild, treeless landscape, the church dates from the thirteenth century, Romanesque in style and surrounded by crumbling fortifications built in 1581. Inside, the frescoes are the work of one Janez of Kastav, and were commissioned in 1490, as shown by the Latin inscription on the north wall. They cover the ceiling and walls from head to toe, rich devotional scenes that depict the Old and New Testaments. In the apse are the *Apostles*, the north wall has an *Adoration of the Magi*, while on the southern wall there's a *Dance of Death*.

Portorož and Piran

Heading west from Koper, the road veers right soon after Izola onto a long, tapering peninsula that projects like a lizard's tail north into the Adriatic. **PORTOROŽ** ("Port of Roses") appears almost without warning, a sprawling resort that by the end of the last century was already known for its mild climate and the health-inducing properties of its salty mud baths. Maladied middle-aged Austrians flocked here by the thousands to be smothered with murky balm dredged up from the nearby salt pans. Up went the *Palace Hotel*, in came the opportunists—and so begun Portorož, a town entirely devoted to the satisfaction of its visitors. After the last war, the transition from health to package resort wasn't hard to make, and it's now one of the ugliest, most developed stretches of coast in all Yugoslavia, a horrible ghetto of bars, chalets, hotels, and *autocamps*. The bay on which it stands preserves a kind of sheltered appeal, and **rooms** are available from both *Generalturist* and the tourist office on the main waterfront, close to where the buses stop. If you want nightlife, too, Portorož can provide it. But otherwise it's a depressing piece of development, worth hurrying on from quickly.

PIRAN, at the very tip of the peninsula three or four kilometers from Portorož's bus station, couldn't be more different. There are tourists here too, lots of them: thronging the main square, packing the ranks of restaurants, milling around the souvenir-stacked harbor. But few actually stay (most are in fact from Portorož's hotel complexes) and the town preserves tangible remnants of atmosphere in its sloping web of arched alleys and little Italianate squares.

The center of town, a couple of hundred meters around the harbor from where the buses stop, is **Tartinijev Trg**, named after the eighteenth-century Italian violinist and composer, Giuseppe Tartini, who was born in a house on the square and is remembered by a bronze statue in the center. Tartinijev Trg is one of the loveliest squares on this coast, fringed by a mix of Venetian palaces and a portentous Austrian town hall. The red-painted corner palace, fifteenth-century and now housing the tourist office, bears the inscription "lassa pur dir" or "let them talk," which legend explains as a retort to nosy townspeople who didn't approve of the owner's more dubious romantic liaisons.

Just off the square there's a small **aquarium**, with a rather sad set of tanks full of the local marine life. Opposite, across the bay of the harbor, the **Maritime Museum** (Tues–Sat 9am–6pm) pays farther homage to Tartini with a copy of his violin and assorted genuine memorabilia, along with an interesting display on Piran's salt industry and a scatter of paintings that includes native ex-votive works by Piran sailors and a listless portrait of the local authorities by Tintoretto. Behind here—follow Rožmanova Ulica—the town's formidable sixteenth-century **walls** stagger across the hill, perforated with the same fairy-tale "Vs" as Koper's Praetor's Palace and with seven towers remaining. You can walk most of the way along these, descending afterward to follow Ulica IX Korpusa to the barnlike Baroque church of **Sv Jurij**, which crowns a commanding spot on the far side of Piran's peninsula. The campanile is visible from just about everywhere in the town and may seem familiar—it's a replica of the one in St Mark's square in Venice. A few dinars gets you a view of the broad swing of the Italian coastline, and behind, green Istria, enclosing the town with clumps of soldierly cypresses. There's nothing much inside, though, and after a quick inspection you may just as well walk farther along the path to the edge of Piran's jut of land and down into the old part of town, picking a way through the dense maze of streets to emerge once again on Tartinijev Trg.

Piran Practicals

The **tourist office** is on Tartinijev Trg, housed in the red Venetian Gothic palace on the corner (Mon–Sat 8am–noon & 5–8pm, Sun 9am–noon), though **rooms** here can be in desperately short supply in high season. Of the town's **hotels**, the *Sidro* on Tartinijev Trg (☎066/75-292) is, amazingly, the cheapest, with double rooms for about $25. The nearest **campground** is the *Jezero*, 2km east of the town, which also has rooms in a small pension (☎066/73-473). For **food**, the seafood restaurants along the seafront are your best bet, though they again aren't cheap; if you're watching the budget, try the self-service place, close by, which serves many of the same dishes for fewer dinars.

Istria's West Coast

Turning south from Piran, you meet the worst part of the Istrian coast—the **west**. In itself it's beautiful enough, with fields of rich red Istrian soil and pinewoods sloping gently down to the sea, but with development at its most intense, package tours filling most of the hotels, and rooms snapped up so far in advance as to make beds on the off-chance a bad joke. All the way down, grim ad hoc resorts have swallowed up the shoreline. Istrian talk about this stretch of coast would put a Texan booster to shame. It boasts a record number of visitors, the biggest hotel in the country, the largest nudist camp in Europe, not to mention the most verdant vineyards and olive plantations. They're impressive statistics, certainly, and of enormous value to the economy of the country as a whole, but the cost to what was once a beautiful part of Yugoslavia has been great.

Umag, Savudrija, Buje, and Novigrad

UMAG is typical of the settlements of west-coast Istria, an attractive town once, clustered on a tiny peninsula but now almost completely surrendered to the holiday business that sprouts mercilessly in a profusion of concrete lidos, vacation chalets and *autocamps*. Most of the development is actually to the north of town in a long string of hotels and tourist settlements that are connected to Umag's center by a regular miniature train, which ferries several thousand people backwards and forwards every day during the summer. In contrast to the brash newness of the resort facilities, the town center is a fairly derelict place, but by day the tourists lend it a semblance of life; come the evening, however, it can be rather dead, the town's visitors making merry in their complexes outside.

If you want to **stay** in Umag, the *Istratours* office on Ulica JNA, right on the harbor, has **rooms**, but they may well be some way out and are in any case hard to come by throughout the summer. The best thing to do is to skip the built-up development immediately north of the town and go straight to **SAVUDRIJA**, a small fishing village about 5km away on the very northwestern tip of the Istrian peninsula. This is reachable by boat from the town and has less of the aura of *KOA* than the other settlements. There are **rooms** available from *Istratours*, and there's a large **campground**, coolly shaded by pines and with some fair stretches of beach (one nudist). You can rent bikes and there are loads of other facilities.

To really escape the crowds, you should head inland to **BUJE**, about 12km from Umag, its old quarter piled up on a hill over patches of newer development down below. Buje was known as the "spy of Istria" for its hilltop site, and it's an almost physical relief to arrive here, the cobbled streets looking out over fertile fields to the distant sea, far away from the packed resorts. The town ramparts, which date from the fifteenth to the seventeenth century, still stand, and enclose a warren-like medieval core that focuses on a lovely central square sided by a Venetian Gothic palace and loggia.

Back on the coast, **NOVIGRAD**, 12km or so south, is prettier than Umag, more tastefully refurbished, and with more of a real-town feel, grouped around its small, pleasure boat-filled harbor. It feels less swamped by tourists than Umag, though there's similarly little to see—only the Baroque church of Sv Pelagij on the central Trg Slobode, and a small lapidarium and museum in a mansion just off the square on Josip Milovac. But the rocks and beaches, which lie to the south of the town, aren't bad, beyond which there's a **campground**, the *Sirena*. If you want to **stay**, *Istratours* on Obala Maršala Tita to the left side of the harbor, has **rooms**.

Poreč and Around

The largest resort in Istria—and, indeed, in Yugoslavia—**POREČ** isn't as bad as you might expect. There is a huge influx of tourists here every summer, occupying a total, it's claimed, of 35,000 beds in the town and around—a staggering figure when you consider that Poreč's true population is just 3000. But the town manages to retain some degree of character, set once again on a small promontory and with an ordered mesh of streets that dates from its days as a Roman encampment. Its main street, Dekumanska Ulica, follows the line of the ancient Roman decumanus, opening out into a square busy with street artists and the summer tourist traffic.

The Town
Aside from its tourist facilities, Poreč has one historic prize: the **Basilica of Euphrasius** (daily 8am–noon & 3–6pm), a sixth-century Byzantine basilica which is reason enough alone for visiting the town, its mosaics claimed by some experts to be comparable with those at Ravenna. Situated just off Ljubljanska, in the center of Poreč, the basilica is actually the center of a religious complex which includes a bishop's palace, atrium, baptistery, and campanile, originally the creation of one Bishop Euphrasius in 543. Entry is through the **Atrium**, an arcaded courtyard that was heavily restored in the last century but still has ancient bits of masonry incorporated in its walls. On the far side, the **Bishop's Palace** is a seventeenth-century building, though on the site of Euphrasius's original residence, while on the left, the octagonal **Baptistery** was also restored in the nineteenth century.

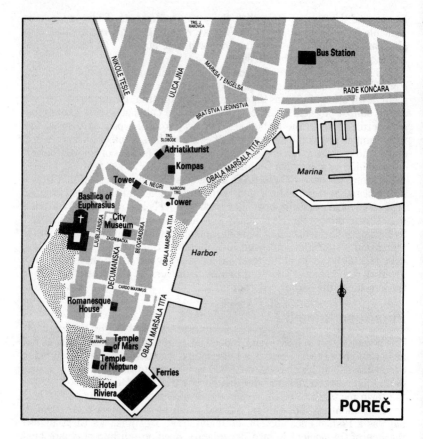

POREČ

As for the basilica itself, it was in fact the culmination of a number of earlier churches, remains of which are still evident. The first, the **Oratory of St Maur** (who is said to have lived in a house on the site), is in scattered pieces on the north side of the basilica, a secret place of worship when Christianity was still a clandestine religion. Fragments of mosaic show the sign of the fish, a symbol of underground Christians at the time. Inside the basilica, the mosaic floor of a later, rather less secretive church has been carefully revealed through gaps in the existing basilica floor.

Otherwise the basilica is a rather bare structure, everything focusing on the apse with its superb late-thirteenth-century ciborium and, behind this, the **mosaics**, which have a Byzantine solemnity quite different from the earlier geometric designs. They're studded with semiprecious gems, encrusted with mother-of-pearl and interrupted everywhere with Euphrasius's personal monogram; he was, it's said, a notoriously arrogant man. The central part of the composition shows the Virgin enthroned with Child, flanked by St Maur, a worldly-looking Euphrasius holding a model of his church and next to him his brother. Underneath are scenes of the Annunciation and Visitation, the latter surprisingly realistic, with the imaginative invention of a doltish, eaves-dropping servant.

After you've seen the basilica, the rest of Poreč can seem rather a letdown, though it's a pleasant enough town to stroll through, with a handful of build-ings that you can structure a walk around, many of them spread along Dekumanska. At one end stands a **Venetian tower** from 1448, now a forum for art exhibitions; not far from the basilica at Dekumanska 9, the **Poreč Museum** (daily 9am–8pm), housed in the Baroque Sinčić Palace, displays archaeological finds, mainly Greek and Roman objects from the surrounding area. Walk west towards the end of the peninsula, and you'll find a distinctive thirteenth-century, so-called **Romanesque House**, with an unusual project-ing wooden balcony—another venue for art shows. Walk much farther from here and you come to **Trg Marafor**, with its remains of Roman temples to Mars and Neptune. Little is known about these and they're really not much more than heaps of rubble, what fixtures they did preserve having found their way to the town museum.

Practical Details: Accommodation, Food, Beaches

Poreč's **bus station** is just outside the town center, just behind the marina on Prvomajska. From here, it's a short, five-minute walk to the *Adriatikturist* office on Trg Slobode, which has a supply of **private rooms**—though expect this to be very low during summer, and don't be surprised if your room is a fair way out from Poreč's center. *Kompas*, at Obala Maršala Tita 16, also has rooms if they've run out. The closest **campgrounds** to Poreč are two at the Zelena Laguna complex, a few kilometers south—*Zelena Laguna* and, farther south, *Bijela Uvala*—reachable on the half-hourly buses which leave from the bus station. There are also hourly boats from the *Riviera* hotel jetty, though they don't take you particularly near either campground.

As for **food**, there's good sprinkling of places in the old town. Cheapest is the self-service restaurant *Peškera* on Nikole Tesle, not far from Trg Slobode, which has an outside terrace overlooking the sea; the *Decumanus*, close by on Dekumanus, is good for breakfast and also serves ordinary meals and pizzas. For evening eating, the *Sarajevo Grill*, also on Dekumanus, is good, offering the usual array of Yugoslav meat dishes; the *Skaleta*, on Obala Maršala Tita, close to the Venetian tower, serves all kinds of food and has a terrace; and the *Istra*, nearby at the junction of Obala Maršala Tita and Bratstva i Jedinstava, also has outdoor seating and serves fish. If you don't eat meat or fish, try the pizzeria *Dal Fuffo* on Osmog Marta, which offers various Italian dishes. If you're staying down at *Zelena Laguna*, the *Zec* complex has a number of restaurants and other eateries, though none of them are cheap.

Generally speaking, the **beaches** around the old town, such as they are, are crowded and unpleasant. As an alternative, some people take a boat from the *Riviera*'s jetty to the island of **Sv Nikola** across the water, though this too is busy with sunbathers from its pricey hotel and the boats there are expen-sive. Better to get right away from the old town and head for the beach near the *Materanda* hotel, half an hour's walk north along the coast from the old town; it's also connected with Poreč bus station by about eight buses daily.

South of Poreč: Vrsar and the Limski Kanal

South of Poreč the tourist settlements and resorts continue, one of the most fashionable of which is **VRSAR**, a tidy fishing village set high above a sheltered harbor. Once the summer residence of the Porč bishops, it's now best known as location of one of the world's largest nudist colonies—**Koversada**, a kilometer down the coast. Established in 1960, this was the first of the Adriatic's naturist communities, and is nowadays a self-contained mini-city, where up to 15,000 can go without clothes for 24 hours a day. Vrsar itself is nice enough, with the eighteenth-century bishop's castle on the hill above, a Romanesque parish church—Sv Marija—and the odd stretch of old town wall. But it gets swamped in summer by the naked enthusiasts from Koversada.

Vrsar sits on the end of the **Limski Kanal**, one of the most popular tourist excursions from Poreč, a fjord which cuts a deep green wedge into the red-earthed Istrian mainland, thick woods rising up sheer on either side and the sea a clear turquoise below. In Roman times this marked the boundary between the Poreč and Pula regions—*Lim* means border or limit; later it became a favorite shelter of pirates, who used it as a base from which to wage war on the Venetians. These days it's a popular spot, not so long ago used as a location for a film about Vikings—the weather's more reliable here than in Norway. There are mussels and oysters cultivated all the way along, which you can sample, along with other fresh fish, in two restaurants on the fjord—the *Viking* and the *Fjord*.

Rovinj and Around

A short way farther south, there are few more pleasant towns in Istria than **ROVINJ**. Delicately poised between medieval port and modern tourist resort, it has managed better than anywhere along this coast to preserve its character by restricting major development to well outside the town center. Its harbor is a likable mix of fishing boats and swanky yachts, its quaysides a blend of sunshaded café tables and the thick orange of fishermen's nets. Spacious Venetian houses and elegant piazzas lend an overridingly Italian air, and the festive mood the tourists bring only adds to the atmosphere. Rovinj is also the most Italian town on this coast: there's an Italian high school, street-names are Italian, and the language is widely spoken in the town.

Rovinj's other claim to fame is as the "Montmartre of Istria"—a tag which stems from the town's painters and other artists, who have gravitated here since the 1950s and every year hold an open-air exhibition of their work in the town. From the main square, **Trg Maršala Tita**, the Baroque **Vrata Sv Križa** leads up to Grisia Ulica, which is lined with ateliers and galleries selling local art. It climbs steeply through the heart of the old town to the **Cathedral** (daily 10am–noon & 4–7pm), dominating Rovinj from the top of its stumpy peninsula. This eighteenth-century church, Baroque in style, has the sixth-century sarcophagus of the saint inside but little else to view beyond its 58-meter-high tower—like the one in Piran said to be modeled on that of St Mark's in Venice. Back on Maršala Tita, the **Town Museum** has the usual collection of archaeological oddments, antique furniture, and exhibitions of Croatian art. North, **Trg Valdibora** is home to a small produce market, from where Obala Palih Boraca leads along the waterfront to the Marine Biological Institute at Obala Giordano Paliaga 5, where there's an **aquarium** (May 1–Aug 30 daily 9am–9pm) with tanks of Adriatic flora and marine life.

Practical Details

Rovinj's **bus station** is five minutes' walk southeast of the town center, just off Trg Na Lokvi, at the junction of Karera and Carduccia. As regards **accommodation**, there are *Generalturist* and *Kompas* offices on Trg Maršala Tita which have supplies of **rooms**. There are two **campgrounds** close by, either side of Rovinj: *Valalta*, about 5km north, and, slightly cheaper, *Veštar*, the same distance away to the south—both accessible on regular buses from the bus station. The *Veštar* camp apparently won the prize for the best *autocamp* in Europe not so long ago, and it has its own beach—though it can get very crowded in summer. Halfway between Rovinj and the *Veštar* camp, *Polari* is an FKK campground. For **eating**, there are lots of fish restaurants around the town for evening meals: try the one the right side of the main square, which has outside seating, or the *Sidro*, by the water on Obala Alda Rismonda.

The two islands just offshore from Rovinj—**Sv Katerina**, five minutes away, and **Crveni Otok** (Red Island), just outside Rovinj's bay—are linked by half-hourly boats from the harbor. Home to a couple of hotels, both are reasonable places to **swim**, with a handful of pebble beaches. Failing that, the Punta Corrente cape, south of town, is pleasant enough, with rocks you can swim from—follow the path around beyond the marina, or rent a **bike** from *Globturist*.

Inland from Rovinj: Bale

About 10km inland from Rovinj, in the direction of Pula, **BALE** is another Istrian hill town, built on the site of a Roman camp and still ringed by walls. Inside the Gothic main gate, the parish church of **Sv Julian** in the central square, is a neo-Baroque nineteenth-century building, but with a Romanesque campanile attached and sixth- and eighth-century fragments from earlier churches on the site in the crypt. Not far away, the **Soardo-Bembo Palace** is worth a look too, a fifteenth-century Venetian-Gothic palace with an elegant balcony built into its towered facade.

Pula and Around

"Pola is a queer old place," said James Joyce at the turn of the century, and even now it's difficult to disagree. In his day, **PULA**—or Pola as it was then—was the chief port of the Austro-Hungarian Empire. Today its strategic location at the head of the Adriatic has made it Yugoslavia's most important naval base; cranes ring the harbor and throngs of sailors crowd the streets, giving it a rough working air that is refreshing after the contrivances of Istria's tourist complexes and cutesy seaside towns. But at the same time Pula belongs to a quite different era, one in which huge tankers and modern warships really have no place. For what distinguishes the town, and forms its main attraction, is the enormous legacy of the Romans.

The Town

Legend has Pula founded by the Colchians, who according to the Argonaut legend, fled here in search of the Golden Fleece; the name stems from the Greek word *polai* meaning "the pursued." The Romans put the city squarely on the map when they arrived in 177 BC, transforming it into an important commercial center, which over the next hundred years, and particularly during the Augustan period, was endowed with all the imperial trimmings appropriate to its rising status. Most dominant of these is the **Amphitheater** (daily 8am–8pm) just north of the center, a great gray elliptical skein of connecting arches, silhouetted against the skyline from wherever you stand in the city. Built towards the end of the first century BC, measurements of 132m by 105m by 32m make it the sixth largest in the world, with space for over 23,000 spectators. Only a small part of the seating remains anything like intact (though with room enough for around 1000), and the interior tiers and galleries were long ago quarried by local people who used the soft limestone to build their houses. But the outer shell is fairly complete.

It's lucky, in fact, that so much survives. The Venetians once planned to dismantle the whole affair and reassemble it piece by piece on the Lido, until dissuaded by the arguments of one of their more enlightened senators. His gallant stand is remembered by a plaque on one of the towers, up which a slightly hair-raising climb gives a good sense of the enormity of the structure and a view of Pula's industrious harbor. You can also explore some of the cavernous rooms underneath—like those exposed under the Coliseum—which would have been used for keeping wild animals and Christians before they met their death. They're now devoted to piles of crusty amphora, reconstructed olive presses, and other lackluster exhibits. The arena itself has been put to good use and is used to stage the Yugoslav film festival, held every year in the last two weeks of August, on the first night of which a firework display shows it to stunning advantage.

South of the amphitheater, central Pula circles a pyramidal hill, scaled by secluded streets and topped with a star-shaped Venetian fortress. Whichever way you walk, if you stay on the main streets and keep the hill on the same side you'll end up where you began. Starting from the main city square of **Trg Bratstva i Jedinstva, Prvomajska** is the axis along which most things happen, running from the **Arch of Sergius**, a triumphal arch erected in 30 BC in memory of a local family of nobles, to **Trg Republike**—the ancient Roman forum and these days the main square of Pula's old quarter. On the far side, the slim form of the **Temple of Augustus** was built between 2 BC and 14 AD to celebrate the cult of the emperor, and is one of the best examples of a Roman temple outside Italy, the high Corinthian columns of its frontage intact and imposing. Inside is a permanent exhibition of the best of Pula's Roman finds, including a lovely set of athletic figurines and tiny sculptures, the sculpted torso of a Roman centurion found in the amphitheater, and a beautifully realized figure of a slave kneeling at the sandaled feet (more or less all that's left) of his master. Next door, the remains of a twin temple to Diana can be seen around the back of the Gothic-Renaissance **Town Hall**, into which it was incorporated in the thirteenth century.

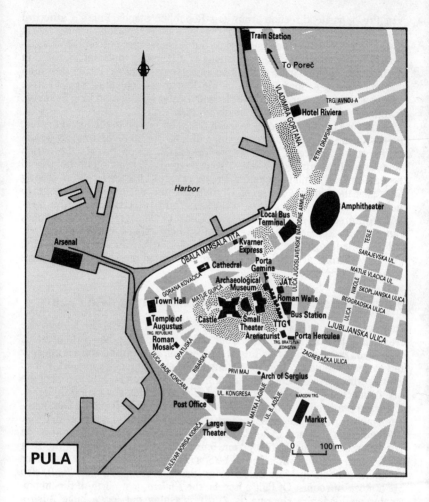

PULA

There are more relics of Roman times back down Prvomajska, where a second-century floor **mosaic** has been uncovered in the backyard of a house by the small park off to the right of the street. Now restored and on permanent display behind a metal grille, it's impressively complete, most of it made up of non-figurative designs—geometric flower-patterns and scrolls—but there's a central panel which illustrates the legend of Dirce and the bull. The story goes that Dirce wronged Antiope and in return was set upon by Antiope's sons, Amphion and Zethus, who tied her to the horns of a bull in revenge. Nearby, in powerful confirmation of the hodgepodge of different eras that makes up Pula, there's a small sixth-century Byzantine **chapel**, part of a mounumental basilical complex long since destroyed.

In the opposite direction from Trg Republike stands Pula's **Cathedral** (daily 7am–noon & 4–6pm), a broad, simple, and very spacious basilica that is another mixture of periods and styles, the Romanesque outcome of a sixth-century basilica built on the foundations of a Roman temple and restored in the fifteenth century with a dignified Renaissance facade. Inside, the high altar consists of a third-century marble Roman sarcophagus, said to have once contained the remains of the eleventh-century Hungarian king Solomon, though there's little else of very much interest.

From close by the cathedral, you can follow streets up to the top of the hill, the site of the original Roman Capitol and now the home of a mossy seven-teenth-century **fortress**, built by the Venetians, which houses the Istrian **Revolution Museum** (daily 9am–1pm & 3–7pm). You can follow the path all the way across the hill from here to the other side of the town center, walking down past the remains of a small **Roman theater**, nestled into the slope, to the **Archaeological Museum** (daily 9am–7pm), which hides in the trees next to the second-century AD **Porta Gemina**. The greater part of Pula's transportable Roman relics have ended up here. There are pillars, capitals and deformed, toga-ed statues mingling haphazardly with ceramics, jewelry, and trinkets from all over Istria: some from the later, medieval period, others from prehistoric times.

Practical Details: Arrival, Accommodation, and Food

Pula isn't particularly beautiful but you do need at least a day here to see everything, and it's a good base from which to explore other parts of Istria. Unless you come during the August film festival, **accommodation** is cheaper and easier to come by than almost anywhere else. The city's **airport**, linked directly with northern Eusrope during the summer season, is 6km east of the city, connected with the bus station by *JAT* buses which coincide with flights. The **train station** is north of downtown at the far end of Vladimira Gortana—a ten-minute walk; the **bus station** is in the middle of town in the fork between Ulica JNA and Mate Balote, a few seconds from the *Arenaturist* on Trg Bratstva i Jedinstva (daily 7am–9pm; ☎052/34-355), which is the best place to ask about **rooms**. The *TTG/Slovenijaturist* office, almost next door to the bus station on Mate Balota (Mon–Sat 7am–9pm, Sun 8am–2pm), also has a stock of rooms. Of Pula's **hotels**, the *Riviera*, just north of the amphi-theater on Vladimira Gortana, is worth splashing out for, a huge Austro-Hungarian colossus with enormous rooms and sweeping staircases where doubles cost about $45 a night. It's also handy for the railroad station. The nearest **campground** is *Stoja*, 3km south of town; take bus #1 from Trg Bratstva i Jedinstva. Failing that there are campgrounds farther south in the resort communities of Premantura and Medulin, or 4km north of the city in the village of Štinjan, where the well-equipped *Puntižela* site has a nice loca-tion on the beach and is shaded by trees. There's also a **youth hostel** at Verudela (☎052/22-617), a couple of kilometers south of the city; take bus #4 from Trg Bratstva i Jedinstva.

As for **eating**, Pula isn't exactly stacked full of decent restaurants. Of the little choice that there is, the *Korzo*, a little way down Prvomajska on the left, is central and cheap; the *Delfin*, opposite the cathedral, is better. Any **night-life** that exists seems to center on the *Jadran Kavana* on Trg Bratstva i Jedinstva.

Listings

Car rental *Kompas Hertz*, Koparska bb (☎052/24-346); *Kvarner Express*, Obala Maršala Tita 14 (☎052/22-519); *Europcar*, Splitska 1 (☎052/34-387).

Ferries From Pula there are weekly connections with Venice, an almost daily service running down to Mali Lošinj and Zadar, plus regular connections up the coast to Trieste. Information and tickets from *Kvarner Express*, Obala Maršala Tita 14 (☎052/22-519).

Film Festival The city's Yugoslav film festival takes place in the last two weeks of August and premieres major new domestic feature-film releases in the Roman amphitheater. Information from ☎052/22-380, though even if your Serbo-Croat is up to the screenings, tickets are hard to come by.

JAT Mate Balote 8 (☎052/23-322).

Post office/telephones The main post office is at Trg Revolucije 4; telephones daily 8am–9pm.

North of Pula: the Brioni Islands

North of Pula lie the **Brioni Islands**, a small archipelago of fourteen islands that was given national park status in 1983, shortly after which they were opened to visitors. There are only two islands of any substantial size, **Veliki Brion** and **Mali Brion**, and you can visit the former either independently by boat from Fažana, reachable on bus #6 from Pula, or on an organized excursion from one of the many agencies offering such things along the city's waterfront. It's one of the most popular trips you can make from the city, not least because of the islands' connection with the late President Tito.

The Brionis' elevation to tourist status isn't anything new. Under the Austrians, and later the Italians, the islands were cultivated as a luxury resort, visited by the cream of Europe's aristocracy. After the war, during which the islands suffered badly, Tito decided to make Veliki Brion one of his official bases, planting much of the island's subtropical vegetation and commissioning a house—called the "White Villa"—in which he could entertain visiting heads of state in the style to which they were accustomed. You can visit this now, laid out as it was in Tito's day, gracefully furnished and decorated with gifts bestowed upon the Yugoslav leader. Organized tours also take in (by miniature train) the collection of wildlife Tito received as presents over the years, herded into a small safari park, together with the considerable remains of an ancient Roman villa which was built on the southern side of the islands in the first century BC.

There's much else to see on Veliki Brion—an ethnographic museum, with a collection of Yugoslav traditional costumes; an exhibition of photos entitled "Tito on Brioni;" and the church of St German, which has a display of frescoes and Glagolitic inscriptions—and the island makes a good day's outing. Sadly it's not possible to visit any of the other islands, though the only one that has anything tangible to see is **Vanga**, an islet to the west of Veliki Brion which was Tito's private residence. It was here, in Tito's luxury villa, that the historic meeting between the Yugoslav leader, Nasser, and Nehru took place in 1956, sealing the formation of the nonaligned movement.

South of Pula: Beaches and Resorts

South of Pula the coast is taken up by new developments of hotels and apartment complexes around the suburb of **VERUDELA**, where there's also a large marina. You might come here for the facilities, which are extensive, or for accommodation—or just to experience relief that you didn't book your vacation here. For a bit more peace, travel straight on through to the resort of **PREMANTURA** (accessible directly from Pula on bus #30 from the bus station close to the amphitheater), where there's a nice **autocamp**, *Stupice*, not especially well shaded but with a young feel and personal facilities for each tent plot. Beyond Premantura, close to **Cape Kamenjak**, the road peters out into a stony track and there are large stretches of open land (owned, apparently, by the army), populated in season by free-lance campers. It's a lovely stretch of coast, with clean, deep water and high cliffs for diving, the rock strata providing natural shelves for subathing privacy—though the possibilities of rough camping are going to dwindle as the authorities clamp down on the practice.

Across the narrow channel formed by the cape, **MEDULIN**, reachable direct from Pula on bus #27 from the amphitheater station, is another fully-fledged resort with a large nudist campground, though more pleasant than Verudela, and one of the principal places people in Pula come to swim.

Inland Istria

The contrast between **inland Istria** and the coast could hardly be greater. You don't need to travel for long before the olive groves and vineyards have given way to an interior that is harsh and unprepossessing, scarred by the wind and dominated completely by gray karst mountains that soak up water as soon as it falls. It's a region accustomed to hardship, but somehow the Istrians have continued to eke a living out of this unyielding landscape, perching their towns and villages high on hillsides alongside life-giving valleys. You will, however, notice widespread signs of depopulation, as many people give up their meager living here for the richer pickings of the coastal resorts.

Motovun, Grožnjan, and Toplice

Perhaps the most famous of the Istrian hill towns is **MOTOVUN**, an unwieldy clump of houses straddling a green wooded hill. Stout ramparts surround the old nucleus of the town, affording fantastic views over the Mirna valley and countryside which produces some of the finest Istrian wines—*Teran* and *Malvasija* are among the better known. Motovun, however, is a favorite with day-excursionists from the nearby resorts, and you even have to pay a small fee to enter the town these days. But the place has a genuine medieval charm, and its main square, fronted by a Renaissance church, a tranquil nobility unequaled in Istria. If you want to stay, **rooms** are available but much sought after, and you'd be well advised to turn up early in the day.

Life in **GROŽNJAN**, about 10km west of Motovun, has been artificially sustained in a similarly entrepreneurial way by the shrewd marketing of it as a hangout for artists and musicians. It's an enjoyable place, though, full of art galleries and busy with people. It's also the setting for regular outdoor concerts. On the other side of Motovun, **TOPLICE** is inland Istria's most popular spa, its sulphurous waters drawing people from all over in search of a cure for their back problems, rheumatism, and so forth.

Beram and Pazin

If Motovun's roots are Venetian, those of **BERAM**, an unspoiled hilltop village a few kilometers south, are quite definitely Slav, with some of the most exciting native art of the whole region. Half a mile north of the village is the chapel of **Sv Marija na Skrilinah** (Our Lady of the Rocks), a diminutive Gothic church with a set of frescoes dating from 1475 and painted by a local artist who signed himself Vincent of Kastav (possibly related to the painter of the frescoes at Hrvastolje, near Koper). Of countless well-executed biblical scenes, two large frescoes stand out. As well as showing a marvelous equestrian pageant, the splendidly rich *Adoration of the Kings* reveals a wealth of fine detail—distant ships, mountains, churches, and wildlife—that strongly resembles early Flemish painting. Similarly, the *Dance of Death* is picked out with macabre clarity against a blood-red background on the west wall: skeletons clasp scythes and blow trumpets in a clarion call to the grave, weaving in and out of a Chaucerian procession of citizens and notables led by the pope and with a rich merchant bringing up the rear, greedily clinging to his possessions and indicating the money on the table he would so dearly love to buy himself out with.

PAZIN, a few twists in the road south of Beram and connected to the village by bus, has little in the way of art treasures but its dramatic setting, dominated by a brooding gray **castle** which sits on steep cliffs plunging around 100m down to the Fojba River, is worth any number of pictures. The castle, originally ninth-century but rebuilt and restructured many times since, literally overhangs the gorge below, where a huge round abyss sucks water into an underground torrent that resurfaces thirty kilometers away in the Limski Kanal. This chasm was supposed to have prompted Dante's description of the gateway to Hell in his *Inferno*, and it inspired Jules Verne to propel one of his characters—Matthias Sandorf—over the side of the castle and into the pit. In the book, Sandorf manages to swim along the subterranean river until he reaches the coast—a feat probably destined to remain forever in the realms of fiction.

Pazin has had a turbulent history, occupying as it does the important junction in the center of Istria which marked the frontier between the Venetian coast and Austrian hinterland. It changed hands several times but usually was ruled by a group of semi-independent local counts. Apart from spectacular scenery and the castle, now housing an **Ethnographic Museum**, there's little of note in the town itself; the museum, however (daily 10am–1pm & 4–6pm) is worth a visit, for its collection of traditional Istrian costumes and handicrafts.

Buzet and Hum

BUZET, the second town of Istria's interior, refused the sort of exploitative help that has been dished out to Motovun, with the result that it's much more unkempt, and more attractive: a typical Istrian hill town quietly decaying while the population moves down to the new settlement below. Buzet was once a Roman settlement and later the home of Istria's Venetian governor, and nowadays its cobbled streets and ruined buildings seem a world away from the new quarter below. On one of its tiny squares, a **plaque** affixed to a house remembers one Stipan Konzul Istranin, a sixteenth-century Croatian writer active in the Reformation in Germany after Luther; he was the first person to translate the New Testament into Croatian. The **town museum** nearby (Tues, Wed, Fri & Sat 10am–2pm) has a small lapidarium, while the view from what remains of the ramparts, over lush green hills to the Ćićeria mountains in the northeast, is lovely.

About 10km east of Buzet, from the village of ROČ, a road leads off right up to **HUM**, the self-proclaimed "smallest town in the world," prettily pyramidal on its hill. The road is famous for the Glagolitic inscriptions that line it on each side, sculpted here by the artist Želimir Janeš in the 1970s in recognition of the importance of the region in Croatian culture. In Hum itself, the parish church of **Sv Jerolim** has a number of frescoes dating back as far as the twelfth century, some of which display a strong Byzantine influence. If you're hungry, there's a small *gostionica*, which serves good Istrian specialties, though it's very popular in summer.

Istria's East Coast

East from Pula, the main road heads inland, cutting off the southeastern rim of the Istrian peninsula and rejoining the coast at Barbanj. Beyond here, the first town of any size is **LABIN**, about 5km inland, on a hill which has been so extensively and carelessly mined that its houses are now considered unsafe; the population has been resettled in the ugly and functional appendage of Podlabin, down the hill. You can walk up to old Labin from the road, though it's now almost deserted, a ghost town whose cracked facades and rubble-strewn streets offer a unique and undisturbed chance to appreciate one of these Istrian hilltop settlements at their silent best. The view from the town walls is superb: sea mist tends to shroud the gulf during the hot part of the day, but when it lifts the mountainous shape of Cres appears, and beyond that Krk and the sinister distant shoreline.

Buses run roughly every hour from Podlabin to **RABAC** on the coast, a fledgling hyper-resort beginning to rival Poreč in magnitude and only slightly trailing in the number of tourists it attracts. It's mainly a modern town, backed up by rows of hulking modern hotels, and in high summer it's worth skipping altogether—though outside this time it's appealing if all you want is a patch of beach to lie on, a reasonable stretch of which lines the bay just to the north. For those prepared to risk it, **rooms** are available from the **tourist office** in the town (though you'll find them much cheaper in Labin), and there's a (usually noisy and crowded) **campground** by the beach.

The road from Labin to Opatija passes through some of the most beautiful coastal scenery in the country, as yet largely undeveloped, Istria's green rim dropping steep and sheer into the sea and permitting few viable places to build. At some points steps have been carved out of the cliff-face; at others a winding donkey track is the only route down, but for the most part the sea is simply inaccessible. **PLOMIN** is typical of the local villages. Ancient and windswept, most of its people have been sucked into the tourist trade on more lucrative parts of the coast and many of its old stone houses are boarded up and empty. Far below, the sea lashes the rocks and the gray outline of Cres looms out of the mist, reachable by regular car ferry from BRESTOVA, a couple of miles farther on.

From Brestova onwards, Istria's seaside industry begins to reappear. **MOŠĆENIČKA DRAGA**, a small village nestled in a bay, has a decent, if often very crowded, beach, as does **MEDVEJA** beyond, though this too can be crammed in season. **LOVRAN**, 5km or so farther on, is just as popular but larger and more elegant, with palatial Austrian villas and grandiose follies, decorated with curly balustrades green with clinging espaliers. There are decent beaches here too, mainly pebble, fringed by hotels and a seafront promenade which you can follow all the way to Opatija, 5km north. Behind the main street, a small old quarter mounts the hill, home to the fourteenth-century church of **Sv Djordje**, which has some frescoes dating from 1479. Beyond Labin there are plenty of small bays, most notably **IČIĆI**, with private rooms to rent and much better swimming facilities than the larger resorts.

Opatija

After Lovran there's no break until **OPATIJA**, longest-established and still one of the most popular of Yugoslav resorts. It's a town in the best tradition of seaside magnificence, a cross between Pismo Beach and Yalta, pretty in an overpowering Austro-Hungarian sort of way, whose nostalgic turn-of-the-century opulence attracts a fair-sized chunk of Istria's abundant tourist fodder. Encouraged by the healthful mineral properties of the water here and the sheltered situation behind Istria's mountains, a Rijeka businessman, Iginio Scarpa, built the first hotel here in 1844. After a visit by the trend-setting wife of the Austrian emperor the town was promoted as a handy health resort for aristocratic Austrians—ironic considering the presence of filthy old Rijeka just a few miles down the coast.

Nowadays Opatija is not especially recommended for a stay. It's crowded and expensive with the only "beaches" being the concrete lidos in front of the main hotels. The only attraction is the **Park 1 Maja**, a botanical garden (close to Scarpa's original *Villa Angiolina*), which boasts a host of subtropical vegetation. **Rooms** are available from *Kvarner Express* or *Generalturist* on the main drag, but these work out extremely pricey in high season—although as most of Opatija's visitors stay in hotels there's normally no problem with availability. For **food**, the *Pivanda* restaurant in Volosko, just outside Opatija on the road to Rijeka, has the reputation of being one of the best restaurants in Yugoslavia, its chef a regular in the gourmet kitchens of Zagreb and Belgrade. Prices are very high by Yugoslav standards, but it's said to be worth it.

travel details

Buses
From Koper to Ljubljana (hourly; 2hr); Poreč (hourly; 2hr); Rijeka (4 daily; 2hr); Trieste (hourly; 1hr); Rovinj (4 daily; 2hr 30min); Piran (4 an hour; 45min).
From Poreč to Opatija (8 daily; 4hr); Pazin (9 daily; 1hr); Rijeka (8 daily; 4hr); Pula (hourly; 1hr 30min).
From Pula to Split (3 daily; 10hr); Pazin (4 daily; 2hr); Zagreb (hourly; 6hr); Rijeka (hourly; 2hr 30min); Vrsar (5 daily; 1hr 30min).

Trains
From Koper to Hrastovlje (1 daily; 17min); Ljubljana (6 daily; 2hr 20min).

From Pula to Pazin (12 daily; 1hr); Ljubljana (5 daily; 5hr).

Ferries and hydrofoils
From Pula (ferry) to Mali Lošinj/Silba/Zadar (6 weekly; 2hr 25min/5hr 20min/7hr 45min).
From Pula (hydrofoil) to Rovinj (1 daily; 45min); Mali Lošinj/Silba/Zadar (1 daily; 1hr 30min/2hr 30min/3hr 45min).

Between March and December a **ferry** *connects the main Istrian ports and resorts with Trieste about four times weekly, though it can't be used to travel between one Yugoslav town and another.*

CHAPTER THREE

THE ADRIATIC COAST AND ISLANDS

F rom Rijeka in the north to the Montenegrin border in the south, the **Adriatic coast** is perhaps Europe's most dramatic shoreline, the sheer wall of Yugoslavia's mountain ranges sweeping down to the sea from stark, gray heights, scattering islands in their path. Not surprisingly, it's the country's greatest attraction, visited by as many as eighty percent of Yugoslavia's foreign tourists every year, and has a reputation for being something of a production line for cheap package tours from Britain and Germany. But its popularity is a deserved one: the coastline is undeniably beautiful, both architecturally and scenically; and, although you'll find the interior of the country less visited, it's the crucial historic heart of the republic of Croatia.

For centuries, the region was ruled by Venice, spawning towns, churches and an architecture that wouldn't look out of place on the other side of the water. All along the water, well-preserved medieval towns sit on tiny islands or just above the sea on slim peninsulas, beneath a grizzled karst landscape that drops precipitously into some of the clearest—and cleanest—water anywhere. There are the usual holiday hangouts, and tourism has mushroomed horrendously recently, but the crowds are rarely difficult to avoid. The abundant Adriatic archipelago can swallow up any number of sightseeing hordes, and on the mainland tourist settlements have been kept away from the main towns.

The coast divides into three distinct regions. In the north, the **Kvarner Gulf** is an introduction to the coast for many travelers, its main town of **Rijeka** Yugoslavia's largest port and a transit point for the whole region. South of here you enter **Dalmatia**, the **northern reaches** of which are probably the least attractive part of the coast—though the two main regional centers, **Zadar** and **Šibenik**, are alluring cities in their own right, and the ancient town of **Trogir**—though similarly not on a particularly appealing stretch of coast—is one of the loveliest towns on the entire seaboard. Continuing into **southern Dalmatia**, **Split**, like Rijeka, is a connecting point for transportation and a major city, but it's worth an extended visit for the prodigious remains of Diocletian's Palace, out of which Split grew. It is also perhaps the most lively town on the coast, with a raw, anarchic feel that merits a couple of days' stay at least. The littoral south of Split, to Dubrovnik, is the most enchanting stretch, the mountains glowering over a series of tiny villages with small pebble beaches looking out at the best of Yugoslavia's islands. **Dubrovnik** itself is touristed out, some say, and certainly the crowds

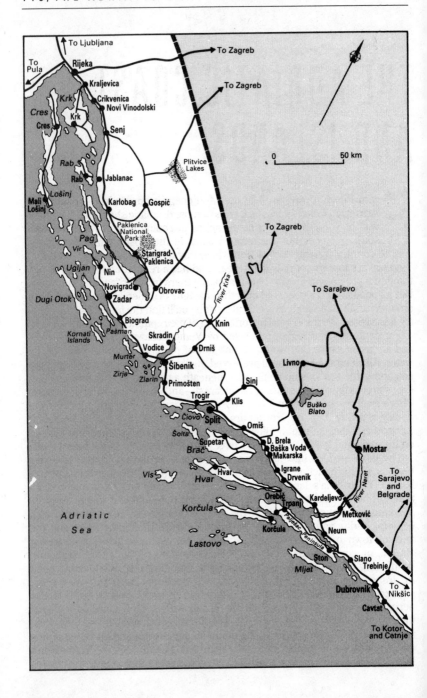

are fairly unavoidable these days. But come outside of high season and you might be pleasantly surprised. Dubrovnik also gives access to more islands, some of which are among the Adriatic's most unspoiled.

Coastal Practicalities

Getting around the coastal region is rarely a problem. There's one main road, the **Jadranska Magistrala** or Adriatic Highway, and **buses** run up and down it with startling frequency every day of the week. All the major centers are connected—you can cover the length from Rijeka to Dubrovnik in one burst of around thirteen hours—and shorter journeys are easy by bus. Beware, though, that picking up buses traveling some of the more major routes can be difficult in smaller centers: even if they have room, they sometimes won't stop, and you're usually better off waiting for a bus that originates at the point you find yourself in.

In addition to buses, at some point you'll almost certainly need to use the **ferries**, run by *Jadrolinija*, the main Yugoslav ferry operator. Just about every inhabited island is connected by some kind of regular **local ferry**, and there's a **main coastal service** which cruises up and down the coast from Rijeka to Dubrovnik around six times a week throughout the summer season, calling at most of the major ports and islands, dropping to twice a week in the winter months. You're allowed stopovers of up to a week at each port of call providing you have your ticket validated on leaving the ferry. *Jadrolinija* also runs services to Corfu and Igoumenitsa in Greece, which stop at many of the same Yugoslav ports and resorts, as does the Greek operator *Strintzis Lines* (see "Getting There" in *Basics* for details on these). Costs are never prohibitive, but it's worth remembering that the long-distance ferry-lines represent the most expensive way of traveling up and down the coast, and if money's an issue you'd be better off using the local island ferries (which tend to be cheaper) and covering longer distances by bus.

Local island **ferry times** are listed in the back of *Vozni Red* (the national rail timetable); timetables for the main coastal ferry and international services are free from tourist offices. Tickets are sold from the *Jadrolinija* offices on every quayside shortly before departure—though for local services it's nearly always possible to buy them on board. On longer journeys, you'd be well advised to take **food and drink** along, as the stuff they sell on board is pricey and sometimes inedible., For a broad idea of frequencies and journey-times, see the "Travel Details" section at the end of this chapter. See also the "Getting Around" section of *Basics*.

As for **costs**, the coast is more expensive than the interior (though no worse than much of the Northwest), but you can still live cheaply, even in the larger tourist centers. The **ferries** are inexpensive, particularly if you're traveling on foot, and the price of private **rooms** won't break the bank—though be warned that you pay around thirty percent extra for staying less than four nights anywhere. Availability, too, can be a problem; during July and August in the more popular centers you'd be wise to reserve in advance, though in the larger cities there's rarely a problem. **Food** is cheap and good everywhere, with an abundance of fish, washed down by the ubiquitous Dalmatian **wines**—crisp, dry whites and heady reds that rank among Yugoslavia's best.

The extreme northern and southern stretches of the Adriatic coast are strictly speaking part of separate regions and are covered in Chapters Two and Four.

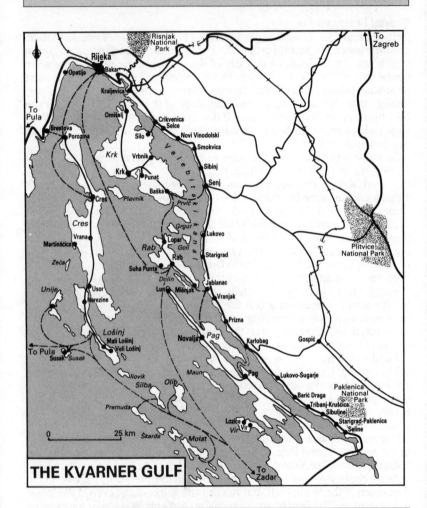

THE KVARNER GULF

THE KVARNER GULF
AND ISLANDS

The **Kvarner Gulf** is the first view of the coast for many visitors, the main roads sweeping down from the cities of the northern interior to converge at **Rijeka**, at the head of the large deep bay which separates the Istrian peninsula from the Croatian coast. Yugoslavia's largest port and a seagoing entry point for many to the country, this is more of a transit point than a stopover in itself, and most people push straight on to the islands that crowd the gulf to the south. Historically this area, though nominally under the sway of the Venetians like the rest of the Adriatic, was ruled for a while by the Frankopans, a family of Croat nobles who through a combination of luck, shrewd judgement, and diplomacy managed to rule here with a fair semblance of independence for several centuries. As a result, a number of towns here are key centers of Croatian national consciousness, the area seen as a free state under the colonial occupier.

Krk is the most accessible of the islands, connected to the mainland by a bridge just half an hour's drive from Rijeka—though the islands farther south, **Rab**, **Cres**, and **Lošinj**, have a feel more estranged from the spread of the city. The coast which forms the eastern side of the gulf is known as the Croatian coast—as opposed to Dalmatia farther southeast—and is not, perhaps, the Adriatic's most interesting stretch. The larger towns here were among the first in Yugoslavia to be developed for tourism—**Crikvenica** and **Novi Vinodolski** are long established and not especially enticing resorts—and it's instead the natural attractions of the area that mark it out. Inland, the **Plitvice Lakes** form probably the country's best-known national park; farther south, the gorge at **Paklenica** provides dramatic opportunities for gentle hiking.

Rijeka

From the sea, rows of hooked, cumbrous cranes and rusty sea-stained tankers front the runaway apartment blocks that make up the bulk of Yugoslavia's largest port, **RIJEKA**—a down-to-earth, unpretentious city and the major transit point for Italy, Greece and the whole of the Adriatic littoral. More backpackers trudge the streets here than anywhere else in the country, and, though it's by no means beautiful and not worth a special journey, if you do end up in Rijeka it's worth dumping your bags (there's 24-hour luggage connections at the bus station) and spending the wait between connections having a look around.

Rijeka, or *Fiume* in Italian (both words mean "river"), is a mixed-up sort of place (some have called it characterless). Decimated by earthquake in 1750, and heavily bombed by the Allies during World War II, its national identity was only assured with the victory of the partisans. Up to then, it had been fought over by the various surrounding states for centuries. From the fifteenth to the eighteenth century, the city was an Austrian possession, a prosperous port that was viewed with suspicion by Venice. Later, Rijeka's strategic significance attracted the attention of Hungary, after which it bounced between Croat and Hungarian sovereignty until the Treaty of London in 1915, which promised Rijeka as a reward to the Italians for joining the war on the Allied side. This was soon annulled at Versailles, but it gave the Italians a taste for a coastline to which they were never entitled—the Italian population here has always been negligible. In 1919 the renegade Italian soldier-poet Gabriele d'Annunzio marched into Rijeka with several thousand men and occupied the city. He was eventually forced to leave, but only after a peace conference that left Rijeka split in two by a new and bitter Italian-Yugoslav frontier.

The City Center

Much of Rijeka was rebuilt after the war, but a surprising amount of its Austrian buildings do remain, many of them in solid ranks along the main **harbor**, where you may well arrive. The bus station lies just back from here, opposite the huge, striped neo-Gothic bulk of the **Capuchin Church**, completed in 1908 and fronted by a large dual staircase. It's said that the Capuchins, in particular the self-styled Saint Jochanza, collected money for the church with public shows of blood-sweating, in the process making the site a minor place of pilgrimage until Jochanza was arrested in 1913.

A hundred or so meters east from here, on the far side of **Trg Togliatti**, the pedestrianized **Korzo Narodne Revolucije** runs the length of the city center, the focus of a vigorous *korso* and a pulsating streetlife. On the left, the **clock tower**, more commonly known in the town as "Pod Uriloj" or "Under the Clock," is the Baroque topping on a much more ancient gateway, up to which the sea came until the city was extended to the present harbor by eighteenth- and nineteenth-century landfilling. The gate gives access to the **Stari Grad** (Old Town), a rather hopefully described area of bombed-out squares, peeling plaster, and shiny black-glass department stores. Through here, the church of **Sv Vid**, a domed Baroque church modeled on Santa Maria della Salute in Venice, has a curious story attached to it. In 1296 a man was losing at cards outside an earlier church and ran inside in a rage, flinging stones at the crucifix, which began to bleed, and he was swallowed up whole by the ground beneath him, except for his hand. The "miraculous cross" stands behind glass on the high altar, and until recently a commemorative bronze hand used to dangle from it; the stone (at any rate, *a* stone) fills a gash in the side of Christ.

Not far from Sv Vid—make a left along Žrtava Fašizma—the town's **History and Maritime Museum** (Tues–Sat 9am–1pm) is another possible stop, housed in the marvelously extravagant nineteenth-century Guvernerova Palace, in which d'Annunzio installed himself during his short period of power. Its huge echoing rooms hold costumes, weaponry, and a lot of eighteenth- and nineteenth-century furniture: most tarnished and faded, some astonishingly kitschy. The park behind, up Šetalište Vladimira Nazora, is home to a local **Natural History Museum**—only worth a stop if you're desperate—while farther up still there are the remains of a stretch of Roman wall, said to date from the second century AD.

Sušak and Trsat

East of here, the thick pea-soup channel of the Riječina once, with the Mrtvi Kanal to the south, marked the Italian border and now defines the edge of the city center, beyond which lies the suburb of **SUŠAK**. Nowadays **Titov Trg** links the two parts of the city, but until 1945 walking here meant crossing

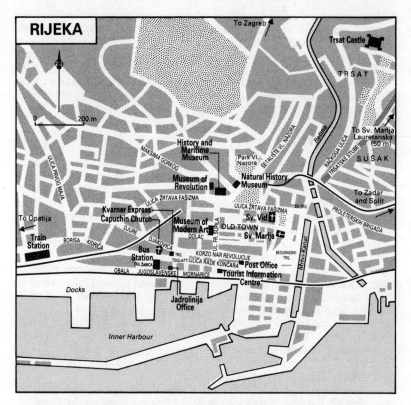

from Italy into the Kingdom of Yugoslavia. On the north side of Titov Trg a Baroque gateway marks the 538 steps that lead up to **TRSAT** (bus #1 or #1a are alternatives), another suburb of the city, and the site, legend has it, where the House of the Virgin Mary and Joseph rested for a few years on its miraculous way from the infidel in Nazareth to safer climes in Loreto in Italy. At the top, the church of **Sv Marija Lauretanska** supposedly marks the spot, a place of almost exclusively female worship and of pilgrimage for women who climb the hill from Rijeka every morning. The church originally dates from the fifteenth century but was enlarged in the mid-seventeenth century and almost completely rebuilt in 1824. At its side is a Franciscan monastery plastered inside with pictures and tapestries, the votive donations of local women.

Across the road from the church, **Trsat Castle** (summer daily 8am–11pm; otherwise 8am–9pm) is an ivy-ed hodgepodge of turrets and towers, walkways and parapets, that looks backwards up the great gray tear in the mountains behind, and forward over Rijeka, which lies under a dim yellowish haze of industrial smog. Beyond slinks the island of Cres, and, to the right, the sheer mountain wall of the Istrian peninsula. Parts of the castle date back to Roman times, but it was primarily a Frankopan stronghold. After their demise an Austrian general of Irish descent, Marshal Laval Nugent, took the place over and restored it in Classical style, constructing the Doric temple in the middle which served as his family's mausoleum. Now, the only thing to admire is the view; in addition, the castle serves as a seasonal restaurant and open-air theater.

Trsat village has **rooms** available (ask at the offices in Rijeka) and a couple of cheap restaurants should you want to **eat**, making it an altogether more pleasant alternative to staying in Rijeka proper.

Practical Details

Rijeka's **train station** lies a couple of hundred meters west of the center on the road to Opatija; the **bus station** is on the edge of the downtown on Trg Žabica, just west of Trg Togliatti. **Local buses**—to Trsat, Opatija, etc—leave from the bus station on the east side of the city center, on Beogradski Trg. Arriving by **ferry** leaves you on the waterfront in the middle of town on Obala Jugoslavenske Mornarice.

Since you're only likely to come to Rijeka to catch a boat there's little point, if you can avoid it, **staying the night**. But if you do get stuck the *Kvarner Express* office on Trg Togliatti (Mon–Fri 7am–8pm, Sat 8am–5pm; ☎051/23-488), has a stock of **private rooms**, and maps and general information on Rijeka, as does *Generalturist*, Supilova 2. The *Turistički Informativini Centar*, Trg Republike 9 (Mon–Sat 7am–8pm, Sun 8am–1pm), also has information and maps but can't reserve rooms. Of the city's **hotels**, the *Kontinental*, just off Titov Trg (☎051/423-477), has doubles for around $40; the *Park*, (☎051/421-155), is slightly cheaper at around S35. There's also a **youth hostel** at Rujevića 58b (☎051/516-977), reachable on bus 6b. If you're **camping**, there are two sites: *Preluk*, about 8km out on the Opatija road, by the sea—take bus #32 from Beogradski Trg; and *Rijeka*, in the opposite direction towards Bakar, approximately the same distance away. Of the two, the former is the nicest.

For **food**, the *Slavica*, overlooking Trg Republike, does decent pizzas, or there's a self-service restaurant on the waterfront. For more exotic fare, try *Tri Palme*, on the front at Ivana Zajca 24. If you arrive late, *Praha* is a 24-hour *gostiona* on Beogradski Trg. Rijeka has a reputation for having a lively **nightlife**, possibly due to the large number of bands to come out of the city during the mid-1980s. Much of this depends on the university, however, and during school-vacation things can seem pretty dead. The **bar** near the church of Sv Sebastijan, in the old town, is about the closest you'll get to carousing during summer.

Listings

Airport Rijeka's airport is sited on the island of Krk, linked with the city center bus station by *JAT* buses which connect with flights. Information from ☎051/841-128.

Car rental *Europcar*, Žrtava Fašizma 26 (☎051/22-371); *Kompas-Hertz*, Zagrebačka 21 (☎051/39-054).

Hospital The closest hospital to the city center is at D. Tucovića 15 (☎051/ 38-333), just past the train station on the right.

Ferries Ferries leave from the quays on Obala Jugoslavenske Mornarice and link Rijeka with Cres, Lošinj, and points down the coast by way of the main coastal ferry, which leaves almost daily in summer. Buy tickets in advance from the *Jadrolinija* office nearby (☎051/22-356).

JAT Trg Republike 9 (☎051/30-207).

Pharmacy All-night pharmacy at Trg Togliatti 1.

Post office/Telephone Rijeka's main post office is halfway down Korzo Narodni Revolucije.

The Coast South of Rijeka: Bakar to Senj

Heading south, it's a while before you feel finally free of the influence of Rijeka's industry, which stretches way down the coast as far as the bridge over to Krk. About 5km out of the city, at the end of a deep inlet, **BAKAR** is a case in point, a pretty place once upon a time, nestled haphazardly around the bay, but nowadays dominated by a vast oil refinery, which casts a sulphurous stench over the surroundings. The town was a Roman settlement originally, and occupied by the Frankopans from 1225; the first naval school on the Adriatic coast was opened here in 1849. Nowadays it conserves its narrow streets and ancient houses, a derelict castle, and a handful of palaces built by local mariners, but as a whole the place doesn't invite much more than a quick hour's wander. Unless, of course, you're looking for a room—Bakar's are around two-thirds the price of those in Rijeka.

Bakarac and Kraljevica

A few kilometers around the bay, the huddle of houses known as **BAKARAC** (literally "little Bakar") makes a better base for swimming, as it is quieter and much more pleasant than its neighbor. Nearby, the high, outstretched ladders are *tunere*, from which fishermen once kept watch for shoals of tuna all along this part of the coast. There would have been a man on these contraptions 24 hours a day, and as soon as a shoal was sighted the entrance to the bay was closed with nets and the fish pulled in. Tuna is still a specialty here, eaten at one time with a sparkling local wine called *Bakarska Voda*. Nowadays, however, this way of fishing has almost entirely died out and most Yugoslavs won't touch *Bakarska Voda*, which has deteriorated markedly in quality. The *Bakarac Motel* (☎051/804-004) has **rooms** available for a low $25–30, as does the nearby *Hotel Neptun* (☎051/804-005), which also has a small **campground**.

KRALJEVICA, just beyond, is another example of an old coastal town almost entirely swallowed up by the industry of the Rijeka hinterland, though it's been an important center in its own right for some time now. The town, which derives from the word for "monarch," was established as a royal port here by Austria, inaugurating a shipping tradition that has lasted (just) until the present day. The shipyards here once employed the young Tito as a steel-worker (he was dismissed for organizing a successful strike), and they now bear his name, although the work they do now is of a largely renovative nature.

Before the arrival of the Austrians, Kraljevica was a Frankopan and, later, a Zrinjski center, and its main historical features are two Zrinjski castles, the **Stari Grad** and **Novi Grad**, around which the rest of the town has developed. The Frankopan and Zrinjski families were families of Croatian nobility, who after enjoying some nominal independence in the 1660s, allied themselves against the Austrians and were executed for their trouble. The castles themselves are far from compulsory stops, and even if entry were permitted, their interest would be strictly limited—a caveat that could be applied to Kraljevica as a whole, and you'd do well to pass straight through, either crossing the impressive **Tito Bridge** to Krk, or pushing on down the coast to Crikvenica.

Crikvenica and Selce

CRIKVENICA (pronounced "Tsrikvenitsa") is the first proper town you reach, a century-old seaside resort that was between the wars one of the more modish playgrounds of some of the ritzier Yugoslavs. It's pretty much package tour country now, spreading along the sea for several miles in a straggle of hotels and tourist facilities, but for unabashed sun and sea it can be a nice place to stop over—certainly better than Yugoslavia's other old-established resort, Opatija (see *Istria*).

There really isn't anything to do but sunbathe and swim. **Strossmayerovo Šetalište** forms the town's liveliest artery, leading along the waterfront from the main **Trg Nikole Cara** in a lazy tangle of hotels, restaurants, and tourist- and seaside-inclined shops and boutiques. The **beach**, extending the length of the seafront, is open to all nearer the town center but private in its more northerly reaches—though the small fee you'll pay for the extra shade on the remotest stretches is worth it. **Rooms** can be had from *Jadran Tourist* (☎daily until 9pm) on Trg Nikole Cara at the center of town, or from their office near the private beaches. For **food**, Stossmayerovo Šetalište has a number of places: namely the *Triton* pizzeria, 100m from the Jadran office; a fish restaurant next door; and several grill restaurants farther down.

Crikvenica **buses** drop passengers behind the *Jadran* tourist office, just around the corner from the main harbor. In July and August there are around ten **ferries** a day to Šilo (on Krk) from Crikvenica.

Selce

From Crikvenica you can walk the few kilometers along the seafront to **SELCE**, a small village almost completely transformed by its function as seaside resort. There's a small beach here, a (grubby) **campground**, and **rooms** are available through the *Turist Selce* office, but it's a crowded, noisy place in summer and not particularly recommended for a stay.

Novi Vinodolski

NOVI VINODOLSKI ("Novi" for short) is another straggly resort town, edging the main road for a couple of miles, though it is of far greater historical significance than might at first appear.* It was here, in 1288, that the so-called Vinodol Statute was signed, the oldest document in Croatian in existence, recognizing the rule of the Frankopans over the surrounding district and the rights of the local citizens. There's not much to betray Novi's independent roots now; it's a dull sort of place, rather suburban in feel, its shoreline lined with large hotels leading up to a scrappy harbor. Up above the main road there's a small old quarter, piled up on the hill, where you can view the minute remains of the thirteenth-century Frankopan **castle** in a central square (in which the document was allegedly signed) and a small town **museum**, with displays relating to the statute (including a photocopy of it) and folk costumes from the surrounding area—though it is often closed.

Down below, there's not much beach to speak of, and the only feasible places to swim off are the concrete platforms near the hotels—though there is a beach at Lisanj, southeast of the town. If you still want to stay, the **tourist office** on the main road, just before the bus stop, has **rooms**. *Snack Bar Zagreb*, on the main road before the tourist office, is a fair place to **eat**, and there are a couple of grill restaurants, with open-air barbecues, between the bus stop and harbor.

Senj

"May God preserve us from the hands of Senj." So runs a popular Yugoslav saying, inspired by the role of the town as a base for a band of pirates known as the Uskoks, who in 1527 made **SENJ** their home and terrorized the surrounding waters for almost a century. Refugees from Omiš to the south, where they had been driven out by the Turks, they at first, with the implicit consent of Venice, harassed only Turkish shipping. But after being disowned by the Venetians, they became less discreet, turning their attention to whoever represented the richest booty. Uskok exploits were, apparently, legendary: they used to taste the blood of their enemies as a pledge of brotherhood, and bloodthirsty tales of them eating men's hearts and dipping their bread in human blood were commonplace. For a while the town attracted adventurers and indolent aristocrats from all over Europe, eager to join in the fun, and for some time Senj was almost wholly devoted to robbery, piracy, and murder. After a time, however, the Uskoks asked to be transported inland and given the chance to live by other means. Each time their pleas were ignored. It suited Austria to leave them be, as a convenient worry to Venetian and Turkish ships and a source of cut-price trinkets for their ladies at home, and it was only after the Uskok War of 1615–17 between Venice and Austria, supposedly brought

---

* Novi was also the birthplace of **Ivan Mažuranić** (1814–90), arguably the Croatian national poet, whose laboriously detailed epic poem, *The Death of Smail-Aga Čengiča*, plays an essential role in the Yugoslav national school curriculum.

about by the continuing atrocities, that the Uskok question was finally confronted. Many Uskoks died as result, hanged or beheaded by the vengeful Venetians, and the rest were exiled to a meager existence inland.

The Town

These days Senj, like Novi Vinodolski to the north, is regarded as something of a cradle of Croatian culture, the Uskoks depicted as brave resistance fighters to years of colonial rule. The quiet little town, however, is a bit of a disappointment, a rather run down-looking place, with not a great deal of interest to see. The main focus of life is the square which opens to the harbor, flanked by peeling palaces and centering on a prominent war memorial. Away from the water is the heart of the old town, around the square of **Velika Placa**, where the fourteenth-century **castle** is a former Frankopan residence, since converted to house a municipal offices. Walking north from here, the town center is bordered by some stretches of fifteenth-century **walls**. Back toward the water, the **Town Museum**, housed in the fifteenth-century Vukasović mansion (daily 10am–noon & 5–7pm), has archaeological fragments and artifacts relating to Senj's place in Croatian culture, together with a collection of ecclesiastical bits and pieces.

The only reminder of the Uskoks in Senj is the **Nehaj Fortress**—literally "fear not" or "heedless"—sturdily safeguarding the town from a rubbly peak to the left of the harbor (daily 9am–3pm); walk out of the old town gate by the castle, do a right and follow the path up the hill. Constructed in 1558 from materials obtained from churches and monasteries destroyed by the Turks, this was the creation of one General Lenković, one of the most famous Uskok commanders, when the Turks were making repeated attacks on the town in the hope of destabilizing the pirates. He did a good job. There's not much to see in the castle itself—just a few photographs, a couple of cannon, and a small lapidarium and restaurant in the basement—but when you climb out on top the logic behind the name becomes clear, the views spreading out so far that it's easy to feel safe.

Practical Details

Buses pull up on the waterfront, close by the main square, opposite which there's a **tourist office** (daily 7am–10pm) with **rooms** and **maps** of the town, though otherwise it seems mainly concerned with advertising Plitvice. On the far side of the harbor there is a **campground**, next to a small **beach**, though the pebble beaches farther north of the town are more pleasant, as are the campgrounds adjacent to them. The busiest time to visit Senj is during **Karneval**, which oddly enough takes place in August and is billed as the highlight of the year. In fact, as the time of year suggests, it's a recently thought-up ruse to attract tourists and not particularly worth making a special trip for.

It's possible to travel on to the **Plitvice Lakes** from Senj. Bear in mind, however, that there is only one bus a day (at 7:54am), though many more up to Gospić, from where there are plenty of connections. If you're eager to see the lakes but want to avoid the hassle of connections, the tourist office in Senj also has information on tours—though they're not cheap.

> ### THE BORA
>
> One other thing Senj is known for is the **Bora**, a wind which is said to be "born in Senj, married in Rijeka, and die in Trieste." A cold, dry northeasterly, it blows across the central European plain and gets bottled up behind the Adriatic mountains, escaping through the passes at places like Senj and, farther south, Omiš. At its strongest, it can overturn cars, capsize boats, and lift you off your feet. When it's blowing, take care.

The Plitvice Lakes

About 40km inland from Senj, and accessible by bus, the **Plitvice Lakes** are one of Yugoslavia's greatest tourist attractions. In summer the road here is a continuous line of German, Austrian, and Italian cars with boats and campers attached, and the whole park has been groomed to be as efficient and orderly as possible. Buses put you down at carefully numbered walkways, boats leave regularly from marked points. None of this lessens the beauty: the sixteen lakes that tumble into each other amid the forests have a minor-key majesty, the same unspectacular loveliness as an ornamental garden. You need a couple of days to see the whole system, and, even if you're not into walking, exploring the lakes seems almost effortless.

Practical Details

Getting to Plitvice from the coast, there are infrequent buses from Senj and Zadar (usually once or twice a day), or connections on from Gospić, which is easier to reach from the coast. The best links are from Zagreb, from where there are plentiful buses. To **leave** can be tricky: theoretically buses pull up at the stops here, but if the bus is full, or the driver doesn't like the size of your pack, they just drive past. This is quite likely to happen to you at weekends, and short of standing in the middle of the road there's little you can do.

There are two entrances to the park. Entrance (*Ulaz*) 1, to the north, is the smaller of them, close to the nearest campground and with a small tourist office stocking rooms. Entrance 2 is the main entrance, and is where the bus driver will drop you if you ask to be put off at Plitvice. Here there's a larger **tourist office** (7am–8pm), which sells entrance tickets (around $10 at last count), has information and maps of the park, and another stock of **private rooms**, though you should bear in mind that these are expensive and increase in price the closer you are to Entrance 2, where most of the main walks start from. On the whole, though, it's best, if you can afford it, to splash out on a room close to the entrance—some can be miles away from the main action. Also close by Entrance 2 is the most convenient of the park's **hotels**, the *Bellevue* (☎048/76-344), which has a few rooms at about the same price you pay for private accommodation (otherwise for around $45) though be sure to phone first to check there are vacancies. If there aren't, you could try the *Villa Poljana* (☎048/76-520) nearby, which has rooms for much the same sort of prices.

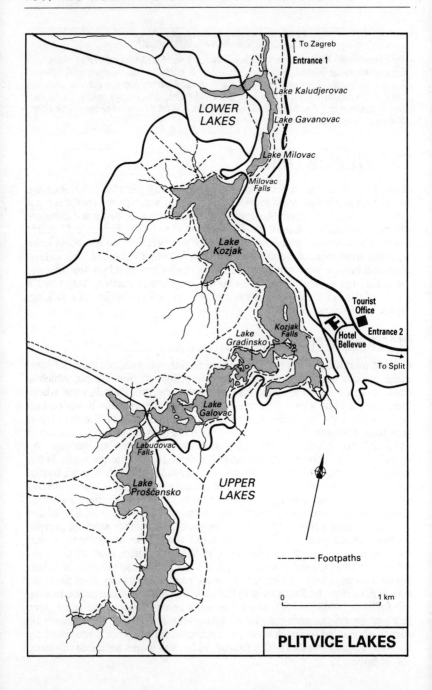

PLITVICE LAKES

You can also rent **bikes** at Entrance 2, and there's a cheap **supermarket** for supplies. Otherwise **eat** at the *Poljana* restaurant here, which has a self-service section. The closest **campground** to the lakes is the *Korana*, about 1km from the northern Entrance 1; you have to ask to be dropped off here as it's not a usual stop. It has a restaurant and a supermarket, and as well as ordinary camping you can rent a trailer for about $25 a night for two.

The lakes: Some Routes

Minerals in the Plitvice Lakes have created an interesting effect, due to the deposition of limestone in the area. In the normal course of events, water eats away at limestone rock forming potholes and caverns, as in the karst formations you find bordering the coast and up in Slovenia. But here the reverse happens. Minerals in the water are picked up by plants in the lakes and turned into stone, shaping coral-like patterns beneath the water.

There are two identifiable sections in the park. Starting out, it's best to do as most travelers do and take the shuttle bus from Entrance 2 to the **southern system**, which starts below Lake Prošćan, the highest of the lakes. Wooded paths follow the succession of lake and waterfall from here back towards the large Kosjak lake and falls, a lovely trip: streams burst out of rocks; brilliant dragonflies hover everywhere; the lake waters shimmer blue and green. The second, more **northerly system** is quieter but every bit as impressive, the lakes narrowing up towards the Plitvice Falls, a high wall of water which, of all the park's attractions, comes closest to the description "dramatic." Paths follow both sides of the water beyond here and past Entrance 1 into the Korana Gorge, where you may be able to swim.

Jablanac, Karlobag, and the Paklenica National Park

Continuing south from Senj, **JABLANAC**, about 4km (an hour's walk) off the main coastal highway, is the ferry-port for Rab and Pag, though otherwise it's not really worth the detour: a tiny place grouped around a small harbor with a pension, a rather dingy campground (quite a walk from the village), and not a great deal else. If you do come here to take a ferry and are on foot, bear in mind that as well as the walk from the main coast road to Jablanac, you may have quite a wait (or walk) at the other end—the ferry terminal on Rab is not much more than a parking lot, with very few connecting buses.

Taking ferries from **KARLOBAG**, about 20km farther south, is somewhat easier; the coast road runs right through the town, and the ferry terminal, serving Pag, is close by the bus stop. Otherwise, though, there's not a lot to recommend Karlobag. It's a slightly desperate place, its meager sights—the remains of a fourteenth-century castle and eighteenth-century Capuchin monastery—not really worth stopping for. If you're catching an early ferry, or arriving off a late one, the **tourist office**, on Trg G. Budako, has **rooms**. From here there's little to detain you before Zadar—about eighty kilometers farther south.

Inland from Karlobag, a road leads up through the bare, rugged karst mountains to **GOSPIĆ**, main town of the Serbian **Lika** region, sited amongst gray parched limestone that stretches as far as the eye can see, speckled with green and the occasional oasis of grass and trees. The people who live in this area are known as traditionally fierce warriors, hardened by life here and somehow managing to squeeze a living out of these sullen slopes. Other than the sheer stark barrenness of the landscape, which can be oddly riveting, there's nothing to stop for, but it's a possible route up to the Plitvice Lakes (see above).

The Paklenica National Park

The **coast** south from Karlobag is similarly sparse on attractions, until you reach the village of **STARIGRAD-PAKLENICA**, a long, rather unattractive place but the handiest base for the **Paklenica National Park**, which starts a few kilometers inland.

This is a beautiful and impressive region consisting of two limestone gorges, grizzled mountains, and caves, and represents perhaps the country's best accessible example of a karst landscape. It's an area that attracts fully-fledged climbers, but it's good, too, for hiking or even gentle walking, with enough trails to keep enthusiasts happy for days at a time.

Paklenica was opened as a national park in 1949, and is geographically part of the Velebit mountain range. The area is prone to three quite different climates—coastal, continental, and sub-alpine—which makes its weather unpredictable, and, at times, extreme. There are two main valleys, Velika (big) Paklenica and Mala (or small) Paklenica, which run down towards the sea, towered over by 400m-high cliffs and cut into by a number of cave systems. It's a stark, bare terrain in places, though green too in others: Paklenica has a better tree cover than most karst areas, with over fifty percent of its area forested.

Practical Details

Buses drop you on the main road close to the gas station, from where getting to the park is easy. Follow the road south just past the *Hotel Alan*, and take the next turning off to the left, which leads to the mouth of the gorge and entrance to the park proper—a four-kilometer walk. There's a parking lot here if you're driving, and an office which will charge you a small fee to get in, and can sell you maps of the cave systems showing marked paths. As for **accommodation** in the area, Starigrad-Paklenica is a tourist resort, with facilities to match, and there are plentiful **private rooms** to be had in the village: either look for the *sobe* signs, of which there are loads, or call the *Turističko Društvo* in advance (☎057/79-040). There's one **hotel** in Starigrad, the B-category *Alan* (☎057/79-036), on the main highway close to the canyon road, a nudist hotel that has double rooms for about $35 and an associated campground. For **eating**, use the *gostiona* on the corner of the Paklenica road and coastal highway, which has seating outside. Incidentally, most people come to Starigrad to **swim**: if you want to join them, there's a thin strand of gray pebble beach just across the highway from the park road.

In the park itself there is one main **refuge**, the *Borisov Dom*, which is open between May and September and has space for around fifty. For details of other refuges in the park, ask at the entrance. If you're walking any distance at all, you'll need stout boots or shoes with thick soles to cope with some of the rocky surfaces. Trails are marked by way of painted-on rocks or trees, and you should always stick to these. Bear in mind, too, that the routes below give rough pointers but are not a complete guide; buy a map if you intend going far, and don't follow anything you're not sure of.

Some Routes

If you're here to walk rather than climb, there are a number of **routes** you can take. Whichever you choose, if you enter the park at the Starigrad entrance, you immediately walk up the **Velika Paklenica** gorge, a gentle climb through the narrow canyon, the well-laid path cutting under dramatic outcrops of harsh rock. After about forty minutes the trail flattens out. Along this stretch there are a number of signposts, giving a choice of three basic routes.

A left fork will take you up, in about 30–40 minutes, to the cave of **Manita Peć**, a complex of caverns about 500m long that is by far the most interesting of the gorge's cave formations. There is a concrete path with steps inside, but although it's safe to enter alone, you should take a flashlight; it's cold too, so wear warm clothing. From here you can either turn back the way you came, or head on for another hour and a half (the path leads from the left of the cave as you emerge), up some fairly steep and none-too-easy slopes, to **Vidakov Kuk**, an 800m-high peak that gives fine views over the coast and islands.

If you hadn't turned off to Manita Peć, you would have eventually reached, after about an hour or so, the *Borisov Dom*. From here a well-marked path leads up in two hours to the **Veliki Golić**, a steep limestone ridge that rises at its highest point to 1285m. The views up here are as marvelous as you would expect. Follow the path along the ridge and it eventually takes you back down (at least another two hours) to join the main path to the *Borisov Dom*.

The third main trail you can follow branches off the central path at much the same point as the others, but heads south, up a steep incline, and across to the neck of the **Mala Paklenica** gorge, which leads down towards SELINE on the coast, opening out about half an hour before the village, where there's another entrance/exit to the park. The canyon is lovely, the trail not too difficult to follow, and the flanks with some impressive rock formations. The whole hike takes about seven hours from entrance to exit, and you can do it in reverse—from Seline—if you so wish.

The Kvarner Gulf Islands

The **islands of the Kvarner Gulf** fill the sea south of Rijeka, a dense concentration and a varied one, ranging from the green wooded hills of Lošinj to the bare, almost lunar environment of Pag. They're popular places in season, and easily accessible from a number of points along both the Istrian and Croatian stretches of coast. Of them, **Krk** is probably the least island-like, connected to the mainland by a bridge and home to Rijeka's airport, and, in its northern reaches, some of its industrial installations. **Rab**, to the south, is quite different, long discovered by travelers, but still retaining some of its unspoiled charm. Farther out, **Cres** and **Lošinj** are one island really, joined by a short bridge, though in landscape they are quite different—Lošinj very green, Cres rather bare. South and west of here, there are a number of much smaller islands, a few of which are inhabited but none supporting a particularly developed tourist industry.

Cres and Lošinj

CRES and **LOŠINJ**—really a single island divided by an artificial channel—were known for a long time as the *Absyrtides*, the place where Jason and his Argonauts fled with the Golden Fleece, and Medea killed her brother Absyrtus as he pursued her. According to the islanders, the story continues with Medea throwing her brother's remains into the sea where two of his limbs became Cres and Lošinj.

Getting to Cres and Lošinj
Ferries run hourly from Brestova, a little way down the Istrian coast from Rijeka, to Porozina on Cres, and this is by far the best way to go if you're with your own car or want to avoid a more lengthy sea crossing. If you're on foot, it's best to take a ferry direct from Rijeka to Cres town (once daily). If you're approaching from the south, Mali Lošinj is linked with Zadar by six ferries weekly—a connection which in the other direction links with Pula, on the southern tip of Istria. Incidentally, island-hopping from either Cres or Lošinj is problematic as neither island has a ferry-link with any of the other major Kvarner Gulf islands. If you are exploring these northern islands and don't want to return to Rijeka, consider taking one of the many excursions to, say, Rab, which is in turn linked with both Krk and Pag.

Cres
On its own, Cres (pronounced "Tsress") is the second largest of the Adriatic islands, only beaten in size by neighboring Krk. It's also one of the barest: a green-gray hunk of land, fairly mountainous in places, spotted only with buttons of gorse and hardy figs and olives, and crisscrossed by stark, white dry-stone walls.

CRES TOWN
CRES TOWN is something of an oasis in Cres's bleak landscape, an oversized fishing village grouped around a small harbor, watched over by the streaky gray hills of the karst. It's still relatively undisturbed by tourism, and has the crumpled look of so many of the towns on this coast: tiny alleys lead nowhere, minuscule courtyards huddle beyond arches, green abundance burgeons over the rails of balconies, and mauve and pink flowers sprout from cracks in walls. **Narodni Trg**, which opens out onto the harbor, is the town center, flanked by a small fifteenth-century loggia and a sixteenth- century clock tower. From here, the main street, 29 Novembra, leads through the heart of Cres, finishing up at the Porta Marcella, a Renaissance gateway from

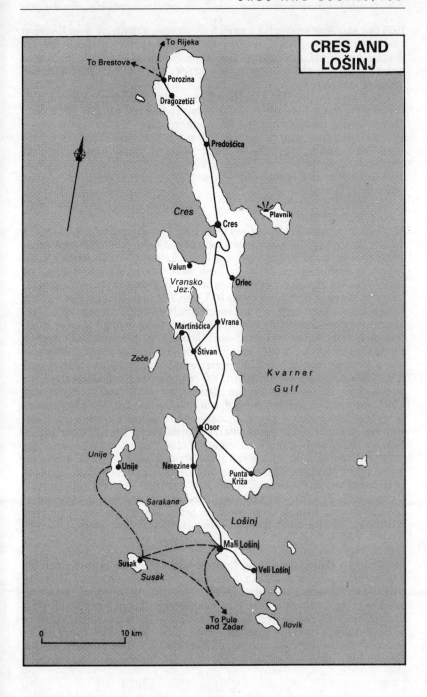

CRES AND
LOŠINJ

To Rijeka

To Brestova

Porozina

Dragozetiči

Predošćica

Cres

Plavnik

Cres

Valun

Orlec

Vransko
Jez.

Vrana

Martinšćica

Zeča

Štivan

Kvarner
Gulf

Osor

Unije

Unije

Nerezine

Punta
Križa

Sarakane

Lošinj

Mali Lošinj

Susak

Veli Lošinj

Susak

To Pula
and Zadar

Ilovik

0   10 km

1595 that stands at one end of a stretch of old town wall dating from Venetian times. Back in the middle of town, the **Cathedral** has a fifteenth-century Renaissance portal, and there's a small **museum** with piles of encrusted Roman amphorae and coins, plus manuscripts and sculpture from Venetian and Austrian days.

If you want to stay, the **tourist office**, on the waterfront, just south of Narodni Trg (daily 7am–1pm & 2–9pm), has **rooms** and will give you a map. There's also a **campground** on the northern edge of town, about fifteen minutes' walk away next to the sea; follow the path west along the water's edge. You can **swim** from close by the campground, or take a boat to the next bay along, where the beaches are better and emptier. Boats leave (early) from the tourist office pier, or they can be rented by the hour or day from the shed below *Hotel Kimen*.

SOUTH OF CRES TOWN

About eight buses a day leave Cres town from near the tourist office to make the trip to Mali Lošinj, a spectacular journey at times when the road drops down directly to the sea on both sides. Not far out of Cres town lies **Lake Vrana**, an emerald-green ellipse of fresh water that supplies both Cres and Lošinj. But for this lake, both islands would be utterly dry. Shortly after, a turnoff to the right runs down to **MARTINIŠĆICA**, a small village with a long shingle beach, a campground, and rooms available from its tourist office—on balance, a better base than Cres if you want to swim, though without much character. At the farthest tip of the island lies **OSOR**, the oldest settlement on either Cres or Lošinj, a once prosperous Roman city of 20,000 inhabitants whose fortunes were checked by a series of sackings and the virulent spread of infection. It's now a small village of 100 or so people, grouped just above the narrow strait that separates the two islands, over which there's a drawbridge which opens at 9am and 5pm every day to let boats through. Not a lot happens here these days, which is part of the appeal, and the streets exude a peace that on a hot summer's day seems utterly undisturbable. On the main square there's a late-fifteenth-century cathedral out of all proportion to the size of the place, and a small museum, housed in the Venetian-built town hall, which has relics of the Roman era. There are **rooms** (ask around in the village), a couple of **restaurants**, and a beautifully situated **campground**, which is smaller, cheaper and—if you do want peace—altogether a better option than the one at Cres. Swimming, though, is not good: the beach area on one side of the town is very dirty, and the other, though cleaner, is rocky.

Lošinj

LOŠINJ is a slim sliver of land hanging limply from the side of Cres. It's smaller, more popular, and has a thick woolly tree cover that comes as a relief after the obdurate grayness of its neighbor. For a long time it was overshadowed by Cres, but after the Venetians' demise it became an important thriving naval island, with a large fleet and several shipyards. By the end of the nineteenth century, it had been developed as a holiday resort—like Opatija on the mainland to the north, a handy vacation spot for the Austro-Hungarian Empire.

MALI LOŠINJ

The island's main center, at the end of a deep sheltered bay, is **MALI LOŠINJ**, larger and more developed than Cres town, with a yachting marina and newly finished bungalows creeping over the wooded points that shelter the town. It's a colorful, flowery sort of place, not as yet spoiled by its popularity with the tourist trade. Slim cypresses nose their way through tiers of peachy cream and orange houses, which drip blood-purple bougainvillea and rhythmic splutters of spiky green palms. The harbor has a tarnished, colonial feel, with its shuttered Austrian palaces lining a busy waterfront behind rows of potted cacti and subtropical plants. Most of the hotels have been kept well out of the way on the Čikat peninsula, together with an enormous campground and the island's most crowded beaches.

Like Cres, once you've clambered around among the stepped alleys and winding streets of the town, there's not much else to do but swim and eat. The Baroque church of **Sv Marija**, on the hill above the harbor, is worth a peep, as is the anti-Uskok **castle** (what's left of it) just behind. But really to wander around any more than this would be to drag Mali Lošinj's cultural attractions to the limit. For **swimming** follow the coastal path to Veli Lošinj, along which there are a number of quiet spots on the rocks, and where you can take all your clothes off, should you want to avoid the populous FKK cove on Čikat.

Mali Lošinj also makes quite a good base for visiting other towns on the islands. A number of private boats offer excursions at reasonable rates and at more convenient times than the *Jadrolinija* ferries. In season, there are trips to Rab and Ilovik three times a week and one daily to Susak.

To **stay**, it's a fifteen-minute walk to the **campground** on the Čikat peninsula; for a **room**, ask at the **tourist office** on the seafront (daily 7am–8pm). The cheapest **hotel** is the *Istra* (☎051/862-151), also on the waterfront, which has rooms for as little as $25 but rumor has it that this also serves as a brothel for the army camp a few kilometers up the road. If you don't fancy chancing it, try the *Alhambra* (☎051/862-022) on the Čikat peninsula, which charges about $40, though bear in mind this will almost certainly be booked up in high season.

For **food**, there's a reasonably priced *gostiona* just off the main drag, behind the line of street artists up some stairs—or, cheaper still, a snack bar which sells ready-to-eat meals on the corner of Trg Moše Pijade.

VELI LOŠINJ

VELI LOŠINJ is a five-kilometer walk from Mali Lošinj—despite the name (*veli* means "big"; *mali* means "little"), a smaller, quieter version of its sister settlement, strung tightly around a tiny natural harbor and dominated by the hangar-like Baroque church of **Sv Antun**, which at the moment is closed due to restoration. You can peer through the portcullis at the frescoes, though you can't get in to see the church's *Madonna with Saints* by Vivarini. Behind the town, a crenellated Venetian tower peers roundly over the waterside houses, but that's about all there is to the place. If you want to stay, the **tourist office** has **rooms**, and there's a **campground**.

Susak

About 9km west of Lošinj, **SUSAK** is one of the more interesting of the smaller Kvarner islands. Geologically, its composition of clay and sand make it unique in the Adriatic. Its isolation, too, has produced a distinctive people and way of life: islanders still speak their own dialect and have retained many old traditions and customs, including an unusual method of singing directly from the throat, and a local costume which consists of gaudily colored green-and-yellow skirts worn with even brighter pink tights. Postcards and guide-books would have you believe you see this all the time; in fact, most of the 200 inhabitants are elderly and rarely dress up in their brightest garb. Instead you'll see a gentler version of the same costume worn, in black or navy. The former industry here, fish-canning, has long since died out and the popula-tion relies on money sent back from emigré relatives to supplement income from sales of, among other things, Susak's good red wine—*pleskunac*.

There's one village on the island, and unsurprisingly little of historical inter-est. You might want to climb up to the church of **Sv Nikola** on top of a nearby hill, inside of which there's a large wooden twelfth-century crucifix, the history of which is disputed. The island gets its fair share of day-trippers, but there's no tourist industry as such, and facilities are minimal. It's possible to get a **room** from the **tourist office**, in the school (daily 9–11am & 6:30–8pm), but due to the water shortage there are no hotels or campgrounds. For snacks and drinks there's a café in the village that serves as the main local meeting place.

Krk

The largest of the Adriatic islands, **KRK** is also one of its most developed, a result, perhaps, of its handy location just a stone's throw down the coast from Rijeka, and its role as the site of the city's airport, more than for any intrinsic attractions. Much of the north is industrial, and generally it's a bare island, without much scenic charm. Krk town is a pleasant place, however, with scraps of city wall surrounding a wanderable old center, and in the south the island's landscape is much more dramatic. Spend a few days here, and move on, perhaps hopping to Rab by way of the regular inter-island ferries from Baška.

In its earliest days, Krk was a Roman base; Caesar is supposed to have had an encampment on the island, and he was defeated by Pompey in a naval battle just offshore. Later Krk fell under the sway of the Venetians, though the island was actually ruled by the Frankopans, the Croat dynasty that reigned over this part of the coast for several hundred years with the tacit consent of Venice. The last Frankopan count to hold any real power here was Ivan. In the late fifteenth century he made Venice his heir as a ploy to ward off his over ambi-tious brothers and went poaching new estates on the mainland. When finally repulsed back to his island, he went mad, upping the taxes, looting the churches and with his armies raping, murdering, and torturing the people. In 1480 the Venetians had no choice but to intervene, taking the deranged man away and absorbing Krk properly into the Most Serene Republic—which is where it stayed until the very late eighteenth century.

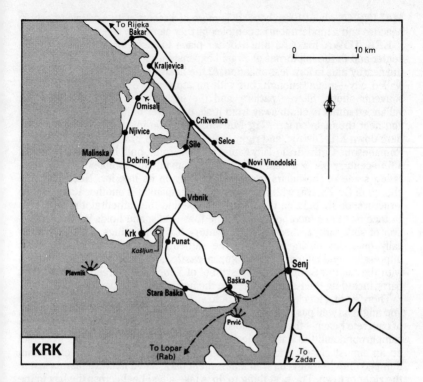

Getting to Krk

There are regular buses from Rijeka to Krk, passing through Omišalj and arriving in Krk town in about an hour an a half, making the island a quick and easy onwards step from the city. You can also reach the island from points on the Croatian coast: ferries run from Crikvenica to Šilo roughly hourly in the summer, and less frequently from Senj to Baška. Baška is a nice place to arrive, but arriving in Šilo, be warned that buses to the rest of the island, including Krk town, are infrequent. At time of writing, the one regular bus to Krk town was at about midday, so try and time your trip accordingly.

Around the Island

Crossing over to Krk by bridge doesn't present a very enticing prospect, and the northern part of the island can seem at first like an extension of the industry that lines the mainland. Broad white drums of oil, pipes, gantrys and smoking chimneys mingle with the scrubby, unalluring landscape—all in all, not a pretty sight.

Things pick up as you head south. **OMIŠALJ** is the first stop of any size, a not-unpleasant village made up of a tiny old quarter heaped up above a newer settlement by the water. There's a Romanesque church here, Sv Marija, which dates from the thirteenth century, but not much else to detain you.

MALINSKA, about 10km beyond, is more of a resort, with a couple of pebbly beaches and a modern tourist complex farther along the coast.

KRK TOWN makes a much better place to head for, the island's main center and in the full throes of a rapid expansion, spreading perniciously over the nearby hills in formless abandon. At the heart of it all there's a small, partly walled city—quaint enough, but with an atmosphere long spoiled by tacky souvenir shops, filigree parlors, and the like. Thin cobbled streets make valiant attempts to climb away from it all, but never quite escape. Buses drop you near the main square, **Trg Maršala Tita**, just inside the walls. Right off here down XIII Divizije, and right again down Petra Franolica, lies the town's Romanesque **Cathedral** (daily 8am–1pm & 4–7pm), built in 1188 on the site of a fifth-century basilica (and before that a Roman bath complex) and incorporating some of the pillars from that building in its interior. Next door, the church of **Sv Kvirin**, with its onion-dome campanile, is another Romanesque structure, oddly built on two tiers, while behind the cathedral, the **Bishop's Palace** has been incorporated into the town walls, and holds inside a collection of sixteenth- and seventeenth-century Italian paintings. This is sporadically open for business—ask in the cathedral—but the building itself is impressive, and adjoins the Frankopan **castle**, a solid structure embellished with the Lion of Saint Mark, the symbol of Venetian sovereignty. The oldest parts, including the Kamplin tower on the north side, date back to 1191.

There's not a lot else to see in Krk town, and it's not great for swimming, so you might as well push off to **PUNAT**, about 4km east, where there's a stretch of concrete beach—though it's normally packed with people from the adjacent campground and the water is decidedly murky. Punat itself is a tiny place, set on an almost closed, tranquil bay, but it's had all the trappings of tourism dumped onto it—souvenirs, an amusement park, and a massive marina just to the right of town. The best thing to do is take a taxi boat across the bay to the sixteenth-century **Franciscan Monastery** on the islet of **Košljun**, which has a chapel with a lovely wooden ceiling, a polyptych by Santa Croce, and a large and dignified *Last Judgement* by Ughetti, not to mention some more off-the-wall exhibits like a cyclops-eyed lamb in a glass case and a two-headed lamb in a bottle. The adjoining **museum** (daily 9am–noon & 3–7pm) has an interesting mish-mash of stuff with no particular connections either: an international selection of banknotes and coins up to a century old, a genealogy of Israel from Adam and Eve to Christ, some ancient typewriters and gramophones.

The southern part of the island is probably the most appealing, with some of the best scenery, rising high above the road up to gray, furrowed peaks before slipping luxuriantly into a darker blanket of pines. **BAŠKA**, at the far southern end and reachable in an hour by frequent bus, is set in a wide bay ringed by stark mountains, a compact old town whose real attraction is its two-kilometer-long stretch of pebble beach, hard under the Wild-West heights of the karst. Baška is an important place in Croat history; it was here that a tablet was found bearing the oldest known text of **Glagolitic script**. This was one of the oldest Slav alphabets—ninth-century, some say—and has had a symbolic importance for Croat nationalists ever since the battles with Rome to use it instead of Latin in a specifically Slav liturgy. The original stone is now in Zagreb, but most places on Krk seem to have sprouted copies.

Krk Practicalities

In Krk town there's a **tourist office** on Maršala Tita (daily 8am–10pm), which has maps (at a price) and **rooms**. *Kvarner Express* on the waterfront also has rooms. There are **hotels** to the left of the town—the *Koralj* (☎051/221-044) and *Lovorka* (☎051/221-022) are the cheapest, with rooms at around $35 a double—and a **campground**, *Jezevac*, ten minutes' walk to the right of town (turn left before the soccer field).

The **beaches** here (rocks really) are well-populated throughout the season; the FKK beach is supposedly the best, although it's also very crowded. You should be able to find somewhere to stretch out on the campground side, but don't expect anything too secluded. For **food** and **drink**, the *Galeb* restaurant is good, and not too expensive, and the *Vaga* bar is a fairly popular drinking spot.

Elsewhere on the island, the swimming is rather better, with the **beach** at Baška by far Krk's best—though again not exactly empty in summer. **Rooms** can be found in all the main centers, in Baška from *Baškaturist* in the middle of the village. There is also a **campground** in Baška, *Zablace*, which is close to the beach.

On from Krk: Grgur and Goli

Moving on from Baška, the ferry journey to Rab is a still, ghostly trip through the gossamer sheen of the Adriatic, past the islands of **Grgur**, with its giant "Tito" and star carved painstakingly out of the rock, and **Goli**, literally "Bare Island," an obstinate hummock of mottled rock that was used as an island-jail for Stalinists and those opposed to Tito after the war. Over a period of five years in the late Forties and early Fifties a total of 15,000 people were allegedly "re-educated" here, most of them for Cominform sympathies. Conditions were harsh, and the prison camp was eventually broken up. Oddly enough, it's currently being converted into a tourist resort, though its reputation as a bleak island gaol lingers on.

Rab

Less than 20km south of Krk lies **RAB**, smallest of the major Kvarner Gulf islands but probably the most beautiful. It's a rocky island too, at least on its eastern side, which rises to a stony gray spine that supports little more than a few goats. But the western side is lush and green, with a sharply indented coast and some good—if crowded—beaches and coves.

Unlike Krk, which enjoyed some measure of independence, Rab was firmly under the thumb of the Venetian Empire for something like 600 years. Venice kept the island poor and dependent in a number of ways: by restricting the supply of salt (which was needed for preserving fish), destroying vast expanses of trees, and insisting that all Dalmatian goods were sold in Venice at fixed prices. In addition, tributes were exacted by the Turks and the island ravaged by plague, leaving the green tip of Rab town's peninsula derelict and abandoned to this day. After the Venetians left the Austrians took over, and things didn't begin to improve for the island until the formation of Yugoslavia earlier this century.

Getting to Rab

You can hop over to Rab by ferry from Krk, which leaves you in Lopar, though bear in mind, if you come this way, that you're a good 10km from Rab town and buses don't always connect with the ferry arrivals. If there is no bus in sight, walk the kilometer or so down to the junction leading to the San Marino beach and pick up one of the more frequent services that pass there. The main coastal ferry calls in at Rab town, though the inadequacy of the harbor can mean bad weather making it impossible to dock. Ferries also run regularly from Jablanac on the Croatian mainland to Mišnjak at Rab's southern tip, though again bus connections make this a chancy way to arrive if you're on foot—and Mišnjak definitely isn't the sort of place you'd want to be stuck for any time at all.

Rab Town

Rab's real pull is its main center, **RAB TOWN**, squeezed onto a slender ridge of land, with its four Romanesque *campanili*—the city's trademark—spaced evenly along the peninsula. On the face of things it's a busy place, very much discovered by tourists. But like so many of the towns along this coast, it absorbs its visitors with ease, retaining its medieval character fairly well, while being a bright, lively place during the holiday season. And the town is genuinely lovely: a tiny city, gray and ocher in color, broken up with gurgles of prickly green palm, huddles of leaning junipers, and sprigs of olive-colored cacti pushing their way between balconied palaces. Somehow, all of Rab's shapes and colors seem just about right.

The city divides into two parts, though you wouldn't immediately realize it: Kaldanac, which is the oldest part, closest to the end of the peninsula; and Novi Grad, which dates from the fifteenth to the seventeenth centuries. The main street, **Ive Lole Ribara**, runs the length of the Novi Grad part of the city, starting from Trg Palih Boraca at the far northern end. Close by the square, the Renaissance **Dominis-Nemir Palace** was the birthplace in 1560 of one Mark Anthony de Dominis, scholar, priest, and sometime Archbishop of Split—until his conversion to Protestantism and move to England where he became Dean of Windsor and Vicar of West Ilsley in Berkshire. While there he wrote his ten-volume *De Repubblica Ecclesiastica*—a vicious attack on the Catholic church—and then headed back to Rome to repent and explain his conduct. He was imprisoned there and subsequently died, his body burnt as a heretic—an ignominious end for a man whose scientific and philosophical work was later to influence figures as diverse as Newton, Goethe, and Descartes. The remains of another part of the Nemira Palace, opposite, are now the *Restaurant Grand*, where bands pump out loud easy listening throughout most summer evenings.

At the other end, Ive Lole Ribara culminates in a small piazza mostly taken up by a Venetian loggia, and, tucked away in the corner, the tiny Gothic church of Sv Nikola. Left of here lies Trg Maršala Tita, where the Venetian Gothic **Knežev Dvor** houses the tourist office. Straight on from the loggia takes you into the older part of town, cutting through the arched street and then climbing up on to the highest part of Rab's ridge of land to the **Cathedral of Sv Marija**, a principally twelfth-century Romanesque church that is a marvelous amalgam of distinct, elegant parts. The west front is striped pale gray and pink, a series of scuffed and hollowed blind arches, cut by a Renaissance doorway that supports a savage *Pietà* of 1414. Inside, the walls are crumbly honey and gray, with, here and there, flecks of the same agate-colored marble. Three aisles look towards a high choir flanked by rich, almost gaudily carved stalls, and, dominating all, a light, delicate ciborium in gray cipollino marble. The plaited slabs above the arches date back to the eighth and ninth centuries; the rest of the structure is contemporary with the church.

The cathedral also harbors the head of Saint Christopher: a powerful relic, visible in the cathedral treasury, that was responsible—so they say—for dispatching Hungarian, Croatian and Norman would-be invaders, though it didn't prevent submission to the Venetians in 1115. Look at the map-picture over the doorway as you go out, of Rab watched over by Christ and Mary. Throughout the years that followed, and the atrocities of marauding pirates and Turks, Rab remained a civilized Christian enclave in barbarous seas. "The community who built this cathedral was so civilised," wrote Rebecca West, "that it could conceive a God who would be pleased not by the howlings of His worshippers and the beating of their breasts, but by their gaiety, by their accomplishment, by their restraint and dignity."

Walk back along the ridge from the cathedral and you pass the first of Rab's *campanili*, the largest and most beautiful, a perfectly symmetrical twelfth-century tower with a bell whose peal was made mellow—legend tells—by gold and silver dropped into the casting pot by Rab's wealthier citizens. The remaining three *campanili* are spaced along **Rade Končara**, which runs north along the ridge towards the park. The first, a smaller tower, is attached to the church of **Sv Andrija**; the second, onion-capped one is that of the church of **Sv Justina**, a small Renaissance church that's now a museum of sacred art, with an assortment of manuscripts, Baroque sculpture, stonework and robes. Amid this look out for a polyptych by Paolo Veneziano (mid-fourteenth-century), a *Death of Joseph* dubiously ascribed to Titian, and the fragment of tombstone by the door—gaze at this long enough and a seemingly worn and incomprehensible script melts into a figure of the Madonna and Child.

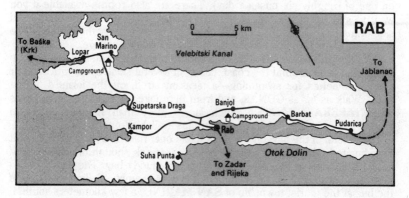

At the top end of Rade Končara, steps lead up to a church on the right with a small **lapidarium** (daily 9am–noon & 6–9pm), from which more steps scale the old fortifications of the city. At the top there are fine views back over the roofs and towers of Rab town.

A gate from the tower gives onto the fragrant **Komrčar Park**, a shady park which provides a leafy route down to the swimming spots below. From here you can stroll to the Franciscan monastery of **Sv Fumija** (daily 9am–noon & 5–7pm), about half an hour from Rab town. Built in 1446, this has a light, delicate cloister that gives onto a small museum in the library above, where you can see illuminated manuscripts, a headless Roman figure of Diana, a fifteenth-century wooden image of St Francis, and some examples of Yugoslav currency through the ages. There's also, in the nearby church, a polyptych by the Vivarini brothers from 1458, and a gory, late Gothic crucifixion on wood. Walk through the cloister and down to the monastery's jetty for views back up the bay to Rab.

The Rest of the Island: Kampor, Supetarska Draga, Lopar, and San Marino

A little way beyond Sv Fumija, on the way to Kampor and easily reached by bus, lies the **Slovensko Groblje** or Slavonic cemetery, close to—and in memory of—the darkened shells of buildings nearby, relics of an Italian wartime concentration camp located here in 1942. Over a two-month period at the camp nearly 5000 Yugoslavs died, deprived of food and water by the Italian officials. The memorial complex remembers it all with depressingly long lines of marked graves—one for each four people that died—and a symbolic mosaic that depicts the war, the suffering, and ultimate partisan victory. Like Istria, this part of Yugoslavia had a hard time of it during the war. Mussolini embraced Italy's long and ill-founded historic claims to this stretch of coast, intending to create a separate Italianate state run on Fascist lines. Anyone who dissented paid a heavy price.

A short walk from the cemetery, **KAMPOR** is a small, scattered village with a fine deep swath of very shallow sandy **beach**, from which you can wade out for several hundred meters. It's not overused, even in high season, and easily reached from Rab town (about an hour's walk walk or ten minutes on one of roughly six buses a day). There are also **rooms** available if you want to stay, from the tourist office/restaurant complex on the right-hand side of the bay. There are a couple of places to **eat**, too; try the *krčma* on the right side of the bay, just beyond the modern part of the village.

Take the path to the left of this restaurant, then fork right, and you pick up a path that leads around the coast, taking in several small spots with sand or shingle **beaches** for swimming—a pleasant stroll, off the island's tourist track. Walk as far as GONAR, and from here take the road inland as far as **SUPETARSKA DRAGA**, a much larger place than Kampor, sprawled around a deep bay and with plenty of rooms available from its tourist office.

The far end of the bay, on the main Rab–Lopar road, is a good place to wait for a bus to **LOPAR**, where the ferry leaves for Krk, though the village itself is just a handful of houses spread around a muddy bay. The sandy beach here isn't particularly picturesque, but it is usually empty. Failing that, get off the bus at the tourist township of **SAN MARINO**, a few kilometers south; if there's no bus, take the road from the crossroads (tourist office), just where Lopar's houses peter out. The beach here, known as **Rajska Plaža** or "Paradise Beach," is very large and again very shallow (you can virtually wade out to the tiny island in the bay), though be warned that it's also Rab's most developed point for tourists. That said, the beach is large enough to always yield a space, even in July and August; there are bars and restaurants and watersports facilities; and it can be an excellent place to bring kids.

Practical Details

You need at least a couple of days to get the feel of Rab town and the rest of the island. It can get crowded, especially in July and August, but not disastrously so, and in Rab town you should normally be able to pick up a **room** either from the hawkers at the bus station or the **tourist office** on Trg Maršala Tita (daily 7am–11pm). There is also a small cluster of private rooms on the opposite side of the harbor, up a track between the yacht club and the soccer pitch; look for the signs. The cheapest **hotel** is the D category *Beograd*, on the seafront (☎051/771-340), which has double rooms for around $30. The *Istra*, on the waterfront on the way to the bus station (☎051/771-134), is slightly nicer and costs about $35–40 a double. The closest **campground** to Rab town is about 2km away in the resort suburb of Banjol, though it's not of an especially high standard; simply follow the sea path south around a couple of headlands, or take one of the plentiful **water taxis** from the rank on Trg Maršala Tita, which will save the thirty-minute walk. Outside Rab town, there's a **campground** at San Marino, the *Rajska Plaža*, which also has beds in its associated pension for around $30 a double. Most of the villages around the island have at least a few private rooms.

For **eating**, the *Ali Baba* on M. Oreškovića, the lower of Rab's three main arteries, does good fish; *Sv Marija*, just beyond the loggia on the right, has a good selection of dishes and a pretty courtyard; the *Paradiso Pizzeria*, up the hill from the loggia on the right, is a good standby for vegetarians. Consider also the *Restaurant Park*, at the far end of Ive Lola Ribara, a reliable eatery with outdoor seating, or the restaurant of the *International* hotel on the waterfront, which has excellent traditional fare. Outside Rab town proper, but worth the walk, there's a restaurant just behind the *Padova* campground on the left-hand side of the road which does omelets, french fries, salads, and large helpings of pasta as well as very cheap drinks. For **drinking**, the slightly tatty *Buffet Alligator*—up a side street opposite the *Restaurant Grand*—is where a good proportion of Rab's youth flock to watch old "Top of the Pops" videos, though it can be rather pricey.

In Rab town you can **swim** from the waterside walkway on the west side of town—take the steps down from beside the church of Sv Justina. The nearest **beaches**, sandy but very crowded, are in the coves towards and around the *Padova* campground. Far better to wade across to the little offshore island, which is quieter and more relaxed. Official **nudist facilities** are the other side of Rab town, round the point of the next bay—again, a taxi-boat ride from Trg Maršala Tita; while the beach at the **Suha Punta** tourist complex farther around the island, in the same direction, is good but again often crowded. Generally, if you want to swim, it's best to go either to Kampor or San Marino.

Leaving Rab, those island-hopping by car and wanting to go on to PAG have no choice but to return to the mainland—to Jablanac—and take a ferry from there. On foot you can either take the twice-weekly ferry to Novalja or pick up the daily boat to Lun, on the remotest tip of Pag island (and strangely enough administratively part of Rab), which leaves at noon. Bear in mind that buses from Lun to Pag town are infrequent and you may have to hitch.

Pag

PAG is a stark and desolate island, a snowy pumice-stone which at first sight looks as if it could barely support any form of life. Around 9000 people live here, looking after three times as many sheep, who scour the stony slopes in search of the rare blade of grass. Hot afternoons always seem hotter here than anywhere else: nothing stirs, seemingly nothing grows—at its greenest the island sprouts no more than a few olives and stumpy, stick-like shrubs—and all around is arid, quasi-desert.

Around the Island

Assuming you're still reading, it would, however, be unwise to write off Pag altogether. The island's capital, **PAG TOWN**, grouped to one side of a deep bay, is one of the most appealing on the coast. A tiny place, it was planned with a tight grid of narrow streets by Juraj Dalmatinac in 1443, after wrangles between Venice, Hungary, and nearby Zadar left the old city of Pag—about 2km south of today's town—virtually a ruin. Dalmatinac laid out the town on a rectangular plan around a central square—**Trg Bratstva i Jedinstva**—and designed the Gothic-Renaissance **Rector's Palace**, now a café and supermarket. The lovely fifteenth-century **Parish Church** on the other side of the square is also his work, a mixture of Gothic and early-Renaissance styles, with vaulted wooden aisles and a flat stucco ceiling, divided by round-arched Gothic-Renaissance arcading. Outside the church, the relief above the door shows the Virgin Mary sheltering the town beneath her cloak.

Tourism is on the increase in Pag: *suven-iri* shops are springing up all over the place, and on Obala Dalmacije there is a sundial—an award from Zagreb Radio to "the best coastal resort of 1986." But for the moment, at least in comparison to the other islands, it retains some elements of a traditional way of life. The red marble Baroque altars in the church, for example, are adorned with examples of the delicate local **lace**, one of Pag's two specialties, a craft that for the moment remains refreshingly unexploited. It's only made in Pag town and is sold by women in the dark, full-skirted local costume, often from their doors; the wearing of the local dress, too, is not an affectation for tourists. Pag's other local claim to fame is its **cheese**, *paški sir*—a hard cheese, salty and delicious—though you find this in other parts of the country. The salty taste is said to be the result of the sea, which taints the low island with its spray. Indeed, Pag is a salty kind of place in general: the precious stuff is the island's main industry, with salt pans stretching out behind the town, and even the tap water tastes slightly brackish.

Three kilometers or so from Pag town, on the far side of the salt pans, lies **Stari Grad**, the town which was evacuated in the 1440s in preference for

Juraj Dalmatinac's new planned community on the bay. There are a few buildings here, mostly in a state of ruin, including the cloister of a Franciscan monastery and a church dating from 1392, which has the very same carving of the Virgin Mary above its door as is on Dalmatinac's church in Pag town.

Eight kilometers north, and connected by around six buses a day, **NOVALJA** is the island's main resort and much more developed and crowded than Pag town. It was a Roman settlement originally, dating from around the first century AD, and has a few ancient remains around to prove it, including a length of aqueduct. But it's primarily devoted to the vacation industry, with features geared accordingly. There's a large **campground** (part nudist), a couple of hotels, and again you will find a plentiful stock of private **rooms**.

Practical Details

If you want to stay in Pag town, the *Hotel Bellevue* near the beach is quite cheap, with doubles for about $25. The **tourist office** (daily 8am–9pm) by the bridge on Jurja Dalmatinca has a supply of inexpensive **private rooms**; there's also a small **campground**. In Novalja, there are a couple of reasonably priced hotels, as well as a much larger and better-equipped campground. The island as a whole is fairly well blessed with **beaches**, and a pebble beach skirts the strip of land that bridges Pag to the other side of the bay. This doesn't get oppressively crowded, and is as good a place to swim as any. If you're in search of more seclusion, there are many short, relatively deserted stretches along the eastern side of the bay, within easy walking distance of Pag town.

NORTHERN DALMATIA

South of the Paklenica national park, the coast bulges out to herald the start of **northern Dalmatia**. In many ways, apart from a few highspots, this is the least interesting part of the coast, and certainly of Dalmatia. There are few beaches worth speaking of, and the landscape is often uninspiring, ranging from the gray, low karst hills spotted with olives in the south, to the bleak flatlands around Zadar. **Šibenik**, and to a great extent **Zadar**, are, nonetheless, enticing cities, among Dalmatia's most important centers and transit-points, and both giving good access to the offshore islands. Of these, **Ugljan** and **Pašman**, which parallel the mainland between Zadar and Biograd, are easiest to reach, and perhaps have the most to offer. Further out, islands like **Dugi Otok** and the **Kornati archipelago**, not to mention the host of smaller, almost completely unknown islands which crowd these waters, demand more time and determination.

Zadar and Around

The ancient capital of Dalmatia, **ZADAR** is a large town of around 100,000 people, but it preserves a relatively small-town feel, with a small historic quarter crowded on to a tapered thumb of land that juts north into the Adriatic.

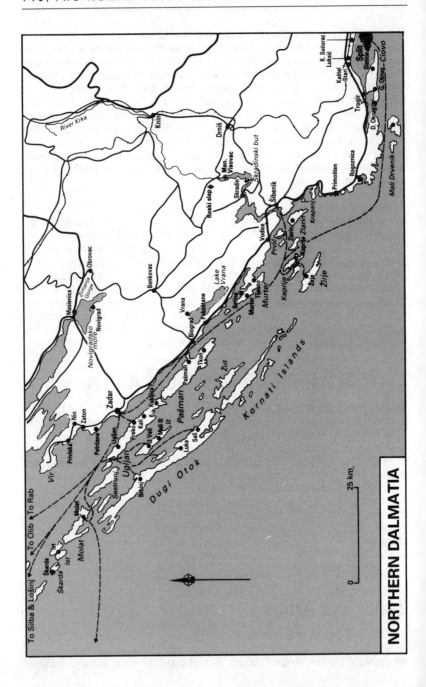

NORTHERN DALMATIA

Pretty comprehensively destroyed in the last war by Allied bombs, it lacks the museum-y, preserved quality of so many of the towns on this coast, and is really much the better for it—a pleasant muddle of architectural styles, where lone Corinthian columns stand alongside rectangular 1950s high-rises, and Romanesque churches compete for space with glassy café-bars.

Zadar was originally a settlement of the Illyrian tribe of Liburnians, but it was colonized by the Romans around the first century BC, who named it Jadera. Later, it became an outpost of Venice, which it remained for close to four centuries, finally becoming reattached to Italy in 1921 under the Treaty of Rapallo as a solitary remnant of Italian rule in Dalmatia. After being bombed no less than 72 times during the war, it was brought under Yugoslav sovereignty in 1947, and, although fast diminishing, you'll find the Latin influence still strong—Italian is widely spoken, particularly by older people, and the place has much of the vibrancy of an Italian coastal town.

The Town

Zadar's street plan survived despite the bombing, and the center of town remains a medieval network of narrow streets, much of it surrounded by walls and barred to motor traffic. The two sides of the peninsula are quite different in feel: the northern waterfront, lined by the most complete set of city walls, busy with the hustle of the ferry traffic:, the southern side, along Obala Maršala Tita, much more peaceful, flanked by gardens and café tables.

The main street, Ive Lole Ribara, cuts through the center of town skirting **Zeleni Trg**, the main city square and the best place to start your explorations. Most things of interest are grouped around here and nothing is more than five minutes' saunter away. It's a messy square, flooded with café-tables together with remnants of Zadar's **Roman forum**. This is little more than a grassy litter of stone really, with a few hastily dumped sarcophagi, the remains of a basilica, and a single-standing pillar which served as a pillory during the Middle Ages.

Much of the forum found its way to the lumpish ninth-century church of **Sv Donat** (daily 7am–8pm), which was built above a couple of altar stones dedicated to Jupiter and Juno by Saint Donat himself, an Irishman who may have been bishop here for a time. A hulking, triple-apsed drum of stone, it's externally not unlike San Vitale in Ravenna, and some maintain it was modeled on Charlemagne's Palatinate Chapel in Aachen, though any comparisons with either building are soon dispelled by the bare, barn-like interior. Past purposes have included shop, military store and museum, but for the moment it lies empty, used only occasionally for summer concerts.

In complete contrast, the streamlined modern **Archaeological Museum** opposite (Tues–Sat 8am–noon & 6–9pm, Sun 9am–noon) has a neatly displayed collection of Zadar's Roman and Illyrian relics; pre-Christian, Roman, and medieval finds from nearby Nin; and fragments of sculpture from most of Zadar's churches. Next door, the church of **Sv Marija** dates from 1066, though its Renaissance frontage was added in 1536 and the interior given a thorough refurbishment in the mid-eighteenth century that left it rather soulless. The Romanesque bell tower, adjacent, was built in 1105 and

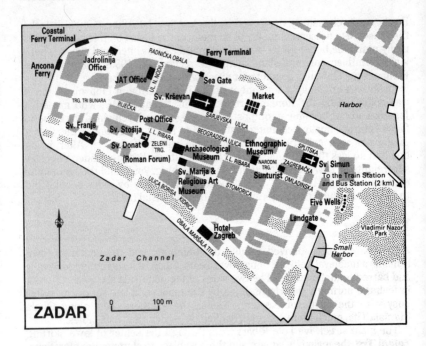

is the oldest in Dalmatia. The adjacent convent is of more interest, recently
converted to house a **Museum of Sacred Art** (Tues–Sat 9am–1pm & 5–
7pm, Sun 9:30am–noon), a positive storehouse of the pick of Zadar's church
treasures and very much the pride of the city. Exhibits vary enormously but
highlights include an early, six-painting polyptych by Vittore Carpaccio; a
large fifteenth-century gang of *Apostles* carved in wood; a soft, resonant *St
Jerome* by Palma the Younger; and, among arm and skull reliquaries too
numerous to mention, some very beautiful and diverse iconic representations
of the *Madonna and Child*. Altogether, it's a fabulous museum, subtly
arranged, beautifully lit, and just small enough to be manageable.

Looking back across the square, the cathedral's **campanile** was only
finished in the last century, by the English writer and architect T.G. Jackson;
if you've been to Rab you may find it familiar—he modeled it on the cathedral
bell tower there. Behind is the **Cathedral of Sv Stošija** (St Anastasia) itself,
a perfect—if late—example of the Romanesque style with an arcaded west
front that echoes the churches of Pisa and Tuscany. Built during the twelfth
century, it's high and capacious inside, basilical in plan, with the nave greedily out of proportion to the narrow aisles hidden away on each side. The lofty
arcade is pretty enough, with pillars picked out in red marble, but it can't help
but look a little lost in the broad expanses of flat, gray stone. At the eastern
end, the ciborium is worthy of close attention, a Gothic work from 1332 with
delicately carved columns.

Following Ive Lole Ribara west from here, and turning left at **Trg Tri Bunara**, given its name by the three eighteenth-century wells on its right-hand side, takes you to the monastic church of **Sv Franje**. This is said to have been founded by Saint Francis himself when he visited Zadar in 1219, and is purportedly the oldest Gothic church in Dalmatia—though actually it's a fairly dull renovation with a flat eighteenth-century roof. You may have to agitate to get the treasury opened, but it's worth it, for its display of thirteenth- and fourteenth-century choral manuscripts, a delicate *Virgin and Child* from the fifteenth century and a remarkable twelfth-century wooden crucifix, the work of a local artist.

The city north of here is enclosed by the longest stretch of city walls. Follow these along to the church of **Sv Krševan** (St Christopher), a more impressive building outside than in (the key is fairly elusive anyway), with a west front similar to the cathedral's and a superb colonnaded east end of three apses—all exactingly proportioned. Farther along, the **market** fills a small square hard up against the walls, the source of any number of dubious items (tortoises and badger fur are just two), beyond which **Narodni Trg** is a second focus for life in Zadar and home of the tourist office and a small **Ethnographic Museum** (Mon–Fri 9am–2pm, Sun 9am–noon). Housed in the former sixteenth-century guardhouse, this displays a selection of ethnic costumes and faded photographs of moustachioed young bucks from hereabouts.

Close by, off Omladinska, the Baroque **Church of Sv Simun** is a seventeenth-century version of an earlier church on this site, and has been recently restored. The previous church was—after the church of Sv Marija—the first resting place of Saint Simun, an obscure saint who is supposed to have held the child Christ in the temple. Inside is his silver-gilt coffin reliquary, held on the high altar by two Baroque angels cast in bronze from captured Turkish cannons. It's an extravagant work of art, executed in 1380 by a Milanese silversmith for the Hungarian Queen Elisabeth out of 250 kilos of silver. The story goes that Elisabeth so wanted a piece of the saint's body that she broke off a finger and hid it in her bosom, driving herself mad until she could replace it; a mixture of awe and horror prompted her to commission the reliquary. The lid shows the bearded saint in high relief, and, on the front, two panels dramatize the legendary discovery of the body in a monastery on the outskirts of Zadar and the triumphant entry into the city of the Hungarian King Lodowick (Elisabeth's husband) after a year-and-a-half-long siege by the Venetians. The center panel is a rough copy of Giotto's fresco of *The Presentation in the Temple* in Padua.

Much beyond Sv Simun and you're on the edge of the town center. Across the square, **Park Vladimira Nazora** occupies the site of the former bastions of the city, the entrance by the five wells that give **Trg Pet Bunara** its name. There's no need to walk any farther south of here unless you're taking a bus or train. A sharp right takes you past the so-called **Landgate**, a construction of 1543, and into the **small harbor**, crowded with pleasure boats. Follow this around and you're back on the Zadar's seaward waterfront, Obala Maršala Tita.

Practical Details

Zadar's **rail and bus stations** are a little way south of the town center, reachable on foot in about fifteen minutes, or by a quick hop on one of the plentiful *Liburnija* shuttle buses. Detailed **maps and information** are available from the *Sunturist* office on Narodni Trg (Mon–Fri 7am–2pm & 4–9pm, Sat 7am–9pm, Sun 7am–1pm & 6–9pm). They're also the best source of **rooms**, and even in high season there are usually some available—though if not, the *Liburnija* office, around the corner on Omladinska, has a small stock. Of the town's **hotels**, the *Zagreb* on Obala Maršala Tita (☎057/25-458), a short walk from Zeleni Trg, is the cheapest and most convenient, a large hotel that normally has space; rooms cost around $40 a double. The nearest **campground** is the *Borik*, open May to September, 4km away at the end of the #5 or #8 bus routes. Nearby there's also a **youth hostel**, open from May until mid-October (☎057/443-145).

As for **food**, a good tip for breakfast is the restaurant in the railroad station, which serves excellent pancakes and cappuccinos—cheap too. For later in the day, there's a self-service restaurant in a small arcade about halfway down Ive Lole Ribara. Moving up a notch, the *gostiona* behind the church of Sv Krševan serves pizzas, a good array of pasta dishes and the usual Croatian meat dishes, and has outdoor seating. On the other side of town, the *Gostiona Stari Grad*, at Sime Matavulja 10, behind the *Hotel Zagreb*, has a standard menu which includes fish and pasta. **Nightlife** in Zadar revolves around Zeleni Trg and the live bands on the terrace of the *Hotel Zagreb*—a good place to drink of a summer evening. Those preferring loud Madonna should try the open-air bar/disco on the city walls just above the ferry terminal.

Plan to spend at least a couple of days in Zadar. The town itself is worth it, there are places to see inland (see below), and an abundance of **islands** within easy striking distance. A dozen boats a day make the half-hour trip to Ugljan, which lies offshore and along with Nin offers the closest and best places for bathing. And there are less frequent connections to the countless smaller and more deserted hunks of land beyond—Iž, Rava, Dugi Otok, Sestrunj, Molat, Silba, and Olib, to name just a few. There are regular **summer connections** too (except Fridays) to Lošinj and Pula, and from there a weekly link to Venice. Three ferries a month link Zadar with Ancona, one a week with Rimini, three a month with Trieste.

Around Zadar: Nin and Novigrad

Inland from Zadar lies an area known as the **Ravni Kotari**, a flat, fertile landscape separated from the Velebit mountain range by the enlarged inlet of the Novigrad Sea. It's a bleak, desolate region, devoid of interest except for a couple of places accessible by bus from the town.

Nin

NIN, about 20km up the coast from Zadar, is probably more exclusively Croatian than anywhere on this stretch of coast. Initially settled by the Romans as *Aenona*, it was for centuries one of the residences of the early

Croat kings and served as the major see of their bishops. It was to Nin that maverick Zadrians fled to escape the harsh rule of Venice, and from here too that in 1059 Grgur Ninski obdurately defended the heretic Glagolitic liturgy against the hegemony of Rome. Nin's period of independence, however, was short lived, and like everywhere else along this coast it eventually fell under direct Venetian rule. Before long, a combination of endemic malaria and Venetian sabotage forced a thriving city into quiet decay, and by the time T.G. Jackson got here in 1887 Nin was no more than a large village whose inhabitants were so wan and unwholesome from malaria that his guides wouldn't let him stay there overnight.

The malaria has gone now, but apart from that Nin can't have changed much since Jackson's day. It's an odd kind of place, ruined in places and rather beaten in spirit. The town is built on a small island and connected to the mainland by two bridges. Scatterings of Roman ruins, solitary arches and mossy, crumbling walls all testify to some sort of past, but there's little other tangible evidence of Nin's former importance. A tiny **Temple of Diana** figures among the scanty Roman remains, and there's a small **archaeological museum** with a few trinkets from the Roman and Croatian eras, though most of the major finds have found their way to Zadar, Split, or Zagreb.

Home to a family of swallows, the small cruciform church of **Sv Križ**, just off the main street, is the oldest intact church in the country, with an inscription on the lintel referring to Župan (Count) Godezav dated AD 800. Get the key from the museum. From the Zadar bus you'll have noticed another tiny church huddled under some slender scotch pines—**Sv Nikola**, an eleventh-century three-apsed church built on an ancient burial mound and fortified by the Turks. Like Sv Križ, there's nothing much here, but the site is impressive, looking over the blustery lowlands to the time-ravaged shape of Nin and the silver-gray ridge of the Velebit mountains, wonderfully unreal in the distance.

PRACTICAL DETAILS: SOME BEACHES
Buses to Nin run approximately every 45 minutes from the main Zadar bus station. Be sure to ask the driver about when you get to Nin as it's off the main road and not clearly marked.

Apart from the town itself, Nin is a good place to come to swim: there's a fine strand of sandy **beach** here on the far side of town, and another stretch in nearby PRIVLAKA, about 5km away.

Novigrad and the Zrmanja Gorge

East from Zadar, the sea cuts deep into the coast, forming the almost entirely enclosed inland expanse of water known as the **Novigradsko More** or Novigrad Sea. The road crosses this at its narrowest point, the Maslenica Canal, a thin blue ribbon of water between banks of parched gray rock, where there's a small motel, the *Plitvice*, at which long-distance buses sometimes pull in for a break.

On the western bank of the Novigrad Sea lies **NOVIGRAD** itself, an hour or so by bus from Zadar. Novigrad heaps up along one side of a wooded, winding inlet, a sleepy place whose castle was where Queen Elisabeth of Hungary was imprisoned and murdered in 1386. The castle is now in ruins, and almost entirely shielded by pines above the town; to get here, follow the broad steps from near the bus stop up past the church, turn left, cut through the houses and take the rough path to the top—about ten minutes' climb in all, and worth it both for the views and the fragrant pine shelter at the top.

If you're here with a car, there are plenty of good places to swim from along the Novigradsko More; otherwise, once you've seen the castle and strolled around the town there's not a lot else to do. On the far side of the inland sea, **OBROVAC** can also be reached by bus direct from Zadar. There's another thirteenth-century castle here, and, just before the town, leading out of the Novigradsko More itself, the **Zrmanja Gorge**—a narrow canyon that is one of the most remarkable karst formations in the country, the rocky sides rising at some points to 200m. There are sometimes organized excursions here from Zadar, though if you can get to Obrovac, it is possible to see some of it on foot. You might also be able to rent a boat or take a water taxi, either from here or in **POSEDARJE**, across the water.

The Coast South of Zadar

The coast road south from Zadar hugs the shoreline, littered with small spots for bathing, at which it's easy enough to stop and take a dip if you're driving. About 30km south of Zadar, **BIOGRAD-NA-MORU** was another capital of the Croat kings, though, like Nin, it has long since fallen on hard times. For years it vied with Zadar for prominence on this coast, holding on to power until Good Friday 1126, when the Venetians razed it to its foundations, plunging the town into a decline from which it never really recovered. The people here still commemorate the fateful day with a special Mass, and by tradition a Black Knight is supposed to emerge from the waves to save the last Croatian queen.

Biograd has recovered its prominence in a modest way as the major resort on this part of the coast, though it's a shabby town, fronted by a marina and some modern hotels. The local **museum** has one or two interesting finds from offshore wrecks, but otherwise the town's main use is as the main ferry-link with the island of Pašman, which lies just offshore.

Farther south, the road touches the edge of **PAKOŠTANE**, a sprawling village that's home to a Club Med camp. Inland from here, **VRANA**, nestled timidly at the top end of the lake of the same name, was the farthest point that the Turks reached in the sixteenth century, evidence of which exists in the shape of a ruined **han** from 1644 which was once the largest in Europe. It's at once the only instance of Turkish architecture on or near the coast, and probably the best example of a *han* in Yugoslavia. The people who used to inhabit this area were known as the *Morlahi*—a wild bunch who, according to one contemporary source, were known for being "fierce, unreasonable, void of humanity and capable of any crime." Nowadays things in Vrana are, mercifully, quieter.

VODICE, fifteen minutes north of Šibenik, is the Adriatic at its worst, a small resort town dominated by a massive marina and the huddles of souvenir stalls here to service the predominantly German and Austrian yachtspeople. Hotels keep a respectable distance on each side of Vodice's bay, and there are **rooms** available from the **tourist office** (daily 7am–9pm), just to the left of the marina, and advertised all over the town. But Vodice is a miserable place to stay on the whole: there are no beaches as such, just rocks and concrete bathing stations, most of which are crammed to the gills throughout the summer and pretty awful; and although the core of the town is likable enough, grouped around a tiny square in the middle of the harbor, it is pretty much swamped by tourists during the peak season. Around ten buses a day pass through the town on their way to the island of Murter, thirty minutes north, but otherwise give it a miss.

Šibenik and Around

Across the broad gash of the Krka River outlet, **ŠIBENIK** can seem like a breath of fresh air after Vodice, a prosperous-looking place with the brash, workaday air of a busy port. It's by no means a resort, and there's not much point in stopping if you're looking for somewhere quiet with a beach. But its cathedral, clasped on the hillside in the heart of Šibenik's atmospheric medieval center, is the coast's finest. And the town makes a good base for a handful of offshore islands, and, inland, the delightful Krka Falls.

The Town

Šibenik's ancient center clings to the side of the hill in a steep tangle of alleys, steps, and arches, its two main arteries, **Zagrebačka** and **12 Kolovoza 1941**, cutting through town from the modern square of Poljana Maršala Tita to Trg Republike, core of the city. Above here, the town's oldest quarters heap up to the **castle of Sv Ana**—the nearest and most accessible of Šibenik's impressive fortifications, built in the twelfth century and reconstructed under the Venetians.

You can walk up to the top if you wish, and the rest of Šibenik's "downtown" provides lots of opportunity for idle wandering, peeking into its innumerable tiny churches, losing yourself in the maze of narrow alleys, and finally emerging on the broad riverfront. But the real focus in the town is the Gothic-Renaissance **Cathedral of Sv Jakov**, the product of a long-running saga that stirred the imaginations and emptied the pockets of the townspeople here during the fifteenth century. Plans for a new cathedral were originally drawn up in 1402, but war, lack of funds and disputes over the site delayed the start of work until 1431, when a group of Italian architects oversaw the erection of the Gothic lower story of the present building. In 1441 a series of scandals and dissatisfaction with the old-fashioned Gothic nature of the design led to the appointment of a new architect, Juraj Dalmatinac (George the Dalmatian). Better schooled in the architectural fashions of the time, Dalmatinac brought lighter, more floral elements to the building, adding a transept to the original basilical plan, and enlarging and raising the choir, which he topped with an octagonal cupola of extraordinary light and beauty. Things went well, but exploitation by Venice, two outbreaks of plague and a catastrophic fire led to frequent stoppages. Dalmatinac died in 1473, and a new mason from Florence, Nikola Firentinac, took over, signing a contract that forced him to follow the existing design, while adding a clear Renaissance strain of his own. Firentinac is known to have been responsible for the whole of the west front.

Entry to the cathedral is via the **North Door**, framed by arches braided with leaves, fruit and swirling arabesques. Two lions roar companionably at each other, supporting the pious, remorseful, and rather crudely carved figures of Adam and Eve. Inside, the church is a harmonious blend of Gothic and Renaissance forms, your eyes drawn towards the raised sanctuary by the sheer space and light of the east end, which streams in through plentiful windows to illuminate the soft gray Dalmatian stone. Follow the stairs down from the southern apse to the **Baptistery**, designed by Juraj Dalmatinac and sculpted by later masons. It's a lovely piece of work, a womb-like cubbyhole of decorated Gothic carving, with four scallop-shell niches rising from each side to form a rich, vaulted roof, beneath which cherubim scamper playfully, upholding the red marble font.

Back outside the cathedral, around the exterior of the three apses, Dalmatinac carved a unique **frieze** of 71 stone heads, apparently portraits of those who refused to contribute to the cost of the cathedral and a vivid cross-section of sixteenth-century society. Certainly you can't help feeling you're looking at real people, some of whom Juraj obviously found ridiculous, some he seems to have actively disliked. On the north apse, beneath two angels with a scroll, he inscribed his claim to the work: "These apses have been made by Juraj Dalmatinac, son of Mate."

Trg Republike itself is lined with historic buildings: a sixteenth-century **loggia**, much restored after World War II bombing, directly opposite the cathedral; and, on its southern side, the fifteenth-century **Bishop's Palace** and **Rector's Palace**. The latter of these is nowadays home to the **Town Museum** (Tues–Fri noon–1pm & 7–9pm, Sat & Sun 10am–noon), which has a display of local archaeological finds from Neolithic to early medieval times, though little English information to help with interpretation. On the opposite corner, the tiny church of **Sv Barbara** has a modest collection of ecclesiastical items, best of which is a small fifteenth-century polyptych by Blaž Jurjev of Trogir, one of the most accomplished of Dalmatian Renaissance artists.

Practical Details

Šibenik's **bus station** is just south of the city center, just off the riverfront on Obala Jugoslavenske Mornarice. The **railroad station**, for what it's worth (trains only run from here to minor inland towns), is a little farther along the waterfront. The **tourist office** on Trg Republike (daily 8am–2pm & 4–10pm) has information and maps, and can help with **rooms**. Failing that, there's a **youth hostel** east of the center in Put Lugusa (follow JNA until it becomes Rade Koncara and turn right), and a central **hotel**, the B-category *Jadran*, on the waterfront, which has doubles for about $45. The nearest **campground** is 8km away in the *Solaris* mega-complex, for which ten buses a day leave the marketplace on Beogradska. Or there's a much more attractive but less

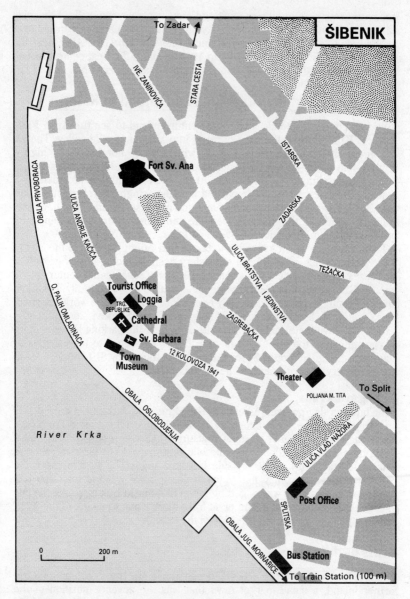

accessible site out near the Krka Falls—in July and August buses run direct, at other times it's a bus to Skradin and a three-kilometer walk. Don't—unless you've reserved ahead—turn up in the latter part of June, when the whole town is taken up with a UNICEF **International Children's Festival**. If you're happy to camp, though, it's an exciting time: events—many in English—play all day long, and in the evening the city's streets and squares are turned over to all kinds of street theater, music, and mime. For **food**, the *Alpa*, near the church of Sv Barbara on 12 Kolovoza 1941, is about the best central restaurant; the *Turist* and *Krka*, near the bus station, are also reasonable.

Around Šibenik: the Krka Falls and Inland to Knin

If you do come to Šibenik, be sure to venture inland to see the **Krka Falls** (Slapovi Krke), where the river narrows into a green, fertile valley. There's one main site, the **Skradinski Buk**, which, while not especially high—around 46m in all—is quietly impressive, cascading frothily over a series of levels through limpid, yielding reeds. At the site everything is provided, with restaurants, cafés, souvenir shops, and not surprisingly there's a lot of tourists. But the location itself is lovely, and you could spend an entire day here, lolling around on the rocks under the tumbling water, sunbathing and paddling in the more docile patches.

From the main falls it's possible to take a **taxi boat** upstream to the islet of **Visovac**, on which a Franciscan monastery nestles among a thick growth of cypresses. The monastery has a small collection of seventeenth-century paintings and, in its valuable library, some incunabula and a beautifully illustrated fifteenth-century *Aesop's Fables*, only one of three like it in the world. Beyond, there's another, less dramatic set of falls, the **Roski Slapovi**, 26m in height. Taxi boats leave the Skradinski Buk site from near the parking lot—the more of you there are the cheaper it is, and they're not eager to take singles or couples—though at around $8 for the boat plus the pricey $10 entrance fee to the monastery, it's not exactly a cheap excursion.

Getting to the Falls
Four buses a day go from Šibenik to the Skradinski Buk direct during July and August; at other times take the Drniš/Knin bus and get off at Tromilja, a crossroads where there's a small restaurant (serving good grilled lamb). From here it's a four-kilometer walk following the road to the river, though you may be able to hitch it. Outside July and August, be sure to check the bus times back—you may find yourself doing more walking than you had bargained for. Another way of getting to the Skradinski Buk is to take the bus to SKRADIN, and walk the 3km or so from there along the bank of the river, bringing you out on the opposite side of the falls.

Drniš and Knin

About 20km on from Krka, **DRNIŠ** doesn't have much to recommend a trip farther inland, a small market town that was the advance position of the Ottoman forces in Dalmatia in the sixteenth century, known as "little Sarajevo" during the time of their occupation. Most of the relics of the Turkish period were obliterated when the Turks were driven out, and the only reminders of those years are a sixteenth-century mosque, since incorporated into the church of **Sv Ivan Krstitelj**, and a minaret—the only one in Dalmatia. There's also a **town museum** which has on display works by the sculptor Ivan Meštrović, who hailed from nearby **OTAVICE**, where he is buried in the **Meštrović Mausoleum**. Built in 1926, and designed by the sculptor for his family, this can be visited—though you'll need to ask around in the village for the key. Meštrović actually died in the United States, where he lived for many years, but his body was flown back here after his death.

Continuing up the same road for another 20km or so is **KNIN**, a Serbian town distinguishable by its Cyrillic street- and shop-signs. The castle on the hill above the town is said to be one of the largest in Yugoslavia, and has recently been converted into a restaurant. Other than that, Knin's only claim to fame is the near-riot which happened here in 1989 during the celebrations to mark the anniversary of the Battle of Kosovo. Serbian nationalism aside, you might arrive here to change trains or buses for the towns of Bosnia, whose border is nearby, in which case there's one accommodation option, the B-category *Dom Penzionara* on Titovo Ulica.

The Northern Dalmatian Islands

The islands of northern Dalmatian considerably less interesting than those to the south; they're a scattered archipelago of small, often bare lumps of land, many of which have so far made few concessions to commercial tourism—though this might be because they have few obvious attractions. **Ugljan** is among the most developed and most inviting, accessible by ferry from Zadar and connected by bridge to the island of **Pašman**. **Dugi Otok**, farther out, shelters the rest of the islands from the open sea with its long bulk, a large barren ridge that spears into the **Kornati archipelago** to the south—an uninhabited scatter of barren rocks that have been designated a national park.

Ugljan and Pašman

UGLJAN is the most densely populated of all the Adriatic islands: a green island, long and thin, linked to its neighbor, Pašman, by a bridge. It's just beginning to discover the commercial possibilities of tourism, but for the moment is largely the preserve of Yugoslav visitors. The Zadar ferry—there are fifteen crossings a day—drops you at **PREKO** (literally "across" from Zadar), Ugljan's largest village, where a *Sunturist* kiosk beside the ferry terminal has a stock of **private rooms**; rooms are also available from the *turističko društvo* in the *Zadranka* and *Preko* hotels. In Preko the locals swim from the harbor or from a thickly vegetated islet in the bay—**Galovac**—where there's a Franciscan monastery that in the days of the Austrian occupation churned out valuable Croatian propaganda on its printing press. Overlooking the town—and deceptively close—is the tenth-century **Fortress of Sv Mihovil**, an hour or so's walk through the central valley and up the ridge on the far side of the island. The fortress, which dates from 1203, is in ruins now, but the views, back over Zadar and the Ravni Kotari, and west to Iz, Dugi Otok, and, on a clear day, Ancona and the Italian coast, are marvelous.

Buses to other destinations on the island normally meet the ferries. On the northern tip of the island, **UGLJAN VILLAGE** has another Franciscan monastery sited right on the harbor, and several **campgrounds** along the road back to Preko. Also accessible from Preko by bus, the village of **MULINE** has three more campgrounds about a kilometer's walk from the bus stop, set side by side amid picturesque woodland, together with a good sandy beach.

In the other direction, Preko runs gently into **KALI**, which crowns a small hillock about a mile down the coast. More immediately picturesque than Preko, it's also firmly and solely committed to the local fishing industry, and you'll find little to do beyond wandering its pinched, slopy streets. Farther south towards Ugljan's southern end is **KUKLJICA**, another small fishing hamlet set in a wide green bay. In season it's normally full of Czechs, who group-reserve the bungalow complex on the pined promontory, but in spite of that things rarely seem too disturbed: there are usually **rooms** available from the tourist office by the church, and there's a good, shallow strip of **beach** (concrete for sunbathing and seldom overbearingly crowded) just fifteen minutes' walk away on the western edge of the island; if you want solitude follow the rough path on the right to the nudist beach, a little way along.

Pašman

About six buses a day ply the route between Preko and the island of **PAŠMAN**, a lengthy string of balding low hummocks, not as green as Ugljan and much less visited, with a tourist industry still very much in its incipient stages. There are very few facilities, and even rooms are scarce.

PAŠMAN VILLAGE, where until recently the main Tkon–Preko bus didn't even stop, is the first real settlement, a faded little place currently enjoying a minor revival in its fortunes, with a tourist office and new supermarket. There's a small stretch of beach, **rooms** are avilaible from the *Jadrantours* office, and there's a **campground**—though the island's best beach is a sandy affair at ŽDRELAC, not far from the Ugljan bridge. Close by, **KRAJ** is noted for its small Gothic Franciscan monastery, dating from 1392, and also has rooms and a campground.

North of Pašman, the Čokovac hill, reachable by taking the first road on the left on leaving the village, boasts a Benedictine monastery built by monks from Biograd that was abandoned when the town was razed by the Venetians. The bus terminates in **TKON**, the island's main center, directly connected with the mainland at Biograd by ten daily ferries. It's a dusty, beleaguered sort of place, with little to recommend it apart from some good secluded beaches just south of town. *Sovinjeturist* (daily 7–11am & 4:30–8:30pm) has a supply of **rooms**, as does *Croatiaturist* opposite, and there's a **nudist campground** a couple of kilometers outside the village.

Dugi Otok and the Kornati Archipelago

DUGI OTOK, literally "long island," is the largest of the islands of northern Dalmatia, 44km long and nowhere more than 5km wide. Parts of it are very remote; some of the settlements are only accessible by sea, and even the main center, Sali, is far more devoted to fishing than any kind of tourism. It is difficult to get to the island outside the summer season, and even during summer there are only a couple of ferries a day, making it impossible to travel without staying overnight, short of taking an organized excursion.

Most ferries dock at Soline in the north of the island, where there's a good sandy beach. Nearby, **BOŽAVA** is a good place to use as a base, a small fishing village with a shingle beach and **rooms** available at the *Hotel Božava* (☎057/86-322), starting at about $25 for a double. Farther south, **SALI** takes its name from the nearby salt beds and is the island's largest village, home of a prosperous fishing industry though with not much else to lure you. **Rooms** are available, should you want to stay, from the **Turističko Društvo** at the *Hotel Sali* (☎057/87-933), which also offers accommodation for around $25 a double. Sali is at least a good springboard for the deep bay of **Telaščica** ("pretty calf"), which cuts into Dugi Otok to the south. Officially part of the Kornati national park (see below), there's a salt lake here, called Mir, that's popular swimming territory. It's full of shrimps which nibble your legs if you stand still long enough—not as unpleasant an experience as it sounds. There's a **campground** at Telaščica, but no other accommodation.

The Kornati Archipelago

Scattered like pebbles to the south of Dugi Otok are the islands of the **Kornati archipelago**, around 125 in all, grouped around the main island of Kornat—at 35km long the largest uninhabited landmass in the Adriatic. The Kornatis form a distinctive environment, the islands rising up out of the sea like gray pimples, harsh bare landscapes almost devoid of any life. During the war the partisans used them as a refuge from the Italians, but since 1980 they've been a national park. They're only inhabited for part of the year, for sheep-raising and tending olives. Apart from the odd memorial from the war years, only a ruined fortress and Christian basilica bear testimony to former habitation, and nowadays the Kornatis are primarily a day-trip destination for tour groups from the mainland, who arrive here in force during the high season.

Much of the land in the Kornatis is owned by the people of Murter (see below), a small nearby island connected to the mainland by road. There are no regular boat connections, but Murter or Dugi Otok are good places to arrange **trips**. Day trips from Murter operate roughly twice a week and cost around $25 per person. Failing that you can simply arrange boats and hut accommodation yourself. There are also local package deals available, with a choice of "Robinson Crusoe"-style holidays on which you get left on the islands with a spartan fisherman's hut and the few essentials necessary to survive; or—less arduously—an organized package based on a nearby island and traveling to the Kornati for a mixture of fishing, diving, and swimming. Contact any of the tourist offices on either Dugi Otok or Murter for more details and exact prices.

Murter

Just north of Vodice, and connected with the mainland by road, **MURTER** is scenically a bare, rather dull island, and another place along this part of the coast which suffers the ritual annual invasion of German and Austrian visitors. The first village you reach, **TIJESNO**, actually straddles Murter's bridge-link with the mainland, a rather nondescript place but with a **campground** 2km beyond, where there's a small pebble beach. A kilometer or so beyond this, BETINA is the next village, which runs almost without a break into **MURTER** village, the main settlement on the island and the place to look for **rooms**. These are available from *Kornatturist*, on the main square of Trg Dalmatinske (daily 7am–9pm), around which what life there is in the place tends to revolve. The nearest **beach** to Murter is Slanica, in a small bay about fifteen minutes' walk from the main part of the village, where there's also a **campground** (though not nearly as pleasant as the one near Tijesno). The beach has a little sand but plenty of rocks, though beware that it does get crowded in summer. You often need to walk around the bay a while to find room. You can rent **canoes** from the beach, or **boats** from the *Kornat Club*, a short walk down Ivana Meštrovića from Trg Dalmatinske. In the evening, life in Murter picks up a little, the ice-cream parlors and cafés around Trg Dalmatinske clicking into action. **Food**, certainly, is no problem: *Gostiona Čadjavica*, a few minutes' walk down Ivana Meštrovića on the left, is good, and the café by the bus stop does pizzas.

Islands off Šibenik

From Šibenik, ferries run out through the thin chink of the river outlet, through a short fortified gorge and out through the scattered remnants of Venetian sea defenses to a small archipelago of tiny islands—though it's probably the least interesting grouping along the coast. **ZLARIN**, reachable on half a dozen ferries a day, is the most accessible and most popular island, twenty minutes away by sea. It has just one village, stippled around a deep bay, which was once renowned for its naval expertise. Women still sporadically wear the local costume and one small workshop is the only reminder of a coral industry long since dead. There are some grubby **beaches** near the village, better ones if you're prepared to walk; a **tourist office** offering **rooms** makes it a feasible alternative to staying in Šibenik. Its sister island, **PRVIĆ**, has rooms available also. Farther out, **OBONJAN** and **KAKAN** are known collectively as the *Otoci Mladosti* or "Islands of Youth," Obonjan for its role as vacation center of the Yugoslav scouts, and Kakan for its function as "seventh continent—a center for the world's children."

South from Šibenik

Immediately south of Šibenik, **BRODARICA** is an undistinguished village that has been principally populated by exiles from the island of **KRAPANJ**, a few hundred meters across the water. This has the odd distinction of being the smallest of the inhabited Adriatic islands, and was known until recently as the home of a sponge diving industry—though this has long since died out. Boats across from Brodarica leave hourly, though unless you've time on your hands a special trip isn't really worth it. The island isn't especially attractive (indeed it's very dirty), and, except for the fifteenth-century Franciscan monastery with its couple of Renaissance paintings and a collection of sponges, there's not that much to see.

Far better to push on south, to **PRIMOŠTEN**, a small town that's the best place on this part of the coast to rest up and do nothing for a while. It's a pretty place, very small, heaped up on an island that's joined to the mainland by a short causeway, though despite its appeal it is by no means engulfed by tourists. Most of what happens in Primošten goes on around the small town square or on the causeway that leads into it. **Rooms** are available from *Dalmacijaturist* (daily 7am–10pm), where the bus stops, and there's a well-equipped **campground**, the *Adriatik*, 3km west of the town on the Punta Maslin peninsula. The campground has its own stretch of beach, but in Primošten itself there are pebble **beaches** flanking the causeway, and on the far side of the wooded promontory to the north of the town, where lurk a number of hotels. If you want to go naked, there's an **FKK beach** at the far end of the promontory, just below the *Hotel Slava*, close to where you can also rent **bikes**. You can rent **boats** by the hour or day from the quayside, just off the main square. For **food**, try the *Villa Fenč*, a little way around the right-hand bay, which has a large terrace and an extra-large variety of fish; the restaurant on the causeway is good, its tables set in a small courtyard. The *Café Calypso*, nearby, serves decent pizzas. Wherever you eat, be sure to try the local Primošten wine, *Babić*—a smooth, dry red.

ROGOZNICA, 10km on from Primošten, was also once an island, though it's a much less enticing place now, its tiny center having become a construction site in anticipation of the tourist boom. **MARINA**, farther on still, is equally small but marginally nicer, with a few compact, if crowded, beaches.

Trogir, Čiovo, and the Seven Castles

Less than an hour out of Split, **TROGIR** is one of the most seductive towns on the Dalmatian coast, a compact brown-beige welter of palaces, jutting belfries and shambling streets fanning out from an antique central square. Yet another island town, connected to the mainland by a short bridge, it lacks the beaches and associated amenities of, say, Primošten, but Trogir's concentration of historic sights can compare with any of the towns on the coast.

Trogir's cosy elegance belies its history. Few Yugoslav towns have suffered so much or so repeatedly as this one, and the long list of invaders includes Romans, Venetians, French, Austrians, Italians, and Germans, not to mention the constant menace of the Turks to the east, attacks by pirates and Saracens, endemic malaria, and, at times, severe internal discord provoked by a rigid class and caste system. The latest invaders are the day-trippers who swarm into Trogir from the surrounding resorts. But they don't stay long, and in the early morning or evening the town reclaims its quiet charm. You can see Trogir in a day and don't need to stay, but it does make a good base for seeing this part of the coast, and Split is only a bus ride away.

Arrival, Accommodation, Food . . . and Leaving

Though some **long-distance buses** do actually stop on the main road opposite the old town, most simply continue on down the main coastal road, which
turns inland to avoid Trogir, so be sure to get down at the turnoff for the
town, around ten minutes away from the old center. The **bus station**, just
outside the town walls, serves local buses only. From here, it's a short walk
across the bridge into the partially walled old town.

Just off Narodni Trg, the main town square, is the **tourist office** (summer
daily 8am–9pm; otherwise Mon–Sat 8am–7pm, Sun 9am–noon), with an ample
supply of private **rooms** as well as maps and other information. The town's
cheapest **hotel**, the *Jadran* (☎058/73-688), which costs about $35 a night for a
double, is a couple of kilometers west of town on the main road near the large
campground of the same name. Closer—and cheaper—is *Motel Trogir*
(☎058/73-424), just a few hundred meters' walk in the same direction, which
has rooms for half the price. There's another, closer **campground**, *Soline*,
close to the old town off the main road, and a third, *Rožac*, twenty minutes'
walk or a short bus ride from town on the adjacent island of Cˇiovo.

Budget **eating** is easy in Trogir: there are dozens of snack bars in the
center serving up lunches for the day-trippers. *Gostionica Trg*, on Narodni
Trg, is as good as any; the *Konoba Fontana*, just off the quayside near the
Kamerlengo fortress, serves better food—though at higher prices. Trogir's
beaches are poor, and the sea around town is murky; if you want a swim
head off towards *Camping Rožac* or to one of the Seven Castles (see below).

Leaving Trogir, bus #37 leaves the bus station every twenty minutes for
the one-hour journey to Split, via the airport and the village-resorts of the so-
called "Riviera of the Seven Castles." In Split the service terminates at the
station on Žrtava Fasižma, ten minutes' walk from Diocletian's Palace. Long-
distance buses are more of a problem—if you stand on the main road expecting them to stop, you could well be in for a disappointment. If they're full, as
they frequently are, they will continue straight on by. A Friday-morning
(6.40am) **ferry** also connects Trogir with Split, an extension of the boat
service to the islands of Mali and Veli Drvenık.

The Town

The center of Trogir is **Narodni Trg**, a creamy-white square flanked by some
of the town's most historic buildings. On the right as you enter the square,
the **Čipiko Palace** is a well-worn fifteenth-century Venetian Gothic mansion
that houses the tourist office, and holds in its foyer a replica of a Turkish
figurehead captured by a ship from Trogir at the Battle of Lepanto. It was
here in 1650 that the codex of Petronius' *Satyricon* was rediscovered. On the
other side of the square, the **Loggia**, with its handsome clock tower, classical
columns, and elaborate detail, dates originally from the fifteenth century
though its pristine appearance is explained by a late-nineteenth-century restoration. The large fifteenth-century relief on the wall of the loggia, the work of
Nikola Firentinac, was damaged in 1932, when the figure of Justice under-

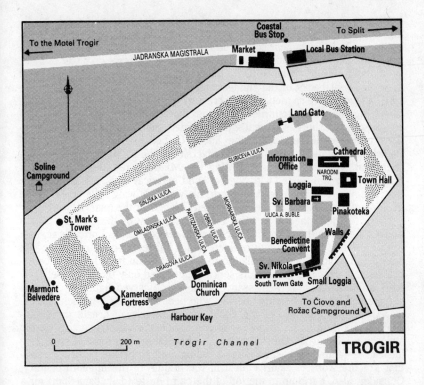

neath the Venetian Lion was dynamited by Yugoslav nationalists. The incident provoked one of the most absurd international crises imaginable, as Mussolini, keen to resurrect territorial claims against Yugoslavia, raged against "Yugoslav barbarism" and forced the Yugoslav government into a groveling apology. As it turned out, the apology did little good, and the Italians were back in force soon after. The panel underneath the lion has since been left blank, and its back wall properly disfigured by a Meštrović relief.

Opposite the loggia, the **Cathedral** (Mon–Sat 9am–noon & 3–7pm) dominates the square, a squat Romanesque structure begun about 1200 and finished some three centuries later with a soaring Venetian-Gothic campanile. Officially dedicated to Sv Lovro (Lawrence), it's popularly known as Sv Ivan after the patron saint of the city, a miracle-working bishop of the eleventh century. The cathedral's most distinctive feature is on the outside, its **west portal**, an astonishing piece of work, carved in 1240 by the Slav master-mason Radovan. Radovan laid claim to his work in an immodest inscription above the door, calling himself "Most excellent in his art"—a justifiable claim when you examine the doorway, which, with a mass of intricate detail, mixes orthodox iconography with scenes from ordinary life and legend, figures of apostles and saints, centaurs and sirens, wood-cutters and leather-workers jostling against each other in a chaos of twisting decoration. Roughly speaking, there is a gradual movement upwards from Old Testament figures at the bottom to New Testament scenes on the arches and lunette. Adam and Eve frame the door and stand with an anxious kind of modesty on a pair of lions, symbols of eternal vigilance. On either side, a series of receding pillars sit upon the bent backs of the "undesirables" of the time—Jews and Turks—while above is a weird menagerie of creatures in writhing, bucking confusion, laced together with tendriled carvings that symbolize the months and seasons. In fact there is no real sense of order, and Radovan and his apprentices only pay lip-service to the linear Catholic certainties of Sin and Redemption, while the intensity and diversity of the carvings hint at a more "heretical" view of the world. During the Middle Ages, the Christianized Balkans were jam-packed with "heresy" and heretical sects, and it's possible that Radovan was influenced by them, his work showing little sense of the triumph of the Gospel and the resurrected Christ over the material world.

Entry to the cathedral is from the rear, by way of the sacristy, which houses the **treasury**—a mundane collection of ecclesiastical bric-a-brac, best of this the fine inlaid storage cabinets and a fourteenth-century Gothic jug, scaled and molded into snakelike form. Continuing on from here, the cathedral itself is dark and gloomy, its sobriety lightened only by the chapel of Sv Ivan, a fine example of Renaissance work with a carved figure of the saint surrounded by torch-bearing cherubs who peep insolently from behind half-closed doors. Look also at the choir, where there's an ornate thirteenth-century ciborium and a lovely set of choir stalls carved in Venetian Gothic style by a local artist. Outside again, the **baptistery** has more Renaissance intricacies—fluted niches, a coffered ceiling, and an ornate puttied frieze—that are the work of Andrija Aleši in the middle of the fifteenth century. Consider, also, a trip up to the top of the **campanile** (daily 8am–9pm) for a view over the town and surrounding area.

Just off the square to the south is the tiny abbey church of Sva Ivan Krstitelj (John the Baptist), known as **Pinakoteka** for its assortment of sacred art from the best of Trogir's churches. Among a number of painted crucifixes and the like, there's some sensitive work by Blaž Jurjev and Paolo Veneziano; canvases of *John the Baptist* and *St Jerome*, painted for the cathedral organ by Gentile Bellini in 1489; and a *Pietà* by Nikola Firentinac, a monumental tombstone carved with a savage realism comparable to Juraj Dalmatinac. Sadly, at the best of times it can be difficult to get into, but the key should be available from the Cathedral.

Nearby, immediately behind the southern town gate, the **Convent of Sv Nikola** (May–Sept 9am–noon & 3–7pm; winter months by request) also has a small treasury, noteworthy for its outstanding third-century Greek *Relief of Kairos*, sculpted out of orange marble and only discovered in 1928. It's a dynamic, intriguing fragment representing the Greek god of the fleeting moment—that favorable instance when all stands at its best. Once past he's impossible to catch, and the back of his head is shaven just to make it more difficult.

Out through the spiked town gate and to the right along the quayside, you'll notice the campanile of the **Dominican Church**, a light, high building with (if it's open) another tomb sculpted by Nikola Firentinac; this one records a woman's lament for her son and husband who died violent deaths in 1469. A lapidarium shelters a rich collection of stone fragments around a delightfully luxuriant courtyard. Farther along, the unremarkable **Kamerlengo Fortress** (no entry) was named after the Venetian official—the "kamerling"—who ran the town's finances. Beyond is the town's soccer field, and, at the far end of the island, Marmont's **Gloriette**. This small stone belvedere was where Marshal Marmont, the French governor here during the early nineteenth century, played cards until Napoleon's harsh Dalmatian policies forced him to resign. Just and progressive, Marmont was probably the best colonial ruler the city ever had and the Gloriette serves as some sort of modest tribute.

Čiovo, and Mali and Veli Drvenik

The coastline around Trogir is bleak, the water polluted by the proximity of Split, and air desecrated by planes landing and taking off at the city's nearby airport. Connected by bridge to Trogir, the island of **ČIOVO** used to be known as "Bua" or "Boa" ("place of the snakes") in the mistaken and rather colorful belief that it was the home of oxen-eating snakes. Today, the most interesting part of this flat and rather drab island is the small town of Čiovo itself, whose ancient twisting streets are home to a shipyard that is the industrial pride of the region. There's nothing else—dreary modern villas line the road both to Slatine in the east and Donje Okrug in the west—though the area near the *Rožac* campground in **DONJI OKRUG**, about twenty minutes' walk from the bridge, is pleasant enough and has a tiny, rocky beach. **SLATINE**, for its part, has a dirty beach that's uncomfortably close to Split. Buses to all places on the island are at best occasional.

Ferries leave Trogir for the two small islands of **Mali** and **Veli Drvenik** every afternoon except Sunday. There's no return service on the same day, so it's prudent to arrange accommodation before you go, though your options are limited—there's nowhere to stay on Mali Drvenik and only a handful of private **rooms** on Veli. Reserve either at the Trogir tourist office or directly (☎058/73-412). That said, neither island has much going for it and only the larger of the two, Veli Drvenik, has any significant settlement.

The Riviera of the Seven Castles

The coastline south of Trogir, swinging around towards Split in a wide curving bay sheltered from the open sea by Čiovo and Split's jutting peninsula doesn't really improve. During the sixteenth century, local nobles lined this broad fertile sweep of coast with fortifications against the Turks—fourteen fortified houses in all, of which seven remain in varying degrees of repair. However, rapid industrial development in the years since has robbed much of the area of its charm, and its latter-day label, the **Riviera of the Seven Castles**, is a flattering one on the whole: the houses aren't really "castles," and the term "riviera" glosses over the residential and industrial sprawl that characterizes much of the area.

The Seven Castles do, however, make the nearest and most accessible places to swim if you're staying in Trogir or Split—bus #37 links them all—and some are better than others. The best thing to do is to follow the shoreline walkway for about about 6km from **KAŠTEL ŠTAFILIĆ**, through **KAŠTEL STARI** and **KAŠTEL NOVI** to **KAŠTEL LUKŠIĆ**, until you spot somewhere you like. Kaštel Novi is perhaps most typical of all four villages—an agreeable if unremarkable little place of ancient houses with a "castle" that's a simple, fortified tower, and not much beach to speak of—though its **tourist office** (daily 7am–noon & 5–7pm) is the place to reserve **rooms** in the unlikely event that you should want to stay. Stari, a short walk away, is better, with a reasonable stony beach—though the water is slightly filmy; Kaštel Lukšić has a mundane rectangular "castle" next to the gaudy eighteenth-century Church of St Mary. Beyond here, **KAŠTEL GOMILICA** has the most impressive of the fortresses, sited on a small islet joined to the mainland by a bridge, but it's the most easterly of the castles bar one, and by the time you get here you're within alarming proximity of Split's industrial installations.

SOUTHERN DALMATIA

The southern reaches of Dalmatia are more dramatic than the north, with lusher, more subtropical vegetation and a terrain that grows increasingly mountainous as you head south, especially around Makarska, where the grizzled peaks of the Biokovo range tower above the small coastal towns and villages. **Split** is the obvious place to head for: it's the major center for the Adriatic coast, and one of Yugoslavia's most vigorous cities; and it gives access to the bulk of the **islands** of southern Dalmatia, a number of which are among the Adriatic's most beautiful. **Brač** and **Šolta** are the nearest, and easily seen on day trips, though the former certainly deserves longer; farther afield, **Vis** and **Lastovo** have recently been opened up to foreign tourists; and **Hvar** and **Korčula** have long been prime—and justified—vacation haunts. You can hop between the islands, rejoining the mainland from Korčula by a short ferry-ride to the **Pelješac peninsula**—an island itself really, joined to the coast proper by a slim neck of land at **Ston**. Failing that, the coast south of Split is easily reached by bus and has a number of tiny villages, most with small beaches, centering on **Markarska**, the largest and probably most enticing center on this stretch. From Ston it's more or less a clear run to **Dubrovnik**, the much-eulogized, ancient walled city, which is a springboard for a handful of smaller islands but is really visited for itself. You won't be alone in doing this, but, out of season at least, it's still unmissable.

Split

By far the largest city in Dalmatia, and its major transit point, **SPLIT** is hard to avoid. Luckily it's also one of the most enticing spots on the coast, with a bustling lack of restraint reminiscent of Naples, a hectic city full of shouting stall-owners, travelers on the move and white-suited sailors, who give it a

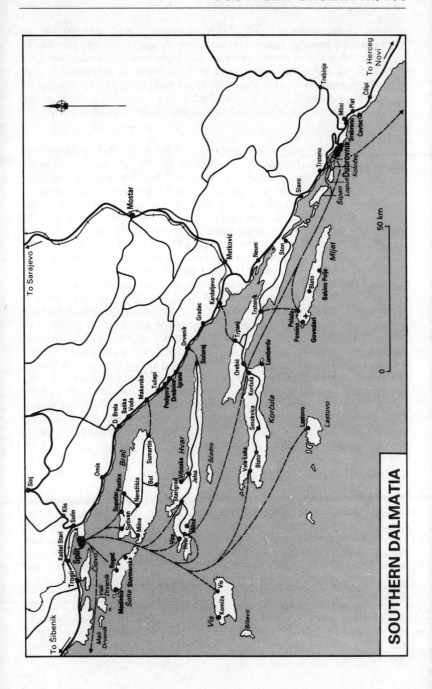

SOUTHERN DALMATIA

vigorous night-on-the-town feel. With a population of well over 200,000, it's also reputedly growing faster than any other Yugoslav city, and its chaotic, often squalid suburbs, where factories and high-rises jangle together from out of an undergrowth of discarded building material, are not the most appealing introduction to the place. But at the heart of all this, hemmed in by the sprawling projects and a modern harbor, lies a crumbling old town and Diocletian's Palace, one of the most outstanding classical remains in Europe.

Some History

It was, in fact, the palace that gave birth to the town. Before the Roman Emperor Diocletian decided to retire here in AD 305 Split didn't exist at all, and the nearest Roman settlement, Salona or *Aspalathos*, was a few kilometers inland. After Diocletian's death in 313, a succession of Roman despots, pretenders and power-seekers used Split as a base, squabbling over the declining fortunes of a divided empire. These were bloody times, and the palace was buffeted into disrepair until—after the fall of Rome—it fell into disuse altogether. In 614 Split was repopulated by refugees from nearby Salona who fled here to escape the Slav invasion, molding themselves a home in what must have been one of the most grandiose squats of all time. They built fortifications, walled in arches, boarded up windows and repelled constant attacks from their enemies. In 1105, the free city was forced to acknowledge the suzerainty of Hungary, a state of affairs which lasted for the next three centuries and during which time the city took on much of its present form. The fifteenth century saw Spalato, as it became known, fall under the rule of Venice, giving way to a period of comparative peace and prosperity until Austria took over in 1797. During all this time, people lived in the palace, propping up the place in return for shelter in a clever and long-lasting symbiosis. After World War II the authorities planned to restore the palace to its former grandeur but had to abandon the idea when they discovered that without the houses, the walls would collapse. Nowadays Split is a port of some size and importance, since the war growing into a boom-town swelled by migrants from all over the country.

Arrival, Information, and Getting Around

Split's **airport** is some 16km west of town towards Trogir. The cheapest way of reaching Split from here is to walk down to the road in front of the airport building and catch bus #37 on its way from Trogir to Split (every 20min, 6am–9pm). It terminates at the bus station on Žrtava Fašizma, ten minutes' walk north of the old center. *JAT* buses also run into town and don't cost a lot more, dropping you right on the waterfront at the airline terminal, but they only connect with scheduled flights. If it's late or you're feeling flush, a taxi into the center of Split will set you back about $25.

Arriving by any other means is more straightforward. The main **bus and railroad stations** are next door to each other on Obala Bratstva i Jedinstva, five minutes' walk from the center, just around the harbor; the **ferry terminal**, for both domestic and international ferries, is a few hundred meters south of here.

For information, the city's **tourist office** is centrally placed at Titova Obala 12 (Mon–Sat 7am–8pm, Sun 8am–1pm; ☎42-142). They have maps of the city, assorted handouts and can reserve private rooms and other accommodation.

As for **getting around the city**, most of the time it's best to walk—indeed that's the only way to see the pedestrianized old center. For journeys out to the Marjan peninsula, and some of Split's museums, you may, however, need to take a bus. The city's buses are frequent, if crowded, and operate between 5am and midnight. Tickets, valid for 45 minutes, can be bought from the driver, or in booklet form in advance (which works out cheaper) from the kiosk at the bottom end of Hrvojeva or others around the city; they should be punched when you board. Most city buses leave from the Trg Republike end of Titova Obala, others from the Hrvojeva end, or from Ive Lole Ribara, just east of here.

> The Split regional area code is ☎058

Finding a Place to Stay

Finding a **place to sleep** in Split isn't usually a problem, even in high season, if you're looking for a private room; hotel beds, on the other hand, are limited, and you should reserve ahead in July and August.

Private Rooms
Arriving at either bus or train station or by ferry, you'll almost certainly be offered a black-market **private room**. There's no reason why you shouldn't accept one of these, but be sure to get the location clear beforehand, if necessary with reference to the map in this book—Split's size means some rooms can be miles from the center. The price, too, should be absolutely clear, and you should be prepared to bargain; reckon on paying the equivalent of about $15 for a double room in or near the center. Private rooms are also available at the tourist office on Titova Obala (see above for full address and opening times), though you'll pay a little more here; *Dalmacijaturist*, a little way along at Titova Obala 5 (daily 7am–8pm; ☎44-666), also has a limited stock of private rooms.

Hotels
You can reserve **hotels** in advance through either the tourist office or *Dalmacijaturist*. At the cheaper end of things, there are only two C- and D-category hotels: the *Slavija*, Buvinova 3 (☎47-053), and the splendidly dilapidated *Central*, Narodni Trg 1 (☎48-242)—though even these cost as much as $50 a night for a double room. Still, they're both smack in the middle of old Split and all its atmosphere. Moving up a price bracket, the B category *Bellevue* is on the edge of the old town at Ante Jonića 106 (☎585-655), and has doubles starting at $65; the *Park*, at the end of Šetalište 1 Maja (☎515-411), is a short walk from downtown near the Bačvice beach and has doubles for $65.

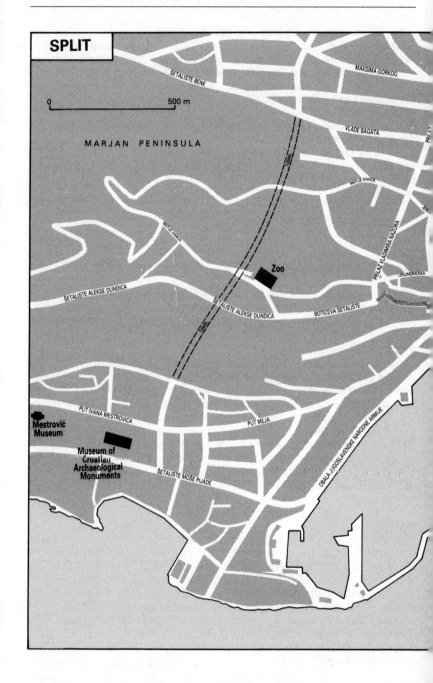

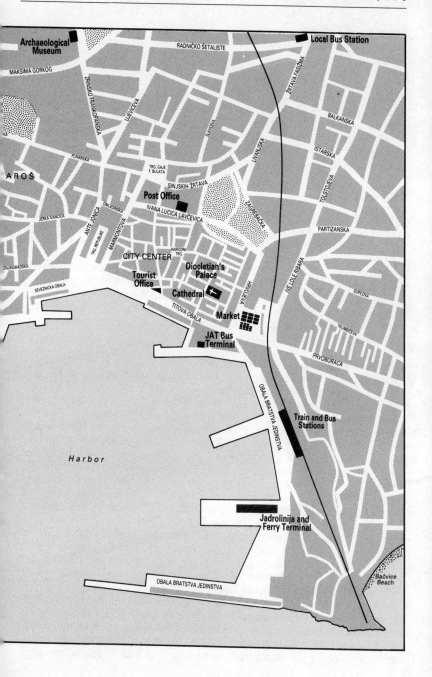

Archaeological Museum

MAKSIMA GORKOG

RADNIČKO ŠETALIŠTE

Local Bus Station

ŽRTAVA FAŠIZMA

BALKANSKA

ŽRINSKO FRANKOPANSKA

UJEVIĆEVA

ISTARSKA

PLINARSKA

TOLSTOJEVA

SLAVKETA

LIVANJSKA

ZAGREBAČKA

TRG. GAJE F. BULATA

SINJSKIH ŽRTAVA

Post Office

PARTIZANSKA

JERKA IVANCICA

IVANA LUCICA LAVČEVICA

ANTE JONICA

ŠUPILOVA

ENJINGRADSKA

TRG. REPUBLIKE

MARMONTOVA

OMLADINSKA

NARODNI TRG.

CITY CENTER

Diocletian's Palace

HRVOJEVA

IVE LOLE RIBARA

SEVEZNICKA OBALA

Tourist Office

Cathedral ✝

TRUMBIĆEVA

Market

TITOVA OBALA

JAT Bus Terminal

PRVOBORACA

Harbor

OBALA BRATSTVA JEDINSTVA

Train and Bus Stations

Jadrolinija and Ferry Terminal

Bačvice Beach

OBALA BRATSTVA JEDINSTVA

AROS

Hostels and Camping

Short of camping, the cheapest option for a bed for the night is to stay at the **Studentski Dom**, open from mid-July until late August. To get there, take bus #17 from Ive Lole Ribara heading west and get off at Spinutska on Marjan—or as near to it as the bus (variable routes) goes. The Dom is down a well-camouflaged right-turn off Bakotićeva, just past the gas station. The nearest **campground**—*Autocamp Trstenik*—is a couple of miles east of the city, adjoining the *Hotel Split*; catch bus #17 east from Ive Lole Ribara and get off at the terminal. Finally, if you're stone-broke, you could slip up to the Marjan Park—though expressly forbidden, it's possible to get your head down if you bury yourself deeply enough in the woods.

The City

Split may be the largest town in Dalmatia, but nearly everything worth seeing is concentrated in the compact **old center** behind the waterfront, made up in part of the remains and conversions of Diocletian's Palace itself, and the medieval addition to the west of it. You can walk across this area in about ten minutes. Outside this central core, Split's peninsula culminates to the west in the **Marjan Park**, almost as large an area as the city itself, its heights giving fine views over the immediate area and beyond and the streets below holding some of the city's prestige museums. You'll have little need to leave the city center in the opposite direction, except perhaps for accommodation or to visit Split's archaeological museum.

Diocletian's Palace: Some Background

Diocletian was born in Salona, the capital of Roman Dalmatia, in AD 245. Though the son of slaves, he proved himself quickly in the Roman military, becoming emperor by the age of forty, in 284. For 21 years he attempted to provide stability, order, and direction to an empire under pressure—goals he achieved with some measure of success, even organizing the last Triumph imperial Rome was ever to see. But Rome was a state in irrevocable decline, and Diocletian remains something of a historical enigma. In the belief that the job of running the empire was too large for one man, he divided the role into four, the **Tetrarchy**, carefully parceling up responsibility among his partners—a decision believed by some historians to be a big mistake, since it led to civil war and confusion. Others claim it enabled the Roman, and resultant Byzantine, empires to endure for another 1000 years. Diocletian was also controversial in his decision to abandon the mock modesty of republican tradition and assume the elaborate court rituals traditionally associated with Eastern despots. Before seeing the emperor, subjects were requested to fall on the ground in submission. And he was one of the emperors most renowned for his persecution of Christians.

Diocletian's Palace was begun in AD 295 and finished ten years later, when the emperor came back to his native Illyria to escape the cares of the empire, cure his rheumatism, and grow cabbages. But this was no simple retirement, and the palace no humble retirement home. Diocletian maintained an elaborate court here, in a building that mixed luxurious palatial apartments with

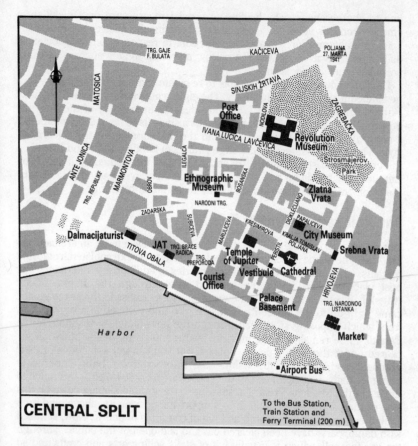

CENTRAL SPLIT

To the Bus Station,
Train Station and
Ferry Terminal (200 m)

the infrastructure of a Roman garrison, with a *decumanus* running east to west across the center, and a *cardo* meeting it at right angles from the north. The building as a whole measured around 200m by 240m, with walls seven feet thick and seventy feet high. At each corner there was a fortified keep and along each of the land walls four towers. Inside, the area north of the *decumanus* was occupied by servants and the garrison; to the south lay the imperial suites and public buildings.

The motives for Diocletian's early **retirement** have also been the subject of much speculation. The simplest reason seems to be the most accurate—he was tired of it all. What he didn't foresee was that his own creation, the Tetrarchy, would come to haunt him. The Tetrarchy had been welded together by interfamily marriage, with Diocletian's daughter, Valeria, staying in Rome after her father's retirement as the wife of one of his partners. Too rich and well-connected to ignore, Valeria became an important figure among the squabbling Tetrarchs: her husband soon died and she was passed from one to another helplessly, leading to consistent pressure on Diocletian to emerge from his voluntary exile. She was continually mistreated, eventually being brutally murdered along with her son. In response to this, Diocletian, daily more involved in the Tetrarchy power struggle, appears to have poisoned himself in despair.

Diocletian may not have been able to re-create a strong, united empire, but he did bequeath a surprising legacy. The eighteenth-century English architect **Robert Adam** came here in 1757 and—despite the hostility of the Venetian governor, who almost had him arrested as a spy—used the palace to produce a set of drawings that were seminal in the development of the "Georgian" style. The Adam brothers rebuilt large chunks of London, Bath, and Bristol on the principles of space, symmetry and grace they had picked up here. If you can, get your hands on a copy of Adam's book—it gives a good idea of what the whole thing must have looked like in the eighteenth century.

The Palace and Central Split

Despite its importance, don't expect Diocletian's Palace to be an archaeological "site"; the shape and style of the palace have to be extrapolated from what remains, which itself is obscured by centuries of addition and alteration. The best place to start is on the seaward side, through the **Bronze Gate** (Mjedena Vrata), a functional gateway which gave access to the sea that once came right up to the palace itself. Inside, you find yourself in a vaulted hall, from which imposing steps lead through the now-domeless vestibule to the Peristil. Little remains of the imperial apartments to the left—they've disappeared under the contemporary houses. But you can get some idea of their grandeur and floor-plan by visiting the **subterranean halls** underneath (summer daily 8am–8pm; rest of the year 8am–noon & 4–7pm)—entrance to the left of the Mjedena Vrata. These—due to the ground sloping down on this side of the palace—were built in to support the apartments above, and until 1956 they remained unexplored and full of centuries of debris. Now, suffused with damp, parts have been cleared out and laid open to the public. Through the vaulted hall, which is usually full of stalls selling arts and crafts and so forth, and up the steps, the **Peristil** was once the central courtyard of the palace complex, opening out from the point where the *cardo* and *decumanus* meet. These days it serves as the main town square, crowded with café tables and surrounded by (considerable) remnants of the stately arches that framed the square. At the southern end, steps lead up to the **vestibule**, a round, formerly domed building that is the only part of the imperial apartment area of the palace that's anything like complete. It was here that subjects would wait in apprehension before being admitted to Diocletian himself.

On the east side of the Peristil stands one of two black granite Egyptian sphinxes, dating from around 15 BC, that originally flanked the entrance to Diocletian's mausoleum, an octagonal building surrounded by an arcade of Corinthian columns that's since been converted to Split's **Cathedral** (Mon–Sat 7am–noon 9 & 4–7pm). Diocletian's body is known to have rested here for 170 years until one day it disappeared—no one knows why or to where. Since then it's been sanctified, a choir has been added, and it's amassed an extensive

DIOCLETIAN'S PALACE

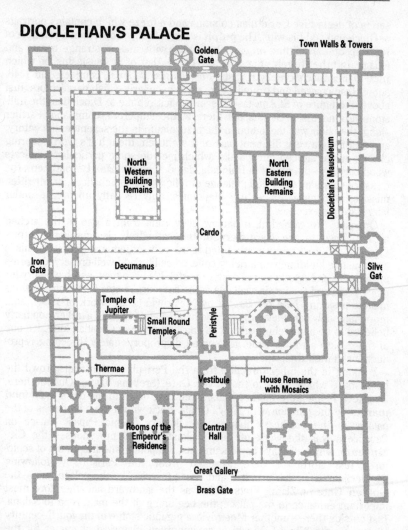

Golden Gate

Town Walls & Towers

North Western Building Remains

North Eastern Building Remains

Diocletian's Mausoleum

Cardo

Iron Gate

Decumanus

Silver Gate

Temple of Jupiter

Small Round Temples

Peristyle

Thermae

Vestibule

House Remains with Mosaics

Rooms of the Emperor's Residence

Central Hall

Great Gallery

Brass Gate

treasury. On the right of the entrance is the **campanile**, a Romanesque structure much restored in the late nineteenth century. The haul up is worth the
effort for the panoramic view over the city and beyond. As for the cathedral
itself, its most immediate feature are the walnut and oak main **doors**, carved
with an inspired "comic strip" showing 28 *Scenes from the Life of Christ*—the
work of local artist Andrija Buvina in 1214. They're scuffed and scraped at the
bottom, but are in fine condition farther up, each of the scenes bordered by a
vine motif that runs all the way up, pawed at by dogs and other creatures.
Inside the cathedral is an odd hodgepodge of styles, the dome ringed by two

series of decorative Corinthian columns and a frieze which contains portraits of Diocletian and his wife. The **pulpit** is a beautifully proportioned example of Romanesque art, sitting on capitals tangled with snakes, strange beasts and foliage. But the church's finest feature is the Altar of St Anastasius, on which Juraj Dalmatinac's cruelly realistic *Flagellation of Christ*, completed in 1448, shows Jesus pawed and brutalized by some peculiarly oafish persecutors. Just above, the figure of St Anastasius is an explicit rebuke to Diocletian: the millstone around his neck was put there at the emperor's command. Farther along, the choir was tacked on to the mausoleum in the seventeenth century, and still feels a very different part of the church, though it's worth peering closely at the latticed choir stalls, which include some particularly delicate wood carving—the oldest in Dalmatia, dated at about 1200. Beyond here, the treasury sports a rather dull melange of reliquaries and chalices, handwritten missals, and thirteenth-century Madonnas, only recently uncovered under later Baroque excesses.

Opposite the cathedral, a narrow alley runs from a gap in the arched arcade down to the **Baptistery** of the cathedral, also originally a pre-Christian edifice, variously attributed to the cults of Janus and Jupiter. This is an attractive building with a richly coffered ceiling and well-preserved figures of Hercules and Apollo on the eastern portal. It's been used as a baptistery for many years and the key is available at the cathedral. Later Christian additions include a skinny *John the Baptist* by Meštrović (a late work of 1954), and, more famously, an eleventh-century baptismal font with a relief popularly believed to be a groveling subject paying homage to a Croatian king. It's one of those pieces whose fame has spread disproportionately, breeding reproductions in their thousands.

Walking in the other direction from the Peristil, market stalls crowd the open space which leads to the **Silver Gate** (Srebrna Vrata). Outside here, **Hrvojeva** holds more market stalls, stretching down to the city's main **food market** by the junction with Titova Obala. Back within the boundaries of the palace, in the northeast quarter, the flowery Gothic Papalić Palace on Papalićeva was the work of Juraj Dalmatinac and now houses the **City Museum**, which displays city documents, weaponry, and fragments of sculpture. Just north of here, reached from the Peristil by following Dioklecijanova, is the grandest and best preserved of the palace gates, the **Golden Gate** or Zlatna Vrata. This was the landward and therefore most important entrance to the palace, the beginning of the main road to Salona. Just outside there's another Mestrović, a gigantic statue of the fourth-century Bishop **Grgur Ninski**. Ninski is an important historical character for the Croats since he fought Rome for the right of his people to use their own language in the liturgy. Incredibly, this mammoth used to stand in the Peristil before it was moved during the Italian occupation. Opposite, the **Museum of the Revolution** (Tues–Sun 9am–1pm) occupies the old city hospital, though it's no great improvement on revolution museums anywhere else in the country.

The east–west axis of the Palace, the ancient decumanus, now Krešimirova, takes you out through the west gate into **Narodni Trg** and the beginning of the later, medieval part of the town center—an irregular web of fascinating, tightly drawn streets and passages that stretches west as far as Marmontova and north to I. L. Lavčevića. On the square itself, which competes with the Peristil for the city's early-evening drinkers, there's an **Ethnographic Museum** (Mon–Sat 9am–1pm & 6–8pm), sited in the old Gothic town hall, with a shabby collection of Dalmatian costumes, more weaponry, and some miscellaneous folk art. Wander down toward Trg Preporodna, where there are a couple of bars and from where you can cut through a fifteenth-century Venetian gateway to emerge onto the waterfront. Amble along to **Trg Republike**, a rather ill-fitting, classically-inspired square, set back from the water beyond Marmontova and one of the city's principal legacies of the Austrians.

North of the Center: the Archaeological Museum

There's not much outside Split's tight old quarter worth making the trip for. The exception is the **Archaeological Museum** at Zrinjsko Frankopanska 25 (Tues–Sat 9am–1pm & 5–8pm, Sun 10am–noon), fifteen minutes' walk from Diocletian's Palace, just north of the Frankopanska/Lovretska road junction. Founded by government decree as early as 1820, the collection is divided into two halves. Inside there are comprehensive, if poorly labeled, displays of Illyrian, Greek, medieval, and particularly Roman artifacts that conjure up some sort of picture of life for your average Salonan noble. Exhibits include delicate votive figurines, amulets, and jewelry embellished with tiny peep-shows of lewd lovemaking. Outside, and rather more interesting, the arcaded courtyard is crammed with a wonderful array of Greek, Roman and early Christian stelae, sarcophagi and decorative sculpture. An excellent guide-book is available, but there are three key exhibits. Two of these, to the left of the entrance, are Salonan sarcophagi, from the third century AD: one represents the tale of deception and unrequited love of the Hippolytus-and-Phaedra legend and is in superb condition—the marble still glistens—while the other is of a Calydonian boar hunt, which in Robert Adam's pictures stood outside Split's baptistery. The third, another sarcophagus, is much later, dating from the fourth century. Latterly labeled *The Good Shepherd*, it has attracted perhaps more than its fair share of academic curiosity because the archetypal Christian motif of the Shepherd is mixed with pagan symbols of Eros and Hades on the end panels.

The Marjan Peninsula: Walks, Beaches, and Museums

Crisscrossed by footpaths and minor roads, the woods of the **Marjan peninsula** are the best place to head for if you're intent on exchanging central Split's turmoil for some peace and quiet. On foot, the peninsula is accessible from Titova Obala via Šperun and then Lenjingradska, which cuts up through the slopes of the **Varoš** district; or you can take bus #12 from the bottom of Trg Republike (every 30min). In summer some of the buses go right around Marjan, but otherwise they stop at its western tip.

Most of Marjan's visitors stick to the road around the edge of the promontory with its infrequent, tiny, rocky **beaches**; the Bene beach, on the far northern side, is especially popular. From the road tracks lead up into the heart of the Marjan Park, which is thickly wooded with pines, rising to its peak at 175m. Just below here there's a small **zoo** and **natural history museum**, though the main historical attractions of Marjan are on the lower, southern edge, along Šetalište Moše Pijade. First of these is the **Museum of Croatian Archaeological Monuments** (Tues–Sat 9am–1pm & 6–8pm, Sun 10am–noon), twenty minutes walk west of the center of town, or reachable directly on a #7 or #12 bus. Housed in a gleaming new ad hoc edifice, with huge open-plan halls and piped-in organ music, this is in a way an ideological museum, an assertion of Croatian culture. The Croats arrived in Dalmatia in the seventh century and enjoyed varying degrees of independence for five hundred years. The succession of conquerors that have swept over Dalmatia since then have obscured this indigenous history and the museum is part of a conscious effort to reclaim this past. Displays include a motley collection of jewelry, weapons, and fragmentary reconstructions of chancel screens and ciboria from ninth- and tenth-century Croat churches, with, as prize exhibit, a ninth-century baptismal font from Nin.

A couple of minutes' walk away, the **Meštrović Gallery**, Šetalište Moše Pijade 39 (daily 9am–6pm), is another Croatian shrine, housed in the ostentatious Neoclassical building that Yugoslavia's most famous and revered modern artist planned as his home, and lived in for just two years. Ivan Meštrović (1883–1962) came from the small Croatian village of Otavice, near Drniš, and spearheaded the Croatian artistic movement of the early twentieth century. Bestknown for boldly fashioned bodies curled into elegant poses and greatly influenced by archaic Greek art, his prowess as a sculptor and grasp of the human form are indisputable. He produced monumental figures, usually to illustrate universal themes, and often on a vast scale (one sculpture exhibited in New York weighed five tons). Above all, Meštrović was the first real *Yugoslav* artist: before the first war he campaigned for a unified southern Slav nation, both through his art and in the political arena. Afterwards, however, the reality of the Yugoslav kingdom made him turn to more specifically Croatian—and later religious—themes, eventually leaving Yugoslavia after World War II to live in America.

Even if you're not mad about Meštrović (and his work can at times appear facile), this is still an impressive collection, and very representative of the artist's output, with a full range, from the relatively early, almost fascistic heads of *Soldiers* and *Heroes*, done in 1908, to the slightly daft *Happy Youth*, from 1946. On the whole, his most successful work is that inspired less by important themes than by people he met and knew. The giant *Adam and Eve*, for example, is ungainly and ridiculous, but the portraits of members of his immediate family are refreshingly direct, especially the honest and sensitive bust of his *Mother*.

Food, Drink, and Nightlife

There are places to **eat** all over town and few are excessively pricey. To **start the day**, you might try the *burek*s at the *Burek Restaurant*, Ilegelaca 13 (open 7am–10pm), whose opening hours make it a budget option for lunch or dinner too. For **fast food** you could try *Buffet Ero* on Marmontova or any one of the several snack bars around about. If you want to sit down, the cheap place to head for is the *Bastion* self-service restaurant 0n Marmontova 9—though it's not the most ambient environment in town. The best place for pizza is said to be the *Pivnica Pizzeria* in the *Koteks* shopping center on Veselina Masleše, east of the city center, though pizzas are as plentiful—and as reasonably priced—as they are everywhere on the coast. **Picnic lunches** are best made up from the delicatessens around Narodni Trg or the market and adjacent shops at the southern end of Hrvojeva.

Otherwise, for a regular **sit-down meal**, the restaurants along the seafront are not at all expensive, and make much the nicest place to eat if the weather's good: the *Adriana*, Titova Obala 7, has good fish. Away from the water, the *Hotel Central* restaurant has an excellent range of cheap day- and early-evening specials. Slightly pricier are the restaurants on Trg Republike. The *Bellevue* restaurant is okay, though overpriced, and it has appalling live cabaret music most nights in summer. Two decent fish restaurants just outside the old center are *Kod Joze*, at Sredmanuška 4, the other side of the park from the Zlatna Vrata, and *Artina*, in the Varoš district at Radmilović'eva 2.

Bars and Nightlife

Nightlife—as ever—revolves around the *korso*, a histrionic affair that packs the blocked-off waterfront to the gills and spills up over Narodni Trg and the Peristil every evening. The atmosphere is exhilarating—friendly and animated. The *Luxor* bar on the Peristil is one of the better **bars** to sit and watch, though later on it becomes a much emptier dive of dubious repute. *Bobis* on Titova Obala itself is good too. Trendier is *Semafor*, opposite the main post office on I.L. Lavčevića, while the art crowd frequents the *Kazališna Kavana*. For late-night drinking and dancing, there's a **disco** by the Bačvice beach, at the end of Šetalište 1 Maja.

The liveliest time to be in Split is during the annual **summer festival**, held between the beginning of July and August 15, when there are outdoor performances of music, drama, and opera all over town. *Dalmacijaturist* can provide details and dates.

Listings

Airlines *Adria*, Obala Lazareta 3 (☎48-753); *JAT*, Titova Obala 9 (☎45-666).

Atlas Preperoda 7 (☎43-055).

Beaches The main city beach is Bačvice, a few minutes' walk south past the railroad station, though despite its convenience this can be grim—small, crowded, and a little too close to Split's polluted harbor for comfort. If you have to go at all, go early and on weekdays to avoid the crowds. Farther on in the same direction, there's a marginally better beach attached to *Split Hotel* and *Trstenik* campground about one mile east of the old town; take bus #17 from Ive Lole Ribara and get off at the terminal. Somewhat better, though still crowded, are the beaches that dent the far edges of the Marjan peninsula—Bene on the northern side, Kašuni on the southern side—though inevitably these involve more walking. Failing that, take a bus out to the Seven Castles (see above) or south to anywhere as far as Omiš.

Books You'll find an eclectic selection of secondhand English books at the *Antikvarijat* bookshop on Ban Mladenova, near Trg Republike. New novels at *Knjižare*, Titova Obala 19a.

Buses Buses to Salona—#1—leave from the Trg Republike end of Titova Obala, along with many city buses. Buses to Omiš leave from the east end of Titova Obala at Hrvojeva. For all points until Trogir go to the station on Žrtava Fašizma, ten minutes' walk north from the palace. For all other destinations use the main bus station on Obala Bratstva i Jedinstva.

Car rental *Kompas/Hertz* and *Inter-rent*, Obala JNA 1 (☎585-840).

Ferry tickets The *Jadrolinija* office (☎43-366) is at the ferry terminal. For the main coastal ferry, advance reservation is prudent.

Hospital Spinčičieva 1 (☎94).

Luggage consignment The most reliable one is at the train station (daily 4am–10pm).

Police Titova Obala 5 (☎49-677).

Post office The main post office is at I.L. Lavčevića 9 (Mon–Fri 7am–9pm, Sat 7am–2pm), which is where you should go to make international phone-calls. There's another post office (same times and services) on Obala Bratstvaa i Jedinstva, just before the bus station.

Sports The excellent *Hajduk Split* soccer team plays in their stadium, the so-called "Poljudska Lepotica," the most modern in Yugoslavia, on the north side of town every other Sunday, Sept–April. Hajduk are currently banished from European soccer for incidents involving their fans (Yugoslavia's worst-behaved) a couple of years back, so this may be the only chance you get to see them. Buses #15 and #17 go to the ground. Consider also a trip to see *Yugoplastika*, Split's basketball team, who won the national championship in 1989. Their stadium is behind the *Koteks* shopping center, not far from the old town.

Trains For information and tickets go to the main railroad station Obala Bratstva i Jedinstva or call ☎48-588, though you might find the lines shorter at *Dalmacijaturist*, on Titova Obala.

ONWARDS FROM SPLIT

Well connected by bus, train, and boat with just about any Yugoslav destination you care to mention, Split is an excellent base to see this part of the country. Apart from the more obvious services into the interior, Split is the Dalmatian coast's main boat terminal with regular **local ferries** to the islands of Brač, Šolta, Vis, Lastovo, Hvar, and Korčula, as well as being a major stop on the summer **coastal car ferry** service, which connects Split with Rijeka, Rab, Zadar, Dubrovnik and Bar. International ferry connections include Pescara and Ancona in Italy, and Igoumenitsa, Corfu, and Patras in Greece. See "Travel Details" at the end of this chapter for more detailed listings.

Inland from Split: Salona, Klis, and Sinj

Birthplace of Diocletian and capital of Roman Dalmatia, the ancient Roman town of **SALONA** gave birth to Split. As administrative and economic center for the region, the town once spread across the northern slopes of the bay of Solin; its population was around 70,000. In the fourth century it became a center of Christianity, but in 614 it was comprehensively sacked by a combined force of Slavs and Avars, and has lain deserted ever since.

The remains of the city are some 6km northeast of Split, easily reached by car but a little tricky by bus. Take bus #1 from Titova Obala/Trg Republike, through the scrawny village of Solin towards Klis. On the far side of Solin the bus starts to climb and veers to the left at a junction; get off here, where a small yellow sign indicates the site. Walk for a little way until you see the entrance on your left, signaled by the *Salona* snack bar.

Though extensively excavated at the end of the nineteenth century, nearly everything of interest at Salona was removed many years ago, and it's a sparse site, with few features of real interest. It is, however, an evocative and peaceful location, its cypress trees and overgrown stones in neat contrast to the hazy industrial suburbs across the bay. The site itself divides into two parts. Closest to the entrance, Manastirine was an early necropolis for Christian martyrs and is piled high with sarcophagi around a fifth-century basilica. Nearby, an eccentric summer villa, the ex-residence of one Professor Bulic (who spent most of his life digging away here) incorporates various other Roman fragments. Below this, you can take the route of the old city walls as they zigzag across scrubby fields through a confusion of ruined basilicas and necropolises. Follow them as far as the second-century AD amphitheater, a largely demolished structure which originally seated some 18,000 spectators and is probably the most extant remain on the site. From here you can leave Salona and walk back east along the main road past a first-century theater on the left, continuing on to the main road back to Split to pick up the bus.

Klis

In Roman times the villas of the wealthier Salonans extended inland as far as **KLIS**, a key strategic point in the defense of medieval Split. The steep rock pinnacle around which the modern town huddles was first fortified in the fifteenth century to keep the Turks from pushing through to the coast. When the stronghold fell after a long siege in 1537, the Turks were able to exert their influence over much of Dalmatia, but although they enlarged the fort—building three sets of battlements as well as a mosque—it still fell to the Venetians in 1648. Subsequently, the mosque was deprived of its minaret and rededicated as a Christian chapel in 1743. The occasional service is still held here.

The castle is remarkably complete—so much so that it is regularly used as a filmset for medieval dramas. It's a stiff climb up from the bus stop, but there's a dazzling view from the top over the plain to Split and out to the islands, and it seems odd that it hasn't been more exploited as a tourist attraction. It's open each day (10am–12:30pm & 2–5pm); **buses** leave from the main station in Split every hour. If you don't care for the climb, bear in mind that there are also buses which run close to the top.

Sinj . . . and on to Sarajevo

From Klis the road (and the same bus) forges across the stony foothills of the Dinara mountains to **SINJ**, a twenty-kilometer trip that, if you happen to be around in August, is well worth making for the **Alka Sinjska**—an annual event which commemorates a day back in 1715 when the locals destroyed a far larger force of Turks. It's actually a sort of medieval joust, but instead of the knights fighting each other they attempt to thread their lances through a series of divided rings dangled from a rope—all at a terrific gallop. The points they score depend on which ring they manage to pierce. It's a riotous, boozy business, involving all the surrounding villages and taking up the whole day in a blaze of color, costume, and procession that builds up to a crescendo when the contest itself takes place.

If you're in the area, the Alka Sinjska is definitely worth the effort. Otherwise don't bother stopping, there's nothing else to see, though if you're stranded the **tourist office** on the main square, Trg Maršala Tita, can fix **rooms**. The seriously hungry will find solace around the corner at *Pizzeria Pivnica*, Narodnik Heroja 23.

From Sinj the road twists and turns its way into the mountains towards LIVNO and on to the turnings for JAJCE or TRAVNIK and **SARAJEVO** (*Bosnia-Hercegovina*). It's a dramatic route, and well worth taking, though not after dark.

The Southern Dalmatian Islands

The coast between Split and Dubrovnik is fringed by Yugoslavia's most concentrated grouping of large islands, from Šolta and Brač, guarding the entrance to the city, out to Vis and Lastovo some way offshore, and Korčula farther south. All are accessible by ferry from Split, and with careful journey-plotting you can hop between most of them, joining the mainland again on the Pelješac peninsula. A couple of these islands—Korčula and Hvar—are also accessible from Dubrovnik. For those islands that are *only* reachable from Dubrovnik, see p.222.

Šolta

Though one of the closest islands to Split, **ŠOLTA** is one of the least developed of Dalmatian islands. It was used by the Romans to dispose of political exiles, and later by the Christian church to banish heretics, and on the face of it seems to have changed very little since either era. A fertile island of red soil, with several large villages and a relatively intact agricultural economy, it's more a place for escape than high-level tourism. Some development is beginning to creep in, notably with the bungalow complex at Nečujam (though this is well away from the main centers of population), which has improved the road system on the island, and connected it to regular water and electricity supplies. The islanders paid dearly for their support of the partisans during World War II—many of them had their crops confiscated and others were either deported or executed.

Two buses meet the ferry at **ROGAČ**, which is little more than a dock and a bar, one heading east towards Maslinica, the other west to Stomorska. Both buses go through **GROHOTE**, the largest settlement on Šolta, perched on a hill overlooking the harbor—a pleasant, peaceful village with private **rooms** (reservable in Split) available. To the west, **MASLINICA** is an attractive fishing village with a couple of restaurants, private **rooms**, and the **pension** *Avlija* (☎058/654-140)—a basic and cheap pension with rooms in its very own Turkish tower.

East of Rogač, the bus passes through the small tourist complex of **NEČUJAM**, a relatively successful development, decked out as a wooded chalet-"hamlet" spreading out from the sandy cove and crystal-clear waters. There's a 24-hour reception, a reasonable restaurant, a regular motor boat service to Split, and all the watersports facilities you'd expect. There's also a plan to expand Nečujam, though for the moment it's the ideal size. If you want to stay here, you only need to pre-reserve during July and August (☎058/585-937). Farther east lies the grim and rather plaintive village of **STOMORSKA**, with a suitably down-at-heel **pension**—the *Olint* (☎058/654-141).

Practical Details

Ferries make the one-hour journey between Split and Rogač around five times daily. Bear in mind, once you're here, that the island bus service is irregular: it only runs to meet the ferry, and you may find yourself doing more walking than you bargained for.

Brač

The third largest island on the Adriatic coast, Brač is another fertile island, though its economy was for centuries underpinned by the export of its famous milk-white marble, which has been used in places as diverse as Berlin's Reichstag, the high altar of Liverpool's Catholic Cathedral, the White House in Washington—and, of course, Diocletian's Palace. In addition to the marble, a great many islanders were once dependent on the grape harvest, though the phylloxera (vine lice) epidemics of the late nineteenth century and early twentieth century forced many of them to emigrate. Even today, as you cross Brač's interior, the signs of this depopulation are all around in the tumbledown walls and overgrown fields.

Brač's first settlers established themselves inland for safety's sake, only moving down to the coast when Venetian control offered a greater degree of security. Nowadays, due to the increase in tourism—Brač has long been a popular day trip and has recently attracted the attention of package tour oper-

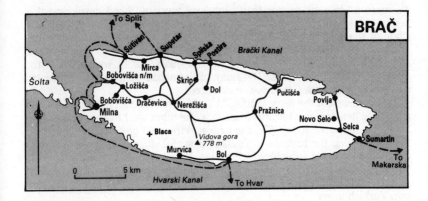

ators—it's the coast of the island which holds the most life, and, with the exception of the inland villages, all the major settlements have come to rely on tourism. At its worst, in Supetar and Sutivan for example, the smaller towns and villages can be simply overwhelmed by the high-season onslaught. But outside these main centers, in Pučišća, Milna, and even the popular Bol, the crush is bearable.

Getting There
The easiest way to reach Brač is by **ferry** from Split to Supetar or Sutivan, a one-hour trip. Ferries leave up to thirteen times daily in summer. You can also take ferries from Makarska to Sumartin, at the east end of the island, but bus connections from here are very poor. There's also a private **boat** service between Jelsa, on Hvar island, and Bol, some six times a week between April and September. Cost is around $5 one-way.

Supetar
Though the largest town on the island, **SUPETAR** is little more than a rather mediocre tourist trap: the old town still clusters around the port, but it's surrounded by an extensive range of hotels, apartments, and chalets and can get crowded in season. There's nothing much here of special interest, but outside July and August at least the stretch of shingle beach is quite pleasant. Just behind here, incidentally, is the Petrinović family **mausoleum**, which pokes a neo-Byzantine ice cream dome above the cypresses a mile or so west of town. The work of an obscure Dalmatian sculptor called Rosandić but Meštrovićian in its monumentality, the mausoleum was built for a rich local family who made their fortune selling British coal to Chile and Chilean nitrates to the Brits. Enterprise indeed.

SUPETAR PRACTICALS
If you decide to stay in Supetar, **rooms** can be arranged at either *Dalmacijaturist* (daily 7am–9pm) or the tourist office (daily 7am–8pm), both in the center of the village by the ferry terminal. They also have detailed

maps of the island. There's a **campground** along the shore some 700m to the east of the quayside. For **food**, there's any number of mediocre restaurants and snack bars around the harbor. For getting out of Supetar, try renting a **bike** from the hotel complex.

West from Supetar: Sutivan and Milna

Fifteen minutes west of Supetar, the village of **SUTIVAN** straggles along the shore behind its rocky beach. Almost everything here is made out of the local marble, and, although there are no special features of interest, it's a pretty enough little place, of narrow alleys and ancient houses only spoiled by the droves of tourists that descend in high season. The **tourist office** near the bus stop (July–Sept 7am–10pm) can arrange accommodation.

The road to the southwest of Sutivan heads inland past the turning for **BOBOVIŠĆA-NA-MORU**, a small village with a marina and rooms, visible way down below at the end of the bay. A couple of miles farther on, buses squeak through **LOŽIŠĆA**, a classically picturesque settlement spread across a steep ravine. There's no tourist office here, but there are a couple of **rooms**, and if you're keen to escape from Brač's more beaten tourist trail, this could be a good place to do it—though you'd be well advised to take your own food. The village of BOBOVIŠĆA lies a kilometer or so to the southwest, beyond which the road crosses the island's empty uplands before twisting down to the sea at Milna.

Used as a Russian naval base during the Napoleonic wars, tiny **MILNA** is a neat and unremarkable port that curves around one of the island's many deep bays. The old village drifts up the hill from the shore, a pleasant enough combination of narrow lanes and stone houses on either side of an eighteenth-century parish church and an adjacent ruined mansion that's curiously known as *Anglešćina* after a fourteenth-century English crusader who once lived there. Otherwise, Milna has a predictable range of restaurants and bars with inflated prices, encouraged by the thriving marina, and an inconvenient, rocky beach a fair walk up along the bay. The **tourist office** (daily June–Sept 8am–9pm) in the main square has plenty of **rooms**, and out of season when this is closed, you can get fixed up at the municipal office around the back of the supermarket near the church (Mon–Fri 6am–2pm). There's also a June-to-August weekly private **boat** service to Split.

East from Supetar: Pučišća

Heading east from Supetar, the bus soon reaches the agricultural center of **POSTIRA** and (usually) continues on up the valley to **DOL**—two villages that together illustrate the movement from the interior to the coast. Dol has a handful of rooms and is pleasant enough but there's nothing much here; Postira is the newer settlement but is of no more appeal. Farther east, at the end of the bus route, the ancient port of **PUČIŠĆA** is built around another of the island's deep natural bays, a pretty little town with a couple of bar/restaurants and a supply of private **rooms** available from the **tourist office** by the bus stop (summer Mon–Sat 8am–1pm & 5–8pm). In the hills behind the town are the island's three main quarries, and the stone is exported from a harbor just along the bay, ensuring that Pučišća is not dependent on tourism, and in fact a good place to escape the crowds. However, there's not much of a beach (rocky strips mainly), and the best buildings are modest affairs—a symmetrical early-nineteenth-century church and the old town hall, pink and Austro-Hungarian.

South from Supetar: Bol, the Mountains, and the Blaca Hermitage

Brač's second town, **BOL** has long been the only significant settlement on the the the island's southern coast, an effectively isolated community stranded on the far side of the Vidova Gora mountains until Napoleon's soldiers built the road across here. In the seventh century, its isolation attracted those Romans who were desperate to escape the Croat invasion; but safety in Dalmatia was never long-lasting, and time and again Bol has been attacked by Turks, pirates, Saracens, and just about anybody else who was passing. Nowadays there's no denying the beauty of Bol's setting, or the charm of its old stone houses. The problem is that it's very small, and is easily swamped by tourists—an influx that grows yearly. But if you can go outside of high season, or are immune to crowds, it's well worth the trip.

The main attraction of Bol is its beach, **Zlatni Rat** (Golden Cape), which lies to the west of the center along the wooded shoreline. This beach is unusual: it's unusually sandy, unusually beautiful and unusually shaped—jutting into the sea in the form of a giant 'Y.' The trouble is that it, too, gets very crowded during summer. When you're through with the beach, look in at the late-fifteenth-century **Dominican Monastery** (daily 5–7pm), perched high on the clifftop just east of Bol's middle. Its location is dramatic, and the monastery museum holds a Tintoretto *Madonna with Child* among its small collection. From here, you can make the steep two- or three-hour hike up to the top peak of the mountains that overlook Bol. There's a fort up here, built by Napoleon's troops, and on a clear days the view is spectacular. Another way to escape Bol's crowds is to make for the hermitage of **Blaca**, tucked away at the head of a valley well to the west of the town. There are two ways of reaching the hermitage: the first and more prosaic route is by following the signposted track off the main road from Supetar to Bol, shortly after Nerežišća; the other, far preferable way is by private boat from Bol—though it's expensive unless you're in a group. It takes about an hour for the boat to travel along the coast to the bottom of the valley, from where there's a track up to the hermitage. Founded in 1588, the last resident was an enthusiastic astronomer who left all sorts of odds and ends, including an assortment of old clocks and a stock of lithographs by Poussin. But the principal attraction is the setting. The hermitage is on the tour guides' itinerary, but the groups don't stay long and the rest of the time you'll have the place pretty much to yourself.

BOL PRACTICALS

Bol's **tourist office** (daily June–Aug 8am–10pm; May & Sept 8am–1pm & 5–8pm; Oct–April 7am–2pm) and **Dalmacijaturist**, both in the center of the village, arrange **accommodation**—though rooms go fast in summer. Alternatively, there are a couple of **campgrounds** and several smart **hotels**. As you'd expect, there's a wide range of **restaurants** and it's easy to rent bikes, boats, cars, windsurfers, etc.

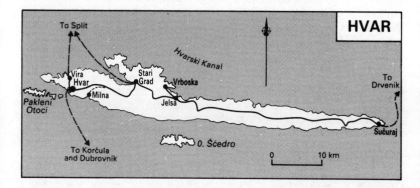

Hvar

HVAR is one of the most hyped of all the Yugoslav islands. People talk of its verdant color, its fragrant air, and mild climate; earlier this century the island's hoteliers even had enough faith in the weather to offer a money-back guarantee if the temperature ever dropped below zero. And Hvar is undeniably beautiful—a slim, green slice of land punctured by jagged inlets and cloaked with hills of spongy lavender. But, unsurprisingly, its main towns have been intensively developed as tourist resorts. Hotels sprawl across the surrounding headlands, loud music pounds from discos and coffee bars, and the July and August air is thick with the guttural tones of English and German. As yet the development hasn't been too crass: no high-rise hotels disfigure the center of Hvar town at least, and the multitude of bistros and bars fit fairly comfortably into the Venetian terraces.

Getting There

Ferries run between Split and Vira, 4km from Hvar town on the mainland side of the island, about three times daily, or to Starigrad, farther east, roughly four times. Vira is no more than a ferry terminal really, and local

HVAR: INLAND TRANSPORTATION

Principal island **bus** connections are as follows.

Hvar town to Starigrad (7 daily, 3 on Sun); Jelsa (13 daily; 6 on Sun); Sućuraj (1 daily; 1 on Sun).

Jelsa to Starigrad (15 daily); 11 on Sun); Hvar town (6 daily; 3 on Sun); Vrboska (2 daily; not on Sun); Sućuraj (2 daily; 2 on Sun).

Sućuraj to Hvar (2 daily; 2 on Sun) via Starigrad and Jelsa.

Starigrad to Jelsa (14 daily; 10 on Sun); Vrboska (4 daily; 2 on Sun); Hvar (6 daily; 3 on Sun); Sućuraj (2 daily; 2 on Sun).

Vrboska to Jelsa (3 daily; 1 on Sun); Starigrad (4 daily; 2 on Sun).

buses meet the boats for onward transportation to Hvar town. Parallel bus services run all the way from Split to Hvar town once daily (July–Aug), and to Starigrad between three and four times daily (all year). The summer coastal ferry (mid-March to mid-Oct) stops at either Starigrad or Hvar town (2–5 times weekly), and connects the island with Split and points to Rijeka in the north, Korčula and Dubrovnik to the south. You can also reach the island by way of ferry from Drvenik to Sućuraj, at the eastern end of the island, five to twelve times daily—though the poor bus connections make this approach only of use if you're traveling by car. Lines build up fast in summer, so arrive early to avoid disappointment. Lastly, throughout the season there's also a private **boat** service from Jelsa to Bol, on Brač, some six days a week.

Hvar Town

Even by Dalmatian standards, Hvar's history seems pretty rough-and-tumble. Originally a Greek colony, the town has been the temporary property of a motley crew of different invaders—Rome, Austria, Hungary, Genoa, Bosnia, and Dubrovnik all had a crack at one time or another—and like much of Dalmatia it only achieved a period of relative peace and stability under the Venetians (primarily 1420–1797). Even this was briefly disturbed, in 1571, when the notorious Algerian corsair Uliz Ali sacked Hvar town on behalf of the Turks and reduced it to a smoldering rubble that had to be rebuilt from scratch. Rebuilt, the town soon reassumed its importance as an entrepot on the East–West trade routes, with the sort of protective harbor favored by sailing ships. Later, the movement of trade to the west and the arrival of steam ships becalmed Hvar town, which drifted into a quiet (but intact) obscurity—until the tourists arrived. Today, the harbor is alive with a constant hum of activity, whether it be the Rijeka ferry lumbering into port, hydrofoils buzzing insect-like around the bay, or tiny water-taxis ferrying people to swim on the Pakleni islands.

INFORMATION AND ROOMS

Hvar town's **information office**, at the bus station (July–Aug daily 7am–10pm; low season Mon–Sat 8am–noon & 6–9pm, Sun 9am–1pm & 5–8pm; closed in winter) can provide all the usual information and advice on **rooms** and supply **maps** of the island. Alternatively, there are a number of tourist agencies five minutes' away along the quayside, all of which have stocks of private rooms. The **tourist office** (summer daily 8am–9pm; otherwise Mon–Sat 7am–noon & 3–8pm, Sun 7–11am & 3–4pm) is a good first place to try. If they have nothing, try either the **private accommodation office** (daily 8am–8pm) or **Dalmacijaturist** (Mon–Sat 8am–2:30pm & 3–9pm, Sun 9am–noon & 6–9pm). Rooms only get tight in July and August. The town **campground** is 300m from the ferry terminal at Vira. When the time comes to leave, Hvar's **Jadrolinija** office is along the quay towards the Franciscan Monastery.

WHAT TO SEE

The best view of **HVAR TOWN** is from the sea, the tiny town center contoured around the bay, grainy-white and brown with green splashes of palms and pines pushed into every crack and cranny. At the center, the creamy-brown triangular main square cuts its way in, flanked by the arcaded bulk of the Venetian arsenal. The upper story of the arsenal was added in 1612 to house the city **theater**, the oldest in Yugoslavia and one of the first in Europe. It's since been comverted to a movie house but the painted Baroque interior has survived pretty much intact (daily 9am–1pm & 8–10pm; winter daily 11am–noon). The piazza culminates in the skeletal campanile of Hvar's **Cathedral** (no fixed opening—try mornings), a sixteenth-century construction with an eighteenth-century facade that's a characteristic mixture of Gothic and Renaissance styles. Inside is routine enough, but the **Bishop's Treasury** (daily 9am–noon & 5–7pm; winter 10am–noon) is worth the entry fee for its small but fine selection of chalices, reliquaries, and embroidery. Look out for a nicely worked sixteenth-century crozier, carved into a serpent, encrusted with saints and embossed with a figure of the Virgin attended by Moses and an Archangel.

The rest of the old town backs away from the piazza in an elegant confusion of twisting lanes and alleys. A little way back from the harbor are the remains of a **Dominican Monastery** (daily 8–10pm), which has a small display of archaeological finds from prehistoric through to Roman times, floodlit to highlight the lines of the walls and scattered sculptures. Up above, the so-called **"Spanish" Fortress** is a good example of sixteenth-century military architecture, though one that has since been rather dubiously converted into a bar/disco/restaurant complex. The views, however, over Hvar and the islands beyond, are well worth the trek to the top.

From the fort you can pick out the fifteenth-century **Franciscan Monastery** (Mon–Fri 9am–noon & 5–7pm), to the left of the harbor, a sliver of white against the blue of the sea. The monastery has a small collection of paintings (mostly obscure Venetian) which includes a tender, dark, and modernistic *Ecce Homo* by Leandro Bassano and a melodramatic, almost life-size *Last Supper* attributed to Matteo Ingoli. Stretched right across the wall, Ingoli's figures seem oddly frozen—a clash between a highly stylized, medieval religious art and the pre-Renaissance realism of some of the body postures. Next door, the monastic **church** is pleasingly simple, with beautifully carved choir stalls and a fanciful partition of 1583; look out for the extravagant dragon candle-holders that push out above the panel detail below.

BEACHES AND BOATS

The **beaches** nearest to Hvar town are rocky, overcrowded and occasionally dirty, and it's best to walk beyond the Franciscan monastery until you find somewhere acceptable. Somewhat better for swimming are the **Pakleni Otoci** ("Islands of Hell"), just to the west of Hvar, easily reached by water-taxi from the harbor (reckon on about $1.50 each way). A chain of eleven wooded islands, only three of them have any facilities (simple bars and restaurants). Jerolim, an FKK island, is the nearest; others are Marinkovac (partly FKK but with a main beach, U Stipanska) and Sv Klement, the largest of the Pakleni, with a limited supply of seasonal **rooms** around the principal Palmižana sandy beach. Water taxis will take you to any of the other islands, but you'll need to take your own food and drink. **Camping** on the Pakleni is forbidden, but easy enough if you're determined. Another alternative is the pretty coastal village of **Milna**, some 7km around the coast from Hvar town and accessible by road (just) and water-taxi, where there's a beach and a few private **rooms** available.

Boats can be rented from several places along Hvar town's waterfront and work out cheaply for groups, though you really do need to know what you're doing to thread your way through the Pakleni.

FOOD AND DRINK

With its dozens of restaurants, **eating** out in Hvar town is not a problem. But it does tend to be expensive, particularly—and predictably—around the main piazza and harbor. For picnic lunches, there's a produce market by the bus station. Also by the bus station is the buffet *Esma*, one of Hvar's more reasonably priced restaurants. *Pizzeria 88*, just behind the arsenal, is a cheap Italian-style bar-restaurant, and there's always the the "tourist menus" provided by several of the hotels—not the most convivial places to eat, but a good bet if you want to hang on to your cash. The *Hotel Slavija*, on the quayside, serves up food as good as any, though on busy nights the service is poor. For something a little different from the usual Yugoslav fare, try the *Creperie Alviž*, opposite the bus station, which has easily the most interesting menu in town.

Starigrad

Some 20km east across the mountains from Hvar town, **STARIGRAD** is Hvar's second fiddle, a popular and busy resort but a much less appealing one, straggling along the side of its deep bay. The old part of Starigrad has been pleasantly renovated, and backs onto the main street as it twists its way along the waterside. The only real sight is the **summer house and garden** of the sixteenth-century poet Petar Hektorović, whose greatest work, *Fishing and Talks with Fishermen*, was the first realistic poem in Croatian literature. Appropriately, the main feature of his house (daily 10am–noon & 5–7pm) is a central cloister with a mullet-packed pond. At the landward end of the main street, the city bus-stop is near to both **Dalmacijaturist** (summer Mon–Sat 8am–10pm, Sun 10am–noon & 6–8pm; otherwise 8am–1pm & 4–8pm) and **Putnik** (similar times), both of whom can arrange private **accommodation**. Starigrad's **campground** is just to the west of what passes for the main square, behind the open-air movie theatre.

Jelsa

The tiny port and fishing village of **JELSA** sits prettily by a wooded bay,
10km east of Starigrad. Tucked away behind a nineteenth-century waterfront,
the old town rises up the hill, a warren of ancient alleys and lanes. Just off the
quayside, the charming, fortified sixteenth-century chapel of **Sv Ivan** is
pushed into one of the old squares, overhung by the balconies of the
surrounding Renaissance buildings. Above this, the town's main **church** is
similarly fortified, and even managed to resist the Turkish attack of 1571,
though it's hard to make out the original design as the facade and bell tower
were added in the nineteenth century.

Such a pretty little place was bound to attract the tour operators, but as yet
Jelsa has not been entirely overwhelmed—and all the new hotels keep a
respectful distance from the center. Jelsa also has a good supply of **private
rooms**, available from the **tourist office** by the bus station (May–Oct daily
8am–10pm; otherwise 8am–noon). For sustenance, there are **restaurants
and bars** all over Jelsa: try the *Konoba Dominko*, a few minutes' walk from
the seafront (signposted).

From the village you can walk along either side of the bay. To the east, on
the headland, the *Hotel Mina* and an adjoining **campground** are close to a
couple of small **beaches**; to the west, the road takes you along the shore,
past the new hotels and onto Vrboska, 4km away. For moving on, bear in
mind that nearly every day throughout the summer a private **boat** service
connects Jelsa with Bol on Brač (about $5 each way).

Vrboska

The sleepy little village of **VRBOSKA** strings along the side of another of the
island's deep bays, about 4km from Jelsa and easily reached by bus or water-
taxi—or just follow the coastal path. The bus stop is on the edge of the old
village, five minutes' walk along the quayside from the **tourist office**, which
has a small cache of **rooms** (daily 8am–1pm & 6–9pm). Vrboska's wooded
campground is behind the tiny boatyard on the other side of the inlet, not too
far from either of Vrboska's two **hotels**. Rock (and concrete) **beaches** line
either side of the bay, a few minutes' walk from the village towards the sea.

The two sides of Vrboska, on either side of the inlet are joined by three
bridges, prompting faintly ludicrous guidebook comparisons to Venice. In
fact, Vrboska's only real claim to fame is the unusual, fortified church of **Sv
Marija** (variable times, try Mon–Sat mornings), which dates from the
fifteenth century and was extensively fortified to resist attacks from pirates
and the Turks. The interior is partly paved with grave slabs and from the
sacristy you can get onto the roof for a closer look at the walls. A couple of
minutes away, the church of **Sv Lovrinac**, also fifteenth-century, has a small
collection of minor art works, including paintings once displayed in Sv
Marija. Best is the polyptych of *St Lawrence* by Paolo Veronese on the high
altar, and a *Madonna of the Rosary* by Leandro Bassano.

Eastern Hvar

South of Jelsa you can drive through the longest road-tunnel in Yugoslavia,
which runs under the mountains to the small, developing resort of **ZAVALA**.

Unfortunately, the tunnel's not wide enough for any of the island's buses, but Zavala does sport some middling beaches and a campground. **East of Jelsa**, Hvar island narrows to a long, thin mountainous strip of land that extends all the way to Sućuraj, linked to the mainland by regular ferries. Poorly served by public transit, all the major villages lie on the main road as it crosses the central plateau, several kilometers from the sea. Anxious to attract some of the tourists, most of them have built some sort of road to the nearest shore—but apart from the scenery and a good degree of isolation, there's nothing special, and without your own car visits are almost impossible. Accommodation is also a problem: few of the inland villages offer rooms and there are hardly any on the coast either. It's possible to find a **room** in **SUĆURAJ** if you're stranded between connections, but otherwise it's a down-at-heel, rather charmless place of precious little interest.

Vis

Situated farther offshore than any other of the Yugoslav Adriatic islands, **VIS** has long enjoyed a unique strategic significance, a fact not lost on a succession of conquering powers. The Greeks, Romans, Byzantines, Slavs, Venetians, Austrians, French, and British have all held Vis at different times, and since the Napoleonic Wars the island has been strongly fortified. Tito made it his base in the summer of 1944 and it was from here that he organized the final stages of the liberation of Yugoslavia. After the war, the island was heavily garrisoned and used for military training; not until the summer of 1989 was it finally opened up to foreigners.

Vis's recent relative lack of accessibility means that the island is, as yet, far from overrun by tourists. What it offers, on the other hand, is wild mountainous scenery, some interesting relics of its history, two good-looking small towns, and a fine local white wine, *Vugava*.

Arrival and Accommodation

Ferries leave Split for the two-and-a-half-hour journey to Vis town once or twice daily all year, though in winter the trip can get mighty rough. An hour or so out to sea, Vis appears on the horizon, looking compact, humpy, and a little forbidding. The **tourist office** (daily 8am–8pm) is just across the road from the dock, and they should have no trouble in arranging private **rooms**, although they'll probably start off by steering you towards the expensive and characterless *Hotel Issa*. Ask at the tourist office for one of their photocopied maps of the island; they're rudimentary but helpful, especially if you intend to do any walking. Unfortunately there's no official campground on Vis, and the island's residual military sensitivity makes rough tent-pitching inadvisable.

Vis Town

VIS TOWN is attractively sited, curved around a deeply indented bay at the foot of a steep escarpment, on the far edge of which are the squat, ruined white sea-forts built by the British when they fortified Vis harbor between 1811 and 1814. The sedate atmosphere of the town is only slightly disturbed by its summer visitors. Walk east along the waterfront—about halfway down is the old church of **Sv Marija od Splica**, which dates from the sixteenth century, crumbling on the outside but worth a look for its collection of paintings. Behind the church is the new **Museum of the National Revolution** (Tues–Sat 8am–1pm & 5–7pm, Sun 10am–noon), which contains an archaeological collection recently assembled from local excavations. It's well organized and emphasises the diversity of cultural influences on the island in classical times. Ask for a copy of the English-language guide. The star exhibit is the bronze head of a Greek goddess, possibly Aphrodite, from the fourth century BC, which is claimed to be by a student of Praxiteles. Downstairs the museum is devoted to the island's role in the struggle for national liberation. Apart from a sizable collection of only mildly interesting military hardware and documentation, there's a large topographical model of the island which shows just how heavily fortified Vis was when it served as Tito's headquarters. For several months in 1944 it was the center of the partisan military machine and nominal seat of the country's political, cultural, and educational organizations, with direct communications to the government-in-exile in London.

Behind Vis town a steep bank is covered with the remains of abandoned agricultural terraces. You can walk up the bank either by road or by a maze of zigzagging donkey tracks: from the top there's a splendid view over the island's central valley—heavily cultivated and the mainstay of the local economy. On the far side rises the peak of **Mount Hum**, at 2000 feet Vis' highest point. Near the summit is the site of **Tito's bunker**, a group of caves which now have the status of a Yugoslav national monument.

FOOD AND BEACHES

Eating is no problem in Vis town. The *Tamaris* restaurant on the seafront serves a conventional but adequate range of food, while the *Lisa Grill* on the left, half a mile down the main street, barbecues fish in the open air right by the waterside. If you've been saving up for an expensive fish-supper you can't do better than the *Restaurant As* in an alley, one block back from the monument by the ferry port. Go early—it fills up fast. Picnickers are handsomely catered for by two well-stocked foodstores.

Vis town's tiny **beach** gets crowded by even a modest influx of visitors. Ask at the tourist office for directions to other quieter coves, though you'll have to be prepared for a stiff walk. The easier option is to go by private **boat**; once again inquire at the tourist office.

Komiža

Three times a day the bus leaves Vis harbor for the 25-minute drive to **KOMIŽA**, the island's main fishing port. It's a pleasant town with the open sea on one side and a ring of mountains on the other. Compact and intimate, the curved harborfront is lined with palm trees and fringed by sixteenth- and seventeenth-century Venetian-style houses with intricate wrought-iron balconies. Dominating the southern end of the harbor is the **Kaštel**, a stubby sixteenth-century fortress, oddly surmounted by a slender corner clock tower. Inside (daily 8am–10pm) is a small collection of works by Djuro Tiljac (1895–1965), a local painter who studied under Kandinsky. At the other end of the harbor, in the tiny market place, is the mid-sixteenth-century **Palača Zanetova**, a stately but dilapidated bulding which was once a ducal mansion. Look out for the carved Virgin and Child high up on the front wall. As for churches, most notable is the sixteenth-century **Gospa Gusarica**, which has an eight-sided well adorned with biblical reliefs set amid trees on the little beach at the northern end of town. Walk out also to the seventeenth-century **Benedictine Monastery**, about a kilometer behind the town in the middle of a large vineyard. There are no regular opening times, but if you can get in around sunset the views from the belfry are spectacular.

KOMIŽA PRACTICALS

Komiža is ripe for development. It's hard to see how its location and charm can fail to be exploited now the island has become accessible to foreign visitors. Hopefully this will be done with sensitivity and imagination. At present there are plenty of private **rooms** available from the **tourist office**, next to the Kaštel (daily 7am–9pm), and no shortage of places to **eat** and drink on the waterfront. The tourist office staff is friendly and helpful and will be able to make suggestions about local **walks**; Tito's bunker is one strenuous option, though minibus trips are available if you want to take it easy. Lastly, the tiny town **beach** soon fills up and if you're after somewhere quieter, you'll be faced with a long walk—unless you can afford to pay for a private boat trip.

Biševo

Each morning small boats leave Komiža harbor for the short crossing to **BIŠEVO**, a tiny islet just to the southwest of Vis. Apart from the wildlife—gulls, lizards, and seals—the attraction here is the **Blue Cavern** (Modra Splija), which can only be reached by sea through a narrow craggy entrance. When the sun is at its height its rays reflect off the seabed and bathe everything in the cavern in an eerie shimmering blueness. The boats that make the journey are well-advertised and the prices are fixed. It's a trip well worth making.

Lastovo

Directly south of the island of Korčula, tiny **LASTOVO** lies at the center of an archipelago of 45 uninhabited islets some five and a half hours from Split. One of the least developed of the Adriatic islands, it is unashamedly short on traditional holiday attractions, but what it lacks in hotels and beaches it more than makes up for in its extraordinary sense of isolation and in its natural, wooded beauty. Aside from anything else, it's a fine place to do some gentle rural hiking.

Lastovo has only one major settlement, Lastovo town, where most of the remaining 2000 islanders live. Remote and virtually self-sufficient in food, Lastovo's history marks it out from the other Adriatic islands, and there's a sense of pride and independence here which is most obviously expressed in the annual **Poklad festival**, held at the beginning of Lent and involving most of the population.

Like Vis, Lastovo was closed to foreigners from the end of World War II until June 1, 1989, because of its military and naval installations. This protracted isolation did little for the island's economy, and depopulation remains a major problem. The anticipated influx of tourists is likely to bring increased prosperity, though at a locally acknowledged detriment to the very qualities that made it attractive in the first place. Lastovo's distance from the mainland, and the lack of beaches, should deter all but the more determined of visitors. But visit soon if you want to catch the island before the rush.

Some History
Like Vis, Lastovo has changed hands many times, and is dotted with the scant relics of a whole variety of cultures. The Romans founded the first urban settlement at Ubli, which remained the main center of population throughout the Byzantine period and the Slav migrations of the eighth century. In 998 the Venetians sacked Ubli to rid it of pirates and the population shifted northeast to what is now Lastovo town. In 1252 the island's ruling class accepted an autonomous role within the Ragusan (Dubrovnik) Empire, with terms and conditions that were defined under a statute of 1310. Sometimes compared to the Magna Carta, this remarkable agreement included provisions banning immigration to the island and guaranteeing women the same rights of inheritance as men.

Despite occasional attempts by Dubrovnik to limit the autonomy of the island, the Ragusan period was a time of stability and prosperity, until the mid-seventeenth century when Dubrovnik fell into decline and Lastovo sank into a remote and impoverished obscurity. Occupied by French and British forces during the Napoleonic Wars, Lastovo was passed over to the Austrians under the terms of the Congress of Vienna in 1815. The Austrians did their best to ignore the island altogether, but the collapse of the Austro-Hungarian state at the end of World War I did Lastovo little good for it was promptly ceded to Italy by the Treaty of Rapallo—an unfortunate quirk of history that was resented by many of the islanders and provoked both defiant expressions of Croatian nationalism and mass emigration to Australia and the USA. Only after the last war was Lastovo returned to Yugoslavia.

Arrival, Accommodation, and Food
Ferries leave Split for the island port of Ubli once or twice daily all year. From September to June most of the boats call at Hvar town and all of them stop at Vela Luka on Korčula island. In July and August they only pause at Vela Luka. Be warned—the crossing can get disconcertingly rough.

After all that time at sea, **UBLI** is a disappointment. Most of what remained from the Roman occupation was carted off to Italy long ago, and all that's left are the relics of a small Christian basilica from the fifth century, lying next to the road a couple of hundred meters inland. Rather than staying here, you're better off taking the connecting bus from the ferry up along the steeply winding road to Lastovo town, on the other side of the island. At Lastovo town, the bus stops right outside the little **tourist office** (variable opening times, but always open when the bus from the boat arrives). Walk right in and ask for a **room**. You'll probably be asked whether you want full board. Consider this carefully. There are precious few eating places on the island, whereas the home-cooking you'll be offered by the people letting rooms is usually of an exceptionally high standard, and served in enormous portions. Needless to say, fish is heavily featured, along with an array of the island's vegetables and wild mushrooms, washed down with local wine.

If you don't want a room, there's an attractively sited **campground** at LUČICA, about 1km away at the end of the road which hairpins down from Lastovo town to the sea. It's primitive, but there are plans to modernize this and build two more campgrounds in the next couple of years. There are no hotels in town. You'll find a a couple of bars, a bank, and a grocery store on the little main street where the bus terminates.

Lastovo Town

Walking back a hundred meters from the bus stop towards Ubli, you have a panoramic view of the whole town built on the steep banks of a natural amphitheater. There's a road at the top and a road at the bottom, and in between a maze of narrow alleys and stone stairways. The buildings date mainly from the fifteenth and sixteenth centuries, and are similar to those in Dubrovnik; depopulation has left many properties empty and dilapidated. The parish church of **Sv Kusma i Damjan** on the far side of town is worth a look. Built in the fifteenth century, the interior is richly adorned with paintings and icons from the sixteenth and seventeenth centuries, including a work by the Spanish master Juan Boschetus over the altar in the south aisle, though the outside has been grotesquely defaced by a neo-Gothic belfry added by the Italians in 1942. Nearby is the site of the new **Museum of Lastovo**, due to open in 1990. Towering above the town is the old **French fort**, built in 1810 above some much older fortifications and now used as a weather station. It's an energetic climb, but the views from the top, of Lastovo on one side and of the coastline and sea on the other, make it worthwhile.

Swimming, Boating, and Hiking

There are no beaches to speak of in Lastovo town, although the little harbor beyond Lučica is ideal for sunbathing and swimming—the water is crystal-clear. Rowboats and windsurfers can be rented at *Hotel Solitudo* right at the other end of the island (reached by a couple of buses a day)—check on price and availability with the tourist office before you set out.

Otherwise, there's plenty of scope for day-long gentle **hikes**. The island is crisscrossed with tracks and paths leading down fertile valleys and up wooded hills. Once you've left town, you're almost guaranteed complete solitude and you'll see a wealth of wild flowers, butterflies and birds. There are over twenty old churches dotted around Lastovo that could serve as targets or reference points. Head for **Sv Luka**, the oldest of all, built in the eleventh century and hardly bigger than a bus shelter, or to **Sv Juraj**, near the summit of Mount Hum—at 1200 feet the highest peak on the island. Alternatively you could make for **Zaklopatica** in the north or **Skrivena Luka** in the south, both of which are tiny rock coves used by fishermen. Get advance directions for these treks from the tourist office.

The Poklad

The annual **Poklad Carnival** takes place on the days leading up to Lent. The climax, on Shrove Tuesday, consists of a ritual that's been closely observed for over 500 years. In this the *Poklad*, a stuffed puppet, is led through Lastovo town on a donkey by the entire population. The donkey ends up at the town center where the puppet is attached to a long rope and hoisted through the air to the top of the town. It's raised and lowered three times while fireworks are let off, and is met at each descent by drawn swords. Finally, the *Poklad* is put back on the donkey and taken to the square in front of the parish church, to the accompaniment of music and dancing. At the end of the evening, it's impaled on a long stake and burned.

Local tradition has it that the *Poklad* symbolizes a young Turkish messenger who was sent by Spanish pirates to demand the town's surrender. The unfortunate young man was executed and the pirate fleet was shipwrecked, though it's likely that the foundations of the ritual are more deeply embedded in the time of year and fertility rites. Whatever the roots of the whole thing, the islanders take the occasion very seriously, and although it's a colorful affair at which traditional costume is de rigueur, it's certainly not enacted for the benefit of outsiders.

Korčula

Like so many islands along this coast, **KORČULA** was first settled by the Greeks, who gave it the name *Korkyra Melaina* or "Black Corfu" for its dark and densely wooded appearance. Even now, it's one of the greenest of the Adriatic islands, and one of the most popular. For many years a limited water supply restricted tourist development, but since the completion of a new pipeline from the mainland in 1986 Korčula town has experienced a boom that has left the old center with spruce new restaurants, doubled the available accommodation, and destroyed much of the town's restrained charm. A chichi new marina, too, adorns the previously quiet old harbor, the subject of a new hi-tech evening *korso* as pedestrians salivate at the sight of the burnished steel and chrome.

The rest of the island is still mercifully untouched, though this is mainly because it's much less obviously open to development—pretty enough, but with no really viable population centers. Lumbarda, just south of Korčula town, is dull and ugly; Vela Luka, on the island's westernmost tip, is crowded and dirty. Blato, the island's largest town, in the western interior of the island, is a possible exception, with tourist settlements at the neighboring villages of Prigradica on the north coast, and, more attractively, Prižba, to the south.

Korčula Town: Arrival and Finding a Bed

Of a number of ways of reaching Korčula town, the simplest is to catch the main coastal **ferry** from Dubrovnik or Hvar/Split (4–7 times weekly; mid-March to mid-Oct), which drops you right at the harbor. There is also the ferry between Split and Lastovo, which stops off at Vela Luka (1–2 times daily with an inconsistent 90min connecting bus service on into Korčula town),

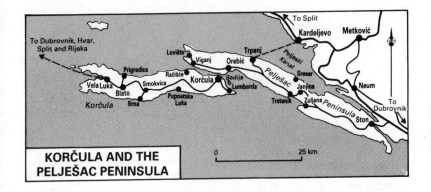

KORČULA AND THE PELJEŠAC PENINSULA

or—the shortest route by sea—the car ferries from Orebić, opposite Korčula town on the Pelješac peninsula (9–14 times daily), but these drop you in Dominće, an inconvenient 3km from town if you don't have car. Failing that there's a **boat shuttle service** for foot passengers only that runs across the narrow straits to Orebić (summer daily 6am–8pm every 1–2hr), or the direct **bus** services that connect Korčula town with Dubrovnik via Ston (2–3 times daily), though this can be time-consuming.

Once you're in town, things couldn't be easier. Korčula's **bus station** and **ferry terminal** are right in the center, a couple of minutes away from the **tourist office** (June–Sept daily 7am–8pm; otherwise Mon–Sat 8am–noon & 5–8pm, Sun 8am–noon). They will phone around to find you a **room**, though these get tight in high season. Try and stay in the old town if you can. The nearest reasonable **campground** is *Autocamp Kalac*, not far from the quay at Dominće, near which there's a **youth hostel** (June–mid-Sept; ☎055/232-132), some 2km out of Korčula on the Dominće road—though you often have to take full board here and the food is inedible. For a regular **hotel**, you could do worse than take a room in the *Hotel Korčula* (☎050/711-078)—doubles cost around $100 a night; if your budget's up to this, be sure to get a room overlooking the sea. If it's not, there's always the D-category hotel *Badija* (☎050/711-115) on the nearby small island of the same name, which has either private rooms for around $20 or beds in rather grim dormitories for less. Beware though: it's normally packed with energetic adolescents.

Korčula Town

KORČULA TOWN sits on a beetle-shaped hump of land, a medieval walled city ribbed with a series of narrow streets that branch off the spine of the main street like the veins of a leaf—a careful plan, designed to reduce the effects of wind and sun. The Venetians first arrived here in the eleventh century, and stayed, on and off, for nearly eight centuries, marking the culture and architecture of the town with their particular style. Here at least they weren't indiscriminate conquerors; they recognized that Korčula's ruling elite were far more apprehensive of their own commoners than of themselves, and the Venetians allowed a good degree of local autonomy.

When the Algerian Uliz Ali turned up outside the town in 1571, the Venetians hightailed it, while the inhabitants put up a brave enough defense to dispatch Ali to destroy Hvar instead.

Korčula's golden age was during the fifteenth and sixteenth centuries, when the town took its present form and most of the main buildings were constructed. Decimated by the plague and left high and dry by the decline of Mediterranean trade, the town slipped into an impoverished, quiet obscurity until World War II, when it was bombed and bombarded no less than 28 times as it was alternately occupied by Italians, Germans, and the partisans.

These days carefully repaired, Korčula town is still a remarkable place despite all its recent development, with a compact, symmetrical beauty that's rarely equaled on this coast. Just up from the quay, the **main gate** into the tiny old town was built to celebrate the victory over the Turks at Lepanto—though the staircase was added and the entrance enlarged in the nineteenth century. Through the gate, the central main street leads through to the **Cathedral of Sv Marko** (summer Mon–Sat 7am–noon & 4–7pm; otherwise 9am–1pm, occasional Sun opening), squeezed into a space between the buildings that roughly passes for a main square; land has always been precious here. The cathedral facade leans away from the rest of the building and is decorated with a gorgeous fluted rose window and a bizarre cornice frilled with strange beasts. In the center, a matronly creature looks anonymously down with half-closed eyes; no one knows for sure who she is, and wild speculations have ranged from the Roman emperor Diocletian's wife to one of a number of Hungarian queens who helped finance the church.

Inside, through a door framed by promiscuous-looking statues of Adam and Eve, the church is one of the loveliest on the coast, a curious mixture of styles developed over the 300 years it took to build. There's a muddled kind of continuity, from the Gothic forms of the nave to the Renaissance northern aisle, tacked on some time in the sixteenth century, the whole appealingly squashed into a space quite obviously too small for it. The clutter of artifacts includes everything from pikes used against Uliz Ali to paintings that include an altarpiece by Leandro Bassano, in the south aisle, and an early Tintoretto—behind the high altar and difficult to make out—although the best of the church's treasures have been removed to the **Bishop's Treasury** (same times), a couple of doors down. This is one of the best small collections of fine and sacred art in the country, with an exquisite set of paintings which takes in a striking *Portrait of a Man* by Carpaccio, a perceptive *Virgin and Child* by Bassano, some Tiepolo studies of hands and Raphael drawings, and a tiny *Madonna* by Dalmatian Renaissance artist Blaž Jurjav of Trogir. There is also a Leonardo da Vinci sketch of a soldier wearing a costume that bears a resemblance to that of the Moreška dancers (see below). Oddities include an ivory statuette of Mary Queen of Scots, whose skirts open to reveal kneeling figures in doublet and hose. How this got here no one knows.

Opposite, in another Venetian palace, is the **Town Museum** (Mon–Sat 9am–noon & 5–7pm), whose more modest display contains a plaster cast of a fourth-century BC Greek tablet from Lumbarda—the earliest evidence of civilization on Korčula—and a room devoted to the liberation struggle, with some faded photos featuring Fitzroy Maclean (skinny, crewcut with a beret). Brigadier Maclean was head of an itinerant Allied mission to occupied Yugoslavia. His job, according to Winston Churchill, was to "find out who is killing most Germans and suggest means by which we could help them kill more." Maclean's reports supported Tito and the Communists, rather than the more reactionary Četniks, and were instrumental in changing British government policy in their favor. Tito was duly grateful, and after the war exempted Maclean from the usual rules on house purchase by foreigners to allow him to buy a retirement home here on Korčula.

Close by the main square, down a turning to the right, is another remnant from Venetian times, the so-called **House of Marco Polo**. Korčula claims to be the birthplace of Marco Polo—a claim not as extravagant as it might first appear. The Venetians recruited many of their sea captains from their colonies, and Polo was indeed captured by the Genoese off the island in 1298, after which he used his time in prison to write his *Travels*. Whatever the truth of the matter, it seems unlikely that he had any connection with this seventeenth-century house, which is these days little more than an empty shell with some terrible twentieth-century prints on the walls. Don't waste your money.

Back down the main street, follow the signs to the **Icon Gallery** (Mon–Sat 9am–noon & 4–7pm), where there's a permanent display of icons in the rooms of the All Saints' Brotherhood. Most of the exhibits were looted from the Cretans in the seventeenth century, and the best is the fifteenth-century triptych of *The Passion*. From here, an enclosed bridge across the street takes you into the church of the brotherhood, **Svi Sveti**, with its brooding Renaissance interior and one of the ugliest altarpieces imaginable—an eighteenth-century *Pietà* enclosed by a fifteenth-century ciborium in imitation of the one of the cathedral.

The Moreška

Korčula town is famous for its **Moreška**, a traditional folk dance and drama that, it's believed, came to the island via Italy from Spain. Its Spanish origins suggest it relates to the conflict between the Moors and the Christians, but in Dalmatia its rise was more likely connected with the conflict with the Turks, in particular the victory over them at the Battle of Lepanto; others have related it to more ancient fertility rites, comparing it to regional English dramas such as the Mumming plays. Whatever its meaning, the Moreška has become a major tourist attraction, and its annual performance on July 27 has been transformed into a weekly summer event, held every Thursday evening between May and September at 9pm on the pitch next to the *Park* hotel. Tickets are on sale at the tourist office, but get them early as they disappear fast.

Basically the dance is the story of a conflict between the Christians (in red) and the Moors (in black). The heroine, Bula (literally "veiled woman"), is kidnapped by the evil foreign king and his army, and her betrothed tries to win her back in a ritualized sword fight that takes place within a shifting circle of dancers. The dance gets gradually more and more frantic, the swords clashing furiously, rising to a climax in which the evil king is forced to surrender while his adversary unchains Bula and carries her off triumphantly.

Food and Drink

Not surprisingly, most **restaurants** in the old town tend to be expensive. One exception is the excellent *Adio Mare*, near Marco Polo's House, one of the best restaurants on the coast and justifiably popular; arrive early to make sure of a table. A good second choice is the restaurant *Planjak*, a couple of minutes from the main gate into the old city, down towards the harbor. If they're both full, try the pizza restaurant at the top of the stairway by the *Hotel Korčula*. Wherever you eat, do try some of the local wines, some of which are excellent. Look out for the delicious dry white *Grk* from Lumbarda, *Pošip* from Smokvica, or the head-banging red *Dingač* from Postup on Pelješac. For **picnics**, there's a fruit and vegetable **market** by the city gate, as well as a couple of supermarkets.

Beaches and Islands

The nearest **beaches** to the old town are on the headland around the *Hotel Marko Polo*, though they're crowded, rocky, and uncomfortable. A better bet is to head off by **water-taxi** from the old harbor to one of the **Skoji** islands just offshore. The largest and nearest is **BADIJA**, where the track from the quay leads, on the left, to the shabby *Badija* hotel and sports complex incongruously sited in a renovated fifteenth-century Franciscan monastery—and on the right to secluded beaches and a couple of elementary snack bars. The waters on this side are crystal-clear and a favorite pastime is making your own "air mattress" from the mass of drying seaweed. Water-taxis also make regular trips to the FKK islet of **STUPE**, where there is a restaurant and a couple of bars. For all the other more obscure islets you'll have to negotiate your own price with the boatman and take your own food and water. Camping is illegal.

Other alternatives for swimming are to take boats either across to **Orebić**, with its long, though overcrowded, shingle beaches, or to the smaller Pelješac resorts of **Kučišće** or Viganj. Boats to Orebić are regular throughout the day, about every hour; boats to the latter two usually leave at about 9am and return in the afternoon—though neither place is of special note. Incidentally, **windsurfing** equipment is available in town at the *Hotel Park* which also organizes lessons for beginners.

Several of the local boat-owners run trips to Pomena on **Mljet**, which can serve as a useful connection as there are no regular ferries. Check your information carefully though—boats only go about three times a week.

Around the Island

The beauty of Korčula town only serves to emphasize just how short on appeal the **rest of the island** is. Closest to Korčula town, **LUMBARDA**, some 8km south and accessible by hourly bus during the week, has the island's best (sandy) beaches but is otherwise a rather drab, modern resort. In the other direction, one road runs the length of the island west to Vela Luka at the far end, and is served by regular bus between four and seven times daily—a ninety-minute journey in all. It passes most of the other major settlements on the island, but, with the exception of Blato, most are similarly uninteresting, bland inland villages usually connected by rough road with a developing set of tourist facilities at the nearest feasible strip of coast. These are usually much the same: tiny modern resorts with a few vacation villas and apartments, some sort of rocky beach, a store and, more inconsistently, private rooms for rent. Most are almost impossible to reach without your own transport.

BLATO is something of an antidote to all this, a faintly old-fashioned country town that's easily the most agreeable of Korčula's inland settlements. First colonized by the Greeks, Blato (literally "mud" or "swamp") is at the center of a wine-growing district and is attractively bisected by a magnificent avenue of linden trees. The town's main claim to fame is another traditional dance, the **Kumpanjina**, held on or about April 23 every year. This is similar to the Moreška, and has it origins in a past victory over the Saracens, but it has the advantage of being much less of a tourist event. Should you want to stay in Blato, the local branch of **Dalmacijaturist** can advise on accommodation, though they'll probably simply point you to the *Lipa* hotel (which is often full anyway), or toward the town's three resorts—**PRIŽBA** and **BRNA** on the south coast, or **PRIGRADICA** to the north. All three of these have **rooms**, but there are only two connecting buses a day.

At the western end of the island, **VELA LUKA** may be your first view of Korčula, but it can be a rather dispiriting one—really it's a place to arrive rather than spend any time in, with crowded concrete beaches around a polluted harbor. If you arrive late and can't get a bus out, there's a **tourist office** in the harbor which has **rooms**.

On from Korčula: the Pelješac Peninsula

Just across the Pelješki Kanal from Korčula, the **Pelješac Peninsula** is a slim, mountainous finger of land some 90km long, extending from Lovište in the west to Ston and the thin stretch of land linking Pelješac to the mainland in the east. Parts of the peninsula are exceptionally beautiful—tiny villages, and sheltered coves rimmed by a shimmering beach. But although it's a reasonably popular holiday area, development is low-key and low-density. The downside of this is that public transit connections are terrible, and unless you're prepared to hitch and walk, most of the smaller places impossible to get to.

Orebić

Towards the western end of Pelješac, the small town of **OREBIĆ** was a subsidiary trading outlet within the Dubrovnik Empire for almost 500 years. Liberated by Napoleon's armies in 1806, independence brought the town a brief trade boom and a period of extraordinary prosperity. Confident of their prospects, the town's merchants set up a Maritime Society in 1865, built a huge church, and constructed their own shipyards to supply an independent merchant fleet. The bubble soon burst and the society and the yards were closed down as early as 1887, allowing Orebić to slip back into a quiet obscur-

PELJEŠAC TRANSPORTATION

FERRIES
Trpanj–Kardeljevo (3–7 times daily)
Trstenik–Polače (Mljet) (2–5 times daily)
Orebić–Dominče (Korčula) (9–14 times daily)
Orebić–Korčula town (every 1–2hr; 6am–8pm, foot passengers only)

Korčula town–Viganj (1–2 times daily, foot passengers only)

BUSES
Orebić–Trpanj (5–6 daily)
Orebić–Dubrovnik via Ston (2–3 daily)
Orebić–Viganj/Lovište (2–3 daily)

ity. But the maritime tag stuck, and, until the arrival of tourism a couple of decades ago, its seafaring tradition was Orebić''s main claim to fame.

Today, Orebić straggles along the seashore on either side of its jetties, an aimless and rather ugly mixture of the old and new. Encased by drab modern buildings, the best part of town is along the seafront, just east of the quays, where several generations of sea captains built a series of comfortable country **villas**, set back behind a luscious foliage of palms, cacti, and subtropical color. Two of these have been opened as small museums (details from the tourist office), with eighteenth- and nineteenth-century period furniture and fittings. And you'd really do better to look in on these than waste time at the official **Maritime Museum** (Mon–Sat 8am–noon & 5–7pm), on the waterfront east of the ferry terminal at 12 Trg Mimbeli, which sports a dull collection of naval memorabilia relating to the Orebić fleet.

Practical Details

If you decide to stay, the Orebić **tourist office** (summer daily 7am–9pm, winter 7am–1pm), next to the landing stages and bus stop, arranges **accommodation**. The best rooms are in a couple of the sea captains' villas, although these are often booked up months in advance. Alternatively a string of **hotels** spreads out west of here and a gruesome campground is just to the east, at Maršala Tita 13. The nearest reasonable **campground** is a couple of kilometers out of town towards Viganj. For **food**, the *Peljeski Dvor* restaurant, by the tourist office, is as good a place as any, and lots of indifferent bars and restaurants line the waterfront. For **swimming**, there's a long shingle beach west of town in front of the hotels, and a few sandy(ish) coves a few minutes' walk east of the tourist office—though all get packed out in the high season. There's also a private **boat** service to the island of Badija (see above) once daily.

West to Lovište

West of Orebić, the road tracks along the coast past the untidy resorts of **KUČIŠTE** and **VIGANJ** before cutting inland across to the seaside village of **LOVIŠTE**. The scenery is beautiful, the blue sea framed by the cool, dark mountains above, but you really need a car to get around. All three villages have private **rooms** and there are ten **campgrounds** in the vicinity.

East to Ston

East of Orebić, the main road twists up into the mountains before the turning to **TRPANJ**, an unremarkable little town where ferries (3–7 daily) cross to Kardeljevo on the mainland proper. If you get stuck here, there's a tourist office with rooms, and, surprisingly, a **youth hostel**—though no other reason to stay.

Farther east, 3km from the main road, the village of **TRSTENIK** is a pleasanter destination, set tight against the hills behind a couple of tiny beaches. It's a quiet place, but it has its own **campground**, private **rooms** from a tiny **tourist office**, as well as ferry links to POLAČE on the island of Mljet several times a day. Beyond Trstenik, the road meanders across the peninsula to the northern shore, passing through the dreary village of Janina before reaching **DUBRAVA**, where a minor road (not traveled by bus) takes you down the 6km to one of the best beaches on the coast at **ŽULJANA**—a tiny resort built round a sheltered bay at the foot of a steep rocky gorge. There's a **tourist office** with unreliable opening times right on the beach, plenty of private **rooms**, and a reasonable **campground**. For **food**, there are a couple of unpretentious bar/restaurants on the harborfront, where you'll also see boats advertising trips to even more remote beaches. Walk back along the bottom of the gorge, through vineyards and vegetable gardens, and you reach the older, less commercialized part of Žuljana. Beyond that is a series of strikingly bizarre rock formations carved by the wind as it blows down to the sea.

Back at Dubrava, the road heads on down the valley to the mainland, flanked by mountains to north and south. About 20km beyond Dubrava, the twin towns of (Veliki) **STON** and **MALI STON** straddle Pelješac at its narrowest point, just before it joins the mainland. Fortified to protect the peninsula from attack from the mainland, these outposts of the Dubrovnik state were connected by a succession of stone walls and towers whose remnants still trail across the adjacent hillsides. Famous for their oysters, and once important as suppliers of salt, both towns are edged by shallow strips of trapped seawater and muddy beach that have deterred the developers.

A favorite half-hour stop on the tourist excursion trail, photogenic **STON** is framed by dramatic and unusually shaped walls, whose apex is on the hillside high above the town's narrow streets. Rebuilt after extensive World War II damage, Ston's old houses mix Renaissance and Gothic styles within a firmly regular grid-iron street plan. Few visitors stay, but there is one **hotel** and the **Turističko Društvo** (summer Mon–Fri 7am–noon & 5–7pm, Sat 7am–noon) have a handful of rooms. Alternatively, there are two **campgrounds** nearby—the dingy *Broce* site 2km to the south, and the much better *Prapratno*, a steep walk down from the main road, 3km to the west. *Prapratno* is situated in its own attractive bay, and has a pebble beach and a comprehensive range of facilities.

MALI STON is far smaller than its sister town, a sleepy little village of old stone houses and farm and fishing outbuildings. Pressed within its ancient walls, it's slowly being restored, but it's all modest stuff and the tourists who drive in soon drive out. There doesn't appear to be anywhere to **stay**, but if you're determined ask at one of the village's two restaurants.

The Southern Dalmatian Coast: Split to Dubrovnik

The coast south of Split is perhaps the country's most dramatic stretch, with some of the best beaches sheltering beneath the papier-mâché heights of the karst mountains, all easily accessible on the frequent coastal bus service. Most of the beaches are pebble or shingle, but some do have sand (a rarity anywhere in Yugoslavia), and all are served by at least one campground and (usually) a stock of private rooms. Development has been underway for some time, and is noticeable, but the steep geography of the coastline has kept it within fairly reasonable limits.

Omiš and Around

The first town of any size south of Split is **OMIŠ**, cowering under the sharp drama of the scenery behind, where the olive-green Cetina River has furrowed a deep gorge, tearing the bone-gray karst into weird, angry shapes. For centuries Omiš was an impregnable pirate stronghold, a menace to other towns up and down the coast. Time and again strenuous efforts were made to drive the pirates out (the pope himself led a Holy War against them in 1221) but without much success. Eventually, in 1444, the Venetians forced a surrender, though the terms they offered were generous, and the pirates simply relocated to Senj, farther north (see p.127).

These days the town is rather dominated by the coastal highway, which passes just south of the old quarter, a huddle of cramped alleys spread out along a pleasant central street—all within the remnants of the old city walls. The new town lies to the south, a featureless stretch of postwar buildings behind the main town **beach**, which is sandy but uninviting. There's one **hotel**, the cheap *Plaza*, and the **tourist office** close to the beach (summer daily 7am–9pm; otherwise Mon–Sat 7am–2pm) has **rooms**. Failing that, you can try the rather dubious delights of the city **campground**, ten minutes' walk away on the other side of the river by the sports stadium. Really, though, the only reason to break your journey in Omiš is to take a **boat trip** up the gorge—a dramatic excursion, with the mountains towering overhead and the river sweeping past below. You can pick these up on the jetty by the bridge most days during summer, or take an organized excursion from the tourist office. You might also stop off here to take a **boat to Brač**—private operators sail there once a week.

From Omiš, the road runs past the village of **PISAK**, which sticks precariously to the side of a steep cliff, a popular resort with a surprisingly large supply of rooms in its tiny tourist office. On from here the road twists around the headlands of the Biokovo mountains, into the expanse of coast known as the **"Makarska Riviera,"** a string of resorts that range from the over-exploited to the relatively unknown. Surrounded by aromatic pine groves, the first settlement is **DONJE BRELA**, which sports a fine strand of beach but is otherwise a spick, span, and antiseptic ad hoc tourist village with pseudo-

Mediterranean architecture and concrete and glass arcades. **BAŠKA VODA**, just down the road, is pretty similar but not quite as successful: the beach isn't as good and the hotels are even more overpowering. If you do come here, two **restaurants** worth eating at for their locations are the *Punta Rata*, about ten minutes' walk north of Brela village, and the *Hotel Berulia* restaurant, which has a lovely elevated position on the beach between Brela and Baška Voda.

Makarska . . . and Connections to the Islands

MAKARSKA, 10km beyond, has on the other hand been around for years—a bright, lively seaside town, ranged around a broad bay, framed by the Biokovo massif behind and two stumpy pinewood peninsulas on either side. There's not a lot to see here. Depsite a 200-year Turkish occupation, it's a Venetian settlement on the whole, but most of this has been lost and the old town is more or less confined to one central square, which slants up, just behind the waterfront, to the Baroque church of Sv Marko. There are two **museums**: a predictable municipal display on the seafront that takes in old partisan relics, and (much better) a small collection of polished sea-shells in a small building on the south side of the old center just off Žrtava Fašizma.

These apart, Makarska's main pleasures are in eating and swimming, and the town's facilities, albeit crowded, are well geared to both these things. Just west of the center, the main **beach** is nearly two kilometers long and you can swim and stroll round either of the peninsulas. For food, the town center has scores of restaurants, not to mention disco bars. Prices are almost uniformly higher than you pay elsewhere; try the *Riva*, just behind the tourist office, which is good value.

The town **bus station** is a five-minute walk from the seafront, up on the main road. The **tourist office**, on the seafront, (June–Sept daily 7am–9pm; otherwise daily 9am–5pm), almost always has **rooms** to spare. Alternatively, the two nearest **campgrounds** are at the far end of the beach near the *Hotel Rivijera*, just beyond which are two **youth hostels** open June to August—the *Goran* (☎058/612-013) and the *Savinja* (☎058/612-112)—though at both of these you'll need to have reserved in advance. Makarska also has two fairly cheap **hotels**—the *Osejava* and the *Beograd*, which face the harbor from either end of the bay—though these too are usually full in season.

South of Makarska

The strip of coast immediately south of Makarska is one of the most intensively developed in all of Yugoslavia, reminiscent of the Spanish *costas*, with hotels and apartment blocks dominating the skyline. **TUČEPI** and **PODGORA**, the first two settlements you reach a few kilometers south of Makarska, are fairly typical: charmless places, ugly and overcrowded, sprawling along the shore behind a stretch of pebbly beach—though rooms go cheap in all but the height of the season from the two tourist offices (both daily 7am–9pm). The obscure, thirty-meter-high monument overlooking the

MAKARSKA CONNECTIONS

Onward bus connections from Makarska are good. So too are ferry connections with the islands. There are links to Sumartin on Brač (3–5 times daily in season), though bear in mind that once on the island bus links to the main towns are very poor. Similarly, precious few buses connect with the ferry from DRVENIK, just south of Makarska, when it reaches SUĆURAJ on Hvar (5–12 times daily). One way around this is to get a place on one of the **boat trips** organized by the Makarska Tourist Office. These leave almost every day between May and October for Jelsa on Hvar and Bol on Brač, and it's easy enough to arrange a one-way ticket; even if this isn't possible it only costs around $8–10 for the round-trip fare. Otherwise, all the major tour operators run day trips by **hydrofoil** to a variety of island destinations including Korčula and Mljet. Once again, it's possible to buy a one-way ticket if there are empty seats; for the longer excursions reckon on about $12.

main road at Podgora is a symbolic seagull celebrating the founding of the Yugoslav navy here in 1942.

Things pick up after Podgora, with **DRASNIČE** the first of several pleasant coastal villages. Tucked away beneath the road and sandwiched against the hillside by the sea, Drasniče was once an isolated fishing and farming community. Today, it's a low-key holiday spot with a mediocre beach, but at least it's managed to keep its character. There's no shortage of rooms— available from the tourist office (summer Mon–Sat 7am–9pm; winter 7am–noon & 5:30–7:30pm)—and in the tiny central square is a graphic mosaic in honor of a local partisan, Zena Biokovka, who was executed by a German firing squad. Up above, on the other side of the road, are the crumbling remains of the old village—a quiet, neglected corner of the coast where you can try to find the paths up the mountain. There's only one **bus** per day from Makarska to the village center; other buses drop you on the main road for the steep walk down.

From Drašnice the coastal highway follows a slim ribbon of greenery between titanic gray mountains and the deep azure of the Adriatic. The best place to stop is **IGRANE**, a cosy headland village spinning away from its ruined seventeenth-century church and spire. A popular, busy little place, Igrane has a tree-lined pebble beach, a tourist office, a tacky modern hotel and plenty of **rooms**. The Makarska Riviera officially ends at neighboring **ŽIVOGOŠĆE**, a tedious new resort that's near the small, unremarkable port of **DRVENIK**, which has a pebble beach, a large campground, rooms, and (most importantly) ferry links to Sućuraj on Hvar.

Farther south, the industrial port of **KARDELJEVO** (formerly Ploče) is one of the Dalmatian coast's few rail heads, and has long been a link town for the interior via the Neretva river valley. Consequently onward **transportation** connections are excellent: trains head off to Mostar, Sarajevo, Belgrade, and Zagreb (five times daily) and dozens of buses go to most major Yugoslav towns, though in season many of the buses for Split and Dubrovnik are full by the time they get here. There's also a ferry to Trpanj on the Pelješac peninsula.

Kardeljevo's **ferry terminal** and the **bus and train stations** are only two minutes apart and few people stop to look around; there is, certainly, precious little to see around Kardeljevo's industrial harbor, whose haphazard high rises give it the look of frontier town. If you miss your connection, the *Hotel Ploča*, near the bus station, has doubles for about $30, and the **tourist office** sometimes has rooms.

Kardeljevo is at the northern edge of the broad delta of the **Neretva River**, once an expanse of marsh and malarial swamp but now—after reclamation— some of the most fertile land in the country. It's a striking landscape of bright green fields interrupted by jagged boulders and dotted with ramshackle, modern villages. Along the rim of the reclaimed land, the old settlements perch on the rocks that once formed the shore-line—impoverished reminders of an even harsher past.

South of the delta the highway twists down to **NEUM**, a brand-new workers' holiday settlement funded by the Bosnia-Hercegovina authorities on their only bit of territory to border the sea. Bosnian fat cats filched money to build themselves luxury villas here—a scandal revealed to the public by the press in 1987. Beyond here, the humped mountains of the Pelješac peninsula close in against the coast until the turning for STON (see above), where the mountains join the mainland and the separating strip of water peters out in a chain of aquamarine salt flats. Fifteen kilometers beyond, **SLANO**, at the head of a beautiful deep bay, was once a port of some importance but has since been overrun by tour operators. There's nothing to see and precious little to do. It has a campground and a tourist office in the main square with rooms. If you need to eat, *Konoba Fanny* has a good selection of food. Just to the south, **TRSTENO** is a far nicer place for a stop. Sandwiched between the road and the sea, it's home to the oldest **Botanical Gardens** in Yugoslavia (daily 7am–7pm). Laid out in the Renaissance manner in 1502, these really are spectacular, and the adjoining **campground** is delightful. From Trsteno the approach to Dubrovnik follows the deep cut of the Dubrava River estuary, passing the city's marina, and the cranes and warehouses of Gruž, the working harbor of the city Byron called the "Pearl of the Adriatic."

Dubrovnik

After Split, the main town of the southern Dalmatian coast, **DUBROVNIK**, is something special, a beautifully preserved fortified town pressed against the sea within magnificent medieval walls. It's also the most popular tourist destination in Yugoslavia, and for much of the summer season its streets are packed with visitors, the town's charm receding under the strain of the congestion. Despite that, no tour of the coast would be complete without a visit, and it's important you don't get turned off to the place as soon as you arrive. Give Dubrovnik time—at least a couple of days—see it in the early morning before most of the tourists have crept out of their hotels, and the city will gradually start to reveal itself. Slowly you begin to see what all the fuss is about.

Arrival and Information

Dubrovnik has no rail connections and **ferries** arrive in the port suburb of GRUŽ, a mile or so west of the old town. The main city **bus station** is a couple of minutes away at the landward end of the quay. From the jetty, buses #1a and #3, marked PILE, will take you to the old town; from behind the bus station, take either #1a, #3, or #6.

Arriving by plane, Dubrovnik's **airport** is situated some 20km south of the city, close to Cavtat. From here there are a number of ways of reaching the city's bus station, which lies about a mile to the west of the old town. You can, most cheaply, catch an ordinary bus from the main road near the terminal building, although local services are infrequent and long-distance buses reluctant to stop—expect quite a wait. Alternatively, there are *JAT* buses (10–15 daily) that deliver you to the *JAT* office behind Dubrovnik bus station, but they're geared to *JAT* flights and you again may have to wait a couple of hours. Failing that, you could, especially if it's late, bargain your way on to one of the tour buses that meet all charter flights. This, however, may prove comparatively expensive and you may face a substantial (steep) walk from the hotels, most of which are on the far end of the Lapad peninsula, to either the station or the old town; obviously clarify before you pay. A taxi to town costs about $30.

For **information**, the **Dubrovnik Tourist Agency** (daily summer 7am–9pm; otherwise Mon–Sat 7am–8pm, Sun 8am–noon; ☎32-108), 50m up the hill from the bus station, has city maps, a small booklet with information on the city and can book private rooms. The **tourist office** (same times; ☎26-354), in the old town by the Pile Gate, offer a similar, but more harassed service.

> The Dubrovnik regional area code is ☎050

Finding a Place to Stay

It's likely that at both the bus and ferry terminals you'll be approached with the offer of a black-market **room**. Late at night and in season this is much the best way of finding accommodation, and is in any case cheaper than finding a room through the offical outlets. Do, however, make sure you know the price and location first: Dubrovnik's a hilly place and you can end up doing a lot of walking. If there's no one around touting beds, make straight for the tourist agency close by the bus station (see above), which has private rooms, as does the tourist office in the old town (again, see above). During July and August you won't be in a position to be choosy, but outside these months try and get somewhere in the district of Boninovo, whose mansions fan out west from the Pile Gate, or in the streets immediately northeast of the old town high above the city beach. At any time of year spaces in the old town are few and far between.

Hostels and Camping

The city also has a number of hostel accommodation possibilities. The **youth hostel**, Vinka Sagrestena 3 (May–Oct; ☎23-241), off Oktobarske Revolucije, some 400m from the bus station, is the most convenient option, though during the summer you'll definitely need to have rewerved in advance. There's also a well-run **International Youth and Student Center** in the suburb of Lapad at Ivanska 14 (bus #4; ☎23-841), and an enormous **campground**, *Solitudo* (☎20-770), reachable on bus #6 from the bus station, at which you can either camp or stay in a cabin for around the price of a private room. There are also campgrounds south of Dubrovnik in Mlini and Cavtat, which the frequent bus services make feasible bases. The completely penurious can bed down—illegally—on the benches in the terraced park overlooking the sea about half a mile up from the Pile Gate on Maršala Tita.

Hotels

Most of Dubrovnik's **hotels** cater to tour operators with the consequence that they're often full and not really a viable option for travelers turning up on the spur of the moment. They're also expensive, and a fair way from the center, most sited way out of town on the wooded Lapad peninsula. The city's cheapest hotels, with double rooms for around $30 a night, are the C-category *Stadion*, behind the bus station (☎23-449), and the C-category *Gruž* (☎24-777) and B-category *Petka* (☎24-933) in Gruž harbor, both of which have rooms for around $30. The *Lero* on Iva Vojnovića (☎32-555) is another option, within walking distance of the old town, with doubles for just under $40. Try also the C-category *Dubravka* (☎26-293), the only hotel in the old town and a gracious place near Sv Vlaho on Od Puča with doubles for $34 a night—though, again, the package-tour trade fills most of the rooms, all summer.

The City

With a population of a little over 30,000, Dubrovnik isn't as large a city as you might think, and although sprawling along the coast for several miles, its real heart is the **old town**. This is where you should head first—it's the site of virtually everything there is to see, and outside the walls the city is much like any other in Yugoslavia. The **Lapad peninsula**, to the west, is home to most of the large package-tour hotels (as well as the campground and youth hostels); just north of here, **Gruž** is the city's port and transit district. These features apart, though, if you spent no time at all in newer part of town you wouldn't really be missing anything.

Some History

Libertas, Dubrovnik's motto, which plasters the sides of buses and the city's tourist literature, says quite a lot about the city's past. For Dubrovnik managed to keep its freedom for several centuries while the rest of this coast suffered under the yokes of various foreign imperialists. Not only is the Venetian Lion of St Mark conspicuous by its absence, but statues of St Blaise, the symbol of Dubrovnik's independence, fill every conceivable crack and niche in the city.

Dubrovnik was first settled by Greek and then Roman refugees in the early seventh century, when the nearby city of Epidaurus (now Cavtat) was sacked by the Slavs. The refugees took up residence on the southern part of what is now the old town, then an island, and gave their settlement the name Ragusa. The Slavs, meanwhile, settled on the wooded mainland opposite, from which the name Dubrovnik (from *dubrava*, meaning "a glade") came. Before long the slim channel between the two was filled in and the two sides merged, taking the name Ragusa, which it kept until this century.

Sandwiched between Muslim and Christian powers, Ragusa exploited its favorable position on the Adriatic with a maritime and commercial genius unmatched anywhere else in Europe at the time, and by the turn of the fourteenth century, having shaken off the yoke of first the Byzantines and then the Venetians, had become a successful and self-contained city-state, its merchants trading far and wide. Its galleons gave us our word "argosy," which means simply "ship of Ragusa." While accepting the nominal suzerainty of Venice, and, later, Hungary, Ragusa somehow managed to stave off direct intervention in its business to remain solidly unattached until the beginning of the nineteenth century and the arrival of Napoleon.

A fire at the end of the thirteenth century, plague in the mid-fourteenth century, and a devastating earthquake in 1667, which left the city decimated by an enormous tidal wave, are just a few of the catastrophes to have threatened this fragile independence—an autonomy which was in any case always menaced by the expansionist superpowers. Fiercely—but shrewdly—Catholic Dubrovnik enjoyed the passive protection of Spain and the papacy, and its skilled diplomats fended off the attentions of the Ottoman Empire with cunning and pragmatic obsequiousness—and regular payment of enormous tributes. Every year two envoys would visit Istanbul, hand over the cash and stay for a year in fawning acquiescence until someone arrived to relieve them. Ragusa's diplomats were renowned for their skill and acumen, and, combined with the republic's respected navy and the city's impressive fortifications, they represented a policy which worked. Meanwhile, Dubrovnik could get on with managing its own affairs, developing a system that, in its Whiggish liberalism, often seems years ahead of its time. In 1417 they passed a law abolishing the slave trade; 1432 saw the establishment of a health service; and three years later came the foundations of a free education plan. Combine this with a town-planning scheme second to none and you're reminded more of the rational humanism of seventeenth-century Holland than the imperial despotism that was the normal state of play in the rest of the Balkans.

That said, Ragusa was by no means a democracy. The organization of the city-state took the form of a rigid oligarchy. There were three clearly defined classes—nobles, commoners, and workers—and marriage or any association between them was severely frowned upon. Not surprisingly, the nobles called the tune. They organized themselves into a grand council of all males over the age of 18, which in turn deputed power to an elected senate that took care of day-to-day business, delegating responsibility to another series of councils who administered the law and the city's purse. Fearful of dictatorship, no personality was ever allowed to emerge from all this to exercise power, and

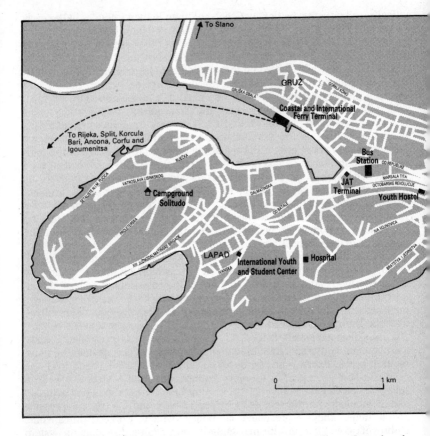

the nominal head of state, the rector (knez), was virtually a figurehead. Elected for just one month, during this time he could only leave his palace for state occasions and, after the end of his period of duty, he was ineligible for re-election for the next two years. This careful system did indeed prevent personalized tyranny, though in reality Ragusa was a much less peaceful place than the neat nature of the system would suggest. With good reason, the nobles were viewed with suspicion by the lower orders, and although everyone had a vested interest in preserving the city's independence (life would have been much worse for everyone under the Venetians or Turks), periods of peace were often punctuated by outbreaks of violent hostility between the classes.

Decline set in with the earthquake in 1667, which killed around 5000 people and destroyed most of the city's buildings. (Ironically much of what you now see dates from the rebuilding after this catastrophe). The city never really recovered from the economic hardships that this brought, a process

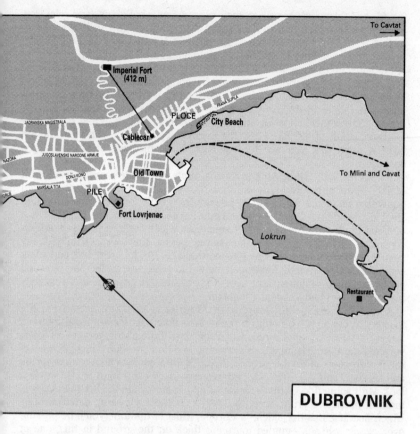

To Cavtat

Imperial Fort
(412 m)

JADRANSKA MAGISTRALA

PLOCE

City Beach

FRANA SUPILA

Cablecar

JUGOSLAVENSKE NARODNE ARMIJE

Old Town

To Mlini and Cavat

NAZORA

DONJI KONO

MARŠALA TITA

PILE

GRUZ

Fort Lovrjenac

Lokrun

Restaurant

DUBROVNIK

hastened by the movement of trade to the west. The city-state survived in diminished form until 1808, when it was formally dissolved by Napoleon.

The Old Town

Dubrovnik's old walled heart juts out from the sprawling suburbs, its walls almost too perfectly complete. All motor vehicles are banned from the center, and buses drop you outside the **Pile Gate**, one of two main gates to the city center, accessible by a stone bridge which dates from 1471. The gate itself is fifteenth-century also, decorated with a statue of St Blaise set in a niche above the arch. Inside, and accessible from the Pile Gate, the best way to get your bearings is by making a tour of the **city walls** (daily 9am–6pm), which stretch all the way around, perhaps the best preserved set of city walls in Europe, 25m high and with all the towers intact. Some parts date back to the tenth century, but most of the original construction was undertaken in the twelfth and thirteenth centuries, with subsequent rebuildings (and reinforcements) being carried out over the years that followed. The walls are a picturesque framing for the city now, but in their day they were literally a lifesaver; one glance at their thickness—up to 6m in places—and the complexity of the gates gives some idea of how seriously the Ragusans took the defense of their city. Of the various towers and bastions that punctuate the walls, the **Minčeta fortress**, which marks the northeastern side, is perhaps the most impressive, built in 1455 to plans drawn up by Juraj Dalmatinac and the Italian architect, Michelozzi. The same architects also designed the **Bokar fortress**, south of the Pile Gate, the interior of which you can visit, though bear in mind that you won't be allowed on to the wall at all carrying a backpack.

Within the walls Dubrovnik is a sea of roofs faded into a pastel patchwork of like colors, punctured now and then by a sculpted dome or tower and laid out with a uniformity of vision that seems incredible for the time. At ground level just inside the Pile Gate, **Onofrio's Large Fountain**, built in 1444, is a bulbous domed object in a small square at which visitors to this hygiene-conscious city had to wash themselves before they were admitted any farther. Badly damaged in the 1667 earthquake, the fountain was part of an elaborate water system developed between 1436 and 1438 that provided public washing facilities right across town—though even in this relatively liberal city Jews had a separate fountain.

Across the street, the **Franciscan Monastery** complex dates from the fourteenth century. The church (daily 9am–noon) is of no special interest, largely a post-earthquake reconstruction, but the cloister, a work of 1348, survives more or less intact, an intriguing late-Romanesque concoction decorated with rows of double arches topped with a confusion of human heads and fantastic animals. The attached treasury (daily 8am–6pm) is also worth a look, with some fine Gothic reliquaries and manuscripts tracing the development of musical scoring. Stop, too, at the apothecary's shop, dated at 1317, which lists itself as the oldest in Europe. Most of the time you'll be peering over people's heads—guided tours are thick on the ground in this, one of their favorite stops—but it's worth the effort for a look at the miscellany of ancient and mysterious jars and utensils.

Placa, Luža, and through to the Ploče Gate

From outside the church, **Placa**, the city's main street, runs straight ahead across the old town, following the line of the original channel that separated the original island of Ragusa from the mainland, and nowadays edged by stately blocks full of tourist shops, its limestone surface polished slippery by the tramp of thousands of feet. Its far end broadens into the pigeon-choked **Luža Square**, the center of the medieval town and even today hub of much of its activity. On the left, the **Sponza Palace** (daily 8am–6pm) was once the customs house and mint, a building which grew in storys as Dubrovnik grew in wealth, with a facade that's an elegant melding of florid Venetian Gothic and quieter Renaissance forms. Dating from 1522, the majestic courtyard inside is given over to a contemporary **gallery** of fine art. A Latin inscription on the far wall refers to the public scales that once stood here, and puts God

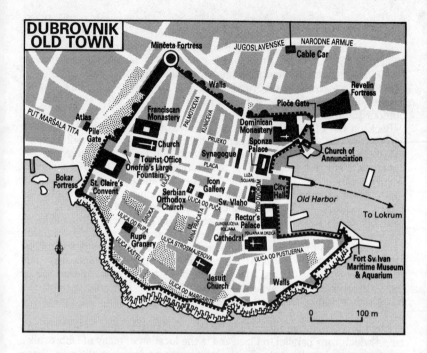

firmly on the side of trading standards: "Cheating and tampering with the weights is forbidden, and when I weigh goods God weighs me." The figures underneath are the sixteenth-century remnants of the old town clock.

Across the square, the Baroque-style church of **Sv Vlaho** (St Blaise) is in graceful counterpoint to the palace, built in 1714 to replace an earlier church. Saint Blaise is said to have appeared in a vision to warn of impending Venetian attack, saving the city and earning himself the title of Dubrovnik's patron saint. His gilded silver figure, above the high altar, holds a little maquette of pre-earthquake Dubrovnik, though it's difficult to get close enough for a good look. Outside the church, smack in the middle of the square, stands the carved figure of an armored knight, usually referred to as **Orlando's Column**. Surprisingly for such an insignificant-looking object, this was the focal point of the city-state; erected in 1428 as a morale-boosting monument to freedom, it was here that government ordinances were promulgated and punishments executed. Orlando's right arm was also the standard measurement of length (the Ragusan cubit); at the base of the column you can still see a line of the same length cut in the stone.

The eastern side of the Luža square is flanked by a loggia and **bell tower**, originally from the mid-fifteenth century but reconstructed earlier this century. The bell, cast in 1506, is the only original part of the tower. On the right is the so-called **Onofrio's Little Fountain**, the work of the same sculptor who did the larger fountain at the other end of Placa, dating from 1440. To the left, a Gothic arch leads to a passage that cuts through to the **Ploče Gate**, a narrow, twisting lane whose recesses were filled in centuries ago to make surprise assault impossible. Ploče is the other main city gate, a larger affair than the Pile Gate, with another statue of St Blaise in the niche above (the oldest in the city) and a bridge across the moat that dates from 1449. The **Revelin fortress**, just beyond, was begun around the same time, but not finished until well into the sixteenth century. It's now used as a venue for outdoor summer concerts.

Back on the other side of the Ploče Gate, on the right, the **Dominican Monastery** (daily 9am–6pm) is approached by a grand stairway with a stone balustrade whose columns have been partly mortared in. Irritated by the loafers who stood at the bottom of the staircase to ogle at the bare ankles of women on their way to church, the monks were themselves responsible for this ill-fitting modification. Entry to the church is through the fifteenth-century Gothic-Renaissance cloister, where Napoleon's soldiers were billeted in 1808. They left an unusual mark: at the base of the pillars on the way to the monastery church, a series of troughs were chiseled with bayonets to help their horses eat and drink. The church itself is a mundane hodgepodge of styles, with Baroque altars, a Gothic apse, and some odd twentieth-century paintings. The best exhibit is a fine pastel *St Dominic* by the nineteenth-century Cavtat artist Vlaho Bukovac. The attached museum has a rather dull collection of manuscripts and incunabula, and a polyptych by Titian.

From the Dominican monastery **Prijeko** leads back west, a dead straight street which runs parallel to Placa and is the location of many of Dubrovnik's most expensive restaurants. On the way it passes Židovska (literally "Jews' street"), one of the many steep lanes which run down from here to Placa and home to a tiny **synagogue** (summer Mon–Fri 10am–noon & 5–7pm, Sat 10am–noon)—said to be the oldest in the Balkans, dating from the fifteenth century.

The Rector's Palace, the Cathedral, and the Southern Part of the City

Beyond Sv Vlaho, on the left, is the **Rector's Palace** (daily 9am–4pm), the seat of the Ragusan government, in which the incumbent rector sat out his month's term of office. The building was, effectively, a prison: the rector had no real power and could only leave with the say-so of the nobles who elected him. He could have spent a month locked in worse places. Built in the fifteenth century by a loose partnership of three architects (which included Juraj Dalmatinac and Michelozzi), the palace is a masterpiece of quiet, unpretentious proportion, not dissimilar to the Sponza Palace, and fringed by an ornate arcaded loggia. Its Renaissance atrium is the site of summer concerts—worth catching if you can—from which an imposing staircase leads up to the balcony, and, off here, the former state rooms, including the rooms of the city council, the rector's study, and the quarters of the palace guard. Today these are devoted to the **City Museum** (daily 9am–4pm), though it's for the most part a rather paltry collection, with mediocre fifteenth-century paintings and dull furniture. The highlight is the work of the fifteenth-century Dalmatian artist, Blaž Jurjev, notably a polyptych of *Our Lady*.

Across the square from the palace, Dubrovnik's **Cathedral** (Mon–Sat 9am–5pm, Sun variable) is a rather plain building, designed by Andrea Bufalini and built between 1672 and 1731, that even the city's official guide admits is a "very unsuccessful specimen of Roman Baroque." The last church was destroyed by the 1667 earthquake, and is supposed to have been funded by a votive gift from Richard the Lionhearted, who may well have been ship-wrecked (and saved) off Ragusa on his way back from the Third Crusade. Excavations of the previous building are going on now—you can't miss the hole in the floor where they're working—but it's unlikely that anything of great interest will be turned up. Otherwise, a couple of Italian paintings, including a polyptych of *The Assumption* by Titian, are about all there is to draw you in to the church itself, though the **Treasury** (same times), hiding behind heavy wooden doors with three keyholes (for three keys held separately by the rector, the bishop, and a nobleman), has a viewable collection. One of the prime exhibits is a twelfth-century skull reliquary of St Blaise, an exquisite piece in the shape of a Byzantine crown, stuck with portraits of saints and frosted with delicate gold and enamel filigree work. Even more eye-catching is a bizarre fifteenth-century *Allegory of the Flora and Fauna of Dubrovnik* in the form of a jug and basin festooned with snakes, fish, and lizards clambering over thick clumps of seaweed. Rebecca West described it as having "the infinite elaborateness of eczema."

From the cathedral, it's a short walk through to the small town harbor, dominated by the monolithic hulk of the **Fort of Sv Ivan** (daily 9am–8pm). The fort has been refurbished to house a downstairs aquarium, full of Mediterranean marine life; upstairs it houses a museum of naval artifacts together with a few rooms with stuffed birds. The exhibits don't really justify the high entrance cost. The harbor was once the main maritime access point to the city, though by the sixteenth century the Gruž harbor had already become Dubrovnik's main port area. Nowadays it's given over to pleasure boats, and the ferries which run across to the island of Lokrum, just offshore.

Walking back east from here, you skirt one of the city's oldest quarters, **Pustijerna**, much of which predates the seventeenth-century earthquake. On the far side, the church of **Sv Ignacija**, Dubrovnik's largest, is the church of the Jesuits, modeled, like most Jesuit places of worship, on the enormous church of Gesù in Rome. The steps that lead down from here also had a Roman model—the Spanish Steps—and they sweep down to **Gundulićeva Poljana**, the square behind the cathedral which is the site of the city's morning fruit and vegetable market. The statue in the middle is of Ivan Gundulić, the early seventeenth-century poet and a native of Dubrovnik who wrote a long poem, *Osman*, on the battles between the Turks and Christian Slavs, and after whom the square is named. From here, Od Puča leads west through the mazy center of the city, stepped alleys branching right to meet the southern seawalls. On the right, there's a nineteenth-century Serbian Orthodox church, and just beyond, a **Museum of Icons** containing fifteenth- to eighteenth-century work by local artists. Make a right from here up Od Domina and you come to the **Rupe Granary Museum**, a municipal grain store from the sixteenth century that contains a dull lapidarium and a reasonable collection of Yugoslav national costumes—though it's currently closed for restoration.

Out of the Old City: Beaches, Islands, and Mount Srdj

The main city **beach** is a short walk beyond the Ploče Gate—despite tremendous efforts to clean it up, grubby, noisy, and crowded thick with radios and flirting adolescents.

There are quieter, rocky spots to swim from on the other side of town near the Pile Gate, close to Fort Lovrijenac (walk up the hill for about 100m; take the turning up the stone stairway by Maršala Tita 27), and you can sometimes swim from the hotel beaches on Lapad, though this can be costly. The best bet is to catch one of the boats from the old city jetty, beyond Luž square, to the wooded island of **LOKRUM**. Boats leave every half hour and take ten minutes to make the crossing (May–Oct 9am–6pm; $1.50 return). Reputedly the island where Richard the Lionhearted was shipwrecked, Lokrum is crisscrossed by shady paths overhung by pines and has a small salt lake smack in the middle. There's FKK swimming on the far side. The remains of a Benedictine monastery house a poor restaurant—better to take your own food—near the Botanical Gardens where odd varieties of giant Ttriffid-like cactus look as if they could swallow you whole. You can't get lost—the whole place is meticulously signposted. One other point: you won't be allowed on to the island with a backpack.

Immediately behind the old town, a **cable car** leaves every half an hour from May to October between 9am and 9pm—otherwise 9am to 4pm—for the summit of **Mount Srdj**, 412m high and crowned by the **Fort Imperial**, built by Napoleon's occupying army in 1808.

Food, Drink, and . . . the Summer Festival

Recent liberalizing measures by the government have probably affected Dubrovnik more than any other city; new restaurants have sprung up all over the **old town**, and prices have predictably shot through the roof. Prijeko, especially, is stacked with restaurants, all of them pricey and many of them indistinguishable from each other. You could try *Konoba Moby Dick*, which is reasonable. Down below Prijeko, the rest of the old town has a handful of cheaper places, particularly around the cathedral. The *Spaghetti Club* on **Gundulićeva** Poljana is deservedly popular, with excellent pizzas, as is *Jug* at Izmedju Polača 6. *Konoba Cavtat* on Od Puč serves good traditional dishes; the *Višnjica* restaurant on Miha Pracata is also worth a try. Nearby, the self-service *Express*, next to Sv Vlaho at Lučarica 2, is the cheapest of the bunch. If you're prepared to travel out to **Gruž** you can get the same food at much cheaper prices. Try the Café-Restaurant *Gruž*, near the ferry terminal on Gruška Obala. There's also a restaurant with a large vegetarian menu on Aleja i Lola Ribara out in **Lapad**.

For picnics, there are produce **markets** every morning (Mon–Sat) on Gundulićeva Poljana and on the waterfront in Gruž—where you can also buy fresh fish as soon as the boats come in. In the old town, there are a number of **supermarkets** on Od Puča, though once again you're better off in the shops around the Gruž harbor—or even along Maršala Tita as it climbs up from the Pile Gate.

The Summer Festival

Dubrovnik's **Summer Festival** (roughly July 10–Aug 25) is a good, if crowded, time to be in town, with concerts and performances in most of Dubrovnik's courtyards, squares, and bastions—sometimes the only chance to see the inside of them. Seats can be pricey, but it's possible to get in free once a performance has begun (say at the first intermission) if seats are available. Further details from the tourist or *Atlas* office at Pile 1.

Listings

Airlines *Adria*, Obala Bratstva i Jedinstva bb (☎581-711); *JAT*, Pile 7 (☎20-055; daily 7am–10pm). *JAT* also has an office behind the main bus station—the main city air terminal.

Atlas Pile 1 (☎27-333).

Bookshops The bookshop around the corner from the tourist office has a good selection of maps and English books on Yugoslav art.

Buses During the summer season and at weekends buses out of Dubrovnik can be crowded, so it's important to get a ticket well before the scheduled departure time. This doesn't apply to buses heading south through Dubrovnik from points north; on these services advance reservations are not possible and tickets only go on sale about one hour before departure.

Car rental There are three agencies close together on Frana Supila: *Alpetour* (☎23-747); *Autotehna* (☎26-477); *Inex* (☎26-917). *Kompas-Hertz* is at Aleja I.L. Ribara 50 (☎23-799).

Ferries There are a bewildering number of ferry connections from Gruž, and a bewildering array of people selling tickets. The main coastal ferry runs south from Dubrovnik to Bar and north to Korčula, Hvar, Split, Zadar, Rab, and Rijeka, between mid-March and mid-October, 3–4 times weekly with occasional onward international destinations. Tickets from *Jadrolinija* at Gruška Obala 74 (☎23-068), by the ferry terminal. For international ferry and other tickets, try *Jadroagent*, behind the Jadrolinija office at Gruška Obala 63 (☎23-464). There are also local ferries from Gruž once daily to Koločep (Donje Čelo), Lopud, Šipan, and Mljet, though the return service from Mljet leaves at 4am Tues–Fri, 3:30am Sat, but at 4pm Sun. The *Hotel Koločep* also runs a small boat service to the villages of Donje and Gornje Čelo on Koločep 3 times daily each way. *Atlas* operate a twice-daily service to Cavtat (May–Sept).

Luggage consignment At the bus station (daily 5am–10pm).

Post office/telephone Maršala Tita 16 (daily 7am–8pm).

Swimming pools There's a municipal swimming pool behind the bus station.

Tourist excursions *Atlas* runs a whole range, including trips to Mostar, Medugorje, Sarajevo, Kotor, Cetinje, Korčula, the Elaphite Islands, and the intriguing "Fish Picnic—clothes optional."

Trains The nearest railroad station is at Kardeljevo, about 60km north.

The Elaphite Islands

The string of islands that crowd the sea between Dubrovnik and the Pelješac peninsula are known as the **Elaphites** or "deer islands," a name apparently first coined by Pliny the Elder in his 37-volume *Naturalis Historia*. Part of the Dubrovnik state from the fourteenth century, the Elaphites were maritime satellites of their powerful neighbor, sharing in its prosperity. In Dubrovnik's golden age their economies blossomed and fleets grew, while rich city merchants dotted the islands with elegant summer villas. The decline that followed was abrupt, and, by the middle of the eighteenth century, many island villages lay abandoned and depopulation had become a major problem. Today, only three of the islands are inhabited—**Koločep**, **Lopud**, and **Šipan**—each of which supports a modest tourist industry, but for which they would undoubtedly be deserted. Of the three, Lopud is perhaps the most developed; elsewhere tourism is fairly low key, with the absence of cars (private vehicles are not allowed on the islands) only contributing to the mellow feel.

Koločep

Just half an hour from Dubrovnik by ferry, the islet of **KOLOČEP** is just one square mile in area, and has a population of under 500 concentrated in two main hamlets, **DONJE ČELO** where the Dubrovnik/Lopud ferry docks, on the north side of the island, and **GORNJE ČELO** to the southeast. There are no special sights on the island, but both villages are pleasant, quiet places that are almost overrun by a mass of fragrant vegetation; the road that connects the two makes for an enjoyable walk. If you want to stay, a limited number of **rooms** are available at both settlements, but in season it's advisable to reserve ahead. Phone the island's one hotel, the *Koločep*, for reservations in private accommodation (☎050/24-244). The **hotel** itself is in Gornje Čelo, but it has an annex, *Villa Lovor*, at Donje Čelo; rooms here cost around $40 a double.

Ferries run once daily from Dubrovnik, and the hotel runs its own private boat service (3 times daily) from Gruž to Gornje and Donje Čelo. Donje Čelo has the better **beach**.

Lopud

In Ragusa's heyday, **LOPUD** was the seat of one of the Republic's vice-rectors, and, with a population of some 4000 (today it's 400), was a favored watering-hole of the city's nobles. As Lopud flourished so the islanders developed their own merchant fleet, becoming famous for their skill as seafarers. They were, however, unable to compete with the larger maritime nations of western Europe, and by the time Napoleon's armies reached Dubrovnik in 1808 Lopud was in decay.

Today, the island's only village straggles around a wide, curving bay behind a long and crowded sandy(ish) beach and enjoys the fruits of a booming package tourist business. Every night throughout the season the water-front crawls with vacationers dipping into pricey bars and bistros. There's only one village on the island, its most prominent monument the fifteenth-century fortified **Franciscan Monastery**, which overlooks the town at the head of the bay. It's mostly a ruin now, and the attached church has a leaky roof and a bad case of woodworm in the choir—though they're both scheduled for eventual restoration. The nearby village **museum** (daily 3–4pm; guided tours on Thurs at 9am) is in a better state of repair, but the exhibits are of little interest, except perhaps for the sailors' votive plates and two large paintings of the town arms: no one's sure whether the snake is eating or regurgitating the boy.

Practical Details

The best thing to do in Lopud village is leave, by way of the easy footpaths that crisscross the entire island. If you're eager to stay, **rooms** are available from the *Atlas* office on the seafront (April–Oct Mon–Sat 8am–noon & 6–8pm). Alternatively, the island has three **hotels**, best and cheapest of which is *Dubrava Pracat* (☎050/87-205), with doubles for $37. The **ferry** to Dubrovnik (and Koločep) only sails once daily but the hotels run additional courtesy services—details in the hotel foyers—plus there's a daily ferry service on to Mljet (Mon–Sat).

Šipan

The largest and least developed of the populated Elaphites, the island of **ŠIPAN** is a delightful combination of craggy hills surrounding a long, fertile plain thick with olive and vine trees and dotted with the occasional hamlet. There are no special sites and there's certainly no nightlife, but if you're after some peace and quiet and some gentle hikes, this is one of the best places on the coast.

There are two settlements on the island: **ŠIPANSKA LUKA** and tiny **SUDJURADJ**. Buried at the end of a deep inlet, Šipanska Luka is a pretty little place with the occasional relic of former glories—best are the remains of the Magistrate's Palace, ten minutes along the road to Sudjuradj. Otherwise, perhaps the most curious building is on the seafront where the neglected remains of a splendid villa, with a balcony supported by carved lions, seems to beg for restoration. The problem is apparently one of ownership; the building was abandoned after the last war and no one has been able to decide what to do with it since.

Practical Details

Ferries from Dubrovnik make the one-hour trip here from Lopud once daily, except on Sunday, calling at both settlements. The island's one **hotel**, the *Šipan*, is in Šipanska Luka (closed mid-Oct–April) and has information on private **rooms**—or you can just ask around. The hotel runs a courtesy boat service to SLANO on the mainland three times daily and sells a detailed guidebook on the Elaphites. The island can only cater to a maximum of 250 tourists and in the evenings you'll find most of them in the hotel restaurant or the couple of bars nearby. The island's main **beach** is a small strip of sand pressed against a thread of rock that separates the sea from the bay, a few minutes west of the hotel. There doesn't appear to be anywhere to stay in Sudjuradj, but it's a lovely seven-kilometer walk away across the island (no buses).

Mljet

Just to the south of the Peljesac peninsula, **MLJET** is a long, thin island, some 32km long and never more than 3km wide. Though almost entirely developed, it's one of the most beautiful of all Yugoslavia's Adriatic islands; very green and exceptionally unspoiled, to the extent that the western section has been designated a national park. Surprisingly, it's largely unvisited and those people who do come are usually on day trips and seldom stay.

Mljet has fair claim to being the island of Melita, where Saint Paul ran aground on his way to Italy and was bitten by a viper before he set sail again. Certainly Mljet did once have a problem with snakes, and a colony of mongooses had to be imported from India to get rid of them. More definitely, the Romans used the island as a place of exile, and finally, in 1333, it was sold to the Ragusans by a Bosnian prince.

Today, the island's tiny villages are dotted along Mljet's only road, as it crosses from one end of the island to the other. The former capital and largest village, **BABINO POLJE**, is about halfway down at the foot of the highest mountain. The best part of the island is the western end, where untouched Mediterranean forest forms the **Mljet National Park** (entry $2) and covers the hills in luxuriant greens and browns. There are three main settlements in the park. **POLAČE** serves as the island's main port, but is no more than a formless sprawl attached to the monumental ruins of a fourth-century AD Roman palace; **GOVEDJARI** is a tiny farmers' village heaped up high on a bluff; **POMENA** is a tourist complex built round the dreary *Hotel Odisej*.

From Pomena you can walk up to the Mjlet's two sea-water lakes, **Malo** and **Veliko Jezero**, Mljet's main attraction and the target in summer of regiments of tourists who arrive by hydrofoil from the mainland. That said, they never get all that busy, and once the day-trippers have gone, you'll have the cool, clear, blue-green waters and the shaded lake-shore walks almost to yourself—and the swimming is delicious. One path leads to an **FKK beach**. There are irregular boat services to the **Hotel Melita**, sited in the old Benedictine monastery on an islet in Veliko Jezero. You can just visit this and leave, but the hotel itself makes for an appealing place to stay, too, its rooms conversions of the old monastic cells. During the day a boat shuttles across the lake to and from the hotel, but at night all is silence apart from the bar and the (reasonable) restaurant.

One other place to **swim** is at the furthest eastern point of the island, beyond the end of the official road, down a track. Here there's a gorgeous long sandy beach—one of the best in the country.

Practical Details

There are two ways of reaching POLAČE by **ferry**: from Trstenik on the Pelješac peninsula (2–5 daily; 90min), or from Dubrovnik and the Elaphites (1 daily, except Sun; 4hr; via the hamlets of Sobra and occasionally Okuklje and Kozarica). At Polače you'll be charged a disembarkation fee for entry into the national park. Incidentally if you come here by car, be sure to fill your tank before you leave—there's nowhere to get gas on the island.

Next to the jetty there's a **tourist kiosk** (July–Aug 9am–8pm; otherwise 9am–11:30am), but, unless you're prepared for a long walk, your best option is to catch the connecting bus from the ferry to POMENA (bus services on the island are almost uniformly terrible.) Pomena has a more reliable **tourist office** (daily in season only noon–5pm), to help arrange **rooms** or **apartments** either within the adjacent *Hotel Odisej* complex (☎050/754-205), in nearby Govedjari or at the *Hotel Melita* (☎050/754-315). The latter's doubles cost around $38, the *Odisej*'s slightly more. The tourist office will also provide a useful **map** of the island. The *Odisej* hotel also rents out **bikes** and has a competent restaurant. The main **campground** is at Govedjari, ten minutes' walk from Pomena, close to the inland lakes. It's a shady place, with a store, great views across the sea, and access to some excellent places for swimming.

If you reach Mljet on a **tourist excursion** from Dubrovnik or Korčula (and this is sometimes a good, and not terribly expensive way of getting here), you'll arrive at Pomena, and this is by far the easiest way to leave. Otherwise, **leaving**, the ferries from Polace to Trstenik are regular; the ferry to Dubrovnik leaves at 4am from Tuesday to Friday, 3:30am on Saturday but a merciful 4pm on Sunday. Negotiating your way onto one of the excursion boats on Mljet, however, can be difficult as no one knows exact times of departures—be flexible or reserve before you come.

Inland from Dubrovnik

Heading inland from Gruž, the Ombla River forms a deep estuary, the **Rijeka Dubrovačka**, a four-kilometer-long channel that was once a favorite resort of wealthy nobles during the period of the Ragusan republic. They built many villas here, a number of which still stand, and the area was much patronized in the nineteenth century by western travelers—though these days the look of the place has been completely spoiled by the modern city's industrial and residential sprawl, not to mention its huge new marina, and bathing was actually prohibited a few years back. Several of the villages along here still sport the odd villa, notably **KOMOLAC** and **ROŽAT**, but it's an area you pass through rather than make a special trip to see.

Trebinje

It's **TREBINJE**, a Hercegovinan Muslim town lying on a *polje* around 30km inland, to which most travelers come, ferried here from Dubrovnik in almost continuous tour-bus parties during summer in the search of the "mysterious east"—a situation that's unfair to both tourists and town. Once an important staging post on the trade routes into the interior, Trebinje sits surrounded by bleak karstland on either side of the sluggish, green Trebišnjica River, spanned by the enormous sixteenth-century **Arslanjić bridge**; since the early days of Dubrovnik's tourist industry it's been promoted as a money-spinning day trip, particularly on a Saturday when its now rather bogus market is held. Basically, if you do want to see oriental towns, save your energy for a deeper exploration of Bosnia and Hercegovina.

It's a drab modern town for the most part anyway, and the only part the tourists come to see is the clumsily fortified **Stari Grad**, with its smattering of eighteenth-century Turkish houses decked out as cafés and restaurants. To make matters worse the cafés are bordered by an apology for a covered bazaar and presided over by a dilapidated white hulk, formerly the Austro-Hungarian barracks. Only a few vestiges of the Ottoman tradition remain; the domeless **Osman Pasha Mosque**, built in the 1720s, is still in use, though it's normally closed, as is the **Imperial Mosque** from 1719, nearby. Outside of the old town and towards the bus station, signs direct you to the **Begova Kuća** or Bey's House, which turns out to be an unremarkable compound whose women's quarters now house a restaurant armed with waitresses in national costume. Surprisingly, the most interesting part of town isn't in the Stari Grad at all, but lies just to the north, near the river, in the labyrinth of tumbledown alleys and lanes of the **Krš**. Fronted by the ancient booths of Gaćinovića, for a moment these shambles give a flavor of what you imagined the "Balkans" to look and smell like—though to the Yugoslavs they're little more than a slum.

South of Dubrovnik: Cavtat and Čilipi

Immediately south of Dubrovnik you run into one of the most heavily developed parts of the coast, purpose-built resorts edging the road and obscuring all sights of the sea. The vast tourist settlement of **KUPARI** might be an alternative **campground** for Dubrovnik but that's about its only positive feature, while the settlements of **MLINI**, **SREBRENO**, and **PLAT** are dreadful blots on the landscape, given over entirely to multinational tour operators. Needless to say, if you do decide to stop, there are hundreds of places to eat and sleep.

Cavtat

Farther on, about a mile off the main coastal highway, lies the tourist resort of **CAVTAT**. Originally the ancient Greek colony of Epidaurus, Cavtat was evacuated in preference for Dubrovnik after a thorough ransacking by the Slavs in the seventh century. It was once a pretty coastal village and a favorite haunt of the wealthy, with a sweet-smelling wooded peninsula and a palm-fringed seafront. But its individuality has been bulldozed into oblivion by the rash of high-rise hotel blocks that has gone up here over the last five years.

Clogged with the extra visitors and disfigured by an excess of gift shops, the only hints of Cavtat's former charms survive in the old part of town, which heaps up the hill behind the waterfront. The showpiece here is the **Račić**

Mausoleum (10am–noon & 3–5pm), built by Ivan Meštrović on a prime spot high above the town for a local shipowning family in 1921. As a meditation on the nature of death it's a depressing sort of monument, with the cool, resounding, and ultimately rather empty kind of grandeur typical of Meštrović. You should also look in at the so-called **Captain's Residence**, which has a collection of engravings and a library of ancient books and manuscripts, and the house of the nineteenth-century Croatian painter Bukovac, which has been turned into a **museum** of his work (Tues–Sat 10am–noon & 4–7pm, Sun & Mon 4–7pm). Nearby there's also a cool but rather ordinary **grotto**.

Practical Details

The best uncrowded **beaches** are at the far end of the peninsula, ten minutes' walk from town, and rocky but well away from the hordes that congregate on the sandy beach in front of the hotels to the east of the center. There are **FKK facilities** just on the other side of the *Croatia* hotel. If you're staying, the town **campground** adjoins the *Albatross*, beyond the large peninsula, or ample **private rooms** are available from a chain of agencies along the waterfront, including the municipal **Reception for Private Accommodation** (daily June–Aug 7am–8pm; otherwise 7am–2pm) and the **Dubrovnik Tourist Agency** (June–Aug 7am–9pm; otherwise 8am–noon & 5–8pm). Cheap **food**, on the other hand, is hard to find, with most restaurants geared up for the more expensive end of the market. The pizzerias on the front are your cheapest option—try the *Amfora*. **Buses** to Dubrovnik leave every half hour.

Čilipi

South of Cavtat, **ČILIPI**, as well as being the site of Dubrovnik's airport, is the main village of the Konavle region, a small area known for the colorful costumes of the people who live here. They're not worn much any more, though Čilipi has become something of an excursion spot for tour operators from Dubrovnik, and buses hustle into the village's creamy-white central square every summer Sunday to catch the people in ethnic dress on their way to Mass. If this sounds appealing, there's a **tourist office** with rooms (daily 8am–noon & 4–7pm), as well as an inconsequential museum and lots of restaurants and bistros, not to mention souvenir shops. From Čilipi it's a short ride through rough-and-ready landscape to the town of HERCEG-NOVI and the republic of Montenegro . . .

travel details

Buses

From Rijeka to Belgrade (3 daily; 9hr); Cres/Mali Lošinj (6 daily; 4/5hr); Koper (4 daily; 2hr); Krk (3 daily; 1hr 30min); Ljubljana (6 daily; 3hr); Postojna (4 daily; 3hr); Pula (hourly; 2hr 30min); Senj (10 daily; 2hr); Rab (4 daily; 3hr); Split (8 daily; 8hr); Trieste (3 daily; 3hr); Zadar (8 daily; 4hr); Zagreb (hourly; 4hr).

From Zadar to Biograd (hourly; 1hr); Nin (8 daily; 45min); Plitvice (5; 3hr); Šibenik (hourly; 2hr); Split (hourly; 4hr); Trogir (hourly; 3hr); Zagreb (4 daily; 5hr).

From Split to Dubrovnik (hourly; 5hr); Klis (half-hourly; 35min); Livno (7 daily; 2hr); Makarska (hourly; 2hr); Rijeka (hourly; 8hr); Sarajevo (5 daily; 6hr 30min); Šibenik (hourly; 3hr); Sinj (hourly; 1hr); Zadar (hourly; 4hr); Zagreb (4 daily; 9hr).

From Dubrovnik to Belgrade (2 daily; 11hr); Cavtat (half-hourly; 40min); Herceg-Novi (15 daily; 1hr); Kotor (8 daily; 2hr); Bar (4 daily; 4hr); Cetinje (3 daily; 3hr); Nikšć (3 daily; 2hr 30min); Orebić/ Korčula (2–3 daily; 3hr); Rijeka (8 daily; 13hr); Split (14 daily; 5hr); Trebinje (hourly; 1hr); Ulcinj (2 daily; 6hr); Zadar (9 daily; 9hr); Mostar (7 daily; 3hr); Sarajevo (5 daily; 6hr); Trebinje (13 daily; 45min).

Trains

From Rijeka to Ljubljana (6 daily; 3hr); Zagreb (4 daily; 4hr 45min).

From Zadar to Knin (4 daily; 1hr 40min).

From Split to Belgrade (2 daily; 13hr); Zagreb (8 daily; 8hr).

From Kardeljevo to Mostar/Sarajevo (5 daily; 50min/3hr).

Coastal ferry

The **main Jadrolinija coastal ferry** sails from Rijeka to Dubrovnik around six times weekly between mid-March and mid-Oct, calling at the following ports: Rab, Zadar, Split, Hvar, Korčula, and, once a week, Bar in Montenegro. Journey-times from Rijeka are roughly: Rab (3hr 25min); Zadar (7hr 10min); Split (14hr); Hvar (16hr); Korčula (18hr 40min); Dubrovnik (22hr).

Local ferries

These details give only a rough idea of frequency and journey durations and should be supplemented with an up-to-date Jadrolinija timetable. Please note that details given are for ferry journeys during the summer season. Outside the June–Sept period, frequencies reduce drastically.

From Rijeka to Cres (1 daily; 2hr 30min); Mali Lošinj (1 daily; 6hr 30min).

From Brestova to Cres (Porozina) (hourly; 15min).

From Mali Lošinj to Pula (1 daily; 4hr 15min).

From Zadar to Silba/Mali Lošinj/Pula (6 weekly; 2hr 25min/5hr 20min/7hr 45min); Ugljan (Preko) (hourly; 30min); Dugi Otok (2 daily; 2hr 30min).

From Crikvenica to Krk (Šilo) (10 daily; 30min).

From Senj to Krk (Baška) (2 daily; 1hr); Rab (Lopar) (2 daily; 2hr).

From Krk (Baška) to Rab (Lopar) (10 daily; 1hr).

From Jablanac to Rab (Mišnjak) (hourly; 30min).

From Jablanac to Pag (Novalja) (6 daily; 1hr 30min).

From Karlobag to Pag (6 daily; 1hr).

From Biograd to Pašman (Tkon) (10 daily; 15min).

From Šibenik to Zlarin (6 daily; 30min); Vodice (4 daily; 1hr).

From Split to Šolta (5 daily; 1hr); Brač (Supetar) (10 daily; 1hr); Hvar (Starigrad) (4 daily; 2hr); Hvar (Vira) (3 daily; 2hr); Vis (2 daily; 3hr); Lastovo (2 daily; 6hr); Korčula (Vela Luka) (1 daily; 3hr 30min).

From Markarska to Brač (Sumartin) (6 daily; 30min).

From Drvenik to Hvar (Sućuraj) (10 daily; 20min).

From Kardeljevo to Trpanj (3–7 daily; 1hr).

From Orebić to Korčula (Dominče) (hourly; 15min).

From Trstenik to Mljet (Polače) (4 daily; 1hr 30min).

From Dubrovnik to Lopud/Mljet (1 daily except Sun; 1hr/4hr).

International ferries

From Rijeka to Igoumenitsa (3 weekly; 36hr).

From Zadar to Ancona (3 times a month; 8hr); Rimini (once weekly; 8hr); Trieste (3 times a month; 9hr).

From Split to Ancona (4 weekly; 8hr); Bari (1 weekly; 10hr); Pescara (5 weekly; 8hr); Trieste (3 times a month; 22hr); Venice (1 weekly; 14hr).

From Dubrovnik to Ancona (weekly; 15hr); Rimini (1 weekly; 26hr); Bari (5 weekly; 8hr); Venice (3 weekly; 24hr); Trieste (3 times a month; 32hr); Corfu (2 weekly; 25hr); Piraeus/Iraklion/ Alexandria (Oct–June only; 1 every 7–10 days).

From Bar to Bari (2 weekly; 10hr).

CHAPTER FOUR

MONTENEGRO

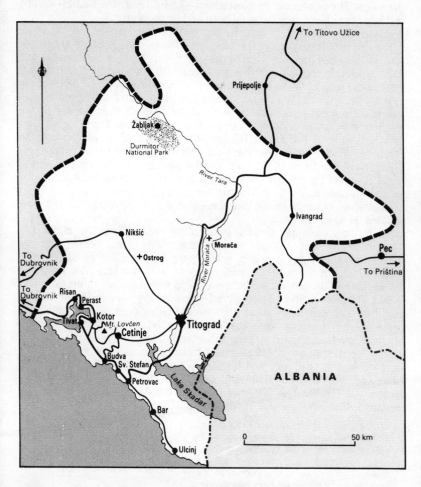

To Titovo Užice

Prijepolje

Žabljak

Durmitor
National Park

River Tara

Nikšić

✝Ostrog

River Morača

✝ Morača

Ivangrad

Pec

To
Dubrovnik

To Prištína

To
Dubrovnik   Risan

Perast

Tivat   Kotor

▲ Mt. Lovčen   Cetinje

Titograd

Budva
Sv. Stefan

Petrovac

Lake Skadar

ALBANIA

Bar

0   50 km

Ulcinj

Smallest of the six republics, **Montenegro** (*Crna Gora* in Serbo-Croat) packs in some of the most stunning scenery in the country, from the wild mountains of the sparsely populated interior to the azure, cliff-edged **Bay of Kotor** and the red coves and weathered rocks round **Budva**. Geographically and historically, Montenegro divides easily into two:

the coastal strip and the interior. With the notable exception of **Ulcinj**, which was for centuries controlled by Turkey, all the principal seaboard towns fell into the hands of the Venetians, whose occupation left its mark in the local culture and architecture. The best preserved are **Perast, Kotor Town**, and more arguably **Budva**. Nearly all of Montenegro's tourists stay on the coast where a rash of tourist settlements, hotels, and *autocamps* push up against the shore. The results can be horrendous—**Igalo, Tivat**, and **Bečiči**—but by and large the older towns have not been unduly disfigured.

Inland, vast mountain ranges rise harsh and rugged against the sky while below the occasional road or track snakes its way through barely accessible terrain—into cavernous canyons or past snow-topped peaks, glacial lakes and deep forests. In this inhospitable land there are few large settlements and most of the smaller towns and alpine-style villages are cut off for much of the year by the snows of the brutal winters. Although tourist facilities are minimal and camping is difficult because of the violent inconsistency of the weather, the interior is not short of particular attractions. These include two excellent national parks, the **Biogradska Mora** near Mojkovac and the **Durmitor Park** near Žanljak; the **Monastery of Morača** (if you're traveling by car); and the drama of the **Tara** and **Rugovo** gorges. By comparison the major towns of the interior are a disappointment except for **Cetinje**, a must for its museums and setting. The trip here from the coast is one of the most breathtaking journeys in the Balkans—and a vivid reminder of just how isolated the town once was.

As for **the people**, there's been more rubbish written about the Montenegrins than almost anyone else. The epic poems of the nineteenth-century Montenegrin ruler Petar Njegoš II carry part of the responsibility for the ludicrous caricatures of "pistol-packing Montenegrin," but in the end the latter have far more to do with a certain romantic vision within Victorian politics. From Byron onwards, key figures in the British establishment were inspired by the nascent nationalism of the south Slav peoples—and not only were the Montenegrins of the day fighting the Muslims, but they were also doing this from a "romantic" mountain fastness in what seemed to be an extravagantly picturesque national costume. They were perfect for their role and it's hardly surprising that after a chat with Gladstone, Alfred Lord Tennyson picked up the theme in his *Ode to Montenegro* (1877). This did more to trap the Montenegrins within the stereotype than anything else. As the poet put it:

> *O smallest among peoples! rough rock-throne*
> *Of Freedom! warriors beating back the swarm*
> *Of Turkish Islam for five hundred years,*
> *Great Tsernogora! never since thine own*
> *Black ridges drew the cloud and brake the storm*
> *Has breathed a race of mightier mountaineers.*

The truth is very different. Cetinje *was* conquered by the Turks, but it was too poor and insignificant to garrison; the Montenegrins *did* fight the Turks, but then they also fought the Venetians *for* the Turks—it largely depended on the bribe. In any case, they were far more interested in fighting against each other—clan against clan, tribe against tribe in an endless series of blood feuds; and finally these "freedom-loving" people had a whole line of autocratic rulers who were resisted either because they proposed to tax everyone or because they were from another clan. These struggles had nothing at all to do with "freedom" (or nationalism) until well into the nineteenth century.

What is remarkable about the history of Montenegro is the early popularity of the Communist Party and its ability to override clan loyalty; during World War II, the vast majority of Montenegrins were supportive of or involved in Partisan activity—which is more than can be said for nearly all the other occupied countries. Neither was this a freak occurrence; as early as 1919 underground Communist Party cells were common in Cetinje, recruiting and organizing workers and peasants.

And this is the rub. The Montenegrins paid dearly for their opposition to Fascism—but it was an ideological struggle, and when the guidebooks reduce these brave people to the status of "indomitable tribesmen" they do them a great disservice. Indomitable they were, but it was for a cause, not because they were born to it.

The Gulf of Kotor

Dominating the Montenegrin seaboard, the **Gulf of Kotor** (*Boka Kotorska*) is undoubtedly the single most impressive coastal feature in Yugoslavia, and in terms of sheer natural beauty is hard to beat anywhere in Europe. More a series of inland fjords than gulf, the green and massive mountains that border Kotor sweep down into the deep clear water, while behind them the stark Njeguši range culminates in **Mount Lovčen**, 1749m high and one of the country's most dramatic peaks. At night the waters of the Gulf lie black and profound, mirroring the star-hung skies that rise above the featureless silhouettes of the mountains, and across the water the sound of birds and boat engines carries clearly for miles.

The Gulf of Kotor is certainly beautiful, but it's avoided the worst excesses of the tourist industry because it has so few beaches. The exception is **Igalo/Herceg-Novi**, at the mouth of the gulf, which with its pebble sea-shore is as crowded a spot as almost anywhere on the coast. The only other comparable resort in the area is **Tivat**, a remarkably charmless and squalid affair a mile or so from the gulf's airport. Of the other three main settlements, **Risan** is a dreary disappointment but **Kotor Town** and tiny **Perast** are delightful, both in their setting and in their ancient buildings—though there's no beach to speak of at either.

The Adriatic Highway runs south from Dubrovnik, past Herceg-Novi, and on to KAMENARI where a shuttle **ferry** crosses to LEPETANE, reducing traffic round the back of the Gulf to a trickle. **Bus** services along the main road are excellent, but Perast and Risan are also easy to reach from Kotor and Herceg-Novi. All five of the main places around the gulf offer **rooms**, though demand tends to outstrip supply during July and August; arrive early to avoid disappointment.

Some History

Such a perfect harbor was bound to attract the attention of the great medieval powers and for centuries Turkey and Venice (among others) sought to wrest control of the gulf either from each other or from the pirates who had dominated the region during the Dark Ages. It was a chaotic conflict, for neither of the protagonists was ever quite strong enough to secure the whole area and, in the prevailing confusion, the gulf's tiny towns kept much of their independence—Perast by loyalty to Venice and Kotor by switching from side to side. By the end of the seventeenth century, the decline of the Ottoman Empire meant that Venice could at last assume control, only to be superseded by the Austrians in 1797. In the nineteenth and early twentieth centuries, an independent Montenegro was desperate to gain access to the sea, and the interminable negotiations with Austria that followed were yet another source of Balkan tension that helped push Europe into war. In 1918 the Gulf of Kotor was joined to the state of Yugoslavia, and it was from here in April 1941 that the royalist Yugoslav government fled into what turned out to be permanent exile.

Throughout these troubled times, the sailors of the gulf maintained a fabulous reputation for their skill and bravery—most notably, the navigators of the victorious Venetian fleet at Lepanto were from Perast, and when Peter the Great determined to build a fleet, he turned to the Gulf for the backbone of his navy. Neither were they abject mercenaries, for the bay's sailors always insisted on a degree of autonomy or at least recognition: men from Perast usually guarded the Venetian battle standard, and in Kotor the Venetian governor handed over the keys of the town to representatives of the municipal fleet for three days every year.

In 1979 the gulf was hit by the most severe **earthquake** in living memory, though the worst of the damage was confined to Kotor town where many of the ancient buildings were reduced to rubble. Since then, there's been an extensive and spectacular program of restoration and—with the exception of Kotor's cathedral—everything is back to normal.

Herceg-Novi

Tumbling down a steep hillside at the mouth of the Gulf, the town of **HERCEG-NOVI** was founded by the Bosnian king Tvrtko in 1382 to give Bosnia access to the sea. Its obvious strategic value ensured the town a stormy history and in a dizzying succession of rulers it changed hands a dozen times, though most of what you see today was built by the Venetians, Turks, and Austro-Hungarians—a mixed heritage that's left a ragbag of styles.

Edged by the tedious modernity of the resort of IGALO to the immediate west, Herceg-Novi boasts a string of new hotels that have made it one of the most popular tourist destinations on the Montenegrin coast. Thronged with visitors, the old city streets are dotted with restaurants and bars, while way down below, the massed hordes press onto the best patches of the rock and pebble beach.

Arrival, Rooms, and Food

Herceg-Novi's **bus station** is on the main coastal road at the edge of town, a few minutes' walk up from the seafront. Services up and down the coast are excellent—especially to Dubrovnik, an hour or so away (see "Travel Details"). Private **rooms** are available from a number of tourist agencies in and around the central square, though the city **tourist office**, *Savina* (daily in season 7am–9pm; otherwise Mon–Sat, 7am–2pm), is on the seafront near the harbor. There's an **autocamp** near the Savina Monastery, some 3km east of the bus station towards Kotor.

For **food**, cheap snacks and giant *burek*s are available at the bus station and ice cream and cappuccino from a number of coffee bars by the harbor. For more substantial meals try the restaurants along Njegoševa as it heads off from the clock tower towards Igalo; *Restoran Glicinija*, opposite the supermarket, is as good as any.

The Town

Twisting down the hill just behind and below the bus station, several paths snake through the **Austro-Hungarian** part of town. Here, faded villas wallow in wisteria, bougainvillea, palms, and orange trees as they explode from every inch of available ground, pricking color against a backdrop of deep, fecund green. Even now these streets hint at the genteel respectability that made Herceg-Novi a favorite holiday spot for the bourgeoisie of nineteenth-century Vienna.

Adjoining this section and halfway between the bus station and the sea, the main square's Ruritanian **clock tower** serves as the promising entrance to the **Old Town**—though what lies beyond is a disappointment. Apart from a few antiseptically restored Venetian houses, there's really nothing of any interest, just an incoherent jumble of city wall and fortification trailing down from the main road onto the shore where a section has collapsed into the sea. High above the town, the sixteenth-century **Spanish Fort** is little better; reduced to a few crumbling heaps of stone by the 1979 earthquake, it's only worth the steep walk for the view over Herceg-Novi and the entrance to the Gulf beyond.

Herceg-Novi's best building isn't in the center at all but lies to the east, a twenty-minute walk away. Head out of town along the shore past the *Hotel Plaža*, cut up the first flight of steps, take the first major right onto Braće Grakalić and the **Monastery of Savina** is dead ahead, on a wooded hillock by the side of the road. Founded in the seventeenth century by refugee monks from Trebinje, the monastery has two churches standing side by side and is dedicated to Saint Sava, the most revered saint of the Serbian Orthodox church. The larger of the two churches is a cheerful meeting of Byzantine and Baroque, with a splendid eighteenth-century iconostasis where Christ looks down from above a rather odd skull and crossbones. The churches are fringed by renovated *konaks*, one of which contains the monastery's **museum** that's stuffed with gold and silver ornaments, it's centerpiece a thirteenth-century crystal cross that reputedly belonged to Saint Sava himself.

Herceg-Novi to Risan

From Herceg-Novi the main road cuts northeast along the side of the gulf to KAMENARI, where a ferry shuttle crosses a narrow neck of water to LEPETANE for the faster route to Kotor town. Bypassed by the ferry, the road around the back of the gulf carries little traffic and is a spectacular trip through a string of hamlets perched nervously between titanic mountains and the sea. **RISAN**, the first settlement of any note, was the one-time capital of the Illyrians and it was here in 299 BC that their queen, Teuta, committed suicide after her defeat at the hands of the Romans. Subsequently attached to the Roman province of Dalmatia, Risan was comprehensively destroyed by the Saracens in the ninth century. The possibility of Illyrian finds attracted archaeologists—Sir Arthur Evans included—though there's remarkably little to show for their efforts; best are the second-century **mosaics** by the entrance to the hospital. For the rest, the modern town is nothing more than new houses and weekend villas sloping down to the sea. **Rooms** are available at the **tourist office** by the shore.

Perast

Two kilometers around the bay from Risan sits **PERAST**, one of the loveliest places in Montenegro and under Venetian control for nearly 400 years. The houses that run by the waterside are toytown Venetian Gothic, with a homey grandeur that's the residue of a magnificent past. For close to half a millennium Perast was the muscle of Adriatic maritime strength, holding forth against repeated Turkish attacks when the rest of the gulf had fallen. The sailors of Venice and later Russia came to the nautical school here and learned the skills of Perast's mariners; its cartographers charted the coasts; its navigators steered the Venetian fleet at Lepanto; its engineers designed ports in the Baltic. Eventually earthquakes, political maneuvering and simple age took away Perast's preeminence and left it to a graceful retirement. A **Museum** (Mon–Sat 8am–1pm; may be closed awaiting restoration) in what was once the palace of the town's leading nautical family keeps a few tokens of naval exploits from later years, but it's not all that memorable. What is is the view of the town, best seen by climbing up the hillside between the decaying houses that are unconcernedly falling back to nature, grass and ivy exploring the front rooms of the seventeenth century. Down on the seafront, captains' houses look confidently out to the entrance of the gulf, and over the red roofs the mountains ring the tranquil sea. Perast is picturesque in the full sense of the word.

You may need to hunt around on the waterfront for someone to take you to one or both of the **islands** that float like rafts off Perast; guided tours are irregular, and it's easier, if a little more expensive, to rent a small boat—going rate for this is about $8. Darkened by cypresses **Sv Djordje** has a much-restored Benedictine abbey and little else. Its companion, **Gospa od Škrpjela** ("Our Lady of the Chisels"), is more interesting. To trace its origins you have to choose your legend. In one, a sailor, shipwrecked in the gulf, clung to a stone here one night, promising that if he survived he'd build a church to the Virgin on the rock. Morning and rescue came; the sailor kept his word and dumped stones until the island rose. The alternative, a little less colorful, is that on July 22, 1452 two sailors found an icon of the Virgin and Child on the rock and took it to Perast; next day it was found that the icon had mysteriously made its way back to the rock, so the Perastians built it an island and fittingly grand church. Though severely battered and rebuilt over the years the church remains, and in the sea-blue and seaweed-green Baroque interior you can still find the miraculous icon, held in a marble altar-piece of great value—for the green Italian marble the Perastians paid an equal weight of silver. The icon was much revered by the gulf's sailors, and round the walls are 2000 silver ex-voto plaques, promised to the Virgin in moments of peril and given on safe return. And in the small museum next door a room is crammed with gifts from those who survived shipwreck; a treasury of everyday objects—plates, cutlery, even sewing machines.

Each year the villagers hold two **celebrations** of the island and its icon, and if you're around these are well worth joining in. On July 22 a great procession—the *fasinada*—sails out to strengthen the island with new boulders, and on August 15 the icon is taken to Perast's church to commemorate a battle with the Turks in which the Virgin appeared in horrific form, scaring off the attackers and saving the day for the Perastians. Less religiously, on June 3 local marksmen enjoy a game called *gadjanje kokota*—shooting the cock. This involves tying an unfortunate rooster to a piece of wood and floating him out into the bay. The locals then blast away with assorted arms, and when the feathers settle someone is declared the best shot and everyone goes off to get drunk. Tough chaps these Montenegrins.

You can see all of Perast in an hour or so, but you'll probably want to stay longer. The **tourist office** seems to have vanished into thin air, but if you're after a **room** you'll probably be approached at the bus stop. Failing that, follow the usual signs around town—though things get tight in high season. There's one small **hotel**, the *Villa Perast* (☎082/72-235; doubles $60), whose **food** is inexpensive, a couple of bar/restaurants, and a good bus service on to Kotor and Herceg-Novi once or twice an hour during the day, less on Sundays. There's no beach.

Kotor

Tucked away at the end of the gulf, the town of **KOTOR** sticks determinedly to the steep sides of Mount Lovčen in one of the most dramatic settings in all of Yugoslavia. First colonized by the Greeks, Kotor flourished from the twelfth century as the chief port of the Serbian state of Raška, though the town was very much an independent commune whose commercial power came to rival that of Dubrovnik. The golden years didn't last long, for the town's position was undermined by the Turkish conquests of the fifteenth century and forced to seek the protection of Venice in 1420—beginning a long and slow decline punctuated by siege, earthquake, and plague.

At 7:19am on April 15, 1979, Kotor's citizens felt the full force of an earthquake that reduced much of their old town to a smouldering heap. Doggedly, the Montenegrins shored up what was left and made a tremendous effort to restore the old town in the minimum amount of time possible. As a result, everything but the cathedral is already back to normal and Kotor is once again one of the best examples of a medieval walled town on the entire coast.

Practicalities

Kotor's **bus station** is a few minutes' walk south of the old town by the road to Budva/Cetinje. Local buses to Perast and Risan leave from outside the main town gate every half-hour or so on weekdays; the Sunday service is poor.

A number of agencies in the old town arrange private **rooms**, including *Montenegro Express* (Mon–Sat 7am–8pm), just inside the main town gate, with a branch office at the *Hotel Fjord* open on Sundays 8am to noon. The unmarked kiosk in front of the town gate is the municipal **tourist office** (opens 9am). Unfortunately there are no rooms in the old town and you'll be condemned to the formless suburbs. Kotor has two **hotels**, the monstrous *Fjord* (☎082/11-113; doubles $70), stuck incongruously on the shore with a sort of concrete make-believe beach, and the over-priced *Vardar* (☎082/16-663; doubles $66), behind the town gate overlooking the main square. The nearest **campground** is about 3km out along the Perast road, in DOBROTA.

The streets of the old town are dotted with snack bars—one of the most popular is opposite the cathedral. On the other hand, **restaurants** are few and far between; the best is the *Galion* (sea-food specialties) near the *Hotel Fjord*. The produce **market** is by the shore in front of the town walls.

The Old Town

Kotor's old town spreads out along the side of the gulf behind its west wall, a confusion of twisting streets and tiny squares framed by a mountain slope, where the thin line of the east wall zigzags up to an apex at the fortress of Sv Ivan. Most of what you see today is Venetian and dates from the fifteenth century, though the ramparts were started by the Byzantines some six centuries earlier.

In an outpouring of revolutionary fervor, the main **town gate** is inscribed with the date of the Liberation and one of Tito's many aphorisms—"What belongs to others we don't want, what is ours we'll never surrender." Inside, the central square is surrounded by an indeterminate mix of buildings including the **Rector's Palace**, the **Town Hall**, the *Hotel Vardar* and a particularly squat **clock tower**—the tower is seventeenth-century, the clock was the idea of the French garrison. An alley on the right side of the square leads through the studied elegance of the mansions of Trg Oslobodjenja and around onto Trg Ustanka Mornara (Square of the Sailors' Revolt) where the Austro-Hungarians held the public trial of the leaders of a 1918 mutiny.

The east side of the square is dominated by the twin towers of the **Cathedral of Sv Tryphon** (closed until 1991), a rather austere structure that's predominantly Romanesque once you get past a fine front added in the seventeenth century after one of Kotor's many earlier earthquakes did away with the original. Just inside is an intricately carved doorway, single survivor of the ninth-century rotunda on which the later church was built. Its open basilica plan is sparse and light, only the ciborium straddling the altar catching the eye; red marble columns support a triangular awning crowned with an angel and richly decorated with scenes from the life of Saint Tryphon. Kotor came to have Tryphon as its patron saint in 890, when a passing merchant ship loaded with relics offered the townspeople a good deal on its most precious object, the head of the saint who'd been put to death 600 years earlier. This bargain was much too good to miss, and Tryphon's head still rests in the cathedral's **treasury** (also closed). Other exhibits include a superb medieval wooden crucifix, as full of the horror of suffering as anything crafted by contemporary German carvers, and dozens of reliquaries like so many dolls' limbs dipped in silver—bits of arm and leg of dubious origin gathered over the centuries: the earlier ones are best.

Another alley leads north from the cathedral square to Trg Bokeljske Mornarice, where the **Maritime Museum** is housed in a refurbished seventeenth-century mansion. A routine display of weapons, model ships, and costumes, nothing really catches the eye except perhaps for the incidental photographs of the turn-of-the-century town. In the center of the next square to the north, the twelfth church of **Sv Luka** (daily in season 9am–1pm & 5–8pm) is Romanesque in conception with a Byzantine-style dome over the nave. Look out for the immaculately restored, golden crucifix above the iconostasis. The north **town wall** is close by, with its tiny gate and attached footbridge spanning the green river Škurda. From the square adjoining the gate you can track around the back of town for the steep climb up to the dilapidated fifteenth-century church of Gospa od Zdravlja and on up to the fortress of **Sv Ivan**—well worth it for the superb views.

For the rest, just go for a stroll . . . you can't get lost.

West of Kotor Town: Tivat

The main coastal road from Dubrovnik to Budva and Ulcinj incorporates the short ferry trip from Kamenari to Lepetane before heading down the west side of the peninsula that is itself west of Kotor town. The principal town on the peninsula is **TIVAT**, arguably one of the most dreadful places on the Montenegrin coast. If for some reason you're forced to stay here, the **tourist office** (daily in season 7am–9pm) is on the seafront five minutes from the bus station and has a good supply of **rooms**. Tivat **airport** is 2km south of town (regular buses from outside the *Hotel Mimoza*), and bus connections include Kotor, Budva, Cetinje (1 daily) and Ulcinj (2 daily). Lastly, of the three islands that lie offshore from Tivat, **Sv Marko** (15 boats daily) is dominated by a Club Med settlement and has the best beaches.

The Road from Kotor to Cetinje

Just south of Kotor town there's a choice of destinations and routes: straight on for Budva and the coastal road to Ulcinj, or left for Cetinje and the Montengrin interior. To get to Cetinje, most buses take the easy and quicker route via Budva; others approach it directly, and these are the ones to catch.

Scaling the heady slopes of **Mt Lovčen**, the trip from Kotor town to Cetinje is one of the most magnificent in Europe and should not on any account be missed. Looking at the mountain it seems impossible that a road could exist, an apprehension that persists when you're actually on the bus snaking your way up. It's a slow crawl, the road winding through dozens of hairpins as the air thins and cools. Below, the gulf spreads out in picture-book clarity, Kotor just a blip at the foot of the mountainside—a superb view that's worth the assault on the nerves as the bus inches its way around rockfalls and the occasional wrecked car. At about 1000m the road runs through the **Lovčen pass** and suddenly you're in the **karst**. Local legend has it that at the Creation, God was flying over the Balkans with a huge sack of stones; the Devil crept up behind and slit the sack open, and what fell out was Montenegro. An appropriate image: the karst is a lunar landscape of crags and boulders, a barren colander that swallows rain and melting snow, repaying the land with thin, patchy vegetation.

Cetinje

Surrounded by frozen limestone peaks and engulfed by snow for up to five months per year, the town of **CETINJE** sits in an isolated valley of alpine beauty—green fields, apple-crumble rocks, and clipped woods. Noted for its museums which chronicle the turbulent history of the Montenegrins, Cetinje is a popular day-trip destination for tourists from the coast—but after they've gone, you have this simple mountain town pretty much to yourself.

Some History

Founded in 1482 by Slav clans in retreat from the advancing Turks, the true history of early Cetinje was deliberately obscured by nineteenth-century Slav nationalists—ably supported by contemporary kings of Montenegro—who were keen to foster the myth of "indomitable resistance." In fact the Turks conquered the region in 1499 but made little effort to keep control; it simply wasn't worth it, and as long as the inhabitants paid their taxes when the Ottomans were feeling assertive, the clans were left pretty much to their own rather unsavory devices. In their turn, the leaders of Cetinje's clans paid the tax when they had to and were quite content to fight for the Turks if the terms were right. By and large, though, they were far more interested in the pursuit of their endless blood feuds and in trying to make a living from their few crops, animal-raising, and banditry. The only unifying force was the Orthodox church whose bishops, based in the monastery of Cetinje, took over what little government there was in 1516. In no sense were the bishops in control of the local clans, but the fealty they owed to their Ottoman overlords was never clearly defined—and this was very handy when their nineteenth-century successors started to claim their right to independence.

Right up until the late nineteenth century Cetinje was an insignificant settlement at the heart of a backward and impoverished region. Little more than a tiny and rather squalid village, Cetinje had no road connections, no hotels, no castles, and hardly any government buildings. There weren't even any effective town defenses—nobody ever had enough spare cash and anyway the geography of the place was usually protection enough—while what central administration there was could not function without the support of the clan elders. Consequently tax collection was usually impossible and Montenegrin rulers came to depend on foreign subsidies.

Nevertheless, Cetinje was to have a major political influence that far outweighed its economic and territorial significance, for the last stages of the decline of the Ottoman state coincided with the rise of Slav nationalism. As the Slavs cast around for symbols of independence they stumbled upon Cetinje with its ready-made dynasty of prince-bishops. The great powers were more pragmatic but they too were forced to accept the inevitability of Turkish collapse, and at the Treaty of Berlin (1878) agreed to give Montenegro the strip of coast from Bar to Ulcinj. At last, Cetinje was the capital of a state of some strategic importance and in a spasm of interest all the major European countries vied with each other in courting the favor of the king of Montenegro from their brand new diplomatic mansions. This is what makes Cetinje rather cock-eyed: at heart it's an isolated, rather insignificant Montenegrin town, but the patina is all nineteenth- and early-twentieth-century extravagance.

The days of glory didn't last long: occupied by the Austro-Hungarians in 1916, Montenegro was shoved into the kingdom of Yugoslavia two years later—only to become a neglected part of what was in effect a greater Serbian state.

Arrival, Accommodation, and Food

The **bus station** is five minutes across town from the main square: if you're offered a **room** here, take it; the **tourist office**, near Nikola's palace, has only a few private places on its books and they're often full. If the tourist office is closed, try the house behind it at Baje Pivljanina 19, which seems to fill some mysterious accommodation function. The only other alternative is the giant *Hotel Grand* where a double room will set you back some $100 during the season. Because of this lack of beds it's best to arrive early so you can continue to Budva if need be—the journey takes about an hour and there are some eight buses a day. Cetinje has few places to **eat**—try one of the cheap and cheerful restaurant-bars on the main street around the tourist office, or the more elaborate dishes of the *Grand*.

The Town

Traveling in the 1930s, Lovatt Edwards described Cetinje as "sleepy and undistinguised, a city of senior citizens," and it's true that Cetinje has few buildings of note and, aside from the setting, is hardly prepossessing. Most of the streets are lined by low, unpretentious pastel-fronted houses dating from the early twentieth century, while the leftovers from Cetinje's eventful past are concentrated in a string of mediocre buildings in and around the main square, five minutes' walk from the bus station.

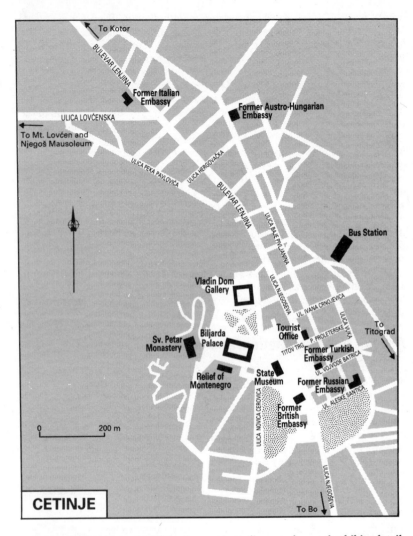

To Kotor

BULEVAR LENJINA

Former Italian
Embassy

Former Austro-Hungarian
Embassy

ULICA LOVĆENSKA

To Mt. Lovćen and
Njegoš Mausoleum

ULICA PEKA PAVLOVIĆA

ULICA HERGOVAČKA

BULEVAR LENJINA

ULICA BAJE PIVLJANINA

Bus Station

Vladin Dom
Gallery

ULICA NJEGOŠEVA

UL IVANA CRNOJEVIĆA

ULICA VUKA

To
Titograd

Tourist
Office

P. PROLETERSKE

Sv. Petar
Monastery

Biljarda
Palace

TITOV TRG

Former Turkish
Embassy

UL VOJVODE BATRIĆA

Relief of
Montenegro

State
Museum

Former Russian
Embassy

UL. ALEKSE ŠANTIĆA

ULICA NOVICA CEROVIĆA

Former
British
Embassy

0   200 m

CETINJE

ULICA NJEGOŠEVA

To Bo

Crammed into these buildings is an extraordinary volume of exhibits detailing Montenegro's history—so much in fact that you could spend a couple of days in the museums alone. Nearly all the displays are labeled exclusively in Serbo-Croat but if you're eager to get to grips with what you see, inquire at any of the museum's reception desks and they should manage to rustle up an English-speaking guide; it's not as expensive as you'd imagine, though the cheapest option is to wait and tag onto one of the guided tours. If you're intent on visiting several of the museums, buy the good-value combined ticket.

The Biljarda

On the right-hand side of the main square, the **Biljarda** (daily in season 9am–5pm; otherwise Mon–Fri 9am–3pm) takes its name from the billiard table that was dragged up here from Kotor at great effort and expense by order of Cetinje's most famous ruler, **Petar Njegoš II** (1803–1851). A squat, two-storyed structure, the Biljarda is neither extravagant nor particularly imposing—which is probably how Petar II, who built it in 1838, wanted it. Petar was in every respect a remarkable man, as interesting as he is unknown outside Yugoslavia: six foot eight inches tall and stunningly good-looking, he was not only a successful secular ruler but a bishop, diplomat, notorious hounder of the Turks, poet of distinction, and a crack shot to boot. The story always told of him, mainly because it was witnessed by an English noble, Sir Gardiner Wilkinson, is that he would frequently call for a lemon to be thrown into the air and shoot it through before it hit the ground—"a singular accomplishment for a bishop" mused Sir Gardiner. Tutored by the Serb poet Milutinović, Petar greatly admired the French Romantics and in his short life—he died when he was 48—produced several major works of his own. Most important of these was an epic drama entitled *The Mountain Wreath*, which is considered the greatest of all Yugoslav epic poems. He also spoke French, German, Russian and Latin, and read their literature, philosophy and jurisprudence in the original.

Considering Petar was such an extraordinary man, the exhibits in the Biljarda are a disappointment: most of the rooms are filled with incidental bric-a-brac from his life and administration, including predictable pictures and portraits, the famous billiard table, and a selection of his reading material which is still on display in the old library. One of the more interesting items is the splendid handwritten **passport** he made for himself when he went to St Petersburg for his investiture as an Orthodox bishop.

In a large glass pavilion attached to the side of the Biljarda, the huge **relief map** of Montenegro was constructed by officers of the occupying Austrian army in 1917. Part of an intelligence-gathering exercise, the map shows just how mountainous Montengro really is, and as you walk around it's fairly apparent why no foreign power ever bothered—or managed—to garrison the country effectively. Lastly, the dashing costumes of the **ethnographic** section of the museum are in the same wing, though they are scheduled for renovation and possible transfer.

The Monastery

Behind the Biljarda, the **Monastery** of Cetinje (daily in season 8am–7pm; otherwise 7am–2pm & 4–7pm) was completed by the founder of the Njegoš dynasty, Prince-Bishop Danilo, in 1701—though it was never meant to be an oasis of quiet contemplation. Part church, part fortress, and part munition store, the monastery buildings housed a rudimentary administration under the aegis of Danilo and his successors, who fused together the functions of prince and bishop to forge a dynasty of theocratic rulers. No one seems to have thought there was a conflict of interests, and Petar II only moved out because it was too crowded.

Built in chalk-colored brick and much modified over the centuries, today's monastery is an inarticulate structure, whose double arcade of cloisters is spoiled by a tacked-on roof and unbalanced by a multileveled tower. A small cruciform chapel contains the tombs of Njegoš notables, including Prince Danilo and Petar I, the uncle of the celebrated poet king. Dull stuff, but the **treasury** has some fine fifteenth- and sixteenth-century icons and religious books, by far the most important of which is *The Octoich of the First Voice*, a gospel dating from 1493. Coming just eighteen years after Caxton's *Histories of Troy*, it's one of the oldest printed books in existence and certainly among the first ever printed in a Slav language.

On the hill behind the monastery are the scant remains of the **Tablja**, a small tower built by Petar II in 1835. When Sir Gardiner Wilkinson was here, he was shocked to see it decorated with Turkish skulls impaled on pikes. Pointing out that this custom deterred foreign visitors, he complained to Prince Petar whom he believed was far too civilized a man to permit such a practice. Petar was not impressed, and when Wilkinson continued his travels into Turkish-held Mostar he found his indignation misplaced: in front of the vizier's palace was another round tower festooned in equally gruesome style—this time with the heads of Montenegrin soldiers; the Turks and the Montenegrins had been swapping heads for decades.

The Palace of King Nikola

Back across the main square, the tiny **church of the Virgin's Birth** was built in the 1880s for the last of the Montenegrin kings, Nikola I, on the site of Cetinje's first monastery. The fifteenth-century foundations that trail around the church have only recently been excavated and restored. Next door, the **Palace of King Nikola** (daily in summer 9am–5pm otherwise Mon–Fri, 9am–3pm) is a long brown-plastered building that looks more like a lesser nineteenth-century mansion than the home of a king. Converted into a **museum**, its interior is an approximation of how it would have appeared in his reign. Like Petar II, his predecessor, Nikola was an unusual man who succeeded where others had failed: during his 58-year reign he brought most of the clans to heel, and in 1878 he managed to extend his territories to the sea when his army occupied the strip of coast from Budva to Ulcinj. As the Ottoman Empire fell to pieces, all the great powers were keen to establish good relations with King Nikola, a situation he exploited skilfully. Cetinje became a capital where all the major European countries felt obliged to establish an embassy or a legation—the former British Legation, in its elegance not unlike the palace itself, still stands on Ulica Njegoševa—and Nikola extracted as much money from them as he could.

One thing that isn't mentioned in the museum is that Nikola was also a pretty detestable creature, with all the ethics of a cornered sewer rat. Throughout his wheeling and dealing reign he used official funds for personal gain while the Montenegrin people suffered intense poverty. As if this wasn't enough, when Russia gave grain to ease a famine, Nikola sold it to the highest bidder and, after 20,000 of his troops had died in the successful siege of Shkoder in Albania, he waited, then surrendered—using his foreknowledge to make a fortune on the Viennese stock exchange. His reign ended in 1916 when, amid accusations of treachery from Serbia, he allowed the Montenegrin army to be captured by the Austrians. He fled to France and there died in exile in 1921, outliving most of the men of his generation.* There's a portrait in the museum showing Nikola smiling the smug smile of a survivor.

The Historical Museum

The **Historical Museum** (daily in summer 9am–5pm; otherwise Mon–Fri and some Sats 9am–3pm) is stuffed into the large yellow building to the right of the Biljarda, just off the main square. Finished in 1910, these government offices were meant to impress, and the building frames a scrubby courtyard with all the static monumentalism you might expect. Inside, a huge collection of Montenegrin artifacts spans the centuries but is based on military trophies—guns, swords, medals, etc. To be honest it all gets rather repetitive—though the simple geometrics of some of the Turkish battle standards are intriguing—until you reach the rooms that house the **Museum of the National Liberation**. The Montenegrins played a vital part in the anti-Fascist war. After Tito's call to arms in July 1941, they rose against the occupying Italian forces with a unity unmatched by any other region. When the Italians issued an order demanding the surrender of all arms, 50,000 heavily armed Montenegrins handed in just two rifles—one didn't work and the other had been "borrowed" from an Italian soldier. The Montenegrins were going to fight, and in the first few weeks they pushed the Italians out of all Montenegro except Cetinje and Podgorica (today's Titograd)—their revolutionary fervour such that they set about constituting soviets on the early Russian models. Montenegro was later partially reoccupied, but never during the whole course of the war was it completely defeated. The cost was horrifically high—proportionally Montenegro lost more of its people than anywhere else in the country. The museum illustrates this in a dispassionate, moving way; the walls are lined with row upon row of pictures of dead partisans, some of the photographs taken from German archives and showing men, women, and children at the moment of execution.

Around Cetinje

On a hilltop high above the Biljarda, the **Mausoleum of Bishop Danilo** is worth the walk for the views over town and a sniff of fresh air. For the more ambitious, the modern **Mausoleum of Petar II** (daily 9am–6pm) is on a mountain top some 20km from town at the heart of the Mt Lovćen National Park. The mausoleum was designed by Meštrović but only completed in 1974 when the components were lugged up from Budva. It's typical Meštrović— magnificent yet humorless—with a massive Petar carved out of a single block

---

* Surprisingly enough, Nikola's remains were returned for burial in Cetinje in 1989 amid much pomp and ceremony from local Montenegrin patriots, and ambassadors from defunct royal families all over the world.

of black granite, symbolically dominating Montenegro below. Petar's body is immediately beneath the sculpture in a dimly lit, dripping tomb. The views are spectacular: you're at the heady summit of the mountains here, and on a clear day you can see the Italian coast. The problem is getting here—if you're driving, finding the right road is a problem as the turnoff (just out of town on the Kotor road) isn't at present signposted. If you're flush, rent a taxi (going rate is the equivalent of $20) or enlist in a guided tour; inquire at the *Grand Hotel*.

Budva

One of the busiest resorts in Montenegro, **BUDVA** straggles along the shore, an ungainly modern mixture of concrete and glass that's edged by its tiny **Old Town**. A favorite destination for British vacationers, Budva is jam-packed with all the predictable paraphernalia of mass tourism—souvenir stalls, pizza bars, and hotel nightclubs—though there's no denying the pretti-ness of the setting or the neat pleasantries of the Old Town, rebuilt from the rubble of the 1979 earthquake. What's more, it's still a good place to stay and its excellent transport connections make it a convenient base for seeing this stretch of the coast.

Some History

In legend Budva was founded by Cadmus, son-in-law of Aphrodite and sower of the famous warrior teeth; more certainly, records show that Budva was an important Greek settlement as early as 500 BC. Dented and damaged, razed and ransacked, Budva struggled through from the collapse of the Roman Empire to the twelfth century when it became a prosperous, semiautono-mous city-state within the Serbian Empire. More problems arrived with the Turks and in 1443 Budva collapsed into the arms of Venice, to become its most southerly Adriatic possession. Some four centuries of Venetian rule gave the town stability and a degree of protection from the Turkish raids that harassed much of the rest of the coast.

From this background a fascinating character emerged. There can't have been many charlatans or impostors who managed to bluff their way to a throne with a name like **Sćepan the Small**. This diminutive character was selling herbs in Budva when a rumor went around that he was really a wandering Polish monk or, more grandly, the Russian Tsar Peter III, deposed in 1762 and presumed murdered. Whether the Montenegrins of the day were particularly gullible or Sćepan extremely personable we don't know, but he was installed as prince in 1766, declaring that although he was indeed Tsar Peter, for convenience's sake his subjects could carry on calling him Sćepan the Small. As it turned out he was a gifted ruler, uniting many of the Montenegrin tribes in concerted attacks on the Turks to the south. And this was to prove his undoing; in 1774 the vizier of Skadar, fearful of Montenegrin solidarity, bribed Sćepan's barber to slit his throat, and Sćepan the Small went to an early (and presumably short) grave.

The Austrians occupied Budva from 1797 to 1918 and did their best to ignore it altogether, despite the town's spirited resistance to the French during the Napoleonic wars; only postwar tourism stopped the rot.

Arrival and Rooms

Budva may have spread far and wide up and around the bay, but the center of town is surprisingly compact. An easy point of reference is the old town, which sticks out into the sea on its own small peninsula. From the large square in front of the old town's main gate, a couple of ribbon-like roads head off around the bay, but all you need in the way of services can be found within the first three or four hunded meters. Budva's **bus station** is here, five minutes from the old town and just behind the shoreline. A stone's throw away, *Montenegro Express* (daily in season 7am–9pm; otherwise Mon–Sat 7am–1pm & 5–7pm) will arrange private **rooms** either directly or through the **tourist office**, a couple of minutes down the road. As you might expect, there are several other agencies, but these two are as good as any. Rooms range from the deluxe and expensive to the basic and cheap but, although there are hundreds, don't leave it too late in high season. Short-stay, single rooms are subject to a variety of surcharges which add about fifty percent to the initial cost. Modern Budva is drab and dreary, so it's worth trying to get a room in the old town, even though these are often filled up months in advance.

The best **campground**, *Autocamp Jaz*, is some 4km from town, just off the road to Tivtat/Kotor (take any bus in this direction and ask to be dropped off). One of the more agreeable of Montenegro's campgrounds, *Jaz* caters to up to 4000 tourists and fans out up a field from a long and pretty beach. Lastly, **hotel** rooms start at about $50 for doubles—the tourist office will provide you with details.

Sights and Beaches

A walled citadel perched on its own promontory, Budva's newly restored **Old Town** was itself built from the ruins of the 1667 earthquake. Entirely Venetian in style and character, the restoration has left it a little too spruce for comfort and there are few buildings of note; the Catholic cathedral of **Sv Ivan** and the Orthodox church of **Sv Trojica** are the possible exceptions. Otherwise, the walk around the town walls is no more than pleasant, and the museum is a waste of time.

Budva's main **beach** curves around the bay from the old town to a headland that edges the resort of Bečići—but it's crowded and uninviting. In the opposite direction, the rocky coves around the cliffs beside the *Hotel Avala* are a better alternative, even if there is an entry charge. Follow the path around the shoreline until you strike sand; the least crowded beach is farthest from the hotel, and you need to climb through a hole in the rocks to get there. Best of all, take a water-taxi from the jetty beside the old town to the island in the bay. Officially called **SV NIKOLA** but known locally as

Hawaii, the west (seaward) side of the island has a long stretch of stone and pebble beach—ideal if you're after a bit of seclusion. At nights (9pm–3am) there's an open-air disco on the tip of the island nearest town.

Eating and Drinking

There are literally scores of **restaurants** dotted all over town, but they're geared to the tourist budget and most are correspondingly overpriced. Two of the cheaper pizzerias, the *Sunce* and the *San Marino*, are just near the bus station, but if you're eating out you'd be better advised to spend a little more because the *Jadran* restaurant—just behind the seafront near the *Sunce*—is one of the best places for seafood on the coast. It has superb cuisine at reasonable prices and is deservedly popular; you'll need to reserve to make sure of a table. If the *Jadran* is the place to eat, the old town is the place to drink, for the narrow streets echo to the sound of pounding music from a string of cramped and modern **bars**—with booze at west European prices.

Budva Environs: South to Petrovac

Readily accessible by bus and water taxi from Budva, the strip of coast down to Petrovac has been intensively developed. Although some of the scenery is undoubtedly beautiful, you'll be hard pushed to escape the hordes of tourists who lie roasting on every bit of beach they can find. Good places to go are few and far between.

One place definitely not worth the halt is **BEČIĆI**, a couple of kilometers round the bay from Budva. Once a pleasant fishing village, it's been crassly developed—massive hotels in front of a large campground—and even the undoubted attractions of its long sandy beach can't redeem the ugliness.

Further down the coast, the overcrowded resort of **MILOČER** is pressed around a tiny red-hilled cove. Very much Bečići's rich uncle, Miločer sucks in Belgrade's monied classes who flock here in summer pushing prices sky-high. The resort's prestige comes from the presence of the Yugoslav royal family's erstwhile **summer palace**, a ten-minute walk away.

This has been converted into the luxury *Hotel Miločer*. Framed by wooded hills and wooded headlands, the palace sits low and flat behind a shingle beach and beside its ornamental gardens. It's a lovely setting and not nearly as crowded as you'd imagine—bring your own food and you'll be set for the day.

Just around the headlands from the palace is the pride of Yugoslav tourism—the absurdly picturesque town of **Sveti Stefan**, photos of which you'll have seen adorning a thousand and one posters. Joined to the mainland by a narrow causeway which arcs out into two perfectly formed sandy beaches, this former island settlement has also been converted into a luxury hotel. Between the wars all the inhabitants left to seek work farther up the coast, and their small red-tiled stone houses—built in the fifteenth and sixteenth centuries—became derelict and unusable. In the early 1950s it was decided to save the buildings, if not the town, by converting each of the houses into self-contained tourist suites. The plan worked and Sv Stefan is now one of Yugoslavia's biggest money-makers, like Miločer its prices beyond most people's reach. For the privilege of seeing how the other half lives, you'll have to pay an entry fee of $5—the idea is to put casual visitors off, not to encourage them. If you do decide to rustle up the money, you'll be disappointed; the old medieval center just doesn't compare with Dubrovnik—or even Budva—and anyway Sveti Stefan's undeniable beauty is much better viewed from the shore.

The resort of **PETROVAC** spreads out around a magnificent, crescent-shaped sandy-ish bay some 8km south of Sv Stefan. Dominated by a string of modern hotels, there's nothing to do but eat, drink, and sunbathe—and that's precisely what hundreds of tourists do every day throughout the summer. Petrovac's **tourist office** has a limited supply of private **rooms**, but they fill fast in season; come early to make sure of a bed.

South to Ulcinj

The drive from Petrovac down to Ulcinj is one of the loveliest in the whole country. The road runs below ranges of sharp summited mountains, green and blue under thin vegetation, occasionally burned bright yellow with broom. By the roadside knarled and wizened olive trees twist and heave in huge groves, some planted in pre-Christian times and as much as 2500 years old. The only problem is accommodation: in July and August private **rooms** go fast, so it's important to reach your destination as early in the day as possible. Campers can be more flexible—the coastal highway is littered with sprawling **autocamps**, though some are amazingly squalid.

Heading south from Petrovac, the first major settlement is **SUTOMORE**, little more than a modern resort strung out around a long sand and pebble beach. About a kilometer to the north, the remains of two **Turkish castles** sit etched into the rocks above the road. Known as *Haj* and *Nehaj* ("Fear" and "Fear Not"), they were built by the Turks as protection against Montenegrin raids on their trading caravans. Sutomore is really rather drab but if you do stop, take a look inside the twelfth-century church of **Sv Tekla**—evidence of an unusual religious tolerance. At the far end of the nave there are two altars, one for the Catholic service and one for the Orthodox, both still in use today.

Much renewed and revamped since the 1979 earthquake, **BAR** is the working port of the Montenegro coast, its importance consolidated by the opening of the spectacular (if slow) rail route to Belgrade. An unengaging mishmash of modern building and oily docks, the only reason to be here is to pick up one of the **ferry links**. Services leave for **Bari** in Italy three times a week, and Bar is the last port of call for the *Jadrolinija* coastal ferry before it moves on to Igoumenitsa and Corfu; tickets from the office overlooking the quay. Bar's **quay** is on the edge of town, five minutes from the main street, but the **bus** and adjacent **railroad** stations are an inconvenient thirty-minute walk away; if it's hot, take a taxi—it's easy to get lost.

If you're stranded the *Putnik* office (Mon–Sat 7am–9pm) by the quay arranges private **rooms**, and you can't miss the town beach close by—it's an enormous rocky strip that heads off up the coast towards Sutomore. At all costs avoid the *autocamp* behind the beach some 2km from town. There's one **hotel**, the expensive *Topolica* (☎085/21-122; doubles $60). What activity there is in Bar's newly-built center revolves round three spaceship-egg boxes that house the town's supermarkets. There's nothing in Bar in the way of antiquities, but about 5km outside town you'll come upon **Stari Bar**, the crumbling ruins of the original old town which was severely battered in a nineteenth-century scrap between the Montenegrins and the Turks. Little remains save bits of a sixteenth-century aqueduct, but it's a lovely setting. To get there, walk straight up from the docks to the main highway to Ulcinj, where a minor road cuts off inland to KRUTE. From here, Stari Bar is clearly visible, overlooking the minor road. Alternatively take a bus from town towards the hospital, from where it's an easier walk.

Ulcinj

ULCINJ is the most southerly town on Yugoslavia's coast and immediately different from anything that precedes it. From Rijeka down to Bar the Venetian influence is universal but Ulcinj, only 18km from the Albanian border, has a marked Oriental flavor: there are few Christian churches, the houses huddled round the bay in the cramped old town are Turkish, and until the earthquake of 1979 the town's six mosques were still in use. Why Venetian influences are excluded here dates back to 1571, when the town was taken over by a party of Algerian **corsairs**—survivors of the great naval battle of Lepanto—led by the Bey of Algiers, Uluz Ali. For the next three centuries it was home to a mixed bag of pirates, thieves, and merchants: buccaneers who plundered shipping in the Adriatic and Mediterranean, burned towns, took slaves and generally did as they pleased so long as they didn't turn their attentions to their nominal allies, the Turks. Gradually these corsairs—Algerians, Moroccans, and Turks—adopted Albanian-style customs and formed a wholly Muslim town. An interesting legacy of their slave dealings is that a tiny proportion of Ulcinj's population—no more than six families—is black, descendants of slaves brought over from Africa in the sixteenth century. The pirating days came to an end in 1878 when the Montenegrin army that reduced Stari Bar to rubble did virtually the same to Ulcinj. From then on, despite various international treaties, the town belonged to Montenegro.

Such a picturesque spot was bound to draw the tourists and today Ulcinj's faded charms recede under the sheer number of visitors; close your eyes and you'd think you were in Hamburg rather than Yugoslavia. Nevertheless, Ulcinj's distinct Muslim character and excellent nearby beaches make it worth a day or two of your time. And, if you have your own transport, it's possible to make some rewarding side trips to the ethnic Albanian villages nearby.

Arrival, Accommodation, and Food

Ulcinj **bus station** is a good twenty-minute walk from the town beach and at least once an hour buses marked 'Lokal' connect the two. En route the bus passes the **local bus depot** by the souvenir stalls at the side of the main drag, Bulevar Maršala Tita. In recent years Ulcinj has mushroomed up the bay from the tiny old town in an explosion of drab modern buildings that straggle inland for several kilometers. Nearly every other house seems to offer **rooms**. The *Neptun* **tourist office** (daily 7am–9pm) overlooks the town beach and can solve your accommodation problems; they have **rooms** and a supply of cheap **apartments**, but if you want to avoid being exiled to some remote suburb, arrive early. Some of the nicest rooms are a stone's throw from the tourist office. Ulcinj has no less than seven large **hotels** and they're almost all expensive. The nearest to the tourist office is the *Galeb* (☎085/81-311; doubles $65), a few minutes' walk east along the shoreline. Cheapest is the *Mediteran* (☎085/81-411; doubles $35). There are two **campgrounds** near Ulcinj, the *Valdanos* to the northwest and the *Neptun* to the southeast; both are accessible by local bus and both are by the sea, but although the *Neptun* (at least 10 buses daily) is behind the gigantic Velika Plaža beach, it's grim and grimy. The *Valdanos* (frequent service summer only) is the better choice.

As you might expect, there are all sorts of **restaurants** and snack bars in the old town, though most tourists eat in their hotels. Three of the better places are on the seafront: the *Sidro* is excellent and not expensive; the *Tri Ribara* is of a similar standard, and the *Složna Braća* next door a bit cheaper and a favorite of the local police.

The Town

The nineteenth-century bombardment did at least concentrate on the fortified citadel high up on the cliffs, and the narrow patternless streets of the **Old Town** below were left largely intact. These cramp into a valley that trickles down to the bay, a chaos of twisting lanes and alleys camouflaged by an abundance of flowers and greenery. It was once a charming spot, but encased in dreary suburbs to the north, flanked by the hotel quarter along the shore to the east, and submerged by crowds of milling tourists, this part of Ulcinj has today unfortunately lost most of its appeal. It's also noticeably short of sights: the **citadel** is little more than a dilapidated ruin—though brand new tourist apartments are to be built within the walls in an attempt to turn the town into another Budva—and none of the **mosques** are open to outsiders. The only other attraction is the Tuesday and more especially Friday **market** which is held in the covered area next to the local bus depot. Even now hundreds of peasants pour in from the surrounding countryside to make this a colorful affair of donkeys, vegetables, and crudely-colored linens. Many of the peasants still wear traditional costume, and though the use of the veil is outlawed, women still pull a scarf or handkerchief across their faces, a vestige of the tradition.

Beaches: Ulcinj and South to the Albanian Border

The gunmetal-gray town beach, **Mala Plaža**, is scrubbed and polished every night and is really rather pleasant, though it does get very crowded, especially from mid-July to the end of August. The main alternative is the **Velika Plaža** (Great Beach) whose fine gray sands run right down to the Albanian border from a point some 4km south of Ulcinj. As it's 12km long, it's always easy to find a secluded spot, though there are complications: the stretch of beach nearest Ulcinj is part of a giant tourist settlement and there's certainly no privacy here. However, this bit of the beach is open to the casual visitor and at least it's well-cared-for—to prove the point it's even fenced off from the rest. The remaining 10km or so of beach has unrestricted access and for years hundreds of visitors have camped on it, driven on it, slept on it, and eaten on it. The results are plain to see; from one end to the other the beach glints with bits of discarded rubbish and it seems that no one has the responsibility to clean it up. If you can ignore the detritus—or find a spot where it's not too bad—then the Velika makes for a pleasant day out, but be warned that for most of its length restaurants are few and far between and anyway most of them are rip-off joints; take your own food. The sands of the Velika Plaža are mildly radioactive, a property that lures arthritis sufferers here for a cure—hence the bizarre sight of people burrowing and scrabbling round in the stuff like a bunch of drug-crazed moles.

From Ulcinj you can **walk** to the tourist settlement at the top of Velika Plaža, starting from the path near the *Hotel Albatros*, following the goat tracks and finally climbing down the rocks at the end of the promontory. This is a bit hairy, but far less mundane than the alternative, catching a **bus** from either the stop by the *Hotel Galeb* or from the bus station. There are two bus services to Velika Plaža from these stops: the first terminates at the tourist village (at least 6 daily) and the other (at least 4 daily) carries on down the military road south to Ada (15km), on the Albanian border. The military road keeps within easy walking distance of the beach via a series of dirt tracks. Both services cross the bridge at the head of the tiny lake just south of Ulcinj. Here you'll see the decaying remnants of an age-old fishing technique— Albanian **Kalimere fishing**, where large nets are lowered by claws into the shallow lakes. This was made illegal in Yugoslavia in 1967 and the deserted apparatus lies rotting away like decomposing stick insects.

The tiny islet of **ADA** sits at the mouth of the Bojana River on the Albanian frontier. A flat and sandy accretion, Ada is connected to the mainland by a bridge and there's an entry fee. Essentially a nudist colony and campground, Ada can get crowded, though it's pleasant enough, well serviced by restaurants, and offers relaxing walks in the greenery that fronts the beach.

If you're traveling by car, it's worth making a tour inland from Ulcinj; the roads through the mountains look out over Albania, and many of the villagers wear traditional costume—here for real and not for the tourists; they most definitely don't like being photographed. A good route would be to SUKOBIN, where a very bored young soldier guards the nation against the Albanian threat, and either along Lake Skadar and west to the coast road, or back to Bar via KRUTE.

Inland Montenegro

Conclusively mountainous, the magnificent Montenegrin interior is one of the least accessible areas of Yugoslavia; much of the country is cut off by heavy snows through the winter, and huge drifts linger well into the spring months. This lack of easy contact with the "outside world", combined with the thinnesss of the soil, has left it in a backward condition, with sheep-farming and a few crops providing a frugal livelihood for the people who weather the harsh winters. It's here you'll find a Degree Zero economy that directives from Belgrade can do little to change; hasty, grandiose attempts at industrialization have only skimmed the surface of the underlying poverty. It's always been like this; independent Montenegro was only ever kept afloat by foreign subsidies.

Nevertheless, the willingness of the bus drivers to cross near-impossible mountain tracks means you can readily take in some of the most spectacular routes—like the **Tara** and **Rugovo** gorges—though to explore more deeply you'll have to resort to walking. If you're using a tent, be careful: even in summer the weather in the mountains is changeable and it can get very cold. Except in the larger towns, tourist facilities all but disappear as soon as you leave the coast.

Budva to Titograd

Montenegro's main interior **highway** runs northward from Petrovac, rising over the coastal ridge of mountains before dipping down to **Lake Skadar**, the country's largest lake, shared half and half with Albania. Enclosed by bare-topped karst mountains, its blue water is tinted with the essential colors of shifting islands of green algae and lilies. There's something magical, almost eerie, about this shallow lake. Through the thin heat-haze that shimmers above it, the mountains recede mysteriously in innumerable shades of gray and in the distance the suitably named Prokleti Gora ("Accursed Mountains") of Albania are just visible. The strangeness extends even to the plants of the lake; a local delicacy is the *kasaronja*, a sort of water chestnut that steadfastly refuses to bear fruit in times of drought, despite unlimited supplies of water in the lake itself. The only settlement of any size is **VIRPAZAR**, which is just off the main road crossing the northwest corner of the lake. Virpazar has one **hotel**, the *13 July* (☎085/71-120; doubles $40), a railroad station, a bus station, and little else. You can drive along much of the western edge of Skadar and pick your spot to get out and walk; without a car, you're sunk. For farther advice and details ask in Virpazar.

North of Skadar a low and featureless plain runs to **TITOGRAD**, modern capital of Montenegro. Formerly known as Podgorica, the town was bombed to oblivion during the war by the Allies—the Italians and Germans had established a command there—and the rapid rebuilding that followed was a gesture of the new nation's pride as much as anything else. This hasty redevelopment has left a characterless agglomeration of high rises, distinguishable only by their flat pastel colors. The bus and train stations are a kilometer or so out of town, but all in all it's better to keep on going: buses from Budva head through Titograd north to Mojkovac and west to Nikšić, but services from Kotor via Cetinje terminate in Titograd and you'll have to change here. If you're stranded, Titograd has three cheap **hotels**, the *Zlatica* (☎081/611-550; doubles $32), the *Ljubović* (☎081/31-503; $36) and, best of the lot, the *Podgorica* (☎081/42-050; $36), right on the river. No one seems to know anything about private rooms.

Titograd to Nikšić

Heading northwest from Titograd, the road reaches Nikšić via the **Zeta valley**. On the way the eighteenth-century **Monastery of Ostrog** can be seen from the road, perched high in the rock and sheltering the remains of one Saint Basilius the Miracle Worker. Though you can clamber up to this place of pilgrimage, it's a long walk from the bus route. To look at, **NIKŠIĆ** seems a much enlarged Cetinje, a flat town cupped on a plateau and rimmed by mountains. But the similarity ends there: a few dull ruins, some forgettable museums, and Yugoslavia's best-selling beer are all the town has to offer, and there's nowhere cheap to stay—the town's one **hotel**, the *Onogošt* (☎083/31-850), will set you back $70 for a double. There's supposed to be a summer bus service from Nikšić to Žabljak for the Durmitor National Park, but if it ever does make the trip, it certainly isn't very often.

Titograd to Mojkovac

Heading north from Titograd the road climbs slowly on a thin ledge beside the river Morača, a few square wooden houses spotted on the valley sides, seemingly primitive but all connected to the electricity grid; bringing the benefits of industrialization to such places is one of Yugoslavia's greatest expenses. As the valley begins to narrow you find the **Monastery of Morača** squatting by the roadside like a gatehouse to the valley beyond. Morača's white and undecorated shape follows the neat rule that height plus width equals length—proportions that give the church its deceptively simple harmony. It is stylistically part of the Raška school, though the frescoes aren't as extensive or as impressive as those of its near contemporaries Mileševa or Sopočani. The few original works that date from the founding of the church in 1253 are mostly in the side chapels, and show scenes from the life of Sv Iljas (Saint Elija), gently colored in the flowing yet monumental style of the court painters, that was to find its greatest expression at Sopočani. Unless you're prepared to get off the bus and hope that the next one along will stop—and this entirely depends on the benevolence of the driver—then you'll have to be content with a glimpse of Morača as you pass. Frustrating, but there are better—and more accessible—monasteries. Beyond, the Morača valley gradually pinches in and the river falls below in the deep gorge. The road passes through rock-hewn tunnels, black and featureless, and for a second it seems you're about to descend into oblivion. At the head of the valley the road snakes up the mountainside and all Montenegro lies below you—then suddenly vanishes as you turn a corner into the upland plain. By now the air is rarefied and even in summer it has a knife-edge chill that hints at the bitter cold of winter, but the landscape is green, even rich, softening the shock of the wind and glimpses of barren-crested mountains.

Ahead is the industrial town of **MOJKOVAC**, a modest sort of place that was once an important mining center. The bus station is in the center of town with the railroad station and the *Hotel Mojkovac* (☎084/72-104; doubles from $40; best place for meals) on the outskirts. There's nothing to see—though the hotel is curiously triangular—but Mojkovac has good transportation connections to Žabljak and is conveniently close to one of Montenegro's best national parks. The **Biogradska Gora** is an invigorating mixture of virgin forest, mountain pasture, and glacial lake just to the south of town: walk 7km back along the main road (if you can avoid being flattened by the oncoming traffic) and take the turning east across the Tara River. The heart of the park is the **Biogradsko Jezero**, 4km along from the turning, and here you'll find a campground, log bungalows, and a restaurant. The small wooden kiosk rents boats by the hour and sells detailed maps of the park if you're looking for serious walking. By Montenegrin standards the walks are pretty easy, but bring your own compass if you intend to be adventurous.

Mojkovac to Žabljak via the Tara Gorge

Three buses a day make the journey from Mojkovac up the **Tara Gorge** to Žabljak. As the road heads north and west the walls of the canyon rise in increasingly steeper gradients from the crashing river below. It's a wild and wonderful spot and at the village of DJURDJEVIĆA TARA, where the road from Mojkovac meets the road from PLJEVLJA, a spectacular bridge spans the chasm below. At the southern end of the bridge there's a memorial to one of the engineers who helped build it. This man, Lazar Jauković, joined the partisans and, with the Italians closing in from Pljevlja, had the rather disagreeable task of dynamiting the central arch; as if this wasn't enough, when he was captured a few months later he was executed here.

Some 30km to the west, the small town of **ŽABLJAK** lies on a wide mountain pasture at the foot of Mt Durmitor which is itself at the center of the Durmitor National Park. The fields around Žabljak have been used for summer grazing for many centuries, but the first people to winter here were the desperate partisans in 1941–2. Indeed, Žabljak became a focal point of resistance to the Fascist armies and was the site of savage fighting right up until its final liberation in 1943. The Italians and their allies, the Četniks, made the local villagers pay heavily for their loyalty to the Communist cause: razed houses, round-ups, and mass executions were common.

Today, Žabljak serves as the springboard for winter skiing in the nearby mountains, but although there are a few ski lifts it's all pretty low-key stuff; in the summer, the town serves as a good base for walks and climbs. Finding **accommodation** is easy: the town has four **hotels**, of which the cheapest are the grubby *Durmitor* (☎0872/88-278; doubles $28) and the more centrally sited *Žabljak* (☎0872/88-300; doubles $40). Private **rooms** are also availa-

HIKING ROUTE: PEĆ TO AUTOVAC (8 DAYS)

Hiking in Montenegro offers endless choice. The interior is laced with tracks linking valley villages and mountain passes, making routes easy to plan. The following hike crosses the republic from east to west with hardly a drop of asphalt in sight. Food is easy to come by and camping never a problem—people are more likely to invite you into their homes than shoo your tent away.

Head west from **Peć** up the spectacular **Rugovo Gorge** (see p.362) for 28km. At **Kučište**, turn right and head north towards Boge on a track that follows the river and takes you through alpine scenery with chalets dotted on the hay fields. Carry on north on a narrowing path that twists to the mountain ridge with great views of the Montenegrin interior. You then drop steeply down through the forest to pick up the valley track and arrive in **Kaludra** (where there's a store). Follow the track into the modern town of **Ivangrad** (stores and services). From Ivangrad take the road to **Pešča**, then continue west on a track deep into the **Bjeslasica Mountains**, at first through forest and then across alpine pasture; families from the valley live up here for the summer with their flocks of sheep. The track becomes a path to cross the wooded col, then drops through the **Biogradska Gora National Park** to the army town of **Kolašin** (stores). Cross the river Tara, then head up the valley track to **Lipovo** with Babin Zub (2253m) lurking to your left. The villages peter out and give way to a steep climb up to the Planina plateau, where there's a Partisan monument and countless farm huts. Continue northwest on the track, then drop steeply down to the next valley at **Krnja Jela**.

Follow the track to **Boan** (hotel), then to **Timar** where you emerge onto the **Durmitor Plateau**, a windswept, treeless place with the mountains of the **Durmitor National Park** rising to the north; it was here that the partisans waited in vain through the bitter winter of 1941 for airdrops of supplies. At **Pašina Voda** leave the plateau to climb the mountain track to **Boricje**. Oxen are still used here to drag sledges of provisions up to the summer pastures in the last of the winter snows. From the col, the mountains can be easily climbed on the marked paths. This route plunges down west for an eternity through villages and woodland to emerge at **Plužine** (stores and hotel), a new and dreary town built to replace the old one drowned by the reservoir planners.

Take the track to **Orah**, then follow the path up through **Lisina** and onto the wooded limestone plateau—beautiful, delicate country, perfect for camping. The final descent is into Hercegovina and the small town of **Autovac**.

ble—ask at the information kiosk by the bus station or at the *Hotel Žabljak*. There's a primitive **campground** on the main road on the edge of town—bring your woolies. For **food** you'll have to rely on the hotels, the produce market, or the two supermarkets.

The Durmitor National Park

Žabljak is on the edge of the **Durmitor National Park**, a mountainous region of glacial lake, steep cliffs, and deep forests. The weather is most unpredictable, so you really do have to know what you're doing if you're going to be walking far, especially since there's no official mountain rescue service; clearly marked paths can, on occasion, simply disappear; and snow hangs round until the beginning of August. But at least the local bears are harmless—according to the official guidebook they are entirely herbivorous.

The park's **information office** (irregular opening hours) is just past the *Durmitor Hotel*, used as a hospital by the partisans, who had their headquarters in the park in 1941. It was into the Durmitor National Park that Captains Bill Deakin and William Stuart, heads of a six-man British military mission, were parachuted in May 1943, to ascertain for Churchill the strengths and allegiances of the partisan forces under Tito. Next door the shop sells an excellent and comprehensive guidebook and large-scale maps.

Most of the walks start from **Crno Jezero** (the Black Lake), some 3km southwest of Žabljak, accessible along a paved road. The shortest and most popular walk in the area is the two-hour stroll around the lake. It's a pleasant way to spend an afternoon and you even get to pass one of Tito's old mountain hideouts marked as "Titova Peć."

North and East of Mojkovac; the Čakor Pass

The road to Belgrade and Priština heads north and east from Mojkovac by the side of the railroad line. The first major turning inland takes you to BIJELO POLJE, the last significant Montenegrin settlement before the Serbian border; from there the road runs on to the village of PRIJEPOLJE for the neighboring Monastery of Mileševa (see p.319) and eventually the Yugoslav capital. If you ignore the turning and continue east, you come to IVANGRAD where you can either stay on the main road to TITOVA MITROVICA in Kosovo or cut off south and then east for PEĆ via the Čakor Pass and the Rugovo gorge—but be warned this is a difficult and sometimes dangerous journey which is bypassed by most of the buses. Thirty-five kilometers south of Ivangrad the road to Peć slips through the village of MURINO where it veers east to snake its way up through Swiss-like alpine pasture to the **Čakor Pass**. At 1849m this is the windswept ceiling of Montenegro and the hair-raising prelude to the Rugovo gorge—for an account of which, see Chapter Eight, *Kosovo*.

travel details

Buses

From Kotor to Budva (2 hourly; 1hr); Cetinje (5 daily; 3hr on the mountain route, 1hr 30min via Budva); Dubrovnik (10 daily; 2hr); Herceg-Novi (3 hourly; 1hr); Peć (1; 7hr); Split (5 daily; 11hr); Titograd (12; 5hr); Tivtat (hourly; 40min); Ulcinj (4; 2hr); Zagreb (1; 16hr); Belgrade (1; 12–14hr).

From Budva to Cetinje (8 daily; 50min); Kotor (7; 1hr); Risan (7; 2hr); Mojkovac (1; 4hr); Titograd (8; 2hr).

From Bar to Budva (hourly; 40min); Cetinje (1 daily; 2hr 30min); Dubrovnik (3 daily; 3hr); Kotor (10 daily; 50min); Ulcinj (hourly; 40min).

Trains

From Bar to Titograd (6 daily; 45min); Belgrade (6 daily; 8hr).

CHAPTER FIVE

BOSNIA-HERCEGOVINA

F orming much of the heartland of western Yugoslavia, **Bosnia-Hercegovina** was the republic that most absorbed the Ottoman Empire, and it still retains a dominant Islamic religion and culture. Over a third of the population are Muslim, descendants of Serbs allowed a degree of freedom if they adopted the faith of their Turkish invaders. And though active worship is now on the decline, the threads of a Turkish past can be seen everywhere: in the mosques of towns and villages, in the costumes, and especially in the food. If you've just arrived from the coast, the difference can be arresting.

Virtually landlocked, Bosnia-Hercegovina's countryside is agricultural and varied. To the north, **Bosnia** has lush mountain pasture interspersed with

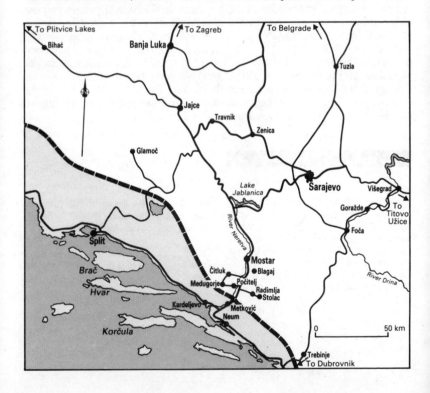

fertile plains, while **Hercegovina**, founded in the thirteenth century by Hercog (Duke) Stefan, comprises wide stretches of gaunt karst gashed by deep gorges—dramatic traveling. The great draw is undoubtedly the capital, **Sarajevo**, a deeply attractive city where the region's three historical ingredients—nationalism, Turkish, and Austrian occupations—underscore a buoyant individualism. It's the target for any trip here. From Sarajevo towns spread out along river valleys in three corridors: north to Croatia via **Jajce**, a compact fortress town of the Middle Ages; southwest to the coast through Turkish **Mostar**, now a favorite tourist spot; and east into Serbia through the **Drina valley**, center for hair-raising raft trips.

Sarajevo

"Mosques, minarets and fezes—holding the gorgeous East in fee while the river cools the air, splashing through the town and the bridge on which whatsisname was assassinated." So wrote Lawrence Durrell, summing up a city it's really impossible to compress into a few impressions. Running alongside the river Miljacka, **SARAJEVO** spreads out like a gesture between the mist-topped mountains; to the west, giant hard-faced skyscrapers of postwar prosperity progress eastwards through the candy-colored buildings of one foreign occupier, the Austrians, to the elegance and decay of another, the Turks. Here, more than anywhere else in Yugoslavia, Islam is evident, an active and integrated culture that generates an exciting oriental feel. Around the **Baščaršija**, Sarajevo's old Turkish Bazaar, are graceful monuments to four centuries of eastern domination, like the stately **Gazi Husref Beg Mosque**, and all over town the untended graveyards filled with *nišans*, tombstones of the faithful, sprout like chalk outcrops, simpler memorials to absorbed invaders.

Of course Sarajevo is associated with the assassination of Franz Ferdinand, but more recently its staging of the 1984 Winter Olympics* was the source of tremendous pride, not only here but throughout the country. *Vučko*, the smug cartoon fox which served as the city's Olympic mascot, continues to beam benignly from windows and billboards over half a decade after the Games. Yet the wrangles continue: was it right to build new skiing facilities in Sarajevo, a town with no skiing tradition? Why not in Slovenia? As everyone paid for the Olympics in extra taxes on food, bus tickets, and the like, how come only Sarajevo reaped the benefits? The usual arguments, but talk to anyone here and they'll tell you with dewy-eyed pride of how every hotel was full, how every telephone briefly and mysteriously worked. Whether Sarjevo can continue to build on this burst of glory isn't clear, but one thing is certain: with its mix of styles and peoples, buildings and customs, and its infamous place in European history, Sarajevo is the most fascinating city in Yugoslavia.

---

* Sports fanatics might like to drop in at the **Olympic Museum**, Nikole Tesle 7 (daily 10am–7:30pm), for its very static array of posters, photos, ephemera and souvenirs of the Winter Olympics. Basically, though, it's little more than a belated attempt to wring the final drops of prestige from the event.

The Sarajevo area telephone code is ☎071

Arrival and Places to Stay

The **bus and train stations** are on the same site, from which it's too far to walk to the center. Instead, buy a flat-rate public transit ticket from the orange station booth—and all over town at newspaper and cigarette kiosks—and jump on a #1 **tram** or any other tram or bus marked *Baščaršija*. Get off at the Princip Bridge (sixth stop from the station), or a little later at the Baščaršija, heart of the old town. If you're only here for the day, there's a **luggage consignment** office at the train station.

If you're after a **private room**, don't be tempted by those on offer from the *Olimpik Tours* office in the train station—they're twice the price of those from agencies in town. Head instead for *Unis Tourist*, Vase Miskina 16 (Mon–Fri 7am–8pm, Sat 7am–4pm), or the faintly intimidating **tourist office** on Jugoslavenska Narodne Armije 50 (daily 7am–9pm), where double rooms cost around $12. Rooms from either office are invariably out of the center; try and ask for somewhere on a bus/tram route. Also, requests for single rooms are unfailingly met with blank stares and suggestions that you look elsewhere. **Unofficial rooms** are found outside the stations, the cheaper hotels, and the tourist offices. Strictly speaking they're illegal, but they tend to be cheaper and more central. It makes a lot of sense to check the precise location, cost, security, and what you're actually getting, right at the outset.

Student rooms work out slightly cheaper but are only available during July and August. Reserve beds via the tourist office or go directly there. *Studenski Dom Stoyanovic* at Radičeva 4d is the most central and hence most popular—from the stations take tram #1 to the fourth stop; walk back down Obala Vojvode Stepe, and it's the third road on the right. The *Student Center* at Aleja Branka Bujica 2 (left off Proleterske Brigade, bus 24 from the station) is farther out but has limitless supplies of rooms.

The **youth hostel**, the *Omladinski Dom* (☎36-163) at Zadrugina 17, is the cheapest place to stay in Sarajevo and lies within easy walking distance of the stations. Cross the large grass circle in front of the train station and walk down Krančeviča; take the first left up Tešanjska, then first right and keep snaking up the hill to the hostel. It gets pretty full during the summer, so phone first from the station. It's a grubby, fairly unpleasant hostel, and the 10:30pm curfew is rigorously enforced, but it is cheap (around $5). Alternatively, the *Dom Odmora Mladost* (☎535-921) is away from downtown but magnificently sited on the slopes of Mt Trebević, fifteen minutes' walk away from the upper cable-car station (for running times of which see "Listings"), or via an infrequent #38 bus that leaves from near the Princip museum (see "The Baščaršija and around"). It's more expensive than the *Omladinski* (around $8) and fills fast throughout the summer; phone first to check room availability.

The nearest place to **camp** is way out of town at **Ilidža**, just off the Mostar road. The campground is part of a massive leisure complex built on the site of an old Hapsburg spa. Take tram #3 or #4 to the end of the line, heading away from the center.

SARAJEVO

If all else fails, the **hotels** *Central* at Ulica Zrinjskog 8 (☎215-515; doubles
$40), *Zagreb*, V. Perića 1 (☎36-830; $34), and *Stari Grad*, Maršala Tita 126
(☎533-394; $28), are cheap enough for a day or so while you hunt down some-
thing less expensive.

Eating and Drinking

Eating is problem-free, with all tastes and budgets well catered for.
Sarajevo's *burek*s are easily the best in the country, particularly the spinach
(*špinat*) variety. As an alternative try the intestine-shaped pastries filled with
spiced meat and/or potato, sold by weight in the Baščaršija. Bear in mind
that the places selling these delights are rarely open after 2pm. The same
district abounds with cheap **kebab places** which will fill you up, with
yoghurt to finish, for a few thousand dinars. More substantial fare in the
Bosnian-Turkish style is to be had from *Aščinica*, whose three branches are
at Maršala Tita 95 and at Barščaršija 17 and 55 (the strip running from the
sebilj metal fountain). Here you're confronted with a dozen or so steaming
pans of stewed meats and vegetables and great basins of salad; it's just a
question of pointing out what you want. End the meal with a plate of *baklava*
oozing with honey and almonds, and don't plan anything energetic for at least
three hours.

Good **pizzas** are reasonably priced at *Dubrovnik Pizzeria* on Halači, straight down Barščaršija towards the river, or at *Pizzeria Monokl* (slightly more sophisticated, and open later) at Zije Dizdevarića 16, on the way up to Vratnik. The food at **self-service** restaurants like *Bosna* (Maršala Tita 36) or *Herzegovina*, by the Catholic cathedral, is dependable but bland. For a real (but by no means expensive) Bosnian-style blow-out, try the wonderful *Morića Han* **restaurant** at Sarači 77 in the Baščaršija, occupying a converted caravanserai (see below). Similar, in that it serves oriental-style food, is *Daire*, Halači 5, housed in a former merchants' warehouse.

Turska kava, Turkish coffee, can be had at any *kafana*. Try *Jasmin* at Remzije Omanović 7, by the *sebilj* public fountain with its speakers blaring Bosnian folk-music. *Café-bar Lisac*, tucked away in the yard behind Maršala Tita 29, is a friendly little place drawing a predominantly young crowd who favor jazz and rock and roll. If it's ice cream you want then make for *Slasticarna Egipat Spaca*, an open-air place halfway down Vase Miskina. Their Egyptian Vanilla Sundae is amazing.

The Baščaršija and Around

The old center forms the eastern part of the city; the four broad streets of Maršala Tita, Vase Miskina, JNA and Vojvode Stepe run parallel to the river, zeroing in on the Turkish quarter, each street with its share of Austro-Hungarian pomposity. A few of the facades are still brightly painted, but most have faded into ornate pastels.

Four hundred years before the Hapsburgs arrived the Turks set up the administrative center of their western possessions here, calling it *Saraj Ovasi* ("the palace-field") and giving the town its name. Ottoman presence was absorbed quickly, and, in a way, turned to the Bosnians' advantage. Heretics called "Bogomils" (see p.264), mostly local nobles, adopted the invaders' faith and became important in the running of the city, so much so that even the power of the sultans was second to their domestic control. In his turn, the vizier of Bosnia was only allowed to spend one night in the town each month and next day he'd be escorted to the city walls and politely ejected.

Today you enter the market center of the Turkish town abruptly; the original **Baščaršija** was flattened in a misplaced fit of postwar zeal and what's replaced it has a decidedly sanitized feel—crowded wooden stalls supplying tawdry scarves and sandals, tin and copper ware. Even so it's a noisy, smoky, hectic place, and everyone colludes in its pretence of authenticity.

The street just above the rose-gardened Baščaršija mosque, **Kazandžiluk**, is one of the most animated parts of the market with the constant tapping of tinsmiths beating out pots and plates. Prices aren't that cheap here, so bargain strenuously—not a practice much admired by the shopowners. On the other hand, no one hassles you and you can look at the goods as long as you wish without having your sleeve tugged or your cash talked out of your pocket.

Helping the Baščaršija get away with it all are the old stone warehouses and *han*s that survived the clean-up, some, like the **Husref Beg Bezistan**, echoing their former use as indoor depositories now that they've been converted into department stores. Local crafts are a specialty and it's a good place to look for souvenirs and presents. But the star of the Baščaršija is the **Gazi Husref Beg Mosque**, built in 1530, possibly by a pupil of the great Turkish architect Sinan. It's the most exquisite mosque in the Balkans, incorporating those elements of Turkish civilization that are most elegant, fresh, and sensuous: a wide tree-lined forecourt with its fountain, the brisk lines of the porch, and inside a crisp geometry of cube and dome, all expansive lightness and miniature color. At one side is Husref Beg's *turbe*, with an epitaph as delicate as the mosque itself: "Husref Beg was overtaken by darkness in a state which was not sleep." Nearby stands the seventeenth-century **Sahat-kula**, the square-based city clock tower, which shows the time in Arabic, or rather the hours of prayer. All through the year, '12' on the clock had to coincide with sunset, the time of evening prayer, a feat so beyond the clockmakers that a man was employed to move the hands round each day. At midday you can still see the *muezzin* climb the minaret and sing (or rather yell above the noise of the traffic) the *ezan*, the nasal whine of the call to prayer: "God is great and there is but one God . . ."

Islamic tolerance of other faiths in Sarajevo was a tradition, and a few minutes' walk from the mosque you find the evidence in a **synagogue** which was the place of worship for Sarajevo's Sephardic Jews, who settled here after expulsion from the Iberian peninsula in 1492. Now a **museum** (Tues–Fri 9am–5pm), it assembles a few pointers to the Jews' past, and, hanging like a black pendulum, the *Book of the Dead*, a massive list of those exterminated by the Nazis. Out of 14,000 Jews in Bosnia-Hercegovina only 2600 were to survive the war, and many left for Israel afterwards; thus closed the sad episode of the Sephardic community. The synagogue's greatest treasure, the **Sarajevo Haggadah**, an illuminated fourteenth-century book of Talmudic writings, is kept and occasionally exhibited in the National Museum (see "West from the Center").

Turn right onto Maršala Tita and you find the Orthodox **Church of Sv Archangela Michala** closeted behind a wall that hid infidel worship from the eyes of Muslim neighbors. Of ancient origin, the church was damaged by fires that struck the city, so the blunt exterior dates from the 1730s. Inside it's all darkness, flickering candles, and mystery, an atmosphere charged with the arcana of Byzantium. On his feast day, the hand of the patron saint is taken from its reliquary and dipped in water, which gains the property of healing the sick; vials are filled with the holy fluid and distributed to be drunk by the congregation. The wooden iconostasis contains icons dating from the fifteenth century, but a better collection of treasures is held in the **museum** next door (Mon–Sat 8am–6pm)—Bibles, silverware, and a beautiful INRI icon near the entrance.

North of the Orthodox church, at Remzije Omanovića 31, the **Town Museum** (Mon–Sat 9am–5pm; ticket includes entry to Svrzo House) reveals the history of Sarajevo through its applied art and handicrafts. The costumes are the best exhibit, though the pseudo-Moorish building with its ornately colonnaded atrium also has its charms. First left up the hill from the town museum and then first right, the **Svrzo House** at Jovan Krsic 5 (Mon–Sat 10am–5:30pm) is an enjoyable example of Turkish domestic architecture dating from the mid-seventeenth century. Built by a wealthy Muslim merchant, it retains the traditional division into male and female quarters connected by open galleried passages. Look out for the rudimentary shower systems set in alcoves in the larger rooms, and for the intricately carved ceilings. Try to get there as it opens—the atmosphere is lost once the crowds move in.

In the nineteenth century the Byzantine style of domestic architecture was revived—albeit in sharply bastardized form. The result in Sarajevo is the lifeless formality of the **Orthodox Cathedral** on Trg Oslobodenja. The cathedral was built in the final days of Turkish rule with donations from rich Serbs, the Russian royal family, and the sultan himself—though his liberalism didn't spread to the local Muslims, whose tolerance ran out when they found the cathedral spire overshadowed the minaret of Husref Beg's Mosque. On the day of its dedication they rose to destroy it, being restrained only by the Turkish police. Subsequently, a more reasonable solution was found—the minaret was raised by a few feet and pride restored.

When the Austrians began their unpopular administration of Sarajevo late in the nineteenth century they built a **town hall** at the end of Vojvode Stepe in kitsch pseudo-Moorish style, thinking it would fit in with the Turkish buildings of the Baščaršija. As a reminder of continuing foreign control under a different name, you can imagine how well *that* went down with the locals. Today it's the university library and, if you look inside to see how Austrian architects imagined a Moorish palace, be inconspicuous—I wasn't and was promptly thrown out. Across the river the **Imperial Mosque** looks cool and magnificent, and faces the town hall with, as Rebecca West put it, "the air of a cat that watches a dog make a fool of itself." Unfortunately neither the mosque nor its **library** are currently open to the public.

East of the town hall the streets climb to **Vratnik**, originally a fortified citadel built after Sarajevo had been sacked by the Austrians in 1697, and now a down-at-heel suburb choked with crumbling Turkish houses along winding alleys. Local law forbade new houses blocking the view of the old, and the result was a chaotic scramble of buildings, each peeping over the shoulders of its neighbor. It's a steep walk up, starting at the *sebilj* and following Kovač and Jekovac up the hill past open spaces full of *stećci*. This part of town feels very different from the commercial bustle of the Barščaršija, only fifteen minutes behind you. There's animated streetlife, but the relative lack of traffic gives it a peaceful small-town atmosphere, while from a multitude of small mosques with wooden minarets comes the call to prayer. The walls of the **citadel** are long gone, though three of the original gatehouses still straddle the streets near the top of the hill. The Austrians built their military command center on the site, a grand yellow building in pavilion style which now houses the Gavrilo Princip barracks. Armed sentries don't encourage you to take a close look. If you climb right to the top—where the houses end and the fields begin—you're rewarded with a spectacular view of the Jahorina and Trebević mountains on one side and of Sarajevo on the other, the Miljacka river running a blue ruled line as accompaniment. "What a city!" wrote Ivo Andrić (see p.267) "a city passing away and dying to rise reborn and transfigured." From high in Vratnik, such effusiveness seems well justified.

The Assassination

The assassination of the **Archduke Franz Ferdinand** in 1914 is one of those schoolbook facts most people store away for future "explanation" of complex events; if the assassination wasn't the reason for World War I it was at least its cause, goes the thinking. But no event in the tortured saga of the Balkans is ever that simple, and Ferdinand's death is one of the most complex—and the most bizarre.

In the 1870s Russia took advantage of weakening Turkish domination to fight and defeat its army. At the Congress of Berlin in 1878 Serbia's independence was recognized, and Bosnia handed over to Austria for enforced administration—a deeply unpopular move that stirred Bosnian nationalist fervor. Secret societies and underground groups spread, and when in 1908 Austria annexed Bosnia, hatred began to boil. After 500 years under the Turks, Bosnians took domination by Vienna with vicious disgust.

Franz Ferdinand was heir to the Hapsburg throne, and an arrogant, widely mistrusted bigot. When wind reached Vienna of Bosnian disquiet he organized a showcase display of Austrian military might on the Serbian border to coincide with the most important day in the Serb calendar, June 28—the anniversary of the Kosovo defeat by the Turks and traditionally a day of mourning. On this of all days the Serb people and Bosnian nationalists needed no reminder from their new dictators, and for the Austrian heir to drive through the streets of Sarajevo was to say the least foolish. To do so without any military force or local police protection virtually suicidal; when Emperor Franz Josef had visited the town a few years earlier, every known anti-Austrian was placed under house arrest and double rows of troops lined the streets. Franz Ferdinand had 70,000 men a few miles away, but not one was with him on June 28, and as he drove down what's now Vojvode Stepe toward the town hall, six Bosnian nationalists were waiting to kill him. Two were schoolboys, the others in their early twenties, and none were proficient with the crude bombs they carried or could hit a brick wall with a pistol. One, Čabrinović, threw his bomb, missed and attempted suicide; the archduke and his wife, Sophie Čoteć, arrived at the town hall shaken but unhurt.

Obviously Franz Ferdinand should never have come to Sarajevo; obviously the trip should have been abandoned. Yet inexplicably and inexorably he progressed towards his fate. An aide suggested diverting the procession away from the dangerously crowded Franz Josef Strasse (now JNA Ulica) and continuing back down Vojvode Stepe to the hotel at Ilidža. This was agreed, but no one informed the chauffeurs. So when Franz Ferdinand's car turned by the bridge into Franz Josef Strasse, an angry aide told the driver he'd taken a wrong turn. The car stopped and a slight young Bosnian called **Gavrilo Princip** stepped out and shot Ferdinand through the heart. Sophie Čoteć leant forward to hold her husband and a second bullet killed her immediately.

There isn't space here to go into the theories of intrigue that have grown out of the assassination; at first glance Franz Ferdinand's unprotected final hours seem almost the offering of a sacrifice, one that could bring Austria into a long-wanted war with Serbia, but the chance aspect of so much of the day's events refutes conspiracy. When Europe had shaken itself after hearing the news, events moved quickly. A month later Austria declared war on Serbia, even though no connection between the Serbian government and the assassins was ever found; Russia refused to countenance Austrian expansion; Germany supported Austria as a pretext for gaining Russian territory and attacking France. The Great War began.

On the corner of the assassination spot the **Princip Museum** (Mon–Fri 9am–5pm, Sun 9am–1pm) has photos of Princip and his co-plotters. Three were hanged, but Princip and Čabrinović were under 21 and were sent to Austrian jails with eleven other Bosnians; only nine survived the war, their diseased prison cells bringing slow, tubercular death. Today they're remembered as heroes, liberators of Bosnia, and lie buried in a little-visited **Mausoleum** on Kralja Tomislava.

The exact spot where Princip pulled the trigger is marked by a slightly comical set of footprints, but as you stand here and look out at what is really just another ordinary street corner, the weight of history, of being at the place where the straining muscles of Europe began to tear apart, hits you very hard.

West from the Center

From the Baščaršija, the broad sweep of Maršala Tita leads back towards the train and bus stations, and through less concentrated, and on the whole more modernized, stretches of town. Just before Djure Djakovića branches north, a small gardened park contains a few ancient *nišans* in what was once a Muslim graveyard. Farther along Maršala Tita, the **Ali Paša Mosque** delights in its miniature simplicity, a pocket-sized late sixteenth-century building surrounded by trees. Sadly, it's currently closed to visitors. Beyond, Maršala Tita passes through a dull expanse of offices and expense-account hotels built to impress during the 1984 Winter Olympics.

Just before, at the beginning of Vojvode Putnika, the **National Museum of Bosnia-Hercegovina** (*Zemaljski Muzej*; Tues–Fri 9am–5pm, Sat & Sun 9–11am; trams #1, #2, #3, and #5 from downtown) displays the republic's archaeological, ethnographic, and natural history collections. The costumes and period rooms of the ethnographic section are fun, but most fascinating are the *stećci*, or Bogomil funerary monuments. The **Bogomils** (the name means "beloved of God") were a mysterious bunch; a heretical sect, possibly of Bulgarian origin, they flourished throughout Bosnia and in parts of Macedonia from the tenth century onward. Not much is known about their beliefs, except what was written by their enemies who accused them of the standard devil-worship and "unnatural" vices—the word 'bugger' is a distortion of *Bulgar*, then the usual term for a Bogomil heretic. Inspired by the teachings of the third-century Mesopotamian, Mani, they believed the devil to be creator of the material world and so denied all things physical, rejecting possessions, the consummation of marriage, the established churches, much of the Old Testament, and the physical presence of Christ. Obviously this brought persecution by both Catholic and Orthodox faiths, and when the Turks arrived at the end of the fourteenth century they shrewdly offered the

Bogomils protection and freedom of worship—so long as they nominally considered themselves Muslim rather than Christian. Since the contemporary policy of the papacy was to have them incinerated, this must have seemed a very reasonable suggestion to the Bosnian heretics and not surprisingly they turned their backs on organized Christianity—and the Turks consolidated their position in the Balkans. Eventually the Bogomils were absorbed into Islam, though not before leaving their *stećci* dotted around Bosnia-Hercegovina as funeral monuments—oddly solid memorials for a faith that revolted against the corporeal. The collection here has some of the best stones, of varying shapes and sizes but usually carved with crude stylized figures. Their Old Cyrillic inscriptions have a peculiar mix of sadness and dry humor:

> *Here lies Dragac. When I wished to be I ceased to be.*
>
> *Here lies Orislav Kopijević. I have been pierced, I have been slashed, I have been skinned, but I did not die of it. I just closed my eyes on the day of Christ's nativity and my lord, the duke, buried me and set up this memorial.*
>
> *I beseech you touch me not. You will be as I am, but I cannot be as you are.*

At Radmilja, near Mostar, you can see a collection of these *stećci* in situ (see p.275).

In the museum's library—though not always on display—is another interesting relic of Sarajevo's mixed religious past: the rare and beautiful *Sarajevo Haggadah*, an illuminated Hebrew codex brought from Spain by the city's Sephardic Jews.

A little down from the National Museum is the **Museum of the Revolution**, Vojvode Putnika 9 (same times as National Museum but open Mon, closed Fri). War museums are a dime a dozen in Yugoslavia, but this one struggles up from the ranks of the ordinary. To comprehend the detailed displays of events from 1878 on, buy the English guidebook: interesting photos, documents, and a fearsome collection of arms.

Listings

American Center Omladinska 1 (Mon–Fri 9am–4:30pm, Sat 10am–1pm). Newspapers, library, weekly films.

Cable car (see map: Mon–Fri 10am–8pm, Sat & Sun 8am–8pm). Whisks you up from the hazy city to the sharp pine air of Mt Trebević. Great views and the quickest way to the *Don Odmora Mladost* youth hostel (see "Arrival and places to stay").

Car rental *Avis*, Obala Pariske Komune 8; *Unis Tourist*, JNA 4.

Folklore Between April and October the *Hotel Bristol* (trams #2, #3, or #5 from the Barščaršija) puts on a display of music and folk dancing in the Bosnian style. It's not cheap and it's aimed specifically at the tourist market, but it's quite fun if you let yourself enter into the spirit of the affair. Prohibitive bar prices may slow down the process.

Gallery of Fine Art JNA 38 (Tues–Sat 10am–1pm & 4–8pm, Sun 10am–1pm). Changing exhibitions on the ground floor and an above-average collection of Bosnian-Hercegovinian art on the first. Highspots are the portraits by Roman Petrović and Pero Popović.

Hospital Moše Pijade 23 (☎94).

JAT Vase Miskina 2. Sarajevo's airport is 12km out, linked by regular *JAT* bus from JNA 24.

Maps The tourist office at Jugoslavenska Narodne Armije 50 sells a more detailed map of the city than we've had space for.

Markets Great produce at the Wednesday market opposite the town hall—try the *borovnica*, wild blueberries. More general produce from the daily market on Maršala Tita; both good for cheap eating.

Police Main station at Augusta Cesarca 18.

Post office Obala Vojvode Stepe 8 is Sarajevo's main office, open Mon–Sat 7am–8pm. There's no effective lining-up system, so you'll be here long enough to appreciate the gilded moldings in this cavernous palace of pretentiousness, built by the Austrians in 1912. Shorter lines and more prosaic surroundings can be found at the substations between the bus and train stations, or at JNA 81.

Radio Sarajevo English broadcasts every day at 11:30am, 91.7FM, 95.3FM, or 98.9FM.

Skiing The 1984 Winter Olympics left Sarajevo with extensive facilities, which it's now trying to fill with tourists. Mount Jahorina is the best equipped with slalom, giant slalom, downhill, and cross-country courses; Mount Bjelašnica also has slalom facilities and moderately expensive pensions. Details, reservations, equipment rental from the tourist office; snow from November to April.

Train tickets *Unis Tourist* (Vase Miskina 16) make internal/international reservations, including sleeping cars.

Northwest Bosnia

The main route **north and west** of Sarajevo runs through some of the most inviting countryside in Bosnia: verdant, copse-patched, and fertile, every small field seems to double as someone's back garden. Cupped in a valley, **TRAVNIK** is the first town you reach, a jumble of houses surrounded by greenery, giving it the look of an untended garden suburb; indeed *travnik* means "place of grass." It's a center for local farmers, whose horses and carts roll in for the Thursday **market**. For this, the day to be here, traditional costume is worn and the whole thing progresses to picturesque effect. But if you miss it there are still a few threadbare leftovers from Turkish times to explore. Outside the *Hotel Orient* on Maršala Tita stand two **turbe**, the mausoleums of the viziers of Travnik. When the Turkish governors were thrown out of Sarajevo, Travnik became the base from which they ruled the rest of Bosnia, and with an iron grip. In the right-hand *turbe* lies Djelaldjin

Pasha, much hated in his day for bleeding the people dry with taxes and ruthlessly removing opponents—he once beheaded 300 dissenters in a single day. The locals still use his name—*Djelali*—as a term of severe abuse. To the east of town the **Many-Colored Mosque** is no longer colorful nor particularly mosque-like, with only the minaret giving it away. On the hillside above, the **Fortress** is firmly locked, awaiting restoration, and there's no low wall to jump over. To get near you need to cross a high flimsy-looking bridge—something bystanders will attempt to dissuade you from doing. Should you want to risk it, grit your teeth and cross, since the view is fine.

If you keep on walking past the mosque out of town, rather than turning up the hill, you reach the ruined **Medressa**, a Muslim school built in 1892 when the new rail line plowed through the old one. A good push at the door secures entry to the building, deserted years ago but with columns and walls still brightly painted, and unperturbed by the weeds that have taken hold. Plans are afoot to remodel it into a hotel, so have a look now while there's still something of the original left.

Travnik's slender claim to recent fame is **Ivo Andrić,** the writer who won the Nobel Prize for Literature in 1961. He was born here and much of his writing concerns Bosnia and Bosnian history—which is probably why most people have never heard of him. *The Bridge on the Drina* is considered his best work, but a number of other books have been translated, including *A Travnik Chronicle*, published in English as the *Bosnian Story* (see "Books" in *Contexts*). Getting into his birthplace, the **Ivo Andrić Museum**, may prove a runaround: first try the door at S. Turudije, but if it's locked go to the town museum just below the *Borac* store off Maršala Tita and agitate for the key. The rewards are a collection of his books and manuscripts, along with photos of the Nobel Prize ceremony. Enthusiasts only.

Unless you're heading up to Vlasić (see below) there's not much point in utilizing Travnik's private **rooms**. If you need to, reserve them at the **tourist office** by the bus station (Mon–Sat 7am–7pm, Sun 8–11am). Roughly twice a day buses leave Travnik for the **ski resort** of **VLASIĆ**; a new road has meant growth but it's still cheap and an excellent if smaller alternative to Sarajevo— prices, ski-rental, and chalet reservations from Travnik tourist office. While you're there try the **cheese** that's known as *Vlasić Sir*, made from the milk of sheep grazing on the mountains' rich alpine pastures, it has a delicious, delicate flavor.

Jajce

Steeped in history ancient and modern, **JAJCE** (pronounced "Ya-it-say") is about the most attractive small town in Bosnia-Hercegovina. Tourist brochures always show the same photo of it: waterfalls of the river Pliva spilling down to the river Vrbas, a sandcastle hill topped with a fortress standing behind. But when you arrive the town looks nothing like this, and to enter Jajce at the **Pliva Gate**, part of the old walls that rim the town's oval mound, is a disappointment—you need to zigzag through the Bosnian-Oriental houses that fight for a place below the fortress to see the town at its best. Now an empty ruin, the **fortress** was once stronghold of the

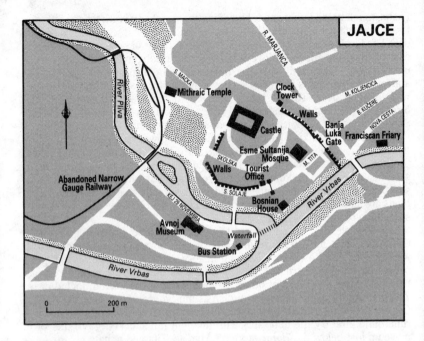

kings of Bosnia: built by the warrior-noble Hrvoke Vukić, it became capital of his successors Stjepan Tomaš and Stjepan Tomašević, on whom it fell to defend Bosnia against the Turks. This proved a lost battle—most of the people adopted Islam in preference to only-recently-arrived Christianity, and the Christian kings needed outside support to prop up their authority. When the sultan started to attack Bosnia he was generally welcomed without resistance, and Tomašević meekly agreed to give himself up if his life was spared; this he did and was promptly executed outside the town. So Bosnia fell to the Turks.

The crypt Hrvoke Vukić had built is one of a couple of subterranean attractions for which you need the help of the **tourist office** to explore; they're at Maršala Tita (Mon–Sat 7am–9pm, Sun 8am–1pm) and also reserve private **rooms**, which fill quickly in July and August. Jajce also has two hotels, both of which charge around $34 for a double room: the *Turist* (☎070/33-268) and the marginally better equipped *Jajce* (☎070/33-285).

For a consideration the tourist office will open the **Catacombs** in the old town. Vukić seems to have left this, his crypt, unfinished; perhaps it was raided by the Turks, possibly because the king had unpopular connections with the Bogomils—some of their symbols are carved on the walls. The catacombs have an eerie, unsettling air that's hard to describe—you get the feeling of something dark and evil going on among the damp black stones, and it's good to get back out into daylight. A short way out of town (a tourist office person takes you there), the **Mithraic Temple** also has its mysteries.

Mithraism was imported to Europe from India and Iran by Roman legionaries, and the carved fourth-century altarpiece clearly depicts the elements of a religion that for a while competed with Christianity—in fact paralleled its mystical elements. Mithras is shown drawing back the head of the sacrificial bull to let flow the blood that forms the earth and its crops, the semen issued in its death throes becoming living creatures. On either side are torch bearers, one with torch uplifted, symbolizing spring and renewal, the other with a torch extinguished: winter and death. The bull's slaughter parodied the crucifixion, and other ceremonies that would have been performed here mirrored the practices of baptism and the Eucharist. Eventually Christianity spread and Mithraism died out—not least because a religion that preaches constant victory and sacrificial death is more likely to be popular with a small group of soldiers rather than the mass of peasant farmers.

In later years Jajce acquitted itself well in resisting invaders. When Bosnia was handed over to the Austrians in 1878 it fought tooth and nail to keep them out, and during World War II it became a **Partisan HQ**, the chiefs of staff holding here the second, 1943 session of their parliament, the Anti-Fascist Council for the National Liberation of Yugoslavia (AVNOJ). Delegates came from all over what would in a few years become Yugoslavia, often traveling for weeks through occupied territory, to declare King Peter and his exiled government divested of authority and raise Tito to the position of Marshal of Yugoslavia. It's for this that Jajce is, to Yugoslavs at least, famed, and naturally there's a **museum** to the event—the actual hall where the meeting was held, decked out as it was at the time with the partisans' slogan *Smrt Fasizumu—Sloboda Narodu* ("Death to Fascism, Liberty to the People") above the stage. Another **museum** (both are open March–Oct 8am–noon & 2–7pm daily) has photos and mementos of the event, including a couple of **Brigadier Fitzroy Maclean**, head of the British Mission, parachuted in near Jajce to liaise with Tito and report back to Churchill on the Balkan power balance*.

Back to the old town, and two final buildings of interest. The **Church of St Luke** makes claim to once have held the body of the saint himself, bought from the Turks who seized it from its original grave in Epirus. When Jajce was about to fall to the Turks the local Franciscan friars hurriedly carried it off to safety in Venice, where they encountered a problem: the Vatican already had a head of Saint Luke, Padua his (headless) body, and in a church in Rome his arm had for some years been curing the sick. After a trial the Papal Legate declared the Jajce Luke to be the genuine item, but the Paduans went on venerating their alternative corpse all the same. Little is left of the church today save a neat campanile, one of the town's landmarks. The Franciscans returned in the nineteenth century and built a monastery and gaudily repellent **Church** east of the center; here a **museum** (daily 9–11am & 2–6pm) sits cluttered with the ribs and bones of Jajce's ruined churches, and what's left of the unfortunate Stjepan Tomašević, whose grave was discovered in 1892.

---

*For a fascinating account of the events that led to the AVNOJ meeting, along with rousing tales of Hardy Boys'-style Balkan exploits, see his book *Eastern Approaches*—detailed in "Books" in *Contexts*.

Jajce's **market day** is Wednesday—which, if you're here that day you won't really need telling, since by 7am the place is swarming with horses and carts all heading to the square on S. Solaje. Here you'll find home-woven clothes that combine incredible toughness with delicate decoration, hand-wrought metalwork, and homemade cheese; and, reminding you that poverty isn't far behind the prettiness, beggars crouch by the roadside plaintively wailing for a few dinar notes. Markets like this are rapidly declining to the tourist bland-outs you find at Mostar; despite the sad edge, don't miss it.

Lastly, a couple of places **to eat**. *Bosanska Kuca*, just left of the Pliva Gate does Bosnian specialties of spiced meats at affordable prices, and *Pizza Fortuna*, on a balcony in the shopping center, has the usual Yugoslav versions of Italian food.

If you're into **camping**, there's a grounds 8km out of Jajce on the Bihac road at the **Pliva Lakes**—an inordinately beautiful place to stay, even allowing for the heavy summer influx of tourists, with dark wooded mountains and deep emerald lakes. The road there takes you past antiquated watermills, tiny wooden boxes strutting above the river like storks and used until recently to grind corn; they seem almost too delicate to have stood the years of use they've evidently had.

Northwest towards Croatia

From Jajce the road follows the **Vrbas Gorge**, the river a green so vivid it seems the color has run down from the forested hills that surround. At the end of the valley **BANJA LUKA**, Bosnia-Hercegovina's second largest city, doesn't have much going for it; flat and faceless, it was extensively rebuilt after an earthquake in 1969. The new town is better than many other recent developments though, and if you do wind up here there's an **Art Gallery** (Tues–Sun 10am–7pm), Trg 27 Mart 2, housed in the town's old railroad museum, and a glossy **Regional Museum** (Mon–Fri 9am–1pm & 5–7pm, Sat & Sun 9am–1pm). If you can get in, the **Ferhad Pasha Mosque** is a self-important sort of building; it was badly damaged in the earthquake, and has been restored with some lavishly colored arabesques—worth seeing. Behind the mosque there's not much left of the fifteenth-century castle, bombarded by the partisans after German troops held out there in the last days of the war; what remained was destroyed in 1969, and all you'll find today is a restaurant and a view of the river. To stay the night in Banja Luka you can get private rooms through the **tourist office** at Trg Palih Boraca 2, the main square in town (from the bus station take a red #10 to the center; Mon–Fri 8am–8pm, Sat 7am–2pm). Or in July and August you might try the *Studentski Dom* on Marx and Engels Trg (bus #10, then #17); best check at the tourist office first as rooms here can prove more expensive than their private accommodation. For nightlife just join the tidal *korso* that sweeps down the Maršala Tita.

From Banja Luka it's an easy leap up to Zagreb or east to the Plitvice Lakes, the latter route taking you through **BIHAĆ**, whose once-Gothic church was transformed into a mosque in the nineteenth century—a fitting hybrid for Bosnia.

The Road to Mostar

The main road from Sarajevo down to the coast follows the **Neretva valley**, a gorge of wooded slopes thinning out to bare karst as you head southwestwards. Road and railway edge the same riverside route, which near Lake Jablanica passes a steel bridge collapsed in the rushing waters. It's the scene of a wartime incident that has become part of Yugoslav folklore. In the winter of 1943 the Germans led a successful offensive against the partisans in Bosnia, forcing thousands of troops and 4000 wounded towards the impassable Neretva valley. Tito immediately had all the Neretva bridges blown up; the Germans, knowing the impossibility of crossing the turbulent swollen river, concentrated troops in southwest Bosnia to ensnare the partisans as they made for Montenegro. But on the night of March 6 Tito ordered a wooden footbridge to be strung across the crippled steel bridge, and succeeded in getting both wounded and partisans safely across. The Germans were left waiting for a retreat that never arrived. It was probably the single most effective withdrawal in Yugoslavia's war; "A fight to save the wounded," Tito called it, "and the most humane battle in the history of warfare." The destroyed bridge remains, a testament to his cunning stratagem, and a heavily-visited **museum** (8am–4pm) displays photos, documents, and weapons a touch more inventively than usual.

After Lake Jablanica the road tracks beside the Neretva along a sheer-walled canyon with peaks rising to 2000m on either side. The diagonal strata of the stark rock walls are clearly visible, punctuated by waterfalls shooting like fingers down the canyon sides.

Mostar

As you approach **MOSTAR** the mountain tops turn silver and the land becomes parched as the valley widens. Summers here are among the hottest in the country, and the town itself lies by the river like burned embers of bone under the sun. Tourists come by the busload from the coast to spend an afternoon in the town: they snap its one attraction, its famed bridge, walk through the market, and promptly disappear. Which is fair enough, really— while an interesting enough place, Mostar isn't going to be the base for anyone's holiday.

Practicalities

If you are going to spend more than the customary afternoon in Mostar, **accommodation** shouldn't be a problem; there's a variety of inexpensive options. For the town's cheapest private **rooms**, head for *Apro Tourist*, about fifteen minutes' walk from the bus and train stations at Kujundžiluk 2 (Mon–Sat 8am–3pm, Sun 10am–noon). Most of the rooms they offer are conveniently central, but if they've run out try *Neretva Tourist* at the *Neretva Hotel* (Mon–Fri 7am–2pm, Sat & Sun 9am–noon). A cheaper alternative during July and August is the **Studenski Dom** at Radićeva 84a (bus #2 or #3 from the stations, or walk down Hercegovačke Brigade until Avenija 14 Februar, then ask). The nearest **campground** is 8km south on the main road at Buna—not ideally sited, but there are several buses a day. Otherwise, the cheapest **hotels** in town are the *Energoinvest*, just down from the stations, and the *Hercegovina* (☎088/21-311), over the river on Moše Pijade. Reckon on $28 for a double room—singles can be a problem.

It's easy to **eat** well and at moderate cost in Mostar, provided you steer clear of the bridge and bazaar, where prices are hiked up by the folklore displays. For light **lunches** try the *Lovac Bife*, Braće Fejića 21, and for **restaurant** food *Mimosa* on Trg 1 Maj (turn left off Braće Fejića after no. 65). Best of all, if a little more expensive, is the *Vlaho* where you can eat on a terrace down by the river (diagonally across the Maršala Tita bridge from the *Neretva Hotel*). *Burek* joints abound in town, and you can buy fruit and local cheeses at the **market** next to the *medresa* (Koran school) at the southern end of Braće Fejića. Spirited evening **drinking** takes off on the terrace of the *Hotel Bristol* and in the *Bife* on Trg 14 Februar. Wine buffs might note that the two main local wines, *Žilavka* (white) and *Blatina* (red) are celebrated in early September each year in the **Festival of the Grape**.

The Town

Mostar developed during the fifteenth century after its annexation by the Turks, who used it as a seat of government for Hercegovina. Meaning to stay, they built mosques, public baths, and caravanserai, but best of all and bang in the middle of the town they built the **old bridge**—the attraction the tourists come to see. The name *Mostar* in fact comes from the word for a bridge keeper and this has to be one of the most elegant spans anywhere, throwing a steep arch over the hurried river below. "Like a rainbow rising up to the Milky Way, leaping from sheer rock to sheer rock," whimsied Evlija Čelebi, passing through in the seventeenth century. Others have seen, in its graceful form, a petrified echo of the Islamic crescent. Today's bridge was built in 1566, but there was already a bridge on the site when the Turks arrived. It was of wood, suspended by chains, and so old and rickety that the inhabitants successfully petitioned Istanbul for a new one. Inevitably, there's an apocryphal tale about the construction of this famous arch: after his first bridge had collapsed, the architect was told by the Sultan to build one that would stand or else lose his head. This rather unusual bonus scheme had a great effect and when the scaffolding was about to be removed, the terrified architect ran off and hid in a nearby village. Even though the bridge held, he never returned—just in case. When you consider that the only mortar used was a composite of eggs and goats' hair, his lack of confidence hardly seems surprising. Hang around the bridge long enough and one of the local lads will take position as if to dive, wait for a hundred or so fingers to hover above shutter releases and then demand a little something to do the deed—at which the crowd disperses. If you want to see less mercenary performances of bravery/stupidity, come on June 4, when the annual diving championships are held.

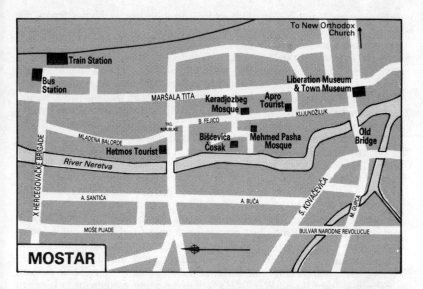

At each end of the bridge stands a large stone tower. On the east side, the **Tara Tower** is a squat semicylindrical building of 1676, whose walls are three meters thick—which is just as well since it was built as the town's gun powder store. At the other end is the **Ćelovina Tower** from 1716, a dour oblong edifice which served variously as a prison and as a barracks.

East of the bridge lies the **Kujundžiluk** or bazaar, originally the market street of the Turkish town. You can still buy crude copper ornaments and jewelry here, as well as brand new "antiques," but it's a charmless place, a series of tourist shop windows rather than a street of artisans. Peruvian woollen caps, Indian carved boxes, and Moroccan pipes all sell well here—and the only visible sign of Turkish influence is an occasional fez donned by charlatan shopkeepers. Put all this behind you and walk on.

Mehmed Pasha's Mosque has something of the true Turkish heritage, its little cobbled courtyard, bubbling fountain, and greenery showing the Ottoman love for things gently sensual. In the middle is a seventeenth-century tomb, elaborate by the standards of Islam, which makes no pretense about death: corpses are brought to the mosque to be washed and wrapped in white cloth, then placed in simple graves, the head turned toward Mecca. *Nišans*, the sugary white gravestones, were simple affairs, a turban representing a man, a sword a janissary, each decorated with a text from the Koran. Disturbance of tombs is forbidden, and all over Bosnia-Hercegovina *nišans* continue to tumble in untended patches. Mehmet Pasha's mosque is itself much like any other—high-domed and patchily decorated—but if you scale its minaret there's a fine view of Mostar old and new; and it's not every day you get to climb a minaret. The other mosque you're steered to (you can get in on the same ticket) is the **Karadžozbeg Mosque**, a couple of minutes' walk away off Maršala Tita. Built in 1557 to a design by Mimar Sinan, it's larger, grander, and less intimate, though the interior is in better repair. A 600-year-old Koran is its prize possession.

If you're into Turkish domestic architecture the seventeenth-century **Biščevica Čosak** stands on Biščevica 14 (daily 8am–7pm), a little too eager to please—dolled up with an excess of carving and decoration in a picture-book idea of what a Turkish house ought to look like. A similar house, the **Kajtazova Kuča** (daily 10am–7pm) on Gaše Ilića, about five minutes' south-east of the old bridge, is older but it has the same artificial look and feel. Neither matches the charm of Sarajevo's Svrzo House (see p.261).

Turkish buildings don't have a monopoly in Mostar. Climb to the top of the hill and the **New Orthodox Church** stands high above the town, built in front of the older church in the 1870s. Cavernous and empty, it's really rather eerie, seemingly built and immediately left to rot, like a ballroom constructed for a single ball. There's also a sprinkling of buildings from the Austro-Hungarian period, notably the **Neretva Hotel** by the river at Trg Republike and the **Municipal Baths** just across the square (useful for a dip if you've been on the road for ages). The **Musej Hercegovine**, just back from the old bridge at Maršala Tita 130, offers predictable, unadventurous fare, including an archaeological section, "Mostar Since the Fifteenth Century," and, as ever, a collection from World War II. For a more moving monument to heroism and sacrifice you should cross town and visit the **Partisan Memorial Cemetery** built into a hillside off Blagoye Parović Ulica.

Towards the Sea: the Neretva Valley

Fifteen kilometers southeast of Mostar, **BLAGAJ** was the region's main town before the arrival of the Turks. It lies at the base of a sheer cliff-face that's splendidly crowned by the ruins of a castle built by Herceg Stefan—he of Hercegovina fame. Right at the foot of the cliff, next to where the river Buna gushes from a rock, stands the **Tekija**, one of the few surviving Yugoslav "monasteries" built by the **dervishes**, an ascetic though fairly liberal bunch of Muslims who founded separate sects in the fifteenth and sixteenth centuries. The Tekija expresses the Islamic style and tradition: a broad-domed *hammam*, arabesque carving, and the *turbe* of an Islamic Saint George, **Sari Saltuk**. According to legend this pious dervish fell madly in love with Herceg Stefan's daughter Milica, so that when the local dragon (who lived in the cave near the Tekija) dragged her to his lair Sari Saltuk leaped forward and killed it, rescuing Milica who duly became his wife. The Tekija, which is supposed to have been built on the site of his conquest, probably bears no similarity to what you see today, which is a recent rebuilding to a nineteenth-century design.

Otherwise, Blagaj has several old Turkish houses and a sixteenth-century mosque but not much else. Nevertheless it makes an ideal day trip from Mostar (3 buses daily). The walk along the river from here to BUNA is very pretty, and you'll probably see eagles wheeling overhead.

The harsh karst limestone of **Mostar** continues along the road to **Listica** and Posušje, where a trip from the road into the hills rewards with strange open wells and vultures flying high. When you reach the wild windswept **Lake Buško**, the landscape changes: a lusher place in summer, a bitter one in winter, this section of the Bosnian interior is bleak and sparsely populated; it was the scene of much fighting and Partisan activity in World War II. **Cincar** (2005m) is a shapely mountain climbed by locals from the *Livno Mountain Club*, but generally the mountains are less spectacular than those to the south. There's little to see in the busy town save a small back street collection of cobblers and a park in which to stretch out your legs. **Glamoć** was the secne of much fighting during the war, and German soldiers destroyed many villages around the *polje*.

From Glamoć on toward **Drvar** the landscape is even more desolate, with villages like **Rore** having a Wild-West air in their ranch-like buildings. The limestone is pocked with deep hollows, often the only parts of the plateau that can be cultivated, the rest being too exposed and the soil too thin. The barren lands end at Drvar, and as Croatia is reached at the pretty village of **Martin Brod**, waterfalls and woodlands take the place of the stark *poljes*, and the colorful dress of Muslim peasants is replaced by the black of Christian Croatian women.

Like Sveti Stefan in Montenegro, **POČITELJ** is the stuff of picture postcards, a fortified Turkish town built into the steep valley-side. With an eye to its obvious tourist potential, the authorities have restored the old houses to a high standard, but although it's picturesque to a fault it's somehow barren and antiseptic. The **Hadji Alija Mosque**, with its richly decorated minaret, is from 1563, while most of the other major buildings—the clock tower, *hammam*, and *medresa*—date from the seventeenth century. The town is dominated by an **octagonal fortress** of pre-Turkish origin. It's not worth an overnight stay (the tourist buses usually give it half an hour) but if you're stranded, or if you just like the place, then there are some pleasant and inexpensive **rooms** in restored houses high on the hill. Details from and arrangements at the *Restaurant Han*—but don't eat there unless you're in the money. Far more reasonable **food** is available at the small unnamed place on the terrace above *Restoran Počitelj*, a great spot to watch the sun set over the river.

Just beyond Počitelj a road turns east towards **STOLAC**, a pleasant little town set in a deep valley with a ruined Turkish castle and some old Turkish houses. Just before you reach the town, the road passes the hamlet of **RADIMLJA**, the most accessible site of the **Bogomil Stećci** found all over Bosnia-Hercegovina (see p.265). There are over 200 monuments at Radimlja, and they come in various shapes—some cuneiform, some like trunk-shaped sarcophagi—but they're all in the local white stone and many are carved with a figure whose right arm is outstretched and exaggerated in a mysterious gesture; other show hunting and dancing scenes. High above the necropolis in the hills to the north lies **Ošanjići**, the remains of an ancient urban settlement of the Illyrians, with walls built of massive slabs and blocks of limestone. It's reached by following the mountain road which snakes north from Stolac—about two hours on foot.

Before June 24 1981, **MEDJUGORJE**, on the high Brotsno plateau on the other side of the Neretva valley about 20km west of the river, was a small agricultural community growing grapes and tobacco. But, on that particular day, a group of schoolchildren reported seeing a vision of the Virgin Mary on a nearby hillside and the village hasn't been the same since. Thronged with hundreds of thousands of pilgrims from all over the world, Medjugorje is now a charmless place of new buildings and fast-food restaurants clustering round the strikingly ugly church of Sv Jakob. Finished in 1969, Sv Jakob offers a multilingual perpetual program of services from dawn till late at night. The main annual pilgrimage takes place in June on the anniversary of the apparition. All sorts of tacky tourist artifacts can be bought here and money-changing is a major industry—if you've been to Lourdes or Jerusalem you'll be familiar with the brisk trade in plastic Madonnas; if not, it all comes as a shock that gives way to mild disgust. Meanwhile, the religious authorities haven't even decided if the visions were genuine—not that it seems to make much difference to the devout. Give the place a wide berth unless you've genuine religious reasons for being here.

To reach Medjogorje you'll ideally have your own transport; otherwise buses run from Mostar, or you can join one of the conducted **tours** from major coastal towns such as Dubrovnik. Accommodation needs are serviced by the **tourist office** on the main road to the church, which has a few private **rooms**, or the *Šuma Grmine* "hotel-village" (☎088/650-005; doubles $35).

If you have your own transportation and a day to spare, press on from Medjugorje towards LJUBUŠKI with its obligatory Turkish fort and dramatic views across the plain to the Biokovo mountains. Just before you hit the town turn left down a narrow road to the **Kravica Waterfalls**. Here the river Trebižat drops eighty feet down a broad horseshoe-shaped pitch. It's a beautiful area, thickly wooded and ideal for swimming and sunbathing. Provided you're discreet, camping's no problem.

Back on the main road, the Neretva approaches the sea and the valley broadens to a brown plain, untidy with dilapidated roadside houses. On the narrow neck of land that is Bosnia-Hercegovina's coastline, **NEUM** deserves mention as the republic's only coastal resort—an exclusively modern ghetto of workers' hotels. To the north, KARDELJEVO (actually in Croatia) is its only port, and the place to head if you're making straight for the PELJEŠAC PENINSULA and KORČULA, or if you're catching the train back to Sarajevo and the interior.

The Drina Valley

South from Sarajevo, **FOČA** is a good place to start exploring the **Drina Valley**—most spectacularly through **raft trips** down it (see below), though to the west there is also the **Sutjeska National Park**, 165 square kilometers of unspoiled, untouristed meadows and forest around the Zelengora and Maglić mountains. In these hills one of the fiercest and most crucial struggles of World War II took place, the 1943 **Battle of Sutjeska**, which saw some 127,000 occupying troops surround 20,000 partisans—nearly a quarter of them suffering from typhus. In the bombardment, Tito himself was wounded, becoming the only commander-in-chief of Allied forces to sustain an injury in combat. The partisans were in serious danger of being wiped out, but with their superior knowledge of the country and skill in movement by night, they managed to find a gap in the surrounding enemy wall. The price was high—a division left behind to hold enemy fire was annihilated, and the immobile sick and wounded were massacred. Altogether 7300 partisans died in the engagement; their memorial stands at TJENTIŠTE, along with a mausoleum and museum.

Foča is rapidly becoming a dreary modern town, though its small Turkish quarter and market (above the main commercial street) have enough residual character to explore while you're waiting for a bus on to Višegrad. Down by the river the **Aladža Mosque** is a small, elegant sixteenth-century structure of delicately balanced line and proportion and refined arabesque decoration. The tireless Turkish traveler of the Balkans, Evliya Čelebi, left his eulogistic comment carved in the decoration: "I have traveled much and visited many cities, but a land such as this I have never seen . . . written by the slave of God, Evliya, in the year 1074." Unfortunately the mosque is rarely open—to see its colorful interior you'll have to content yourself with peering through shuttered windows.

By **raft trips** down the Drina the tourist people really mean raft, simply logs tied together and piloted by an experienced *triftar*, whose skills are traditionally passed down from father to son. Since the dam below Višegrad tamed the lower stretches of the Drina it's not as dangerous as you might think— more of a gentle drift down to Višegrad, overnighting at a hotel in GORAŽDE en route. Trips run from the beginning of July to the end of August, leaving Foča at noon each Saturday; details from the *Zelengora Hotel* or *Unis Tourist* nearby. For really living dangerously, a longer alternative is the run down from DJURDJEVIĆA TARA in Montenegro via the river Tara—a four-day journey described by the tourist board as "intended for courageous people." Details from the tourist office at Djurdjevića Tara or most local travel agents.

North of Foča the Drina Valley is more scenic than spectacular, though it has its moments as the road rises high above the river, flashing through rock-hewn tunnels. Slowly the steep defile's sides widen and at the end of the gorge **VIŠEGRAD** spreads along the broadened valley, the mountain ranges running down in random scribbles to the river. As at Mostar there's just one thing to see, and you see it right away—the **bridge**. Built by the Turks in the sixteenth century, it's as tidy as a draftsman's drawing, strong yet graceful on its ten arches. Ivo Andrić's book about it—*The Bridge on the Drina*—is just as famous, though his subject is really the story of Bosnian families from the time of the building of the bridge to World War I. Višegrad itself is a small, uneventful, but likable town, a useful stopover with cheap **private rooms**— available from *Panos Tourist* at Maršala Tita 24 (Mon–Fri 7am–7pm, Sat 8am– 2pm, Sun 8am–noon)—and a good **restaurant**, *Ušće*, at the jetty (follow the signpost from the end of main street). If you arrive by bus, get off in the center; when you leave buy your ticket from the station, which is a short way out of town. The choice of routes is to Serbia and Titovo Užice, on the main Dubrovnik–Belgrade road that rises steeply from the town to cross the **Zlatibor mountains**, or to Sarajevo via ROGATICA—both half-day journeys.

South of Foča the road down to the coast skirts the Sujetska National Park, before an unmemorable journey down to Trebinje and then Dubrovnik. At Trebinje you can cut east into Montenegro via Nikšić, but it's not the best approach and public transit connections are dreadful.

travel details

Buses

From Sarajevo to Banja Luka (5 daily; 4hr 30min); Belgrade (5 daily; 8hr); Dubrovnik (3 daily; 5hr); Foča (3 daily; 2hr); Jajce (5 daily; 3hr 30min); Kardeljevo (8 daily; 3hr 30min); Mostar (4 daily; 2hr 30min); Skopje (2 daily; 11hr); Split (4 daily; 5hr); Travnik (5 daily; 2hr 30min); Višegrad (4 daily; 2hr 30min); Zagreb (4 daily; 8hr).

International buses

From Sarajevo to Istanbul (1 daily; 33hr).

Trains

From Sarajevo to Belgrade (5 daily; 6hr) and to Kardeljevo (9 daily; 4hr) via Mostar (2hr).

International trains

From Sarajevo to Stuttgart (1 daily; 22hr).

CHAPTER SIX

SERBIA

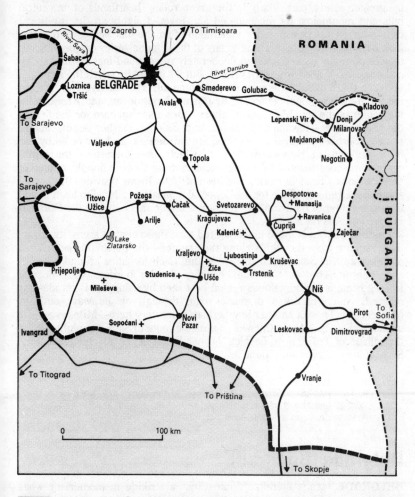

T hough the largest, and arguably the most diverse and beautiful of the Yugoslav republics, **Serbia** is one of the more neglected parts of the country. If people come here at all, most only spend a couple of nights in Belgrade before heading south for the better-publicized charms of Greece or the perennially well-patronized Adriatic coast. This is a shame, as Serbia's attractions can easily match those of the rest of Yugoslavia; and because it is so undervisited, it's also one of the cheapest regions of the whole country.

Serbia sports few appealing towns: **Belgrade**, despite a recent refurbishment and a vibrant feel, is a drab city by most people's standards, and most other places similarly bland and modern. But scenically the republic boasts far greater assets, particularly in the green rolling heartlands of its central hills and mountains. Its most touted and revered sights are its **medieval monasteries**, the best possible illustration of an age that Serbs, even today, look back on with pride. Getting to any of these monasteries can be difficult; they're normally tucked away in deliberately remote and inaccessible spots, and often you'll need your own vehicle. But it's generally worth the struggle, both for the buildings themselves and some superb scenery. The triangle formed by the regional centers of **Kruševac**, **Kragujevac**, and **Kraljevo**, in the center of the republic, collectively provides a springboard for the first of the monasteries—Ravanica, Manasija, and Kalenić. Farther south, among some of Serbia's loveliest landscapes, are **Studenica**, an hour or so by car from Kraljevo, or **Sopoćani**—both of which have marvelous thirteenth-century frescoes painted by master-painters from Constantinople, center of the Orthodox Christian world. The town of **Novi Pazar** provides the best—and most intriguing—base for the Sopoćani monastery, a Muslim town that is the main center of the Sandžak: the former buffer area between the Ottoman Empire and Austria-Hungary.

Eastern Serbia is more undiscovered than these central areas, its attractions ranging from the sights along the Danube—the Mesolithic settlement of Lepenski Vir, Smederevo castle—to the Vlach localities around Negotin and Zaječar. The west of the republic, on the borders with Bosnia-Hercegovina, is a mountainous region best seen by using the Belgrade–Bar railroad, which carves a dramatic route through on its way south to Montenegro. There's another key Serbian monastery here—**Mileševa**—just outside Prijepolje. Also in the west, a possible route to Sarajevo might take in the village of **Tršić**, near Loznica, former home of the nineteenth-century Serbian literary giant Vuk Karadžić.

The two autonomous provinces of **Vojvodina**, to the north, and **Kosovo**, to the south, though technically part of Serbia and with their share of key Serbian sights, are covered under separate chapters, which follow.

Belgrade (Beograd)

BELGRADE means literally "White City," a striking misnomer for what must be one of the grayest of European capitals. Occupying a strategic point on the junction of the Danube and Sava rivers, it was the property of a warlike succession of Celts, Romans, Huns, and Avars until the Turks wrenched it from the Hungarians in 1521, from when it formed the northernmost point of their empire. The Kalemegdan fortress—from which the modern city has

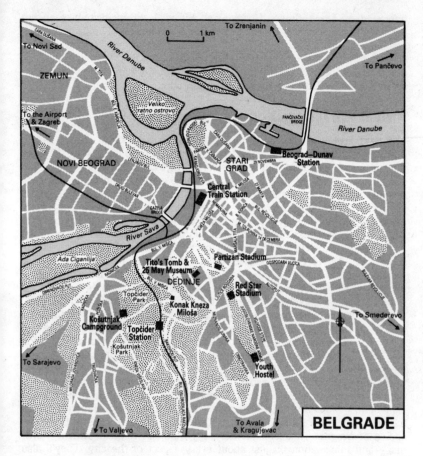

grown—sweeps around a wooden bluff overlooking the wayward swerve of the Danube, quiet now, but for years the frontier between East and West, and at the very crux of Balkan squabbles and struggles for influence.

Towns as strategically important as this are rarely beautiful, and Belgrade is no exception; a couple of Muslim shrines and a dilapidated mosque are the only traces of 350 years of Turkish rule, while heavy shelling in the last war left virtually no street unscathed. A few museums, the Kalemegdan Park, and the raw vigor of its streets make it worth two or three nights, but it's a city that's soon exhausted, and until recently even the most fanatically loyal Belgrader wouldn't have advised you to stay any longer. The last few years, however, have seen a massive effort to clean up the capital—a move given impetus by the hosting of the nonaligned movement conference here in September 1989. Old buildings have been renovated, new ones pushed up with speed, and the public transit infrastructure has begun to work with unprecedented smoothness. How long all this will last remains to be seen, but the days of playing ugly sister to the likes of Zagreb and Ljubljana to some extent seem to be over. Above all, the city these days seems very consciously the *capital* of both the country and the Serbian republic: the Cyrillic script dominates more than ever before, and Serbian history and culture is played up and exalted—features which in a way only add to its charm.

Arrival and Information

The city's **rail and bus stations** are situated next door to each other, in downtown's most run down and dilapidated area; **arrival** here is not the easy, European-style initiation it is in the west of Yugoslavia, but the busy, Balkan atmosphere of the area, with its *burek* stalls, gypsies, and cheap stand-up restaurants, is an invigorating one. Both stations have luggage-consignment facilities should you want to dump your bags while getting oriented or accommodated (see "Listings"). Arrival at Belgrade's **airport**, at Surčin 18km northwest of the city, doesn't necessarily let you off the hook: buses run between 5:15am and 9pm every 15–20 minutes from the airport to the railroad station, some going on to Slavija Square, others to the JAT terminal on Bulevar Revolucije (the former leave from the arrivals hall, the latter from the domestic departures hall); journey-time to the railroad station is roughly 25 minutes. Taxi fares between the airport and the city center run to around $25, though be prepared to bargain, and for drivers to attempt to put you together with other passengers to share a vehicle.

For **information**, there is a booth at the airport (daily 8am–9pm) which has basic brochures and maps and will phone hotels to check on vacancies; the kiosk at the railroad station (daily 7am–9pm) is normally far too stressed to provide much more than a map. Usually it's far better to wait until you're in the city center proper, and visit the main **tourist information center** (daily 8am–8pm; ☎635-622 or ☎635-343) in the subway under Terazije (entrance on the corner of Knez Mihailova). They have the usual free maps of Belgrade, copies of *Beograd*—a useful monthly city guide in English, with a transit map—and information on just about every aspect of the city. They'll also check on availability of accommodation.

Getting Around The City

Belgrade spreads untidily for miles, but most things of interest are either in the center or within easy reach of it by public transit. The city is served by a comprehensive and efficient, if slightly confusing, system of **buses, trams, and trolley-buses**. Each stop has a baffling plan of all routes attached, but where it's advisable to use public transit, we've indicated which route to take; the *Beograd* monthly has a plan of routes. There's a flat fare – tickets are bought from the driver, or, more cheaply and conveniently, in strips of six from most tobacco kiosks; punch them yourself on entering. Services run from around 4am until midnight, after which a series of night buses takes over.

Inspectors are so rare that many Belgraders (particularly young ones) simply travel without tickets. You can try this if you're so inclined but be warned that offenders are fined on the spot—and the old trick of pulling out a foreign passport and pleading ignorance doesn't cut any ice at all.

Belgrade's unplanned and sprawling nature means that there are few points at which public transit lines converge. However, there are a few useful points of reference. Slavija Square is the biggest interchange for the south and southwest; the road above Zeleni Venac market is where buses pass north–south on routes between Novi Beograd and the city center; the railroad station stop plugs you into most destinations on the tram system.

The Belgrade area telephone code is ☎011

Finding a Place to Stay

Accommodation in Belgrade is expensive for what you get, with even budget choices and lower-category hotels charging way above the norm for the facilities they offer. Paying through the nose to share a room with an overgrown cockroach is still, unfortunately, a common experience. The Terazije tourist information center will phone up hotels and student hostels for you but doesn't handle private rooms.

Private Rooms, Student Hostels, and the Youth Hostel

Often the cheapest alternative, **private rooms** can be had at the *Lasta Turist Biro* (Mon–Sat 7am–7pm; ☎641-251), conveniently placed opposite the railroad station, though its staff are unusually abrupt and the rooms sometimes placed way out of the city center. Failing that, you can bargain independently with the people hanging around outside, an often cheaper option, but don't count on anything turning up.

If you don't want a private room, the *Pansion Centar*, just a few doors along at Trg Bratstva i Jedinstva 17 (☎644-055), has dorm beds for just a little more, and though often booked solid by groups is worth a try. If it's full, the *Mladost* **youth hostel** is another option, though far from downtown at Bulevar JNA 56 (☎465-324)—a fifteen-minute journey on tram #9 from the railroad station and then two minutes' walk down Kapetana Zavišića. Dormitory beds here cost $8–10 per person (depending on YHA membership), including a frugal breakfast, and there's no curfew.

If all else fails—or if money is tight—there is normally **student accommodation** available from the beginning of July until the end of August, though year to year this can be something of an unknown quantity. The main student settlement, *Studentski Grad*, on the fringes of Novi Beograd at the end of the #65 bus route from Zeleni Venac, was renovated in the summer of 1989 to house the army of journalists covering the nonaligned summit and it could be that this will be the regular host facility from now on. Ask at the tourist information center for up-to-date details—it could well be the cheapest option of all.

Hotels

Belgrade's **cheapest hotels** tend to be a little way out of the center. The *Taš*, Borisa Kidriča 71 (☎343-507), beyond the Tašmajdan Park, has doubles for $40, though it's small—best reserve in advance; the *Dom Prosvetnih Radnika*, Cara Haila Selasija 30 (☎685-6969), is a cosy place behind the Slavija Square with doubles for the same price; while the most inexpensive hotel in the city is the *Trim*, at Kneza Višeslava 72 (☎558-128), south of the center, charging just $30 for a double. Take bus #53 from Kneza Miloša or bus #23 from Takovska. Equally cheap, but even farther out, are a couple of hotels in Zemun, the *Grand*, Maršala Tita 31 (☎210-536), and the *Central*, Maršala Tita 10 (☎191-712), both of which have doubles at around the $25–30 mark.

Otherwise the city's regular **hotels** don't vary much in either price or amenities, and you can expect to pay around $50–60 for a double room in a B-category hotel somewhere downtown. If you're loaded down with luggage and aren't up for a walk, closest to the railroad station is the *Astorija*, at Milovana Milovanovića 1 (☎645-422), which has doubles for $55; farther up toward Terazije, the *Prag*, Narodnog Fronta 27 (☎687-355), charges $60; in the opposite direction, at Sarajevska 37 (☎682-855), the *Turist* is slightly cheaper at $50. Cheaper still, though more of a hike from the railroad station, the *Balkan*, Prizrenska 2 (☎687-466), rents out some double rooms for as little as $40. About as centrally placed as it's possible to get, the *Kasina*, Terazije 25 (☎335-574), above the self-service restaurant and café of the same name, has doubles for $55. The *Toplice*, 7 Jula 56 (☎626-426), is more peacefully situated not far from the Bajrakli mosque and costs about the same.

If money is no object, the *Moskva*, opposite the *Balkan* at Balkanska 1 (☎686-255), provides the most atmospheric place to stay in Belgrade, though its double rooms weigh in at a hefty $120 a night; similarly consider the *Palas*, Topličin Venac 23 (☎637-222), which costs $110.

Camping

If you're **camping** there's a choice of two main grounds, best of which is *Košutnjak*, Kneza Višeslava 17 (☎555-127), south of the city center in the Košutnjak Park, which has bungalows as well as plots for caravans and tents—though the tent spaces are only available during the summer; take bus #53 from Kneza Miloša as far as the *Trim* hotel. The *National* in Novi Beograd costs slightly less—bus #74 from the Tašjmadan Park.

The City

The central core of Belgrade occupies the nub of land that marks the junction of the Sava and Danube rivers, spreading out from the remains of the Kalemegdan fortress, the original heart of the city. It ranges from the oldest, most residential quarter, immediately below Kalemegdan—so-called "**old Belgrade**"—to the busier, more commercial sector farther south, around **Trg Republike** and **Terazije**, where you'll find the bulk of the city's shops and restaurants. Farther south still are the main buildings of the federal and Serbian **government**, from where a number of wide boulevards spear out south and east through the city's amorphous suburbs. Much of the **southern**

outskirts are green parkland, and worth visiting as such; west, across the Sava, lies the quarter known as **Novi Beograd**—a new, planned district of wide boulevards and spanking new skyscrapers, conference centers and hotels. Beyond Novi Beograd, **Zemun** is nominally a separate city, its old quarter of low-slung houses and hilly streets quite at odds with the enforced modernity which you pass through to reach it.

The Old Center

The wide swathe of **Terazije** slices through the central and commercial hub of Belgrade; ask a taxi driver to take you to the city center and he'll drop you here. Hardly elegant, it's nonetheless the place Belgraders come to do their shopping, with the main city branch of *Robna Kuća Beograd* and many other stores besides. Opposite *Robna Kuća Beograd*, the art nouveau **Hotel Moskva**, built in 1906 for an insurance company, makes for a distinctive— and distinguished—landmark, its large terrace and fountain presiding over Terazije's bustle. Underneath the street, a profusion of underground walk-ways, leftovers from the city's half-finished metro and filled with shops and bars, mirror the busy life that goes on up top.

Walk west from Terazije, towards the Bratstva i Jedinstva bridge over the Sava, and you come to the city's main central food market, **Zeleni Venac**, an aromatic and atmospheric introduction to the city, and one of its main focal points for transport. To the north, Terazije leads into the busy, pedestrianized street of **Knez Mihailova**, centerpiece of Belgrade's extensive late-Eighties facelift. Once-grimy facades have been sandblasted, new paving stones have been laid, and the street has been filled with ersatz turn-of-the-century street lamps, mailboxes, hexagonal newspaper kiosks, and bollards covered with advertising stickers. Whether Belgrade actually ever looked like this, or whether it's just an appealing piece of kitsch, is open to debate; but the locals are exceedingly proud of the fact that their city (or its core at least) has at last been turned into something at least part-way attractive.

Most of the **fountains** that line the street are modern, but one, on the corner of Zmaj Jovina, has a grain of historical authenticity; it's a reconstruc-tion of a fountain which originally stood in the middle of Terazije but which mysteriously disappeared after the war. During the renovation procedure and the attendant concern with all that was connected with "old" Belgrade, local journalists led a campaign to find out what had happened to it, coming to the conclusion it had been bulldozed to make way for a postwar partisan parade.

Encroaching on Knez Mihailova from the east is **Trg Republike**, a mixed-up square flanked by glassy modern high rises and spruced-up classic remnants from more monumental architectural times. The equestrian statue is of Prince Mihail Obrenović, hailing him as liberator from the Turks. He points meaningfully south, to the lands still to be extricated from the infidel.

Behind Obrenović looms the **National Museum**, accessible by way of the entrance on V. Čarapića (Tues & Wed 10am–5pm, Thurs 10am–7pm, Fri & Sat 10am–5pm, Sun 10am–2pm)—a collection of art and archaeology founded in 1844 and installed here in 1946. By European standards its collection is of vari-able quality, but there are one or two specifically Yugoslav exhibits it would be a shame to miss. The ground floor holds a fairly ordinary, though extensive,

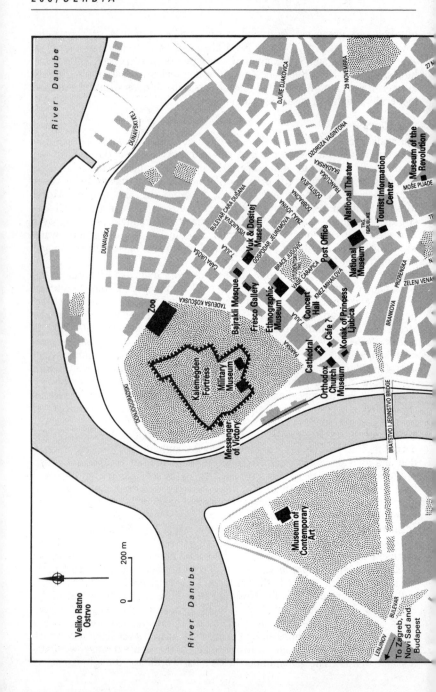

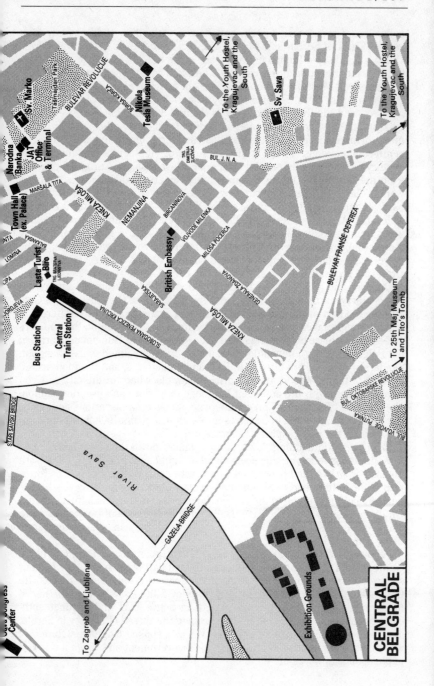

CENTRAL BELGRADE

Town Hall (ex. Palace)
Sv. Marko
Narodna Banka
JAT Office & Terminal
Tašmajdan Park
BULEVAR REVOLUCIJE
BOMSKA KOBIĆA
Nikola Tesla Museum
Sv. Sava
To the Youth Hostel, Kragujevac and the South
To the Youth Hostel, Kragujevac and the South
MARŠALA TITA
KNEZA MILOŠA
NEMANJINA
TITA DIMITRIJA TUCOVICA
BUL. J. N. A.
BIRCANINOVA
VOJVODE MILENKA
MILOŠA POCERCA
GENERALA ŽDANOVA
BULEVAR FRANŠE DEPEREA
BAKANSKA
LOMINA
OPA
...NTA
British Embassy
SARAJEVSKA
KNEZA MILOŠA
Lasta Turist Biro
TRG BRASTVA JEDINSTVA
...JDREVA
SLOBODANA PENEZICA KRCUNA
Bus Station
Central Train Station
To 25th Maj Museum and Tito's Tomb
BUL. OKTOBARSKE REVOLUCIJE
BUL. VOJVODE... PUTNIKA
STARI SAVSKI BRIDGE
RIVER SAVA
GAZELA BRIDGE
To Zagreb and Ljubljana
Exhibition Grounds
...va Turjess Center

collection of prehistoric, Greek, and Roman antiquities—finds mainly from various parts of Serbia and Macedonia, including Greek gold jewelry from Ohrid, a good set of Roman figurines, and some delicate Roman jewelry. Look out also for the work of the country's best-known and most prolific modern sculptor, Ivan Meštrović, notably his strident figure of Miloš Obilić—a central character in medieval Serbian history, especially the poetry of the Battle of Kosovo—and Vuk Karadžić, creator of the first Serbian alphabet (see below). Upstairs, the first floor is devoted to medieval and later Serbian art, with fragments of monastic frescoes and an exhaustive series of seventeenth- and eighteenth-century icons. There is also an array of eighteenth- and nineteenth-century Serbian paintings, while the floor above displays European painting from the fifteenth to the twentieth century, together with modern Yugoslav works. There's a fine self-portrait by Moše Pijade, a prominent figure in the partisan movement, and canvases by Yugoslav Impressionists like Milan Milovanić. Among works from abroad, there's a thin scattering of Venetian work, some middling Dutch and Flemish pieces, and a number of slightly more promising nineteenth- and twentieth-century rooms, where most of the more major European figures have their say: Renoir, Degas, Pissarro and Utrillo are represented by a painting or two each.

Opposite the museum, the **National Theater**, dating from the end of the last century and recently restored, occupies the site of the old Istanbul Gate into the old part of the city behind. Following Francuska east from here and making a right takes you into the **Skadarlija** area, centering on the pedestrianized throughfare of Skadarska and once known as the Bohemian quarter of old Belgrade, though now little more than a brightly painted tourist hangout. Skadarska especially is lined with bars and restaurants, and the food served at most of them is good, but it's pricier than elsewhere in the city and you have to put up with the attendant trappings of folklore and pseudo-tradition. No doubt the *Tri Šešira* (Three Hats) café did once harbor artists and poets, but today it's mainly full of travelers in search of a quaint Balkan Montmartre and some of the more aspiring Belgrade trendies.

If you're not into sitting down, simply wander down the street and sample the snacks on offer at the stalls on the right-hand side: rolls filled with goulash or *kajmak* and paper cones filled with deep-fried sardines. The **fountain** at the bottom end of Skadarska is a copy of the one in Sarajevo's bazaar quarter, a gift presented to the city on the occasion of the nonaligned summit. On the opposite side of the road, **Bajinova Pijaca** is one of Belgrade's more animated markets, watched over by a somber Protestant church currently being converted to a theater complex.

Following V. Čarapića up towards Kalemegdan from Trg Republike, **Studentski Trg**, on the right, cuts into the old part of town, a neatly laid-out square opposite the main buildings of the university—hence the name. The florid statue on the right is of Dositej Obradović, the so-called grandfather of modern Serbian literature, who played an active part in the nineteenth-century nationalist movement by encouraging the spread of literacy in Serbia, and the use of Serbian as a written as well as a spoken language. Obradović was minister for education in Karadjordje's government and wrote a number of philosophical works in Serbian.

On the northern side of Studentski Trg, the **Ethnographic Museum** (Tues, Wed, & Fri 10am–5pm, Thurs 10am–7pm, Sat 10am–5pm) covers all the regions of Serbia, from the Vojvodina in the north to Kosovo in the south, with reference to—and examples of—costumes, carpets, agricultural tools, and domestic effects. Fairly recently upgraded, and with English translations throughout, it's an excellent museum, imaginatively laid-out and easily digested, and if you're at all interested in any aspect of Serbia, a must. On the eastern side of the square there's a small Muslim **turbe**, the late-nineteenth-century tomb of one Sheikh Mustapha and one of the very few Islamic structures left in Belgrade, most of which either burned down or were destroyed after Serbian independence. The faithful still push money through the grills in homage to the dead man. Beyond here, on Gospodar Jevremova, is another Muslim remnant, the **Bajrakli Mosque**, or "Flag Mosque." This is Belgrade's only surviving mosque and is still used, though it's unlikely that you'll be able to see any more than the small courtyard.

The house Dositej Obradović opened as Serbia's first proper school in 1808, at Jevremova 21, is now a **museum** (Tues–Sat 9am–1pm & 4–7pm, Sun 9am–1pm). The building was in fact the home of a local Turkish official, and as well as material on Dositej and Vuk Karadžić, the scholar who phoneticized the Serbian alphabet and recorded and collected their previously oral folk poems, with whom Dositej worked, there are items relating to the Turkish period in Belgrade. See also the section on Vuk's birthplace, Tršić, on p.316.

There is another reminder of Vuk Karadžić west of here, at the other end of 7 Jula, where the grounds of the nineteenth-century **Cathedral**—a fairly undistinguished neo-Baroque edifice that went up in 1830 after the Turks relaxed their ban on church-building—contain Vuk's body. In a way the church is a center for Serbian patriotism; the relics of Prince Lazar were brought here soon after its completion and are still venerated today—though its role has recently been usurped by the completion of the enormous new shrine of Sv Sava south of the city center (see p.292). Opposite the cathedral is another surviving Turkish building, the **Cafe?**, which used to be called the "The Cafe at the Cathedral" but after complaints of impiety from the priest-hood opposite had to change its name to the present enigmatic alternative—something which attracted more clientele than ever and helped fuel the bar's reputation as the number-one haunt of Belgrade Bohemians. These days it's still a good place to drink (and eat).

Just around the corner, the **Konak of Princess Ljubica**, at Knez Sime Markovića 8 (Tues–Fri 10am–5pm, Sat & Sun 9am–4pm), belonged to the wife of the nineteenth-century Serbian leader Miloš Obrenović, whose jealousy for her husband became so legendary that it was said she hounded the women of her husband's court literally to death if they were unfortunate enough to catch his eye. The house she lived and raised her family in is today hers in name only, its interior a reconstruction of typical rooms of the upper classes at the time, with their blending of the eastern influence of Turkey and the formal rigidity of western salons. Oriental touches—the Turkish bath and window seats—and the Ottoman sense of spaciousness and light prevent any stuffiness.

The Kalemegdan Park

Just north of here, the **Kalemegdan Park** covers the area from which Belgrade began, sited on the exposed points at the top of the city's horn of land and commanding long views over the confluence of the city's two rivers. It was a natural place to build a fortress, and the current structure and its various occupiers are almost a microcosm of Serbian history itself. To Rebecca West, Kalemegdan "meant life to those who held it, death to those who lost it," and high up here it's easy to understand what she meant: across the sluggish waters of the Danube the ruthlessly flat Pannonian plain stretches north, deep into Hungary; behind, the gentle hills of central Serbia roll south, forging into the mountainous backbone of the Balkan peninsula.

The first fortress at Kalemegdan was built by the Celts, expanded on by the Romans, and rebuilt in the Middle Ages by Stefan Lazarević—one of the last medieval Serbian leaders, who clung to power in the face of unyielding Turkish expansion. The medieval town of Belgrade grew slowly within the castle walls, but with the coming of the Turks the whole place fell into neglect. Most of what you see now is the result of a short-lived Austrian occupation in the early part of the eighteenth century. Then, and into the next century, European travelers regarded Kalemegdan as the beginning of their travels in the Orient, its mosques and minarets signaling to them as they crossed over from the Austrian side of the river. A. W. Kinglake saw in the fortress a final, brooding frontier, the very end of Europe before the "splendor and havoc of the east," and James Fraser, writing a few years earlier, felt crossing the river was "like quitting the living for the dead."

Nowadays Kalemegdan is mainly taken up by a large park. This is both the main haven of peace and quiet in central Belgrade and a scarred and explorable testimony to Belgrade's historic ups and downs, scattered with ruins, passages, sections of wall, and the like. The southern side is shadily planted and partly-cultivated, the venue of impromptu chess games, but for the most part it follows the old ramparts in overgrown abandon.

Make straight for the Sava side for its views over the river to Novi Beograd opposite. A little way up, four marble **tombs** marked by the words "Death to Fascism" commemorate some of the biggest heroes of the Yugoslav revolution, two of whom—the party's leading Marxist theoretician, Moše Pijade, and Tito's dashing young right-hand man, Ivo Lola Ribar—are names you'll see honored all over the country in street names and squares. Walking north from here, through the late-seventeenth-century King's Gate into the fortress proper, you'll find a **Roman well**, a dark, dank place with a sheer and slightly frightening brick hole full of water. Up above, Ivan Meštrović's **Messenger of Victory** is another patriotic monument, originally supposed to stand in the city center but put up here after protests from more puritanical Belgraders about the figure's full-frontal nudity—it is quite obviously male. Something of a symbol for the city (it's depicted on almost all the tourist handouts), the perching falcon symbolizes Slav freedom and the sword the defense of peace—notions made all the more poignant by the subsequent horrors Belgrade underwent in the last war.

The **Military Museum** (Tues–Sun 10am–5pm), housed in the labyrinthine interior of the main fortress building, is the one thing in the park you shouldn't miss. It's a marvelous museum, well laid out and easy to follow despite largely Serbo-Croatian labeling, at once a strong reminder of the past and a hopeful epitaph to it. Billed as a visual narration of Yugoslavia's wars—another way of saying a history of Yugoslavia itself—it is a story of occupation and resistance under Turks, Austrians, and, later, the Nazis. The outbreak of World War I is vividly illustrated by mugshots of Princip and his cohorts, and of the luckless Franz Ferdinand shortly before his assassination. But the main focus of the museum is the war of liberation, with stark black and white photographs that help to bring home the brutality of the era. In one a young partisan boy, Filip Filipović, raises his arms in a final gesture of defiance before being hanged by the Germans—a much reproduced photo that became *the* symbol of partisan heroism. The museum comes to a climax with the flags of each partisan brigade set above piles of captured enemy weapons. After the crimes you have just seen, it's a fitting conclusion.

Not far from the museum, below the battlements, are two small **churches**, still very much in use. The ivy-covered and larger of the two, the Ružica church, holds blackened frescoes on the far wall, away from its soldier-flanked entrance, showing the donor holding his church. The smaller church, Sv Petka, down another flight of steps, has gaudy mosaics and is busy on Sundays with ailing Belgraders here to drink the waters of the holy spring on which the church is built. East of here there's a Baroque **gateway** which dates from 1717, erected by Eugene of Savoy to commemorate his victory over the Turks. Farther east still, in the corner of the park, is Belgrade's **zoo** (daily 8am–7pm), until recently a much neglected institution with a limited variety of beasts, though recently the recipient of a degree of investment and thoughtful renovation. The recent well-publicized escapes of "Sammy the Chimp," whether genuine or stage-managed, helped to hype the zoo locally and make it popular again with the locals, and the emphasis is these days on making the zoo a bearable place for the animals as well as an interesting place for humans. All in all, along with the nearby amusement park and model train-rides, (and indeed the rest of the fortress), it's a good place to bring the kids.

East from Terazije

Heading east from Terazije, a left turn brings you to **Trg Marksa i Engelsa**, an austere, concreted square that's home to some of the city's socialist institutions: the gray arc of the *Dom Sindikata* or Trade Union Hall, now largely used as a concert hall; the offices of the Socialist Alliance's newspaper, *Borba*; and the Museum of the Revolution—on the face of it a convincing piece of Fifties socialist monumentalism, though actually built for the Agrarian Bank in 1933.

The square opens out onto Bulevar Revolucije and, on the left, the domed bulk of the **Skupština** or Federal Assembly, fronted by Toma Rosandić's unusually sensuous horse-wrestling statues, placed here in 1939. The Federal Assembly is in effect the country's parliament, and is elected every four years; it is divided into two bodies, one federal chamber and another made up of delegates elected from the individual republics and provinces, and it has the power to elect the government cabinet or Federal Executive Council.

Opposite the assembly building, at the head of massed ranks of flower-beds, is the **Gradska Skupština**, Belgrade's city council building and in former times the royal palace. Originally attached was a building known as the prince's residence; this was demolished in 1904 after the violent events of the preceding year, when the bloody feud of Serbia's squabbling dynasties came to a head. In a palace revolution designed to put a Karadjordje back on the throne, a group of army officers murdered King Alexander Obrenović, together with his queen Draga, with a brutality that sent a shudder of fear and revulsion through the other crowned heads of Europe.

Beyond the Skupština, the uncompromising Renaissance-style building which houses the main post office and the National Bank shields the church of **Sv Marko**—until the building of the shrine of Sv Sava to the south, Belgrade's largest church, a solid neo-Byzantine structure built between the world wars on the model of the church of Gračanica in Kosovo province. It's a rather bare shrine inside: the ornate sarcophagus on the left houses the supposed remains of one of Serbia's greatest empire-builders, Dušan IV; the simpler tomb on the right, bearing the inscription "I sleep, but my heart is still awake," is in fact empty, awaiting the demise of the current religious patriarch.

From Sv Marko east, Bulevar Revolucije runs parallel to the grassy lawns of the **Tašmajdan Park**, a popular promenading place named after the Turkish quarry once situated here (in Turkish, *taš* means stone, *majdan* an open space)—the hollowed-out bowl of which now holds a sports stadium. Beyond Tašmajdan, the grimy, traffic-clogged ribbon of the boulevard stretches far into the city's suburbs, flanked by peeling Neoclassical edifices, some of which house the technical faculties of the university.

Nearby, underneath the trees, there's a statue of **Nikola Tesla**, the Yugoslav-born inventor who spent much of his career in the USA, working for the likes of Edison and Westinghouse, and making several important discoveries in the field of electrical engineering. Tesla is very much the forgotten man of modern science, Edison and Marconi getting the credit for many things on which Tesla was concurrently working. He actually courted obscurity, declining the Nobel prize when offered it in 1912, claiming he wasn't interested in meaningless accolades. Nearby, a house has been opened as the **Nikola Tesla Museum** (Tues–Sat 10am–noon & 4–6pm, Sun 9am–1pm), and gives a quick educational jaunt through his life; it even contains his funerary urn. One thing you won't find any reference to in the museum is the oft-repeated story of his do-it-yourself castration—an attempt to free himself from all potential distractions in the pursuit of science.

A hundred meters beyond the university buildings, a small **park** contains a statue to language reformer Vuk Karadžić, the traditional meeting-point for laborers and itinerant craftspeople from the south, who hang around waiting to be taken on as casual labor. Beyond here you are unlikely to wander.

Maršala Tita, Slavija, and Beyond

Bulevar Maršala Tita is an extension of Terazije, a busy shopping street that heads straight as an arrow towards the southeast of the city. There's little of outstanding interest along its one-kilometer length, and the boulevard is more a prime example of how Belgrade's climate and air pollution (a mixture of traffic emissions and the widely used brown coal) has reduced the city's architecture of all styles and periods to the same crumbling grayness. It's an effect that can also be observed in the streets to the west of Maršala Tita—**Kneza Miloša, Nemanjina,** and around—where the buildings house government departments that are the model of bureaucratic mock-grandeur and facelessness.

Close to the Terazije end of Maršala Tita there's one historic building of lukewarm appeal, the elegant **Kršmanović mansion** at no. 34 (Tues–Fri 10am–4pm, Sat & Sun 9am–3pm), named after its wealthy merchant-owner who donated it to the Serbian nation on his death in 1914. It was here that the Kingdom of Serbs, Croats and Slovenes was proclaimed on December 1, 1918, and you can peek inside the so-called "Hall of Unification" where the event took place, as well as at a rather schoolmasterish exhibition detailing the revolutionary movement in Belgrade between the wars.

At the top of Maršala Tita, past the city's newest landmark, the proud, dark Beogradjanka building, trams and trolley-buses rattle around the cobble-stones of Trg Dimitrije Tucovića, a vast traffic circle known to everyone by its prewar name—**Slavija**. Tucović, whose bust stands in the middle of the square, is another of modern Yugoslavia's secular saints. A prime mover in the turn-of-the-century Serbian social democratic movement, he died in battle in 1914. Otherwise, the main features of Slavija are the high-rise hotel of the same name and Yugoslavia's first *McDonald's* restaurant, housed, rather incongruously, in a squat Balkan-style building from the nineteenth century.

From Slavija, Bulver JNA heads south across Vračar hill, the site of Karadjordje's peasant army's encampment outside the besieged city in 1806. An impressive, sword-brandishing statue of Karadjordje marks the spot. Behind this, the **Serbian National Library** is one of the city's most attractive modern buildings. But the thing that dominates the skyline on Vračar is the huge gilded dome of the new **Hram Sv Sava**—the shrine of Saint Sava, which when completed will be the largest working Orthodox church in Europe. Sava, born around 1175 as Rastko, the youngest son of the medieval warlord Stefan Nemanja, was the virtual founder of the Serbian Orthodox church, and the medieval state's first archbishop, crowned in 1219. As head of the new national church, he crowned his brother Stefan as the first, imperially sanctioned, king of Serbia—known afterwards as Stefan Prvovenčani or Stefan-the-First-Crowned.

By the time of his death in 1236, Saint Sava was already the focus of a powerful cult, and became the symbol of Serbian national identity after their fall to the Turks. Sixteenth-century Serbian rebels carried images of Saint Sava on their banners, something that worried the Turks so much that they had the saint's bones transported from their resting place at Mileševa monastery to Vračar, where they publicly burned them on May 10, 1594. The Turks hoped that the flames that rose from the hill here—visible for miles around—would signal the final defeat of the Serbian people.

The construction of the shrine, funded by contributions from Serbs all over the world, has been nothing if not problematic. Originally conceived at the end of the last century, war and economic slumps prevented the scheme from getting off the ground properly, and at the time of the German invasion the building had risen a mere seven or so meters. After the war, when the land here was nationalized, legal wrangles again delayed the project, and it was only in the mid-1980s that bureaucratic channels were unblocked and the construction work resumed in earnest, spurred on by the recent upsurge in nationalism in Serbia, which—as in Croatia—is closely aligned with the church. At time of writing the *hram* was still a construction site, with guided tours offered daily on the hour between 9am and 4pm. But it's due to be finished in 1992, by which time it will be a fully operational church complete with underground concert hall, library, crypt, and a chapel devoted to Prince Lazar, the martyr of Kosovo (see "Kosovo Polje" in the *Kosovo* chapter).

Outside the church there's a small colony of souvenir kiosks, developed by the enterprising Serbian Church's tourist company, *Ras Tourist*—a colony which will only grow as the building becomes more renowned. Behind lies the suburb of **Crveni Krst**, an area of quiet backstreets lined with the ivy-covered bourgeois residences of the nineteenth century, most of which were taken over by the state and coverted to apartments at the end of the last war.

The City Outskirts: the Southern Suburbs, Novi Beograd, and Zemun

Most people find enough in the middle of Belgrade to occupy them for the length of the average two- or three-day stay, and you probably will too. But if you're here for any longer, or are simply eager to escape the grime of the city center, there's plenty worth traveling out to, especially in the park-filled southern fringes.

THE SOUTHERN SUBURBS
Belgrade's main recreation spots are way to the south of the city, separated from downtown by the concrete ribbons of the *autoput* and the innumerable interchanges and overpasss that feed it. **DEDINJE** has always been a well-to-do suburb, settled by the wealthy middle classes in the inter-war period and still dotted with elegant villas and mansions, the preserve of the Party aristocracy since the war. Tito lived down here, and he's remembered by the **Josip Broz Tito Memorial Center**, at Botićeva 25, just off Bulevar Oktobarske Revolucije (Tues–Sun 9am–4pm; bus #42 from Tgr Republike), which overlooks the city from the site of his former residence. Closest to the road, the **4 Jula Museum** occupies the house of the former editor of *Politika*, Vladislav Ribnihar, where Tito officially called the Yugoslavs to arms against the Nazis in 1941, though there's not much to see here now. Climbing the hill up from here, the **Museum 25 Maj** was opened in 1962 to display items from around the world that the Marshal had received as presents from various world leaders on his adopted birthday, May 25. A little way up the hill from here is **Tito's Mausoleum**—otherwise known as the *kuća cveće* or "house of flowers"—where the great man's tombstone stands in a cool hall surrounded by flowers and a very stiff guard of honor. As you might expect, it attracts a steady stream of Yugoslavs, though reactions seem more restrained than, say, those at Lenin's tomb. Adopt an appropriate air of reverence and follow the arrows.

The mausoleum is tastefully understated, but the same doesn't go for the rest of the memorial complex, which exudes some of the luxury of which Tito is said to have been so fond. Another **museum**, a circular white marble structure built for the ailing president in 1979, contains yet more gifts bestowed upon him, while a **hunting lodge** around the corner was presented to Tito by the Slovene people on the occasion of his sixtieth birthday in 1952.

Beyond Dedinje, **Topčider** (tram #1 or #3 from the railroad station) is a popular destination among Belgraders for weekend outings. It was laid out as a park during the reign of Miloš Obrenović, who built himself a residence here at the same time as his wife Ljubica's house went up in the city center. Miloš's **konak** is less pretty, but displays the same marriage of Turkish and central European styles. When refurbished, it will resume its role as Museum of the First Serbian Uprising.

From Topčider tracks lead up into **Košutnjak**, a wilder, less cultivated wooded park, ideal for directionless wandering. Northwest of Košutnjak, **Ada Ciganlija** (literally "Gypsy Island") is a favorite target in summer, a long wooded strip stretching along the bank of the Sava River, and joined to the south bank by a short artificial causeway. Ada's sandy beaches offer ample opportunity for swimming, and you can also rent boats or windsurfers, or just hang out in the island's numerous cafés and restaurants, many of which specialize in fish. The water on the southern side of the island, between the island and the east bank of the Sava, is apparently checked and filtered regularly so it's quite clean for swimming; there's a nudist area at the far southern end. Take bus #53 from Zeleni Venac or #37, #56, or #58 from Kneza Miloša.

NOVI BEOGRAD AND ZEMUN

Unless you're going to visit the contemporary art museum or are staying at one of the city's plush futuristic hotels, there's no real reason to go to **NOVI BEOGRAD**. But you might want to follow the southern bank of the Danube along to **ZEMUN** just beyond, a pleasant walk, partly through a park; bus #15 also makes the trip in fifteen minutes from Zeleni Venac—get off at Karadjordjeva Trg. Zemun, originally a Roman settlement, was once a separate city from Belgrade but is now no more than a suburb, though parts of it still have a feel distinct from the city. The district closest to the water, Gardoš, is due for a revamp, after which it may be one of the trendier outposts of the city. For the moment it's a peaceful escape from the city center – a good place to come and eat (see below), and to wander the winding streets, lined by low nineteenth-century houses, which give some idea of how Belgrade must once have looked. There's a local **museum**, on the main Maršala Tita (Tues–Fri 9:30am–12:30pm, Sat & Sun 9am–1pm).

Belgrade's Smaller Museums and Galleries

Belgrade has an exhaustive number of **museums and galleries**, on many different subjects, some of which are too specialized—or too far out from the city center—to easily slot into any of the above accounts. What follows is a round-up of the best of them.

ART AND VISUALS

Gallery of Frescoes

Cara Uroša 20. Tues & Wed 10am–5pm, Thurs 10am–7pm, Fri 10am–5pm, Sat 10am–5pm, Sun 10am–2pm.

Excellent and convincing replicas of medieval frescoes from the more important Serbian and Macedonian monasteries—a good introduction, and incentive for visits, with all of the principal frescoes in one place helping to put things in perspective. Among the copies on display are the stirring and monumental *Dormition of the Virgin* from Sopoćani, perhaps the finest of all Serbian frescoes; the rich blue *Crucifixion* from the Virgin's Church at Studenica; and the buxom peasant *Virgin* from Peć, oddly enough framed by a cast of Radovan's exuberant west door from Trogir's Catholic Cathedral. You can also get a good close-up of what's left of Mileševa's *Deposition* (in the monastery it's too high to study in any detail) and the famous *White Angel* from the same church. Don't forget to ask for the multilingual guidebook.

Museum of African Art

Andre Nikolića 14. Tues–Fri 10am–6pm, Sat 10am–7pm.

Based on the private collection of one Zdravko Pečar, and with some mildly interesting assortments of wood carving from West Africa.

Museum of Applied Art

Vuka Karadžića 18. Tues–Fri noon–7pm, Sat 10am–7pm, Sun 10am–2pm.

Ceramics, porcelain, and glass from the nineteenth and twentieth centuries.

Museum of Contemporary Art

Novi Beograd. Daily 10am–5pm, closed Tues; bus #16 or #36 from Zeleni Venac.

A disappointment. Well-arranged in a spacious modern gallery, these two collections of paintings—1900–45 and 1945 to the present day—are a generally dull and derivative bunch. Yugoslav interpretations of major European trends such as Cubism, Constructivism and Modernism are apparent in the work of Tone Kralj, Ignat Job, and Sava Šumanović, as is the perspective of the politically committed art of the 1930s, which was to develop into the limp propaganda of the 1950s. But the later works of the 1960s and after chase just about every pop and post-pop fashion in a depressingly directionless manner. From all this one or two paintings stand out—the skilled and sensitive self-portraits of the statesman Moše Pijade, the surrealist work of Milena Pavlović-Barilli, and the dark, hypnotic Primitive paintings of Ivan Generalić—though it's a comment on the disparate and ultimately pointless diversity of twentieth-century Yugoslav art that so large a gallery should have so little of value .

HISTORICAL AND RELIGIOUS

Historical Museum of Serbia

Nemanjina 24/VII

Largely ignored until its recent renovation, which was part of the latest resurgence of Serb nationalism, and devoted to a proud collection of artifacts related to the early-nineteenth-century Serbian uprisings. Prize exhibits are the personal effects of Karadjordje.

Jewish Historical Museum
7 Jula 1a (first floor). Opening times uncertain.

Detailing the history of the Jews in Belgrade and Yugoslavia as a whole, this museum's most interesting and saddening sections inevitably concern the war years, when 67,000 of the country's 82,000 Jews were murdered by the Nazis and their collaborators. Many of the photos here show the concentration camps of central Europe—well known but no less horrifying for that. Another section proudly recounts the activity of Jewish fighters in the war, with many pictures of Moše Pijade, most senior of the Jewish partisans and vilified by Nazi propaganda. A moving museum with good English information.

Museum of the Banjica concentration camp
Veljka Lukića Kurjaka 33. Tues–Fri 10am–4pm, Sat & Sun 9am–3pm.

Housed in the actual former army barracks that were the site of the Nazi concentration camp, this place really speaks for itself. Eight thousand people were either exterminated or left to die here between July 9, 1941 and October 3, 1944.

Museum of the Illegal Party Printing Works
Banjički Venac 12. Tues, Thurs & Fri 11am–5pm, Sat & Sun 8am–2pm.

Much the same kind of agitprop material you find in revolution museums all over the country.

Museum of the Serbian Orthodox Church
7 Jula 5. Tues–Sat 10am–5pm, Sun 11am–3pm.

Situated through a maze of first-floor corridors in the home of the patriarchate of the Serbian Orthodox Church, this is a mixed selection of icons, devotional objects, robes, and vestments. Labeling in Cyrillic and a disappointing lack of medieval items, most of which were destroyed by the rampaging Turks, make it a museum for only the most devoted or interested.

National Museum of the Revolution
Trg Marksa i Engelsa 11. Tues–Sun 10am–5pm.

Now that the party is well installed in spacious offices across the Sava, the former headquarters of the Communist Party's central committee has become host to a permanent record of the revolution, with photos, documents, and bits and pieces relating to the Yugoslav struggle—the blueprint for countless exhibitions like it throughout the country. An informative experience, though frustratingly labeled exclusively in Serbo-Croatian.

MISCELLANEOUS

Forestry and Hunting Museum
Kalemegdan Park. Tues–Sun 9am–6pm.

Yugoslavia's forests and mountains are full of wildlife—wild boar, wolves, and bears still abound—and displayed here are trophies bagged by hunters and stuffed versions of animals so scarce you nowadays find them only in zoos. The formidable array of weaponry on show goes some way to explaining why.

Ivo Andrić Museum
Andrićev Venac 8. Tues–Fri 11am–5pm, Sat & Sun 8am–2pm.

This museum honors the Yugoslav Nobel prize-winning novelist with a few of his personal knickknacks. For more on Andrić, see *Contexts*.

Natural History Museum
Ivana Milutinovića 57. Tues–Sat 9:30am–5pm, Sun 9:30am–1pm.

The usual forlorn grouping of bits of rock and stuffed beasts.

Pedagogical Museum
Uzun Mirkova 14. Tues–Sun 10am–5pm

Dull collection of old textbooks and ancient educational trappings.

Postal Museum
Majke Jevrosime 13. Mon, Wed, & Thurs 9am–3pm, Tues & Fri 11am–7pm.

What you'd expect from the title—and no more.

Railroad Museum
Nemanjina 6. Mon, Tues & Fri 9am–2pm, Wed 9am–6pm.

Situated close to the railroad station, a predictable collection of railroad memorabilia.

Red Star Museum
Ljutice Bogdana 1a. Tues & Thurs 10am–5pm, Fri 10am–2pm.

Soccer fanatics only.

Food, Drink, and Nightlife

Belgraders tend to prefer **eating and drinking** in the open air, and the city is really only at its best for these activities in summer. Between May and September both Knez Mihailova and Skadarlija are full of life until midnight and beyond; as soon as it rains or the weather gets cold, however, people opt for an evening at home.

Breakfast, Street Food, Self-service Restaurants, and Pizza

It's possible to eat very cheaply in Belgrade. Stand-up snacks and street food feature highly around the city, and there's no excuse for going hungry. For **breakfast**, you could start the day as many Serbs do, with a *burek*. The *pekarna* (bakery) on Studentski Trg, opposite the Ethnographic Museum, serves possibly the best *burek* in town, as well as a wide range of delicious pastries made on the premises. The booths attached to the *Inex* bar on Trg Republike also serve filo pastry squares, rolls filled with *kajmak*, and other such dainties. Failing that, there are any number of *burek* stands around the railroad station, most serving yogurt to help it down with. Also, some restaurants will serve a light meal of cheese, tomatoes, hard-boiled eggs, and bread, and for something more substantial the self-service restaurants (listed below) open early in the morning.

For a quick **lunch on your feet**, you could try the snacks along Skadarska, or one of the ubiquitous plastic kiosks selling *pljeskavica*. In moments of desperation there's always Belgrade's branch of *McDonald's* on Slavija Square (a new branch is due to open soon on Terazije). Marginally more appetizing are the stand-up joints around the railroad station (the area as a whole is a good source of cheap food), though to **sit down** there are a number of **self-service restaurants** that don't cost a lot more: *Kasina*, Terazije 25 (open 7am–10pm), and *Zagreb*, Obilićev Venac 29 (open 6am–10pm).

Pizza is another inexpensive alternative, cheap and filling and usually a reasonable interpretation of the Italian standby. *Atina*, Terazije 28, is a long-established and basic pizza restaurant, closely followed by *Stari Grad*, Vasina 9 (closed Sun), which is good value and popular. Others include *Pod Lipom*, Makedonska 4; *Šumatovac*, Makedonska 33; and *Freska*, Vuka Karadžića 12, the latter a new privately-owned place with opulent wood-paneled decor. Slightly farther out, near Slavija, *Cortina II* is small and poky but youthful and atmospheric, while *Vladimir*, Bulevar Revolucije 43, has outdoor seating.

Restaurants

Belgrade is packed with cheap, unpretentious grill **restaurants** serving basic Serbian fare for very low prices. Eating cheaply of an evening is never difficult. The *London* restaurant, on the corner of Maršala Tita and Kneza Miloša, is a large and good-value alternative, with both Serbian specialties and pizzas. If you want a little more atmosphere and don't mind spending a tad more, *Vuk*, Vuka Karadžića 12, and nearby *Proleće*, at no. 11 on the same street, are both excellent and central Serbian eateries.

More interestingly, *Klub Književnika*, part of the Serbian Writers' Union at Francuska 7, attracts a wide range of artists, literati, and foreign diplomats, and is open until 2am; the more straightforward *Srpska Kafana*, Lole Ribara 25, serves good home cooking to aspiring thespians. The outdoor terrace of *Madera*, Bulevar Revolucije 43, is another well-known meeting-point for people with cultural pretensions—though its former role was quite different. It acted as headquarters of the newly victorious Yugoslav Communist Party after the war; taking over this bastion of bourgeois social manners was a good way of showing who was boss at such a sensitive time.

Two other eateries worth visiting as much for their clientele as the food are the *International Press Center*, Knez Mihailova 6, and the *Klub Privrednika* (literally "businessmen's club"), Terazije 34, both of which are open fairly late and are relatively upscale places to watch the new Belgrade middle classes at play. One place that defies any categorization is the *Klub Prosvetne Zajednice* or "educational community club," Obilićev Venac 27 (first floor; daily 6pm–1am), which draws a wide spectrum of Belgrade intelligentsia to something resembling a nineteenth-century literary salon in atmosphere. It's intimate and civilized for a quiet drink or slap-up meal.

There's not much in the way of **overseas cuisine** available in Belgrade (though possibly slightly more than in other Yugoslav cities). Two names stand out: *Peking*, Vuka Karadžića 2, serves rather average Chinese food; and *Troika*, Triše Kaclerovića 2, just off Bulevar JNA close to the bridge across the expressway, is a camp Russian restaurant where waiters in peasant smocks juggle with the china (tram #8, #9, #10 or #14 from Slavija). Consider also a trip to *Vltava*, Maršala Tolbuhina 81, whose selection of Czech specialties is limited but where you might be tempted by the excellent beer.

If you have still more money, Belgrade's best-known restaurants cluster together in the so-called Bohemian quarter of **Skadarlija**, but although the food in most of them is very good (and authentic), prices are higher than in the rest of the city and they're far from peaceful—live music is a feature of most of them, usually nineteenth-century Serbian folk music played by traditionally clad trios or quartets. Four restaurants you might try are the *Tri Šešira*, Skadarska 29; *Dva Jelena*, opposite at Skadarska 32; *Ima Dana* at Skadarska 38, and *Skadarlija*, Cetinjska 17. Most of these are enormous places, with lots of outdoor seating on an array of terraces, and you'll invariably be squeezed in a corner somewhere well away from a waiter, but it's all part of the atmosphere. Another part of the city Belgraders specifically head for to eat is **Ada Ciganlija** (see above), an island in the Sava southwest of the city center, where a number of permanently moored barges on the northern side of the island hold some good fish restaurants. *Arka* is one of the best, with a wide range of both river- and sea-fish dishes—and you don't pay a lot extra for the location. **Zemun**, too, by the Danube on the far side of Novi Beograd, draws people out for food: try the *Venecija*, also housed in a boat moored on the river, or the *Šaran*, a little farther along on the waterfront—both of which serve decent river-fish.

Cafés and Bars

Belgrade has a number of **cafés**, many with outdoor tables, that are good for sipping coffee and taking a break from sightseeing to watch the passers-by. It's certainly worth sticking you head around the door of the *Hotel Moskva* lounge, which is renowned for its cake trolley and where evenings especially are a near-pastiche of fin-de-siecle elegance, complete with obsequious waiters and string quartet. *Kod Spomenika*, on Trg Republike next to the Obrenović statue (the name means literally "at the monument"), is also known for its cakes and sweets; *Zagreb*, on the corner of Knez Mihailova and Obilićev Venac, and *Mažestik*, just behind, are also good; and *Kolarac*, at Knez Mihailova 46, is a young animated place that's good for a drink in the evening too (it's open until 1am). It also has a small restaurant.

Around the corner from *Kolarac*, the *Cafe?* in 7 Jula, opposite the cathedral, is one of the best places to drink in the city and probably the city's most famous bar. It's also intimate, serving drinks at prices that haven't risen with its notoriety and with an affordable restaurant attached. In the other direction, slightly out of the city center towards Slavija, *Manjež* on Njegoševa, overlooking the flower market halfway up Maršala Tita, is a popular traditional *kafana* open until 1am. *Poslednja Šansa* in Tašmajdan Park, open until 3 or 4am, is the last refuge of the city's café society and low-life.

A new habit is to put cafés and bookshops together. The best are at the *Jugoslavensko Dramsko Pozorište* (Yugoslav Drama Theater), on Maršala Tita, and *Café Čitilište*, Zmaj Jovina 1, an ivy-clad courtyard behind the city library reading room.

Pubs and Bars

As well as the more traditional cafés, Belgrade has a number of more western-style **bars or pubs**; indeed private bars are springing up all over the city. There's not always a great deal to choose among them: all tend to be small, are usually very crowded, and serve a wide range of pricey imported beers and spirits to the accompaniment of loud rock music. Fashions change quickly, and the popularity of certain bars with them, but the following all have well-established reputations.

Trozubec, Nušićeva, just off Terazije through a passage underneath *Robna Kuća*, is a good place for a daytime cappuccino. *Galerija*, just off Vuka Karadžića; *Cvetić*, on Njegoševa; *K.B.*, Bulevar Revolucije 38; *I.T.D*, Bulevar Revolucije 130; and *Café-restoran D & B*, Bulevar Revolucije 140, are all noisy, smoky places that come alive at night. The *Partizan Café*, at the tennis club run by the soccer team and sports club (Humska 1), is considered to be quite chic.

Nightlife

Away from the bars and cafés, Belgrade's best **nightlife** has always revolved around the student clubs based in the university faculties. Entrance is limited to members, but it's often possible for foreigners to bluff their way in waving a passport or some sort of ID, especially if they're female. Bear in mind, though, that June to September is a dead period, with very little happening.

The best-known clubs are *Akademija*, on the corner of Raićeva and Knez Mihailova—run by students of the Fine Arts Academy—and *Bona Fides*, Bulevar Revolucije 67, below the law school. You could also try *Stupica*, behind the Yugoslav Drama Theater on Maršala Tita. More easily accessible is the *Jazz Club* at the *Dom Omladine* (literally "house of youth") on the corner of Moše Pijade at Makedonska 18. The *Dom Omladine* also has a late-hours bookshop and small bar, and stages sporadic gigs. The *SKC*—student cultural center—on Maršala Tita also hosts bands during the semester, and organizes a variety of film shows and exhibitions.

Shops and Markets

Belgrade's main **department stores** are *Robna Kuća Beograd*, at Terazije 25 and Knez Mihailova 5, and *Beogradjanka*, Masarikova 5—both good for picking up toiletries and other essentials, though their ranges of ordinary consumer items are run-of-the-mill and far from cheap.

For food shopping and picnic lunches there are large **food halls** under both *Beogradjanka* and the Knez Mihailova branch of *Robna Kuća Beograd*, as well as a small supermarket in the subway under Moše Pijade—open until 10pm during the week. There's also a *"Dragstor"* for late-night shopping at Zeleni Venac 3, open until midnight. Fresh produce is best bought from the **Zeleni Venac market**, at the top end of Narodnog Fronta—a riot of fruit, vegetables, meat, and fish that is Belgrade's best, and most evocative, food market.

For **souvenirs**, the *Narodna Radinost* chain sells pricey folk kitsch—tablecloths, coffee grinders, coffee sets, and the like – and has branches at

Terazije 43 and Knez Mihailova 2. Genuine Orthodox church paraphernalia can be had from the church shop, *Zadruga Pravoslavnih Sveštenstva*, at Bulevar Revolucije 26 and Generala Ždanova 27.

Most of the city's **record shops** have uniform collections of Yugoslav and western rock, but it's worth looking out for more specialized places like *Jugoton*, Nušićeva 27, and *Muzička Kuća*, Makedonska 21, which have collections of folk music and authentic Serbian Orthodox church music. Records by western artists are usually made here under license and, although cheaper, be warned that the same standards of quality don't necessarily apply.

English-language **books** can also end up being cheaper here, due to the exchange rate. There is a good selection of paperbacks at the *Mladost* bookstore in the SKC; the adjoining *Srećna Galerija* photographic gallery can be a source of arty postcards. *Prosveta*, at Terazije 16, has a stock of Penguins, while *Jugoslavenska Knjiga*, at the head of Terazije (Knez Mihailova 2), has a fine array of books on Yugoslavia. The *Kulturni Centar Beograd*, on Trg Republike, stocks English books and a variety of foreign magazines, and has a quiet upstairs reading room. For secondhand English books, try either *Prosveta*, Knez Mihailova 35, or *Matica Srpska*, Knez Mihailova 40.

Sport

Belgrade's two main **soccer** teams are *Crvena Zvezda* (Red Star) and *Partizan*, the army team. The latter has always been associated with the postwar Yugoslav order, while the former attracts support from the old prewar bourgeoisie. Rivalry between the two sets of fans is still fanatical: Red Star supporters are known as *cigani* or gypsies, those of *Partizan* as *grobari* or gravediggers. Matches are normally played on Sunday, and local derbies—sometimes switched to Saturdays—are not to be missed. Red Star plays at the massive Marakana stadium, at Ljutice Bogdana 1a, south of downtown on Bulevar JNA; *Partizan* is just up the road at Humska 1. Both forums can be reached by trams #8, #9, #10, or #14, or bus #47 or #48, from Slavija.

Belgrade's other teams are *Rad*, based in Banjica, near the terminal of the #9, #10, and #14 tram, and *OFK Beograd*—based at the Omladinski stadium on Mije Kovačevića (tram #3 or #8). However, neither have much of a following, and apart from the occasional run in the top flight are firmly second-division material.

The city's other main spectator sport is **basketball**, in which the two main rivals are the same as those in soccer (they're general sports clubs really). Red Star plays at Hala Pionir (tram #3 or #8); *Partizan* plays at the Dom Sportova, in Novi Beograd.

Listings

Airlines *JAT*, Maršala Tita 18 (inquiries ☎642-773; Yugoslavia and Europe reservations ☎131-392; America and Australia ☎138-416), also at Bulevar Revolucije 17 (☎343-443); *Adria*, Kolarčeva 8 (☎629-699); *British Airways*, inside the *Hotel Metropol*, Bulevar Revolucije 69 (☎333-160); *Pan Am*, Hotel Slavija, Svetog Save 1 (☎444-3470); *Swissair*, Terazije 3 (☎326-751).

Airport inquiries Phone ☎601-424, 601-431 or 601-439. 24-hour service.

American Center Čika Ljubina 19, just off Knez Mihailova. Library, exhibitions, and one of the few places in town to get your hands on an English-language newspaper. Open Mon–Fri 8am–7pm, Sat 8am–1pm.

Atlas Zmaj Jovina 10 (☎183-062).

Automobile club The Motorists Association of Yugoslavia (**AMSJ**), Ruzveltova 18 (☎440-185). Phone ☎980 for traffic information; ☎987 for breakdown assistance.

British Council Knez Mihailova 48. Library and reading room with English-language books and newspapers—usually a week old. To borrow books you need proof of permanent residence. Open Mon–Fri 10am–4pm.

Bus station Železnička 4, behind the railroad station. It can be horribly confusing at first, but it's really quite organized once you've worked out the timetables and destinations, which are all in Cyrillic script. Tickets and timetable information for southbound buses are available from the north side of the station, vice versa for northbound buses. Tickets for international destinations are bought from *Basturist*, office at the station entrance (☎627-146). With your ticket you'll be given a small metal disc—don't lose it, it admits you to the forecourt where the buses leave. Bus information ☎624-751 or ☎627-049; reservations ☎644-455.

Car rental *Avis*, Obilićev Venac 25 (☎620-362); *Unis*, Cara Uroša 10 (☎634-766); *Kompas-Hertz*, Hotel Jugoslavija, Bul. Edvarda Kardelja 3 (☎692-339); *Globtour-Emona*, Gospodar Jevremova 30 (☎642-488); *Putnik*, Kneza Miloša 82 (☎641-556). Most of these firms also have offices at the airport.

Car repair Austin, Rover, Renault, Peugeot at Laze Simića 17 (☎650-022); Audi and Volkswagen at Vojislava Ilića 145 (☎488-2500); Citroen at Dimitrije Tucovića 155 (☎411-730); Ford at Omladinskih Brigada 31, Novi Beograd (☎156-660); Volvo at Svetozara Markovica 12 (☎320-901).

Pharmacy There are 24-hour services at *1 Maj*, Maršala Tita 9, and *Savski Venac*, Nemanjina 2.

Embassies *Australia*, Čike Ljubina 13 (☎624-655); *Canada*, Kneza Miloša 75 (☎644-666); *United Kingdom*, Generala Zdanova 46 (☎645-055); *USA*, Kneza Ilosa 50 (☎645-655); *Netherlands*, Simina 29 (☎626-699); *Norway*, Kablarska 30 (☎651-626); *Denmark*, Neznanog Junaka 9a (☎667-826); *Sweden*, Pariska 7 (☎626-422).

Emergencies Police at Ulica 29 Novembra, near the bus stop (☎92); ambulance ☎94.

Flea market This is pretty inaccessible, just off the main *autoput* to Niš at the junction with Kružni Put, the city beltway. Arrive early on a Sunday morning and you can pick up just about anything—providing you've got the hard currency to pay for it.

Hospitals The Boris Kidrič Health Center, Pasterova 1 (☎683-755); for teeth, try the dental polyclinic at Ivana Milutinovića 15 (☎443-491).

Lost and found Central office for lost items found anywhere at Cara Dušana 43a (☎624-877)—open Mon–Fri 7:30am–3:30pm. Property known to belong to a foreigner is usually handed right over to the relevant embassy.

Newspapers English-language papers are available from the kiosks outside the *Hotel Moskva* and *Robna Kuća* on the opposite side of the street. *Prosveta* bookshops stock occasional copies of *Time* and *Newsweek*.

Photographic equipment *Cinephoto*, Knez Mihailova 2 (☎623-348); *Fotoservis*, Terazije 31 (☎332-492).

Post offices For general postal services and poste restante (general delivery) the main post office is at Takovska 2 (Mon–Fri 7am–8pm, Sat 9am–4pm). To make international calls go to the post office in Zmaj Jovina, open 24 hours, or the third large post office in central Belgrade, next door to the train station, open Mon–Sat 7am–8pm; telephones Mon–Sat 7am–midnight, Sat 7am–10pm.

Radio *Radio Belgrade* broadcasts daily in English at 12.02 VHF 88.9 and 95.3 MHz. Tune in also to *Studio B*, which broadcasts in English and French daily at 8–10am, 2–3pm, and 5–6pm on 94.9 MHz and 333m AM, and has details on events, exhibitions, food, nightlife, sports, weather, etc.

Railroad station Trg Bratstva i Jedinstva 1a (information ☎645-822). Trains for Romania leave from the Dunav Stanica or Danube Station, on the other side of town at Djure Djakovića 39 (information ☎763-880). Lines for tickets at both stations can be a nightmare, so buy yours in advance from *KSR*, Maršala Tita 25. Bus #34 links the two stations.

Sightseeing tours Ask at the main tourist information center or go direct to *Putnik* (Terazije 27 or Dragoslava Jovanovića 1) for information on their three-hour coach tours of the main city sights; weekend ten-minute helicopter flights departing from Ušće, the confluence of the Danube and Sava; day trips to Avala; or daily river cruises, usually involving either lunch or dinner. *Ras Tourist*, an offshoot of the Serbian church, at Katanićeva bb (☎444-4333), organizes guided trips out to the Serbian monasteries.

Swimming The most centrally located pools are those in Tašmajdan (outdoor in summer, indoor in winter). In Novi Beograd try the pools at the *Intercontinental* or *Jugoslavija* hotels. You can also swim from the beaches of Ada Ciganlija (see above).

Taxis Can be hailed or found in long lines outside the railroad station, on Terazije, Trg Republike, or other central spaces. Alternatively telephone ☎444-3443 or ☎630-555.

Telephones Tokens or *žetoni* are available from post offices or kiosks in sizes A, B, or C. A is sufficient for a local call, B for outside Belgrade, C for international. Phonecards are being introduced, but slowly—again available from kiosks and post offices.

Travel agents *Karavan*, the Belgrade branch of the national youth travel organization, is at Takovska 12 (Mon–Fri 7:30am–8pm, Sat 8am–4pm), and is the best source of discount flights, ISIC cards, etc.

South from Belgrade: Through the Šumadija

South of the city, Belgrade's bleak high rises soon give way to an undulating countryside of patchwork pasture and arable land, dotted with orange roofs. About 20km from the city, the road passes the wooded pyramid of **AVALA**, a forested hill 511m high that's a favorite picnic spot of Belgraders. It's topped with a giant radio mast and Ivan Mestrović's **Tomb of the Unknown Soldier**, a monumental memorial to World War I, in hulking gray granite and decorated with imposing caryatids. This can't help but seem a futile gesture, and not a little ironic—it was finished in 1938 and Italy and Germany both donated wreaths. But the paths that wind around the hill itself are pleasant enough—though they can be crowded on summer weekends—and the place as a whole is easily seen on a day trip from the capital.

Beyond Avala the road cuts through the **Šumadija** or "wooded land," stretching out either side in quiet forested folds and flanked far to the west by the distant hills of western Serbia and Bosnia. It's an almost English landscape, but wilder, less cultivated, not quite so neatly arranged. The area was a base for the early-nineteenth-century Serbian uprisings against the Turks, the first instigated by the great Serbian leader, **Karadjordje**, or "Black George," a pig-farmer-turned-peasant-commander who united wayward bands of rebels, planned forays into Turkish-held territory, and drafted the constitution of an independent Serbian state. Though still seen by the Serbs as the original founder of their liberty, Karadjordje was a moody, unpredictable man, and in 1813, when faced with an Ottoman army of unbeatable proportions, he deserted his men and fled across the Danube to the safety of the Fruška Gora. No one ever found out why, but on his return from exile Karadjordje was assassinated, shot down by the new darling of the Serbs, Miloš Obrenović.

Fifty or so kilometers on from Avala, **TOPOLA** was Karadjordje's campaign headquarters, an undistinguished little town today, but, as Milovan Djilas writes, "one of the most powerful and venerated shrines in the Serbian national consciousness," since it remembers not just Karadjordje himself but the dynasty to which he gave birth—which later went on to provide the majority of the unified Yugoslav kingdom's monarchs. Just above the town, a short fifteen-minute walk, the hill of Oplenac holds the relics of Karadjordje's short period of power. In a set of public gardens stands the fortified Balkan-style **konak** where he lived, now a small museum, together with the church where he worshipped, and a guardhouse, now converted to a restaurant. Close by is the **Karadjordje Mausoleum** (daily 8am–7pm), a Byzantine-style church built in 1912 by Peter I—the first of the Karadjordjes to resume the throne in 1903—that's an unashamed attempt at glorifying the dynasty, linking its greatness to the magnificence of medieval Serbia under the Nemanjas. The great man's bones are installed in the south apse, traditionally the resting place of the medieval Serbian kings, and the mosaics that cover the interior are gaudy copies of frescoes from the Serbian monasteries—superbly worked, but rather empty in their self-conscious ostentation. The tombs downstairs were installed to receive later representatives of the family line, but most of them are empty, only emphasizing the rather miserable failure of the Karadjordjes to hang on to power.

Kragujevac and the Morava School Monasteries

From Topola it's a short trip down to **KRAGUJEVAC**, one-time capital of Karadjordje's rival, Miloš Obrenović, now the home of Zaštava cars and a dusty modern town with little to tempt you to stay. During the last war it was the scene of one of the Germans' most vicious atrocities, when, on October 21, 1941, 7000 people were shot here by the Nazis as a reprisal for Partisan activities in the area (100 males for each German soldier killed in an ambush); to make up the numbers children from the local school were marched out as well. On the outskirts of town is a memorial park and museum, but more than anything the memory lives on in the people here: there's a paranoia of foreigners that you won't find anywhere else in Yugoslavia, and it's the only town in the country that accepts no responsibility for the safety of German tourists.

There's not a lot to see downtown, and not much to suggest Miloš Obrenović's occupation of the place between 1819 and 1839. There are two Balkan-style konaks that date from the period: the **Amidžin konak** on Vuka Karadžića west of Maršala Tita, built by Miloš for his cabinet chief Sima Milosavljević in 1823, and the next-door **Knez Mihailov konak** built for Miloš's son. Together they form a town museum and modern picture gallery, though opening times are erratic. The **Šumarice** memorial park, half an hour's walk west of the city center, where the main strip of Maršala Tita becomes 21 Octobra and climbs through the suburbs onto the pastoral, sun-bleached highlands, forms the main interest. It's a huge place, with cemeteries, monuments, and memorial sculptures strewn over a wide area. Best known of the sculptures is the massive concrete V-shape, the work of Miodrag Živković in 1963, which has almost become a symbol of the town, and there are more sculptures and other artwork inspired by the reprisal housed in a memorial **museum** on the site (daily 8am–4pm). On the far side of Šumarice there's also an **"ethno-park"** of reconstructed Šumadija houses, which shouldn't be missed if you've made it this far.

Practical Details

Kragujevac's **rail and bus stations** are just southeast of the town center, across the Lepenica River. To reach the center, walk down to the end of Šumadijska, turn left into Djure Djakovića and cross the bridge at the end into Trg Narodna Fronta, where the main street, Maršala Tita, begins. There's a **tourist office** at Maršala Tita 98, just above the offices of *Kragujturist*, where you can ask about **private rooms**. Otherwise the cheapest rooms in town are at the *Hotel Sloboda*, just off Maršala Tita at Lenjinova 1 (☎034/63-035), with rooms at $20 a double, closely followed by the equally central *Dubrovnik*, on Save Kovačevićeva (☎034/60-137), with doubles for $26. For **food** there is a wealth of grills and *kafane* throughout the town, all offering good, cheap Serbian fare. *Pizzeria Big*, 27 Marta II, is an alternative if you don't take a shine to any of them, while there are a few privately owned bars and bistros on the upper reaches of Maršala Tita—*Vojvoda* and *Enrico* are just two—which are handy for a bite to eat on the way to or from the Šumarice park.

Kragujevac makes the best base for the **monasteries of the Morava School** (see below), principally Ravanica, Manasija, and Kalenić, which are scattered around the countryside to the south and east. Bear in mind, though, that without your own transportation you'll need a full day for each one—and even then you will have to set out early if you want to be back by evening. There are two or three buses a day to DESPOTOVAC, main point of departure for Manasija; otherwise take one of the twelve daily buses to SVETOZAREVO, an hour and a half away, and change there, either for ĆUPRIJA for Ravanica, or OPARIĆ for Kalenić.

The Morava School Monasteries

The monasteries of the **Morava School** were the latest of the medieval Serbian churches, dating from the period after the Serbian defeat by the Turks at the Battle of Kosovo in 1389, when the Serbs had relocated north to the region around the Morava River and its various tributaries for safety. A particular style of painting – more decorative and less monumental than before – developed, along with a distinctive architectural style that owes much to examples of Mount Athos. For more on the Morava School style, see "Serbian Monasteries and their Frescoes" in *Contexts*.

The Monastery of Ravanica

A ten-minute bus ride from the town of Ćuprija, **RAVANICA** is perhaps the most accessible of the monasteries of the Morava region, the first of the religious communities that rose here in the late fourteenth century as the last fling of the dying Serbian Empire. It was founded by Prince Lazar and finished some time in the 1380s, and after his death at the Battle of Kosovo in 1389, his body was brought back here and the monastery became center of the cult that mushroomed around him. According to the heroic poems of the battle, Lazar lay decapitated for forty years on Kosovo field, until one day his head and body fused together again and he announced where he wished to be laid to rest:

> *He preferred his splendid Ravanica,*
> *At the foot of the high mountain Kuchaj,*
> *For Lazar built there to God a temple,*
> *While he lived and ruled amongst his people,*
> *Built a church for his own soul's salvation,*
> *Built with his own bread and his own treasure,*
> *Not with the tears of widows and orphans.*

The greater part of the battlements has been destroyed, but the ruins still ring the monastery buildings, enclosing a peaceful complex inhabited by a handful of nuns. The **church** is the most low-key of the Morava School churches, a stocky, five-domed honeycomb of different shades of brown, molded with the characteristic patterning of the period. Inside, the frescoes in the narthex date from an eighteenth-century rebuilding, after the monastery had been plundered by the Turks; the abbot responsible for this—Stefan—is shown on the west wall. In the nave the medieval frescoes are disappointingly shabby, and those that are left dull and pockmarked.

Apparently the Turks can't be wholly blamed for this—the plaster is said to have been badly prepared and so the colors faded quickly. Best of a rather sad lot are the *Cycle of Miracles* on the south wall and the *Entry into Jurusalem*, curving round the southern apse. On the west wall you will see the badly mutilated figure of Lazar standing next to his wife Milica. Rather than let them fall into the hands of the Turks, his mummified remains were removed to safety in the Vojvodina in 1683, and since the war they've been in Belgrade.

The Monastery of Manasija

Squeezed into the narrow Resava valley (and walkable from Despotovac village), **MANASIJA** is a slightly younger monastery than Ravanica, built in 1406–18 and once the artistic center of Lazar's son Stefan's kingdom and a seat of learning. It's circled by massive outer walls that give it a doughty fortress-like solidity—a defense it needed badly as the Turks pushed relentlessly north. Even when building began, Stefan knew the days of his Serbian kingdom were numbered, although no sense of uncertainty mars Manasija's marble church. From the outside it's a solid and simple building, with just a frill beneath the eaves for ornament, while inside some of the splendor of the medieval court is revealed in frescoes, painted by master painters from Thessaloniki and Athos, that are much better preserved than those at Ravanica. These paintings show the furthest refinement of Serbian realism, the virtuoso use of color—particularly blue—and delicacy of detail creating beautifully expressive portraits. Only a third of the original frescoes remain, but in their treatment of biblical themes all reflect a world urbane, rich, and courtly. Badly damaged, Stefan's portrait as donor looks out from the west wall, surveying the church he built as his mausoleum. The aristocratic *Warrior Saints* of the north wall (perhaps the finest of the paintings) could just as well be holding books of poetry as swords, and the guests in the *Parable of the Wedding Feast* in the northern apse are Byzantine nobles eating the finest food from opulent dishes.

The Monastery of Kalenić

The monastery church of **KALENIĆ** is the culmination of the Morava School style. Finished around 1413 by a Serbian noble known as Bogdan, and wrapped in an exuberant, almost candy-striped skin, this is the style at its decorative, expressive best, adorned with lions, gryphons, and birds in relief and chessboard geometric designs that rise to a high, central cupola. Inside, the **frescoes** are, on the whole, well-preserved, and represent some of the finest achievements of Serbian art. The painters worked to a rigid plan which—since a thorough 1950s restoration—you can still make out, with the proportions of the paintings deliberately coinciding with the dimensions of the building; thus they are painted larger the farther away they are from the viewer. In the narthex there are scenes from the life of the Virgin; the apse holds a depiction of the *Communion of the Apostles*; while, in the southern apse, the *Marriage at Cana* is perhaps the most striking work, in fact an exquisitely arranged tableau of a medieval Serbian wedding, complete with the dress and custom of the period. Look closely and you will see that the groom is about to prick the finger of the bride, a blood-mixing pledge that was part of Serbian marriage ritual. You may notice, too, that each figure is eating with a knife and a fork—evidence, Serbs say, of the high degree of refinement in Serbian society before stagnation as part of the Ottoman Empire.

Sadly Kalenić is also one of the most difficult Serbian monasteries to get to, even with your own vehicle. This is as remote a part of Serbia as you're likely to travel through, and the roads beyond Oparić are not good, and can degenerate into unpassable mud tracks if it rains. On foot you can try hitching from Oparić, which is reachable by bus from Svetozarevo, but expect quite a wait, and perhaps to cover the 10km or so in more than one ride. By car, just follow your nose—and keep asking the way; everyone knows the monastery.

Central Serbia: Kruševac, the Morava Valley, and Kraljevo

Around 25km south of the Kalenić monastery, the provincial center of **KRUŠEVAC** is another possible base for the Morava monasteries, though a much less appealing one even than Kragujevac, its center redeveloped with the spacious characterlessness typical of so many Serbian towns. There's precious little evidence of it now, but this was Prince Lazar's capital when he lost the Battle of Kosovo, and his former **fortress**, on the corner of Cara Lazara and Pane Djukića, a short walk from the main Trg Maršala Tita, is now a small park, littered with rubble and stretches of wall and turret. The **Lazarica church** in the middle dates from 1380, a fussy, well-kept specimen of the Morava School, with delicate tracery, rose windows, and a typically polychrome exterior on which checks, crosses and weird dragon-like creatures predominate—though the frescoes which once adorned the interior have since been lost.

Close by, among the exhibits of the **National Museum** (daily 8am–6pm) is the gown that Prince Lazar is supposed to have died in on Kosovo Polje, and a number of other artifacts relating to Lazar and the Serbian Empire, as well as later items from the nineteenth-century struggle against the Turks. Here too is a model of Ivan Meštrović's *St Vitus' Day Temple*, which was going to be erected on the Plain of Kosovo in memory of the battle—a massive (250m long, 100m wide) and oddly fanatical work by the Croatian sculptor.

Kruševac practicals

If you have to **stay** in Kruševac—and there's little to hold you except bus connections—the B-category *Hotel Europa* has rooms for about $30, but is nearly always packed out with student groups. It's also the most central place to **eat** cheaply, though don't expect *haute cuisine*.

The Morava Valley: the Monastery of Ljubostinja

The main road forges west from Kruševac towards Kraljevo, following the wide floodplain of the Zapadna (or Western) Morava River. **TRSTENIK**, lying about halfway between Kruševac and Kraljevo, is a small town that's worth a stop for a look at another Morava School church, that of the **Monastery of Ljubostinja**, about 3km to the north. It's well signposted from the town, which drags along the road and fizzles out just before the monastery – an easy walk, but if you don't feel up to it one of seven buses a day will ferry you there.

Ljubostinja feels very much a working monastery, a small palatial estate centered on a large *konak* in which the nuns make their own honey and wine. It was founded in 1395 by Prince Lazar's widow, Princess Milica, who retired here—to the spot where, it's apocryphally claimed, she first met Lazar—with other gentlewomen to mourn her husband's death and the eclipse of medieval Serbia. The church, ouwardly at least, is quite different from the other Morava School structures, with a whitewashed exterior that displays none of the fussiness of Kalenić or the Lazarica church, though the decoration around the arches and windows is impressive. Inside, it's a homy church, with a welcoming feel quite at odds with the usual Orthodox mystery. Few frescoes survive, but you can just make out the portraits of Lazar and Milica on the west wall of the narthex and—in better condition—those of their sons, Stefan and Vuk, on the other side of the door.

Kraljevo and the Monastery of Žiča

Half an hour on from Trstenik, **KRALJEVO** is an industrial town mostly destroyed in the last war and largely rebuilt to a new plan. It's a self-satisfied little place, mainly residential, arranged around a shopping precinct which culminates in the inevitable overstated war memorial and a combination arena-square where the evening *korso* becomes a spectator sport. With a car you could use Kraljevo as a base for some of the monasteries, but it's not one of the best places; indeed it's better left as a stopover on the way south. Only the Žiča monastery is best seen from here, and once you've seen that, aside from the **Muzej-Galerija Fresaka**, Karadjordjeva 3, which has copies of frescoes from the surrounding monastic churches, there's nothing to keep you from moving on.

The Monastery of Žiča

The monastery of **Žiča** lies about 4km outside Kraljevo, easily accessible by hourly bus (direction Mataruška Banja); its cupolas, painted a rusty red in imitation of those on Mount Athos, crown the brow of the hill. This was once among the grandest of all the Serbian monasteries, founded by Saint Sava—patron saint of the Serbian people—as head of the new Serbian Patriarchate when he returned from Athos to sort out the wrangles of his brothers. Local tradition has it that he was led to this site by a golden thread, which is what the name of the monastery means. Žiča was the fulcrum of his masterplan to establish the great and holy kingdom of Serbia as a force to be reckoned with in Europe: he crowned his brother Stefan here, and in 1220 gave the monastery a charter that made it the owner of land as far away as Lake Skadar. If medieval Serbia reached a graceful conclusion in the monasteries of the Morava valley, Žiča was one of the places that its glories began.

The church has been heavily restored over the years, the last time in 1954, which has left it bare and soulless. The frescoes, sadly, are in a sorry state of repair; most of the originals were lost to plundering Bulgarians in 1290, and all that survives from Sava's time are patches around the cupola and the *Crucifixion* in the south transept—difficult to see as the transepts have been sectioned off as choir stalls. The other remaining frescoes are fourteenth-century, best the rather stiff, stylized *Dormition of the Virgin* on the west wall.

Practical Details

Staying at Kraljevo isn't recommended, but if it's late and you're needing to stop, the *Turist* **hotel**, on the main square (☎036/22-366), is adequate and has rooms for around $20. Failing that, the nearby spa town of MATARUŠKA BANJA, a little way beyond Žiča, has **private rooms** available from its *Centralna Recepcija*, as does the *Putnik* office, Maršala Tita 1, in the spa center of VRNJAČKA BANJA—back towards Trstenik. For **food** there's a reasonable restaurant on Kraljevo's main square.

South to Studenica

South of Kraljevo the road weaves its way around the sleek, wooded spurs of the **Ibar valley**, the landscape growing more dramatic by the minute. On the left, about 20km on, the castle of **Maglić**, the early-fifteenth-century stronghold of a Serbian archbishop concerned to protect himself from marauders, peers proudly down from a flattened peak on the east bank of the river. This was a task well accomplished, and from this side only those with time and energy on their hands (and their own transportation) will be able to even contemplate scaling the hill to the top. The river is far too deep and fast to wade, and the nearest bridge is 3km back towards Kraljevo, where the railroad crosses the water.

The Monastery of Studenica

The road continues down to USĆE, where a smaller road branches off to make the half-hour climb up to the monastery of **Studenica**, a lovely, quite spectacular journey up the forested valley, high above the river which froths and foams far below. The monastery sits primly among the thickets of pines and Alpine pastures, deliberately remote and inaccessible, the first and greatest of the Serbian monasteries and originally established at the end of the twelfth century by Stefan Nemanja, founding father of the Nemanja dynasty; when the archbishop of Canterbury visited Yugoslavia twenty years ago it was here he came to preach. At one time the complex had nine churches, of which three are left, standing in an oval paddock framed by the monastery's secular buildings, which help to give Studenica the feel of a workplace as well as religious retreat. It's one of the most thriving of the monasteries, certainly, and although the flow of tourists never amounts to very much, its one hotel and handful of additional buildings—a post office, a couple of restaurants—indicate a complex much more discovered than most of its counterparts in the rest of the republic. It also has many more monks than other monasteries, and ownership of a fair amount of land. The monks are usually glad to show you around if they're free, and although no one actually speaks English, you could try asking for Brother Jovan, who speaks German.

The Monastery Churches

Center of the monastic group is the church of **Sv Bogdorica** or Church of Our Lady, built in the Raška School style during the closing decades of the twelfth century. It was founded by Stefan Nemanja, who abdicated here before retiring to the Hilandaríou Serbian monastery on Mount Athos. After his death his body was brought back here, where it lies still, the subject of a major pilgrimage on his feast-day—May 24.

From the outside Sv Bogdorica is a Romanesque church in style, with exterior decoration—vine leaves, figures, and strange animals adorn the doors and windows—that is reminiscent of many churches you see on the Adriatic coast. The clumsy exonarthex was added by King Radoslav in 1230, a later Nemanjic ruler who spoiled the smooth polished serenity of the original marble structure with the plain and rather savage extension. This is in effect the entrance hall of the church and holds its treasury, which includes various fifteenth- and sixteenth-century liturgical items and the elaborate nineteenth-century Viennese coffin of Stefan Nemanja's son, Stefan Prvovenčani—a popular figure locally. Its lid is littered with the gifts of local people, and articles are often placed underneath to soak up healing power.

Beyond this point, in a marble tomb in the inner sanctum of the church, lies Stefan Nemanja, below a fresco which shows him being presented to Christ and the Virgin; with Nemanja, the southern corner of churches became the traditional resting place of Serbian rulers. The frescoes in here are contemporary with the completion of the church in 1209, and although few remain especially intact, those that do represent the first flowering of Serbian fresco painting: calm, monumental works, with a new emphasis on the human form. The *Crucifixion*, on the west wall of the nave, is remarkably well preserved; Christ hangs against a background of deep blue, flanked by the bowed figures of the Virgin and Saint John, the painting colored with rich blues, golds and maroons. It's a formal painting—Christ's body is gracefully draped, His hair hangs in ringlets, and blood falls symmetrically from His wounds—but also an emotional one, and it's hard to come away unmoved.

The tiny **Kraljeva Crkva** or "King's Church," next door, is a much later structure, built in 1314 by King Milutin. It's nothing special architecturally but its frescoes are impressive, displaying a humanism and narrative detail characteristic of Serbian painting at its best, not least in the fresco of the *Birth of the Virgin* on the north wall. Certainly there's a keener interest in contemporary detail, even a degree of realism, than in the paintings of Sv Bogdorica. On the left a woman holds a tray of surgical instruments; to the right the figure of Destiny fans the new-born babe; in the foreground a woman tests the water with the back of her hand before bathing the baby.

The third and final remaining church of the monastic complex is that of **Sv Nicolas**, close by, built at the beginning of the thirteenth century and a very simple building that's often closed up. If you can get in, a couple of frescoes have been preserved, one showing the *Entry into Jerusalem*, the other *Three Marys at Christ's Grave*.

Practical Details

Getting to Studenica (or leaving) isn't difficult: buses leave for the monastery throughout the day from Ušće, which is in turn connected by frequent bus to both Kraljevo and Novi Pazar. And thanks to the newly asphalted road, the journey up here is a lot quicker—and smoother—than it used to be; reckon on about 30 minutes. Once here, it's a good idea to **stay** and lap up some of the monastery's peace. The *Studenica* hotel (☎036/836-222), a short walk beyond the monastery, is beautifully situated and not too pricey at $30 for a double; it also has a decent **restaurant** with a terrace.

South to Novi Pazar

From Ušće, the road winds south, following the route of the Ibar River. Ten kilometers or so after you cross the river for the second time, a rough dirt road leads off right to the monastery of **GRADAC**, 12km or so up the hill. It's not an easy ride, but the monastery's Church of the Annunciation, another example of the Raška School, is worth the detour if you have your own (sturdy) set of wheels. The church was founded in 1275 by Queen Helen of Anjou, wife of Uroš I, and with its blind arcading and sculpted doorways is reminiscent of the churches at Studenica and Dečani. Its frescoes, sadly, are in poor condition; those that remain illustrate the *Communion of the Apostles* among other things—but the site, high on the exposed hilltop, is lovely.

Moving on from Gradac, the road pushes southeast toward Titova Mitrovica and Kosovo, a short way before the border of which a minor but well-paved road branches off at **RAŠKA**—a long, straggling industrial community useful for its train station and bus connections but no more. If you're heading south and don't want to go to Novi Pazar, this is the place to change. After Raška you enter the **Sandžak**, a remote Muslim region of low mountains and few drivable roads that remained a solitary island of Turkish rule and a buffer between the states of Serbia and Montenegro until the late nineteenth century (*sandžak* was the Turkish term for Ottoman administrative provinces).

Novi Pazar and Around

NOVI PAZAR was the capital of the Sandžak, and an important stopping-off point on the caravan routes between Dubrovnik and Constantinople until the annexation of Bosnia by Austria-Hungary cut it off from the coast. Its position lent it obvious strategic importance for the early Serbian rulers, and Stefan Nemanja established his first capital nearby, where it remained until King Milutin moved operations to Skopje. You can still see the ruins of Nemanja's palace at Ras, a few kilometers west of town—though it's the later monastery of Sopoćani that brings people to Novi Pazar, with what is by common consensus considered to be the finest extant example of Serbian fresco painting.

Notwithstanding these historical associations, Novi Pazar itself has little to remind one of the Serbian era, and its most immediate features are an odd mixture of Turkish and modern, with a downtown that blends a small Turkish-style bazaar quarter with a complete Seventies renovation. Concrete high rises have ripped the heart out of its old center, which focuses on a main square that's more parking lot than central meeting-place, flanked by a department store, a Turkish *han*, and the neo-orientalism of the massive new *Hotel Vrbak* complex.

The town's main street leads east from the central square, its Turkish dwellings, tea-houses and noisy bazaar atmosphere about as close to the East in feel as you get in Serbia, at least outside of Kosovo. Relics from Ottoman occupation dot the middle of town. The old **fort**, close by, was built in the fifteenth century as the headquarters of the Sandžak region and now doubles as a quiet, shady park. At the far end of the main street, the **Altum Alem Mosque** is a small and intimate sixteenth-century structure with a gaily colored *mihrab*—though it's clearly seen better days; bash hard on the door (no. 79) and you should be let in. There's more evidence of the influence of Islam in the town on view at the **town museum** (daily 7am–3pm), just off the main square, which has a collection of artifacts and craftwork relating to the Turkish period.

Around Novi Pazar: Sv Petar and Djurdjevi Stubovi

Apart from the Sopoćani monastery, there are a couple of other sights worth seeing around Novi Pazar. The first, the church of **Sv Petar**, a circular plan building with radiating apses and a high central cupola, is walkably close, situated on a grassy mound about 2km north of town, beyond the bus station. Stefan Nemanja held an early council here that outlawed the Bogomil heresy in Serbia, and some sources claim it was in this building that he abdicated, though in fact the church is much older than this would suggest; indeed it's said to be the only surviving Serbian church to predate the era of Stefan Nemanja. Its nucleus dates from the ninth century, and the site is probably a good deal older; in the 1950s the grave of a fifth-century Illyrian prince was discovered here, together with royal burial accoutrements that have since found their way to Belgrade. There's nothing much to actually see, only some badly chipped frescoes from the thirteenth century, but the sense of age inside the building is potent. To get in, pick up the key from the house nearby.

The other thing worth venturing out of Novi Pazar for, and clearly visible high on the hill from everywhere in the town, is the church of **Djurdjevi Stubovi**, though you really need your own transportation to get here. It's only about five kilometers' walk, but quite a climb to the top—strictly for the fit and energetic. The church is actually in ruins now, with only the shell of its cupola and nave still standing, focus of a peaceful ring of grassy stones, enclosed by trees. Again there's not much here beyond the occasional faded fresco, but on a clear day with no other visitors (and the site is never overrun), the place has a solitary, windswept atmosphere that's appealing, and the views, across the rolling mountains for miles in all directions, are marvelous. Just below the church, a museum contains a model of the church as it would have looked, together with pieces rescued and reconstructed with plaster.

Getting to Djurdjevi Stubovi isn't as obvious as it seems from Novi Pazar. To do it, head west down the main street, turn right by the *Jugogas* garage, and take the first left by the building marked "Jošanica."

Novi Pazar Practicals

The only place **to stay** in Novi Pazar itself is the *Hotel Vrbak* (☎020/24-844), which has rooms for around $50 a double. Cheaper, though a bit isolated without your own transportATION, are two motels out on the road to Sopoćani: the *Motel Ras* (☎020/25-892), close to the ruins of old Ras (buses every hour), and the *Tourist Dom* (☎020/22-014), near the monastery itself (buses every three hours), both of which have double rooms for about $40. All three hotels have **restaurants** too, so you needn't go hungry, though if you're not averse to diet of *ćevapčići* there are plenty of grill restaurants and snackeries in the center of Novi Pazar.

The Monastery of Sopoćani

You'd be mad to visit Novi Pazar without seeing the monastery of **SOPOĆANI**, about 16km west of town on a road that cuts deep into the remote heart of the Sandžak. King Uroš I built the church here as his mausoleum, a Raška School foundation that stands out strong and white against the green woolly hills that surround it. Until fifty years ago it was little more than a ruin, and its frescoes had seen two centuries' exposure to the elements; since then it has remained—despite its relative fame—something of a retreat, a resting place where a few elderly nuns work out their days in an atmosphere of real tranquillity.

The church's exonarthex was added in the fourteenth century by Dušan and except for the campanile has subsequently collapsed. But the rest of the building, dating from 1263 and in typical Raška style, is intact. Uroš planned the church as much as a celebration of his family as of God, and the frescoes, in the narthex at least, show the Nemanjic dynasty in its full glory. The figures of Uroš and Dragutin rear up in front of you, on the right; on the east wall, the thirteenth-century council of Stefan Nemanja has been added to a depiction of the seven ecumenical councils; while on the north wall a fresco representing the death of Uroš's mother, Anna Dandolo, painted above her sarcophagus, gets the sort of treatment normally reserved for depictions of the Virgin.

Uroš himself lies in the nave, where the frescoes, finished around 1265, are very different in both style and intent to those in the narthex, the work of master painters from Constantinople working to a scheme that is a moving affirmation of faith and Christianity. The best-known piece, the *Dormition of the Virgin*, covers the west wall, a traditional placing that doesn't take away from its power; it depicts Christ serenely central over his mother's bier holding a swaddled babe—the soul of the Virgin about to ascend to Heaven—while the Apostles stand silently by, a human, dignified grouping, posed in eloquent, almost musical relation to each other. Colors are muted green and gold, or maroons mellowing to powdered pink, and only the women wailing from the balcony behind add a discordant note. The other frescoes echo the painting of the Dormition, its lines of Apostles answered by the rhythmic parade of bishops in the apse, its sad, handsome figures reflected by the strong, stooping Christ on the north wall reaching down to haul up souls from Purgatory. There are other figures worth studying, not least that of John, on the right in the north transept, but really it's the church as a whole which impresses. In their grandeur, emotion, and originality, these paintings are hardly bettered anywhere in medieval art, and it is tempting to speculate (as Serbs do) on just what degree of civilization was undermined by the Turkish conquest a century later.

West from Belgrade: the Road to Tršić

The road southwest from Belgrade follows the meanders of the Sava River, a dull trip across featureless terrain, taking in the unremarkable spa town of OBRENOVAC on the way. It's the slow way to get to Šabac, and on public transit you'll almost certainly cover part of the distance on the east–west *autoput*—a much quicker route in the long run.

ŠABAC is a dusty, dirty town scarred by railroad sidings, with very little of interest by any standards. There's a small overgrown Turkish fortress here, dating from the fifteenth century, and a handful of mediocre nineteenth-century buildings, one of which holds a local museum. But really the only time it's worth being here is for the **Šabački Vašar**, an enormous fair held every year on September 21. Somewhere between a folklore festival and an agricultural show, it's the biggest annual event in Serbia, pulling in hordes of people from the villages around and culminating in a massive concert of ethnic music.

Beyond Šabac the road skirts the **Mačva**, marshy lowlands that mark the junction of the Drina and Sava rivers. Geographically speaking this is the southernmost point of the Pannonian Plain, and the villages of the Mačva are similar in character to those of Slavonia and the Vojvodina to the north: endless strips of colorwashed houses standing end on to the road, edged by tidy gardens and lawns.

LOZNICA is neater than Šabac, but has even less to offer, and the main attraction here is the village of **TRŠIĆ**, 5km southeast, the birthplace of one of Serbia's most important historical figures—Vuk Stefanović Karadžić. Hailed as the founding father of the Serbian literary language, his portrait, with drooping white moustache, is a familiar sight all over the republic.

Vuk Karadžić was born in 1787 to a poor family of local farmers, and, with the help of local monks and some comparatively well-off relatives, taught himself to read and write in a society where illiteracy was very much the norm, especially in the countryside. After the Serbian national uprising of 1804 his skills were much sought after to help in the administration of the fledgling state. With the Turkish reconquest of Belgrade in 1813, Vuk fled to Vienna, where he began a career publishing (previously oral) Serbian folk tales under the guidance of the court librarian, the Slovene Jernej Kopitar. At a time when the Romantic movement was sweeping Europe, many people were enthralled by Vuk's stories of the plucky Serbs battling against their Turkish oppressors, and the tales made him into something of a celebrity—though Vuk's ambition was as an educator, and his intention was to use the Serbian folk tales as a way of bringing literacy to the villages they originated in. He spent the rest of his life traveling the lands of his people, writing down the oral and folk literatures he found. His most important contribution, perhaps, was, along with his colleague and mentor, Dositej Obradović, to adapt the Cyrillic script to the specific needs of the Serbian tongue, producing a supremely logical alphabet in which each letter corresponds to a precise sound—a rarity in the babel of European languages.

Vuk's reconstructed **birthplace** lies at the end of a one kilometre-long trail through the well-preserved nineteenth-century village. Tablets bearing Vuk's proverbs line the route up from the coach park—cloying homilies for the most part, such as *zlo činiti a dobro se nadati nije moguće* (it's impossible to do bad and hope for good), but folk wisdom that struck a chord with the Serbian peasantry. The house itself is a fake, a typical whitewashed structure common to these border regions between Bosnia and Serbia, built in 1933 on the supposed site of the original dwelling, but its reconstruction has been undertaken with such a close attention to period detail it's hard not to be impressed. Inside are the few simple items Vuk's family would have possessed, and no more: a bed, a cauldron, the random cooking utensil, and a shin-high table surrounded by tiny three-legged stools at which the family would have squatted in order to gulp down their humble fare.

There's no English information, and everything is (not surprisingly) labeled in Cyrillic. But the place speaks for itself really. Close by, look also at the *saborište*, a natural terraced amphitheater fitted with wooden benches in which the annual *Vukov sabor* or Vuk's assembly is held, on a mid-September Sunday.

As for the rest of the village, it's inevitably rather touristy, but things are done fairly tastefully, with the accent on authentic period re-creations. There's a nineteenth-century watermill selling its own corn, a *biljana apoteka* or herbal apothecary where you drink herb tea and buy natural remedies, and a café at which you can sit on reproductions of the Karadžić's lilliputian furniture. There's also a good **restaurant**, the *Šator*, beside the village green, which serves tasty Serbian specialties and home-baked bread.

Practical Details . . . and into Bosnia

Tršić is a feasible day trip from Belgrade, even on public transit, or a potential stop-off on the way into Bosnia. There are about five buses a day from Loznica to Tršić, though check with the driver about getting back; some buses back to Loznica skirt the town center without going to the bus station.

Beyond Loznica the road follows the Drina upstream, the hills closing in as you cross the border. The first taste of Bosnia is the town of **ZVORNIK**, cowering under the ruins of a medieval Turkish fortress, from where it's up into the mountains of eastern Bosnia and across to Sarajevo, some two hours distant.

Western Serbia: the Road to Mileševa

Following the Zapadna Morava valley west from Kraljevo takes you into the westerly reaches of Serbia, a green, increasingly mountainous area, through which the **Belgrade–Bar railroad** cuts a lovely route, via Valjevo, Titovo Užice, and Prijepole, making a possible, if slow, way to see the region.

Around 40km due west of Krajevo, **ČACAK** is the first large center, a cheerless town with little to hold you—though the Djetinja valley just beyond is worth a look, a steep gray defile dappled with occasional trees. On the far bank, a number of seventeenth-century **monasteries** shelter beneath precipitous heights, simple, sober buildings from a time when believers were forced to hide themselves away in the remotest places.

The Monastery of Arilje

A little farther on, in POŽEGA, a road branches south for the village of **ARILJE**, whose creamy domed church is the only remnant of a monastery founded by King Dragutin at the end of the thirteenth century. Dragutin was one of the least competent of all the Serbian monarchs. A Catholic zealot of the most fanatical kind, his overthrow of his father, Uroš I, and subsequent attempts to establish the Catholic church in Serbia led to his forfeiture of vast tracts of the empire and forced abdication in favor of his brother Milutin. This church is a rare reminder of his short reign, with frescoes showing Dragutin, Milutin, and Dragutin's wife Katelina—rich, royal representatives, studded with jewelry and finery, hardly aware of the tiny figure of Christ behind— together with others depicting the Sacrifice of Abraham and Tree of Jesse.

Titovo Užice

Back on the main road, it's another short hop on to **TITOVO UŽICE**, a go-ahead modern town punctured by skyscrapers and spread across the spacious valley of the Djetinja River. Užice, as it was formerly known, has always held a strategic importance. It was here, in the autumn of 1941, that the Užice Republic was declared—the first free partisan state, which lasted just 67 days until the town was forcibly taken back by a German strike force 10,000 strong. For those 67 days the war effort was run from here: a provisional government was set up, factories produced munitions, and party presses turned out newspapers and propaganda daily. Its eventual evacuation—a chaotic, hurried affair—was the first and one of the greatest partisan defeats; casualties were grotesque, and the unit that defended the town fell to the last man, spurring Tito to offer his resignation as party leader.

These days the town is of more interest for its history than for anything specific to see, though a **museum**, about ten minutes' walk from the bus station, documents the events of 1941, with displays on the republic and its tragic aftermath. There are weapons, photographs, and you can visit Tito's office, preserved as it was left on the day of the evacuation. Outside, the primitive munitions factory brings home the makeshift nature of the whole affair.

In the center of town, the main square, **Partizan Trg**, is dominated by an austere greatcoated Tito—one of very few public statues of the late leader in existence (there's a copy of this one at Kumrovec, his birthplace)—while all around award-winning architecture sneers at the Nazis' short-lived victory. Its location is attractive enough, but otherwise the town isn't especially appealing, though it does make another good journey-breaker if you're heading west into Bosnia.

Practical Details . . . and the Zlatibor Mountains

If you want **to stay** in Titovo Užice, the *Hotel Palas* (**☎**031/21-752), five minutes' walk from the **bus and train stations**, close to the river, has doubles for around $50. For **food** there are a couple of cheap self-service restaurants, or you could try the restaurant in the *Zlatibor* hotel, just off the main square.

South of Titovo Užice, beyond Čajetina, lie the high, treeless pastures of the **Zlatibor mountains**, a favorite among Yugoslav health resorts, speckled everywhere with winter chalets. **PARTIZANSKE VODE**, situated at a height of 1000m, is the main concentration, with hotels, ski-lifts, and any number of medical services for the treatment of ailing Yugoslavs. Incidentally, southeast of here, at **KAPAONIK**, near Ras, is the republic's major winter-sports area, with spanking new facilities for skiing laid out at altitudes of between 1600m and around 2000m. Before long you're descending through a heavily wooded valley, and, beyond the twin lakes of Radoina Jezero and Zlatarsko Jezero, entering Prijepolje.

Prijepolje and the Mileševa Monastery

PRIJEPOLJE, around 60km south of Titovo Užice, is scenically situated where the Lim valley has flattened out into a broad bowl. It's on the Belgrade–Bar railroad line and is the best, or at least the nearest, base for the monastery of Mileševa, where you can see one of the most important Raška School churches.

The Monastery of Mileševa

MILEŠEVA was founded around 1218 by Vladislav, grandson of Stefan Nemanja, who became king of Serbia in 1234 and planned the church as his mausoleum. Historically it's an important church for the Serbs, best known as the last resting place of Vladislav's uncle, Saint Sava, founder of the Serbian church. The cult that flowered around Saint Sava locally attracted Christians and Muslims alike, a precedent that so worried the Turkish authorities that in 1594 they had his bones taken to Belgrade and burned: devout Serbs still tell how on that day Saint Sava's body rose above the pyre and hovered in the stormy sky. Narthex and nave have together formed the main body of the **church** since the collapse of the dividing wall, though they're still known respectively as the blue and gold parts of the church—labels that refer to the predominant colors used in the frescoes. The collapsing wall left half a monkish portrait of Stefan Nemanja, heading a parade of the Nemanjic dynasty from Saint Sava to Vladislav, who, as donor, clutches a model of his church. On the south wall of the nave a fresco of the *Angel at the Tomb* gazes coolly down, serene yet strong, his eyes gently accusing. This may ring a bell: it's probably the most famous of all Serbian fresco paintings, an image which first became more widely known when it was projected across the Atlantic as part of the first USA–UK satellite link-up, and for a while it was one of the emblems of the United Nations. The other frescoes are no less impressive. Just above, though rather difficult to see, is a lovely *Deposition*, with a shadowy, limp Christ tended by the Virgin and Mary Magdalen; next door is a demure Virgin in an *Annunciation* scene.

The monastery itself is a shadow of the community it was; only two monks remain and, in a region predominantly Muslim, this is one of the poorest of Serbian monasteries. Visible from here, high on a crag and accessible, is a **castle** of disputed origin. The local story is that it's the idle boast of a rich woman who didn't know what to do with her money; more likely it was an outpost of medieval Bosnian kings.

Practical Details ... and South through the Lim Gorge

Prijepolje's **bus and train station** are situated together on the west side of the river, ten minutes' walk from the town center. If you have your own transportation it's best to see Mileševa and move on; if not you'll probably need **to stay**. The *Hotel Mileševa* (☎033/21-078), close to the bus and train stations, has double rooms for about $28 and probably the town's best **restaurant**—a focal point of life in the evenings, with live music. To **get to Mileševa**, about 6km outside town, you can either take a bus (four a day from Prijepolje bus station) or walk—about 45 minutes to an hour; turn right by the Turkish clock tower in the middle of town and follow the (good) road to the end.

South of Prijepolje, towards BIJELO POLJE, is a spectacular trip by road, the last stretch, after Brodarevo, weaving its way through the **Lim Gorge**. The sheer, craggy rock towers menacingly high above, with trees sprouting in nooks and pockets, to provide a feathery cover of green up top. The railroad follows the same route, and although much of the time you're in a tunnel, the track emerges now and again to some superb views. Beyond the gorge you're in Montenegro and, before long, the dull town of Bijelo Polje— the place to change buses if you're heading into Kosovo from here.

Eastern Serbia and the Danube

From Belgrade routes lead east into one of Serbia's most beautiful and certainly most remote corners, enclosed by the frontiers of Romania and Bulgaria. It's an area of rugged, gold-bearing mountains traversed by dark forested valleys, the difficult topography of the region ensuring the survival of archaic traditions and rich folklore. The tourist industry is very unevenly developed, and although attractions like Lepenski Vir and the Djerdap Dam have prompted the building of modern hotels, there are few private rooms and very little understanding of the concept of independent travel. In some places you may be considered an oddity.

Despite this, most of the major centers of Eastern Serbia—such as there are—are well connected with Belgrade by bus. And although the once-daily hydrofoil services down the Danube itself to Kladovo have been indefinitely suspended, it's worth inquiring at *Djerdap Tourist* in Belgrade (Vuka Karadžića 4; ☎185-135) for any bus trips that might be going. Trains, on the other hand, though they run to both Negotin and Zaječar, are tortuously slow and worth avoiding altogether.

Down the Danube

As always, the **Danube** provides the most obvious spur into Eastern Serbia, a river not so much blue as a muddy brown, forming a wallowing border between Yugoslavia and Romania. Once a perilously fast stretch of water, since the building of the Djerdap Dam, farther downstream, this part of the river has become in effect a placid, slender lake, at times as much as a mile wide, its silty waters forming long wooded islands and fertile banks of green. One other effect of the dam has been to reduce the Danube's efficiency as a waste disposal system for central European industry; pollutants from upstream now collect along this stretch of the river, depleting fish stocks and withering the local flora.

Half an hour out of Belgrade, taking the minor road that parallels the river, is the small riverside town of **GROCKA**, where vine-covered hillsides slope down towards the sandy banks of the river. Twenty kilometers beyond, **SMEDEREVO** was where the last ruler of medieval Serbia, Djordje Branković, holed up when the Turks had occupied most of the rest of the country and he had been forced to cede Belgrade to the equally expansionist Hungarians. His **fortress** sprawls along the south bank of the river, a last retreat, once hemmed in by hostile Turks and Magyars and now framed by a modern patchwork of cranes and tower blocks. Smederevo is an unappetizing place, with a massive steel mill to the south, and a big rail shunting yard separating the town center from the castle itself, which was blown up in a munitions explosion in 1941—a blast which also killed thousands of local people. But the remaining shell is still impressive, stretching along the banks of the river for half a kilometer. Branković was safe enough walled up here— the Turks did capture the castle in 1439 but oddly enough let him have it back again—and he ruled until his death in 1456. Smederevo fell three years later and remained in Turkish hands until the nineteenth century.

From Smederevo the road heads inland across the dusty arable Morava plain to the small agricultural center of **POŽAREVAC**. Known to history by its German name—Passarowitz—it's here that the Austrians and Turks came to terms in 1718, signing a treaty which confirmed Hapsburg conquests as far south as Belgrade. From here, the road doesn't really rejoin the Danube until **GOLUBAC**, where it passes right under the arches of the splendid medieval **castle** of the same name—a more romantic sight than Smederevo, clinging to a craggy outcrop and guarding the entrance to the narrower stretches of the Danube. Built by the Hungarians, it was subsequently commandeered by the Turks but abandoned in the eighteenth century when their frontiers altered.

From Golubac onward, the river is more appealing, and the road hugs the bank, only dodging away for short stretches to climb up into the rolling hills of the valley. **DONJI MILANOVAC**, about 40km on, is a new town entirely rebuilt after former settlement disappeared under the lake formed by the dam. Though itself without interest, people come here for the excavations at **LEPENSKI VIR**, a large Mesolithic and Neolithic settlement which was discovered here in the mid-Sixties and is reachable from the town by bus.

It was exploratory digging for the Djerdap Dam which uncovered the first of the remains. A year later the greater part of the settlement was excavated, and in 1967 a number of monumental stone sculptures were found—the oldest Mesolithic sculptures yet uncovered in Europe, dating back to 6000 BC. The site itself—before it was flooded—seems to have been a logical place for people to live: up on a raised shelf away from the capricious waters of the Danube (*Vir* means "whirlpool"), and with a ready supply of fish in the river and wildlife in the forest. Some seventy houses were found in all, and in 1970 the finds were transferred to a plateau a little farther up, which was roofed over and converted to a small **museum**. This is where you can see most of the major objects now. The stone sculptures especially are remarkable, mainly life-size heads, intricately and individually carved and implying (along with the planned nature of the village) a well-formed civilization, with an art and culture of its own. Originally assumed to be a fishing village, experts have since mooted ideas that Lepenski Vir was some kind of religious center: the bones of fish and deer that were found could be the remains of sacrifices and the heads depictions of primitive gods. This remains a matter for debate, however, and many anthropologists still maintain that the heads represent actual inhabitants of the village.

Sadly it's not really possible to see Lepenski Vir as a day trip from Belgrade without your own transport. The daily bus from the capital to Donji Milanovac leaves about 6am, and by the time you arrive it's almost time to catch the bus back again. Consequently you'll need to **stay**: the ultra-modern, A category *Lepenski Vir* hotel (☎030/86-131) has doubles at varying levels of luxury starting at $40 apiece, and a wealth of recreational facilities including yachting.

From Donji Milanovac the Danube pushes sluggishly through the sheer **Kazan Gorge** to TEKIJA, where there's a bus up to the **Djerdap Dam**, a Yugoslav-Romanian venture meant to tame the angry waters of the Iron Gates of the Danube and replace the more exciting rapids as a tourist attraction. Before, the river cut through here with ruthless speed, its syrupy waters swirling and eddying dangerously, forcing barges and ships to navigate a narrow channel close to the right bank, where the water was still so fast they had to be towed by steam train. Now, thanks to the dam, which is said to be the third largest in the world, the water is quiet, the river wide and serene, and there's not a hint of white water anywhere.

You can visit the **hydroelectric station** on the Yugoslav side (produce your passport and don't take photos), in the company of a guide, for plentiful statistics and a short film outlining the history of the project. Outside the complex stands the **Tablet of Trajan**, recently moved from its position high on the riverbank upstream. Dating from AD 102, it celebrates the completion of a road along the narrow Danube defile by the Emperor Trajan—a road that common Roman consensus had agreed impossible, when it was abandoned some eighty years earlier. According to the tablet, the emperor was considerably more determined than his compatriots, and he "defeated both the mountain and the river" to finish the work.

Trajan's concern for the area's infrastructure was prompted by his interest in conquering the kingdom of Dacia, now Romania, on the other side of the river. To facilitate his campaigns he built a **bridge** across the river 15km south of Djerdap, just beyond the dull modern town of **KLADOVO**. The whole thing was demolished two centuries later when Dacia fell and belligerent forces began to use the bridge against the Romans. But a couple of stone pillars are still visible on the Yugoslav side, along with the remains of a fortress built to protect the bridge.

Kladovo itself is known for its caviar and not much else, a desperate, beaten sort of place with only the modern *Djerdap* hotel to tempt you. On the northern side of town is the Turkish castle of **Fetislam**, but it's overgrown with weeds, and on the whole a smaller-scale, less dramatic version of things already seen at Kalemegdan.

South of the Danube: the Road to Negotin

An alternative to following the Danube is to cut straight across country towards Negotin. The mountains south of the river contain an incongruous mixture of Transylvanian wilderness and heavy industrialization, with grim mining communities nestling secretively in deep, densely forested valleys.

Many of the people here are **Vlachs**, migratory shepherds who belong to the same ethnic stock as the Romanians, speak a dialect of Romanian, and can be found in isolated pockets all over the Balkans. Here the Vlach population is largely settled, their remote villages occupying an arc of territory from Kučevo in the northwest to Negotin in the southeast. They divide into two groups: the *ungureani*, who live in the highlands, and the *carani*, who settled earlier and live on the plains, and are much more integrated with the Serbian population around them. The *ungureani* are still very much an independent people, with their own mythology and ancient pagan beliefs. In the village of Duboka, 10km northwest of Kučevo, women are said to fall into painful trances at Whitsun and communicate with the dead. They have distinct traditions in folk music too, relying heavily on the eerie panpipes common in neighboring Romania. And their influence can be seen in the cuisine of eastern Serbia, a soft, fatty, piquant cheese made from ewe's milk replacing *kajmak* as the region's staple dairy product.

KUČEVO, 50km beyond Požarevac, is a dusty characterless place, but may be a useful base for excursions into the neighboring **Homoljske Planine**—desolate moors dotted with isolated hamlets where old people still wear traditional dress. Beyond Kučevo, the wide, maize-covered valley floor gives way to a narrow, winding gorge. Increased roadside sightings of rusting industrial machinery and abandoned concrete slabs are signs that you're close to **MAJDANPEK**, a tough, hardworking town that's a major center for copper and, in former times, gold mining. The Pek River is still panned for gold by a few semiserious locals, and the tourist authorities are beginning to plan such trips for visitors.

Mining apart, Majdanpek doesn't have much in the way of distractions, though its location, surrounded by a rim of craggy peaks, is a dramatic one. The mine is noticeable at once, a massive wedge cut into the earth on the town's northern side, its slag stretching endlessly down the valley. About a kilometer outside the town are the **Rajkova Pecina** caves (April–Oct daily 9am–6pm), several kilometers of stalactite-filled caverns that served as a refuge for resistance fighters against the Turks in days gone by. There's been some effort to develop these for tourism over recent years, but they're still almost completely unknown. Their travertine floor is unique.

Shortly after Majdanpek you can either branch north across stark mountains up to Donji Milanovac, or south to the dour copper-mining town of BOR, though the latter is worth avoiding. The best route, though, is straight ahead, gently descending through the forested Šaška valley. Rocky cliffs tower above small roadside hamlets, the farmers managing to squeeze tiny patches of crops into the narrow valley floor. After an hour's drive across a plateau there's a sudden drop into the Timok valley and the secluded provincial town of Negotin.

Negotin

Arriving at the bus or train station (together on the western fringes of the town on 27 Septembra), you'd be forgiven for thinking that **NEGOTIN** is yet another of Yugoslavia's uninspiring postwar conurbations, an impression that the twenty-minute walk to downtown does little to dispel. However, Negotin is full of surprises, its center a sunbaked grid of nineteenth-century Balkan-style houses zeroing in on Trg Maršala Tita, a tranquil square lined with birch trees. Pride of place on the square goes to an equestrian statue of **Hajduk Veljko**, a mysterious figure whose exploits fighting the Turks during the first Serbian uprising are a legend around these parts. Around the side of the Nova Crkva on the square is his so-called *barutana* or powder store, a poky cellar which used to stand in the corner of a long-demolished defensive tower; out towards the main road to Vidin and Bulgaria a red marble memorial marks the spot where he died defending Negotin in 1813.

The regional **Muzej Krajine**, down Vojvode Mišića (Tues–Sat 9am–6pm, Sun 9am–1pm), has, along with Roman finds from the surrounding area, a display of weapons from Veljko's time, together with a reconstructed peasant house and a few Vlach costumes. Close by, the low, elongated form of the **Stara Crkva** was built in 1803 after the Turkish authorities gave permission for its construction on the condition that it be built slightly below ground level and with no outward beauty. Two tablets in the wall mark the last resting place of the ubiquitous Veljko, exhumed and reburied here by his brother in 1844. The graveyard is full of exquisite peasant headstones from the eighteenth and nineteenth centuries, a local craft quite unlike anything else in Yugoslavia. These are made from soft stone carved into arabesques or sun motifs and surmounted with clusters of tiny crosses—largely abstract designs but often featuring line drawings of the deceased. The bright colors they were painted in originally have faded, but you can still make out traces of deep blue, the traditional color of oblivion and forgetting. These stones were moved here from the surrounding villages, but you can still see some examples in situ in a hillside cemetery above the village of Plavna, 20km west of Negotin.

Back towards the main square is the birthplace of **Stefan Mokranjac**, a nineteenth-century composer renowned for his liturgical music based on Serbian Orthodox hymns. Kitchen, living room, bedroom, and personal effects are preserved in the two-story house, along with a display charting Mokranjac's career—something celebrated locally once a year in September, with a series of concerts.

Practical Details . . . and Negotin's Fair

Negotin's only **hotel**, the B-category *Krajina*, Trg Moše Pijade (☎019/52-852), is reasonably priced, with doubles for $20. For **food** there's not much choice: Borisa Kidriča has two lively eateries—*Pizzeria Julia* at no. 11, and the *Tandem* fish restaurant at no. 14. Otherwise nightlife revolves around the restaurant in the *Krajina* hotel, a depressing place full of TV screens. The best time to be in Negotin is the end of September, when the town is taken over by one of Serbia's oldest and best-known **fairs**. Officially scheduled to last three days, it invariably goes on for two weeks, with entire families from the surrounding villages taking up residence here. The folkloric element is dying out, though, and what would have been traditional costume a few years back is gradually being replaced by the Benetton-clad kind of cruising you find everywhere in Yugoslavia.

Around Negotin

The area **around Negotin** is noted for its wine-producing villages, many of which still have ancient *pivnice* or wine cellars, hollowed out of the earth and lined with stone to keep them cool. RAJAC and ROGLJEVO, 10km south of Negotin near the Bulgarian border, are the best-known villages. Another possible trip out is to the valley of the Vratna River, 20km northwest, a narrow chasm in which the rushing torrent of the river has carved three natural "gates" out of the rock. They are spread over three kilometers, upstream from the Vratna monastery, where the road ends.

Zaječar

Plentiful buses run down from Negotin to the main town of the region, **ZAJEČAR**, zigzagging across a plateau overlooking the Timok River. Although still fairly remote, Zaječar is a larger, more cosmopolitan place than Negotin, nowhere near as pretty, and the visitors that do come here are usually most interested in the ruins of the Roman citadel of Gamzigrad, 13km west of the town. Most Yugoslavs know Zaječar for its crystal glass, a product that's hightly thought of locally but which more often than not ends up as a free giveaway in northern European gas stations.

The Town

Arriving at Zaječar bus station, walk through the market behind into Moše Pijade and the main town square, to the right of which is Maršala Tita, the town's commercial center. It's a modern, rather characterless scene, and there are few remnants of the town's Turkish period except for **Radul Beg's Konak** on Ljube Nesića, built by a local Turkish official for his son with money filched from the local population. Inside is a collection of furniture, housed in a series of reconstructed nineteenth-century parlors that reflects something of the tastes of the provincial bourgeoisie.

Back on the main square the town **museum** (Mon 6:30am–2:30pm, Tues–Fri 6:30am–7pm, Sat 6:30am–2:30pm) has finds from Gamzigrad, including a well-preserved mosaic of Dionysus with a leopard, and a model of how the fortress originally looked during the Byzantine period. There are also Vlach costumes and a display of *trvelj*, a local headdress which consisted of a series of woollen strips tied into the hair and left for long periods. It was banned at the turn of the century because it was unhygienic.

Practical Details

If you're wanting **to stay**, the *Hotel Srbija* on Moše Pijade has doubles for about $20. Daytime **eating and drinking** spots, however, are hard to find, and it's best to search out the privately owned bars and restaurants that have sprung up here in recent years. Best is the strangely named *Big Ben Cafe*, Ljube Nesića 111, a riotous and friendly place packed every evening with the local beau monde. Also good, with excellent home cooking, is *Luna*, at Cara Dušana 40.

A rather lackluster **pop festival**, the *Gitarijada*, takes place annually in Zaječar's soccer stadium on the last weekend of August. Attracting a mixed crop of domestic bands, it apparently drew an audience of 40,000 in 1989, a large proportion of which stayed in a makeshift campground on the fringes of town. There's also the *zaječarski vašar* or **fair**, held at the beginning of September; largely overshadowed by the Negotin fair, this is a kitsch event, dominated by cotton candy and amusements.

Gamzigrad

There are about seven daily buses from Zaječar to **GAMZIGRAD**, though they're arranged to suit local people rather than tourists: three run early morning, three early evening, and only one in the middle of the day – check in the town for exact times. The Roman **citadel** (daily 10am–4pm) is just short of the village; the bus driver will deposit you by the roadside 1km away from the site, from where you take a farm track across fields to the remains themselves.

The difficulties of getting to the site in mind, it's not surprising that there's not much here, and certainly no facilities for tourists. The outer shell of the ruin dates from the sixth century, a Byzantine rebuilding after an Avar sacking, but most of what's left beyond here is part of the once-opulent third-century palace of the emperor Galerius, spread over several acres of rubble-strewn meadow. Galerius named the palace *Romuliana* apparently in remembrance of his mother. Its most impressive feature now is a collection of **mosaics**, striking geometric designs largely covered in sand now to protect them from the elements. Largest is the ten-meter-long mosaic in the so-called Great Hall, immediately opposite the entrance, which features a labyrinthine floor-plan of the palace itself. Most of the figurative mosaics, however, have either been carted off to Zaječar or Belgrade. There's much that hasn't been unearthed (perhaps three-quarters of the palace still lies below the surface), but the site has been so plundered over the years, both by raiders and local peasants looking for building materials, that it seems unlikely that there would be much of value.

South to Niš

Beyond Zaječar routes head west over the Rtanj mountains to join the main Belgrade–Niš *autoput*, passing the village of **BOLJEVAC**, which contains a small but informative museum. This is housed in the former jailhouse on Dragiše Petrovića and devoted to the history of the **Timočka Buna** or Timok uprising—the biggest rebellion in the history of the Serbian state. The uprising was sparked off by a central government decision in 1883 to collect all privately held weapons in the outlying regions only recently ceded from Turkey. The independently-minded peasants of the Timok region were outraged, and King Milan Obrenović was forced to send in the army to enforce his rule, precipitating a bloodbath. Eight hundred of the insurgents were marched in chains to Zaječar, and after a series of kangaroo courts a number were sentenced to death and shot on Kraljevica hill, just outside the town (where a memorial still stands).

There's another museum to the uprising in **KNJAŽEVAC**, 20km south of Zaječar, but most people (at least Yugoslavs) make for **SOKOBANJA**, on the far side of the Rtanj mountains, one of Yugoslavia's premier spa resorts, and with an air of retired gentility more reminiscent of Vichy or Bath than the wild remote countryside you've just traveled through. If it's the end of the day and you're tired, there are hotels aplenty in the town, and some of Serbia's very few private rooms. But you'd really do better to head straight through.

Niš and Southeastern Serbia

The largest town of southern Serbia, **NIŠ** grew up as a Roman settlement, and was an important staging post on the route between Belgrade and Constantinople. It claims to have been the birthplace of the emperor Constantine, and is still a crucial center, home to a large university and much heavy industry. But it's probably the last town in Yugoslavia that anyone would want to visit. The grubby buildings of its center play variations on the colors of its river, the Nišava, and the surrounding industry has left a thick layer of dirt and depression over the town. However, as Niš is the main junction of the E5 *autoput*, you may arrive with time to spare between connections.

The Town

What life there is in Niš mills around **Trg Oslobodjenja**, a grim square of seedy 1960s development with a ghetto of hotels at one end and the uninteresting remnants of a large Turkish fortress at the other—the **Tvrdjava**, built between 1690 and 1722. Inside this there are public gardens, a mosque, and an arsenal coverted to a gallery of modern art. The town center's other main sight is the **Archaeological Museum** on Kongresa KPJ (Tues–Sat 9am–4pm, Sun 9am–1pm), which has local finds, best of which are those from Byzantine times.

Niš's real attractions are outside the center of town, though most are as morbid as the town itself. The **Crveni Krst Concentration Camp** on Bulevar 12 Februar, on the same road as the bus station but walking away from town (Mon–Sat 9am–4pm, Sun 10am–2pm), is the most powerful and interesting sight; originally built as an army depot, it's a somber gray memorial to the bravery of its inmates—partisans, Communists, gypsies and Jews rounded up prior to their torture and execution or deportation to the death camps of the north. On February 12, 1942 a suicidal escape attempt left fifty prisoners machine-gunned on the walls—the bullet holes are still visible—but also saw a hundred managing to scale the barriers in one of the biggest breakouts of the war. Today there's little in the buildings save old photographs of prisoners, their smiling jaunty expressions horribly at odds with the pall of misery that still hangs over the place.

Altogether 30,000 people passed through Crveni Krst, and many met their deaths at **Bubanj**, a hill to the southwest of town. It was here that the Nazis committed one of their worst atrocities in the final stages of the war. As the tide turned in favor of the partisans mass executions were carried out to cover traces of the occupiers' crimes, with upwards of 1000 people, mostly local peasants, being shot each day. No one knows the exact total, but it's reckoned that at least 12,000 bodies lie below the crest of the wooded hill. An inelegant concrete **memorial** commemorates the dead, "fists of defiance" rising brutally from the earth. It's clumsily done but the symbolism is moving, as is the inscription on the wall nearby:

From the blood of Communists and Patriots they grow.

Fists of Revolution,
Fists of Rebellion,
Fists of Freedom.

They executed us
But they never killed us,
Never subjugated us.

We trod on darkness
And made way to the sun.

Niš's other gloomy relic is on Brace Taskovića, a #24 bus ride from the center—the **Ćele Kula** or tower of skulls (Mon–Sat 9am–4pm, Sun 10am–2pm). It's the result of a typically Serbian gesture: surrounded by the Turkish army on Ćegar hill in 1809, one Sindelić and his men chose death before dishonor and ignited their gunpowder supplies, blowing to pieces most of the Turks—and all of the Serbians. To let the locals know who was boss, the Turkish pasha later ordered around 1000 Serbian heads to be stuffed and mounted on the tower. After much souvenir-hunting in the nineteenth century, only about sixty skulls remain to return the tourist's stare, and though at the time they must have been a grisly statement of Turkish sovereignty, today the whole thing looks curiously like a fruitcake.

Just beyond the Čele Kula are the excavations of the Roman town of **Mediana**, an imperial settlement of several villas that was occupied until the sixth century AD. There's a museum which contains a fine floor mosaic but otherwise the remains are definitely scanty.

Practical Details

It's best not to get stuck in Niš overnight—there's no private accommodation and the **hotels** are wildly overpriced. The B-category *Centroturist* (☎018/22-477) is about the cheapest, with double rooms for as little as $20 (though often much more). Failing that, the **tourist offices**—*Srbijaturist*, Vozdova 12, and *Putnik*, Vozdova 2—will point you to rooms in the spa resort of NIŠKA BANJA, 10km away to the east, where a room at the cheaper *Institut za Srčana Oboljenja* (☎018/860-004) will set you back around $28. If you're **camping**, *Motel-Camping Nais*, about 5km out of town on the Belgrade road, is the closest grounds, very well-equipped and reasonably priced.

Southeastern Serbia

There are three main routes out of Niš by road, one heading east to Bulgaria, the other two south to Kosovo and Macedonia.

East to Bulgaria

Heading east from Niš down the E80 leads to the **Bulgarian border** through the wilds of southeastern Serbia, though they don't have much to offer. **PIROT**, the first town of any size, has had a tradition of carpet-making since Turkish times—bargain hard in the market and shops and you might pick up a bargain. East of Pirot the road falls into the Nišava canyon before reaching the border town of **DIMITROVGRAD**, the best place to find out about occasional buses and less regular trains into Bulgaria and, some 30km or so hence, to Sofia. In Dimitrovgrad you're also close to the monastery of **Poganovo**, about 10km south, very close to the border. Built in the fifteenth century, this is hard to get to, but the journey itself, following an unpaved track from the village of Vlasi, 5km off the main road into Bulgaria, is worth it. The church has well-kept frescoes dating from the 1490s and is fronted by an odd Balkan-style gallery giving access to its bell tower.

South to Kosovo and Macedonia

There's a choice of two roads south from Niš. One, the E80, leads down into Kosovo, passing through the small towns of **PROKUPLJE**, dominated by its Byzantine castle on the hill above, and **KURŠUMLIJA**, where there are two twelfth-century churches built by Stefan Nemanja.

The other route heads more directly south down to Skopje and Macedonia, first crossing a dull plain to **LESKOVAC**, a textile town that describes itself as "the Manchester of Serbia." Conceivably, you might want to come this way to see the remains of the sixth-century Byzantine town of **Caričin Grad**, 20km away close to the village of LEBANE, though you'll need your own transportation to make it this far. The rewards are fairly slight, but the site is a large one (and is still being excavated), and it holds some extensive basilicas as well as a number of patchily preserved mosaics showing early Christian iconography—the Good Shepherd and the like—and more ancient mythological scenes like the battle of amazons and centaurs.

From Leskovac the road slowly rises from the plain to follow the river Morava, the steep sides of its wooded valley intensely green. Where the valley broadens, small settlements scatter their paprika roofs below the mountain crests, the road and rail routes tracing the course of the river. Below Vladičin Han the valley widens out, its sides flanked by ragged strips of cultivation—wheat, barley, and grass merging into each other like a badly tended truck farm. Most of what there is in **VRANJE** – a broad area of houses on the riverside, populated by oxen, ox cart,s and their drivers – can be seen as the bus descends from the *autoput*. There's a small Turkish quarter, with a large house that once accommodated the pasha's harem, a note of the increasing Turkishness found as you continue toward Macedonia. **KUMANOVO**, in Macedonia, was the site of a Serbian victory over the Turks in the First Balkan War. It has several mosques and a large Muslim population, though little seriously to detain you apart from the Matejce monastery (see p.389). Mountains beyond form the backdrop to an arid, bitty landscape, their heights topped with snow for much of the year—a grand and fitting prelude to Skopje.

travel details

Buses

From Belgrade to Novi Sad (hourly; 1hr 30min); Subotica (hourly; 3hr); Vršac (hourly; 1hr 30min); Zrenjanin (hourly; 1hr 15min); Sombor (10 daily; 2hr 30min); Zaječar (6 daily; 3hr 30min); Šabac (hourly; 1hr 15min); Loznica (10 daily; 2hr 15min); Zagreb (hourly; 7hr); Ljubljana (4 daily; 10hr); Rijeka (2 daily; 11hr); Split (2 daily 13hr); Dubrovnik (3 daily; 14hr); Sarajevo (5 daily; 8hr); Skopje (4 daily; 9hr); Kragujevac (hourly; 2hr 30min); Kruševac (6 daily; 3hr); Kraljevo (hourly; 3hr); Niš (8 daily; 4hr 30min); Titovo Užice (6 daily; 4hr); Novi Pazar (12 daily; 6hr); Priština (2 daily; 8hr).

From Kruševac to Kragujevac (2 daily; 2hr 15min); Titovo Užice (4 daily; 4hr); Niš (10 daily; 3hr).

From Novi Pazar to Priština (4 daily; 4hr); Skopje (2 daily; 6hr).

From Novi Sad to Subotica (6 daily; 1hr 30min); Zagreb (4 daily; 7hr 30min).

Trains

From Belgrade to Novi Sad (5 daily; 1hr 15min); Subotica (4 daily; 3hr); Niš (7 daily; 4hr 30min); Titograd/Bar (6 daily; 8hr 45min/9hr 30min); Zagreb (7 daily; 6hr); Ljubljana (4 daily; 7hr); Kosovo Polje (4 daily; 7hr 10min); Sarajevo (6 daily; 7hr); Zaječar (2 daily; 7hr 30min); Skopje (7 daily; 7hr); Titovo Užice (3 daily; 2hr 30min); Split (2 daily; 12hr); Negotin (1 daily; 9hr 30min).

International Trains

From Belgrade to Budapest (3 daily; 6hr 30min); Bucharest (1 daily; 14hr); Sofia (1 daily; 10hr); Istanbul (1 daily; 25hr); Athens (3 daily; 24hr); Prague (2 daily; 19hr); Moscow (1 daily; 42hr); Paris (1 daily; 28hr).

CHAPTER SEVEN

THE VOJVODINA

T he land that stretches north of Belgrade across the Pannonian Plain to the Hungarian border is known as **The Vojvodina**—like Kosovo an autonomous province within the Serbian Republic. The name means "the duchy," as for years the region was part of the Austrian Empire. Keen to create a defensive front here after the retreat of the Turks in the seventeenth century, the marshland was drained and settlers encouraged; among the first to arrive were 40,000 Serb families, fleeing the south in fear of Turkish resurgence. They were allowed freedom of Orthodox worship, establishing a new patriarchate in the town of Sremski Karlovici, and soon migrants from all over central Europe came to farm the rich land.

The last great migration to the Vojvodina took place after 1945, when over half a million ethnic Germans (known as *Volksdeutscher*) were ejected from their homes for alleged mass collaboration with the Nazis. Their rich farmlands lands were shared out among landless peasants and poor smallholders from Yugoslavia's more barren regions, priority being given to communities that had excelled themselves in the partisan struggle. Although the majority of newcomers were Montenegrins and Serbs, families were deliberately drawn from all over Yugoslavia in an attempt to strengthen yet farther the multinational, genuinely Yugoslav nature of the Vojvodina.

Today, more than anywhere else in the country, the Vojvodina contains a disparate mix of peoples: in addition to the sizable Hungarian minority there are Romanians, Ruthenians (Ukrainian Russians), Slovaks, Croats, Gypsies, even Greeks. Everyone speaks Serbo-Croat, but in a laudable attempt to preserve cultural diversity children can go to schools where lessons are taught in their own ethnic language. Providing elementary and secondary education in Hungarian, Slovakian, Ruthenian and Romanian costs a great deal of money but, as the Yugoslavs point out, a fortune can't buy tradition, though it may just save it.

It was Vojvodina's unique position as a patchwork of nationalities that assured it autonomous status within the republic of Serbia after the war. But this was always a potential bone of contention, with Serbs complaining that the autonomy enjoyed by the Vojvodina (and Kosovo) went too far, putting Serbia at a disadvantage in relation to other republics. Things came to a head in 1988 when a reinvigorated Serbian leadership under Slobodan Milošević, struggling to regain control over wayward Kosovo, attempted to reintegrate both autonomous provinces back into Serbia. When the Vojvodina leadership tried to put up a fight, Milošević exploited popular discontent to get rid of them. Accusations that Vojvodina's leaders were no more than corrupt bureaucrats trying to hang on to their power and privileges struck an immedi-

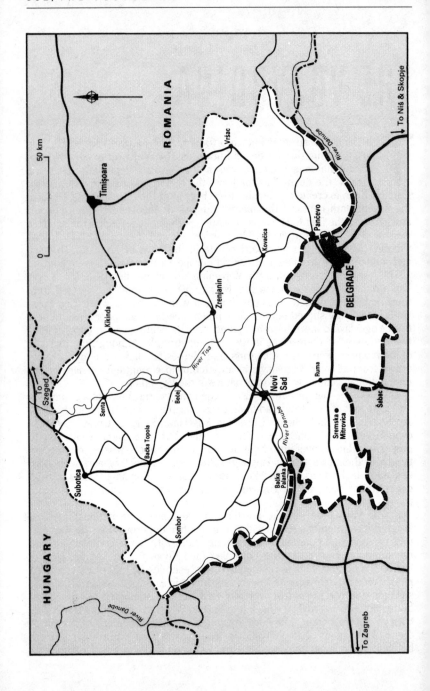

ate chord among a population suffering a variety of economic and social ills. In October 1988, big stage-managed demonstrations in Novi Sad swept the Vojvodina fat cats from office, replacing them with a new, more pliant leadership. Currently, with Serbia resurgent, relations between the Vojvodina's ethnicities are a little less easy than in previous years, but the atmosphere of multicultural tolerance still holds.

The Vojvodina's jumble of people lives in one of the most uniform areas of the country. Mile after mile the flat, fertile plains roll north, endless expanses of wheat, corn, sunflower, and soybeans flashing by with hypnotic regularity—the rich land of the Vojvodina has the capacity to provide enough crops to feed the whole country. Oddly, the vastness and similarity of the landscape never grind down to monotony: pastel-painted towns and villages dash color on the horizon, and in the middle of it all an island of low hills, the **Fruška Gora**, provides the single interruption to the level skyline. It's this area and the nearby town of **Novi Sad** that are the highlights of the Vojvodina; the other private little towns, though pretty enough, aren't really of much interest.

> The Novi Sad area telephone code is ☎021

Novi Sad

Grand capital of the Vojvodina, **NOVI SAD** is the best base for excursions into the Fruška Gora, and worth a day or so in itself—a small but likable old center and the massive fortress of Petrovaradin being the main treats.

Practicalities

Arrive at the bus or train station and you're some way out of downtown. A #8 bus from the train station forecourt takes you in, and a few minutes' walk away, the **tourist office**, Dunavska 27 (Mon–Sat 8am–7:30pm), will furnish you with a map or leaflets and direct you to *Putnik* at Narodinh Heroja 8 for private **rooms**. These are mostly on the outskirts of town and evaporate quickly at weekends, especially in summer, but there's a reasonably priced **campground** on the *Ribarska Ostrvo* ("Fisherman's Island"). **Hotels** are a pricey alternative: most central are *Vojvodina* at Trg Slobode 2 (☎622-122) or *Putnik* at Ilije Ognjenovića 26 (☎61-555), both of which cost around $70 for a double. The *Tvrdjava Varadin* hotel inside the Petrovaradin Fortress (☎431-122) offers a taste of *Mitteleuropa* highlife for $70–$90.

Eating and Drinking

By the end of 1990 there'll be a *McDonalds* on Trg Slobode; if your conscience won't let you eat there, the best sources of cheap food are the self-service restaurant at *Hotel Vojvodina*, or at *Café Zagreb* in Katoločka Porta, a quiet courtyard behind the Catholic cathedral.

If you want to dine in style, there's a handful of excellent **restaurants** serving delicious local food, usually to the accompaniment of live folk music. Two highly regarded places in the old town district offering Serbian dishes are *Fontana* on Svetozara Markovića, a pleasant garden restaurant with a front-room café that resembles a Victorian gin palace; and *Lipa*, on the corner of Miletića and Markovića, a warren of rooms which again features a garden at the rear. Try *Piroš Čizma*, Lasla Gala 34, for Hungarian food, or *Marina*, Trg Lenjina 4, for Slovak fare. *Sečuan*, the Chinese restaurant at Dunavska 16, is reasonably priced and excellent quality.

On the other side of the river in Petrovaradin you pay for the view at the *Terrace Restaurant*, in the fortress itself, but there's an above average pizzeria, *Sremac* at Matije Gubca 19, in the main street below.

For **nightlife**, the cluster of cafés at the bottom of Dunavska is the place to head for in summer. There are plenty of privately owned bars elsewhere in the center, far and away the most popular being *Atrium*, on Svetozara Markovića immediately opposite the Orthodox Cathedral. The arched roof and wooden benches of its smoke-filled cellar attract the more stylish of the city's youth.

The Town

Novi Sad developed in tandem with the huge **Petrovaradin Fortress** on the Danube's south bank. There had been fortifications here ever since the Romans built an encampment on the hill to keep the Avars at bay, but the fortress took its present shape in the eighteenth century when the Austrians turned it into a barrier against Turkish expansionism. Shaken by the siege of Vienna in 1683, they took advantage of a lull in fighting to build an invincible last defense on the Danube to keep the Turks out of central Europe. Designed by the French military architect Sebastian Vauban, it was a truly vast enterprise, and took a hundred years to build. It has four independent subterranean levels with a total of sixteen kilometers of tunnels; if the garrison was attacked 30,000 men could shelter underground and cover every inch of the surrounding land by firing through 18,000 loopholes—of which officers were normally acquainted with just a small section, the overall plan of the fortress being a closely guarded secret. The convicts forced to build it called it the "Castle of Death"—as many as seventy a day died of overwork and disease.

The irony is that Petrovaradin became unnecessary even as it was being built. After a final bash in 1717 the Turks withdrew south to consolidate their hold on Serbia, the threat subsided, and Belgrade took over Petrovaradin's strategic importance. No assault was ever made on the impregnable fortress, and the only time shots were fired was in 1848 when the Hungarian garrison revolted and bombarded the city for several months. When they were eventually tricked into surrender, two-thirds of the town had been flattened, which accounts for the lack of earlier building today. The fortress eventually became a jail, its most celebrated occupant being the youthful Tito, briefly imprisoned when, as a young NCO in the Austrian army, he was charged with propagating socialist ideas. The trip through the maze of passages is fascinating and shouldn't be missed—**tours** (Tues–Sun 9am–4pm) aren't regular so you may have to wait and tag along with a group.

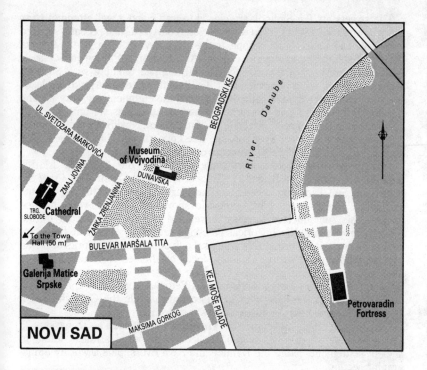

Above ground the best thing is the view, Novi Sad's onion-bulbed skyline corralled by the modern town and the broad, silent Danube, making its way south in the foreground. Enjoying the protection of the fortress, Novi Sad flourished in the late eighteenth and early nineteenth centuries. Serbs and others traveled north to escape the Turks and the civilized capital somehow earned itself the title of "Serbian Athens," the relative benevolence of Hapsburg rule enabling Serbs to establish a whole plethora of cultural and literary organizations. The 1848 bombardment only temporarily upset things, and today there's no better example of a flourishing bourgeois provincial town; its broad streets are sided by nineteenth-century houses, small parks, and tidy squares, and an air of pleased prosperity abounds.

Hub of the city is **Trg Slobode**, a spacious square with an ostentatious town hall on one side and the brick-clad **Catholic Cathedral**—an unadventurous piece of pseudo-Gothicism—slipped in on the other. Facing the cathedral, Ivan Meštrović's **statue** of nineteenth-century nationalist leader Svetozar Miletić raises an angry fist to the local pigeons. Miletić managed to upset everybody in the course of a long and turbulent political career. His Serbian freethinking Peoples' Party vigorously opposed Magyar dominance in the Vojvodina, royal dictatorship in the fledgling Serbian State to the south, and priests everywhere—Catholic and Orthodox alike.

The streets off Trg Slobode are closed to traffic and a well-attended *korso* flows down **Zmaj Jovina**, lined with spacious courtyards and recently spruced up private cafés and clothes shops, to the oldest part of town. At the head of the street stands the nineteenth-century **Archbishop's Palace** (now part of Novi Sad's university), a curiously fanciful red-tiled building with Moorish arched windows and a pinnacled roof. To the left, Svetozara Markovića leads past the Serbian Orthodox cathedral towards the eighteenth-century trading quarter of the city, a grid of crumbling narrow streets as yet untouched by renovation. In the opposite direction lies **Dunavska**, Novi Sad's most popular hangout, where summer evenings see free concerts and film shows, and, if you can squeeze in, lively performances of local folk dance.

One of Novi Sad's two worthwhile museums, the **Gallerija Matice Srpska**, Trg Proleterski Brigada 1 (Tues & Thurs 8am–7pm, Wed, Fri & Sat 8am–3pm, Sun 9am–1pm), celebrates an early upsurge of the arts in the Vojvodina. There's much work by Paja Jovanović, 98 years old when he died in 1957, his romanticized idealism developed in youth unaffected by the modern movement. His historical paintings are pretty dire, but there are some fine portraits of proud Edwardians. Look out too for the works of Stefan Aleksić, whose *autoportraits* chillingly focus on themes of drink and death. Two lesser collections are to be found on the same square as the Matice Srpska: the **Galerija Pavla Beljanskog** (Wed–Sun 9am–5pm) concentrates on Serbian art of the early part of this century, while the **Galerija Rajka Mamuzića** (same hours) houses a postwar collection.

The town's other museum, the **Vojvodjanski Musej** at Dunavska 35 (Tues–Sun 8am–3pm), has a good collection of burial artifacts found in ancient settlements along the Danube and Sava rivers, plus a worthy ethnographic section.

Finally, if you're here in summer, there's an area popular for **swimming and sunbathing** along the banks of the Danube about a mile south of the city center, where Bulevar 23 Oktobra (the long strip heading down from the station) crosses the new road bridge over to Sremska Kamenica. You pay to enter, but once inside there's a good sandy **beach** and extensive lawns, all served by a range of cheap cafés, restaurants, and snack kiosks. The river is tested each day, and signs are posted advising on how clean it is.

The Fruška Gora

Just about anywhere in Novi Sad you can look south to the low rolling hills of the **Fruška Gora**—pretty tame compared to the mountains elsewhere in Yugoslavia though no less likable. Densely wooded, the hills have upland plains of wheat and vines, and on summer evenings a heavy, heady air hangs over the land, its dusty crimson sunsets somehow out of place this far north.

This is ideal **walking country**—which is just as well, as there's no other way of getting around without your own transportation. You can only get a bus from Novi Sad (direction Šabac or Sremska Mitrovica) as far as IRIŠKI VENAC, site of an impressive monument to the partisans who fought from these hills. The monasteries south of here form handy stepping stones for wanderings; there are over twenty dotted around, built when the Turks clamped down on Orthodox worship after taking the nearby patriarchate of Sremski Karlovici. The best three are close enough for a long day's walking: Hopovo, Krusedol and Vrdnik.

HOPOVO, off the main road before the village of IRIG, is the most Byzantine in style, frescoed with the seventeenth-century works of an unknown monk-artist from Mt Athos, and decorated outside with a graceful twelve-sided dome supported by columns. A buzzing and verdant farmyard backwater 8km away, **KRUŠEDOL** monastery's church dates from the sixteenth century, though most of its frescoes are from the mid-eighteenth, as the Turks burned the original building. The interior's a little too rich, like an over-tattooed body; the best frescoes are the oldest, sixteenth-century survivors in the style of the Russian school. The war years saw Krušedol used by the Ustaše as a prison in which partisans and their supporters were tortured and murdered. Bodies were burned around the monastery, and afterwards a tiny paper note was found hidden in the hair of one of the victims, a woman:

> *Jelica, my love my strength, forgive Mother, I am separated from you, Mother gives you three thousand kisses on your little chin, God go with you, my child, dear living sweet heart, Mother is waiting for them to shoot her.*

Krušedol has its ghosts.

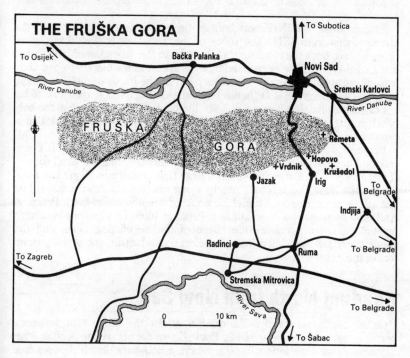

THE ZOGRAFI: THE LOST PAINTERS OF THE BYZANTINE ERA

The churches and monasteries of Vojvodina are rich in the work of the *Zografi*, itinerant artists and craftspeople who established an artistic tradition quite different from that of the rest of Serbia. Arriving in the great migrations of the late seventeenth century, the earliest *Zografi* were steeped in the Byzantine traditions of Serbian religious art, but contact with the wide world of Hapsburg Europe transformed their work. The end result was an intriguing mixture of late Byzantine and early Baroque that is rarely found anywhere else except in this fascinating backwater bypassed by the rest of European art. They were also the last in the medieval artisan tradition, handing down skills within the family and traveling across the region to complete small-scale commissions for a church that was struggling to establish itself in a new environment. As the Orthodox church got richer towards the nineteenth century and increasingly turned towards academically trained painters, the *Zografi* died out, and with them, the last remnants of Byzantine art.

Principal centers for the *Zografi* were the Banat towns of Veliki Bečkerek (now Zrenjanin), Modoš (now Jaša Tomić) and Temešvar (now Timişoara in Romania, but at that time an informal focus of Serb culture), but their works are also scattered throughout Vojvodina. The best places to see them are the Fruška Gora monasteries of **Hopovo** and **Krušedol**, the **Matice Srpska** gallery in Novi Sad, and the monastery of **Bodjani** (70km west of Novi Sad beyond Backa Palanka), which is resplendently decked out with the frescoes of one of the few *Zografi* whose name hasn't been lost, the eighteenth-century master Hristofor Zefarović.

Farther west, **VRDNIK** was built in the sixteenth century, though the church dates from 1811. The relics of the great leader Tsar Lazar were brought here from the monastery of Ravanica in the migration of 1683, out of fear that they would be desecrated by the Turks. Lazar's black wizened body was moved again during the war to keep it from the hands of the Ustaše, and now lies in Belgrade's Orthodox cathedral. The monks' quarters today contain a hospital, but you can still see the church. Vrdnik also has the only hotel in the area, the *Banja Termal* (☎022/465-429), with doubles at a reasonable $44.

Between the Fruška Gora and Novi Sad, **SREMSKI KARLOVICI** is a refined little town with a cluster of Baroque buildings around a small square. If there's time, the **Cathedral** sports a large rich iconostasis, all gilt and floral scrolls, the **New Patriarchate** nearby vying with it for sumptuousness. Just out of town, a **Peace Chapel** commemorates the short-lived Peace of Karlowitz between the Austrians and Turks in 1699. This curious building's bell-topped rotunda echoes the shape of the negotiating table, and the windows are cut like Union Jacks, in deference to Britain, one of the guarantors of the treaty's terms.

Heading North from Novi Sad

Heading north across the **Pannonian Plain** the Hungarian influence becomes more and more apparent. Horse-drawn fiacres are the popular form of transport, and the little villages preserve a Hapsburg dictate: houses face the main street end-on with a single "gossiping window," the idea being that doorways on the streets were hot-spots of seditious chatter, and therefore banned. It's also in this region that you'll find what's left of Yugoslavia's **Communal Farms**, part of a project which ran briefly thoughout the country in the 1940s and 1950s. They were created immediately after the war, when land was taken away from the big property owners and shared out among the peasants and small farmers, who were then urged (if not forced) into collectives. This didn't work; early bad harvests and opposition from the peasants to working in such large units forced Belgrade to rethink. The traditionally less-developed areas like Macedonia and Bosnia, already struggling with the problems of centralized production in a region riven with natural barriers, were allowed to revert to smaller units where new technology and farming methods could be introduced gradually. Only in the flat arable fields of the Vojvodina, which actually benefited from the use of such methods, did communal farming take any hold.

Half an hour beyond Novi Sad the road forks at Srbobran, presenting two potential routes northwards into Hungary. You could head northwest to the serene market town of Sombor, before crossing the border to MOHACS, or you could take the other route due north to the bigger regional center of Subotica.

Sombor

Although the long rows of grimy apartment blocks in the outskirts may initially lead you to think otherwise, **SOMBOR** is in fact one of the few towns in the Vojvodina which hasn't been blighted too seriously by postwar architecture. Downtown at least, an almost archaic atmosphere of central European gentility has been left virtually untouched. It's a town of wide, tree-lined boulevards and well-tended parks, with carefully pruned hedges and shrubs crammed into every available space. The town center (from the bus station a ten-minute stroll down Staparski Put) is ranged around three parallel squares, Trg Oslobodjenja, Trg Republike, and Trg 7 Jula. The last-named is the most picturesque, dominated by the old **Town Hall**—a quaint, bright yellow Neoclassical oddity which is now home to the *Gradska Kafana*. Opposite the town hall you will find the **Galerija Milan Konjović** (Tues & Thurs 7am–noon & 5–7pm, Weds & Fri 7am–2pm, Sat 7am–1pm, Sun 9pm–noon), devoted to the Sombor-born artist who was something of a rarity in twentieth-century Yugoslav painting. Rather than merely copying the currently favored western European styles he molded them into a colorful, expressionistic style that was entirely his own. The wild brushstrokes and bright hues of Konjović's Vojvodina landscapes portray the plain as something turbulent and brutal, never dull. Sombor's attempts to associate itself with the art world extend to the **Town Museum** at Trg Republike 4 (Tues–Thurs 8am–5pm, Fri 8am–noon, Sat & Sun 10am–1pm), where modest touring exhibitions in the upstairs gallery do something to enliven the dull agitprop display of war and revolution below. Another gallery, **Likovna Jesen** at Laze Kostića 5, between Trg Republike and Trg 7 Jula, displays work invited to the annual autumn art festival of the same name.

Sombor is full of the yellow ocher facades common to all the former Hapsburg territories; one building that stands out is the **Županija** or former county hall, on the corner of Staparski Put and Venac Stepe Stepanovića. Built to serve as the Austrians' seat of local government in the last century, it's a typical example of the kind of imperial architecture found in the eastern half of their empire, the concave roofs and eccentric Gothic ornamentation belonging to what was subsequently termed the Transylvanian style.

The town is quickly exhausted—you don't need more than a couple of hours to see everything—but the **tourist office** at Trg Republike 2 has private **rooms** should you need to stay. Failing that, the *Hotel Sloboda* (025/ 24-666) across the road has overpriced but comfortable double rooms for $60.

The countryside around Sombor is given over to herds of grazing horses and lonely, isolated farmsteads known as *salašsi*, usually long, single-story whitewashed buildings with thatched roofs grouped around a *djeram*—a traditional well where water has for centuries been raised by using the leverage of a long wooden pole. West of Sombor the plain fades into extensive marshlands along the banks of the Danube, a paradise for wildlife and local hunters alike.

Subotica

SUBOTICA, 37km from Hungary, is a large town with little to recommend it. Throughout its history it has been shifted from one side of the border to the other, with the result that the majority here speaks Hungarian as their first language. The Hapsburg influence is here too, in the famous and frivolous **town hall** of 1903, a lumpish and graceless building, its rhythmless curves and awkward angles splashed with once-gaudy colors, the interior a sea of toilet-green tiles and floral decoration. If you like such things it's possible to explore, visiting an above-average **Ethnographic Museum** as you go (Sat & Sun 9am–1pm, Tues, Wed & Fri 9am–3pm, Thur 10am–6pm). Best by default of Subotica's other buildings is the **Palata Likovnog Susreta** opposite the train station. Though small, it manages to combine elephantine clumsiness with the ostentatious decoration of its larger neighbor; the kindest thing to be said of it is that it's not bland.

Subotica isn't a place to spend more than a couple hours, and if you're heading north to Hungary it's not worth breaking the journey. If you do wind up here the **tourist office** at Nusičeva 2 (☎024/274-342; turn left off Kidričeva by the *Putnik* office) boasts some of the country's cheapest **rooms**, but they're often full—phone ahead to inquire. Cheap **food** is supplied by a couple of express restaurants in the streets around the town hall in Trg Slobode; both do a good cheap Hungarian goulash. There's a **campground** 8km farther north, in the small resort of PALIĆ, whose lake provides swimming and the rent of all sorts of watercraft; frequent buses run from Subotica.

Eastern Vojvodina: North from Belgrade

The area of the Vojvodina between the Tisa River and the Romanian border is known as the **Banat**, named after the ban or governor chosen from among the indigenous Serb population by the ruling Hapsburgs, who allowed the area a certain degree of autonomy in the last century. The best way to explore it is to follow the main road east from Belgrade towards the frontier town of Vršac, a 75-minute bus ride through the familiar endless maize fields and sleepy villages colonized by huge flocks of geese. **PANČEVO**, just across the river from Belgrade, is a rather drab and uninspiring town whose character has been destroyed by postwar development. The **National Museum**, on Trg Borisa Kidriča 7, has a few interesting relics from the prehistoric site at Starčevo, 16km from Pančevo on the banks of the Danube. Thirty kilometers north of Pančevo, accessible by local bus, is the Slovak village of **KOVAČICA**, Vojvodina's most important center for naive art. Many of the peasant artists (Jan Sokol and Zuzana Halupova seem to be the best names to drop) welcome visitors into their homes, but the town's **Dom Kulture**, at Maršala Tita 46, has a small gallery. Beyond Kovačica, **UZDIN**, has a similar reputation; here the inhabitants are ethnic Romanians, and traditionally the artists are women.

Traveling east from Pančevo you encounter a series of dusty and unkempt villages whose Dust-Bowl feel is the result of a combination of the dry, windy climate and the sandy soil. Indeed, 20km east of Pančevo lies the **Deliblatska Peščara**, almost 300 square kilometers of sand dunes and barren heath. Local tourist literature describes it as the "European Sahara," and though it's nothing so dramatic, it's a fascinatingly desolate region and a paradise for wildlife—although you need to get away from the main road to appreciate it at its most bleak. Continuing northeastward towards Vršac, the rural population is predominantly Romanian. The Romanian Orthodox churches in the roadside villages of Nikolinci and Ritiševo present the bizarre spectacle of garish green and red brickwork surmounted by bright blue roofs and domes, like the picture on a badly tuned TV set.

Vršac

VRŠAC is 10km from the Romanian border and the main crossing point if you're traveling to Timişoara. In the nineteenth century Vršac was an important center in the Serbs' political and cultural struggle against Hungarian domination, and it is still the seat of the Serbian Orthodox archbishopric for the Banat. Nowadays Vršac has the air of an isolated provincial backwater on the edge of civilization—which perhaps goes some way to explaining why it competes with Maribor in Slovenia for the highest suicide rate in Yugoslavia. Nevertheless, it is this apparent isolation, coupled with the stark Deliblatska Peščara, which gives the Vršac region its distinctive character.

Vršac is an important agricultural center, surrounded by a patchwork of golden maize fields and dark green vineyards. It is one of the most important wine-producing centers in Yugoslavia—mostly white wine of the Riesling variety—although the accent is on quantity rather than quality. The best time to visit is in September, when the whole town is taken over for three days (usually Sept 21–23) by the *Vašar* or fair in honor of the grape harvest. Festivities include peasants dressed in medieval costumes, pageants, gypsy brass bands, the occasional dancing bear, and a good deal of serious drinking.

The town center is compact and easy to cover in a short time. It's full of intriguing, if modest, eighteenth-century buildings, and the obvious place to start is Trg Save Kovačevićava, the site of the bus station. At no. 15 is the **Zgrada Dva Pištolja** ("House of the Two Pistols"), a mid-eighteenth-century building and formerly an inn which acquired its name when, according to legend, the leader of the first Serbian uprising, Petar Karadjordje, found refuge here and, being rather strapped for cash, paid his bill with two pistols. The front of the building is nondescript—it's best admired from the courtyard in the back. The house at no. 11, **Sterijina Kuča**, was the the birthplace of Jovan Serija Popović, one of the founding fathers of Serbia drama (if anyone's interested). Pride of place, however, goes to the **Archbishop's Palace** on Maršala Tita 20—a rather pompous building dating from 1759, and fronted by an equally incongruous ornamental garden. Almost exactly opposite the palace is the **Orthodox Cathedral**, which houses a spectacular iconostasis with intricate engraving work by eighteenth-century craftsman Aksentije Marković.

The **National Museum** is on the town's dowdy main street, Andje Ranković 19. It's largely devoted to materials relating to Vršac's most famous sons: the aforementioned Sterija Popović and the painter Paja Jovanović, a dry academic realist whose vast canvases depicting the struggles of Serbian history can be seen in Novi Sad, Pančevo, and Belgrade. His monstrous *Vršac Triptych* stands in the museum, a lionization of the local peasantry harvesting the fruits of the land.

Overlooking Vršac on a rocky hill is a solitary tower or *kula*, the only surviving remnant of a medieval fortress that changed hands constantly between Hungarians, Serbs, and Turks. Beyond this is a range of wooded hills, the **Vršac Planina**, which lead up to the Romanian border, crisscrossed with paths and bridleways, and commanding panoramic views of the surrounding countryside.

Should you wish to stay the **tourist office** at Trg Podobed 1 should be able to find you a **room**, or there's the *Hotel Srbija* (☎013/815-545), with doubles for $60.

Zrenjanin

Seventy-five kilometers north and west of Vršac, **ZRENJANIN** is the largest town of the Banat, a drab and charmless place with a largely postwar center, its outskirts dominated by grain stores and food processing plants. The town was once as cosmopolitan as anywhere in the Vojvodina, with immigrants pouring in during the eighteenth century from as far away as Italy, France, and Spain—minorities that have long since been assimilated and disappeared.

Buildings of interest are thin on the ground; the main square, Trg Slobode, and main shopping street, Maršala Tita, are both unhappy mixtures of dilapidated nineteenth-century and faceless modern. Only the **Županija**, (town hall) stands out, the usual mixture of late Baroque and neo-Gothic; the red star and a hammer and sickle perched on top of the clock tower somehow add to its charm. Down from the square, the **town museum** at Subotićeva 1 has an exceedingly gloomy picture gallery, with murky portraits of local church dignitaries and businessmen.

travel details

Buses

From Novi Sad to Belgrade (hourly; 1hr 15min); Subotica (6 daily; 1hr 30min); Vršac (6 daily; 2hr 15min); Zrenjanin (hourly; 30min); Zagreb (4 daily; 7hr 30min).

From Zrenjanin to Belgrade (hourly; 1hr 15min).

Trains

From Novi Sad to Belgrade (5 daily; 1hr 15min); Subotica (4 daily; 1hr 50min).

From Subotica to Belgrade (4 daily; 3hr).

CHAPTER EIGHT

KOSOVO

T echnically part of the republic of Serbia, the Socialist Autonomous Province of **Kosovo** is less explored, more politically unstable, and immeasurably poorer than anywhere else in Yugoslavia. Around eighty percent of its two million citizens are ethnic Albanians, descendants of the Illyrian peoples who spread throughout the east of the Adriatic centuries before the Roman conquest. Despite a history of cultural repression, Albanian has at last become the official language here—though nearly everyone speaks at least some Serbo-Croat; today there's an Albanian newspaper and university and street signs are bilingual. In some towns, like Prizren, where Turkish is spoken, signs are trilingual, while TV stations in Priština broadcast in four languages, including Romany and Macedonian. Although there's a substantial number of Catholic Albanians, most are Muslim; many of the older men still wear the beige felt skullcap, or *plis*, which is the symbol of Albanian manhood, while most of the women wear their heads covered. In the countryside, particularly around Prizren, traditional costumes are still fairly common.

Few people know this portion of Yugoslavia. Its landscape varies from the flat dullness of its central plain to the snow-capped heights of the mountains that skirt its borders, climbing west into Montenegro and south into Macedonia. There are few large centers apart from **Priština**, the capital, where government money and a fast-rising population (Kosovo has the highest birthrate in Yugoslavia) have made a brash, modern town with little to tempt you. Around Priština stretches **Kosovo Polje**—the Plain of Kosovo— site of the battle which signaled the downfall of the Serbian Empire in 1389 and an important historic site for Serbs, though there's not that much to evoke the battle now. The monastery of **Gračanica**, in the opposite direction, is a more intriguing Serbian site, one of the greatest of the medieval dynasty's monasteries. Away from Priština, to the south, the smaller town of **Prizren** has a more picturesque, minaretted charm, as well as another key Serbian church. **Peć** in the east, was for several hundred years the headquarters of the Serbian Orthodox church and retains a complex of impressively frescoed churches just outside town, not to mention a run-down but evocative old bazaar quarter. Peć is also a good jumping-off point for traveling through the **Rugovo Gorge**, a sheer, Nosferatu-like chasm that makes for a superb route west into the mountains of Montenegro.

Some History . . . and the Political Present

One of the things it's most important to note about Kosovo is the delicate **political situation**. The province is a veritable sea of conflict and contradiction. Slav tribes penetrated Kosovo in the seventh century, driving the indige-

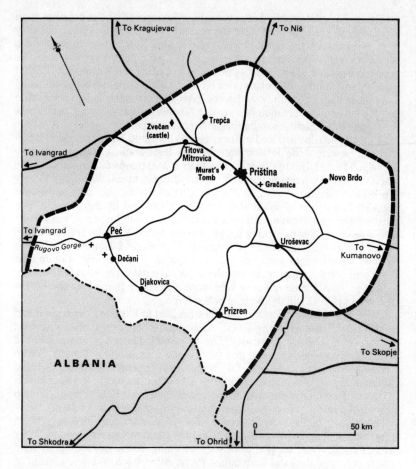

nous people into the mountains to the south and west. The Serbs built their monasteries and established their principalities here, the area becoming a power base of the Serbian Empire until it in turn was overrun by the Turks in the fourteenth and fifteenth centuries. The key engagement—psychologically if not militarily—was fought near Priština on Kosovo Polje in 1389, when the Serbian Prince Lazar was defeated and killed. Rather than accept Turkish control, many Serbs moved north and the vacuum was filled by Islamic settlers of Turkish and Albanian origin. The Albanians had an ambivalent attitude to their new conquerors: on the one hand they were hated invaders; on the other they became co-religionists, marginally less hostile than their Serb neighbors. The Serbs were not impressed by this ambivalence and to them the defeat of 1389 represented, and remains, a potent symbol of territory lost and culture attacked.

Within this context, the Serbs were bitterly opposed to the creation of an independent Albanian state after the second Balkan war in **1913**, but they were overruled by the Great Powers, who passed Kosovo over to Serbia as a sop. The region became a backwater of the emergent Yugoslav state, its people despised and exploited as peasants and Muslims. World War II didn't help. Many ethnic Albanians viewed the collapse of Serbian-dominated Yugoslavia with equanimity, and some even supported the Italian occupation and the subsequent creation of a greater Albania in 1941—though perhaps as many joined the partisans to fight against the occupiers.

In **1945** the Albanian leader Enver Hoxha accepted Tito's request to incorporate Kosovo into the postwar state of Yugoslavia, leading to an armed uprising which forced Tito to divert no less than 30,000 troops to Kosovo at a time when they were needed to pursue the retreating Germans. With Tito's victory (on both fronts) Kosovo again became part of Serbia, this time within the Socialist Federation of south Slav peoples. Embittered by the uprising, Tito crushed any sign of nationalist opposition and filled all the region's key posts with outsiders, later tightening his grip on the region after the break with the Soviet Union—Albania remained staunchly Stalinist and Tito feared a border incident which might justify Soviet intervention. The Yugoslav Communist Party's notional commitment to ethnic parity must have sounded strange indeed to an Albanian minority who were alternately harried by the UDBA (the secret police) and the Serbian police force.

In the **mid-1960s**, Tito and his allies decided to liberalize the regime and reform the UDBA. With the lid off, Kosovo exploded, and 1968 saw serious rioting—events which persuaded Tito to rethink his policy and institute a series of reforms designed to give back some measure of autonomy. Aid to Kosovo was increased, and the region was re-constituted a "Socialist Autonomous Region" and given priority over other regions in the distribution of central funds. Over the next two decades cash from Belgrade poured into Kosovo at a rate fifty percent higher than anywhere else in Yugoslavia.

The money made little difference. The population remained very poor, unemployment stayed absurdly high, and the gap between Kosovo and richer areas, like Slovenia, seemed to be ever widening. Many blamed the system; others criticized the local Communist Party, either because it was corrupt or because it wasted money on instant prestige projects rather than improving communications or developing the exploitation of Kosovo's considerable mineral wealth. Whatever the reason, the lives of ordinary people were little affected by Belgrade's ostentatious—and expensive—displays of concern, and in the **spring of 1981** student demonstrations ignited concealed economic and ethnic resentments that had been smoldering away for years. The result was rioting that left 11 people dead and over 200 badly injured. Belgrade reacted forcefully: local government and party officials were purged and the army sealed off the whole area, carting over 1000 activists away to prison—where some 400 remain, serving terms of 15 years or more.

The **mid-1980s** were a period of repression, Belgrade stepping up efforts to stifle all nationalist opposition in the province but doing little to solve the underlying problems. Periods of unrest were met by heavy-handed policing, while financial subsidies continued to increase. Above all, the central government was anxious to avoid driving the reformist majority into the arms of the nationalist minority, concentrated at the university of Priština—a rather limited strategy that really only held off the inevitable. As the economic crisis in the country as a whole deepened, and dissent over solutions grew throughout Yugoslavia, so conditions became ideal for a resurgence of Serb nationalism under the Serbian party leader, Slobodan Milošević. Serbs living in Kosovo claimed that they were harassed by the Albanian majority; the Albanians denied this and the two sides drew farther apart. Since then, central government has resorted to a policy of severe repression (some would say occupation); dozens have been killed, hundreds have been arrested, although the anti-Serb movement in the province is anything but subsiding. In November 1988 there were mass demonstrations in Priština to protest against the forced resignations of two local party leaders, Azem Vllasi and Kaqusha Jashari. February 1989 saw the protests continue with an underground sit-in and hunger strike at the Trepča mines, near Titova Mitrovica. Close to 1500 miners took part, and the strike only ended with the resignation of three local top officials perceived to be Serbian stooges. A month later, Kosovo's regional government was forced to surrender much of its autonomy to Serbia, sparking off a long series of protests, riots, and strikes that left police as well as demonstrators dead—and, Belgrade's nightmare, uniting nationalist and reformist elements against the re-emergent Serbian hegemony.

More recently, in June 1989, the Serbians rubbed salt into the Albanians' wounds by staging a massive demonstration to commemorate the six hundredth anniversary of the defeat on Kosovo Polje itself—a gathering attended by over half a million Serbs, drawn here by the sledgehammer nationalistic rhetoric of Milošević. Meanwhile, long-term—and constructive—solutions have taken a back seat. Past experience shows that Milošević cannot pulverise the Albanians into submission indefinitely, and that sooner or later there has to be a negotiated compromise. But the higher reaches of the Communist Party (and many Yugoslavs, not just in Serbia), have lost patience with the Albanians to the extent that repression in the region has become almost institutionalized. For their part, the Albanians maintain they have a right to autonomy as a separate republic. Figures bear this out: Macedonians and Montenegrins both have their own republics, yet the Albanians, who are numerically superior, don't. Belgrade argues that republic status would give Kosovo the right to secede from the federation, possibly even to join an independent Albania—something they couldn't possibly tolerate. Kosovo Albanians say they wouldn't withdraw—why should they? Most of them believe in the Yugoslav ideal, and want to remain part of it, just as long as they can secure parity with the republics. Serbia especially is not inclined to take the chance, and anyway, to come full circle, the Serbs will not contemplate losing control of the symbol of their nationhood for a second time. It's an almost impossible situation, and one which will have to see some very great compromises from Serbs and Albanians alike before there's even the remotest chance of a settlement.

Titova Mitrovica, the Trepča Mines, and Kosovo Polje

TITOVA MITROVICA—formerly known as Kosovska Mitrovica, and a rather ugly blanket of modern buildings through which peeps the occasional minaret—is the first town you reach if you come down to Kosovo from the north. There's no need to stop here, other than to change buses for Peć; the town center preserves a handful of Turkish-looking buildings but is for the most part functional and modern. But it's a prosperous place by Kosovo standards, and has been an important one in the country at large for some time, the lead and zinc mines at **Trepča**, just outside town to the east, producing close to half of Yugoslavia's total. Perhaps because of this crucial role in the country's economy, the mines are among the most politically delicate spots in an ultra-sensitive region, and they have played an increasingly prominent role in the unrest in the region, forming the focus for protests not only against the parlous state of the economy but also in reaction to the increasing centralized Serbian influence in Kosovo's affairs. Early in 1989 miners here staged a sit-in hunger strike demanding Albanian autonomy, provoked by the sacking of the local party leadership. Later in the same year the mine was again occupied to coincide with the trial of the former party boss, Azem Vllasi, for counter-revolutionary activities.

There's nothing to see at Trepča, only a large memorial to a group of miners who sabotaged a railroad here in 1945, and you get a more than adequate view of this from the town. But it's worth making the short walk three kilometers west of the town to the castle of **Zvečan**, originally a Roman fortress, but rebuilt under the Turks. Although it's pretty ruined now, Stefan Nemanja lived here for a time, and it was in the castle, supposedly, that in 1331 Stefan Dečanski was imprisoned and strangled by his son, Dušan IV. North of the town, too, there's another medieval Serbian relic, in the form of the church of St Stephen at the **Banjska** monastery—though this is only really reachable if you have your own transportation or are fond of walking. Built in 1315 as the resting place of King Milutin, it was modeled on the monastery church at Studenica, and although it has no frescoes, its situation, at the foot of the wild Rogozna stretch of mountains which reaches back up to Novi Pazar, is lovely.

Kosovo Polje

South of Titova Mitrovica, the Plain of Kosovo or **Kosovo Polje** spreads out from either side of the road, ablaze in spring with the red peonies that are said to blossom from the blood of the thousands of Serbs who died in battle here on June 15 1389—St Vitus' day. This, the **Battle of Kosovo**, marked the beginning of the end for medieval Serbia, whose army—a mere 30,000 men against around twice that—was no match for the Ottoman Turks, who had swept across the Balkans to probe their defenses. The Serbs didn't go down without a fight, however: the Ottoman leader, Sultan Murat, was in fact killed during the battle, by the Serbian noble, Miloš Obilić, who was anxious to clear his name of treachery. But the sultan's son, Bayezid, took command on his death, murdering his brother and rival to the title and going on to thoroughly rout the Serbs. Lazar was taken prisoner and decapitated, and the Serbian Empire, already in decline, was in effect at an end.

Delayed by the determination of the Byzantines to hold on to Constantinople (it fell in 1453), the Turks took another century to consolidate their control of the southern Slavs; oddly enough, in this atmosphere of accelerating apocalypse, with the Turks pushing slowly but relentlessly north, Serbia's cultural flowering to some extent continued, even prospered. But by the end of the fifteenth century any vestiges of Serbian independence had disappeared, from which time the Turks remained in control for four, generally oppressive, centuries. Taxation was high, and the Turks put little into the local economy in return; all those who would not convert to Islam were made *rayah* or "livestock" (*rayah* means "cattle")—prohibited from riding a horse, wearing green or carrying arms. Males were forced to join the Ottoman army, as janissaries.

Perhaps because it marked effectively the end of Serbia as any kind of recognizable state, Serbian epic poetry—oral songs collected and written down in the nineteenth century—wove heroic tales of chivalry and honor around the circumstances of the battle. There is a cycle of four epic poems, and it is partly through them that the battle is remembered, a mix of fact and fiction that engendered a romantic sense of Serb nationalism which remained throughout the Turk occupation, and is still strong even now. Before the battle, Prince Lazar was given two choices by God: should he choose an earthly kingdom he would win a great victory; should he plump for a heavenly one, he must build a church to God on Kosovo field and perish with his army, so making the outcome of the battle almost inevitable. As the poems point out:

> *All was done with honor, all was holy,*
> *God's will was fulfilled upon Kosovo.*

According to the poems, Lazar lay here for forty years before he was taken north and laid to rest in the monastery of Ravanica. Legend has the news of Lazar's death brought to his widow Milica by blackbirds, but the truth is that news of the battle took time to filter out, and was confused by Murat's death: at first it was thought that the Serbs had won a decisive victory, but as the reality of defeat became known fear and panic spread throughout Christian Europe, expectations of a push farther north and west were growing to alarming proportions.

Today the battle remains *the* most important date in the Serb historical calendar, something which makes the current provincial problems here even more intractable. For Serbs, Kosovo is of key historical importance in the history of their republic (it's sometimes referred to as Stara Srbija or "Old Serbia"), and it remains perhaps the most potent symbol of Serbian nationalism—when the Serbs won back Kosovo Polje from the Turks in 1912, their army knelt and kissed the sacred ground. Recently, some of the republic's most intensely nationalistic rallies have been held on Kosovo Polje, not least on the sixth hundredth anniversary of the battle in 1989, when well over half a million ardent Serbs turned up to hear Slobodan Milošević speak and watch a ceremony presided over by the patriarch of the Serbian Orthodox church and 300 priests.

All this said, there's not much on the plain to see, and most people drive straight through or just come out here to catch a train at Kosovo Polje station—the closest to Priština. A stone **tower** on the left side of the road, a few kilometers north of Priština, remembers the heroes of the battle; on the other side, as if in opposition still, stands the **tomb of Sultan Murat**. Curiously, only Murat's intestines were left here; the rest of his body was taken back to Turkey.

Priština and Around

PRIŠTINA was once yet another capital of the Serbian kings, and is nowadays the administrative and cultural heart of (Albanian) Kosovo. It's an odd city, one of Yugoslavia's most heavily changed over recent years: one half sports some of the country's most radical-looking modern buildings, while the other is a shapeless muddle of red roofs, topping the decrepit old quarter. With Skopje, Priština's city center ranks as among the most modern in Yugoslavia, but here there was no earthquake to justify the demolition. Rather, Priština is an example of the efficacy (or not) of regional aid, more than anywhere else in the province displaying the efforts at regeneration that Belgrade has attempted for Kosovo, and the money that has been poured into the region. But the surrounding hovels shame the new buildings of the city center (the gleaming *Grand Hotel*, a space-age university library)—white elephants which, the local joke goes, only lack the commodities they're supposed to have: the banks have no money, the library has no books, and the hotel rarely puts up any guests. The other feature of Priština is the army, whose members you'll see on the streets here and there. Priština, with its Albanian university, is the center of the nationalist cause in Kosovo, and the town these days can't help but feel a little like a place under occupation.

Maršala Tita is Priština's main street, a pleasantly planted thoroughfare that winds up from the *Grand Hotel* to **Trg Bratstva i Jedinstva**, where a huge abstract statue resembles an inverted clothes peg. From here, the main street bends aimlessly into the old town close by a trio of ancient mosques. The third one along, the fifteenth-century **Imperial Mosque**, is fronted by an attractive little water fountain and inside are some elegant (restored) murals. There's nothing else: a small **museum**, devoted to the history and culture of the Kosovo region, has been closed for restoration for as long as anyone can remember, and the other old mosques are in a bad state of repair and seem to be kept permanently locked. As for the **Old Town** itself, it's not hard to see why people here are bitter, the miserable shambles of mud shacks and broken-down row-houses with cracked and subsiding façades in marked contrast to the high rises on the main street. In the market lean peasants perch on crates to sell handfuls of tattered produce. This is indeed another country from Slovenia in the north, and funds from Belgrade seem to have made little difference to the region's economy.

Practical Details

Arrive by **bus** and you'll find yourself on the outer fringes of town, behind an unpromising panorama of apartment blocks; from here it's either a bus or short taxi ride to the center. **Trains** run only to Kosovo Polje, 8km west of the city, from where the connecting bus service to town—#1—is both infrequent and unreliable. If you want to stay in Priština your choices are limited: there are no **private rooms** and only two **hotels**—the *Grand* (☎038/20-211), which costs about $60 for a double room, and the cheaper *Božur* (☎038/24-400), which costs about $25—both on Maršala Tita. For **food**, there are lots of places in the old town that lay out tempting spreads in big steaming pots— no language problem, just point to what you want. Alternatively, try the wooden booths that line the streets opposite the university for a promising variety of *bifes* and *grills*. The town **information center** is at Maršala Tita 25 (Mon–Sat 8am–8pm). In the evening, entertainment centers on Maršala Tita, where the unusually populous evening **korso** is justly famous for miles around and probably Priština's main excitement. If you get tired of walking up and down, the ground-floor coffee bar of the *Grand Hotel* is equally popular and just as friendly.

The Monastery of Gračanica

If Priština is itself something of a disappointment, the **Monastery of Gračanica** (Mon–Sat 8am–5pm), 8km to the south, in part makes up for it, and makes a night in the city one well spent. Built between 1315 and 1321 by King Milutin, its church—the only part of the monastery buildings to have survived—is externally one of the most impressive of all Serbian Orthodox churches, and the best example by far of the Serbo-Byzantine school. Crouched behind trim boundary walls, its gentle succession of curving roofs build up pyramid-like to four small cupolas and a high, raised dome; herring-bone and cross-stitch patterns decorate the pale pinkish stone of the facade in a mixture of dazzling exuberance and almost geometric precision.

Milutin was one of the most notorious of all the medieval Serbian monarchs, a rather unscrupulous, much-married womanizer, sometimes compared with England's Henry VIII, though all in all he was a relatively successful and enlightened ruler. He came to the throne in 1282, and after moving the Serbian court from Ras to Skopje, expanded the Serbian Empire several-fold, making his kingdom into the model of a Byzantine mini-empire. His portrait, holding his church and clad in the stiff jewel-studded regalia of his office, occupies a pillar inside. His fourth wife Simonida is opposite, her eyes scratched out by centuries of peasants who powdered and swallowed the mixture of plaster and paint as a cure for weak eyesight—eyeless saints are common in Balkan churches. Simonida seems a timid, frail creature beneath her robes, and a sad one once you know her story. The daughter of the Byzantine emperor (the marriage was a diplomatic coup for Milutin), she was sent to Serbia at the age of six to be the king's wife and to seal a treaty between the two rulers—an agreement which gained the Serbian king a huge expanse of territory. Milutin, who was about fifty years old at the time, consummated the marriage too soon and left her utterly barren. Isolated, fearful, and infertile, Simonida tried to run away while attending her mother's funeral in Constantinople, and begged Milutin to let her become a nun, but it was all to no avail, and she was still his wife when he died. Indeed he was said to be so jealous of her that he had a staircase built inside one of the columns up to a gallery above the narthex, from which she could watch the proceedings without being stared at by lusty courtiers.

The church's other frescoes are very fine indeed, the lower reaches of the nave plastered with royal images, revelations of the rich world of Milutin's Byzantine court. Above these rise frescoes that show the more devout side of the era, with a mystical realism some have compared to Blake, others to El Greco—though the *Last Judgement* on the west wall is a macabre piece reminiscent of Bosch, full of strange beasts and reptiles. The *Dormition of the Virgin* on the southern wall is also an impressive painting, a fluid work, not unlike the painting of the same subject at Sopočani. In the side apses the comparison with Blake becomes clearer: *John the Baptist* in the north chapel is a severe figure, fiercely ascetic; in the southern apse *Elijah* sits in his cave, more interested in a life of contemplation than the food—a symbol of the Eucharist—offered by the raven.

Outside the church, the exonarthex was added later and bricked up not long after, but it has since been opened up again and serves as a small porch. The frescoes here date from the late sixteenth century. The church is still very much in use and there's a small religious community in the monastery compound. Aged nuns guard the entrance and one or two of them do a brisk trade in cakes and brandy.

Getting to Gračanica

The monastery isn't at all far from Priština but it can be difficult to reach without your own transportation. In theory bus #5 makes the ten-kilometer journey to the village from behind the *Grand Hotel* every hour or so, but frequencies are erratic; check times and details at the tourist information office, especially for the return trip. It's possible that asking around in town about how to get to the monastery may elicit a hostile response so this is best avoided. Taking a taxi is, of course, possible (try picking one up outside the *Grand*), and may just be easier than taking your own car—Gračanica is a Serb village and the signpost from the main road (first left heading south out of Priština) frequently disappears.

Novo Brdo and on to Macedonia

It's no accident that Gračanica and Priština were key nuclei for the Serbian Empire—the area as a whole was an important one during medieval times. Topping a hill about 20km from Gračanica in the direction of Gnjilane, up a tiny road to the left, the gold and silver mines of **NOVO BRDO** extracted a healthy living for the Nemanja despots, and in its heyday supported a population of some 40,000. The Nemanjas minted their money here, and it was described by one contemporary observer as "a city of silver and truly a city of gold." Nowadays it's derelict, having fallen into ruin after the Turkish occupation (although the Turks continued to work the mine until the seventeenth century), but you can still see the remains of the impressive fortifications: six stout square towers arranged symmetrically at the top of the hillside.

Otherwise, from Priština it's an easy drive down to Skopje and Macedonia across the rest of Kosovo Polje, following the Lepenac River and passing through the grimy settlements—UROŠEVAC is one—that lie along it. Failing that, the hour-and-a-half bus journey down to Prizren in the southwest of the province is a pleasant trip, through the wooded hills that form the valley of the Sitnica River.

Prizren and Around

If Priština ranks as a bustling city, **PRIZREN**, around 75km southwest, is a small, sleepy town, and as such it makes a much more appealing base from which to explore Kosovo. The dilapidation that distinguishes the province as a whole is still apparent here, but the town has a picturesque quality that Priština lacks, with its core, huddled around the bubbling Bistrica River, retaining much of its Turkish architecture and feel. Prizren was originally the Roman settlement of Theranda, and later an important center during the Byzantine era. Afterwards, the town became a seat of Serbian kings, which it remained for 200 years, a prosperous and wealthy city protected by King Dušan's monumental fourteenth-century fortress high above the town. Today, few traces of the Serbian era remain, wiped out by 400 years of Turkish rule and replaced by a muddled hodgepodge of brown roofs, slender minarets, and the pepper-pot domes of Turkish baths. Houses clamber up the hillside towards the fort, clutching the green in ragged tiers.

Above all, Prizren is a mixture: there's a sizable Serbian community here, the spoken language is as much Turkish as Albanian, and street signs are in all three languages. In spite of this, though, there's little of the tension that exists in Priština. Wednesday—**market day**—is when people from the surrounding villages surge into the place, some in traditional dress. Many of the men wear the traditional Albanian beige felt costume of hipster trousers, waistcoat, and skullcap; Muslim women stroll in *dimije*—baggy trousers gathered at the ankle; Catholic Albanian women don a gaily colored affair of white cotton and candy-stripes, with pleated aprons and a bustle at the back of the skirt. The women of some of the more remote mountain villages wear brightly colored skirts supported by an extraordinary hoop/corset.

Practical Details

Arriving in Prizren by **bus** leaves you in the thick of dusty suburbs about ten minutes' walk from the center. **Accommodation** isn't hard to find, but there's not a huge choice and it doesn't come cheaply. The *Hotel Theranda*, right in the middle of town (☎029/22-292), charges around $30 per person per night; failing that there's the run-down but very reasonable *Hotel Turist*, also downtown, which has double rooms for around $20. Cheaper still, there's a primitive **campground** some 2km southwest of Prizren, on the road to Albania, that has a small hotel—and of course space for camping. **Food,** as ever in this part of Yugoslavia, is no problem: everything's cheap and all the restaurants display what they've got in the window—Turkish style—so there's no difficulty choosing. The hotels, namely the *Theranda* and *Turist,* also have decent restaurants. Prizren has no official **tourist office,** but *Kosova Turist* and *Putnik* (Mon–Sat 7am–7pm) are right in the center, by the river, and should be able to help with most queries.

The Town

The center of town is dominated by relics of the Turkish era, not least in the fifteenth-century **bridge,** which crosses the river, and the early-seventeenth-century **Sinan Pasha Mosque** on the far side, built, apparently, with stones from the Sveti Arhandjela monastery just outside town (see below). An apocryphal tale tells how the Christians here thought Sinan Pasha's behavior in doing this so outrageous that they went all the way to Constantinople to complain to the Sultan, who sent them back to Sinan Pasha with a golden thread and an ultimatum: either he hanged himself or rebuilt the monastery. Somewhat fanatically, Sinan Pasha chose the former, leaving the monastery in ruins and the mosque intact, a graceful domed structure with a single minaret. It is supposed to house a small museum of oriental manuscripts, but you'll be lucky to get into any part of the building, since it's very rarely open even for prayer.

There are more Turkish remains in the opposite direction, in the form of the **Mehmed Pasha Hamman** (daily 7am–3pm), just beyond the *Hotel Theranda.* This has recently been converted to an art gallery, but you can still get an impression of the intricacy and extravagance of the former baths. There are also dozens of old and elegant Turkish **mansions** dotted around town, some of which are painted on the outside to celebrate pilgrimages to Mecca.

But Prizren's most famous sight is tucked away in the rabbit-warren of lanes and alleys behind the market—the **Church of Bogorodica Ljeviška,** or Our Lady Falling Asleep (Tues–Sat 10am–noon & 2–4pm), an early-fourteenth-century structure built by King Milutin on the site of a Byzantine basilica as a monument to the glory of his court and empire. It's a grand church, with five cupolas, three apses, and five aisles, perfect for state processions and grand occasions, though it was only one of 360 monasteries and churches that used to stand in Prizren. Though built by Milutin the church saw most service under his grandson, Stefan Dušan, who had his capital here. Dušan was every bit as dynamic a ruler as his grandfather. Like him he was eager to expand the boundaries of the Serbian Empire, and during his reign successfully invaded parts of what is now northern Greece; he also drew up a new legal code, the *Zakonik,* which incorporated elements of Byzantine and Roman law. Sadly, the church isn't looking its best these days: its frescoes once ranked among the finest of the medieval Serbian age, but most were lost when the church was converted to a mosque, and those that

THE PRIZREN DERVISHES

One peculiarity of Prizren is its **Dervishes**, a Muslim sect that, in Britain at least, tends to be associated with the fanatical Sudanese tribesmen who fought against Gordon at Khartoum. Actually dervishes are always peaceable groups, a mystic Muslim offshoot who preach universal love and recognize the teachings of both Christ and Mohammed—with the consequence that they're shunned by Christians and Muslims alike. Their name derives from the Arabic for mendicant or beggar. They're probably best known for their frenetic ceremonies—here called *zirkas*—where they work themselves into a frenzied, trance-like state by howling, whirling or dancing. Victorian travelers wrote of dervishes reaching such a mystical pitch that they could swallow white-hot coals, eat broken glass, and walk through fire without any ill effects.

In Prizren the dervishes, who divide into eight active sects, howl, chanting the names of God to an ethereal accompaniment of pipe and drum, until they reach a trance. One of the eight sects—the *Halveti*—also practices flagellation and cheek-puncturing, the latter a bloodless (and supposedly painless) process meant to enable the release of bodily tension and therefore help attain a more spiritual state. Not surprisingly, the authorities aren't keen on the dervishes in general, and information is hard to come by—certainly it's not a tourist attraction of any kind. The *Halveti* do meet regularly in the Halveti Hall, close to the town center, but this is only likely to be open to the public at *Nevruza* (the Festival of Spring), on or around April 21.

weren't are so pocked by Turkish plaster (removed in the 1950s) that the subjects look as if they are emerging from a snowstorm. Most of what you can see dates from 1310 to 1313. On the west wall are the *Founders of the Nemanjic Dynasty*—Stefan Nemanja, Saint Sava, and Stefan-the-First-Crowned—appropriately regal representatives of a royal line that was in its prime when this church was built. In the apse, the *Communion of Apostles* has a grace on a par with the frescoes at Sopočani. And there's a delicately rendered *Virgin and Child*, one of nine depictions of the Virgin in the church. Otherwise, though, you'll have to hunt around quite imaginatively to find anything all that fine.

The painter of the frescoes, the Greek artist Astrapas, is remembered, with the architect, on the east wall of the outer narthex in an inscription which details the contract drawn up between them and Milutin; for their pains they received a monthly salary of four buckets of flour, some salt and a bucket of ale. On the other side is another inscription, in Arabic this time, made by a traveling Turk deeply impressed by the church: "The iris of my eye is the nest of your beauty."

Finally, Prizren has two small museums of middling interest if you have a spare half-hour. There's an **Archaeological Museum**, housed in another old *hammam* behind the Ljeviška church (daily 9am–5pm). And on the other, eastern side of the town center close to the river there's the **Prizren League Museum** (daily 6am–10pm), which has a small collection of documents and artifacts relating to the role played by the league in organizing Albanian resistance to the Turks in the nineteenth century. Times with both, however, are erratic—don't assume they'll be open even when they're supposed to be.

On from Prizren: the Višegrad Fortress, Sveti Arhandjela, and Into the Šar Planina

There are more holdovers from the pre-Turkish era in Prizren just outside the town center. Closest and most accessible are the ruins of the *kaljaja* or **Višegrad Fortress**, a fourteenth-century structure that overlooks the town. In its time, it must have been a considerable stronghold, guarding the craggy Bistrica pass as it heads off through the Šar Planina mountains and on into Macedonia. Today, little is left except the setting, but it's a fine one, giving fabulous views over Prizren and beyond—although the trek to the top is as lung-bursting a process as you might expect. On the way, stop off at the tiny (and again ruined) church of **Sv Spas**, the other surviving medieval Serbian church in Prizren, built during the reign of Stefan Dušan and—though partly roofless now—retaining some badly damaged fourteenth-century frescoes.

Overlooked by (but not accessible from) the fort is the ruined **Monastery of Sv Arhandjela** (Holy Archangels)—about 3km out of town along the Brezovica road. Built within the lower part of the original fortress by Stefan Dušan in 1348, and intended as his burial place, the monastery is set in a clearing under the majestic gray rock of the Bistrica gorge. Recently excavated, its massive complex of church, palace and chapels was substantially destroyed by the Turks under Sinan Pasha, who used the stones to build his mosque back in the town center (see above). There's not much to see here now, but it's an evocative site, worth strolling out to; and you can clearly make out, in floor-plan at least, the church and the monastic buildings that once surrounded it.

The Šar Planina

The journey east from Prizren, through the Bistrica gorge and the **Šar Planina** national park, is worth making for itself. The Šar Planina is a solid mountain range which divides Kosovo from Macedonia to the southeast. Stretching for some 120km, from Uroševac to Debar in western Macedonia, its highest point is Titov Vrh at 2703m. Snow stays on the peaks well into the summer months, and this, together with the proximity to the Albanian border, lends the area a remote and wild air. Villagers on both sides of the range will tell you of the dangers posed by wolves, Albanian border guards, and the elements. Tracks and paths lead into the mountains from villages perched on the steep valley sides. Once above the tree-line the stark rocky summits emerge in luxuriant Alpine scenery. The paths are not waymarked, but are well-trodden by shepherds and their flocks.

The most accessible point if you're not hiking is **BREZOVICA**, at an altitude of 900m Kosovo's prime—indeed only—ski resort, about 20km east of Prizren. There's not much of interest in the village itself, but there are a couple of reasonable hotels to service the skiing and (in summer) the hiking trade, and one hotel at the ski slopes themselves, 1750m high, 30min by bus from the village. It's really a resort in its infancy, mainly used by Yugoslavs. At the slopes there are five chair lifts and three drag lifts, though breakdowns, and therefore lines, are common. In the village, best place to eat is the *Brvnara* restaurant, where you can cook your own meat or fish at an open grill.

Peć and Around

Once a key outpost on the frontier of the Ottoman Empire, and before that a center of the Orthodox church in Serbia, Kosovo's third sizable center **PEĆ** is another of the province's towns that once enjoyed a measure of prestige but has now fallen on relatively hard times. It has neither the high-rise good intentions of Priština, nor the low-key prettiness of Prizren, its sprawling suburbs zeroing in on a center that's a muddle of rickety low-slung clapboard rows and concrete. But this isn't to say you should avoid Peć altogether: the town's ramshackle charm and tumbledown bazaar quarter could never be described as dull, especially on market day (Saturday); and its setting, surrounded by some of Kosovo's most breathtaking mountain scenery, partly snow-capped for much of the year, is Kosovo's loveliest. Also, the complex of the old Serbian Patriarchate just outside the town provides a cultural focus, not to mention the superbly frescoed monastery of Dečani to the south, for which Peć is much the most sensible base.

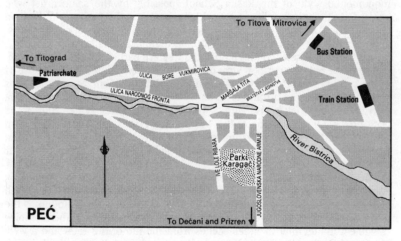

The Patriarchate

Peć became the headquarters of the Serbian church in 1253, and remained so, on and off, until the latter part of the eighteenth century. It was moved here from Žiča by Archbishop Arsenius, who anticipated trouble from restless Bulgars and Magyars to the north and in 1346 was granted autonomy by the emperor Dušan. The lands of the patriarchate extended west to the coast and north as far as Budapest, and this was—at the time anyway—the safest of sites from which to oversee them, well clear of the vicissitudes of history (and invasion) at the mouth of the narrow Rugovo Gorge, which in those days was almost impassable. Peć prospered, even through the most difficult centuries of the Turkish occupation, and was a center of national resistance and identity during the occupation.

The patriarchate of the Serbian church is now in Belgrade; the old patriarchate lies just outside the town, a twenty-minute walk through Peć's scruffy suburbs. All that remains of the original monastic buildings is a complex of churches, one of which dates back to the original move to the site. Otherwise the bishop's palace is gone, as are the other structures, although the community of thirty or so nuns that lives here in the enormous *konak* looks to be thriving.

The churches are connected by a long **narthex**, a hall-like structure added in the fourteenth century and originally an open loggia; it was walled up in the mid-sixteenth century and decorated with frescoes, although the family tree of the Nemanjas dates from the original structure. The original church of **Sv Apostola** (Church of the Apostles), built by Arsenius in the mid-thirteenth century to a plan of Saint Sava, is the central, largest, and most interesting of the churches: a dark, mysterious place, full of nooks and corners. It was modeled on the church of Sion in Jerusalem, the traditional site of the Last Supper, and the earliest of its frescoes, painted in the austere monumental style of the Raška School (possibly by the same artist who worked at Studenica), follow a set scheme, based on the frescoes in the Sion church. The *Ascension* in the cupola is a swirling, visionary work, with Christ sitting calmly on high, above some strong, dignified Apostles and an earthy, peasant Virgin. Elsewhere, high up in the western part of the church and difficult to make out, is a cartoon strip of *Christ's Passion*, painted in the later part of the century, each frame full of the drama of the moment. Strain your eyes and you can pick out a number of familiar events: a sycophantic Judas cynically clutches Christ to kiss Him; a worried-looking Peter denies Him as the cock crows. On either side of the west door are later frescoes, dating from the fourteenth century—a *Virgin and Child* and *St Nicholas*—giant, solemn figures that make you feel you're being watched even when you turn your back.

The two other main churches of the patriarchate, either side of Sv Apostola, were added by later archbishops in the first half of the fourteenth century. **Sv Dimitri**, on the left, built in 1324 by Archbishop Nikodim, is the more rewarding of the two, its frescoes freely arranged with a liberal choice of subject matter that includes scenes from the life of the saint and a well-preserved *Birth of the Virgin*. You may have to ask for it to be opened since it also holds the patriarchate treasury, which includes ancient manuscripts, various icons, and the like. **Sv Bogorodica** (Church of Our Lady), on the southern side of the complex, was finished around 1330. It's a grand, open, and well-lit church, with none of the pitchy mystery of the other two, but its frescoes are definitely worth a peep—realistic scenes, full of details of landscape reminiscent of the craggy terrain around Peć. The scenes from the *Life of the Virgin* stand out, notably those showing the Virgin's birth. Look closely too at the *Raising of Lazarus*, where you can clearly see the grave openers' appalled faces as the stench from the tomb reaches them. Be sure, also, to look in on the small chapel of **Sv Nikola**, off the southern side of the church, built in 1337 and decorated with paintings showing the story of the saint (the precursor of Santa Claus) over three hundred years later by Radul, a Serbian artist of the day.

THE PATRIARCHATE OF PEĆ

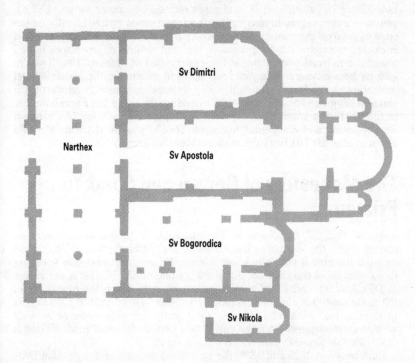

The Rest of the Town . . . and Practical Details

There's not much else to Peć, but the town is an evocative place to wander through, especially if you're here for its Saturday **market**, which is a lively and authentic affair thronged with people from the surrounding villages. The small bazaar quarter or **Baščaršija**, between the main street and the bus station, is also worth a browse, as are the town's mosques if you can find them open. The fifteenth-century **Bajrakli Mosque** is the most interesting, in the heart of the bazaar quarter and one of the oldest mosques in the country.

In any case, if you're heading west into Montenegro (or east to Macedonia), Peć makes a good place to break your journey – **accommodation** is inexpensive and relatively easy to find. Of the town's **hotels**, the unpretentious and very central *Korzo* (☎039/22-423) was until recently the cheaper, but it's currently undergoing a renovation designed to improve its (admittedly spartan) facilities; before this happened doubles cost about $30 a night. The alternative, the *Metohija*, almost opposite (☎039/22-424), was always a much nicer place to stay in any case and isn't greatly more expensive at $45 for a double room. Alternatively, there's a **campground** in the Karagač park, just south of the town center, though prices here aren't that much cheaper than the hotels. Nearby, the *Karagač* **youth hotel**, at Ive Lole Ribara 76 (☎039/21-864), is cheaper with double rooms for about $25; if you have a car you might also try the *Dardanija* motel (☎039/21-612), on the edge of town on the road to Priština, which has doubles for around $30. **Food** is cheap; there are lots of *grills* and *bifes* and several cheap places dotted round the railroad station and at the eastern end of Maršala Tita. If you're looking for a bit more variety and can afford to splash out, the *Metohija* hotel restaurant is good, and although pricey by local standards, well worth it if you're feeling hungry. For night-time **drinking**, try either the *Korzo* hotel bar or the bar-restaurant at the campground—the latter something of a hangout for the locals and open until midnight. Should you need them, *Metohija Turist* in Maršala Tita has **information** (Mon–Sat 7am–7pm).

The Monastery of Dečani and South to Prizren

South of Peć, the flat plains of the **Metohija**, or "churchlands," were so named when the town was the center of the Serbian church. You'll pass through the area if you're heading down to Prizren, and generally speaking that's what most travelers do. But worth getting off the bus for is the village of **DEČANI**, around 45 minutes from Peć, close to which the monastery of the same name shelters in a secluded enclosure just where the plain begins to steepen into forested mountain. It's a pretty three-kilometer or so walk west to the monastery from the village bus stop on the main road, making it easily feasible to see Dečani on a day trip from Peć.

Built between 1327 and 1335, the monastery was founded by Stefan Uros III Dečanski, a Serbian king who afterwards took the name of this, his greatest creation. Dečanski was the son of the formidable King Milutin, and he was (rather mistakenly) coerced into rebelling against his father by his stepmother Simonida—who had a real and understandable interest in deposing her tyrannical husband. Dečanski was still a young man, and Milutin had no trouble brushing off his rather half-baked rebellion, blinding his son as a punishment and dispatching him to exile in Constantinople. By some trick of fate, or more likely just plain bribery, Stefan managed to retain his sight, and after spending six years in Constantinople was eventually pardoned and allowed to return to Serbia. Feigning blindness, he wasn't considered much of a threat in the Serbian court and managed to survive until Milutin's death, when he discarded his bandages and assumed the throne—an eager and well-intentioned but fundamentally incompetent ruler. During his reign the empire foundered, the economy stagnated, and Serbia's borders were threatened. His position was coveted by his half-brother Constantine, whom he had crucified and sawn in half for daring to depose him. His son, Dušan, was more successful: with the nobles behind him, he had his father imprisoned and later strangled—an ignominious end, but for Serbia a fortuitous one. Under Dušan the golden age could resume.

Despite their differences, the monastery's **church** is very much a joint effort of the two rulers, Stefan and Dušan, who crown the door through to the nave, making their offerings to the enormous *Christ Pantocrator* above them. The church was completed during the reign of Dušan, and it was he who was responsible for most of the frescoes. The exterior of the church, however, is all Dečanski. Begun in 1327 as his private mausoleum, he rented an architect from Kotor on the Adriatic coast, a Franciscan monk called Fra Vid, to design the building, which explains its Romanesque, more western appearance. It has the same fine chiseled quality as Studenica, its stripes of marble and stone weathered to a smooth, creamy lilac and beige; sloped roofs decorated with blind arcading replace the cupolas of Gračanica and Prizren; doorways and windows are pilastered and in relief. Above the main door especially, the workmanship is of a very high quality, with a relief of Christ between two angels and the signs of the zodiac above. Unusually, Dečani suffered little under the Turks: it was to have been turned into a mosque, but legend asserts that an *imam* was killed by a piece of falling stone as he approached the monastery and the plan was abandoned. More feasibly, the monastery was probably spared because the neighborhood around was responsible for breeding falcons for the sultan.

Because of this, Dečani's **frescoes**, most of which were finished in the late 1330s, are perhaps the most complete you'll find in Yugoslavia. There are more than a thousand paintings altogether, and going inside is like walking into an enormous pop-up book of the Middle Ages, the formal monumentalism of Studenica and Sopoćani replaced by complicated attempts at narrative rather than symbolism—multifarious cartoons that illustrate the calendar, the miracles and parables of Christ, and the exotic, colorful world of Dušan's court. There's a mass of familiar subject matter, in colors that glow clear and precise. Byzantine bishops crowd the vaults, in their strict black-and-white formalism more reminiscent of the paintings of Mondrian than anything else; the Nemanjic family tree in the narthex shines turquoise and gold; and there's also a pictorial calendar, with 365 frames depicting the days of the year. Dečanski lies in the nave, certainly an ineffectual monarch, but canonized after his death for the healing powers his coffin became known for among local peasants—Christian and Muslim alike. They still come to his resting place, often crawling underneath the coffin to absorb as much of the saint's blessing as possible.

If you want to **stay over**, you might be able to put up at the monastery itself; inquire of one of the monks. If that's not possible, there's a small tourist complex near the monastery, off to the right of the road back to the village, which includes a tiny **campground** and the reasonably priced *Visoki Dečani* **hotel** (☎039/61-442), with rooms for around $40.

About 25km on from Dečani lies the dull little town of **DJAKOVICA**, not much in itself and offering absolutely no reason to stop, but interestingly home to the remnants of a sect of dervishes known as the *Bektashi*, which has a belief that mankind is reincarnated as animals. This in mind, the more devout among them are supposed to wear bells on their feet to warn small creatures of their arrival—though frankly you're unlikely to see any of this nowadays.

West to Titograd: the Rugovo Gorge

From Peć, the most obvious route is on to TITOGRAD, and thence to the Montenegro coast. Buses tend to take the easier, though less direct of the two routes west, north into Montenegro by way of ROZAJE, then heading west to IVANGRAD across high mountains where the snow is thick throughout the summer. Try if you can, though, by changing at Ivangrad, to experience the other route, which heads directly west from Peć through what's left of Kosovo, twisting a tortuous course up the spectacular **Rugovo Gorge**. This is a startlingly deep, breathtakingly sheer chasm through which the road hairpins and hesitates, sometimes lost in semidarkness, sometimes emerging to face a horrific, almost bottomless drop and pulling out of what seems lemming-like suicide just when you think it's too late. Far below the river Pecska Bistrica rushes viciously through its narrow valley, the sides plunging straight and sheer, streams of water and shattered trees falling to the torrent below, the summits too high above to be seen. The bus drivers swing the wheel with absurd confidence, climbing up above the summer snowline to the 1849-meter Čakor Pass, where the road enters Montenegro. On the subject of Montenegrin drivers, it's worth quoting Rebecca West:

> *The Montenegrins are a race of heroes, but since the Turks have gone they have nothing to be heroic about, and so they are heroic with their motor cars. A Montenegrin chauffeur looks on his car as a Cossack or cowboy looks on a horse, he wishes to do tricks with it that show his skill and courage, and he is proud of the wounds he gets in an accident as if they were scars of battle. It is a superb point of view, but not for the passengers.*

It was through this gorge that the second **Serbian army** retreated in the winter of 1915, long before there was even a road. Heavily defeated by the Austrians and Germans, they had decided to march over the mountains in the expectation of reaching promised British and French supplies on the coast. The weather was atrocious and food nonexistent; what little the Montenegrins had they were forbidden to sell to the troops since their king, Nikola II of Cetinje, had made a secret and treacherous deal with the Austrians. Of the 250,000 troops who began the march, 100,000 fell by the wayside from disease, malnutrition, exposure, and the sheer exhaustion at having already fought a three-year war of attrition. When the survivors reached the sea the essential Allied help wasn't there and they were forced to continue their long march down to the town of Durazzo on the Albanian coast. Eventually Britain and France agreed to re-equip the Serbs on the island of Corfu, but those too far gone for medical aid were were sent to die on nearby Vid—still known as the "Island of Death." En route another tragedy took place that's a microcosm of the disparateness and suffering of the south Slav peoples: when the boats left for Corfu, the sea was filled with bobbing loaves of bread, flotsam from a supply ship torpedoed that day. Most of the young, starving Serbians had never seen the sea before, knowing only the shallow streams of their native country. They leaped out of the boats to wade across to the food and sank like stones. Their companions from the north and south who knew the Danube or the Macedonian lakes tried to hold them back, and in the scuffles the boats capsized and hundreds drowned.

travel details

Buses

From Peć to Dečani (hourly; 45min); Skopje (5 daily; 5hr); Titograd (4 daily; 6hr).

From Priština to Belgrade (2 daily; 8hr); Novi Pazar (2 daily; 3hr); Peć (every 2hr; 1hr 30min); Prizren (every 2hr; 1hr 30min); Skopje (hourly; 2hr 30min); Titograd (5 daily; 10hr).

From Prizren to Belgrade (2 daily; 10hr); Peć (half-hourly; 2hr); Priština (every 2hr; 1hr 30min); Skopje (3 daily; 3hr); Titograd/Ulcinj (summer only 1 daily; 10hr/15hr).

Trains

From Kosovo Polje (Priština) to Peć (4 daily; 2hr 30min); Prizren (2 daily; 3hr); Skopje (3 daily; 2hr 30min); Titova Mitrovica/Raška/Kraljevo/Kragjuevac/Belgrade (4 daily; 30min/1hr 40min/2hr 40min/3hr 40min/6hr 10min).

From Peć to Kosovo Polje (1 daily; 2hr); Metohija, change for Kosovo Polje and Prizren (7 daily; 20min).

From Prizren to Metohija (4 daily; 1hr 5min).

CHAPTER NINE

MACEDONIA

They say **Macedonia** "exists behind God's back"—an apt description. Tucked away down in the south far from coast and capital, this has long been one of the poorest parts of the Balkans, its sovereignty shunted around between Turkey, Greece, and Bulgaria, its people long dependent on the lowest of incomes from farming. Its present boundar-

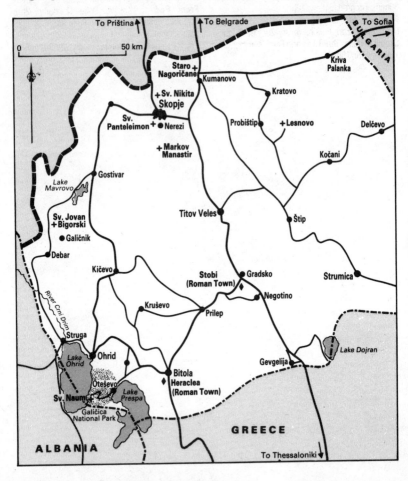

ies are essentially arbitrary—an uneasy compromise between surrounding states—for Macedonia has few simple ethnic divides, though Macedonian Slavs are in the majority. Neither is it much visited by tourists: all most people know of the region is the run down to Greece by road or rail, a journey that takes in some of the poorest and drabbest agricultural areas and gives a distorted picture to those who don't stop off. For Macedonia, at its best, is magnificent. In the south **Ohrid** has a clutch of superb churches that date back to the tenth century, and the lakes there and at nearby **Prespa** are a prime—though not overvisited—target. **Skopje**, the capital, along with **Bitola** and **Prilep**, are the towns to head for—in fact the only main towns, for Macedonia is a land of villages.

Summers here are the hottest in the country and in July and August the lowland plains of tobacco field and opium poppy bake in an intense, brittle heat with escape to the mountains and lakes a priority. Agricultural development is slowly pushing the region out of centuries of poverty, but the tourist industry is in its infancy. This can lead to problems in traveling—**buses** are sparse and irregular in the east and there are few private rooms or (official) campgrounds. **Hotels**, however, often provide a cheap and viable alternative, and the area to the west of the E-5/E-75 *autoput*—the most interesting part of the republic—is easy enough to get around. It's possible to make round trips here from Skopje to the lakes, and then head on down to Greece.

Some History

The Yugoslav province of Macedonia is a truncated version of a greater Macedonia that covered parts of what are now Albania, Bulgaria, Yugoslavia, and Greece from the decline of Alexander the Great's empire until the Second Balkan War of 1913. This greater Macedonia became a key province of the Roman Empire as roads across it were the fastest way of reaching Constantinople from the Adriatic and Rome. Perhaps surprisingly, it survived Rome's collapse but was still left high and dry—for the Byzantines it could never be more than a buffer against the Slav tribes to the north. The **Turks** arrived in the fourteenth century and colonized the region more thoroughly than any other part of their European empire. Their 500-year domination transformed the character of the province and marked every town, but by the end of the nineteenth century it was obvious that the Ottoman Empire was in its turn coming to an end. The Russian victory over the Turks in 1878 started a spiral of confused events as Russian, Austrian, British, and independent Balkan governments intrigued for control of parts of the disintegrating empire including Macedonia—a spiral that was eventually to precipitate World War I.

The Turko-Russian Treaty of San Stefano (1878) handed Macedonia to the new state of Bulgaria, but this was scotched by the other great powers who left it under Turkish rule. Frustrated, the Macedonians set up **IMRO** (the Internal Macedonian Revolutionary Organization), a guerilla-style unit which campaigned for an autonomous Macedonia. Following an uprising (known as the Ilinden rebellion) in 1903, the Turks replied with a harsh policy of repression, and for years Macedonia was condemned to internecine civil war punctuated by brutal massacre. Sickened by the murder of their fellow Christians, annoyed by the inactivity of the world powers, and keen to extend their boundaries, Serbia, Bulgaria, Greece, and Montenegro finally managed to combine into the Balkan League of 1912. In a rare display of unity they joined forces to drive out the Turks (the **First Balkan War**, 1912), but at the height of their triumph Bulgaria made one of the most reckless policy decisions imaginable and laid sole claim to Macedonia. Infuriated, Bulgaria's former allies went on the offensive against her and won a quick victory to end the **Second Balkan War** (1913). As a result, Macedonia was redivided—part went to Serbia, the south to Greece, and a fraction to Bulgaria—though IMRO, which was still intact, was not consulted and now turned its attention to the new oppressor, Serbia. Depressingly, a new cycle of insurrection and repression began, for the Serbs responded to opposition with measures as harsh as any before—it even became illegal to mention the word "Macedonia" on the streets.

World War I led to more Balkan blood-letting and the creation of an independent Yugoslavia. Dominated by Serbs, the new royalist government ignored the province and left it to rot in its own poverty. With the outbreak of World War II, trouble broke out yet again as Bulgaria joined the Axis and marched into Macedonia. A few IMRO members fought alongside the Bulgarians—seeing alignment with Bulgaria as a blow to Serbia—but many joined Tito's partisans, and in 1943 Macedonia was given republic status in the plans for a postwar state. After the war, the Macedonian language—more like Bulgarian than Serbian—was allowed to be used for the first time in centuries.

Following decades of neglect and underinvestment, combined with rampant inflation and the factionalization of the republics in recent years, the economic contrast with richer regions in the north of the country has led to wholesale **migration** out of Macedonia. Tired of being the economic underdogs, hundreds of thousands of Macedonians have voted with their feet—and moved to wealthier republics in search of a better standard of living.

Skopje

Hurrying down to Ohrid or Greece most people bypass **SKOPJE**, which is a mistake: no other town in Yugoslavia is anything like it. Encircled by a broad sweeping bowl of dark snow-capped mountains, it stretches out across a panorama of decaying minarets and futuristic slabs—a mix of ancient and modern, which resulted from the worst **earthquake** in recent Yugoslav history. The earthquake, on June 26, 1963, saw 1000 dead, 3000 injured, and 100,000 homeless. Macedonia, poorest of the republics, reeled, turning to the world for aid and getting it on a grand scale: Russia sent a special clearing unit, America a complete military hospital, and as they worked side by side Tito declared the rebirth of the city a symbol of international unity and co-operation. Rebuilt, Skopje boasts showpiece Western structures that can, it's claimed, withstand force 10 on the Richter scale, and a consumerism more extreme than anywhere else in Yugoslavia. Sleek showrooms sell video recorders and state-of-the-art stereos, and kids on the street wear up-to-the-minute fashions. Alongside this Slav-inspired modernity is a traditional Islamic community that makes the city a vibrant meeting place of cultures, apparently confident of the future; in Skopje at least, you feel the Yugoslav ideal has a chance.

The Skopje area telephone code is ☎091

Arriving and Finding Somewhere to Stay

Arrive in Skopje by bus and you couldn't hope to be more central. The **bus station** is at the entrance to the old bazaar, the Čaršija—though there are vague plans to move it to the new **train station**, some fifteen minutes' walk south of the center, an easy taxi or #5 or #7 bus ride away. A regular bus service also connects Skopje **airport** (16km east) to various points in the town center and the JAT office.

Whichever way you arrive, the best place to head for is the **tourist office** (daily 8am–7pm), a couple of minutes from the bus station on the new pedestrian bridge that serves as the entrance to the Čaršija and crosses above the main city boulevard. They have a limited supply of private **rooms** at about $9 per person per night and an efficient reservation service. They will also phone ahead to see if there are vacancies at the tiny **hotel** attached to the Monastery of Sv Panteleimon (see p.372). This really is *the* place to stay—the cool air of the hills; lovely views; simple, unpretentious rooms and a bargain at about $25 per double. The only problem is access—as it's 10km out of town, you really have to go by taxi. By comparison, Skopje's other hotels are pretty mundane though not especially cheap; least expensive is the rather glum *Jadran*, opposite Maršala Tita by the post office (doubles $30). The most convenient are the utilitarian *Bristol* on Maršala Tita (☎239-821; doubles $48), the *Turist* at Džuro Strugar 11 (☎236-753; $42), and (more expensively) the *Grand* (☎239-3111; $50–80) at Moša Pijade 2. Once Skopje's premier hotel, the *Grand* does at least have a certain faded charm. Cheaper hotels tend to be farther out of town—try the *Panorama* (Donje Vodno, Triglavska; ☎231-976; doubles $34), nicely situated on a hill at the start of the road to Sv Panteleimon. Cheap **rooms** are available in July and August only from a couple of *Studentski Dom*s including the *Goce Delčev Center*, west of the city at Taftalidže 11—but check with the tourist office first as host facilities sometimes change. At other times of the year it's a toss-up between the cramped **youth hostel**, 500m from the train station at Prolet 25, or finding an unofficial private room by being as conspicuous as possible at the bus station. Be warned that these aren't as easy to come by as in other cities—and that if you arrive in town after the tourist office has closed your only option may be a hotel. There's also a large **campground** near the soccer field in Gradski Park, a twenty-minute walk from the center; follow the Vardar River upstream and it's on the southern bank.

Eating and Drinking

There's no shortage of places in which **to eat**. For cheap snacks and light meals, try the *Pelister self-service* at Maršala Tita 50; on the same street the *Hotel Tourist* has a reliable restaurant. The *Hotel Bristol*'s restaurant is similarly good—and popular—while the *Menada*, just by the tourist office, serves up a superb range of Macedonian dishes: try the *argatska zakuska* (meat and mushroom pie) or the *čaršiska vešalica* (pork and mushrooms). In the Čaršija, outdoor grills sell cheap snacks such as *tavce gravče* (spiced beans) and *tavce gravče pleskavica* (with meat) alongside the more usual *palačinki* (pancakes) and *burek* with *sirenie* (cheese), *španać* (spinach) and *meso* (meat). The best places to drink are also in the Čaršija, and among the cafés that flank Ploštad Maršala Tita—but be warned, Skopje closes early and most restaurants don't stay open much after 10pm.

About Town

The murky river Vardar divides the old town from the new and, broadly speaking, the Christians from the Muslims, who in turn subdivide, with the ethnic Turks to the north and gypsies to the northwest. At the center the Vardar is straddled by the *Kameni Most* or stone bridge, an ancient Roman structure, though much remodeled subsequently. In the old days the Turks would tie Macedonians to tables in the middle of this bridge, then charge from either side, slashing them with spears as they rode past. Fine sport.

Today the bridge is a more mundane focus of life. On the near side **Ploštad Maršala Tita** marks the new center—a broad, café-lined square, much like any other but forming the pivot for an impressive *korso* that rebounds across the bridge in the evenings, its destination the **Čaršija** or bazaar. This is Skopje's old Turkish quarter, built (more accurately, thrown together) in the years of Ottoman domination, and ironically the area least damaged in the earthquake. By night it's a ramble of low, mottled buildings holding cafés and bars; by day some of the intimacy and a lot of the romance disappear—like the bazaar in Sarajevo the Čaršija has outlived its original purpose. The shops have been superseded by supermarkets, the craftspeople get a better living working in the factories, and the whole thing is beginning to be preserved for tourists. A few years ago each of the narrow streets had its own trade or craft, and carpenters, tailors, tinsmiths, even scribes did business on clearly defined territories; now it's mostly souvenir and jean shops, and the craftsmen only knock together sandals and shoddy leather goods—you need to look hard to find anything you can't buy at a California flea market.

For all this, the Čaršija keeps its noisy, earthy atmosphere, especially on weekends when the adjoining **Bit Pazaar** (Flea Market) sprawls out its wares and all the tribes of Macedonia gather to sell their produce, from rough hand-woven fabrics to poor handfuls of crops. This, one of the largest markets in the country, has a variety of goods matched by the diversity of the people who come to sell them. Muslims, ethnic Albanians, village Macedonians, and especially gypsies flock in from the surrounding countryside, a tradition unchanged by earthquakes or modernization.

Just at the entrance to the Čaršija is the **Daut Pasha Hamman** (Tues–Sat 7am–5pm), a Turkish bath built by a fifteenth-century grand vizier and now home to an art gallery. Forget the paintings: humped and solid outside, cool and spacious in, it's the building that's the treat, its high, broad-domed interior decorated with almost edible facing, and silhouetted stars that beam down from stylized firmaments. Under the lower, lesser domes are a few medieval icons, sternly beautiful and ill-at-ease in this sensuous eastern building.

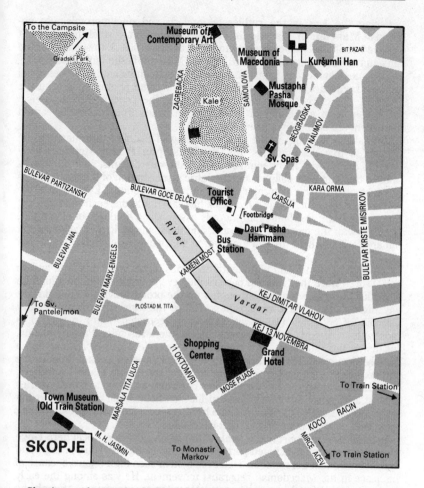

Skopje owed some of its wealth to being a staging-post on the Dubrovnik–Constantinople trade route, and in the **Kuršumli Han** or "Bullet Inn" (theoretically Mon–Fri 7am–3pm; often closed) above the Čaršija, merchants and their entourage of servants, horses and camels would spend a night on their travels. A sort of medieval motel, these *hans*, known farther east as *kervansaray*, once littered the trade routes of the Islamic world, though only a few survive in Europe. The Kuršumli Han itself was severely damaged in the 1963 earthquake, but a thorough restoration has helped it regain much of its original stronghold appearance; a *han* needed to protect both merchant and the valuable goods he carried, hence the lack of windows on the ground floor. Inside the tidily arcaded courtyard a collection of statues fills the rooms, but like the Daut Pasha Hamam it's the building, not the exhibition, that pleases.

Facing the *han* is the ruthlessly modern and uncompromisingly un-Turkish **Museum of Macedonia** (Tues–Sat 9am–5pm), which houses what survived of Skopje's several museums destroyed in 1963. Two sections of the museum are currently open: the Historical Museum is the more interesting, with some magnificent icons, a gold-edged sixteenth-century processional icon, and, upstairs, a group of particularly gruesome photographs from the years of the fascist occupation. Highlight of the concise Archaeological Collection is an exhibition of fishlike stone heads from the 9000-year-old settlement at Lepenski Vir (see p.322).

Behind the museum is the most imposing of Skopje's mosques: it's the decoration that distinguishes this, the **Mustapha Pasha Mosque** (daily dawn to dusk), with its fifteenth-century arabesque designs, stylized inscriptions of the four great caliphs, and the intricate decoration of the mausoleums of Mustapha and his daughter in the mosque's grounds. Even before the earthquake many of Skopje's mosques had fallen into disrepair, and you get the feeling that the Islamic faith here is essentially a holdover of past times. Only a few of the mosques are in use, and muezzins no longer call from the minarets—if you hear the call to prayer at all, chances are it'll be coming out of a loudspeaker*.

In the seventeenth and eighteenth centuries things were different, and so self-assured were the Ottoman powers they even permitted the building of a Christian church in the city—though with the proud proviso it shouldn't be any higher than their own mosques. Hence the little seventeenth-century **Church of Sv Spas** (Tues–Sun 7am–7pm; restricted hours in winter) is mostly underground, tucked away below the Mustapha Pasha mosque. Inside, its tiny, shadowy *naos* contains a masterpiece of peasant carving, a naively decorated **iconostasis** whose biblical scenes snake around the screen, full of the detail of everyday life. Its carvers, the Filipović brothers, placed biblical figures in Macedonian costume, and enacted their stories against a background of local peasant life—an honest and curiously moving act of faith. As a kind of signature, the brothers included themselves, working away with an apprentice on the right-hand side.

In Sv Spas's forecourt is the tomb of the much-celebrated local hero **Goce Delčev**, whose moustachioed portrait you'll find alongside Tito's in cafés and shops throughout the republic. Delčev is held in such high regard because of his place in the Macedonian separatist movement. He was among the early leaders of IMRO, the revolutionary Macedonian movement, though he opposed the Ilinden rising against the Turks that IMRO engineered in 1903—fears well founded, for Turkish suppression was immediate and savage. An enlightened and astonishingly liberal revolutionary, Delčev fought to overthrow Ottoman domination of Macedonia, refusing to attack local Turks, declaring that they too were victims of Ottoman oppression. Delčev didn't live to see the results of the Ilinden rising: he was killed in a chance run-in with Turkish troops a few days beforehand.

---

*The Mustapha Pasha mosque, incidentally, has one of the few **minarets** in Yugoslavia that visitors are allowed to climb. Whether this is local liberalism or an attempt to draw visitors is unclear.

More or less opposite Sv Spas is the entrance to the **Kale**, site of Skopje's ancient citadel, whose few remains survived various fires and attacks from the sixth century onwards, but couldn't withstand the drubbing of the earthquake. There's little to see nowadays save the random crumbling gateway, but the view is the best you'll find—beyond the ramshackle minarets and the Čaršija, Skopje's skyline rolls out like downtown Dallas, its chocolate-brown TV building and the concrete ski-slope arts center angular interruptions beneath dark mountains. From the Kale, Skopje's mediocre **Museum of Contemporary Art** (Tues–Sat 10am–7pm) is a climb up the hillside and, if it's a burning hot Macedonian day, one not worth losing the sweat for. Largely a collection of local art, it's weakly spiced with the work of a few modern masters—after the earthquake the museum's curator appealed to the world's most famous artists to donate a painting, though judging by what's here his enterprise seems to have been uncharitably rewarded. Only a *Head* by Picasso is of any note.

Back across the river, it's fair to say that once you've recoiled from the shock of the new, Skopje's center isn't all that diverting, and once you've made a tour of the old part of the city (which could occupy a lazy day) you could cover the rest of the new town in a couple of hours. The single thing to see is the **Town Museum**, which documents the city's history in a dull collection of exhibits, the best those concerning the earthquake. But the building itself, fashioned in austerity-measure gray, tells the story more powerfully. It's the shattered remains of the old railroad station, now a memorial to the disaster—the hands of the station clock frozen at 5:17, the time the first tremors of the earthquake shook the city. A sobering reminder, nudging you into uneasy speculation about what will be left standing after Skopje's *next* earthquake.

Listings

Car rental *Putnik*, Grand Hotel, Moša Pijade 2 (☎239-925); *Kompas*, *Kontinental Hotel*, Bulevar Jugoslavija (☎220-122).

Consulates *Greek*, Straše Pindzura (☎223-133); *Turkish*, Samoilova (☎211-810).

Hospital City Hospital, 11 Oktobra 53 (☎221-133).

JAT Bulevar Partizanski Odredi 1, Mon–Sat 7am–7pm, Sun 7am–2pm (☎239-623). For airline information ☎231-028.

Post office Main office with international phone facilities at Kej 13 Novembra (daily 7am–8:30pm); other office on Mito Hadživasilev Jasmin Mon–Fri 7:30–8pm, Sat 8am–noon.

Taxis Taxi ranks at train and bus stations, and on Trg Maršala Tita. Or phone ☎261-908.

Travel agent *Karavan Youth Travel Office*, Gradski Trgovinski Center (☎213-213). Sells *ISIC* cards and has details on cheap flights.

Around Skopje: Sv Panteleimon and Other Monasteries

The mountains around Skopje are dotted with fascinating but thoroughly inaccessible medieval monasteries. Only one, **Sv Panteleimon**, 10km away near the small village of NEREZI, has a decent road to it, and even then requires some effort to reach. If you're driving, take the road adjoining the *Hotel Panorama* (south down JNA and keep on the main road; the turning is signposted). Without your own transportation the only option is to fall back on taxis; to keep the fare as low as possible (around $12), take a #57 bus to the end of the line and catch one from there. Alternatively it's a couple of hours' exhausting walking up the mountainside, or chancing your luck hitching a ride at the junction by the *Panorama*. Once up at the monastery, it isn't difficult to find a lift back into town—so long as you're not in too much of a hurry.

It's worth making the effort: Sv Panteleimon sits neatly on a high bluff, Skopje almost unreal miles below, submerged on summer days beneath a sweltering haze of heat and smoke. Of the monastery only the church survives, a tiny, homy affair built by the Byzantine prince Alexis Comnenos in 1164, with a typical floorplan from what's known as the Comnenian Macedonian period: a cross around a central domed square. But if the setting of Sv Panteleimon is breathtaking and the church itself harmonious, miniature, and lovely, its **frescoes** are magnificent. Covered by overpainting until the early part of this century, their discovery revealed some of the finest Byzantine art of the twelfth century, startling in its fresh and realistic representation and breaking with the rigid stylization of earlier Byzantine works. The most famous of the paintings, *The Virgin Embracing the Dead Christ*, is as sensitive, immediate and expressive a depiction of sorrow as anything in Byzantine art. The others share an easy precision and refined coloring; best perhaps the *Nativity of the Virgin* above the entrance to the *naos*—the women excited, questioning, huddled in a doorway—and the portrayals of the saints, particularly Sv Panteleimon himself, dapper and majestic by the iconostasis.

Be warned that entry into the church can be a bit haphazard. The man with the key is supposed to be there seven days a week (9am–7pm) during the season and beyond, but if he's called away for army maneuvers or has an emergency, he takes the key with him.

In the last few years the monastery complex has been restored, and the church now adjoins a restaurant and a small **hotel** (April–Oct)—a bargain at about $25 for a double. Surprisingly, the hotel is little known and there's a good chance of getting a room at the last minute, though it's best to reserve from the tourist office at Skopje first.

The best of the other monasteries, **Markov Monastery**, can only be reached by car. Drive 9km straight out of town down Ulica 11 Oktomvri; turn right down the new road signed "Nova Breznica" and some 8km beyond is a signposted country lane marked "M. Markov"—the monastery is a couple of kilometers down the lane. Surrounded by solid walls and entered by an ancient gate, there's nothing touristy here—the monastery is the heart of a busy farm and the ramshackle, balconied conventual buildings are very much lived-in. The monastic church is fourteenth-century with a dark and mysterious interior ringed by vigilant frescoes: look out for the *Procession of the Angels* on the lower half and the *Passion* above.

Fifteen kilometers northwest of Skopje, the **Monastery of Sv Nikita** is again only accessible by car, and it's best to ask at the tourist office in Skopje for precise directions on how to reach it. Built in the early fourteenth century by the Serbian king Milutin, the simple Serbo-Byzantine-style church has frescoes by Mihail and Eutije, who also painted those of Sv Kliment in Ohrid and Staro Nagoričane near Kumanovo. Least accessible of all are the monasteries of Matka and Sv Andrejaš, lying on the Tetovo road about 18km out of Skopje. **Matka**, on the left bank of the river Treska, was built in the mid-fourteenth century, though its rather dull frescoes date from 1497. If you're here, it's worth continuing a kilometer or so to the late-fourteenth-century **Sv Andrejaš**, picturesquely sited on the banks of a lake by a gorge.

Western Macedonia: Skopje to Ohrid

Five buses daily make the four-hour trip from Skopje to Ohrid via the main road through KIČEVO, and in July and August you'd be well advised to buy your tickets beforehand as buses are often full. The more interesting, slower route cuts off to the west just south of GOSTIVAR to pass through the mountains and lakes that border Albania—but the problem here is lack of transport. You can get dropped off pretty much anywhere, but after DEBAR buses are few and far between and, at the more remote spots, drivers are reluctant to stop and pick you up. Four buses a day head off from Skopje to Debar (2hr) and there are two a day from Skopje to Ohrid via MAVROVO and Debar (5hr).

Out of Skopje the road to Tetovo crosses the scrub-covered flatlands until all at once the mountains appear, their snowcapped summits suspended mirage-like above the horizon. This is the **Šar Planina** range that separates Macedonia and Kosovo, and at its foot **TETOVO** just about merits a stop if you're not reliant on buses. Much of it is familiar high-rise construction, but the suburbs have a village-style prettiness with gardened *konak*s, camouflaged in August and September by a cottage industry of tobacco-drying. In the center of town is the **Šarena Džamija** or Coloured Mosque of 1495, covered with decorative panels outside and postcard views of Istanbul in. It's an odd mosque, but then some of Tetovo's Muslims were far from orthodox: as at Prizren there's a strong dervish tradition and the seventeenth-century **Tekija**, a couple of miles away, is a restored whirling dervish ceremonial hall, now Tetovo's museum. Hard to find (drive on from the mosque, take the first major right, and you're about 1km away), and frankly not really worth the effort, the Tekija is surrounded by a stone wall, surmounted by a watchtower, and has a cluster of sleeping and eating quarters inside; the ornate pavilion near the fountain is best.

From Tetovo the road cuts through the **Vardar plain**, small villages hung like rockpools on the mountainsides, their Muslim influence always apparent in the white minarets that spike the greenery. **GOSTIVAR** is the first town you reach, an undistinguished place but the stop to decide on a route south. Most of the fast buses from Skopje to Ohrid take the **eastern route** via

HIKING ROUTE: GOSTIVAR TO SKOPJE (4 DAYS)

From Gostivar take the Lakavica road south and, after 2km, turn left up the track to BELVISTA. Wooded hills crossed with sandy tracks rise behind the village: you need to ask for the path to TRNOVO, then follow the easily discernable, scenically stunning route that twists east through oak trees up into the SUVA GORA. Camping here is no problem, but, as ever, you should be circumspect and choose an out-of-the-way location in which to pitch your tent. After roughly 10km Trnovo is reached, a wild, friendly ethnic Albanian village scattered up the mountainside. Ask here for directions to RASTEŠ and climb steeply northeast across open moorland to reach a track that runs across your path; the track rises to a col, then falls east to Rasteš itself. In front of the town the shimmering rocky ridges of the Jaku Pica mountain range rise up, while behind the Šar Planina mountains can be seen.

From Rasteš you'll need to ask local directions in order to find the footpath to TROBELOV; leading east, it's a perfect hiking route, a cobbled path still used by villagers in the absence of a road. Winding between fields and alongside streams, it's an ideal stretch for finding somewhere to camp. Eventually you reach Trobelov, a village steadily depopulating as its young move out to larger towns nearby in search of work, leaving only a shrinking population of old people. Continue east up to the bare mountain ridge that provides exhilarating views of the mountain ranges to the east—today occupied by the military and strictly out-of-bounds. A twisting rock-strewn path plunges down the seemingly impossibly steep slope to the temptingly cool **Treska River**, oasis-like in the arid limestone scenery. Pick up the valley track, turn left and head northeast to Skopje over the KULA PASS (good camping), through NOVA BREZNICA, SOLNE, SOPIŠTE and past **Markov monastery** (for an account of which, see p.372). An excellent and easy hike, and one that cuts a great swathe through the Macedonia hidden behind the mountains.

Kičevo—a pleasant if unremarkable journey, alternating between mountain and plain and passing ancient Macedonian hill villages with their strong, rectangular stone houses.

The **western route** via Debar is far more dramatic, the road twisting through mountains where autumn trees turn shades of red, yellow, and gold. Unfortunately, bus connections on this longer, slower route are few, and you'll need to make an early start to avoid getting stuck for the night. There's no organized accommodation save at the village of **MAVROVO** on the edge of **Lake Mavrovo**. Dammed in the 1950s to provide Macedonia with badly needed cheap power, the lake is surrounded by a singularly beautiful forest that's been incorporated into a national park. It's popular as a summer picnic spot and the hills around are the heart of a thriving winter sports industry. Unfortunately, without its snow cover the village looks rather bedraggled and efforts to turn it into a mountain walking center have been a total failure—though as a result, summer full board comes at bargain-basement prices at the modern *Hotel Bistra*, in the village by the bus stop (doubles $35).

Fifteen kilometers away, high up in the mountains, perches the hamlet of GALIČNIK, famous for miles around for its **wedding ceremonies** held on or around July 12. For many centuries Galičnik's villagers have been stock farmers, scratching a precarious existence from the thin mountain soils. The poverty forced many of the men to travel to find work, often ending up abroad. By tradition the migrant workers returned home each July to see their families or marry en masse. It's still done—though it's become something of a tourist spectacle—and special transportation is provided from Mavrovo and occasionally Skopje (check with the Skopje tourist office). The ceremonies are highly ritualized affairs of tokens and symbols and form a preliminary part of the marriage contract; custom dictates that other parts include the chaining of the bride to the hearth and a post-consummation announcement by the groom that he found the bride to be a virgin. Ancient customs aren't usually very enlightened.

At other times of the year it's only possible to reach Galičnik by car, and the village remains a remote, rather desolate place, stretched aimlessly along the mountain slopes. There's one **hotel**, the *Neda*.

Back along and tucked in beside the road to Debar, the monastery of **Sv Jovan Bigorski** (St John the Baptist; daily 9am–6pm) consists of a series of broad wood-and-brick-balconied *konak*s from the nineteenth century that frame an eighteenth-century church, traditionally founded 500 years earlier by Stefan Nemanja. The *konak*s are in pristine condition and the best part is the palatial dining room overlooked by portraits of past *igumen*s (abbots). Meanwhile, the entrance to the church is almost engulfed by a primitive cartoon strip of frescoes with a centerpiece depicting the *Last Judgement*: the saved shuffle off to the left and, just above, Patient Women, Ascetics and The Just are transported to safety in what appear to be inverted hats. On the right, devils herd the damned towards Beelzebub, who sits in the gaping jaws of a nasty-looking dragon. In case anyone misses the point, the various categories of sinner are clearly labeled: robbers, heretics, liars, and so on.

Inside, the tremendous walnut **iconostasis** was carved in the nineteenth century by the Filipović brothers (of Skopje's Sv Spas fame). This is a larger, more mature piece, and in many ways finer: each of the panels depicts biblical themes, the pillars thick with human figures and small creatures scaling upward. It's a vivacious, complex work of extraordinary intricacy, "signed" by the brothers with carved self-portraits to the lower left. The church has one other surprise—the drab silver **icon** of St John that's housed in a sort of grandfather clock halfway up the nave is one of the oldest in the Balkans (1020); as is the convention, Saint John holds his head under his arm.

After your visit, you'll need to rely on the good humor of the bus drivers to pick you up. A dangerous but usually effective technique of stopping the bus is to stand square in the middle of the road and make an unequivocal "stop" gesture; the only alternative is to join one of the "West Macedonia" tours at either Skopje or Ohrid.

Ten miles farther on, the tatty "Albanian" town of **DEBAR** sits high in the hills and hard by the border. Before the road to Albania was closed, it was a flourishing little place whose metal-workers were famous for their delicate wares. That's all gone—but in the unlikely event you decide to stay the *Hotel Venec* is on the main street.

From Debar the road curls around the power station and therapeutic sulphur springs on DEBARSKO JEZERO, before it starts its dramatic run down to Lake Ohrid, edging all the way alongside the river Crni Drim—the "Black Devil." Lacing through the mountains, it's an exhilarating journey—and at the end of it all lies OHRID.

Ohrid

OHRID has a beauty that is little short of magnificent. The old town, medieval center of the Serbian Orthodox world, sits threaded on a hillside, a maze of Turkish architecture studded with some of the finest and best-preserved churches in the country. Below, the lake gleams limpid and warm, with good beaches and bordering a national park. By anyone's standards Ohrid is compelling—and you'd be mad to miss it.

But, like some of the coastal resorts, Ohrid's unchallenged popularity is steadily causing its downfall. In recent years weekly charter flights have started to arrive from Scandinavia, Germany, and The Netherlands, and in summer months the town can be packed solid with tourists doing the rounds of its sights. Not that this should put you off—Ohrid has yet to become another Budva—just to say that if you have a choice, time your visit out of season (April to May or September to October). Ohrid's churches will be less crowded, accommodation easier to come by, and the town at its peaceful best.

Practical Details

In recent years the modern part of Ohrid has spread, but the old town is quite small—it's possible to walk around it in under an hour—and using the lake as a guide it's easy to find your way about, however tortuous the streets become. **Bulevar Boris Kidrič** is the main thoroughfare, running straight down to the harbor and neatly dissecting the town into old and new. The **bus station** is smack in the middle, a block behind the waterfront on Partizanska, with services to most principal Macedonian destinations and Ohrid **airport**, 10km west.

The **tourist office** (summer daily 7am–9pm; otherwise 7am–2pm) is at Partizanska 3, virtually next door to the bus station. They'll help with **private rooms**; go for "Category 1" addresses as they're most central, and more specifically try to get somewhere in **Kaneo**, an attractive part of the old town, hard by the lake. Prices are reasonable ($10–16), though if you want something cheaper you might try STRUGA, 14km away to the northwest and a tourist center in its own right. Ohrid's rooms are of a high quality, something that can't be said for the **youth hostel**, *Mladost*, which is in any case often full; for the committed it's 2km out of town on the Struga road (Goce Delčev) and open from April to October. Alternatively there are four **campgrounds** (May–Sept) within easy striking distance. The nearest is the *Andon Dukov*, 5km away on the road to Struga; another is *Sv Naum* at the southern end of the lake, 29km out of Ohrid and 2km from the monastery of Sv Naum—though this is rather run-down. Reach it by taking the bus towards the monastery and ask to be let off at the *autokamp Andon Dukov*. Also along this road are *Elešec* (10km out of Ohrid; grim) and *Gradište*, 16km out of Ohrid (6 buses daily; ask to be let off), which has a good range of facilities including inexpensive rooms in bungalows and fixed trailers, reservable at the tourist office. At the other end of the market, a string of **hotels** with doubles at $40–50 line the lake shore around to the east at Sv Stefan. Most are away from the center and few have any charm; a miniature electric train links the waterfront *Putnik* office to the hotels.

Though accommodation of some sort should be available year-round, rooms fill fast in late August during the **Ohrid festival**, a series of folk dance performances and concerts with the Cathedral of Sv Sofije as one of the venues. Tickets and programs are available from the tourist office or *Putnik*, who also provide transportation to the more inaccessible venues.

Eating and Drinking

For cheap food, try the cluster of cafés and grills on the main waterfront square; best, if a little tacky, are the pizza places. Other inexpensive options are the *Self-Service* behind the *Lentica* restaurant, across the road from the bus station, and the café directly opposite the university building at Dimitar Vlaxov 54, which offers snacks to the town's students. Much more trendy is *La Piovra*, an Italian restaurant about 100m down Partizanska from the bus station—great food (including vegetarian dishes), cheap prices and decent decor means it's packed out most nights; you may have to reserve. For more authentically Macedonian cuisine, washed down with *T'ga Za Jug*, the best Macedonian wine, try the *Klimentov Konak* or the *Ohridska Kuka*, both on Car Samuil, or *Klimentor Konak* on Nada Fileva (under the old clock tower)—all are good places to try the fabled **Ohrid trout** or *pastrmka*. This species of trout has been around almost as long as the lake itself, and is

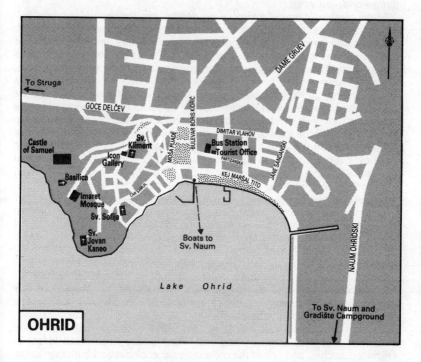

found only here, in Lake Prespa, and in Lake Baikal in Siberia; it's best eaten *à la Ohrid*—stuffed with vegetables and paprika, and grilled on charcoal. When caught young the trout is known as *belvica* and has a more delicate flavor; it's not as common on menus as *pastrmka*.

Lake Ohrid's other specialty is its **eels**. Before the Crni Drim (the only exit from the lake) was dammed these swam 5000km to the Sargasso Sea to spawn and die, the elvers continuing the cycle by returning to the lake. Nowadays special trucks ferry the eels from river mouth to lake and back, an experiment that, it's hoped, will save the eels. Occasionally you'll see them on menus as an expensive seasonal delicacy (look for *jagula*).

The Old Town and Its Churches

Clinging to a promontory at the north end of the lake, most of Ohrid's **old town** isn't really all that old—the wooden houses that overhang the narrow streets in a delicately colored shambles of white walls and pale stone date from the nineteenth century—but the story of the town, steeped in the history of the early Christian church, goes back a lot farther. Ohrid owed its early growth to the Via Egnatia (the Roman road that linked the two great cities of Rome and Byzantium), and was settled by the migrating Slav tribes in the sixth century, who gave the town its present name from their description *vo hrid*—on a cliff.

In the ninth century the arrival of two monks saw the beginning of a scholarly and monastic tradition that was to last for 600 years. The monks, **Kliment** and **Naum**, were disciples of the missionary brothers Cyril and Methodius, and it's possible that the Cyrillic alphabet used by the brothers to translate the Bible into the Slavonic language was first fully worked out here. Certainly Kliment and Naum introduced Christianity to the Macedonian Slavs, making the town a base for missionary excursions throughout the Balkans and a home for monastic learning comparable to Mount Athos. Its territories were vast, stretching from the Danube to Salonica and westward to the Adriatic, and the most brilliant church dignitaries, theologians, and artists gathered here, instigating a near-frenzy of monastery building that gave the town over 300 churches—a supreme position that lasted until the arrival of the Turks in the fourteenth century. Many of these churches have survived until today, though all too often forgotten and neglected, encrusted into the hill like rotting teeth.

Entering the old town from the square alongside the jetty, **Car Samuil** bends its way past a string of prestigious merchant houses built in the "Ohrid Style," with overhanging upper storys dangling delicately over the street. This is an embellishment of the traditional Macedonian stone house, and there are plans to turn the best examples into a museum—if the money ever materializes. In the meantime, look out for **Sv Nikola Bolnički** (St Nicholas's Hospital) and **Sv Bogorodica Bolnička** (The Hospital of Our Lady), fourteenth-century churches decorated with frescoes and, in Sv Bogorodica, an elaborate iconostasis.

Straight ahead, the **Cathedral of Sv Sofije** (summer daily 8am–8pm; otherwise 9am–4pm; closed occasional Mon) is the largest and oldest of Ohrid's churches, and one of the most majestic ecclesiastical buildings in the

Balkans, marking a high point of early-medieval church architecture. The basilica church has seen many alterations and additions since its foundation in the ninth century—most damagingly, transformation into a mosque—but what remains today has an austere splendor and above all a sense of light. The broad nave and aisles have none of the shadowy, lugubrious mystery you associate with the Serbo-Byzantine style, and the arches and vaulted roof continue the simple but firm feel of illuminated space. There's no iconostasis for the mysteries of the Communion to hide behind either—it was removed by the Turks; the *minbar* you see today was their addition, a stylish piece of oriental craftsmanship that holds its own in the ancient surroundings. The inscription on the side reads

> *The man who believes in Allah is like the fish in the sea*
> *The man who does not believe is like a bird in a cage*

Despite structural alterations everything still focuses on the apse, where the **frescoes** are the earliest in the Byzantine tradition in the country, contemporaries of an eleventh-century rebuilding. A monumental, stylized *Virgin and Child* fills the altar apse, towering over the *Apostles' Communion* that runs below, while a procession of angels, sharp-winged and severe, move toward the Virgin, kneeling in homage. Some of the biblical scenes depicted here went on to become motifs in Serbo-Byzantine painting; others, like the *Scenes from the Life of Abraham* on the south wall, and the north wall's *Dream of St John the Divine*, are unique. Look out too for the *Fiery Furnace* and *Jacob's Ladder*, illustrations that must have filled their early viewers with awe. Indeed, this was one of their main purposes: an illiterate audience needed visual prompts, and the more impressive the better. In keeping with the Byzantine tradition there's a formal hierarchy to the frescoes, with ecclesiastical figures on the lower bands, biblical scenes in the center, and the Kingdom of Heaven surmounting all—an ordered spiritual world, defining the position of man and his Maker. Before you leave the cathedral, climb up to the superlative **exonarthex**—two levels of slenderly columned arcades that formed an exterior porch to the church.

Straight up the hill from Sv Sofije, past the remains of a Roman ampitheater, a small plateau ends in the **Gorna Porta** (upper gate), which was locked at dusk right up until 1912. Just to the right, **Sv Kliment** (summer daily 8am–8pm, frequently closed Mon; otherwise Tues–Sun 9am–4pm) differs greatly from Sv Sofije both outside and in: a low wedge hugging the earth, the lines of the Macedonian-style church have been distorted by a nineteenth-century porch and it's hard to make out the original building that rises as a series of peaked brick fans. Built in 1295, it became a storehouse for Ohrid's treasures when the Turks entered the town, the most valuable of which were the relics of the saint himself, transferred for safekeeping from the church of Sv Panteleimon. The treasures have long since gone and once more the reason for visiting is the **frescoes**.

Hidden under soot from centuries of incense and candles, a thorough cleaning in the 1950s revealed some spectacular late-thirteenth-century works executed by the masters Mihail and Euthije. They mark a break from static Byzantine iconography, bringing new elements of folklore and medieval life into their interpretation of biblical stories. It's as if the frescoes of Sv

Sofije have suddenly come alive; the brilliantly colored illustrations are full of vitality, movement, and individuality, with a skilled handling of perspective that rivals that of their Italian contemporaries. The *Garden of Gethsemane*, finest of the works, show this to perfection; in a complex composition the disciples huddle as a sleeping group, each set apart by his posture and gesture. The *Lamentation* opposite has the same vigor, with the artists' observation of folk custom apparent—to the left four professional mourners chat among themselves, resting before the next bout of wailing. Really, there's more to both church and frescoes than can be said here. If you're interested, pick up the informative booklet on sale in the church and continue across to the **Icon Gallery** (same hours), which has works from the twelfth to nineteenth centuries—though their age is discernable only by their condition, such was the little-changing style of icon-painting. Best of the rich, aging images are a stern fourteenth-century *Sv Kliment* and the *Evangelist Matthew*, both by Mihail and Euthije, a couple of processional icons from the same period, and a number of lurid representations of Saint Marina, being alternately burned, stretched, and sliced up.

As you climb above the town, Ohrid's web of wandering streets and secret hillside alleys suddenly makes a lot more sense—and from the **Castle of Samuel** it seems almost ordered, the terraces of houses moving down in ranks to the lakeside. Save for the view and a few nervous lizards there's nothing within the ragged castle walls—they were systematically raided for building materials after the fall of the emperor Samuel. Samuel, energetic son of a local prince and self-styled "Czar of the Bulgars," retook most of Macedonia a few years after its capture by the Byzantine Empire in 968, and from the castle controlled his territories for forty years. Sensing dangerous power taking root, the Byzantine emperor Basil the Bulgar-Slayer galvanized his forces to crush Samuel, and beat him in a decisive battle at Strumica. By Basil's vicious and salutory order, all Samuel's 14,000 men had their eyes put out, save one in every hundred who was left with the sight of one eye in order to lead the others back home.

Following the path that runs down from the castle, you come upon the stumpy remains of an **early Christian basilica:** carefully brush away the protecting sand and you'll find the original fifth-century mosaics. The church was excavated recently, and it's reckoned that its size and rich materials would have made it one of the most important of the time; nowadays the local kids use it as a soccer field. Just below, and derelict from the outside, is the **Imaret Mosque**, where Kliment built his original monastery and school. Determined to erase the Slav tradition, the invading Turks had it demolished and built a mosque on the site—the *turbe* nearby is of its benefactor, Sinan Yusuf Chelebi. Evidently they did a good job of razing the monastery, for modern excavations have revealed only the foundations and empty tomb of Saint Kliment, his bones hurriedly removed to prevent desecration.

Come to the lower end of the path and you're facing one of Yugoslavia's most famous postcard scenes: **Sv Jovan Kaneo**, a tiny cruciform church which perfectly fulfills the unwritten rule that Byzantine churches should not only be beautiful but beautifully sited. Balanced on a cliff above the serene blueness of the lake, the church meets both conditions, even though its interior has been stripped of decoration. Just below, a complement to Sv Kaneo's tinyness, the minuscule **Kaneo beach** is the best in town and—as you'd imagine—crowded throughout the summer.

Though you don't need an interest in churches or frescoes to soak up the feel of Ohrid, they add direction to your walks, and other specific sights are few. Away from the old town, locals gather around the bars and cafés along Goce Delčev, where you're quickly reminded of just how poor the province can be: scruffy handicraft and junk shops front cracking and crumbling hovels, a world away from the glossy shops around the corner on Moša Pijade.

Lake Ohrid and Sv Naum

At the foot of Ohrid town and rimmed by mountains, the waters of **Lake Ohrid** have an almost Aegean clarity—largely because of an expensive UNESCO-sponsored clean-up project involving (in a rare act of co-operation) both Yugoslavia and Albania, whose border the lake straddles. The result is that on a good day the waters—among the deepest in Europe—are transparent to a depth of 21 meters, which must in itself be some sort of record. Though this crystal-clear water is ideal for swimming, **beaches** are not the lake's strong point, other than the tiny strip at Kaneo in Ohrid. For the nearest of any size you need to make for the hotels on the eastern side of the lake at **Sv Stefan**, an area that's fast growing into a self-contained resort—the farther you get from town the more secluded and generally better they are. It's easy enough to reach the main hotels (such as the *Gorica* and *Park*) and their beaches via the electric train (see above), or, more enjoyably, by boat taxi (see below); ask an accommodating taxi pilot to drop you off at one of the small rocky inlets if you want solitude. Apart from the excellent sandy beach near the *Sv Naum* campground, all are pebbly.

However, don't miss a trip to the **Church of Sv Naum**, at the lake's southern end. While it's possible to catch one of six daily buses from the station in summer to make the sticky thirty-kilometer journey, it's far better to take the **boats** which leave daily from the seafront at 8am, returning at 3pm (tickets from *Palasturist*, 120 Moše Pijade), or bargain with one of the private operators. The trip to Sv Naum takes around ninety minutes.

Founded by Saint Naum in the tenth century, the monastery reclines comfortably in its own wide paddock, looking out across the lake to the Albanian town of Podgradec. In a way the church is a bit of a fake: what you see today, a squat stone building with two raised cupolas, was assembled in fits and starts from the sixteenth to nineteenth centuries, the porch a modern addition. Its frescoes are nineteenth-century imitations and there's piped muzak, but for all this the church and its grounds are almost soporifically beautiful, and only the most priggish purist could fail to enjoy them. As well as the impressive iconostasis, take a look at Saint Naum's tomb in a shallow side chapel where frescoes illustrate his life. One tells the story of a peasant on his way to market who was attacked by a bear. The bear killed his ox but Saint Naum, having a way with woodland creatures, intervened and commanded it to pull the cart—a homespun miracle if ever there was one. Naum is also held to be a sort of patron saint of the mentally ill, and still greatly venerated locally; if you're reading this near July 3, try to make it for the **celebrations** of his saint's day. Feasts are held in the grounds and pilgrims bring gifts to the church, carrying them three times around in supplication for a mentally afflicted friend or relation. Until quite recently the monks ran the monastery lodgings as an asylum; today they house vacationing tourists and though forming a real bargain between June and August, when rooms are available, do rather spoil Sv Naum's tranquil atmosphere. Alternatively, there's the *Sv Naum* campground a couple of kilometers back up the road. For somewhere to eat, try the restaurant below the monastery; it's one of the best in Macedonia, serving up *pastrmka* in a lakeside setting.

A discreet army camp behind the monastery reminds you that the border with Albania is only a couple of kilometers away, and a broad swath cut in the forest marks the frontier of the countries. Albanians attempt to cross fairly frequently, though an agreement between the two countries allows for the repatriation of criminals, which the Albanian government automatically invokes. The Yugoslavs use their discretion. Border guards on both sides are reputedly bored and trigger-happy—walking in the area isn't advised.

West from Ohrid

To the west of Ohrid an uneventful fourteen-kilometer road trims the lake shore to the unremarkable and unpretentious town of **STRUGA**. Falling either side of the river Drin as it briskly decants itself into the lake, Struga is a brisk ethnic Albanian and Turkish town with a colorful Saturday market and an old section spreading out on either side of the pedestrianized main street as it nears the river. Recently renovated, this part of town is a pleasant mixture of styles (Macedonian, Turkish, Albanian, Italian) and makes for an interesting exploration—which is more than can be said for the macabre collection of stuffed animals that make up the dusty **Natural and Scientific Museum** on Kej 8 Novembri. Struga now serves as an accommodation center for Ohrid, so development seems to be diluting its once-earthy character.

West of Struga, Lake Ohrid is disfigured by a long line of charmless modern hotel complexes. The only conceivable attraction is the **church of Sv Bogorodica** that's attached to the *Hotel Bistra*, ten minutes' walk along the shore from the village of **KALIŠTA**, 6km south and west of Struga. The church has been badly restored, but perched in the rocks above is a tiny frescoed **cell** once used by an ascetic order of monks; with the winter wind howling in off the lake, the dank stone floors must have mortified the sternest of flesh. Entry is via the hotel.

Practicalities
Should you ponder a day trip to Struga, the frequent buses from Ohrid will land you at the **bus station** just off Maršala Tita, a stone's throw from the **tourist office** (high season daily 7am–8pm; otherwise Mon–Sat 7am–3pm) which provides private **rooms** at about half the Ohrid price. The best rooms (you'll have to specify) overlook the lake and the expanse of pebbly beach that fronts the town. A string of routine **hotels** straggle along the lake and the **campground** is at the start of town as you approach from Ohrid. Struga is also the venue for an international **poetry festival** at the end of August— worth checking out as some eminent poets come to recite their works.

East of Ohrid: Lake Prespa

Only a few kilometers from Lake Ohrid, **Lake Prespa** is quite different. It's a wilder, more elemental place, if anything even more magnificent—the pale mountains that run down to Greece plunge sheer and massive into its waters, and the whole area has a feel of rugged, rather frightening isolation. The problem is lack of public transit—it's awkward to get to and difficult to travel around without a car. One solution is **to hike**, starting from Sv Naum or Ohrid and crossing the **Galičica National Park** that straddles the mountain range between the two lakes—great views and easy walking through woods and alpine pasture.

The obvious target is **OTEŠEVO** on the western shore of Lake Prespa, which can also be reached by taking a bus from Ohrid and changing at RESEN. Oteševo is one of only two places on the lake that offers **accommodation** (one hotel, the *Oteševo*, ☎096/41-803, doubles $38; one campground), although the main reason for its popularity is its **beach**. Conducted boat trips leave Oteševo for tours of the lake that include the tiny island of **GOLEM GRAD** and its ruined monastery of Sv Petar.

From Oteševo it's possible to hike or drive to Lake Prespa's star attraction, the church of **Sv Djordje**, providing rain hasn't made the track impassable. To get to the church, head northeast from Oteševo around the lake to MAKAZI (18km), where a right turn at the main junction will take you down the east side of the lake; just after the first turning for Pretor, follow the signs for KURBINOVO, a couple of kilometers away in the foothills.

You couldn't get a more traditional farming village than Kurbinovo, and if you ask around the farmhouses the custodian of the church will appear with the key. Key and custodian stick together and it's another rather tricky two kilometers up a dirt track to the church. Sheltering in a wooded valley, Sv Djordje has beautifully vivid late-twelfth-century **frescoes** painted by the same school of artists who worked on Sv Panteleimon near Skopje. Highly stylized, the figures have a brooding simplicity that can verge on the surreal—for example, the witnesses in *The Assumption* and the onlookers in

---

HIKING ROUTES: RESEN TO OHRID THROUGH GALIČICA NATIONAL PARK (2 DAYS)

From Resen and Carev Dvor (the last stops for supplies), head for the village of EVLA and pick up the track alongside the stream that heads west into the mountains. After a couple of kilometers of gentle rising the path veers to the right at a junction of streams and twists up through deciduous woodland, emerging from the thick woods to climb up above the dizzying limestone peaks to the lip of the plateau. A massive spring, some 30m across, erupts from the limestone here, the water cascading down the mountainside; it's a perfect camping place, with views down over Lake Prespa. Continue across the plateau on any of a number of paths heading west to Ohrid; at the plateau's western edge a well-made mule track drops down steeply to the edge of Ohrid. A couple of words of warning: marked footpaths up to the mountains are few and hard to find; and the locals claim that wolves lurk in the thick woodland that cloaks the lower slopes. . . .

Jesus Enters Jerusalem—though as you bump your way back down the track it might not seem entirely worth the effort. If you're traveling on, note also that the **Greek border** just to the south is closed.

As an alternative base to Oteševo, the straggling settlement of **PRETOR** does have good beaches, box bungalows, a youth hostel, and a campground—but the bus service is dreadful and you really do need to hike to get here.

Bitola and the Ruins of Heraclea

The main road east from Ohrid snakes through high wooded hills, past the ski resort of MOUNT PELISTER, before tracking down to the fertile Plain of Pelagonia, a flattened expanse of land beside the Reka River. On the western edge sits **BITOLA**, Macedonia's second city, which was once a playground of the local rich (their decaying mansions still dot the suburbs), but is now simply a pleasant provincial town. It's worth visiting for two reasons: the remains and mosaics of its ancient city, Heraclea Lynkestis, and the chance to catch a train to Greece.

A town has existed here since the time of Philip of Macedonia, but it only became a city of substance when the Romans made it capital of one of the four districts into which Macedonia was divided and ruled. The Bulgars and the Slavs added little to the one-time capital and the Turks did little more until the nineteenth century, when they established their premier military academy here—Kemal Atatürk was its most famous student. Downtown, on the edge of the old Turkish quarter and by the main street, Bulevar Prvi Maj, a conspicuous seventeenth-century **clock tower** adjoins what little remains of the covered **bazaar** or *bejistan* that kicks into life on Tuesdays. Nearby are the nineteenth-century church of **Sv Dimitrija**, one of the largest Orthodox churches in the country, and the twin main **mosques**—one still in use but in a state of poor repair, the other recently renovated and used as an art gallery. Though the paintings are forgettable, the sixteenth-century **Ajdar Qadi Mosque** is a grand assertion of Ottoman wealth and power where the simple, expressive lines of the building are offset by the delicacy of the geometric frescoes inside. At the junction of Partizanska and Titova Ulica the **Archeological Museum** has bits and pieces unearthed during excavations of the Heraclea—a useful introduction to the site.

The rest of the town is a moderate collection of routine modern and crumbling nineteenth-century buildings. The center rises to a small-town prettiness of mustard-painted houses on geometric streets, their regularity upset by carelessly placed mosques, and evocative of the years before this century's upheavals, when Bitola (then called Monastit) was a secure and affluent place. The grand *konak*s of Maršala Tita still confront modern traffic with closed-shuttered propriety, though these days Bitola is really a fairy typical Macedonian town around a fairly typical Macedonian market, and you're better off heading out to the Roman ruins, a twenty-minute walk away.

The **ruins of Heraclea Lynkestis** (turn left out of the bus and railroad station and head away from town until you see the sign; 1km) date mainly from the Roman occupation, when the city was an important staging post on the Via Egnatia that connected Rome and Byzantium. They're still being excavated and archaeologists are confident of more intriguing finds; so far an amphitheater, two basilicas, and an episcopal palace have been unearthed, though the best discoveries are undoubtedly the **mosaics**. The finest of these, in the Great Basilica, are from the early Christian period of the fifth century. At first they seem simply decorative, but a complex symbolism lies behind the designs—vines represent Christ growing from the spring of life, stags the constancy of faith, and peacocks eternal life. Elsewhere scenes of hunting in paradise show the influence of earlier Hellenistic themes, all immaculately preserved. Enough remains of the town's foundations to give an idea of what it must have been like and, encircled dramatically by distant mountains, it's an evocative and atmospheric place.

Practical Points . . . and Connections to Greece

Bitola's **bus** and **train** stations are next door to each other and a ten-minute walk from both Heraclea (to the left; signposted) and the town center (to the right). The most convenient place to **stay** is the *Hotel Epinal* (☎097/24-777; $40 per double), right in the middle of town or, for the energetic, there's the far cheaper **Studentski Dom** (July–Aug), a fair walk out at Studentska 2; head away from the bus station to town, turn left on Partizanska and ask directions. No one there speaks English and the idea of foreign travelers wanting a bed strikes them as very odd—but it is possible. There's no tourist office as such, but you can garner what information you need at the travel agencies, and city **maps** are available at the kiosk in front of the *Epinal* (invaluable if you want to find the *Studentski Dom*). The center has the usual array of **cafés** and **restaurants**—the *Epinal*'s is better than most, as is the pizza place next door—and you could wash pretty much anything down with the local brew, **Bitola beer**, made from the town's especially soft water.

Bitola is only 18km from the **Greek border**, but reaching northern GREECE isn't as easy as you'd think. The nearest local bus service gets is 5km from the frontier—but then there isn't a connecting service from the border anyway. Consequently it's a question of walking or hitching some 22km to the first major Greek town, FLORINA. Trains do leave from Bitola for Florina and SALONIKA infrequently (one a day, late afternoon) and at a speed that makes you think it'd be quicker to walk. A better idea all around is to get there from the TITOV VELES junction to the northeast, last stop for the southbound "express" trains.

North from Bitola: Prilep and Around

North of Bitola the road bobs through the vaguely English landscapes of the Pelagonian Plain, fields of crops rashed with poppies, straggling behind low hedgerows. **PRILEP** is the most important of the towns here, gathered under a wild ragged outline of mountains, as dark and brooding as El Greco's Toledo. A workaday sort of place, it's the center of Macedonia's tobacco industry, helping to supply the country's not inconsiderable need for nicotine. Six hundred years ago it was also the home of **Prince Marko**, son of King

Vukašin and a Serb noble who fought at Kosovo. This much is fact, but a great tradition of epic poetry and folklore myth has attached itself to Marko and elevated him to the rank of medieval superhero—a sort of Robin Hood, King Arthur, and Saint George in one. He lived till the age of 300, having slaughtered innumerable Turks and other sundry villains, aided by his horse Sarač, a remarkable creature that not only had the gift of speech and could outrun all others, but also shared its master's prodigious appetite for wine. Like Arthur, historic reality reveals a more pragmatic character: Marko was defeated by the Turks and kept his princedom of Prilep only as the sultan's vassal, ending his days fighting for the Turks *against* the Christians.

The forbidding **Castle** on top of the mountains is part of the legend, though it was in fact the second stronghold of the unfortunate King Samuel, who alternated his court between here and Ohrid in the tenth century. It's difficult to give precise directions to the castle (roughly, turn left off Maršala Tita onto Markova and follow your nose up the hillside) but don't miss it—caught among the granite outcrops, it's an eerie, desolate set of ruins, much more the home of a defeated king than a warrior prince. Dotted around are ancient **tombs** cut into the rock and several early Christian burial chambers—the mountain seems to have long held special significance for the people who lived on the fertile plain below.

Tucked in a narrow niche on the southern side of the mountain, the **Monastery of Sv Archangel** is rapidly crumbling away to complete destruction, and any future restoration will mean a total rebuilding from its rotting fourteenth-century timber foundations upward. If you do get inside look for the *Tablet of the Thracian Rider* which has somehow intruded into the church. It shows a pre-Christian deity, possibly Rhesus, and goes some way to explaining the ambivalent nature of Marko's legend. The Roman legionaries of Thrace and southern Macedonia brought worship of the god into the area, and when Christianity drove the faith underground the memory of the warrior-god remained—and was syncretized with the real character of Marko.

The monastery is the biggest of fourteen **churches** in Prilep, the majority of which are in the old *Varoš* or suburbs that lie between the mountain and the new part of town. Most are normally kept closed, but **Sv Dimitrije** (near where Markova becomes a track) is accessible, with remarkably well-preserved and exquisite thirteenth-century frescoes in a church so square and simple it's like a gallery of medieval art. To get in, ask the caretaker in the hut nearby—he'll probably show you his own primitive carvings.

Prilep's **bus station** is a few minutes' walk from Maršala Tita (aim up the hill towards the nineteenth-century watchtower), where you can find the town's single budget **hotel**, the *Lipa* (☎098/24-140; doubles $38–50), and the **tourist office** (Mon–Sat 7am–7pm). It doesn't take long to realize that Prilep isn't exactly geared up for tourists: the office can't even offer a map, but (for a fee) might just be able to find someone to guide you around the mountainside attractions. Other than getting drunk, Prilep's single evening entertainment is the pleasant evening *korso* that runs on Maršala Tita.

From Prilep, it's feasible to make a day trip by bus west across the Pelagonian Plain to **KRUŠEVO**. Though the town itself, lying on the slopes of Mount Busava, is unremarkable, it was here that IMRO, the Internal Macedonian Revolutionary Organization, organized an abortive uprising

HIKING ROUTE: PRILEP TOWARDS KAVADARCI (2–3 DAYS)

Within a day's walking of the burning heat of Prilep is a cool, moist oak forest with springs and lush grassy clearings—the ideal antedote to the aridity of Prilep and a perfect stretch for both hiking and camping. Follow the Kavadarci road east out of Prilep and after 5km swing left (northeast) onto a dusty track to OREHOVEC, an affluent little village beyond which the track narrows, the subsequent villages become increasingly deserted, and the shimmering limestone mountains loom nearer. Butterflies (and other less friendly insects) seek your sweat, falcons swoop, and the air cools as the mule track twists up the limestone escarpment on a series of well-graded hairpins. Eventually you reach a limestone plateau with great views out to the weird hills that back Prilep and to Mount Kozjak in the south. This lovely open landscape is enhanced by the thick deciduous woodland that the path plunges into on its descent towards NIKODIM. Springs and grassy glades abound in a moist microclimate that comes as a real and refreshing surprise after the crucible-like exhaustion of the scorching lowlands. Should you camp here, the ideal spot to overnight, watch out for bees—they seem oddly attracted by tents.

The path continues, lurching over limestone once again, to Nikodim, a nearly deserted village, whence tracks lead through scrubland and vineyards, follow the stream, and rejoin the Kavadarci road, the heat, and the dust. From KAVADARCI, a small, busy market town, buses connect with NEGOTINO (where there's a campground) and the E-5/E-75 *autoput*.

against the occupying Turks on St Elijah's Day, August 2, 1903. Known as the **Ilinden rebellion** from the Macedonian name for the saint, it was brutally supressed by the Turks after just eleven days; so severe were their reprisals that the international superpowers of the day forced the sultan to curb his excessive repression of Christian subjects. Today, the anniversary of Ilinden is Macedonia's national day.

Stobi and Titov Veles

From Prilep, the road north to Stobi and Titov Veles passes through the **Babuna Mountains**, medieval fastness of the heretical Bogomils, and on across some of the best countryside in Macedonia—lowland bowls of shimmering heat in summer, the mountains sharp with crystal air—until it reaches the E-5/E-75 *autoput* which separates east and west Macedonia*. To get to Stobi from Prilep, catch a bus towards Titov Veles and ask to be set down at GRADSKO (make sure the driver will do this first), then walk 3km to the site. Alternatively (and a bit of a long shot), head for NEGOTINO, 17km away, and catch an (irregular) local service.

---

* Running from Skopje to Gevgelija, the **route of the E-5/E-75 autoput** (and the parallel railroad line) follows the path of the river Vardar as it heads into northern Greece. This was once the main highway for a series of invading armies that dogged Macedonia's history, but today tourists and heavy traffic thump through to the south, largely oblivious to what lies on either side. Dotted with motels, the E-5/E-75 is well-served by express bus (4 times daily).

STOBI is one of the most important archaeological sites in Macedonia. Spreading out from the road, it's easy to reach by bus (or car) but more difficult to leave. Long-distance buses will whizz past rather than stop, and the local services to Gradsko and Negotino are unreliable and inconclusive—the express buses don't call in at either and you certainly wouldn't want to get stuck there. The best bet is to catch the **train**—surprisingly Stobi has its own railroad station and certain trains from Skopje and Gevgelija stop here; further details from Skopje tourist office.

One of the four capitals of Roman Macedonia, Stobi was strategically positioned on the Via Egnatia, and grew in size and wealth until severely damaged by an earthquake in the sixth century. It then went into decline, and was finally abandoned in the fourteenth century; the ruins were only rediscovered in 1861 and digging didn't start until the 1920s. Even now the excavations are incomplete, though work continues and there are elaborate plans to build a restaurant and employ a team of guides for passing visitors—but as it is you'll have to rely on the minimal signposting.

Greek in its conception, Roman in its development, and Christian by conversion, Stobi was also popular with the Slavs who arrived in the seventh century and built their mud walls on top of the remaining stone blocks—you can still see bits of their handiwork. But the best finds come from the earlier periods: sixth-century animal mosaics in the **House of Psalms**, the fourth-century geometric patterns of the **Theodosian Palace**, the remains of a massive amphitheater, and a complicated series of **church buildings** dating from the fourth to the sixth century. Cramped and crowded fourth-century geometrics from an early **basilica** push up against a beautifully symmetrical sixth-century **baptistery** that is itself framed by vivid mosaics; as at Heraclea, each motif has a careful symbolism. Before you go, have a look at the site **museum**; a lot of it is incomprehensible bric-a-brac, but the **terra-cotta figures** from pagan burial ceremonies are extraordinary.

South of Stobi, the E-5/E-75 road cuts through the wild defile known as the **Demir Kapija** (the Iron Gate) before rushing down to the border town of GEVGELIJA and on into Greece. To the north it's a quick 27km to **TITOV VELES**, which huddles on either side of the Vardar River, its Turkish houses rising on rambling and precarious tiers. It's a pretty-looking place, especially at sunset as the light cuts across the valley, but really only worth interrupting your travels if you want to pick up the (daily) train down to THESSALONIKI or ATHENS. Cheapest accommodation is at the *Jovče Čučuk* hotel, near the bus station—doubles around $25.

Eastern Macedonia: Kumanovo and Kratovo

Eastern Macedonia hardly figures in Yugoslav tourist literature, and for good reason. What places of interest there are tend to be awkward to reach, some of the larger settlements are amazingly squalid, and accommodation is sparse. On the other hand, the region has several fine monasteries and churches, a smattering of intriguing old towns, and rolling plateaus and uplands that remain some of the most remote parts of Europe—where you're still likely to see costume and custom dating back centuries. To get something out of this you really need your own transportation and some knowledge of Serbo-Croatian or Macedonian/Greek, and travel details outlined in this section should be double-checked before you make a journey—busing it in the east is a hit and miss affair.

First an exception: 35km east of Skopje, the town of **KUMANOVO** is painlessly reached by bus (hourly; 40min) and was the site of the definitive Serb victory over the Turks in the First Balkan War of 1912. An unremarkable place, Kumanovo has a routine modern center and a grubby town **hotel**, the *Kristal*. There's no tourist office and no city maps, but if you want help *Palasturist*, just up from the bus station, will do their best.

Kumanovo is the easiest springboard for one of the region's star attractions, the church of Sv Djordje, more familiarly known by the name of the nearby village, **STARO NAGORIČANE**. The problem is getting there: the village is only 12km away but it's so small that few buses go direct and your alternatives are pretty doubtful. If you take one of the buses to KRATOVO (every 2hr), make sure the driver will set you down at the turning on the main road, from where it's a dusty four-kilometer walk. The return journey is even more difficult; short of lying in the road, it's difficult to get any of the buses to stop.

If you do make it, the reward is a tiny cupolaed **church** (Mon–Fri 7am–5pm), built from graying stone and battered by later facing. It's all that remains of a grand monastery established by King Milutin in 1314, who also commissioned Mihail and Euthije, decorators of Sv Kliment in Ohrid, to paint its **frescoes**. Like the Ohrid works their compositions here are vital and elaborate—best are the *Scenes from the Passion* and the *Life of St George*—and continue the move begun in the fourteenth century towards a narrative explanation of biblical themes. As well as the religious images there's a sympathetic portrait of King Milutin as donor, and his young wife Simonida.

If you're traveling by car you can carry on up the road past the village to the **Monastery of Prohor Pčinjski** (20km), right on the border with Serbia. The monastery dominates the surrounding valley with elegant lines of whitewashed walls and gilt cupolas rising well above the trees. There's nothing touristy here—the monastery is part of a productive farm, its balconied *konak*s are still lived in, and purposeful bearded monks crisscross the courtyard. On feast days local villagers gather at the monastery bringing gifts and in return receive food and accommodation; it's an older world where you're very much the outsider, the object of only mild curiosity. This rural idyll is, however, already tarnished by the hydroelectric workings just around the river bend, and other plans are pending. The monastery was the site of the first formal meeting of anti-Fascist groups during World War II, and the government, which partly pays for the upkeep of the buildings, is eager to convert part of the complex into a hotel; the monks aren't enthusiastic.

Kumanovo is also the starting point for trips to the **Monastery of Matejić**, on the eastern slopes of the Skopjska Crna Gora. To find it you'll most definitely need a guide (ask at *Palasturist*) and your own transportation. The church, completed around 1360 and a center of learning throughout the next century, is a small, elegant affair of brick, whose central dome is topped with a rare twelve-sided drum. Inside it's bright and airy, but the frescoes, painted just after completion, are in poor, faded condition.

It takes about an hour for the bus from Kumanovo (every 2hr) to travel the fifty kilometers east to the mountain town of **KRATOVO**. Hanging precariously on the sides of a steep ravine, Kratovo is a splendid shambles of ragged storage towers and high-arched Turkish bridges over the murky Tabačka River, which twists between a chaotic mixture of housing dating from at least the seventeenth century. Despite its isolation, Kratovo is one of the oldest settlements in the Balkans, at the heart of mountains that were once rich in gold, copper, and bronze. A mining boom town during both the Roman and Turkish occupations, by the sixteenth-century Kratovo yielded the sultans a revenue of 70,000 ducats a year; the poet Zaifi impiously suggested his countrymen should make their pilgrimages here rather than Mecca. It all came to an abrupt end in the eighteenth century. The Slav miners had always been ruthlessly exploited by their Turkish masters, and when an Austrian force showed the fragility of Ottoman control by a successful incursion into Macedonia, they rose in revolt. The Turks took a terrible revenge: the miners' leader was dismembered on the Kameni Most in Skopje, and Kratovo was flattened. After this violence it was hard for the Turks to find replacement miners and Kratovo never really recovered.

Some lead-mining still goes on around Kratovo, but it's a far from prosperous place, where fanciful plans to turn old workings into tourist attractions seem absurd—if not lethal. A rough-and-ready town, there's one **hotel** (the *Kratis*, right in the center) but no private rooms.

From Kratovo you'll need a car with a good suspension and possibly a guide to reach the remote **Monastery of Lesnovo**—roughly, head south on the more easterly of the roads out of Kratovo, passing through DOBREVO (9km). After another 6km you'll reach a T-junction; turn left here for the village of ZLETOVO (1km), where you'll need to seek help and/or a guide—the monastery, a stiff two hours' walk on a hill high above the village, is unreachable without one or the other. Built by the Despot Oliver in 1341, the church's **frescoes** were painted by a local artist, Michael of Lesnovo, who included an intriguing sequence of works that show contemporary peasant customs; one frame is a group of men with interlaced arms dancing the *oro*. On the northern wall there's a portrait of the richly armored Despot Oliver as donor. The carved **iconostasis**, the work of the Filopović brothers, rivals their more famous work at Sv Spas in Skopje.

Finally, back on the main Skopje–Bulgaria highway, the road continues east through the dull ugliness of KRIVA PALANKA, up to the Bulgarian frontier and on to SOFIA.

Southeast Macedonia: Strumica and Lake Dojran

The road from Skopje to Strumica cuts off from the E-5/E-75 road at Titov Veles and heads off east to **STIP**, a ramshackle, scruffy little town that straggles along the sides of a steep curving ravine. The only interesting part is the gypsy town that runs up the hill to the northeast of the town center. Otherwise there's no reason to linger; there's one **hotel**, the *Astibo*, if you do.

HIKING ROUTE: ŠTIP TO DELČEVO (3–4 DAYS)

Start from the back road to Karbinci, a quiet, tarmacked road passing collective farms, and leave it when it swings south to RADANJE. Take the dust track that heads east along the valleyside through a string of bustling villages. While it's easy to camp anywhere around here—and the locals helpful and eager to talk—the only place you may arouse the interest of a bored policeman is VINICA, a small market town that marks a change in the nature of the walk. Pick up the old German-made army track that leaves the Vinica/Istibanja road to rise up onto the mountain plateau. The track contours east across the barren upland, past occasional farms with views down to the valley and ahead to Bulgaria. As you descend to DELČEVO you enter thick woodland filled with flamboyant bee-eater birds.

From Štip you can travel northeast, along the course of the Bregalnica River, to Bulgaria via the remote towns of KOČANI and DELČEVO, or continue southeast to **STRUMICA**, a garrison town and one of the ugliest places in Yugoslavia; the single **hotel**, the *Esperanto*, may be the only one in Europe with a rusting car abandoned outside the front door. The town's only other claim to fame was the Battle of Strumica in 1014, where the Byzantines destroyed the army of Czar Samuel of Ohrid (see p.380) and where 14,000 of his men were blinded to deter further Slav ambition. The monastery of Vodoča, near Strumica, overlooks the scene of the atrocity from which it takes its name—*vadi oči*, to put out the eyes.

The triangle of land between Strumica, Štip, and Delčevo is one of the most barren, isolated and sparsely populated areas of the Balkans. On these wasted uplands, the **Ovče Polje** or "Sheep's Field," fertility rites and ritual sacrifices took place right up until World War II—analyzed in one of the most brilliant passages of Rebecca West's *Black Lamb and Grey Falcon*, which sees the ceremony as a negation and distortion of the "life force".

South of Strumica (44km)—and east of Gevgelija (37km)—the waters of **Lake Dojran** are split between Greece and Yugoslavia. Marginally more interesting to read about than to visit, the lake is unusual because it's never more than ten meters deep—a fact which has encouraged its fisherpeople to adopt a fishing technique rarely seen outside of China. For centuries cormorants with clipped wings were used to drive the fish into the nets, though recently some of the younger men have decided dynamite is less of a problem. The birds are still in use but only when the fishing is right—in November and December—and the nearest a visitor usually gets is a smoky fresh fish tourist lunch on one of the wood and reed **stilt-houses** near the lake shore. These were the traditional living quarters of the tribes of the lake and Herodotus described their customs when he visited the area in the fifth century BC: toddlers had string attached to their feet to stop them falling into the water while, in this polygamous society, each set of three stilts signified a wife.

Best time to visit the lake is in spring or autumn, for in the summer months this is one of the hottest places in Yugoslavia . . . and the heat's absolutely murderous. The tiny main settlement, **STARI DOJRAN** (a couple of kilometers farther on from the even tinier village of NOVI DOJRAN), is the place to head for, a popular holiday spot for Greeks and Yugoslavs with a moderate **bus** service from both Skopje and Gevgelija. There's no tourist office as such but an **information kiosk** (summer only 7am–9pm) can be found near the bus stop on the main street. A wide range of **accommodation** is available, including private **rooms** and a large **autocamp** on the Greek frontier (2km south): the town's two hotels are the *Galeb* and the *Polin*, similarly priced at $15–40 for doubles. Just up from the bus stop, the *Hotel Galeb* is as good a place as any to try the local delicacy, the superb scaly *linis* fish; best grilled, the *linis* is peculiar to Lake Dojran. Long stretches of shingle beach surround the lake, but it's too shallow and muddy to appeal for a swim. Finally, although the **Greek border** is so near, the bus service on into Greece is atrocious—it's quicker to go back to Gevgelija or try to hitch a ride on one of the local tourist excursions to Thessaloniki.

travel details

Buses

From Ohrid to Struga (every 30min; journey time 45min); Resen (every 2hr; 1hr) with Resen to Oteševo (7 daily; 1hr); Bitola (10 daily; 1hr 45min) with Bitola to Prilep (10; 2hr); Prilep to Titov Veles (10; 2hr 30min); and Bitola to Skopje (10; 3hr).

From Skopje to Belgrade (9 daily; 7hr); Dubrovnik (1; 14hr); Gevgelija (4; 4hr); Kumanovo (16; 40min); Niš (7; 4hr); Ohrid (7; 4hr); Ohrid (via Mavrovo and Debar) (2; 5hr); Peć (5; 5hr); Priština (6; 2hr 30min); Prizren (5; 4hr 30min); Strumica (10; 3hr); Tetovo (10; 1hr); Titov Veles (7; 1hr).

From Skopje, international buses to Sofia (1 daily; visa in Belgrade only), Istanbul (2–3 times weekly) and Greece (4 weekly). The length of the journey depends on frontier formalities, but reckon on 24hr to Istanbul.

Trains

From Bitola to Florina (1 daily; 2hr).

From Skopje to Belgrade (2; 9hr); Niš (2 daily; 5hr).

From Skopje, international trains to Athens (2 daily; 14hr); Thessaloniki (2; 8hr).

PART THREE

THE

CONTEXTS

THE HISTORICAL FRAMEWORK

Balkan history is almost inpenetrably complex—and that of Yugoslavia especially so. The country as it exists today dates only from 1945, and well into this century the modern republics—Serbia, Croatia and Montenegro—were each independent states. What follows is necessarily a simplified (and brief) account, and it is intended primarily to provide a general framework for the more detailed accounts in the text and individual chapter introductions.

BEGINNINGS: ILLYRIANS, ROMANS AND SLAVS

Although recorded history of the area now covered by Yugoslavia begins with the arrival of the Greeks in the seventh century BC, recent archaeological finds have revealed settlements stretching back to the **Bronze Age** and beyond. Remains of one of man's earliest forerunners—*Homo Krapinesis*—have been found in Croatia, and discoveries at the Grapčeva Cave in Hvar along with stone forts in Istria show that a well organized form of society had reached the coastal areas by 4000 BC. Inland, ruins of a developed civilization have been found at Lepinski Vir on the Danube, dating, by general consensus, to around 6000 BC, making it one of the earliest permanent settlements in Europe.

From these isolated beginnings the tribes scattered over the country, gradually coming together in two broad groupings: the **Illyrians** in the west, and the **Thracians** in the east. On the coast, around 700 BC, they were joined by colonies of **Greeks**, who had been trading along the Adriatic almost since they learnt to navigate. Their influence never spread far inland, but by the third century BC it was extensive enough to provoke an Illyrian backlash, a confederation led by the semi-legendary King Agron, and later his widow Queen Teuta, driving them from everywhere except Vis.

The Illyrians, however, had little time to consolidate these gains. To the east came progressive incursions of **Celtic** peoples, peaceable at first but soon creating a territorial threat that led to battle; in the south spread the **Macedonian Empire** of Alexander the Great; while across the Adriatic the balance of the whole area was beginning to change with the campaigns and colonizations of **Rome**. The Yugoslav-Illyrian coast was an inevitable target for early Roman expansions, and, using as their pretext defense against Illyrian piracy, the second and first centuries BC saw almost constant warfare between the two powers, culminating in AD 9 with the formal Roman annexation of the region under the emperor Tiberius.

Roman occupation lasted a little under three centuries, its influence largely confined to the main coastal cities and provincial capitals (a pattern continued by later occupiers) but extending beyond these in the programs of road building and tax collection. The fighting qualities of the Illyrians, which delayed Roman subjugation for so long, were turned to good effect in the Imperial legions. Discovery of large metal reserves made Dalmatia an extremely profitable area for the Romans, and the colony also provided several emperors—Claudius, Diocletian and Maximilian among them.

Traces of the Roman presence are still visible throughout Yugoslavia, and there are three major sites: the Pula amphitheater, the remnants of Salona, and, most importantly, Diocletian's palace at Split. This was for a long time the eastern base of the Roman Empire, after Diocletian's division of the territories in AD 285—a division, into the two rival empires of **Rome** and **Byzantium**, that had significant shaping influence on the fragmentary development of Yugoslavia. The dividing line ran up from Budva through Montenegro to Belgrade—a line which you can still draw today to mark quite distinct regions. To the west, which followed Rome, the Latin alphabet is used and the people are predominantly Catholic; to the east, Byzantine-controlled into the Middle Ages, the Christian faith is Orthodox (as in Greece) and the alphabet Cyrillic.

The disintegration of the Roman Empire in the fifth century corresponded with a series of raids into Yugoslavia by central European tribes: the **Barbarians**. Goths and Huns both penetrated the country, but most powerful and wide-ranging were the **Avars**, who for a time controlled lands as far as Constantinople (Istanbul), and the **Slavs**. The Slavs came originally from the Carpathian mountains, on the borders of what are now Romania and the Soviet Ukraine, from where they were driven by Avar—and Bulgar—raids. Unlike most of the other Barbarian tribes they had no real homeland to return to and settled with tenacity in Illyria-Yugoslavia. They had a particularly strong social structure, the *zadruga*—a system of extended families holding land and social responsibilities in common which survived Turkish occupation and could still be found in outlying areas until World War II—and they entered the Balkans in three highly individual groups. In the north settled the **Slovenes**; in the west, the **Croats**; and in the lands south of the Danube, the **Serbs**. These, along with a group of Romanized peasants known as **Vlachs**, who occupied the mountains around Kosovo and northern Macedonia, either absorbed or displaced the Illyrians throughout the country, only a small coastal strip retaining their former Latinized character.

THE REPUBLICS—AND TURKISH OCCUPATION

The three Slavic peoples—**Serbs**, **Croats** and **Slovenes**—originally shared a single common language, and, to an extent, an identity. Their distinct patterns of settlement, however, soon forged very different dialects, and the mountainous nature of their territories an isolated fragmentation. This, combined with the region's vulnerability, ensured their separate and highly individual development. At the beginning they were divided by the Catholic-Western and Orthodox-Byzantine spheres of influence, later as independent kingdoms and republics.

Perhaps the most unifying strand in medieval Yugoslav history—and indeed that of the Balkans as a whole—is the **Turkish Ottoman occupation**. Even this, however, affected the republics in very different ways and degrees. The Turks held longest sway over Macedonia, parts of Serbia, Bosnia-Hercegovina and the fiercely independent mountain vastness of Montenegro. But save for a brief period in the fifteenth and sixteenth centuries, Croatia, Slovenia and Dalmatia all remained Christian and European, under the rule of Austrians, Hungarians and, on the coast, Venetians. The unity, in fact, is more a result of the ending of Turkish rule than anything else. In 1877 the Turks were defeated by Russia, and under the **Congress of Berlin**, held the following year, Serbia and Montenegro gained independence, helping to increase the pressure towards some kind of Slav unity.

CROATIA

The Croats were the first Yugoslav people to form an independent political unit, throwing off their allegiance to the Byzantine Emperor in 924 with the creation of a **Croatian kingdom** and royal dynasty by one **Tomislav**. This continued, unbroken, for going on for two centuries, and Croatia developed into a well organized medieval state, extending for a time to control of the Dalmatian coast. In 1089, however, the dynasty's last king, Kresimir, died without a successor and control passed to the neighboring and related King Ladislas of Hungary.

Croatian history remained interwoven with that of **Hungary** for the next eight centuries, sharing its monarch, although being governed more or less autonomously by a *Ban* or Viceroy. It was a classic feudal state, the medieval Croatian nobles exercizing influence at the Hungarian court, and remained so well into the nineteenth century. Control, however, shifted slightly with the Turkish advance into Europe, which in the sixteenth century spread **Ottoman** power right across Croatia and into the Hungarian plains. But defeats at the siege of Vienna (1683) and again at the Battle of Zenta (1697) forced them into retreat, ceding Croatia-Slavonia to the Hapsburg Prince Eugene of Savoy under the Treaty of Karlwitz.

Hapsburg rule saw a return to power of the Croatian nobles, who played off the Austrians and Hungarians in their factional struggles, but little change for the enserfed mass of the people. The period was marked by a series of violent **peasant revolts**, forcefully put down. The most famous—which figures prominently in socialist accounts of Yugoslavia's history—was led by the legendary **Matija Gubec** in 1573. This, however, unlike the others, presented no great difficulty to Hapsburg power. Gubec being publicly executed along with some 6000 of his followers. It was only in 1848, with the revolutions in Austria-Hungary, that Croatian serfdom was finally abolished and an elementary bourgeois justice imposed.

After the defeat of Austria by Prussia in 1866, the Hapsburg Empire was transformed into a **dual monarchy**—Croatia and Slovenia remaining part of Hungary, and Dalmatia going to Austria. This allowed Croatia to regain something of its old autonomy, though its *Bans* were still appointed by Budapest, and, like Hapsburg Slovenia, it slowly became a focus for aspirations towards southern Slav unity.

DALMATIA

Although now part of Croatia, Dalmatia's development had been very different, and, through its tempting geographical position, perhaps more complex than any other part of Yugoslavia. It was the region most extensively settled by the Greeks and Romans, and has been conquered and controlled in turn by Byzantines, Hungarians, Slavs from Croatia, Serbia and Bosnia, and (in part) by the Turks. Its most important and long-standing influence, though, was **Venetian**. Dubrovnik—or *Ragusa*—was one of the wealthiest Venetian city states, generally independent but closely linked to the great maritime empire in both its politics and trade. And all along the Dalmatian coast there are cities stridently Venetian in their architecture, built on the proceeds of similar contact.

Venetian power emerged in the thirteenth century and lasted, somewhat shaky and decadent in its final stages, until subjugation to **Napoleonic France** in 1797. For Dalmatia, this at first meant stretches of the coast ceded to Austrian rule, but after Napoleon's subsequent defeat of Austria at Austerlitz, the region, along with Istria and parts of Croatia, was incorporated into a single French-governed region known rather fancifully as the **Illyrian Provinces**.

French occupation was brief—after Napoleon's defeat Dalmatia was reassigned to Austria and Croatia-Slovenia to Hungary—but the experiment with unity, and an accompanied improvement in the economy, was a powerful stimulus to the subsequent movements for Slav unification. So too was Austrian oppression, which held on to the feudal society that had underpinned the Venetians' commercial success and moved hard to counter Dalmatian political aspirations towards a united Croatia.

SLOVENIA

Slovenia has affinities with both Croatian and Dalmatian history, though in comparison it's unusually straightforward. The Slovenes failed to set up their own medieval state, the Turks never reached this far north, and from the eighth century until its incorporation into the Hapsburg Empire in the sixteenth century the region was ruled from **Germany**. Over the years there were various attempts to "Germanize" the people, but the Slovenes retained both their language and cultural identity. The former found fortuitous encouragement during the Protestant Reformation, the church authorities promoting its use to the point of printing the Old Testament in Slovene—and they too had the first Slavic grammar and dictionary.

Napoleon's occupation here was a favorable influence, with **Ljubljana** becoming capital of the "Illyrian Provinces," an event which contributed significantly to nineteenth-century struggles for unity.

BOSNIA-HERCEGOVINA

In its early development Bosnia-Hercegovina is again quite close to that of Croatia. A territory of the early medieval **Hungarian Empire**, it emerged as an **independent kingdom** towards the end of the twelfth century. Its founder, **King Kulin**, ruled from 1180 to 1204, an important period which saw the emergence of **Bogomilism**, whose ascetic—and heretic—"spiritually pure" lifestyle was adopted by the king and most of his nobles. Subject to hostility from both Catholic and Orthodox churches, the Bogomils were frequently persecuted from across the borders, and even subjected to a Hungarian-led crusade. The sect survived, however, and medieval Bosnia rose to considerable power in the last half of the four-teenth century under the expansionist King **Stefan Tvrtko**. At his death in 1391 the king-dom included large parts of Serbia and Dalmatia—though much of this was in reality semi-autonomous, controlled from a series of isolated mountain castles by one of the Middle Ages' most ruthless and exploitive feudal nobles.

This feudal savagery had unusual, if not perhaps surprising, effects with the **Turkish invasions** of the fifteenth century. Confronted by a religion which decreed that no believer should be enslaved to another, and (in theory at least) that no man should own more land than he can farm, thousands of Christian Bosnian peasants converted to **Islam**. So too, for equally pragmatic reasons, did much of the Bogomil nobility, who were offered freedom of worship for (nominally) considering themselves Muslim "Begs" or *Beys*. To begin with, this seems to have marked a general improvement in conditions, Ottoman rule being conservative and sometimes severe, but by contemporary standards fairly just. With the decay of the Ottoman Empire in the eighteenth and nine-teenth centuries, however, the Bosnian ruling elite drifted back towards the corruption and tyranny of their Bogomil predecessors, and a particularly harsh tax collection system (imposed as in Serbia by the *Janissaries*) provoked a number of **Peasants' Revolts**. The most serious of these broke out in Hercegovina in 1874, spreading to Bosnia the following year, and its effects (and the conditions which had produced it) gained a certain notoriety in "liberal" European circles. From the end of the nineteenth century, the **"Bosnian Question"** began to figure in Central European power poli-tics. **Austria-Hungary** was given the right to administer the region—first through a neutral-ity pact with Russia, later, after Turkish defeat, under the Congress of Berlin. Conditions began to improve, with industry and mineral exploita-tion dragging the lands into the modern age, though the feudal land system remained virtu-ally intact in the countryside. It was to be in the Bosnian capital, **Sarajevo**, that Slav national-ism finally burst on to the European stage—culminating, with the assistance of the assassi-nation of Archduke Franz Ferdinand, in World War I.

SERBIA

By far the greatest of the medieval kingdom-republics, Serbia emerged as an independent power at much the same time as Bosnia-Hercegovina. For five centuries after their arri-val, the Slavs of Serbia had been engaged in factional struggle between rival tribes—each led by a *Župan*, or chieftain,—and had seen considerable threats of absorption, initially by the Bulgars, later as part of the Orthodox Byzantine Empire. At the end of the twelfth century, however, these pressures had receded, and a dominant *Župan* family emerged. This was the **Nemanjić dynasty** founded in eastern Serbia by **Stefan Nemanja**—a towering figure in Serbian history, who gathered about him a court as sophisticated as any in contemporary Europe and extended Serbian control over Montenegro and parts of what is now Albania.

The dynasty lasted over two centuries—a "Golden Age" which plays a vital part in Serbian national consciousness, and which forged the Serbs' strongest links with the Orthodox church. Stefan himself went into retirement at a monastery and his son, the monk **Saint Sava**, established in 1219 the **Serbian Orthodox Church**. It was above all this religious identity which characterized the Serbs, and which survived the fall of the secu-lar state after the death of the last great Serbian king **Stefan Dušan** (1331–55), in whose time Serbia was the most powerful nation in the Balkans. Prior to Stefan's death, and the sudden Turkish advances, Serbia had spread to occupation of Macedonia, all of Bulgaria and the greater part of northern Greece. In 1355 the Serbian armies stood at the gates of Salonica, poised to extend to the east and perhaps Constantinople itself. Nothing, however, came of this, as under Stefan's successors Serbia went into rapid and drastic decline. By 1389 **Lazar**, the last Serbian prince, was grouping the nation's forces for a last counter-attack and show of resistance to the Turks at the **Battle of Kosovo**. The result of this battle, in which he and most of the Serbian nobility were killed, was decisive. A few of the northern Serbian territories contin-ued under isolated Christian rule, but in 1459 the last of these fell to Ottoman control—a state in which they were to remain for the next four centuries.

In keeping with Islamic tradition, the **Ottoman**-conquered lands were held to belong to God—which in practice meant the Sultan, his earthly designate—and were allocated to Muslim knights. Some of the Serbian Slavs converted, avoiding subjugation as serfs or *rayah*, but most did not and in the early years at least were not persecuted for their religion beyond the normal demands of feudal society. There was, however, heavy Serbian emigration—one of the most enduring effects of Turkish occupation—and Serbian communities were established in Dalmatia, Montenegro, Slovenia, Bosnia, and across the Danube in the then Hungarian-controlled lands of the Vojvodina.

It was the seventeenth century which really signified the beginning of Ottoman decadence—in Serbia and throughout much of the Empire—and a particular resentment which surfaced was the growing recruitment and power of the **Janissaries**. These were Muslim converts, taken forcibly as children from Christian families and trained into crack regiments of troops. At first they were simply an instrument of the Sultan's military will, but in time they became a self-perpetuating elite, protecting their own position with unsurpassed savagery and exploiting the local peasantry through traditional feudal taxation. In opposition to them—and to the *Spajis*, Turkish cavalry units who played a similar role—there slowly emerged groups of Serbian rebel bands. These, known as the **Hajduks**, had existed as early as the fifteenth century, but in the later years of Ottoman rule they grew in force, conducting significant guerrilla campaigns from mountain and forest strongholds. As in Greece, where similar bands of *Klephts* harried the Turkish administrators, it was many years before they gathered into any kind of unity and national opposition to Ottoman rule, and when they did, in the **National Revolt** of 1804, they were at first easily put down.

The National Revolt, however, led by a former pig-farmer called **Petar Karadjordje** ("Black George"), took root among the Serbs and found support among their Russian Orthodox co-religionists. The revolt broke out into a full scale **War of Independence**, and Belgrade, Smederevo and other northern Serbian towns fell under Hajduk authority. Things were halted only by the wider events of

European politics, Napoleon's invasion of Russia leading to the withdrawal of their troops in eastern Europe and leaving the Ottomans a free hand to crush remaining Serbian resistance. Karadjordje was forced to flee across the Danube, and re-occupation savagely enforced.

MONTENEGRO

A part of the medieval **Serbian Empire**, Montenegro managed to carve out its own identity after the Serbian defeat at Kosovo, and in the face of the Turkish conquest. Because of the mountainous nature of its terrain, the Turks here were unable to gain full control, and the rebels waged a ceaseless guerrilla campaign throughout the last years of the fourteenth century and for most of the fifteenth. Towards the end of this period **Ivan Crnojević**, a Montenegrin Hajduk leader, welded together the anti-Turkish tribes to form a small **independent principality** with a capital at Cetinje—a territory which was ruled after his death by a series of Bishop-Kings. Of these, the most culturally distinguished was **Petar Petrović Njegoš II** (1830–50), a legendary fighter and a fine poet, whose *Gorski Vijenac* ("Mountain Wealth") is one of the great epic works of Yugoslav literature.

The collapse of the Turks, and the 1878 **Congress of Berlin**, gave Montenegro vital access to the coast and official recognition of its independent **sovereignty**. In the years before the Balkan Wars it was perhaps the most peaceable of all the Yugoslav territories, even experimenting with parliamentary democracy for a short period. Economically, however, it has always been one of the poorest Slavic regions and throughout the nineteenth century saw substantial emigration—particularly to North America.

MACEDONIA

Macedonia's history—which has spawned one of the most complex political problems of all the republics—was until this century largely a question of two Imperial occupations, first under the **Byzantines** (who controlled the area, sporadically, from the sixth to the fourteenth century), then under the **Ottoman Turks**, who remained here longer than in any other part of modern Yugoslavia, leaving only after the Balkan Wars of 1912–13.

Within these periods, the region also saw a brief phase of **Bulgar** rule—under **King Samuel** at the end of the tenth century—and a longer one as part of **Stefan Dušán**'s **Serbian Empire**. On these two turns of history, and on the Greeks' ancient links with the region under Philip of Macedon (and emotional links as part of Byzantium), rest the modern claims to the area, asserted by all three nations after the Ottomans had finally been driven out. To this confusion, with its various terrorist factions of the late nineteenth century, must be added the last century's rivalry between **Austria** and **Russia**, each of whom had vital trade routes and sea access through the region. It was as much through conflicting and insoluble ambitions that Macedonia remained under official Turkish control for so long, the Great Powers being unable to come to any deal with each other at the 1878 Congress of Berlin, and **Ottoman rule** being extended, for three more decades, by default.

THE BALKAN AND FIRST WORLD WARS

The various strands of the Slavic kingdoms and republics begin to gradually interweave towards the end of the nineteenth century, and with the Russian defeat of the Ottomans and the momentous **Congress of Berlin** in 1878, they started to take shape as a nation of South Slav peoples. As outlined above, the Berlin treaty recognized the sovereignty of Montenegro, and it also gave formal independence to the by now well-established **Serbian kingdom**, with whom the Montenegrins were moving towards permanent union. Southern Slav tensions inevitably were to focus on **Macedonia**, with its continued Ottoman presence, and under the inspiration of King Peter I of Serbia, a League for the Liberation of the Balkans from Turkey was formed, with the unique co-operation of Bulgaria and Greece with Serbia-Montenegro. The result, in 1912, was the short and successful **First Balkan War**, forcing the Turks to concede to Serbia both Macedonia and the Albanian-dominated region of Kosovo. Rather than consolidating their gains to the east, however, where Greece and Bulgaria both laid claims to parts of Thrace (and Greece to Constantinople), the allies fell out over control of Macedonia, Bulgaria eventually attacking both Greece and Serbia for sole

possession of the Macedonian territories. This was the **Second Balkan War**, which ended within a single year—in 1913—with the entry of Romania on the side of Greece, Serbia and Montenegro. Its result was a patched-up adjustment of frontiers at the **Treaty of Bucharest**, unsatisfactory to all sides, and not least to the divided Slavs of Macedonia. Serbia, though, came out a significantly consolidated Slav state, acquiring western Macedonia and the greater parts of lakes Ohrid and Prespa. It was a triumph of a sort, and a spur to Slav nationalism in the north, where Austria-Hungary continued to hold power.

The position in the north, and on the coast, was again complex and fragmentary, but pan-Slav ideas and pressures were developing at a similar pace. In **Croatia**, which was under Hungarian jurisdiction, and **Slovenia**, under the Austrians, nationalists were divided between those who favored an "ethnically pure" Croat state—precursors of the Croatian Fascists of World War II—and the dominant advocates of unity with the south. This culminated in 1905 with the majority of the Croatian and Serbian political parties forming a Croat-Serbian Alliance. They were joined in their agitation by the Dalmatian delegates to the Austrian parliament, all of whom favored Slav union.

As ever, things were more complicated in **Bosnia-Hercegovina**, part of the old Ottoman Empire but governed since the Congress of Berlin by Austria and formally annexed by it in 1908. Discontent, after this, became increasingly vociferous and Bosnian pan-Slavic movements mirrored similar activity elsewhere around the principle of union with Serbia. Austria, however, was determined to maintain its territories and began putting pressure on Serbia in order to crush the potential of—and aspirations towards—a pan-Slav state. On June 28, 1914, the **assassination in Sarajevo** of Archduke Franz Ferdinand, heir to the thrones of Austria and Hungary, gave them the excuse they had wanted. Although the Serbian government was unconnected with the incident (the assassin was a member of the "Young Bosnian" nationalist movement—see p.263), Austria issued it with an impossible and uncompromising ultimatum, and in July invaded. From the convolutions of Bosnian nationalism, **World War I** had begun.

The Serbian armies proved greater opposition than Austria had envisioned, forcing back the original offensive. But it was an unequal struggle and the Serbs' part in the war consisted mainly in helping to uphold the Salonica front. Away from the fighting the South Slav movement had its focus in the **Yugoslav Committee**, based first in Paris and later in London. Comprised mainly of nationalist politicians from Croatia and Serbia, the Committee ceaselessly lobbied the Allied Forces for the inclusion of a united South Slavic state in any peace settlement. These hopes seemed initially dashed when, by the secret Treaty of London in 1915, Italy was persuaded to join the war on the Allied side in return for a substantial slice of the Adriatic, including Istria and Trieste. In the end, however, the American president, Woodrow Wilson, came out in favor of independence for the Austro-Hungarian minorities. And so it was, that on December 1, 1918, the **Kingdom of Serbs, Croats and Slovenes** came into existence, its territories uniting those named republics along with **Montenegro** and **Bosnia-Hercegovina**.

SERBIAN MONARCHY AND WORLD WAR II

The new Slav state—renamed **Yugoslavia** in 1928—was faced with as many problems as it had solved. It came into existence, under western supervision, as a monarchy, headed by the Serbian prince **Alexander Karadjordje**, and was subject from the beginning to claims of Serbian domination. These in fact had good basis. The Serbs favored a centralized state, and pressed hard towards this end when a coalition of the parties met to promulgate a constitution in 1921. Opposition came, above all, from Croatia, and from Stjepan Radič's **Croat Peasant Party**, which refused to vote on any proposals and withdrew to Zagreb. The constitution as a result was even more centralist than it might have been, and in its eight years of existence was constantly dogged by Croatian attempts to make it unworkable and have it overthrown.

Things came to an initial head when in 1928 Radič was assassinated by a Montenegrin with Serbian political sympathies. The following January King Alexander dissolved parliament and imposed a **Royal Dictatorship**. This was a disaster. Nothing was done to bring Croatians

into any positions of power, and significant numbers of them joined a new, underground nationalist organization—the proto-Fascist **Ustaše** led by a lawyer called **Ante Pavelič**. The Ustaše in 1934 assassinated King Alexander, who was succeeded on the throne by his son Prince Peter, at the time just ten years old. Authority passed to a regent—King Alexander's brother, **Prince Paul**—whose regime merely escalated anti-separatist repression.

These years, however, also saw the emergence of a new force in Yugoslav politics, the **Communist Party**, which had the potential, at least, to cross regionalist divides. Established in 1920 on a wide base of revolutionary elements within the peasantry, and to an extent among the developing industrial working class, the Party had won a considerable number of seats in the early municipal elections, gaining control in both Serbian Belgrade and Croatian Zagreb. However, a short time before entering parliament they found themselves, along with all communist organizations and trade unions, proscribed by the national government. Driven underground, they regrouped, and worked to establish closer links with the Soviet Union. **Josip Broz** or **Tito**, who had worked in Moscow with the Third International on his release from Yugoslav imprisonment, was the motivating force, and was in 1937 elected General Secretary of the Party.

The royalist government meanwhile had veered between alliance with its central European neighbors—forming the "Little Entente" with Romania and Czechoslovakia—and increasing involvement with Nazi Germany, whom it saw as protection against the "Bolshevik threat."

When **World War II** broke out, Yugoslavia initially proclaimed itself neutral, but by 1941 Prince Paul was formally aligning his government with the Italian-German Axis pact. It was a move which sparked immediate rebellion—Communist-supported but led primarily by Air Force officers who arrested the regent and put a young **Prince Peter** on the throne. Hitler's reaction was to bomb Belgrade—on April 6, 1941—and to send his armies, with those of Mussolini's Italy, across the borders.

The Yugoslav forces opposed the **Axis invasion** but with little chance or hope of success. Within eleven days they had capitulated and once again the country was occupied and partitioned by foreign powers. **Germany** annexed most of Slovenia; **Italy** took Montenegro and the Adriatic coast; **Bulgaria** moved into much of Macedonia. In Croatia and Bosnia-Hercegovina, which with Serbia were allowed to remain individual puppet states, the Germans placed in power Ante Pavelič and the **Ustaše Fascists**: here, in a region which included two million Serbs, some of the worst persecution of the war was set in motion— Pavelič at its conclusion having slaughtered over 600,000 of their number.

RESISTANCE: THE PARTISANS AND CETNIKS

Resistance groups were at first splintered among the country's various regions and political groups but within a few months two organizations stood out. These were the **Cetniks**— pro-Serb, anti-communists led by Colonel **Draža Mihailovič** and supported by King Peter's "government in exile" in London—and the Communist **Partisans**, led by **Tito**. The Četniks' sporadic resistance soon ended in the face of savage German reprisals, and effective resistance passed to the Partisans. While Mihailovič's inactivity quickly led to accommodation, and often collaboration, with the Germans, Tito called for an all-out struggle regardless of the consequences. Despite horrific reprisals Tito's policy proved far more effective, with the result that many non-communists joined the Partisans. Mihailovič, who himself was probably never guilty of collaboration, met with Tito on several occasions in 1941 but rejected all offers of joint resistance. It was a tragic decision, which almost inevitably precipitated fighting between the rival organizations: this broke out in November 1941 and a Četnik-Partisan **Civil War** was to last, in varying degrees, until the country's liberation in October 1944.

Through 1942–3 Tito's Partisans constantly engaged the occupying forces. Twice they came close to annihilation—the first time being forced by the Germans to retreat from Croatia into the mountains of Bosnia and Montenegro, the second undertaking a legendary retreat, carrying their wounded across the Sutjeska valley—but these events only served to increase their national popularity and standing, attracting many to their ranks. In the areas

that were liberated from effective Axis control they had the support and authority to set up a local *de facto* form of government—the **AVNOJ** (Antifascist Council of the National Liberation of Yugoslavia), which was in effect a direct challenge to that of King Peter, still exiled in London.

In September 1943, a full-scale British military mission led by Brigadier **Fitzroy Maclean** was attached to Tito's HQ. With so many German divisons being tied up in Yugoslavia, the Allies had to decide which resistance group to support: Maclean concluded that the Partisans were the only group worthy of help and as a result of the Tehran Conference the Allies withdrew all support from Mihailovič and began to provide material aid to Tito. This established, the Partisans moved towards power, eluding a last German attempt to liquidate Tito at his island headquaters of Vis, and as 1944 progressed playing a major part in forcing an Axis retreat from the central Balkans. With an eye to the future Tito met secretly with Churchill, and later concluded an agreement with the Russians, inviting Soviet troops onto Yugoslav territory to take part in the **liberation**. This came about within months. On October 22, 1944, Partisan troops, together with Red Army units, entered Belgrade, and by the following spring Tito's Communists were in political and military control of the whole country—its territories much the same as before the war.

Even by the standards of Central Europe it had been an incredibly bitter and costly struggle. An estimated 1,700,000 Yugoslavs— nearly a tenth of the country's population—had been killed.

TITO'S YUGOSLAVIA

During the last months of the liberation, King Peter's emigré government had reached agreement with Tito, recognizing his temporary authority as leader. Towards the end of 1945, however, the country moved towards democratic **elections**, hurriedly arranged in order to give the Communists maximum advantage. Most of the country's political parties were encouraged to join the People's Front, an organization dominated by the Communist Party. Those that declined were effectively prevented from campaigning. Although the ballot was nominally secret, those wishing to vote against the Popular Front had to push their ballot papers into a separate box—sufficiently intimidating to ensure that most people didn't take the risk. Faced with these conditions, any remaining royalist members of the provisional government soon resigned. However, such was the need for a strong and united government capable of rebuilding Yugoslavia's shattered economy, most of these irregularities went unnoticed by the international community. Packed with the Communists and their supporters, the National Assembly voted unanimously to declare Yugoslavia a republic on November 29, 1945. The king stayed in exile, and his remaining ally inside the country, Mihailović, was eventually captured and executed. A new Soviet-inspired constitution was adopted, creating a federation of six national republics—the rigid discipline of the Communist Party holding the whole structure together.

Before long, large estates were confiscated, currency reform destroyed the financial base of the bourgeoisie and a Five Year Plan with the emphasis on heavy industry was instituted. To finance the plan, Yugoslavia's economy was closely linked with the **Cominform**, the Soviet-controlled organization of European Communist countries. However, in June 1948 Yugoslavia's links with the Soviet Union were drastically severed: Tito refused to bow to Soviet pressure over several major ideological issues and began to develop his own line in foreign policy. Yugoslavia was expelled from the Cominform and the Soviets made an unsuccessful appeal to Yugoslav party members to overthrow Tito. A period of acute tension between the two countries followed, with the threat of Soviet invasion very real, yet Yugoslavia refused to respond to provocation—which included shelling of Yugoslav positions from Albania and Bulgaria—the country under Tito beginning the process of evolving its own form of socialism.

Stalin's economic blockade, coupled with a string of bad harvests brought about by bungled attempts at collectivization, led Yugoslavia to the brink of economic collapse. A drastic rethink was needed, and a rigorous critique of Stalinism in the next two years led to a communism based on Yugoslavia's specific needs. The party itself was renamed the League of Communists, as if to suggest that it would play a less overbearing, more informal role in future. The ever-present nationalist question was dealt with by a loosening up of the **federal system**,

whereby each republic enjoyed autonomy in its own affairs. This autonomy was tempered by the guiding role of the party and—increasingly—by Tito's own personal authority, but it was far more substantial than anything inside the Soviet bloc. Another major innovation was the introduction of the **self-management system** based on workers' councils in factories and producers' councils in schools, hotels, and the like, controlled not by the state but by the people who work in them—on the positive side this means diversification and a degree of competition; on the negative side it can lead to inefficiency and wasteful duplication. Nowadays self-management is increasingly seen as a hindrance to effective economic reform, and, with more power being given to industrial managers, it seems to be slowly on the way out.

With the reforms of the 1950s Yugoslavia developed into the most liberal of all the established Communist states. Its innovations on the domestic front were mirrored in international relations with Tito championing the nonaligned movement worldwide. Treading a delicate line between the superpowers gained Yugoslavia international credibility far in excess of its size or power.

Internal politics didn't always run so smoothly. The immediate aftermath of the Tito/Stalin split was characterized by a wave of arrests of so-called **Cominformists**, who were carted off to endure years of harsh treatment on the infamous Goli Otok or "Bare Island." In the 1950s things eased up, and the security forces were in fact used to rein in those who were beginning to take the new liberalism too far. Federal vice-president and wartime leader **Milovan Djilas** was thrown out of the party in 1954 for suggesting that the renunciation of Stalinism ought to be followed by a gradual abdication of the entire Communist bureaucracy. He remained Yugoslavia's most notorious dissident—whenever Tito felt the need to improve relations with the USSR, he packed Djilas off to jail as a sign of Yugoslavia's continuing Communist orthodoxy.

In the 1960s, the quickening pace of economic liberalization created a rift between the conservative Communists and their more reform-minded colleagues. Tito initially sided with the reformists, purging another of his former wartime comrades, Aleksandar

Ranković, the feared head of the secret police, on the charge that he had filled the President's office with bugging devices. Yugoslavs were generally pleased to see Ranković go, but the democratization expected to result from his fall never really got under way—petering out instead in a morass of inter-republican disputes. The phenomenal economic growth of the 1960s had created tensions within the federation: the highly developed northern republics of Slovenia and Croatia wanted to reinvest their new-found wealth free from the interference of central government, and produced a new generation of nationally-orientated politicians capable of arguing their case. By 1971, in Croatia, this had mushroomed into a mass movement campaigning for greater autonomy, and, fearing disintegration of the federation, Belgrade opted for a crackdown. Another purge followed a year later, this time getting rid of a dangerously independent Serbian leadership. Everywhere republican leaders were replaced by more pliant, mediocre men, who could be trusted not to rock the boat, and calls for farther democratization were discouraged.

The remainder of the 1970s were years of stability, but also of great stagnation. A new constitution in 1974 helped solve a few of Yugoslavia's nationality problems by giving the republics more control over internal affairs and the two provinces of Vojvodina and Kosovo more autonomy. But this only stored up trouble for the future, Yugoslavia's federal units emerging in the early 1980s as eight warring mini-bureaucracies, with little common will to fight the growing economic and political crisis.

YUGOSLAVIA AFTER TITO

Yugoslavia's success in moving away from the Soviet model and achieving a semblance of balance between its various nationalities had a great deal to do with the personal authority and charisma of **Tito**. When he died in 1980 many observers predicted the imminent collapse of the system. This didn't happen: before his death Tito laid down plans for a power-sharing leadership that would, politically at least, ensure the survival of the federation, and prevent, as he put it, the emergence of a Stalin after his Lenin. A new collective presidency was introduced, chairmanship passing yearly from republic to republic. Yugoslavia's new leaders (for the most part anonymous time-servers who had been the ageing president's yes-men) were, however, soon overtaken by a host of intractable economic problems—high unemployment, a massive foreign debt, and an inflation rate which currently stands at some 2000 percent. Their failure to find any **solutions** soon revealed the weaknesses of the system Tito had bequeathed. Economic reforms aimed at making Yugoslav industry more competitive were sabotaged by conservatives in the party bureaucracy, who feared an erosion of workers' rights, or even worse, a return to capitalism. And provincial power barons everywhere abused the autonomy given to them by Yugoslavia's decentralized system to protect local industry against central government's efficiency drives.

Economic differences soon translated themselves into regional disputes, with different republics pursuing their own interests regardless of central government. Yugoslavia's north-south divide has proved particularly damaging: the more developed northern republics stand to gain from the introduction of a more competitive, market economy, while the more backward south fears that its state-subsidized industries will be decimated by any such shakeup. Many Croats and Slovenes increasingly resent channelling funds southwards to (they claim) prop up the less-developed areas—a resentment that feeds a much more ominous, separatist sentiment. In these conditions, faith in communism has dwindled: membership of the League has rapidly declined, the standing of its leaders has been tarnished by a series of corruption scandals, and republican communist organizations are increasingly appealing to nationalist feeling in an attempt to bolster their flagging popularity.

THE POLITICAL PRESENT

All of these developments have been thrown into stark relief by the problem of **Kosovo**, where the Albanian majority have long demanded full republic status. In 1981 their demands boiled over into full-bloodied riots which were suppressed only after tanks moved in. The Albanians have a strong case for full status, but the authorities cannot grant it for fear the new republic will take advantage of the constitution which allows republics to cede from the federation. The army's tanks only served to mute the unrest, driving it underground for a few years with the heavy hand of the secret police, and 1988 and 1989 saw a dramatic worsening in relations between Serbs and ethnic Albanians in the province, with more riots, strikes and protests.

Long-standing differences were exacerbated by the rise of **Slobodan Milošević**, leader of the Serbian Party, whose dynamic personality and uncompromising political views rocketed him from comparative obscurity to the position of president of the Serbian Republic. Milošević, whose speeches have become increasingly anti-Albanian, argues that Serbia contains forty percent of the country's population and a third of its land, yet in the federation of republics that constitutes Yugoslavia, is only one voice among eight—including two autonomous provinces. During 1989, his speeches stirred up nationalist sentiment all over Serbia, playing on the notion of the Serbian Golden Age and culminating in June with a celebration of the six hundredth anniversary of the Battle of Kosovo on Kosovo Polje that was attended by at least half a million people.

Milošević's popularity in championing the cause of the minority Serbs in Kosovo, combined with a hard-line approach to any minor civil disturbance by Albanians, led to an underground **hunger strike** by 1300 miners at the Trepča zinc mine near Priština in February 1989. After occupying the mine for eight days, the miners gave up their strike when several prominent Kosovo Communist Party officials were removed from office. In the meantime, the Yugoslav president had sent in a large number of troops, realizing that if any of the miners died (and many were close), Kosovo could well have seen a full-blooded rebellion.

The following weeks saw an unprecedented backlash against the Albanian community throughout the whole of Serbia. Massive **demonstrations**, often led by students, took place in Belgrade, and Novi Sad, capital of Serbia's other autonomous province, the Vojvodina, had the largest demonstration in its history. Milošević-inspired demonstrations also focused dissatisfaction with the worsening economic situation, dislodging the party leaderships in the Vojvodina and Montenegro. On February 23 the Serbian government passed amendments to the constitution effectively **removing Kosovo's autonomy**: Serbia gained

control over the police, courts and civil defense, and moved 100 tanks and 15,000 troops into the region to underline its control. **Riots** broke out in Uroševac, the police stormed the university at Priština and surrounded the Kosovo national assembly. A few days later the inevitable happened and demonstrations by ethnic Albanians turned into pitched battles with the police: two senior police officials were killed (one an ethnic Albanian, the other a Serb), and, officially, 29 other people were shot dead by police, though the true figures may be much higher. From that date, Kosovo has effectively been under Serbian army occupation, and though the atmosphere has calmed, it seems likely that it could flare up again at any moment.

The Kosovo question has crucial implications for the Yugoslav federation. With the hugely popular Milošević apparently pursuing the formation of a Greater Serbia, in direct opposition to the tenets of Titoism, the outlook for the country is bleak. Party officials in Croatia, Serbia's old enemy, were quick to voice support for draconian anti-Albanian measures, but the feeling on the streets of Zagreb is of support for the ethnic community against what is seen as Serbian bullying: the Croat Communist Party newspaper, *Vjesnik*, even likened Milošević's recently-published memoirs to *Mein Kampf*. Meanwhile Montenegro and Macedonia bear the brunt of the country's increasingly dire economic situation, while the richer republic of Slovenia seems to be steadily turning its back on the rest of the country, looking economically, culturally and touristically to the north.

It does seem as if the old guard is on the way out, in spite of Milošević, and that most people think the only long-term economic solution is to shake up the country's inefficient and often corrupt system. There has lately been talk of joining EFTA, perhaps even later the EEC, and the current federal government under Ante Marković is keen to pursue liberalizing economic measures—and pluralistic political solutions. The republics of Croatia and Slovenia recently voted to hold free elections, probably with non-Communist candidates standing, in mid-1990. However, this is likely to be resisted by Serbia and the southern republics, and the austere emergency economic solutions that will have to be imposed in order to stem the country's rampant inflation (and to gain support from the IMF) are likely to prove deeply unpopular in the country as a whole. For the moment, the future of Tito's great ideal of unification, and indeed of Yugoslav Communism itself, now seems fractured and deeply uncertain. As a Croatian journalist wrote, "We have had two beautiful dreams imposed upon us, Communism and Yugoslavia. Perhaps even one of them would have been too much."

ARCHITECTURAL CHRONOLOGY

6000BC	Earliest settlements along the Danube.	Archaic village of **Lepenski Vir**—discovered in 1965—oldest known Neolithic settlement in Europe.
12th C BC	Illyrian and Thracian tribes inhabit the Balkans.	
8th–6th C BC	Coast colonized by Greek trading ports.	Few existing remains: small finds, jewelry and artifacts.
4th C	Greek cities spring up along trade routes.	**Stobi** and **Heraclea** founded in 350 by Philip II of Macedonia. Trogir's *Relief of Karos* shows Hellenistic decorative style.
229 BC	**Roman conquest** of Balkan and Illyrian tribes begins.	**Pula's amphitheater** built in grand Imperial style—rich arcading and decoration. **Salona** (Solin) typical of early Roman towns.
AD 285	Diocletian divides his empire into east and west.	**Diocletian's Palace** at Split: monumental and lavish complex of temples, apartments and garrison built as retirement home for the emperor. **Heraclea** shows the zenith of Roman art: mosaics on early Christian themes combined with Hellenic styles.
6th–7th C	**Slav migration**. Slav culture established in the Balkans. First influence of Christianity through missionary teaching.	Slav tribes raid and destroy Roman towns and establish their own settlements. The **Basilica of Bishop Euphrasius** in Poreč is the finest early Christian building on the coast—elaborate mosaics.
9th C	Cyril and Methodius initiate conversion of Serbs to Eastern (Orthodox) church in Macedonia. Cultural influence of **Byzantium** spreads. **Serbian state** founded in defiance against Byzantine expansionism.	Earliest Byzantine churches at Cyril and Methodius' base, Ohrid, later destroyed by Turks. In **Zadar**, **Sv Donat** has elements of Byzantine and Carolingian style.
10th–11th C	Ohrid becomes center of early Christianity and Byzantine influence.	Ohrid's **Sv Sophia** (1040)—has rich representational frescoes—the first two-dimensional religious art of the Christian era in the Balkans. **Sv Panteleimon** (1164) at Nerezi perfects the Byzantine fresco style.
Late 12th C	**Nemanja Dynasty**	**Studenica** (1209) is the first great monastery church of the Raška style. Following the fall of Constantinople the greatest fresco artists of the period leave the city and work on the Raška churches, producing the highly decorated monasteries of **Sopoćani** (1265) and **Mileševa** (1234).
13th C	Serbian Patriarchate established at Peć.	Building of churches at Peć begins; **Church of the Apostles** completed c. 1250. The monastery churches of Gračanica (1314), Staro Nagoričane (1318)

13th– 14th C	Golden era of Serbian state. Domestic architecture flourishes under Serbian kings.	**Stecci**, Bogomil memorial stones, scattered over Bosnia-Hercegovina. Main concentration at Radimlja near Mostar.
1389	Battle of Kosovo: beginning of Turkish hegemony in Balkans.	Spread of **Ottoman Empire** into Balkans brings Turkish-style architecture. Serbs are pushed north, the Morava valley becoming the final site of monastery building, **Manasija** (1418) and **Kalenić** (1413) strongly defended against Turkish attack. Serbian lords build castles in defensive positions at **Smederovo** (1430) and elsewhere.
1420	**Venice** occupies the coast.	**Romanesque architecture** includes the cathedrals of **Rab** and **Zadar**. **Venetian-Gothic** buildings spread down the coast: the cathedrals of **Split** and **Trogir**; countless **campanili**.
Mid 16th C	**Dubrovnik** achieves *de facto* independence as a city-state.	Italian architects (such as Michelozzi) employed to build Dubrovnik's palaces and churches: they work with local architects, notably Jurai Dalmatinac, who also designed **Šibenik cathedral** (begun 1413) and **Pag's old center**.
16th– 17th C	**Turkish presence** in Bosnia-Hercegovina strengthens.	**Gazi Husref Beg mosque** in Sarajevo (1531). Bridges at **Višegrad** and **Mostar** are good examples of Turkish architecture.
1690	Serb migration into the Vojvodina	**Vrdnik** and **Krušedol** are among several Baroque-Byzantine monastery churches founded by migrant Serbs in the Fruška Gora.
1697	Prince Eugene of Savoy liberates parts of the north from the Turks; they become part of his **Hapsburg Empire**.	The great fortresses of **Kalemegdan** and **Petrovaradin** are built to protect Austria from Turkish threat.
18th C	Continuous skirmishes between Turks and Serbs. Further movement of Serbs north.	The Italian Francesco Robba designs Baroque churches and monuments in Ljubljana. His pupils are responsible for highly ornate buildings throughout Slovenia.
1877	End of Turkish hegemony: **Austria-Hungary** takes control of **Slovenia**, **Bosnia**, the north of **Croatia** and **Serbia**.	Austrian-style town houses built; civic architecture follows Classical or pseudo-Moorish themes. New road and rail systems open up the country.
1920	Establishment of monarchist Yugoslav state.	
1945	Liberation from occupying Fascist forces; beginning of the Socialist Federation of Yugoslavia, led by Tito.	Repair to damage caused by Allied and Axis bombing; postwar housing shortage met by rapid building of high-rise blocks. Spate of monumental memorials to the war of liberation.
1963	Earthquake in Skopje	Much of modern town destroyed. International style designs used for new center include rail station, arts center and post office.
1980	Death of Tito.	
1985– 1989	Worsening of the economic crisis; ethnic tensions in the country as a whole deepen.	The resumption of the construction of the **Shrine of Sv Sava** in Belgrade, scheduled for completion in 1992.

SERBIAN MONASTERIES AND THEIR FRESCOES

This is intended as a brief background to Eastern Orthodoxy, its architecture, frescoes and the styles of medieval Serbian church building. Throughout, Serbia refers to at least the area of the present-day republic: more often than not, it includes today's Macedonia and sometimes the greater part of the Balkans themselves. Dates after churches refer to the completion of the frescoes; completion of the church could have been anything up to a decade earlier.

BACKGROUND AND BEGINNINGS

Built by the medieval kings of the Nemanjić dynasty, which flourished from the late twelfth century until the early 1400s, and richly decorated with frescoes, Serbia's monastic churches represent some of the finest achievements of the Byzantine era. First and most astute of the Serbian monarchs was **Stefan Nemanja** who, through a series of pacts and cunning alliances, broke free from the sway of the Byzantium in 1190 and forged an independent Serbian state, initiating an age which Serbs, even today, look back on with pride. It was, apparently, a civilized time: one story goes that when initialling a treaty with the Holy Roman emperor, Frederick Barbarossa, Nemanja signed himself with a rich, flowing hand while the emperor could only manage an oafish thumbprint; and the explosion of Christian creativity that accompanied it has been compared to the Italian Renaissance. Serbia developed a sophisticated oral literature and a national art and architecture, its monarchs producing a spate of small but richly decorated churches to house their bones for posterity. The peripatetic nature of the Serbian court led to a broad scattering of these monuments, and deliberately isolated monastic churches perch in supremely remote spots all over the east of the country. When the Turks

arrived in the fifteenth century, they either demolished them or converted them to mosques, covering the frescoes with plaster. Few survived intact, and it was only this century that the churches were restored, the plaster chipped off their frescoes and the buildings once again turned over to monastic communities.

Serbia took its Christianity—**Eastern Orthodoxy**—from Constantinople: only the Orthodox church could offer the Serbs a Patriarchate of their own, and anyway the country's ties with the East had always been stronger. The contemplative nature of Orthodox Christianity has always been important, shaping a monasticism more concerned with "communion with God" than the pastoral nature of western monastic orders. Prayer and meditation could be undertaken either solitarily—which led to the ascetic leanings of Orthodox monks—or communally, in a meditative monastic order. Center of Orthodox monasticism is the Athos peninsula in northern Greece, where a number of monasteries make up an autonomous republic. The early Serbian rulers looked to here for inspiration and enlightenment, often retiring in old age to *Chilandar*—the Serbian Orthodox monastery on Athos which still exists today.

Orthodox **churches** differ from those in the West in a number of ways. Nave and choir are replaced by a centralized circular or square plan, frequently domed (an intimation of Heaven) following the inspiration of the emperor Justinian's cathedral of St Sophia in Constantinople. There are no seats—the congregation always stands—and the apse is separated from the main body of the church by an *iconostasis*, a heavy screen pierced by doors and richly decorated with the icons that form an integral part of Orthodox worship, acting as a sort of visual aid to the liturgy. Behind, a priest prepares bread and wine before the liturgy is sung.

But the most distinctive feature of the medieval Serbian church is its **frescoes**—attempts to encompass the entire heavenly kingdom as a background against which man could achieve ultimate union with God and so be cleansed of all sin. Frescoes were the medieval alternative to mosaics, which until then had been the principal form of church decoration. They had a number of advantages: not only

SERBIAN ORTHODOX MONASTERIES

River Danube

Novi Sad

Fruška Gora +Remeta

VOJVODINA

ROMANIA

Vrdnik+ Hopovo+ +Krušedol

BELGRADE

River Danube

0 ____ 50 km

Kragujevac ●

Kalenić+

+Manasija
+Ravanica

Paraćin ●

BULGARIA

Kraljevo ●   Ljubostinja
Arilje+   +Žiča
            Kruševac ●
Studenica+   +Lazarica
Gradac+

River Morava

Mileševa+

SERBIA

Djurdjevi
Stubovi ● Novi
Pazar
Sopoćani +

River Ibar

● T. Mitrovica

+ Peć

● Priština
+Gračanica

+Dečani

Titograd ●

KOSOVO

BULGARIA

● Prizren
+Ljeviska

Sv. Nikita
+

● Kumanovo   Staro
             Nagoričane

Skopje ●

+Lesnovo

Sv. Panteleimon

Markov+

River Vardar

+Sv. Jovan
Bigorski

MACEDONIA

● Prilep
+

ALBANIA

Sv. Kliment
+ Sv. Sophia
+ Ohrid
Sv. Naum

Lake
Ohrid

Lake
Prespa

GREECE

were they considerably cheaper, they also lent themselves to a similarly monumental style and were almost as durable if executed properly. Painters would work quickly, usually in pairs, one grinding pigments while the other plastered the walls. The first step was to apply several coats of lime plaster—usually four—and after the penultimate one was dry, trace on a rough cartoon of the intended work. This was covered with a final coat and the diluted pigment painted straight on while the plaster was still wet and absorbent, so that the paint fused with the wall itself rather than just remaining a surface layer; only later touching-up would have been done on dry plaster. Frescoes, then, for all the preparation involved, were a quick and spontaneous medium, much less deliberate than mosaics. Finished, they were meant to be seen not as individual works, but as part of the scheme for the church as a whole, and conventions had to be observed in their arrangement. *Christ Pantocrator* (Christ as Ruler of All) commonly gazes majestically from the central dome; the Virgin ascends to Heaven on the west wall of the nave; saints line the apse; and, in Serbian churches at least, it was normal to paint a portrait of the dead king/donor being presented, with his church, to the Virgin.

To the Byzantines, images were seen as paralleling the physical manifestation of God on Earth in Christ, so experiments in style were dangerous and rare. Nevertheless, distinct stylistic developments, not only in Serbian architecture but in painting too, fall into three separate but related categories—the Raška, Serbo-Byzantine and Morava Schools. Pre-Nemanjić foundations went up mainly in what is now Macedonia: Sv Sophia (1040) in Ohrid, and Sv Pantelemeion (1164) in Nerezi near Skopje, are the best surviving examples.

THE RAŠKA SCHOOL

The **Raška School** style dates from the foundation of the Serbian state in the late twelfth century to the closing years of the thirteenth. Named after the capital of the early rulers, it's more western, more estranged from Byzantium and consequently the most Serbian of the three schools—Nemanja's early kingdom was in many ways just as attached to Europe as to Constantinople. The influence of Romanesque architecture is unmistakeable, with blind arcading and sculpted animal, human and vegetable decoration around doors and windows; the lunettes above the portals often contain compositions—pietàs, nativities—in high relief. All churches were built of stone and a few, richer creations have facings of highly polished marble. Inside they're characterized by an absence of aisles, a central apse and raised dome, with deep side recesses that would later become transepts. Frescoes were kept deliberately simple, both in style and subject matter,

STUDENICA

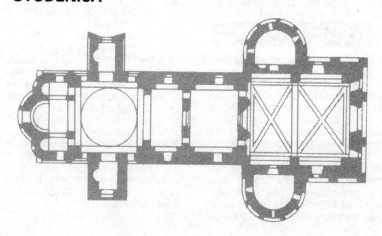

GRAČANICA

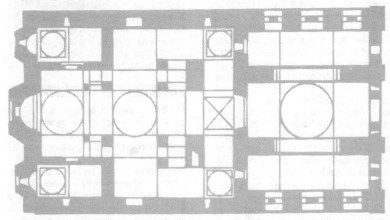

the technique monumental, focusing on well-known motifs from the Gospel—the *Last Supper*, the *Crucifixion* and particularly the *Dormition of the Virgin* were popular scenes. As time went on, ancillary buildings (narthex and outer [or exo-] narthex) came to be adorned with "profane" subjects—representations of kings and queens and historic events—but in the nave a strict iconography continued to be observed. Principal Raška School churches still standing include Studenica (1209), Žiča (1219), Mileševa (1237), Sopoćani (1265), Peć (1263), Morača (1252), Gradac (1275) and Arilje (1295).

THE SERBO-BYZANTINE SCHOOL

As King Milutin extended Serbia into a fully-fledged empire, so architecture took a new turn, resulting in the creations of the **Serbo-Byzantine School**, which flourished from the late thirteenth century until Serbia was forced to yield to the Turks and flee north. Under Milutin and his immediate successors, Serbia was stronger than it had ever been, extending its boundaries south and regaining the Byzantine strain it had to some extent lost. More than any other, the Serbo-Byzantine School retains clear links with Eastern tradition, turning the cruciform plan into a cross-in-square and topping churches with a profusion

of domes and cupolas; important churches have four cupolas crowding around a central dome. The external sculpting so prevalent in Raška School churches is almost completely lacking here. Instead, facades were striped with alternately colored bricks and slats of stone, combining with the tiers of roofs and cupolas to produce a rich, exotic and markedly more oriental effect.

The Gospels were still the chief source of inspiration for fresco artists, but were now combined with apocryphal stories, lives of saints, scenes from the church calendar and freer depictions of royalty—a new variety of material that led to less monumental scenes, breaking up church interiors into smaller, more varied panels. It became more important to tell a story than to move the viewer, and the serene figures of Studenica and Sopoćani gradually gave way to livelier, expressive characters, captured in a landscape or standing in front of buildings. Dečani is probably the best example of this narrative form still standing—though its architecture is much more Raška in style. Major Serbo-Byzantine churches still standing include Gračanica (1320), Bogorodica Ljeviska in Prizren (1307), the Kralja Crkva in Studenica (1314), the later archbishops's additions to Peć (1324/27), Lesnovo (1349), Staro Nagroičane near Kumanovo (1318) and Sv Kliment in Ohrid (1295).

THE MORAVA SCHOOL

After the death of Stefan Dušan, the Serbian Empire slowly began to fall away, until the very existence of the Serbian state itself was threatened. The Turks swept relentlessly north through Macedonia, defeating the Serbs at the Battle of Kosovo in 1389 and forcing them to take refuge way north in the hills around the Morava valley—safe, for the moment at least, from the invading armies. This signalled a fresh era in architecture—the **Morava School**—in which the Serbs continued, bloodied but unbowed, to build churches until the Turks were virtually on their doorstep. Church exteriors continued the candy-striped brickwork of the Serbo-Byzantine School but added touches from Raška, sculpting animal and vegetable motifs in low relief on doors and windows, and making first-time use of baked clay as well as of stone. Buildings also kept their multiple domes, but were cut into a three-apsed trefoil plan that had arrived via Macedonia from Mount Athos. On the whole, the churches of this period are simpler, less grandiose than their predecessors, almost as if in their quietness, they anticpate and symbolize the eclipse of the Serbian state. Frescoes, too, were in some ways a meeting of previous styles, combining the inquisitive invention of the Serbo-Byzantine artists with the calm, restrained technique of the Raška School painters. Characteristics include accomplished drawing, imaginative use of color and a spirited adaptation of subject-matter; urbane warrior saints and Christ's miracles became popular subjects, but in many cases painters were content to produce placid evocations of their age. Principal Morava School churches include the Lazrica church at Kruševac (1370), Ravanica (1381), Kalenić (1413), Manasija (1418) and Ljubostinja (1405).

AFTER THE MORAVA SCHOOL

With Serbia firmly under the Ottomans, Christian art and creativity stagnated. Morava School styles found their way to nearby Orthodox countries—Russia, Greece and especially Romania—and in the late seventeenth century the monks and Christian artists and architects of the monasteries fled north of the Danube to the Hapsburg Vojvodina, where they built new churches and monasteries—nostalgic communes that echoed those of Serbia's golden age. Hopovo, Krušedol and Vrdnik are three examples. Later, while the rest of the country suffered under the Ottoman occupation, the Vojvodina became a flourishing center for Serbian culture and the arts, crucial in reawakening Serbian national consciousness.

KALENIĆ

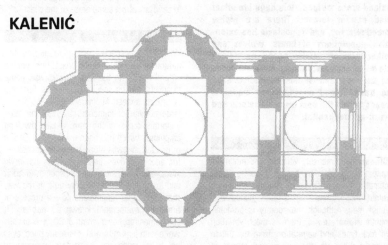

YUGOSLAV WILDLIFE

The view of Yugoslavia that many visitors get is one of bare, almost desert-like mountains stretching precipitously down to a brief area of maquis vegetation and a blue sea. But the increasingly developed coastline is only one, rather atypical aspect of the country, about three-quarters of which is covered with mountains, mostly of karst limestone and rich in plant species. Unlike the coastal ranges, which were accessible to ships and logged out hundreds of years ago, many inland areas still maintain huge broadleaf and conifer forests. There are alpine meadows, too, and Yugoslavia has extensive populations of bears, wolves and other large mammals. Indeed, as holiday developments swallow up more and more of the coast and islands, naturalists have to travel inland up the steep mountain roads to find the best areas of natural and semi-natural habitat.

BACKGROUND

Climate is immensely variable, the mountain ranges and interior basins creating local climates. **Geography**, also, is more varied than might be imagined from a quick glance at a relief map. Although the country is predominantly **mountainous**, there is much variation of rock types and vegetation, from the Julian Alps in the north, through several ranges of

Dinaric mountains stretching parallel to the coast, to the huge and immensely rugged areas of limestone in Montenegro and Macedonia, which are essentially Balkan and contain many relict and endemic species. The **karst** areas are probably the most exciting, both from a natural history perspective and because of the amazing scenery. The mountains are spectacular and there are also high plains, covered with grotesquely shaped rocks which look like virtual moonscapes, unlike anything else found in Europe.

Wetlands are the most disappointing habitat in the country. The shortage of agricultural land has meant that, with exception of a handful of nature reserves, virtually all marshy areas have been encroached on or destroyed by **drainage**. Over most of the country **agriculture and forestry** are the predominant factors influencing wildlife. Upland areas are often heavily grazed by goats and sheep, and the vegetation is usually impoverished even in existing oak and beech forests. Many of the upland meadows, on the other hand, are harvested for hay, and in consequence maintain a good plant population. Though many forest areas have been maintained, it's claimed that about three hundred miles of the coastal forests south of Trieste were felled to build Venice. Since then, grazing and, in the past, cultivation on terraces, have both helped to impoverish the landscape. More recently, pollution from industry and from sewage has started to seriously affect some areas of the coast.

SLOVENIA

While not an especially exciting region for the naturalist, Slovenia does boast one unique natural feature in the **Postojna caves**, home to several unique species of animals. Postojna is around sixteen kilometers long and has a large number of immense caverns. The most important focus is the **olm**, a cave-dwelling amphibian which has been living here—and in other cave systems along the Adriatic coast—for aeons. It lives permanently in its larval state, and never matures to become an adult and lose its external feathery gills in the way that most other amphibians do—a process of arrested development known as *neoteny*. It sometimes reaches a length of 30cm, is usually white with pink gills, and is virtually blind, eyes not being much use in its dark underground home. Finding wild specimens is said to be very difficult, but there are captive olms to be seen in the caves.

Other specialized cave dwellers are found in the system as well. There are several species of **crustaceans**, including some relatives of the common pond slater. There is also a cave harvestman, along with cave spiders and moths. Despite the commercialization of some areas, many of the caves have never been explored, and biologists believe that other unique life forms could come to light.

CROATIA

Much of Croatia belongs to the coast, and this is where the most interesting areas for the naturalist lie. At the most westerly end of the Dinaric mountains about 30km inland from Rijeka, the **Risnjak National Park** is a mountainous country of karst limestone, with large forest areas and upland meadows. Large areas of the forest have never been exploited, and have the status of a strict nature reserve. From the village of Crni Lug, a marked forest track passes through the dominant forests of mixed beech and fir, transitional woods of oriental hornbeam and hop hornbeam *Ostrya carpinifolia*, finally ending up in thickets of dwarf mountain pine *Pinus mugo*, and a characteristically alpine form of beech forest.

One of the most striking karst features is the 200m-deep funnel on Mount Risnjak, itself the highest peak in the park at 1528m. Known as **Viljska Ponikva**, the funnel creates a **temperature inversion** which in turn gives rise to an inversion of vegetation zones. Hence there are beech forest species at the top of the funnel and higher ridges, and dwarf mountain pine on the lower slopes—a remarkable reversal of the normal zonation.

Above the tree line, the **alpine pasture** has colorful and scarce plants such as the alpenrose *Rhododendron ferrugineum*, a bushy shrub with bright pink flowers, black vanilla orchid *Nigritella nigra*, the orange lily *Lilium bulbiferum* and a blue gentian *Gentiana symphyandra*. Highlights among the park's **bird species** include an extraordinary array of woodpeckers, including most of the European species, and both red-breasted and collared flycatchers; honey buzzards are a common predator, and there's a faint chance of a glimpse of the rare and local Ural owl, right at the southern edge

of its range. Almost the size of an eagle owl, it often hunts by day, feeding off animals as big as the red squirrel.

Further south, the spectacular karst mountains of the **Central Velebit range** tower above the Adriatic, with vast tracts of almost primeval beech, pine and fir forest covering peaks up to 1700m high. It has been minimally affected by human interference, and is rarely visited by tourists, mainly because of its inaccessibility. Two places to aim for are the lumberjacks' huts at Strovaca, deep in the heart of beech and pine forest, and the logging village of Krasno, following a route up from the *garrigue* and *maquis* areas of the coast to mountain pasture and meadows, oak woodland and beech forests—a superb **habitat cross section** of the Croatian coast. In the mountains, dense beech, fir and patches of spruce forest leave little light for anything else to grow, though the area is rich in bulbous plants. The flowering season falls between February and May, and there's a wonderful and bewildering array of **crocuses** and their relatives. The tiny yellow flowers of *Sternbergia colchiflora* and the pink or white *Colchicum hungaricum* appear in spring while *Colchicum visianii* flowers in autumn. The pale lavender *Crocus dalmaticus* and the deep purple *Crocus reticulatus* both appear at lower altitudes in spring. *Crocus vernus* prefers the top of the Velebit range in deeper soils around trees.

At the southern end of the Velebit mountain range, the **Paklenica National Park** is the only national park on the Croatian coast. Its easy access from the coastal plain, but difficult entrance, make it both accessible to visitors and difficult to exploit, a situation which has preserved both its beauty and diverse plant and animal life. Despite being so near the coast, it has the distinctive vegetation of upland Yugoslavia. The transition from the baked coastal plain and *garrigue* vegetation to beech-clad valleys and rocky limestone peaks is impressive. Climbing up through the narrow gorge entrance, whose limestone and dolomite rocks rise 400m, you pass through woodlands of white oak *Quercus pubescens*, manna ash *Fraxinus ornus*, oriental hornbeam *Carpinus orientalis*, and finally extensive beech *Fagus sylvatica*. There are two notable bellflowers in these rocks and cliffs: *Campanula fenestrellata*, with blue goblet-shaped flowers, and

Campanula waldsteiniana. Around half the area of the park is beech, oak and black pine *Pinus nigra* forest. Beech is most dominant in the northwest and the longitudinal valley of Paklenica towards Ivine Vodice. The most beautiful pine forests are located in the area of Mocila. **Birds of prey** are common in Paklenica. They include golden eagle and eagle owl, a permanent community of griffon vultures living in Mala Paklenica, and several species of falcon. The rock nuthatch, blue rock thrush, black redstart, wallcreeper and several species of warbler are all common in the park. The brown bear is extremely rare, but the fox, wild boar, roe deer and weasel are all relatively numerous.

DALMATIA

Although the whole **Dalmatian coastline** is of interest to naturalists, the north has been badly affected by deforestation and the effects of the coast road. But farther south offers good opportunities to observe some of the region's typical habitats, namely the **Balkan maquis**, and to spend some time looking at Yugoslavia's still-excellent **marine life**. There is a good selection of **passerine birds**, especially in the summer, although as always they are most active early or late in the day. Look out particularly for the colorful green and yellow **bee-eater** and the bright blue **roller**, best spotted on telegraph wires beside the road, or, in the case of the roller, indulging in the spectacular tumbling display flight which gives it its name. The lesser gray shrike is still common in Yugoslavia and is fairly easy to spot because it perches in places where it can overlook a large area. Watch out for the red backed shrike as well. There are relatively few species of **warbler** in the *maquis* compared to wetland areas or forests, although the Sardinian, barred, orphean, sub-alpine and olivaceous warblers can all be found breeding in places. Apparently olive tree warblers also extend north at least as far as Dubrovnik, but are not common.

Birds of prey are also likely to be seen along the coast, including the ubiquitous kestrel and the lanner falcon. During the spring and autumn, you can watch the migration of parties of gray and purple herons, little egrets, squacco and night herons, red footed falcons, collared flycatchers—and, sometimes, Mediterranean gulls.

Despite the damage done by the wildlife trade, there are still quite a few **tortoises** to be seen in Yugoslavia, although they are never particularly easy to spot unless they move. Unfortunately, the easiest way to see them is when they are (suicidally) crossing the road. There are many species of lizards as well, including the spectacular green lizards *Lacerta viridis* and *L.trilineata*.

The **maquis vegetation** is well worth a careful look. Throughout most of the Yugoslavian coastal area, *maquis* is the result of degradation of the original forest. Although it appears very similar to that found throughout the Mediterranean, and contains many of the same species, the Balkan *maquis* is easily recognized as a distinctive habitat. South of Cavtat there are extensive areas of scrub containing, among others, the strawberry tree, *Arbutus unedo*; the laurel *Laurus nobilis*; *Phillyrea latifolia*, another small evergreen shrub; the downy oak *Quercus pubescens* (also known as the white oak); Kermes oak *Quercus coccifera* with its spiny leaves; large stands of the prickly juniper, *Juniperus oxycedru*; and, a long way from home, the Spanish broom *Spartium junceum*. Below these there's another layer dominated by the heather *Erica manipuliflora*—much taller than northern European species. Many of the bushes are heavily armed with spikes and thorns, so forcing a passage off the path isn't easy.

MARINE LIFE

The **Adriatic seashore life** is quite different from that found in northern Europe. Generally there aren't the large masses of brown seaweeds, and the virtual lack of tides means that rock pools and intertidal areas don't really exist in the same way. This means that you have to go into the sea itself: a mask is essential, a snorkel desirable, and flippers a bonus. Diving down, there's a sudden drop in temperature after a few feet, and this cooler water changes the marine life as well.

Immediately noticeable, even from the shore, are two very distinctive species of algae—the **peacock's tail** *Padina pavonia*, which has a white and brown striped fan a few inches across, and the **mermaid's cup**, which looks like a tiny white toadstool. Both are often abundant in shallow water and around clean harbors. There's also a bewildering array of red algae, and, especially in polluted water or where freshwater streams flow into the sea, abundant growth of the sea lettuce *Ulva lactua*.

Among the most obvious marine animals is the **black sea urchin** *Arbacia lixula*, which is usually common on any rocky area of shore. Although the spines are not poisonous, they can get deeply embedded in the soles of your feet so it is worth wearing sandals or canvas shoes. There is also a range of other sea urchins in deeper water, along with their relatives, brittle stars and starfish.

Some of the **marine worms** are spectacular, even in quite shallow water, building calcareous tubes several inches high, pointing upwards and with the beautiful fan of the worm itself visible so long as it is not alarmed, when it will retreat convulsively into its tube. **Molluscs** are abundant, including the only European species of the tropical *Conus* shells. Like many *Conus*, this one is poisonous and can sometimes be fatal. The large and brightly colored **top shells** are also common, along with such Mediterranean specialties as keyhole limpets, which are small limpets with a notch on the top of the shell, abalones, and many bivalves. On the seabed, a range of **sea slugs** browse away at the algae and general detritus. There are also some very large sea hares, *Aplysia spp*, so called because they are brown and have two tentacles like long ears.

One of the most unusual species on the sea bottom is the **sea cucumber**. The most common sort is usually about 25cm long, dark brown and with slightly spiky skin. It lies around on the bottom looking like a slightly obscene sausage and apparently spews its stomach out as a form of aggression if provoked (it later grows a new one).

A couple of tips for the shorebound. **Lights on the water at night** can attract a whole range of animals, including fish and the black sea urchins, and an evening walk along the seafront can sometimes reveal schools of fish and literally dozens of urchins in the pool of light created by a harborside street lamp. Areas where trash has been dumped in the water provide food for many scavenging creatures like the octopus and squid. You almost certainly won't spot these superbly camouflaged creatures unless they move, so be prepared to settle down for a few minutes in a likely looking spot and watch for a slow creeping or the blink of the octopus's baleful orange eye.

In southern Dalmatia, Cavtat and Mljet are good places to observe some of this wildlife, Mljet especially for its stands of forest and areas of flowering shrubs, and the several species of **butterfly** you can see here. Common are the Cleopatra *Gonepteryx cleopatra* and the southern white admiral *Limenitis reducta*. **Reptiles** include the Turkish gecko *Hemidactylus turcicus*, the sharp-snouted rock lizard *Lacerta oxycephala*, which is a typical small lacertid lizard with distinctly blue underparts, and Dahl's whip snake *Coluber najadum*, a very slender non-poisonous snake with characteristic dark spots on the side of its neck. Snakes were in fact once a problem here, to the extent that mongooses were imported to get rid of them. These have now become a pest at the expense of other animals.

BOSNIA-HERCEGOVINA

Inland from the coast, the **Neretva valley and delta** district is one of Yugoslavia's most important areas for migratory and wintering birds. There are several small lakes connected to the sea at Kardeljevo which are flanked by reedbeds, marshland and highly productive farmland, providing ideal conditions for waterfowl in places. Not surprisingly, the area has come under intense pressure for drainage and conversion to farmland. Nowhere is this more so than **Hutavo Blato**, a nature reserve 5km north of the town of Metkovic. Although this wetland area is only a shadow of its former self, it remains an important and exciting reserve, and well worth visiting for the spring or autumn migrations.

Around 235 bird species have been recorded in the wetlands of the Neretva valley, mainly **wintering and migratory species**. These include the pygmy cormorant, purple, squacco and night herons, spoonbill and great white egret. Numerous species of waders including the marsh sandpiper and Temminck's stint are not uncommon. Bean geese have also been reported during hard winters. There are also about 500 species of **flowering plants** recorded from the area, along with many species of lichens, mosses etc. Many of these may have disappeared under the drainage schemes, although there are still large areas of reedswamp remaining.

Further inland, the **Sutjeska National Park**, on the border with Montenegro, is home to the **Perucica** forest, one of the best known and richest virgin forests in Europe. Perucica forms a strict 1434-hectare nature reserve within the park itself, and attracts many visitors because of a magnificent waterfall which can be seen from a small path leading off halfway up the main track through the nature reserve. The trees themselves are outstanding. The forest is immensely dense and productive, and it is claimed that the best parts have over 1000 cubic meters of timber per hectare. There are 143 deciduous species known, and 12 conifers, and the trees are markedly zoned with altitude, with broadleaves gradually giving way to stands of evergreen. Among the most notable are the eastern beech/silver birch *Fagus orientalis/ Betula pendula* community which dominates the lower slopes, the spruce *Picea excelsa*, which is found farther up, and the dwarf mountain pine *Pinus mugo*, which extend almost to the summit. There are also a number of rarities. These include the Tartarian maple, *Acer tataricum*, which is distinguished from other maples by usually having unlobed leaves; *Spiraea chamaedryfolia*, a rare shrub in the rose family; a number of species of *Cotoneaster*, and *Petteria ramentacea*, a legume shrub confined to a few areas of southern Yugoslavia. The forest is unusual in including several species of small trees or shrubs more normally found in central Europe, including the false medlar *Sorbus chamaemespilus*, the elder *Sambucus nigra*, and spurge laurel *Daphne laureola*.

Partly because of the magnificent forest, and also because hunting has been more successfully controlled in the area, this is also the place to come and try to spot **large mammals** such as wolves, bears and chamois. This said, although they are present they're certainly not easy to see, and you may be disappointed. The **bird life** is more visible, and includes breeding honey buzzards overhead, while capercaillies stalk the forest floor.

MONTENEGRO

Inland, Montenegro is perhaps the most spectacular Yugoslavian republic, with huge areas of karst limestone mountains and large forests. **Lake Skadar** is the most famous wetland in Yugoslavia for birdwatching and one of the key sites for any serious naturalist. It is also the largest lake in the country, set among spectacular, bare, mountain scenery, and with a fair proportion of its shoreline in Albania. **Water birds** are the main reason to come. It is most famous as the breeding site, perhaps the last in the country, of the **Dalmatian pelican**. However, there are numerous other unusual and exciting water birds, including pygmy cormorants, glossy ibises, squacco and purple herons, great, white and little egrets and ferruginous ducks. Whiskered terns quarter the shoreline in places, and there are many waterfowl in the winter. Coots and moorhens are abundant along the water's edge and little grebes and black-necked grebes are both much in evidence.

The woods along the shore, and the extensive areas of reedswamp, provide good habitat for **small birds**. Among the warblers you might see are moustached, wood, Savi's and Cetti's warblers. There are also vast numbers of red rumped swallows in the breeding season, flickering over the water's surface catching mosquitoes. Birds of prey seen at the lake include the common black kite, and lesser spotted and Bonelli's eagles, hunting over the lake from their breeding sites in the **Moraca gorge**, just to the north of the lake.

North of Skadar, the **Lovčen National Park** is one of the most accessible upland hill areas for people traveling on the coast, only a few kilometers outside Kotor. The park is mountainous and mainly **forested.** The lower slopes are dominated by hop hornbeam *Ostrya carpinifolia* and the same downy oak *Quercus pubescens* found in the coastal *maquis*. Above about 1000m there is a forest zone of eastern beech *Fagus orientalis*, which has leaves like western beech but branches which slant upwards, giving the impression of a whole forest of trees standing with their arms in the air. There are many other tree species, including the Montpelier maple *Acer monspessulanum*, turkey oak *Quercus cerris*, whitebeam *Sorbus aria*, mountain ash *Sorbus aucuparia* and hazel *Corylus avellana*, along with numerous pine species.

Although the forest has apparently suffered from heavy grazing underneath the trees, there are over **1200 different plants** recorded, including some which are endemic to the area, such as *Lamium lovenicum*, a local species of dead nettle. The mountain meadows are rich with a wide range of plants, some of the most noticeable being the bright blue globe thistle *Echinops ritro*, several species of pinks *Dianthus spp*, and many bellflowers including the large *Campanula latifolia*. Although early summer is the best time for plants, there are still many in flower in late July and August.

Lovćen is also home to several **birds of prey**, including the imperial eagle, buzzard, peregrine (unusual in Yugoslavia) and the griffon vulture. The imperial eagle can be distinguished from other large eagles by the white flashes on its shoulders, although these are less obvious in this eastern species than in those found in Spain. Alpine swifts scream over the village and jays are common. Rock partridges can be seen on the higher ground.

Further inland, the **Durmitor National Park** is divided into two parts, a mountain massif and a gorge, and is a United Nations World Heritage Site. The **massif**, which reaches up over 2500m high, has a mixture of conifer and broadleaf forest, along with huge areas of upland, Alpine-type meadows, which are still grazed in the summer by sheep and cattle. The **flowers** are exceptional. Even fairly late in the summer, it has a rich, Alpine-type mixture of plants including many endemic or relict species, such as the saxifrage *Saxifraga preuja*, a unique figwort *Verbascum durmitoreum*, and a local trefoil *Trifolium durmitoreum*. Quite apart from the rarities, there are a whole range of commoner species, including *Polygala major*, the largest of the milkworts, *Linum capitatum*, a flax with clusters of bright yellow flowers and *Gentiana utriculosa*, the small annual gentian.

The park has been fairly unregulated with respect to hunting until quite recently, so that large **mammals and birds** are still scarce, although now hopefully increasing. There are plenty of ravens and hooded crows, the latter taking over from the Western European carrion crow throughout Yugoslavia. There are also a number of birds of prey and game birds, including peregrines and black grouse.

MUSIC

You're likely to hear a refreshingly wide variety of music in Yugoslavia, the clash between western consumerism and indigenous styles throwing up fascinating by-products in all spheres of music. A great deal of musical entertainment takes place out of doors; and concert tickets and records are comparatively cheap.

FOLK MUSIC

Yugoslavia is perhaps unequalled in Europe in terms of the sheer wealth of diverse traditions to be found in such a small geographical area. Much of it either originated from—or was influenced by—outside cultures: Serbian and Macedonian music have much in common with Near and Middle Eastern styles; in Bosnia much of the music is pure Turkish; elsewhere, you can detect melodies common to the whole Slav cultural region, while Italian influences creep in on the coast. Each area has retained its regional peculiarities, although the last century has seen a lot of levelling out. Many traditional instruments have been abandoned in favor of new, mass produced accordions—now the dominant instrument in all areas, often joined by clarinet, a range of percussion, and, increasingly, electric bass guitar. Spontaneous village music is now hard to find, but traditions are everywhere kept alive by local, state-financed organizations, prominent among them the *KUD—Kulturno-umetnicko drustvo* or cultural-artistic society. Most towns have one of these, and many factories have folklore troupes. There are also regular programs of folk performances in many major cities and tourist centers.

SLOVENIA

Slovene folk music generally belongs to the alpine, Austro-Bavarian cultural sphere, the dance music mainly polkas and waltzes played by groups containing clarinet, accordion and brass. In fact, so similar is it that the largest-selling *ländler* ensemble in southern Germany is that of the Slovene Avsenik brothers. Apart from this, there are still some remnants of older styles that survive in isolated areas, for instance in Rezija near the Austrian border and Prekmurje in the southeast, where the music of Goslarije (Beltinška Banda are one exponent) shades into that of neighboring Croatia.

In the summer and autumn it's possible to hear Slovene folk music at Gasilske veselice ("firemen's balls"), held outside local fire stations—which, with their combination of open space for dancing with a building from which to sell food and drink, are considered the best place for a town party.

CROATIA AND THE VOJVODINA

Elsewhere in the north, one traditional instrument that hasn't been replaced is the *tamburica*, a mandolin-type instrument of Eastern origin, brought to Europe by the Turks in the fifteenth century. Carried northwards by successive streams of migrants, it's now common to a wide swath of territory from Vojvodina in the east to the Adriatic coast in the west. *Tamburica* orchestras are particularly common to Slavonia in Croatia, and the Backa in northern Vojvodina—an area populated by patches of Catholic Croats, known as the *Bunjevci* and *Sokci*, who came here in the eighteenth and nineteenth centuries. *Tamburica* playing is usually awesomely fast. Also in Vojvodina, Hungarian and Slovak music figure prominently, while over on the other side of northern Yugoslavia, you'll find big choral groups on the Dalmatian coast.

Also on the coast, in Istria and around the Kvarner area, you can hear a kind of music notable for its extreme dissonance and unusual scale. The *sopile* of this area (folk oboes) are always played in pairs, one large and one small, creating a music unparalleled in Europe in its chromaticism.

SERBIA

The vast majority of **Serbian music** is characterized by jolly dance tunes oriented towards collective merry-making. More lyrical are the so-called *starogradske pesme* or old town songs, a product of the awakening urban culture in the last century. If you're eating or drinking in Belgrade's so-called Bohemian quarter, Skadarlija, you'll hear a lot of these, along with songs reflecting Serbian national consciousness. These were rarely heard in public until a few years ago. Of a number you might hear are *Mars na Drinu* ("March to the River Drina"), *Tamo Daleko* ("over there, far away"), both traditionally connected with the heroic retreat of the Serbian army in World War I, and a song of much more recent vintage, penned in response to the new nationalist upsurge—*Ko to kaze ko to laze, da je Srbija mala* (roughly "anyone who says Serbia is small is a liar").

The typical Serb instrument is the *frula* or *svirala*, a type of flute or whistle. Vlado Baralić is one of the most exciting young performers and is rumored to be making a CD for a Dutch company. The Serbian style of accordion playing, with its fast-repeated notes and involved ornamentation, is derived from the technique of the *frula* (just as that of Macedonia has developed out of pipe techniques). The characteristic dance form in Serbia is the *kolo*, a circular dance with a fast two-beat rhythm often played with exceptional virtuosity and alarming speed. Ljubiša Pavković, Mirkom Kodić and Branimir Djokić are the players to look out for.

In the northeast of Serbia, in the **Vlach** areas, the music is very different, related to that of neighboring Romania. Even the fast dance melodies are tinged with melancholy, and the long ballads, sometimes connected with the old pre-Slav forest and snake cults, can be quite heart-wrenching.

It's probably among the **Albanian** population of Kosovo (and to some extent western Macedonia) that the traditional music of the area is most alive. Most young people can sing at least a few local folksongs, or maybe even play the *cifteli*, a type of two-stringed lute of Turkish or Persian origin which is used both as an instrument for dancing to and for driving along the ballads, mostly about the heroes of the past and their noble deaths. If you should happen to buy a *cifteli* (they're often sold by makers who come down to the markets in Priština and Prizren), be aware that the scales of Albanian music don't correspond to those of a piano keyboard.

MACEDONIA

Macedonia is probably the richest of the republics when it comes to musical folklore. Village musicians play the *gajde* bagpipe and *kaval* (a long rim-blown flute), and although a good deal less common than they once were, there are still players about. In the towns, groups of clarinet, violin, kanun zither and lute, known as *čalgii*, play a music influenced by oriental models. Until recently no wedding was complete without a pair of *zarli* (a *zarla* is a large, loud primitive oboe), and the big double-headed drum, the *tapan*, and it's still possible to hear these groups at festivals.

Macedonian rhythm is complex, and at first listening can be baffling to outsiders. But once you've learned a few dance steps (which any Macedonian will be delighted to show you), they begin to make perfect sense. Musicians to watch out for are, the doyen of bagpipers, Pece Atanasovski and his group, the clarinetist Tale Ognenovski, and the representative of a newer style, the saxophone and clarinet player, Ferus Mustafov, who is considered the hottest of the younger generation and plays in a wild, improvisatory fashion showing influences from Turkey, Bulgaria and Greece—as well as his home area of Strumica. He frequently plays in a restaurant on the kale above Skopje.

BOSNIA

Bosnia has nurtured a tradition of mournful, introspective café songs good for drowning your sorrows to: best exemplified by the work of a popular singer and serious musicologist, Himzo Polovina. More dramatic are the extraordinary, hauntingly beautiful *sevdalinke*, old Turkish songs of unrequited love (*sevdah* means yearning, and is derived from the Turkish word for love). These are supposedly sung in walled gardens by young girls eager to attract lovers, although there are male-sung versions as well, usually accompanied by *saz*, a lute-type instrument introduced by the Turks. Watch out for Hašim Muharemović and the younger Halid Musić.

In the villages there is a style known as *Izvorna muzika* or "music from the source," consisting of very odd melodies, often sung in two parts with the lower part either a drone or shadowing the upper voice a tone below, accompanied by two violins and a *saz*. It's usually pretty rough, but groups such as the young Zvaci Zavičaja have a punkish energy that's appealing.

MONTENEGRO

Montenegro's musical traditions largely coincide with those of Serbia, outlined above, but contain one important remnant of times past, the *gusle*—an antiquated leftover from an age when wandering minstrels and storytellers roamed the entire Balkan peninsula. Until this century the majority of Yugoslavia's peoples were illiterate, and history was handed down in the oral tradition through songs of great exploits—especially important for a defeated nation attempting to preserve a semblance of national pride and identity while subdued under Turkish rule. The Battle of Kosovo and the doings of folk heroes were recounted in epic poems, often thousands of verses long, memorized and performed by itinerant *guslari*—named after the single-stringed *gusle*, a lyre played with rudimentary bow, on which they accompanied themselves. Though originally found throughout the Montenegrin and Serbian populated areas of Yugoslavia they're now especially rare, although many village houses still have a *gusle* hanging from the wall—and perhaps an older member of the family who can actually play it. Outside a few isolated Montenegrin villages, you're very unlikely to find spontaneous *gusle* performances today. Professional *guslari* still give concerts and record albums, often updating their texts with tales of the Partisan war, but the basic musical structure is faithfully preserved—an extended, monotonous wailing, accompanied with the cat-gut screech of the *gusle* itself. It's not to everyone's taste, but is undeniably powerful.

ROMANY MUSIC

Much of the live music you're likely to hear during the course of your travels will be performed by **gypsies**, who have provided the Balkan peninsula with many of its professional musicians since their arrival in the region six centuries ago. A feature of southern Serbia and Macedonia is the preponderance of gypsy **brass bands**—often family affairs, making a living by providing the entertainment at local weddings. The material they play—largely chosen to please the local audience—consists of the usual *kolos*, *oros* and *cocteks*, supplemented by souped-up versions of modern international hits. Everything is played with the characteristic gypsy virtuosity, and showy instrumental solos abound.

Similarly hybrid is the music played by gypsy bands in the cafés and hotel bars of the south and east. Again these are conversant with many styles in order to entertain a diverse public, picking up Serbian, Macedonian, Albanian and Greek characteristics. Many gypsy performers have added synthesizers and electric drums alongside the more traditional instruments—the result an intoxicating cultural mix of ancient eastern melodies and the sounds of modern technology. Southern bars are good places to hear this kind of music, or wherever there's a large Romany population, and in the markets of Skopje, Priština and Niš you can pick up any number of home-recorded cassettes. You also might hear the true gypsy-style haunting female-sung songs, often performed within the Romany community itself or at one of their festivals—the annual *Djurdjevdan* in early May being the best-known.

NEWLY-COMPOSED FOLK MUSIC

Most of the "folk" music you hear on the radio and find in record shops is in fact a modern popular variant increasingly referred to by the epithet *novokomponovana narodna muzika*, or newly-composed folk music—based on traditional styles and themes but played with modern electronic instruments. It's very big business all over Yugoslavia, its role and popularity comparable to Country and Western music, with its own family of exceedingly wealthy, extravagantly dressed megastars, whose lives are endlessly paraded through the gossip columns. Its main heartland is Serbia and Bosnia, and many of the best exponents come from here, their ululating vocals echoing the influence of the east. Look out for records by undoubted queen of the genre, Lepa Brena, a more refined older generation of singers such as Vesna Zmijanac, Miroslav Ilic and Tozovac, and a whole horde of leering Bosnian medallion-men headed by Halid Muslimović and Rifat Tepić. Again, picking up cheap cassettes sold on market stalls is a good way to amass a representative collection. And watch out for posters advertising gigs in Belgrade and Sarajevo.

POPULAR MUSIC

Yugoslav **popular music** is musically insipid and derivative, and, for a foreigner with no knowledge of the language, without any real point of access. A popular singer/songwriter tradition goes back to the 1960s, when names like **Arsen Dedic** and **Djordje Balasevic** dominated the airwaves with lilting, "easy listening" ballads similar to Russian chansons. This minstrel tradition subsequently found its way into the mainstream of Yugoslav rock, a conservative, unchallenging movement that still very much endures. Two names stand out, both musically unoriginal, but national institutions just the same. The first of these, Sarajevo's **Bjelo Dugme** ("White Button"), have covered the whole gamut of styles from Blues to Eurodisco during the course of their twenty-year career, although leader Goran Bregović's recent attempts at writing film scores seem much more original than the often overtly plagiaristic material he writes for the group. The Serbian band **Riblja Corba** ("Fish Soup") are the other, their lead vocalist Bora Djordjević held in great esteem as something of a people's poet and spokesman of the nation's youth, with songs charting the decline of the Yugoslav ideal throughout the 1980s recently published in book form under the title *Hej Sloveni*: name of the country's national anthem. Bora's erstwhile sidekick **Bajaga** now inhabits more commercial pop-rock territory - described as the Yugoslav Paul McCartney, which sums up his style of inoffensive mediocrity better than anything.

Southern Yugoslavia grimly clung on to these rather conservative rock traditions throughout the Eighties, while northern cities increasingly came under the influence of New Wave, New Romanticism and European synthipop. Punk did cause the odd ripple in Belgrade, the seminal but short-lived **Sarlo Akrobata** spawning two groups that endure to this day: **Ekaterina Velika** (Catherine the Great), who began as Talking Heads copyists but moved on to develop a distinctive if rather unchallenging commercial rock style; and **Disciplina Kicme** (Discipline of the Backbone), who have attained much more critical respect for their anarchic punk/jazz fusion, driven by the manic bass-playing of anchorman Koja.

The Zagreb music scene proved much more productive, throwing up a host of style-obsessed but essentially superficial bands grouped together under the banner *Zagrebački novi val* or Zagreb New Wave. Raising their heads above the general mediocrity were **Azra**, although again the words were always more interesting than the music, with songs such as "68" and "Poland in my heart."

Despite remaining under the dominance of dinosaurs such as Bijelo Dugme, Sarajevo was by no means bypassed, producing the intriguing punk/folk fusion of **New Primitivism**—a movement which extolled the virtues of Balkan peasant culture. Leading lights were **Zabranjeno Pusenje** (No Smoking), best summed up by the opening track of their debut LP *Das ist Valter, Anarchy in the Baščaršija.*

LJUBLJANA, LAIBACH, AND NSK

Of all the Yugoslav cities, **Ljubljana** is the only one to have developed a strong home-grown scene of its own. Since the onset of punk and the birth of the movement's most significant band, **Pankrti** (The Bastards), Ljubljana became an important bastion of Yugoslav counter-culture. It was supported throughout by the pioneering efforts of Student Radio and the Student Cultural Center, SKUC, which promoted gigs before diving into independent record production; and displayed surprising longevity—mutating into hard-core, thrash and speed-metal as the 1980s progressed.

The Ljubljana punk scene didn't produce much of musical value save for Pankrti themselves, but was of incalculable importance as a social catalyst, its development going hand-in-hand with the republic's new social movements. The authorities were sufficiently worried by the growth of the apparently nihilistic subculture to instigate what became known as the "Nazi-Punk affair" in autumn 1982, when it was claimed that punk contained strongly fascistic elements (one notorious group of the time called themselves the "Fourth Reich," although they never played a note in public). The scene's main impressario, DJ and Pankrti manager Igor Vidmar, even spent a much-publicized spell in jail for displaying a swastika on what was in fact an anti-Nazi lapel badge. The affair soon blew over, but remained in the public mind long enough to greatly affect the early career of **Laibach**.

Like the Sex Pistols in the UK, Laibach became notorious throughout Yugoslavia before most people had heard a single note of their music. Laibach were both a product of Ljubljana's alternative scene and a rebellion against its values, their interest in systems of control and the link between art and totalitarianism lending them a much more authoritarian, anti-liberal, uniformed image than their contemporaries. This wasn't all. Earliest influences were modern German groups like Kraftwerk and DAF, and their name (the German name for Ljubljana) soon had them banned from playing on home turf by the sensitive city authorities.

All of this was sufficient to attract the attention of local TV presenter Jure Pengov, who propelled them to nationwide stardom in 1983 by branding them as enemies of the people on his popular weekly TV program. The daily press followed suit, and Laibach were denied the chance to defend themselves in print—a crackdown which only intensified their ideas on (and exploitation of) totalitarian imagery.

In 1983 Laibach teamed up with the fine arts collective *Irwin* and the drama group *Gledalisce Sester Scipion Nasice* (The Theater of the Sisters of Scipion Nasica—later re-named Red Pilot) to form **Neue Slowenische Kunst** or **NSK** (New Slovene Art). The use of the German language again raised a few eyebrows, though NSK argued that Slovene culture was by its very nature the result of outside, largely Teutonic influences, and there could be no specifically "new Slovene" culture without returning to these predominantly Germanic origins. This theme was investigated in NSK's most important project to date, *Baptism Beneath Triglav*, a stunning multi-media spectacle staged in 1987 which dealt with the conversion to Christianity of the Slovene nation in the early Middle Ages—and its simultaneous subjugation to the Germanic culture that had brought the new faith to them. Much of NSK's imagery, seen in Laibach's record covers and the paintings of Irwin, mixes Nazi and Socialist Realist art as if to say both systems are inherently the same. The rigid collectivism of the NSK structure ("The individual is an invention of the humanist

liberal" they proclaim) gives a strong impression of authoritarian nationalizm, but it's full of elements of pastiche. Diagrams of NSK's organizational structure bear a striking resemblance to those in Yugoslav school textbooks which aim to explain the country's bafflingly complex system of political representation.

By helping to blow the lid off an uptight society, NSK played no small part in speeding up the democratization process in Slovenia. Whatever their original intentions, the shock value of their imagery forced many in Slovenia to take up positions on the question of artistic freedom, with the result that the authoritarian group's most vociferous defenders were liberals. The crunch came in 1987 when NSK's graphic design subsidiary, New Collectivism, won a Yugoslavia-wide competition to design a poster advertising the annual Day of Youth—a typical socialist manifestation of support for the regime which was being increasingly questioned by the official youth organization in Slovenia. When an observant member of the public noticed that NSK's poster plagiarized a work by 1930s Nazi artist Richard Klein, pressure was put on the Slovene public prosecutor to take action. The fact that he eventually refused to do so was an important watershed in modern Slovene history.

Laibach's musical output has always given the appearance of conforming to a preconceived plan. Their earliest works were avant-garde, experimental exercises: *Nova Akropola* ("New Acropolis") was the first LP to be released in the West, and made hard listening, but its use of images of Slovene folk culture (stags and hay ricks for the most part) seemed to establish Laibach as spokesmen for the small Alpine nation. Their subsequent releases, the 1987 album *Opus Dei* and 1988's cover of the Beatles' *Let it Be*, marked their transition from avant-garde provincials to international popstars, and a new-found legitimacy as one of Yugoslavia's main cultural exports. No longer considered the bad boys at home, their records are now released under licence by the state record company. Their sound is still uncompromising—pompous, repetitive arrangements and raw, growling vocals—with projects like *Let it Be* seeming to confront the very notions of western pop music, plundering the past and so drawing attention to the essentially moribund and nostalgic condition of the medium.

RECORDS

Records in Yugoslavia are usually limited to very short pressings which quickly sell out. There's therefore not much sense in providing listings of records other than those released outside the country. If you can't find enough in your local record store, get a catalog from *Monitor*, in New York, *Rounder* in Boston, or from Chicago-based *Wax Trax*. It's worth knowing also that much folk music is—bizarrely—easier to find in Munich, West Germany, than in Yugoslavia itself. The large gastarbeitten community has led to a dense concentration of specialist record stores around the city's train station.

Folk

Jova Stojiljković and his brass band *Blow Besir Blow* (Globestyle). Gypsy brass band music from southern Serbia.

Vujicsics *Serbian Music from Southern Hungary* (Carthage). Music from the Vojvodina performed by contemporary Hungarian musicologists.

Various Artists *Narodna* (Touch; cassette-only release). A largely exploitative collection playing on the western consumer's desire for exotica, though it features some exciting Serbian orthodox hymns from the Middle Ages.

Yougoslavie 1: Serbie orientale; les bougies du paradis (Ocora). Vlach music from northeastern Serbia, around Negotin and Zaječar. Predominantly village dance music featuring fiddles and bagpipes, and music to accompany pagan ceremonies connected with death.

Yougoslavie 2: Macedoine; Polyphonie Tosque; Sous les peupliers de Bilisht (Ocora). Southern Albanian three- and four-part choral music, supplemented by a few bagpipes.

Yougoslavie 3: Macedoine—melodies guegues; bessa ou la parole donnee (Ocora) Typical northern Albanian repertoire of heroic songs from region arpound Debar and Kicevo, *cifteli* music.

Folk music of Yugoslavia (Topic/Rounder). Wide-ranging anthology put together by veteran musicologist Wolf Dietrich.

Musica populare di Yugoslavia (Albatros). Another wide-ranging collection, mainly Slav, from Istria, Macedonia, Croatia, Slovenia.

Orient-Okzident: Sud-ost Europa 1 (Musuem Collection—Berlin West). Again compiled by Wolf Dietrich. Yugoslav, Greek, Turkish, Romanian music, and very good sleeve notes.

Rock

Laibach

There are several early releases, now extremely hard to get hold of, charting Laibach's early, more avant-garde, phase. Prominent among them are two Dutch-produced live cassettes, two albums released in Yugoslavia by SKUC (and featuring a mixture of material from other sources, including John Peel sessions), and two albums released by Walter Ulbricht Schallplatten of Hamburg—the 1985 live LP *Neu Konservatiw*, and *Rekapitulacija*, a boxed set of four 12" singles covering early works 1980–1984. Otherwise the available works are as follows:

Panorama (Wax Trax, 12" single) 1984
Die Liebe (Wax Trax, 12" single) 1985
Nova Akropola (Wax Trax, LP) 1985
Opus Dei (Mute, LP) 1987

Baptism (Soundtrack to NSK's 1987 theater performance of same name) (Sub Rosa, 2-LP boxed set) 1987
Sympathy for the Devil (Mute/Enigma EP) 1988
Let it Be (Mute, LP) 1988

Borghesia

Ljubav je hladnija od smrti (Love is colder than death) (SKUC/FV, LP, Yugoslavia only) 1987
Escorts and Models (Play it Again Sam, LP) 1988
Resistance (Play it Again Sam, LP) 1989

Miladojka Youneed

Miladojka Youneed (NL Centrum, LP) 1988

AFTER LAIBACH

Laibach demonstrated that Yugoslav groups could compete with the West on equal terms rather than endlessly imitate, and their success

has been paralleled by a growth in the range of production facilities available to Yugoslav groups, and a new sensitivity towards media marketing. The Student Cultural Center (SKUC) in Ljubljana continue to gather various facilities under their wing, including a new marketing agency, Dallas, and the long-standing independent record label *FV*. The latter especially has inspired the growth of a whole plethora of small, often cassette-only labels financed by local organs of the youth league. The outlook for further development is, however, far from rosy, with the ever worsening financial crisis making funds short to support either new record labels or an extensive gigging circuit. State-owned record labels are also cutting back enormously, and are very unwilling to sign all but the most commercially insipid material, concentrating their efforts instead on releasing American and British material under licence from western companies.

However, there are a couple of groups achieving some sort of breakthrough outside Yugoslavia, all of them from Slovenia. The leather-clad disco-oriented rockers, **Borghesia**, are the most prominent, with a string of releases on Belgian-based label *Play it Again Sam*. Despite their aggressive, martial image, Borghesia are keen to dissociate themselves from the authoritarianism of Laibach and emphasise instead an almost anarchist individualism, placing them firmly in the tradition of Ljubljana's early punk subculture. The powerful rock/jazz fusion of another Ljubljana group, **Miladojka Youneed**, has been released in Holland. In Yugoslavia itself there's not much of an avant-garde left, but you could do worse than look out for concerts or recordings by Slovenian techno-samplers **Demolition Group**, or two rather heavy, gothic, doom-laden outfits—Rijeka's **Let 3** and the Macedonians **Mizar**. Local pop groups aiming for teeny audiences abound. Two of the more bizarre are Zagreb's **Psihomodo pop**, whose entire repertoire consists of rehashing the early work of the Ramones, and the Slovene band, **Agropop**, who absurdly mix cretinous Eurovision-style melodies with politically committed lyrics.

YUGOSLAV FICTION

BOSNIAN STORY

Born in 1892, IVO ANDRIĆ is possibly Yugoslavia's best known author. Despite writing almost exclusively on his own country—particularly his native Bosnia—Andrić's insight into a people under foreign domination brought international critical praise, culminating in the Nobel Prize for Literature in 1961. The Bridge on the Drina, a fictionalized history of the town and people of Visegrad, established his reputation. A Travnik Chronicle, published in 1961 as Bosnian Story is perhaps the most accessible of his works, analysing the effects and intrigues in the Turkish controlled town. Ivo Andrić died in 1975.

At the beginning of the year 1807 extraordinary things began to happen at Travnik, such things as had never been known before.

No one in Travnik had ever supposed that the town was made for an ordinary life or for the trivial daily round—no one, not even the humblest true-believer in the backstreets. This basic feeling, that they were in some way different from the rest of the world, created and called to something better and higher, entered into every single human soul with the cold wind from the hillside, with the running waters of Sumec, with the sweet flavored corn from the sunny fields about the town, and it never left them, even in sleep or poverty or in the hour of death itself.

This was true in the first instance of the Moslems who lived in the town. But even the lesser breeds of all three religions, scattered about the steep slopes or crammed together in a separate suburb, were filled with the same feeling, each man after his own fashion and according to his station in life. This was also true of their town itself which had something in its situation and plan which was peculiar, personal and proud.

Travnik was, in point of fact, a deep and narrow gorge, which successive generations had in the course of time built over and brought under cultivation, a fortified passageway in which men had settled down to live permanently, adapting themselves to it and it to themselves as the centuries went by. On both sides the hills divide steeply, crowding close together at a sharp bend in the valley, where there is barely room for the meager river and the road beside it. The whole shape of the place is like a half-opened book, both pages of which are, as it were, illuminated with gardens, streets, houses, fields, graveyards and mosques.

No one has ever worked out the number of hours of sunshine of which Nature has docked this town, but undoubtedly the sun rises later here and sets earlier than in any other of the many towns and townlets of Bosnia. Even the people of Travnik do not deny this, but they add that while the sun does shine over their town, it shines as it does nowhere else.

In this narrow valley, in the bottom of which the Lasva flows and whose sides sparkle with springs, runlets and streams, a valley full of damp and draughts, there is hardly anywhere a straight road or a piece of level ground where a man can set his foot freely and without taking heed. Everywhere it is steep and uneven, tangled and intertwined, wound about and split up by private roads, fences, blind alleys, gardens and wicket gates, graveyards or places of worship.

Here, by the side of the water, that mysterious, unstable and powerful element, the generations of Travnik are born and die. Here they grow to manhood, sickly and pale, but tough and equal to anything life may bring. Here they live, with the Vizier's Residence ever before their eyes, proud, neat, fastidious and sly; here they work and thrive or sit idle and grow poor. Invariably canny and reserved, they never laugh aloud but they are not incapable of a smile; they talk a little and prefer to talk scandal in whispers. And here, in waterlogged graveyards, they are buried when their time comes, each after his own faith and custom, and give place to a posterity like themselves.

Thus the generations change, transmitting one to another not only a peculiar personal heritage of body and mind, but a country and a religion; not only a hereditary sense of what is right and fitting and an ability to recognize and distinguish all the various paths, gateways and alleys of their intricate town but also an inborn aptitude for knowledge of the world and of men in general. All these qualities are the endowment of every Travnik baby as it comes into the world, but above all the quality of pride. *Pride is their second nature*, a living force which never leaves them but governs them and sets upon them a visible mark by which they may be known from the rest of mankind.

Their pride has nothing in common with the simple bumptiousness of prosperous peasants or of small country townsmen who, when satisfied with themselves, swell visibly and are loud in self-congratulation. On the contrary, the pride of Travnik is all within; *it is more like a burdensome inheritance*, a painful duty towards oneself, one's family and one's town, or, strictly speaking, towards the exalted, lofty and unapproachable idea which the people of Travnik have of themselves and their city.

Still, every human emotion has its proper limits, and so has the feeling of one's own greatness. Certainly Travnik is the *seat of a Vizier* and its people are well-kept and well-bred, sensible and wise enough to talk with kings: but there came days when, even to them, their pride became a millstone about their neck and they could have wished to live instead, peaceful and carefree, in one of those obscure and ordinary market-towns which do not figure in the calculations of kings or in the quarrels of states and do not lie within the range of world events nor in the path of renowned and powerful men.

By now the times were such that there was no hope of anything at all agreeable and absolutely no expectation of positive good. For that reason the shrewd and self-reliant men of Travnik hoped that in fact nothing would happen and that life would go on, as far as possible, without change or surprises. What good could come of a time when kings were falling out, nations were giving each other bloody noses and whole countrysides were in flames? A new Vizier? He would be no better and no worse than the one before and his staff would be unknown men, numerous, ravenous and possessed with God knows what new forms of covetousness. "The best Vizier we ever had," they used to say, "was the one who got as far as the frontier, then went back to Stamboul and never set foot in Bosnia." Some stranger, a distinguished traveler, perhaps?— But we know what that means. They leave a little cash and a few presents in the town but after them comes retribution or, next day at least, a police inquiry and investigation. Who were they, what were they, where did they

spend the night, who did they talk to? And in disentangling and clearing yourself, you lose ten times over any amount you may have made. Well then, a foreign spy? or some confidential agent, of unknown authority and dubious intentions? The fact is you never can tell who is what, what he may have on him, or whose outrider he may be.

In short, there's no luck to be had these days. Still, here's bread and here's one more day left to a man to eat and live through in peace in his finest of all the towns on earth, and God keep us from the public eye, from distinguished visitors and from great events.

Such, in these first years of the nineteenth century, were the inmost thoughts and wishes of the leading men of Travnik, but it goes without saying that they kept them to themselves: for in Travnik there lies between a wish or a thought and its visible or audible expression a long and devious road which is not easily traversed.

In recent times, at the end of the eighteenth and the beginning of the nineteenth century, there had been events and changes enough a great many in fact and in every direction. Events came pouring in from all sides, they clashed and eddied all over Europe and the great Ottoman Empire, and penetrated even into this little pocket of earth and collected there like floodwater or the silt of streams.

Ever since the Turks had withdrawn from Hungary, relations between Moslems and Christians had grown steadily worse and more involved and, in general, more bitter. The soldiers of the great Empire, the *Agas* and *Spahis*, who had been forced to leave their rich settlements in the fertile plains of Hungary and to return to their own poor, constricted country, were full of rage and illwill against everything Christian; at the same time they increased the number of mouths to be fed, while the number of hands to labor remained as before. On the other hand, these same wars of the eighteenth century which had driven the Turks out of the neighboring Christian lands and sent them back to Bosnia had aroused bold hopes in the subject Christians and had opened up prospects hitherto undreamt of; and this too was bound to have its effect on the attitude of the *rayah* towards his imperial overlord the Turk. Both sides—if one may talk of two sides at this stage of the struggle—both sides fought after their own manner and employed whatever tactics opportunity and the time might offer. The Turks resorted to repression and force, the Christians to passive resistance, guile and conspiracy, or readiness to conspire. The Turks fought in defense of their right to live and their own manner of life, the Christians for their own attainment of that same right. The Christians felt that the Turks were becoming steadily more oppressive and the Turks observed with bitterness that the Christans were beginning to give themselves airs and were no longer what they used to be. Out of this conflict of such opposite interests, beliefs, aspirations and hopes, there grew a painful tension which the long Turkish wars with Venice, Austria and Russia continually heightened and concentrated. In Bosnia the atmosphere grew heavier and darker, clashes became more frequent and life more difficult; everywhere there was less order and less assurance. The opening of the nineteenth century had brought the rising in Serbia as the visible sign of a new era and with it new tactics. The tension in Bosnia grew sharper and tighter still.

As time went on, the revolt in Serbia caused increasing anxiety, dissension, damage, expense and loss throughout Turkish Bosnia, and consequently to Travnik as well, though more to the Vizier, the authorities and the other Bosnian towns than to the Moslems of Travnik itself. They were not prepared to consider any war great or important enough to warrant their contributing their wealth, let alone their persons. Of "Karageorge's rising" the Travnik Turks spoke with a rather forced contempt, just as they always found some disparaging word for the forces which the Vizier sent against

Serbia and which the irresolute and squabbling local commanders assembled, slowly and in disorder, in the neighborhood of Travnik.

Napoleon's campaigns in Europe had long been a favorite subject of conversation in the town. At first men had talked of them as of distant events which might be explained and described but which had not, and could not have, any connection with their own daily lives. The arrival of the French army in Dalmatia suddenly brought this legendary "Bonaparte" a good deal nearer to Bosnia and Travnik.

At the same time there came to Travnik a *new Vizier, Husrev Mehmed Pasha*, bringing with him a deep admiration for Napoleon and an interest in everything French, and that, as Travnik found, in a far higher degree than was fitting for an Osmanli and for a high official of the Turkish Empire.

All this disquietened and annoyed the Moslems of Travnik and they began to express their feelings about Napoleon and his exploits in short, non-committal sentences or simply by a lofty and contemptuous pursing of the lips. Even so, none of this could entirely remove and protect them from this same Bonaparte and from the event which, like fire or the plague, overtook alike the man who ran from them and the man who sat still at home. This invisible and unknown conqueror plunged Travnik into unrest, commotion and excitement, as he did so many other cities of the world. For years to come the stern, resounding name of Bonaparte was to fill this Bosnian valley, and whether they would or no the people of Travnik were often to mouth its knotty, angular syllables; it was long to echo in their ears and hover before their eyes. The "Consular Age" had arrived.

ALBANIAN TALES FROM KOSOVO

Before 1945 the Albanian language was outlawed in Kosovo, and any literature was purely oral— tales, riddles, poems and proverbs told by villagers gathered together on winter evenings, and often accompanied by the one-string lahuta or two-string cifteli. Often stories would be moral messages, others recall with pride the old patriarchal society, but many are simply and deeply humorous and meant to entertain. As men and women never mixed together in company, they *developed separate literatures: the tales that follow are men's stories, translated by John Hodgson from the collections of Anton Cetta, a folklorist who has worked for over thirty years to preserve in written form the declining oral tradition.*

YOUR WISHES ARE GRANTED

Once, in the old time of the king, three soldiers set out from the town of Prizren. When they reached Sopia bridge, heavy rain began to fall, and the soldiers took shelter under the bridge.

When the rain stopped, the Pasha left the town to see what damage the rain had done to the crops, for it was harvest time, When he reached the bridge, he paused to look at the fields. He heard the soldiers talking and stopped to listen. The soldiers were asking each other: "What would you most like to have in this world?"

One said: "I would not ask anythng from God except to be able to go home for two hours to see my father and mother."

"The only thing that I would want in this world would be to have the Pasha's daughter for my wife."

The third said: "I would ask God to have all my debts paid, so that I wouldn't owe anybody a penny."

A few days later, the Pasha summoned the soldiers before him, and said to them: "What did you each say under Sopia bridge that day of the heavy rain?"

At first the soldiers did not want to speak, but the Pasha forced them and in the end they told him exactly what they had said.

To the first soldier, who had only wanted to go home for two hours, the Pasha gave a month's leave.

To the second, who had wanted his daughter for his wife, the Pasha said: "I'll call for her at once, and I wish you joy of her."

He asked the third: "What did you ask for?"

"I asked for enough to be able to pay my debts, so as not to owe anybody a penny."

The Pasha said: "Debts are with us until the day we die."

And he took his sword and cut off the man's head.

Told by Selim Bucaj,
from the village of Llodrovc.

THE POOR BOY WHO CHEATED THE WHOLE VILLAGE

In days long ago there was a poor boy who lived with his mother. They possessed nothing but a single cow. One day, he said to his mother: "Let's kill the cow and ask the whole village to dinner, and give what's left of the meat to our neighbors. We have plenty of neighbors, and they always have animals to kill. And when they slaughter their cows, then they'll invite us to dinner and give us meat, and we'll live a little better than with our dry bread."

So they slaughtered the cow, cooked a big dinner, and gave away the rest of the meat. A few days went by, and they waited for invitations, but none came. They waited for presents of meat. Nothing. They hadn't a bite in the house. So the boy took the hide of their dead cow and carried it to the city to sell. But nobody offered a single penny for it. He walked the city streets all day and towards dusk left the town and set off again home. But he was sorry to return empty-handed, and thought that he would stay in the town one more night, take the hide to market again the next day, and perhaps sell it. And he wrapped himself up in the skin and lay down to sleep in a meadow outside the town. At dawn, the crows saw the hide and thought it was a dead animal. They swooped down upon it. The boy reached out one hand and grabbed a crow. He got up and, carrying the hide in one hand and the crow in another, went back to the city. He carried the two about all day, but still nobody would give him a single penny for his hide. Night fell, and the poor boy wanted somewhere to sleep. He knocked at some gates. A lady appeared and asked him: "What do you want?"

"Can I sleep here? I'm not asking for a room or anything decent—just somewhere in the yard where the dog won't eat me."

The woman invited him in and allowed him to sleep on the porch.

So the boy wrapped himself in his hide again and lay down to sleep. But after a short time there came another knock at the gates. The woman appeared and opened the door. It was not the master of the house. The boy emerged from his hide and peered through a chink in the door. So this was the woman's lover. The man had brought a roast chicken, fruit, brandy, tobacco and other things—an entire spread. The couple ate and ate and then went to bed. But just as they were settling down, the lady's husband knocked at the door. Her lover didn't know what to do—but the woman said: "Quick into the wardrobe."

So he hid himself in the wardrobe, and the woman hid all the food in chests and cupboards around the room—some in one place and some in another. She went outside to open the gates, and at once rushed back and huddled under the blankets. The boy lay there wrapped in his hide, as if he had seen nothing. But the master of the house tripped over him as he passed through the porch, and said: "What are you doing here?"

"I'm just a poor man. I've brought this skin to sell and I'm going round town with this crow, that knows how to tell fortunes."

"But does this crow know anything?"

"He knows all the affairs of your household," said the boy. "He knows the past, the present, and the future."

"Well, come in, and let's hear what he says."

So they sat down on comfortable chairs, and the master of the house said: "Tell my fortune."

"This crow only speaks when you give him a sovereign."

The gentleman gave him a sovereign, and the boy hit the crow on the head. "Ngek," went the bird.

"What does he say?"

"He says there's a roast chicken, some bread, and some other things in that chest over there."

"What? We don't keep food in here. We have a kitchen."

"That's what the crow says. Maybe he's lying, but I don't think so."

Then the gentleman got up, and when he looked in the chest, there was the roast chicken, the roast meat, and the bread. He put them on the table, and the two ate together.

"All right," said the gentleman again. "Tell me something else."

"He wants another sovereign."

The man handed over another coin, and the boy said: "In that cupboard over there, there's some brandy and tobacco."

"That can't be," said the master of the house. "I only keep brandy in my tavern in town."

"That's what the crow says, and I don't think he's lying."

The master of the house went to look, found the brandy and tobacco, put them on the table, and the two drank together.

"All right, all right. Tell me something else."

He handed over another sovereign. But the boy didn't hit the crow very hard, and the bird made no sound.

"What does he say?" asked the gentleman.

"One sovereign's not enough."

The man put another sovereign on the table, but the boy still didn't hit the crow hard enough, and not a sound came.

"It must be something very important."

The gentleman began to worry. He forked out still more sovereigns—one, two, three . . . At the tenth, the boy decided to call a halt, and hit the crow. "Ngek," went the bird.

"He says there's a man in that wardrobe."

The gentleman got up and opened the wardrobe, and found his wife's lover standing there.

"Who on earth are you?"

The man in the wardrobe simply shrugged his shoulders sheepishly and the master of the house shut the door on him, leaving him still inside.

"Sell me that crow," he said to the boy in great consternation. "I work alone down in my tavern, and I want that bird to tell me what's going on in my house. It seems to know everything."

The boy wanted to sell the crow, but saw it was still dark. So he hesitated, and bargained until morning, and in the end asked for fifty sovereigns.

The gentleman thought this was a gift, and handed over the money. So the boy left the house, threw the hide to the street dogs, and set off home. When he was near his village, the neighbors saw him.

"Did you sell the hide, then?"

"I certainly did," said the boy, "As soon as I arrived in town! and what a crush! I sold it for sixty sovereigns, and could have made more! But I though they were joking when I asked them how much they'd give, but they said sixty, so I accepted the first offer. Some merchants have come from the coast, and they're looking all over for cowhides. If you get there quickly, you can ask up to two hundred!"

So the villagers upped and killed all their cows and oxen and collected great piles of hides and tons of meat. They loaded up the hides on carts and set off for town. When they arrived, nobody would give them a penny for their skins.

"Why in heaven's name have you brought all these hides?" asked the townspeople.

"A boy from our village told us there were merchants from the coast looking for hides. He sold his for sixty sovereigns."

"That was a lie."

The villagers were furious, and swore they would kill the boy when they got home again.

But by chance, that night the boy said to his mother: "Mother, I can't sleep very well in this bed over here. Let's change beds, just for one night."

His mother agreed. In the middle of the night, the neighbors burst in with axes and attacked the old woman, leaving here dead. Shortly before dawn, the boy got up and placed his mother on the back of a donkey, took a basket of eggs, and set off again for town.

When he arrived in the city he took his mother's body and propped it up against a wall; he placed the basket of eggs beside her, and stretched out her hand, as if she were selling. He withdrew to the other side of the street and waited, watching. It was not long before a rich man came along and asked the old woman: "How much are the eggs?"

The woman, of course, did not reply.

The rich man asked once again and, thinking the old woman was asleep, reached out and shook her, as if to wake her up. When he touched her, the body fell sideways, and the boy leapt from his hiding place: "Aah! You've killed my mother!"

"Don't shout like that," said the rich man. "You'll bring everybody running!."

"Don't shout? I'll fetch the town guard and tell them you've killed my mother!"

"Wait!" said the rich man. "I'll give you anything you want. Just don't tell anyone!"

"Only if you give me a hundred sovereigns and help me bury the old lady."

"Here you are," said the rich man. "Just leave me in peace."

So he handed over a hundred sovereigns and they took the body to the mosque and buried it, the rich man paying the fee. The boy mounted his donkey and set off for his village. When he arrived home, the neighbors saw him, and said: "What? Still alive?"

"I certainly am, and in fact you've killed my mother, and I took the body to town. There were some merchants there from the coast, who asked me what I had on my donkey. I said "An old woman, a corpse," and at once they asked, "How much do you want for it?" I thought they were joking, so I said, "A hundred sovereigns," and at once they forked out the money. They took the body, loaded it on a cart, and set off, and told me to tell people I met that if anybody had any old people's corpses, they should bring them to town and ask anything they wanted for them. And believe me, I could have got three hundred for mine."

So the villagers upped and got out their axes and set about killing all their old folk. They gathered the corpses, loaded them onto a cart, and took them to town.

At the entrance to the city, however, the town guard stopped them, and asked: "What's going on with all these corpses? What's happened?"

"A boy told us that merchants from abroad have been looking for corpses. He sold his own mother for a hundred sovereigns."

"And did you kill all these people?"

"Yes, we did."

So the guardsmen leapt onto the villagers and put most of them in prison. But a few escaped and ran home. And when they found the boy who had cheated them they jumped upon him and tied him in a sack.

Now near the village there was a deep pothole. The villagers argued among themselves, and at last decided to throw him in this cave, and to let him die a horrible death. So two young men took hold of the sack, carried it to the pothole, and threw it in. But the sack stuck half way down, and wouldn't fall any farther.

"We'll have to push it down," said the two young men. "Let's go and fetch a plank and give it a shove."

And off they went. Meanwhile the boy in the sack began to sing a popular song of the mountains. A goatherd nearby heard him, and asked: "What's all that noise for?"

"I'm singing."

"Why?"

"In the village they told me I have to get married tonight, and I don't want to. "Get married, or else!" they said, and I said, "No!" And they put me in this sack and left me here for an hour to think about it. "Think hard," they said. "If you want to get married we'll take you back home, and if you don't we'll push you down the hole." But I still don't want to get married. And now they're going to kill me."

"I'd really like very much to get married," said the goatherd. "Can I take your place?"

"If that's what you want, untie the sack," said the boy.

At once the goatherd set to work on the knot. The boy climbed out, and the goatherd took his place. The sack was tied up again, and the boy took the herdsman's cape and staff and climbed up the mountain, whistling as he went.

When the two villagers came back they simply gave the sack a push without asking any questions, and down it went into the depths of the earth, goatherd and all. Then at dusk the boy reappeared in the village, cape over his shoulders, staff in hand, whistling cheerfully, and leading a great herd of a hundred goats. The villagers watched in bewilderment.

"You back again? Didn't we throw you down that pothole?"

"You did, and what a good turn it was. At the bottom there was an old fellow, two parts beard and one part man, who caught me in his arms and took me out of the sack and gave me something to eat. He had about two or three thousands goats. He asked me if I wanted to go back up, and I replied that I did, and then he asked me how many goats I wanted to take. I

said, "Twenty," but he said, "No, no, take some more" and he forced me to accept a hundred. I didn't want to take them, but he was trying to make me take about a thousand. Goats down there grow like weeds up here."

"So there must be some left," said the villagers.

"What else do you think? Anybody who gets there early can bring back at least five hundred."

So down they went, young and old, into the pothole. Only the women were left at home.

They did everything they could to get rid of that boy, but in the end he won. And he became a rich man, with plenty of land, and livestock, and all the good things of life.

Told by Ramadan Gjoka,
from the village of Terstenik.

THE TAILOR'S DUMMY

More a poet than writer of fiction, VLADA UROŠEVIĆ was born in Skopje in 1934 and led a group of writers who discarded local and national themes for a greater involvement in the mainstream of European literature. This is one of his few short stories.

At midday the writer carried the dummy across the square. It was an ordinary tailor's dummy with a wooden base and no head. The beggars and town loafers abandoned their places in the shade and stared after him for a long time.

The writer had a hard time getting the dummy upstairs. "Who're you carrying that thing for?" asked his neighbor, passing on his way out to the market. "Nobody," the writer panted, dragging the dummy along as one supports an unconscious man, holding it around the waist. The staircase was narrow, and the climbing became more and more difficult; the base of the dummy kept bumping against the bannisters. Finally the writer reached the door of his garret flat. He leaned the dummy against the wall and took the key from under the doormat.

"It's shameful," said Lilla when she came to visit him that afternoon. "Who said you could use my dresses like that?" The writer was standing in the middle of the room, surveying his work with satisfaction. The dummy was dressed in various odds and ends Lilla had left

behind in his flat one day at the end of spring after she brought them back from the dry cleaner's. On the stump of the neck the dummy now had a plaster cast of the head of Aphrodite. Adorning the head was a large, black straw hat.

The writer was highly satisfied with what he had done. The head had been set slightly askew so the hat partly obscured the face, and the dummy looked out from under the brim as though it were trying to win affection. Lilla shrugged, made a grimace of disgust, and turned away. "You might use your time more intelligently," she said. "You haven't written a thing for ages. Instead of writing you just act the fool."

"Go and find me if you can," the writer began reciting sadly, "a word as simple as a stone..."

Lilla was becoming impatient. "I don't understand you," she said. "I don't understand this joke of yours with the tailor's dummy."

"Charming," said Lilla. She decided to take away the pieces of clothing that were hanging on the tailor's dummy, but in the end she changed her mind. Outside, the city was choking orange-colored dust, in the stench from the rubbish bins and the heavy smell from the shrunken river. She crossed to the door and went out onto the balcony. Down below, in the back yard, on the stark white concrete, some half-naked boys were sitting and cracking apricot pips. The other part of town, across the river, was the yellowish color of faded postcards.

A tiny figure was walking along the street waving its arms and looking up. "Here comes the painter," said Lilla. "We can't hide from him; he's seen me. Now he'll stay till midnight."

The painter was delighted with the dummy. "It's superb!" he shouted, gesticulating extravagantly. "It reminds me of my student days. When I was at the Academy we never had any money for models, so we had to paint tailor's dummies. There are some dummies!"

The painter stayed a long time. The stars were hardly visible in the summer sky; they were smothered by the exhalations of the city, the moisture hanging in the air, the smoke. "That's the constellation of Sagittarius," mumbled the painter, pointing vaguely somewhere above the tops of the skyscrapers.

Then the three of them went out together. The painter was in raptures over the dummy and promised to paint it. He was sweating. The city was trapped beneath the stifling heat, and the baked air that had been sealed into the walls all day was only now escaping through the bricks. The people walked with difficulty along the streets; there was a sickly gleam in their eyes, and they were jumpy and irritable.

The following day, when Lilla went to visit the writer, she met his landlady on the staircase. "I've had just about as much as I can take of all this!" shouted the landlady, flushed and panting. "As much as I can take. First it's a girl, and now it's some kind of ghost and a tailor's dummy!" The landlady turned around as Lilla squeezed past her. "Find somebody else!" she shouted. "That man of yours is undressing a freak up there, an antique freak!"

"What's going on?" asked Lilla as she walked into the room.

The writer smiled bitterly. "It's all so stupid," he said. "First thing this morning, in came the man to collect for the electricity. I was on the balcony. Suddenly he screamed and ran down the stairs. A little later the landlady suddenly appeared. I was just setting up the dummy when she came in." The dummy was wearing a theatrical wig. The long red hair tumbled down in waves over its shoulders.

"How's the story getting on?" asked Lilla.

"I'm still mulling it over," said the writer. "It'll be an excellent story. D'you feel like going out?"

As they were saying goodbye, the writer asked Lilla for her sunglasses.

The following day Lilla found the dummy wearing her sunglasses. The dark glasses made a strong contrast with the white plaster head; it seemed as though from behind them the dummy was keeping an eye on everything that happened in the room. "You're crazy," said Lilla. "I won't allow you to use my sunglasses like this."

The writer tried to calm her. "That's you," he said, pointing to the dummy. "When I'm writing about the dummy, I think about you. It's your twin."

"Don't you mix me up in all this," said Lilla. "I don't want to be replaced by anybody—no matter who. I hope you don't take it to bed with you!"

"Don't be such a little goose," smiled the writer. "It's only a dummy."

"You're beginning to frighten me," said Lilla. "I don't understand you any more."

""Go and find me if you can,"" the writer began reciting, ""a word as simple as a stone...""

"All the same," said Lilla, "I don't like this game of yours with the dummy."

"The story'll soon be ready," said the writer soothingly. "It'll be a splendid story. A young man who falls in love with a tailor's dummy. You'll see what a sensation it will be."

"Are we going out tonight?" asked Lilla. "There's a good Greek film showing at the open-air cinema."

"All right," said the writer. "I just have a little more to add." He stuck some cheap, shiny buckles into the dummy's hair, stepped back a few paces, and surveyed it with satisfaction. Then he jotted down something in his notebook. "It gets more and more beautiful, don't you think?" he asked. Lilla was silent. She made a point of facing the other way.

In front of the open-air cinema they met the painter. He was eating peanuts. "How's the story getting on?" he asked at once.

"Splendidly," said the writer. "I've worked out a new ending. It'll be a kind of absolute story."

"Let's hurry," said Lilla. "It looks as if the tickets are nearly all sold."

The writer said he was going to work for the following few days. Lilla did not come to visit him. Only when she finally got bored of going to the cinema alone did she climb up to his garret flat one evening. The dummy was standing in the middle of the room. The writer was lying on his bed. The light was not switched on.

"It's terribly stuffy in here," said Lilla. "You never air the place. Have you been out at all?"

"I've been busy writing," he answered. "The story's almost finished."

Lilla made a wide detour around the dummy, stopped by the bed, and sat down. "Now that the story's almost finished, will you clear that dummy out of here?" One could detect in her voice a scarcely concealed note of hatred toward that wooden figure dressed in her clothes.

"Don't be impatient," said the writer. "The dummy should be allowed to stay for a while. The young man in the story is very much in love with it." The half darkness that filled the room was thick and sticky. There was a smell of unwashed clothes, of sweat. The fetid air hung in the limp rags.

"Are we going to go anywhere?" asked Lilla.

"Not this evening," said the writer.

"Tomorrow?" asked Lilla.

"Yes tomorrow," said the writer with a sigh. "I still have something left to write this evening."

"All right," said Lilla, rising. "Wait for me tomorrow in the café on the quay."

The first person Lilla met the next day was the painter. He told her he had seen the writer in the café on the quay. "What happened to the dummy?" the painter shouted after her when they had already said goodbye.

"Nothing," said Lilla. "But something's going to happen soon."

She climbed up the staircase, afraid that the landlady might spot her. She found the key under the doormat and opened the door. The dummy was standing in the middle of the room. Lilla walked up to it, slowly and cautiously, as though she were approaching a living being. She was overwhelmed with a sense of disgust and tore the wig from the plaster head. The bald plaster crown shimmered in the moonlight.

She quickly undressed the dummy. The brooches and buckles tumbled to the floor, where they cracked and shattered under her feet. Her hands trembled as she burnt the wig and the pieces of clothing in a small stove full of old papers. The room smelt of smoke.

She took the plaster head, opened the balcony door and leaned over the rail. The white

blob of the head described a neat arc in the twilight; then there was a light explosion as the plaster shattered on the concrete paving of the yard. The cats fled from the rubbish bins, meowing with fright.

Lilla then threw the dummy itself from the balcony. The wood clattered loudly on the ground. A light was turned on outside, somewhere in the yard. An elderly voice could be heard shouting: "Have you gone mad? I'm going to call the police!" Lilla quickly left the room, closed the door, and ran downstairs.

Excited voices could be heard in the yard. Doors were being opened. She thought she glimpsed several people gathering. She ran out into the street and kept running until she reached the corner. Then she walked slowly.

She had already recovered her calm by the time she came to the quay. She had seen the writer from a distance; he was sitting in front of the café, drinking beer.

"Hot isn't it?" she said as she sat down.

"Terrible," said the writer. "Do you want a beer?"

"If it's cold," said Lilla . "I'm terribly thirsty."

"I've finished the story, you know," said the writer. "It's ready at last. I wrote the end yesterday. D'you know how it finishes?"

Lilla drank her beer and simply raised her eyebrows curiously.

"The girl who loves him," said the writer, "goes to his place when he isn't there and destroys the dummy."

Lilla lowered her unfinished glass.

"It's a strange story," the writer went on. "A kind of absolute story. This young man who falls in love with the dummy is writing a story. The story is about how a young man, who is in love with a dummy, writes a story. And he writes the story." The expression on Lilla's face was cold. Under the neon light her face had a lifeless sheen as though it were made of plaster.

"Hurry up," said the writer. "Drink your beer. I want to go back to my place and read you the story."

Lilla managed to speak only when they reached the staircase. "What happens at the end of the story?" she asked.

"Oh," said the writer as he unlocked the door, "when the writer sees that she's destroyed his dummy, he strangles the girl. Funny isn't it?"

BOOKS

TRAVEL

Rebecca West *Black Lamb and Grey Falcon* (Penguin $14.95). A remarkable piece of writing, erudite and all-embracing, and really the definitive work on Yugoslavia before the war. This is the sort of book you can dip into again and again, and it's only spoiled by some naively optimistic conclusions on a country that was, at the time (1937), a dictatorship. If you can't get hold of it *Rebecca West: A Celebration* (Penguin $9.95) includes a fairly representative chunk.

Edith Durham *Through the Lands of the Serbs.* Edith Durham was one of the most intrepid of women explorers and her (numerous) adventures through the Balkans in the early years of this century make for captivating reading. Something of a folk heroine in Albania, where streets are still named in her honor, her *High Albania* (Ayer Co. Pubs. $23.50) contains a fair portion on Kosovo.

Sir Arthur Evans *Through Bosnia and Hercegovina on Foot during the Insurrection* (Ayer Co. Pubs. $31). An exciting and humorous account of a difficult and eventful trek by the youthful Evans as Turkish control crumbled. Buoyantly written, and good for Islamic background.

Sir J. Gardiner Wilkinson *Dalmatia and Montenegro* (Ayer Co. Pubs., 2 vols., $30 each). Another stalwart nineteenth-century Brit braves what were then wild and unknown lands and unearths some interesting tales and facts.

Abbé Fortis *Travels into Dalmatia* (Ayer Co. Pubs. $37.50). Bigoted but entertaining eighteenth-century Venetian on a voyage around the colonies.

Evelyn Waugh *The End of the Battle* (Little, Brown o/p). Evelyn Waugh was sent to Yugoslavia as a liaison officer in the 1940s, and fictionalises his distaste for Partisan reprisals in this, the final volume of the *Sword of Honor* trilogy. If you can stand his politics, the acid style is brilliant.

Sir Fitzroy Maclean *Eastern Approaches* (Atheneum $10.95). Fitzroy Maclean led the British mission to the Partisans during the war, and he's now held in some esteem throughout Yugoslavia. Basically an autobiography, this includes a racy account of the wartime struggle—compulsory reading for anyone remotely interested in the period or the country, or just Maclean himself. His *Disputed Barricades*, long out of print, is an excellent biography of Tito and altogether a cogent resumé of twentieth-century Yugoslav history.

HISTORY AND POLITICS

Fred Singleton *A Short History of the Yugoslav Peoples* (CUP $13.95). The most complete history of the country you can buy.

Phyllis Auty *Tito* (UK edition only, available in libraries). Probably the most thorough—and impartial—biography of Tito by an English-speaking writer.

Milovan Djilas *Tito* (Harcourt Brace Jovanavich $9.95). By Yugoslavia's most famous dissident and sensationally subtitled "The Story from Inside," this is fascinating—especially after the adulation heaped upon Tito from other quarters. Djilas's rambling reminiscences present a fumbling military commander and scheming politician, motivated more by self-interest and a lust for power and luxury than anything else. By the same author: *Memoirs of a Revolutionary, Wartime,* and *Rise and Fall* (all Harcourt Brace Jovanovich) are autobiographical accounts of life in the prewar underground, the Partisan movement, and his fall from grace in the postwar order respectively.

Duncan Wilson *Tito's Yugoslavia* (CUP $37.50). An easy-to-read, largely sympathetic overview of Yugoslav history since the war; written by an ex-ambassador to Belgrade.

John Phillips *Yugoslav Story* (Jugoslovenska Revija). John Phillips was a *Life* magazine photo-journalist who reported on Partisan activities during the war. He was also a friend of Tito's, and this book of photos and remembrances begins with Phillips's account of his funeral in 1980. Particularly interesting for the author's powerful wartime photographs, the book is often available cheaply in Yugoslavia.

Dennison Rusinow *The Yugoslav Experiment 1948–1974* (University of California Press o/p). Dense, scholarly account of Yugoslavia's hybrid political system and her experience with self-management.

Milojko Drulović *Self-management on Trial* (State Mutual Book $40). A worthy attempt to explain Yugoslavia's complex system of workers' self-management. Written in the 1970s though, it holds few pointers to why the system has now all but fallen apart.

Nora Beloff *Tito's Flawed Legacy* (Westview Pubs. $25.50). Breezy, journalistic polemic which argues, in essence, that Tito was not such a good chap after all and the West was wrong to lend him so much money.

Stevan K. Pavlowitch *The Improbable Survivor: Yugoslavia and her problems 1918– 1988* (Ohio State University Press $25). Largely critical overview of modern Yugoslav history by a veteran emigré historian. More up to date than the other selections here, it's very good on the deepening crisis of the Eighties.

Gertrude T. Robinson *Tito's Maverick Media: The Politics of Mass Communications in Yugoslavia* (University of Illinois Press $24.95). A good and readable examination of the Yugoslav media. Deals well with the interplay of different ethnic differences in Yugoslavia's somewhat de-centralized media, as well as with aspects of ideology and modernization.

ART AND ARCHITECTURE

T.G. Jackson *Dalmatia, the Quaterno and Istria.* First published in 1887 and unavailable now outside the better-stocked libraries, this is an illuminating three-volume guide to the art and, particularly, the architecture of the Adriatic coast.

Anne Kindersley *The Mountains of Serbia* (Transatlantic o/p). Highly personal but packed with information—a fine book if you want to

read about the Serbian monasteries, and one that formed an invaluable resource for our own research.

David Talbot-Rice *Art of the Byzantine Era* (Praeger o/p). Informed and comprehensive appreciation of Byzantine icons and frescoes, with a chapter specifically devoted to Serbia.

Desmond Seward and Susan Mountgarret *Byzantium: a Journey and a Guide* (State Mutual Books $70). Though much of this is not surprisingly devoted to Greece, there are a couple of chapters on the Serbian and Macedonian monasteries.

SPECIFIC GUIDES

Piers Letcher *Yugoslavia: Mountain Walks and Historical Sites* (Bradt UK). Useful walking routes through the country alongside a fairly useless guide. Nevertheless, an invaluable book if you're intending to head off the beaten track.

Oleg Polunin *Wild Flowers of Greece and the Balkans* (Oxford UK). Contains an excellent description of the flora of Yugoslavia's many National Parks.

LITERATURE

Milne Holton (ed.) *The Big Horse and Other Stories of Modern Macedonia* (University of Missouri Press $26). Broad selection of contemporary Macedonian short stories, one of which is reprinted on p.433.

Ivo Andrić *The Bridge on the Drina* (University of Chicago Press $8.95). The most widely read work by Yugoslavia's Nobel Prize winning novelist. Others published in the US but now out of print include *Devil's Yard* (Grove Press), and *The Pasha's Concubine and Other Tales* (Knopf). *The Woman from Sarajevo* (Knopf o/p) is a superb story of a miserly woman and her greed and loneliness, set against a colourful background of the Balkans in the first half of the twentieth century. For more on Andrić, and an extract from his *Bosnian Story*, see the preceding section "Yugoslav fiction."

Celia Hawkesworth *Ivo Andrić: Bridge Between East and West* (Humanities $29.50). An academic overview of the work of Ivo Andrić.

Danilo Kiš *Garden, Ashes* (Harcourt Brace Jovanovich $2.95) and *A Tomb for Boris Davidović* (Harcourt Brace Jovanovich o/p).

Two rather turgid novels by one of Serbia's most highly regarded modern writers. A far better introduction to his work is the more recent short-story collection *Encyclopedia of the Dead* (Farrar, Straus and Giroux $17.95). A brilliant, kaleidoscopic mixture of factual history and fiction, it starts as an enquiry into anti-semitism but ends up in a maze of books and tales, questioning the authenticity of the written word as we accept it.

Milorad Pavić *The Dictionary of the Khazars* (Hamish Hamilton UK). Something of a post-modernist cult novel, tracking down the history of an obscure east European tribe by means of obscurantist, alphabetically arranged encyclopedic entries. There are two versions of the book, one male and one female: just one vital paragraph differs.

Ivan V. Lalić *Last Quarter* (Longwood Publishing Group $6.95), *Roll Call of Mirrors: Selected Poems of Ivan V. Lalic'* (Wesleyan University Press $10.95). The only accessible Yugoslav poet in translation, Lalić's work explores the "disintegration and entropy" of the end of the century in a metaphysical, lyrical style.

Aleksandar Tišma *The Use of Man* (Harcourt, Brace Jovanovich $19.95). The tortured existentialism of Tišma, up till now little known outside Yugoslavia, is well showcased here in an account of the lives of four friends during the brutalities of World War II, and the boredom that follows.

Milka Bajic Poderegin *The Dawning* (Honeyglen UK). A populist, historical family saga set in turn-of-the-century Montenegro. Don't let the poor English translation put you off; it's actually quite good for local color.

Vasa D. Mihailovich *The Little Box* (Charioteer $7.50). Prose poetry by major Serbian poet, softly drawing on Serbian history and folklore; his themes are both patriotic and humanistic.

B. Mikasinović (ed.) *Introduction to Yugoslav Literature* (Twayne o/p). A good selection, with writings from Serbia, Croatia, Slovenia and Macedonia. *Modern Yugoslav Satire* (Cross Cultural Communications $12), also edited by Mikasinović, is a good, representative selection of postwar satirical prose, ranging from the humorous to grotesque. Charts the shift from the 1970s onwards towards wider criticism of Yugoslavia's emerging consumer society.

TRAVEL ONWARDS

Few countries border so many, and such a disparate mixture of, countries as Yugoslavia—seven in all, varying from the recently opened-up states of the Eastern bloc to the more discovered nations to the west.

ITALY AND AUSTRIA

North and west are **ITALY** and AUSTRIA—the most obvious targets. **Venice** is just a short hop across the border from Ljubljana, and is the first of a rich chain of historic towns that arc across the north of the country towards Milan—**Padua**, **Vicenza**, **Verona** and **Mantua** all merit a stop. Further south, frequent ferries to **Ancona** offer a way into Tuscany; ferries to **Pescara** land you in the Abruzzi and not far from **Rome**; and those to **Bari** open up **Naples**, **Sicily** and the whole of the Italian south. For the complete picture see the *Real Guide:Italy*. You may not want to linger in **AUSTRIA**, at present Europe's most expensive country, but it's worth at least considering stopping to sample the imperial elegance of **Vienna** and the medieval center of **Graz**, just 50km across the border from Maribor; **Salzburg**, much touted and exceptionally beautiful, is also correspondingly pricey, and normally packed to bursting with tourists.

HUNGARY, BULGARIA AND ROMANIA

With the gradual disintegration of the Iron Curtain the "Eastern bloc" countries that ring Yugoslavia's north and eastern borders are becoming increasingly accessible and provide an opportunity for exciting travel at a time of dramatic change. Since it's possible that liberalization within the countries will lead to more relaxed visa requirements in the next few years, you should keep an ear close to the ground for latest developments.

HUNGARY offers the easiest introduction to the region, with its capital **Budapest** a cheap, convivial and cosmopolitan city you'd be silly to miss if you're in the north with time on your hands. Nationwide, the IBUSZ (tourist organization) sorts out rooms for around $5 a head and there are plenty of student hostels and a good range of campgrounds. You'll need to apply for a visa at least ten days before you set off; these cost around $15–30, are valid for thirty days and can be obtained from Hungarian consulates. The *Real Guide: Hungary* has all the details.

ROMANIA veers from the craggy beauty of the Transylvanian Alps to relatively unexploited resorts on the Black Sea. Its capital, **Bucharest**, is connected by daily train from Belgrade—a 14-hour trip that must rank as one of Europe's slowest and most dismal train journeys. Following the downfall and death of hated leader Nicolae Ceauşescu, travel in the country should be an easier and more pleasant experience, though you'll almost certainly have to exchange a certain amount of money each day, and pay a lot for accommodation. Romania sports few bottom-rung hotels, private rooms are illegal and student hostels, where they exist, tend to be full to the gills throughout the summer months. For the latest information, contact the national tourist organization *ONT*, at 573 Third Avenue, New York, NY10016 (☎212-697 6971) and offices in most European capitals.

Easier, and certainly worth a stopover if you're making for Istanbul, or (circuitously) northern Greece, is **BULGARIA**, and **Sofia** in particular—an attractive city, well loaded with the relics of Ottoman occupation, and linked to Belgrade by a twice-daily train. Thirty-hour transit visas are usually issued on the spot at Bulgarian consulates for around $12; full entry permits can take anything up to a week to get and cost $16.

ALBANIA

The unbending isolation of the late Enver Hoxha's regime in **ALBANIA** produced what is by far the least visited nation in Europe. Though travel restrictions have loosened slightly since his death, it's still impossible to visit individually, you can't get in at all if you're American and independent travel on from Yugoslavia is out of the question. Any trips have to be organized in advance, and if you decide to go, remember that you can't get in if you are dressed outrageously, nor if you flaunt a copy of the Bible or Koran. Once there your tour will most likely take in the ex-Turkish outpost of **Shkoder**, the Adriatic port-resort of **Durres** and the capital **Tirana**, by all accounts the dullest of cities.

GREECE

By far the largest proportion of people who visit Yugoslavia go on to **GREECE**. The main *Jadrolinija* ferry sails down as far as **Corfu** and **Igoumenitsa** (around 3 times weekly in summer) and trains run the tortuously slow haul from Belgrade to Thessaloniki and Athens three times daily; if you're in Macedonia a daily connection from Bitola to Florina makes short strides over the border quite feasible. **Thessaloniki** is Greece's livelier and less polluted second city and a good spring board for the various delights of northern Greece: the islands of **Thasos** and **Samothraki**, the **Athos** peninsula and the monasteries of **the Meteora**; plus it's another viable journey-break before Turkey. From **Athens** ferries will transport you to just about any **Aegean Island** you care to mention. Whatever you plan, the *Real Guide: Greece* seems an obvious investment.

LANGUAGE

Yugoslavia is harlequinned with languages—Hungarian, Greek and Albanian all get a look-in—but the country's principal language is Serbo-Croat, a Slav tongue akin to Russian which splits into two major dialects: Serbian and Croatian.

Unless you're here for some time you're not going to make any great inroads into it; better brush up instead what German, Italian and French you can muster, in roughly that order. German is widely spoken in the north and by returned *gastarbeiter* everywhere; Italian is universally understood on the coast; and French was taught in schools in the 1950s: fish around and you should find a *lingua franca*.

Outside the main tourist centers English is fitfully spoken (although fast becoming the most fashionable language to learn amongst the young) and what Serbo-Croat you pick up in one place won't necessarily help you out in the next—Slovenia and Macedonia both have their own languages, and though nearly everyone understands Serbo-Croat, regional pride dictates that the local alternative gets priority. But sally forth with the words and phrases listed on the next page: even the barest knowledge makes for easier and more rewarding travel.

THE CYRILLIC ALPHABET—AND PRONUNCIATION

Used more or less everywhere outside Croatia and Slovenia, the Cyrillic alphabet is easily learned despite its somewhat daunting appearance. Get to know it as soon as possible, if only to read the signs on buses and train schedules.

А а	a	as in farm
Б б	b	as in but
Ц ц	c	like the "ts" in cats
Ч ч	č	as in check
Ћ ћ	ć	a bit harder than the "t" in picture
Д д	d	as in Dylan
Џ џ	dž	as in the "j" of jaundice
Ђ ђ	D, d or Dj, j	a softer dz, like the "d" in verdure
Е е	e	as in bed
Ф ф	f	as in food
Г г	g	as in got
Х х	h	as in hat; before a consonant, like a softer "ch" in chutzpah
И и	i	like the "ea" sound in pea
Ј ј	j	"y" as in youth

К к	k	as in kiss
Л л	l	as in lost
Љ љ	lj	like the "lli" in colliery
М м	m	as in map
Н н	n	as in nut
Њ њ	nj	like the "ni" in opinion
О о	o	always short, as in hot
П п	p	as in pin
Р р	r	as in rip, but sometimes rolled
С с	s	as in super
Ш ш	š	the "sh" sound in shoot
Т т	t	as in tea
У у	u	like the "oo" in boot
В в	v	as in vat
З з	z	as in zip
Ж ж	ž	like the "s" in pleasure

Each letter is pronounced, never silent—*knjiga* (book) is pronounced *ker-nyee-ga*. Similarly, vowels are sounded separately: eg *trinaest* (thirteen)—tree-na-est. The combination **aj** is pronounced like the end of the English sigh, **ej** like the end of stay; and **oj** like toy. **Stress** is important; a slight misplacing of the accent renders the word unintelligible. We've marked the stress accent but remember two rules: the last syllable of a word is never stressed—so in words of two syllables the stress always falls on the first, eg, Zagreb.

SERBO-CROAT WORDS AND PHRASES

Basics

Do you speak English/ German/Italian/ French?	*Góvorite li éngleski/ némački/italijanski/ fráncuski?*	good evening	*dobro veće*
yes	*da*	good night	*laku noć* (this is said only when leaving)
no	*ne*	how are you?	*kako ste?*
I don't understand	*ne razúmem*	fine, thank you	*dobro hvala*
I understand	*razúmem*	today	*danas*
OK	*u redu*	yesterday	*juče*
please	*molim (prosim in Slovenia)*	tomorrow	*sutra*
thank you	*hvala*	the day after tomorrow	*prekósutra*
two beers please	*dva piva molim*	in the morning	*újutro*
hello	*zdravo*	in the afternoon	*posle podne*
goodbye	*do vidjénja*	in the evening	*úveče*
	more colloquially *ćao*	now	*sada*
	more formally *zbogom*	excuse me	*izvínite*
good morning	*dobro jutro*	sorry	*opróstite*
good afternoon/day	*dobar dan*	here you are	*izvólite*

Questions and Answers

To ask for something in Serbo-Croat, use the third person singular of the verb to have—*ima*, and the interrogative particle *li*. Eg "Do you have any fish?"—"*Ima li riba?*." "Is there a train to Belgrade?"—"*Ima li voz za Beograd?*" This construction stays the same whether the subject is singular or plural. The answer you'll get will either be *ima* (yes) or *nema* (no), perhaps the most irritating little word in the language.

I want	*Zelim*	why	*zašto*
I want to go	*želim da idem*	good	*dobro*
how much is it?	*kóliko košta?*	bad	*loše*
it's too expensive	*to je préskupo*	here	*ovde*
anything cheaper?	*nešto jefti'nije?*	there	*tamo*
cheap	*jéftino*	is this seat free?	*slóbodno?*
expensive	*skupo*		
I'm not paying for this	*ne plaćam za ovo*	**Some useful pairs**	
I want a room for one/two/three/four	*želim sobu za jedan/dva/ tri/četiri*	big—small	*véliko—malo*
where	*gde*	more—less	*više—manje*
how	*kako*	quick—slow	*brzo—sporo*
when	*kad*	early—late	*ano—kasno*
		beautiful—ugly	*lepo—ružno*

Directions

Where is...?	*gde je...?*	straight on	*desno*
how far is it to...?	*kóliko je daléko do...?*	is it near/far?	*pravo*
where can I get a bus to...?	*gde mogu da uzmem auto- bus za...?*	ticket	*da li je to blizu/daléko?*
bus/train/car/ferry/ taxi/foot	*autóbus/voz or vlak/kola/ trajekt/peške*	return ticket	*karta*
		station	*póvratna karta*
how do I get to...?	*kako mogu da dodjem do...?*	bus stop	*stánica*
left		is it going to Belgrade?	*autóbusna stánica*
right	*levo*	I'm lost	*da li ide za Beógrad?* *ja sam se izgubio*

Signs

entrance	*ulaz*	hot	*vruće*	departure	*pólazak*
exit	*izlaz*	cold	*hladno*	police	*mílicija*
toilet	*toálet* or *W.C*	open	*otvóreno*	hospital	*bólnica*
men	*muški*	closed	*zatvóreno*	no smoking	*zabránjeno púšenje*
women	*ženski*	arrival	*dólazak*	no entry	*zabránjen ulaz*

Numbers

1	*jedan*	11	*jedánaest*	40	*četrdéset*	500	*pet stótina*
1 and a	*jedan i*	12	*dvánaest*	50	*pedéset*	600	*šest stótina*
half	*po*	13	*trínaest*	60	*šezdéset*	700	*sedam stótina*
a half	*pola*	14	*četrnaest*	70	*sedamdéset*	800	*osam stótina*
2	*dva*	15	*pétnaest*	80	*osamdéset*	900	*devet stótina*
3	*tri*	16	*šesnaest*	90	*devedéset*	1000	*híljada/tísuća*
4	*četiri*	17	*sedámnaest*	100	*sto*	10,000	*deset híljada/*
5	*pet*	18	*osámnaest*	101	*sto jedan*		*tísuća*
6	*šest*	19	*devétnaest*	155	*sto pedéset*	100,000	*sto híljada/tísuća*
7	*sedam*	20	*dvádeset*		*pet*	1,000,000	*milíon*
8	*osam*	21	*dvádeset i*	200	*dve stótine*	2,000,000	*dva milióna*
9	*devet*		*jedan*	300	*tri stótine*		
10	*deset*	30	*trídeset*	400	*četiri stótine*		

When discussing simple numbers or prices in spoken Serbo-Croat, the final *stotina* is often dropped: eg 700 dinars becomes *sedam,* and even more confusingly, 100000 becomes *deset stotina* (literally, "one hundred hundreds").

Days of the Week

Sunday	*nédelja*	Thursday	*četvŕtak*	day	*dan*
Monday	*ponédeljak*	Friday	*petak*	week	*nédelja/sédmica*
Tuesday	*útorak*	Saturday	*súbota*	month	*mesec*
Wednesday	*sreda*		Days aren't capitalized.	year	*gódina*

To continue your language studies, the most useful of the available **phrase books** is *Harrap's Serbo-Croatian Phrasebook* (Prentice Hall $4.95). For a detailed glossary of food items, see *Basics;* for a glossary of Yugoslav terms and acronyms, see overleaf.

GLOSSARY

APSE Semi-circular recess at the altar end of a church.

AUTOCESTA Freeway (Slovene).

AUTOPUT Freeway.

BAN One-time military governor of Slavonia, Croatia and parts of Hungary.

BASILICA Church with nave, aisles and clerestory, based on Roman-style building.

BEG Minor official in the Ottoman empire.

BEŽISTAN Turkish covered market.

BORA Chill, intense northeasterly wind that blows across the north Adriatic coast.

BYZANTINE EMPIRE An empire that ruled much of the southern part of Yugoslavia from Byzantium (Istanbul) from the seventh to twelfth centuries.

CARDO Cross street of a Roman town.

CARŠIJA Bazaar.

CESTA Street (Slovene).

ČETNIKS Military group led by Draža Mihailović in World War II; initially fighting against Axis powers, they expended most of their later energies on the Partisans, tacitly supported by German and Italian troops.

CIBORIUM Canopy fixed over an altar; often decorated.

CLERESTORY Arcade of windows in the upper storey of a church.

DECUMANUS Central street of a Roman town or garrison.

DZAMIJA Mosque.

EXONARTHEX Short porch before the narthex of a church.

EZAN Islamic call to prayer, sung by the muezzin from a minaret.

FKK Abbreviation for the Yugoslav Naturist Association. Resorts and beaches so labeled are nudist.

GLAGOLITIC A Slavic alphabet found only in certain Roman Catholic liturgical books in the Croatian coast and islands.

GOSTILNA Restaurant (Slovene).

GOSTIONA Restaurant.

GRAD Name given to central part of a town; eg *Stari Grad*—Old Town, *Donji Grad*—Lower Town, *Gornji Grad*—Upper Town.

HAMMAM Turkish baths, today often converted into galleries, restaurants, etc.

HAN Hostelry, usually small, once used by travelers on trade routes.

HRAM Temple, shrine or church.

ICONOSTASIS Decorated screen in Orthodox church containing tiers of icons that separates sanctuary from nave and priest from congregation during Eucharist.

IMAM Approximate Islamic equivalent of a Christian priest (Islam has no clergy).

INCUNABULA A book printed before 1500.

JANISSARY Soldier of the Sultan's personal guard, often taken from Christian family as a child and brought up as Muslim. In the later years of the Ottoman Empire they became a dangerous religious/military autonomous power.

JNA Abbreviation of *Jugoslovenske Narodne Armije*, a common street name.

KARST Name given to typical scenery of a limestone region: landscape is generally bare, with disappearing rivers, gorges and caverns. See p.51.

KOLO "Walking dance," often performed at weddings and celebrations.

KONAK Turkish-style villa.

KORSO Often the main social event of a town, the *Korso* generally happens early in the evening: crowds of people stroll between two roughly fixed points, meeting and chatting in a casual procession that can involve most of the town. The farther south you go, the better attended the *Korso*.

KRČMA Small inexpensive restaurant.

KUĆA House.

LAPIDARIUM Collection of sculpture.

LOGGIA Covered area on the side of a building, often arcaded.

LUKA Harbor.

MIHRAB Niche in the wall of a mosque indicating the direction of Mecca and prayer.

MINBAR Pulpit from which the imam delivers and leads prayers.

MUEZZIN Singer who delivers call to prayer.

NAOS Innermost part of an Orthodox church, lying below the central cupola and in front of the iconostasis.

NARTHEX Entrance hall of Orthodox church, often decorated with frescoes on secular subjects.

OBALA Broad street, normally facing sea.

OTTOMAN EMPIRE Turkish empire which ruled most of Yugoslavia (except Slovenia and the coast) from the fourteenth to the nineteenth centuries.

PARTISANS Guerrilla groups instrumental in liberating Yugoslavia from Axis powers in World War II. Led by Josip Broz Tito, their Communist organization founded the postwar Socialist Federation of Yugoslavia.

PASHA High-ranking official of the Ottoman Empire.

PATRIARCHATE Controlling office of a see of the Orthodox church.

PERISTYLE Colonnade surrounding a court or building.

POLJE A fertile depression in a karst landscape, often supporting a settlement or crops.

PUT Road.

RAYAH Subject class of Ottoman colonies.

SABORNA CRKVA Orthodox cathedral.

SETALISTE Boulevard.

STOLNICA Cathedral (in Slovene).

SVET Saint, such as Sveti Stefan—Saint Stephen. Abbreviated Sv.

TURIST BIRO Tourist office.

TURISTIČKO DRUŠTVO Tourist office.

TRG Square; *Trg Bratstva i Jedinstva*—Square of Brotherhood and Unity.

TURBE Small mausoleum of a Turkish dignitary, usually found near a mosque.

ULICA Street, often named after a Partisan hero, such as Ul. Ive Lola Ribar.

USKOKS Piratical group that terrorized the northern Adriatic in the late sixteenth century.

USTAŠE Croatian Fascist group led by Ante Pavelic; during World War II they fought alongside Italians, committing many atrocities against the civilian Serb population.

VIZIER Below the Sultan, the most important official in the Ottoman Empire.

VRATA Gate.

INDEX

HELP US UPDATE

We've gone to a lot of effort to ensure that this edition of the Real Guide: Yugoslavia is completely up-to-date and accurate. However, things do change—hotels and restaurants come and go, especially in the larger cities, opening hours are notoriously fickle, and there are yearly subtle variations in bus and ferry frequencies that can spoil the best-laid travel plans. Any suggestions, comments, or corrections toward the next edition would be much appreciated. We'll credit all contributions, and send a copy of the new book (or any other Real Guide, if you prefer) for the best letters. Send them along to:

Martin Dunford and Jack Holland, The Real Guides, Prentice Hall Trade Division, A Division of Simon and Schuster Inc., 15 Columbus Circle, New York, NY 10023.